ECLIPSE OF THE ASSASSINS

ECLIPSE OF THE ASSASSINS

The CIA, Imperial Politics, and the Slaying of Mexican Journalist Manuel Buendía

Russell H. Bartley *and* Sylvia Erickson Bartley

THE UNIVERSITY OF WISCONSIN PRESS

Publication of this volume has been made possible, in part, through support from the Anonymous Fund of the College of Letters and Science at the University of Wisconsin–Madison.

The University of Wisconsin Press
1930 Monroe Street, 3rd Floor
Madison, Wisconsin 53711-2059
uwpress.wisc.edu

3 Henrietta Street, Covent Garden
London WC2E 8LU, United Kingdom
eurospanbookstore.com

This book may be available in a digital edition

Library of Congress Cataloging-in-Publication Data

Bartley, Russell H., author.
Eclipse of the assassins : the CIA, imperial politics, and the slaying of Mexican journalist Manuel Buendía / Russell H. Bartley and Sylvia Erickson Bartley.
pages   cm
Includes bibliographical references and index.
ISBN 978-0-299-30640-3 (cloth : alk. paper)
1. Buendía, Manuel, 1926–1984—Assassination. 2. United States—Foreign relations—Mexico. 3. Mexico—Foreign relations—United States. 4. United States. Central Intelligence Agency. 5. Espionage, American—Mexico. 6. Drug traffic—Mexico. I. Bartley, Sylvia E., author. II. Title.
E183.8.M6B375   2015
327.73072—dc23
2015008379

CONTENTS

ACKNOWLEDGMENTS

Charles Bowden (†)
John Womack Jr.
George Marshall Davis

(readers)
Michael de la Cruz, Mark Ruedrich, David J. Springer, Stuart L. Wagner, Charles Wollenberg

(research assistance)
José A. Barrón, Manuel Becerra Acosta (†), William Benemann, Julián Cardona, Adrienne Hunter, Lionel Martin, Edward M. Medvene, Molly Molloy, Bill Mulvihill, Fernando Ramírez de Aguilar, Carlos Ramírez Hernández, John Ross (†), Matthew Rothschild, Miguel Ángel Sánchez de Armas, Peter Dale Scott, Maryellen Sheppard, Gary Webb (†)

(informants)
María Dolores Ábalos Lebrija (†), Adolfo Aguilar Zínser (†), Héctor G. Berréllez, Ángel Buendía, Jorge A. Bustamante, Miguel Ángel García Domínguez, Lawrence Victor Harrison, Kathleen A. Henson (†), Michael Keith Hooks, Phil Jordan, Michael Levine, Rafael Loret de Mola, William Robert "Tosh" Plumlee

(logistical support)
Richard and Julie Steckel
Harold (†) and Jackie Wollenberg

(institutional support)
Fundación Manuel Buendía
University of Wisconsin–Milwaukee

Any undertaking of this complexity and duration generates many debts of gratitude, only a portion of which can ever be duly acknowledged. In the present instance, we must commence with author Charles Bowden and Harvard University historian John Womack Jr. Our indebtedness to both men for their insights, unstinting support, and encouragement over the past decade is beyond measure. Each read and critiqued every chapter as we drafted them, more than once obliging us to revise, expand, or otherwise hone our account. They likewise actively advocated for the book's publication. To our great sadness, Charles Bowden did not live to see our book's physical birth under the imprimatur of his own graduate alma mater, the University of Wisconsin. We were still going around with him about interpretive issues in our epilogue when he failed to awake from an afternoon nap on the last Saturday of August 2014.

We are equally indebted to George Marshall Davis (aka Lawrence Victor Harrison), without whose courage and principled determination we could not have exposed the perverse political agendas responsible for the murders of Manuel Buendía and U.S. Drug Enforcement Administration agent Enrique Camarena Salazar. His assistance has come at a grievous personal cost, itself a reflection of those same perverse agendas. In part, this book is his as well as ours.

Likewise, we express special thanks to the five readers named in addition to Bowden and Womack. They were selected as a representative sample of the book's eventual readership, persons of intelligence and diverse educational backgrounds but without specialized knowledge of the topic. Doubting at times that they had anything helpful to contribute, they nonetheless read the entire manuscript and in doing so provided us with useful insights into how best to frame this multifaceted account for general interest readers as well as regional and international affairs specialists.

The list of individuals who assisted us with research tasks for this book is not exhaustive but does recognize those who facilitated our work in especially significant ways. For the most part, we note their respective contributions in the text. Several, however, deserve additional comment. Maryellen Sheppard graciously documented real estate histories related to matters discussed in chapters 15 and 16. Bill Mulvihill expertly transferred recorded interviews and television news reportage to CD and DVD formats for ready consultation and long-term preservation. Lionel Martin and Adrienne Hunter facilitated our Buendía inquiry in Cuba. Border and Latin American specialist Molly Molloy at the New Mexico State University Library (Las Cruces) secured key documentation and, together with Charles Bowden, engaged us in insightful dialogue based on firsthand knowledge of and personal contact with several key informants discussed in the epilogue. José Barrón, webmaster for convicted Camarena case defendant René Verdugo Urquídez, facilitated our access to a veritable treasure trove of trial and law enforcement documents assembled by the Verdugo legal defense team and made publicly available as an online digital archive at a website devoted to the defense of Verdugo's innocence (http://reneverdugo.org/docs.html).

We are, of course, grateful to all our informants but wish to express special gratitude here to those who ran personal risks in talking to us or who simply shared what they knew in the hope that it would help expose the true perpetrators of the Buendía assassination and the related murder of DEA special agent Enrique Camarena Salazar.

Given the time that has elapsed since we commenced this inquiry, some of the informants listed here have since died. Where we know this to be the case, we so indicate with the symbol †.

During the final decade of our Buendía investigation, the Wollenbergs and Steckels provided welcome shelter in the San Francisco Bay Area and Southern California whenever we were on the road conducting interviews or related research. For their warm generosity and logistical support, we remain ever grateful. We also wish to acknowledge the institutional support we received during the first dozen years of this project from the Department of History and the Center for Latin America at the University of Wisconsin's Milwaukee campus, which enabled us to conduct key portions of our investigative work in Mexico. In this same vein, we express our deepest gratitude to University of Wisconsin Press Editorial Director Gwen Walker, who together with Senior Editor Sheila McMahon and their skilled staff deftly shepherded our manuscript through the multiple stages of publication to the final book.

ABBREVIATIONS

AMI	Agencia Mexicana de Información (Mexican Information Agency)
ARDE	Alianza Revolucionaria Democrática (Democratic Revolutionary Alliance, a Costa Rica–based Nicaraguan *contra* force)
BBCF	Bartley Buendía Case Files
CAL	Confederación Anticomunista Latinoamericana (Latin American Anti-Communist Confederation)
CIA	Central Intelligence Agency
CISEN	Centro de Investigación y Seguridad Nacional (Investigation and National Security Center, Mexico)
Comintern	Communist International
CONACYT	Consejo Nacional de Ciencia y Tecnología (National Council of Science and Technology, Mexico)
COPPPAL	Conferencia Permanente de Partidos Políticos de América Latina (Permanent Conference of Latin American Political Parties, Mexico)
DCI	Director of Central Intelligence
DEA	Drug Enforcement Administration
DFS	Dirección Federal de Seguridad (Federal Security Directorate, Mexico)
DIA	Defense Intelligence Agency
DISEN	Dirección de Investigación y Seguridad Nacional (Investigation and National Security Directorate, Mexico)
ENM	Escuela Nacional de Maestros (National Teachers School, Mexico)
FBI	Federal Bureau of Investigation
FDN	Fuerza Democrática Nicaragüense (Honduras-based Nicaraguan *contra* force)
FEG	Federación Estudiantil de Guadalajara (Guadalajara Student Federation, Mexico)
FEJ	Federación Estudiantil de Jalisco (Jalisco Student Federation, Mexico)
FELAP	Federación Latinoamericana de Periodistas (Federation of Latin American Journalists)

FEMACO   Federación Mexicana Anticomunista (Mexican Anti-Communist
           Federation)
FER   Frente Estudiantil Revolucionario (Student Revolutionary Front,
           Mexico)
FMLN   Frente Farabundo Martí de Liberación Nacional (Farabundo Martí
           National Liberation Front, El Salvador)
(FNU)   first name unknown
FOIA   Freedom of Information Act
FSLN   Frente Sandinista de Liberación Nacional (Sandinista National
           Liberation Front, Nicaragua)
GNR   Government of National Reconstruction (Sandinista)
G/S   Group Supervisor (DEA)
ICE   Immigration and Customs Enforcement
INTERPOL   International Criminal Police Organization
IPS   Dirección General de Investigaciones Políticas y Sociales (General
           Directorate of Political and Social Investigations, Mexico)
LC23S   Liga Comunista 23 de Septiembre (September 23rd Communist
           League, Mexico)
MFJP   Mexican Federal Judicial Police (*see also* PJF)
NAFTA   North American Free Trade Agreement
NSA   National Security Agency
NSC   National Security Council
OAS   Organization of American States
OIG   Office of Inspector General (CIA)
OSPAAAL   Organización de Solidaridad con los Pueblos de Asia, África y América
           Latina (Organization of Solidarity with the Peoples of Asia, Africa and
           Latin America, Cuba)
OSS   Office of Strategic Services
PAN   Partido de Acción Nacional (National Action Party)
PEMEX   Petróleos Mexicanos (Mexico's state-owned oil and gas industry)
PGJDF   Procuraduría General de Justicia del Distrito Federal
PJDF   Policía Judicial del Distrito Federal (Federal District Judicial Police,
           Mexico City)
PJF   Policía Judicial Federal (Federal Judicial Police, Mexico City)
PJJ   Policía Judicial de Jalisco (Jalisco Judicial Police; *also* Jalisco State
           Police)
Politécnico Instituto Politécnico Nacional (National Polytechnic Institute, Mexico
           City)
PRD   Partido de la Revolución Democrática (Party of the Democratic
           Revolution, Mexico)
PRI   Partido Revolucionario Institucional (Institutional Revolutionary
           Party, Mexico)
RAC   Resident Agent in Charge (DEA)
RCRMC   Riverside County Regional Medical Center, Moreno Valley, California

RNC   Radio Noticias del Continente (Continental News Radio, Costa Rica)
S/A   Special Agent (DEA)
SETCO   Servicio Turístico; *also* SETCO Air (Honduran airline contracted by
           the CIA)
SIPE   Sistema de Información y Promoción Editorial (Editorial and News
           Promotion System, alternative Mexico-based Latin American news
           service)
SISMI   Servizio per le Informazioni e la Sicurezza Militare (Military
           Intelligence and Security Service, Italy)
STPRM   Sindicato de Trabajadores Petroleros de la República Mexicana
           (Oil Workers Union of the Mexican Republic)
TASS   Telegrafnoe Agenstvo Sovetskogo Soiuza (Telegraph Agency of the
           Soviet Union)
UAG   Universidad Autónoma de Guadalajara (Autonomous University of
           Guadalajara)
UNAM   Universidad Nacional Autónoma de México (National Autonomous
           University of Mexico, Mexico City)
UPD   Unión de Periodistas Democráticos (Democratic Journalists Union,
           Mexico)
VOA   Voice of America
WACL   World Anti-Communist League

ECLIPSE OF THE ASSASSINS

Droll illustration of Manuel Buendía by Mexican caricaturist Rogelio Naranjo, matted and displayed by Buendía in his private study. (Courtesy of María Dolores Ábalos Lebrija, widow of Manuel Buendía)

INTRODUCTION

Journalist Down

Investigating and exposing the men and activities of the CIA in Mexico is one of my most important tasks as a journalist. It is a personal endeavor in which I am of course joined and assisted by, as well as indebted to, many other Mexicans. We share the belief that if a foreigner devotes himself to spying, assassination, subversion, deception, and corruption, then he is a dangerous enemy who must be exposed, denounced, and, if possible, caught, so as to have him expelled from the country.

—Manuel Buendía, *La CIA en México* (1984)

WITH HIS DISTINCTIVE VISAGE, thick-framed glasses, and receding curly hair, Manuel Buendía Tellezgirón was the delight of Mexican caricaturists. Always ready to share a good laugh at his own expense, he had a refined sense of humor that permeated both his personality and his politics. Following his violent death in 1984, colleagues memorialized him with a delectable little volume devoted to "The Humor of Manuel Buendía."[1] The book's cover exhibited an appropriately playful illustration by "El Fis-gón" (Rafael Barajas Durán), one of Mexico's leading political cartoonists. Buendía's personal favorite in this genre was a brilliant depiction of himself in full reportorial attire drawn for him by the equally renowned caricaturist Rogelio Naranjo. It had resided on a bookshelf facing Buendía's desk in the private study of his Mexico City home.

An agile wit and master of repartee, Buendía also enjoyed the distinction of being Mexico's most influential contemporary journalist. His Red Privada ("Private Network") column was obligatory reading for politicians, diplomats, and virtually anyone concerned with current Mexican affairs. When he was brazenly murdered on 30 May 1984 in downtown Mexico City, it was an event of historic proportions that reverberated well beyond Mexico's national frontiers. Some welcomed his death in the U.S. District of Columbia.

That final Wednesday in May found Buendía immersed in his daily journalistic routine. It was a strange day punctuated by a solar eclipse, itself obscured by clouds and smog blanketing the ancient Aztec capital. Something terrible was going to happen, darkly predicted one of Buendía's associates. The night before, Don Manuel had dined at an upscale restaurant in Mexico City's fashionable Pink Zone (Zona Rosa) with the head of the country's secret police, José Antonio Zorrilla Pérez, and three press officials. "Pepetoño," as Zorrilla was familiarly known, took that opportunity to give Buendía a new .45 caliber semiautomatic pistol in a red velvet case.[2]

At midday Buendía met for lunch with Undersecretary of Foreign Relations Víctor Flores Olea, also in the Zona Rosa within easy walking distance of his office at 58 South Insurgentes Avenue. For some time he had been preoccupied with American efforts to pressure the Mexican government to align its policies with U.S. regional interests and likely discussed those concerns with Flores Olea. With the advent of the Reagan administration and its foreign policy establishment of neo–cold warriors, no issue concerned him more than the increasingly strained relations between Mexico and the United States. They defined his politics and contextualized his demise.

Buendía's office occupied a cramped sixth-floor space in a drab eight-story edifice at the eastern edge of the Zona Rosa, across Insurgentes on the even-numbered side of the avenue. To the left of the entrance was the Librería Hamburgo, with Buendía's recent book on the U.S. Central Intelligence Agency (CIA) prominently displayed in the window. Immediately to the right was a little pastry shop, then a parking structure where Buendía would leave his gray 1982 Ford Mustang. Returning from his luncheon engagement with Flores Olea, he walked through the small lobby, past the glass-encased directory with its humorous sixth-floor listing for the "Mexican Intelligence Agency," and ascended the stairs to his MIA office. The building's elevator was out of order.

The Agencia Mexicana de Información (AMI), which syndicated Buendía's daily column nationally, paid his rent and office expenses, including secretarial help. At the moment he was without a secretary and waiting for AMI to assign him a replacement. Additionally, he had two assistants, young men he was mentoring in the techniques and practice of journalism. The older of the two, Luis Pablo Soto Olguín, had been with Buendía for sixteen years and related to the columnist more as a stepson than his assistant. He was responsible for Buendía's extensive reference files. The younger lad, seventeen-year-old Juan Manuel Bautista Ortiz, was just beginning his journalistic apprenticeship. He ran errands and did other routine tasks. Soto had left for the day when Don Manuel returned from lunch, but Bautista was in the office.

Buendía spent the rest of the afternoon making phone calls and working on his column. Around 6:30 he made ready to leave. He stuck the semiautomatic that Zorrilla had given him the night before into his waistband, placed the weapon he normally carried in his desk drawer, threw his James Bond–label trench coat over his shoulders, and, accompanied by Bautista, descended the six flights to the lobby. Juan Manuel was on his way to a nearby copy center. As they exited the building and turned toward the parking structure, the lad hurried ahead to pay the attendant so that Buendía would not have to wait for his vehicle. Just as he reached the attendant's booth he was stunned by the deafening report of a firearm. Turning, he saw his mentor collapse to the sidewalk as a revolver-wielding assailant fired three more shots into him at point-blank range.

The gunman displayed the agility and assurance of a trained assassin. Witness accounts place him at the scene for some time before Buendía left the building and describe his movements in considerable detail. He was of medium stature and athletic build, had a full mustache, and wore a black leather jacket, green pullover, blue jeans, tennis shoes, and a white baseball cap with the visor pulled down to conceal his facial features. He approached his victim from behind and fired the first fatal shot into Buendía's lower right back, angling the bullet's course upward through the liver and lung. He immediately grabbed the hem of Buendía's raincoat with his free hand, pulled it up, and fired three more shots into the journalist's upper torso. The force of the bullets' impact, combined with the victim's defensive reflexes, made Buendía rotate to his right, with the result that the entry wounds advanced progressively from back to front, passing beneath his right arm, the final shot severing the fountain pen he carried in the left inside pocket of his jacket and impelling him backward. He fell faceup with his head oriented toward the parking garage, his feet—toes pointing outward—toward the entrance to 58 South Insurgentes.

Having assured himself that Buendía was down for good, the gunman moved quickly away through stunned onlookers. He was briefly pursued by an agitated Bautista, who had grabbed Buendía's pistol and given chase, but easily eluded the journalist's young assistant. Stopping to fire at his pursuer, he collided with a startled pedestrian, missed the shot, and quickly resumed his flight along Insurgentes to the corner of Havre Street, where he doubled to the left, then continued running southeast along Havre. In the block between Liverpool and Marsella, Buendía's assailant climbed behind a waiting accomplice on a black-and-white Honda motorcycle, and the two sped away into the evening pall.

Three additional motorcyclists had been positioned nearby, although no one perceived that they operated in concert. Witnesses did report the presence of other persons whose demeanor suggested prior knowledge of the crime, among them a shadowy figure with a handgun who materialized out of the gathering cluster of onlookers, approached the inert body on the sidewalk, and peered at the open but now sightless eyes, then calmly walked away. It would later be learned that officers of Mexico's Federal Security Directorate (DFS) had been posted in the area before the shooting and that the motorcycles were operated by agents of the directorate's Brigada Especial. One Special Brigade operative notably present that day was Víctor Manuel Gómez, "El Gringo," as he was familiarly called by his associates. He had phoned in sick and supposedly did not report for work, yet was observed "constantly at Zorrilla Pérez's side" while Zorrilla was overseeing the crime scene. Among the small fraternity of Mexico City police reporters, El Gringo was thought to be the liaison between the DFS and the CIA.[3]

When Juan Manuel Bautista recovered his wits after his nearly fatal pursuit of the gunman, his first thought was to inform Luis Soto. He reached his office mate from a mezzanine phone inside the 58 South Insurgentes building and quickly recounted what had transpired. Soto, in turn, immediately thought to inform DFS chief Zorrilla Pérez and asked Bautista to get him Zorrilla's private number from the office upstairs, which Juan Manuel did in a few brief minutes. After receiving Soto's call, Zorrilla notified Secretary of Government Manuel Bartlett Díaz, who instructed the DFS chief to take charge of the crime scene and to keep him updated on subsequent developments. It is probable that Zorrilla had been informed of the shooting by his own operatives before Soto called. It is also likely that the Mexico City CIA station had been apprised

MANUEL BUENDIA, PERIODISTA MEXICANO.

Surveillance photo of Manuel Buendía from the files of a political police unit attached to the former Federal District Delinquency Prevention Investigations Department. (Courtesy of María Dolores Ábalos Lebrija, widow of Manuel Buendía)

58 South Insurgentes Avenue, Mexico City. The third row of windows from the top was Manuel Buendía's office. (Sylvia E. Bartley)

Manuel Buendía at work in his South Insurgentes Avenue office, 1982. (Courtesy of the Fundación Manuel Buendía)

Buendía assassination site, east sidewalk of South Insurgentes Avenue, by the entrance to the parking garage. The entrance to number 58, where Buendía had his sixth-floor office, is just outside the left edge of the photograph. (Sylvia E. Bartley)

of Buendía's slaying, either through established liaison channels or directly by one of its own agents.

What happened next was as improbable as it is revealing. Within twenty minutes of the shooting, Zorrilla arrived on the scene accompanied by more than twenty heavily armed DFS agents, who quickly cordoned off the area. Almost immediately there was a confrontation between Zorrilla's people and the Federal District Judicial Police (PJDF), which came perilously close to a shootout when a DFS *comandante* put his gun to the head of the *judiciales'* commanding officer. At issue was crime scene jurisdiction, which constitutionally fell to the capital city's PJDF but in this instance was disputed by national security personnel under explicit orders from the secretary of government. In point of law, the DFS had no constitutional authority to exercise police functions. As in other countries, however, the institutional boundaries between law enforcement and national security blurred on the ground, and throughout its thirty-eight-year history DFS agents regularly ran roughshod over such juridical limits.[4] No doubt invoking orders from Bartlett Díaz, Zorrilla managed to defuse the confrontation with the *judiciales*, then impose his own authority over the crime scene and adjacent area.

Equally noteworthy was the way Zorrilla took charge of and orchestrated all funeral and interment arrangements for Buendía. Taking advantage of the distraught widow's inability to focus on the practical details of the moment, the DFS chief arranged for the body to be viewed at the spacious Gayosso mortuary, Mexico City's most prestigious funeral venue, located far across town from the Buendías' Lindavista home and clearly selected for Zorrilla's own ulterior purposes. As described by former Buendía intimate Miguel Ángel Granados Chapa, Zorrilla presided over all the funereal rites "as though he were the primary surviving relative," making sure to be seen as a grand friend of the deceased and thus above suspicion as having had anything to do with the killing. He also arranged for Buendía to be interred in the stately Jardines del Recuerdo cemetery and to have a single graveside speaker, journalist León García Soler, who could be counted on to make no inconvenient allusions in his final remarks. Zorrilla paid all funeral and burial expenses out of the DFS budget. His primary purpose in making himself so visible at Buendía's funeral, Granados Chapa surmised, was to have President Miguel de la Madrid, in the emotion of the moment and witnessed by those who had come to pay their last respects, assign him primary responsibility for conducting the official inquiry into the deceased's murder, "despite the fact that the DFS had no institutional authority to do so."[5]

The practical consequence of Zorrilla's actions was to compromise the criminal investigation of the Buendía homicide. From the outset, DFS agents grossly violated crime scene protocols, manhandling the body, searching the victim's pockets, and rifling through drawers and files in Buendía's office. Witnesses were sequestered and interrogated for days and weeks on end before being released to the proper investigative authorities. Purported suspects were physically abused in unsuccessful attempts to secure confessions of guilt, while key items of physical evidence disappeared, including the victim's clothes. All of this hopelessly vitiated what five years later would be presented to the public as the official resolution of the Buendía assassination.[6]

At the time of the Buendía slaying, Russell was a senior faculty member in the Department of History at the University of Wisconsin's Milwaukee campus. He was also a contributor to the Mexico City daily *unomásuno*, one of a new breed of periodicals spawned by government interference in the management of Mexico's leading newspaper, *Excélsior*. A core group of *Excélsior*'s most accomplished journalists had been forced out in July 1976 by the administration of President Luis Echeverría Álvarez (1970–1976) in a heavy-handed attempt to muzzle an increasingly critical press. Among those ousted were the paper's managing editor, Julio Scherer García, and its assistant managing editor, Manuel Becerra Acosta, each of whom would soon found their own publications: Scherer García the combative newsweekly *Proceso*, and Becerra Acosta the alternative daily *unomásuno*.

Both publications reflected a newly emergent journalistic style inspired throughout Latin America by the tumultuous struggles of the 1960s and 1970s, one characterized by reasoned, fact-based analysis and a determination to hold power accountable. Because the assault on *Excélsior* had come at the end of Echeverría's presidential term and, in the face of a public outcry, could be disavowed by his successor, it had the unintended effect of opening a new space for critical journalism in Mexico. That space soon came under renewed attack and by the 1990s would again be severely restricted, but for the decade 1978–1988 it allowed committed media professionals to engage in serious journalism. *Excélsior*'s decision to carry Manuel Buendía's Red Privada column on its front page less than a year after its own internal purge was no doubt part of a management strategy to repair the paper's damaged professional image. Buendía, for his part, chose to publish in *Excélsior* for strictly pragmatic reasons of exposure and dealt indirectly with the paper through the AMI.[7]

Russell had started writing for *unomásuno* in 1980 and would contribute current affairs articles, feature interviews, historical essays, and investigative pieces over the next decade. Sylvia joined him early on in these journalistic endeavors and developed her own relationship with *unomásuno* as a photojournalist. It was in these circumstances that we became involved in the Buendía case. Although we were foreign nationals, we shared a professional bond with our Mexican colleagues and experienced the same outrage as they when Buendía was killed. His death was an offense to the sensibilities of all who value an open society and constitutionally protected citizen rights.

It was also a major political event with ramifications reaching far beyond downtown Mexico City. Indeed, the thought that crossed many of our minds at the time was that Buendía might have been felled by operatives of the CIA. There were, of course, other possible culprits, most of them Mexican, but a number of circumstances made it difficult not to place the American administration of Ronald Reagan high on the list of suspects. Because our U.S. citizenship afforded certain advantages for this type of inquiry, we decided to focus our investigative efforts on the possibility of a U.S. link to Buendía's death. This book recounts that investigative journey as it unfolded over the better part of three decades.

For many readers this will be exotic and alien terrain where a few guideposts may be helpful. It is well at the outset to note that historically there has always been a dark side to the conduct of U.S. foreign relations, especially with those countries closest to our national territory. When in the mid-1970s the Senate Select Committee on Intelligence, chaired by Idaho senator Frank Church, held open hearings on assassination as an instrument of American foreign policy, the public was awed by its revelations of CIA plots to kill Cuba's Fidel Castro and other foreign leaders. The hearings culminated in a theatrical display of exotic assassination weapons choreographed for the television audience and punctuated by committee members' expressions of disbelief and chagrin over such aberrant government behavior.

There was nothing aberrant about it, however, only the fact that it had come to such public light. Yet in that light, the damage was adroitly contained by limiting discussion to plots against foreign leaders, disavowing the practice of targeting heads of state as inherently un-American, and lamenting those few documented instances where this had occurred as egregious policy lapses. When the final Church report was released, with its litany of James Bondish misdeeds, many Americans congratulated themselves for having confronted the error of their ways, breathed a collective sigh of relief, and then got on with their lives.[8]

Political assassination by governments, however, has never been directed primarily at heads of state, but rather at significant actors of lesser rank who can be physically eliminated with minimal risk of exposure. Actual numbers defy tabulation, but they are elevated, for this is part of the universal calculus of power to which every government has occasional or frequent recourse, including the United States. Nothing that transpired in the post-Vietnam CIA assassinations scandal altered that fact. To the contrary, the Church Committee was in the end an effective device for lulling the general public back into a state of comfortable delusion about our exemplary morality and the righteousness of national purpose and behavior.[9]

Presidential prohibitions notwithstanding, this country has long had recourse to assassins and has deployed them more often than law-abiding citizens would care to imagine.[10] While the assassins' victims have not usually been heads of state, invariably they have been persons of actual or potential influence. Nor have such victims always been foreign nationals, for governments—ours included—will terminate their own whenever secrecy or covert purpose requires.

Eight months after the assassination of Manuel Buendía, U.S. Drug Enforcement Administration (DEA) special agent Enrique "Kiki" Camarena Salazar was abducted in Guadalajara, Mexico, brutally interrogated about his undercover work, then killed by his captors. The Camarena murder had an immediate impact on U.S.-Mexico relations and for the next several years would be used as a bludgeon by the Reagan administration to cudgel Mexico into line with U.S. regional interests. While at first blush the Buendía and Camarena killings seemed to be unrelated, they turned out to be closely connected. Both crimes were officially attributed to local villains, but in each case we find the long arm of the United States. Evidence we have developed strongly suggests that the two men, a prominent Mexican newspaper columnist and an American narcotics agent, were silenced on orders from Washington to prevent them from compromising U.S. covert operations in Mexico and Central America. Their deaths are emblematic of premeditated murder as an instrument of foreign policy and remain one of the Cold War's closely held secrets.

Assassinations, former CIA covert operations chief Richard Bissell once remarked, should only be carried out if they can be accomplished "in the deepest, most permanently impenetrable secrecy." A political assassination, he emphasized, "should never be discovered or even suspected, ever!"[11] Few secrets remain "permanently impenetrable," however, and over the years the carefully contrived official versions of the Buendía and Camarena killings have gradually unraveled. The process began in the Mexican press, where tenacious colleagues of Manuel Buendía relentlessly exposed efforts to cover up the motive and responsible parties behind his violent demise. It would unfold most intensely in the five years following Buendía's death, then continue tortoise-like out of public view for another two decades. Kiki Camarena's murder likewise has begun to be exposed through its linkages to the Buendía case.

Despite obvious inconsistencies and lingering doubts, once Mexican authorities made their case, interest in the Buendía affair quickly waned. The public's attention span is typically short, while police investigators tend not to pursue crimes over excessively prolonged periods. Time is considered the criminal investigator's enemy. Memories blur, witnesses die, trails fade. The longer a crime goes unsolved, common wisdom holds, the less likely it will be solved. For the most part, Buendía's media colleagues likewise turned their attention to other stories, either accepting the official version of events and considering the case closed or simply yielding to the practical imperatives of having to earn a living.

Our perspective was different. As an academic historian with a regular income, Russell was both inclined and in a position to approach the Buendía case with a view to the long haul. For us time was a favorable element, not an enemy. Our purpose was not to bring guilty parties before the bar of justice, nor were we constrained by the often arbitrary rules of evidence applied to judicial proceedings. We sought rather to place Manuel Buendía in proper historical perspective, to explain why he was murdered, and to expose for the historical record those who were behind his homicide. If time erases clues and muddles recollections, it also contextualizes past events and often brings to light new evidence. Given enough time, tongues frequently loosen and knowledgeable informants talk. Eventually they talked to us, shining a small but bright beam of light down the rabbit hole into Richard Bissell's dark netherworld of black ops.

We worked both sides of the U.S.-Mexico border and pursued leads in other countries as well. Our Mexican press credentials, coupled with the personal endorsement of *unomásuno*'s managing editor, Manuel Becerra Acosta, opened doors to us that normally would not have been accessible. We were especially fortunate to have the cooperation of *unomásuno*'s own reportorial staff, whose members readily shared their investigative insights and on more than one occasion provided us with significant leads. We were also welcomed into the circle of Buendía's professional associates and enjoyed a particularly fruitful relationship with the Fundación Manuel Buendía, the foundation created in the months following the assassination to perpetuate Buendía's legacy and promote professionalism among Mexican journalists.

Our method consisted of combining traditional gumshoe investigation with engaged journalism, in which we would publish articles about the Buendía case designed to elicit responses from knowledgeable, perhaps even complicit, readers. The technique

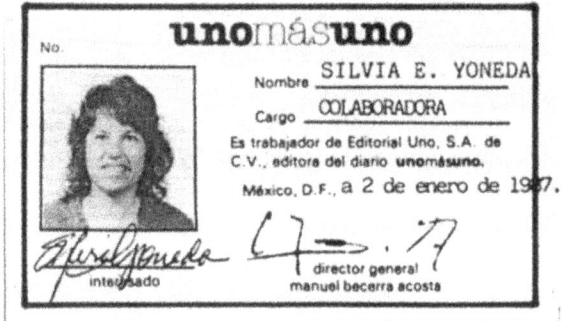

Authors' Mexican press badges (*charolas*) from the daily newspaper *unomásuno*. Sylvia E. Bartley used a former married name in the 1980s.

Manuel Becerra Acosta, founding editor of *unomásuno* and a key supporter of the authors' Buendía investigation. (Courtesy of Manuel Becerra Acosta)

was what an ex-CIA agent and pivotal informant would describe to us as "dropping tokens"—in other words, floating loaded, but always incomplete, information for the purpose of provoking readable reactions. We did this with some success and actually became something of a thorn in the side of Mexican authorities, who communicated their displeasure to us in a variety of ways. For a time we actually found ourselves in the curious role of convenient foil where, as U.S. nationals, we were able to say things in print that our Mexican colleagues may have felt constrained to leave to someone else. This was true as well of *unomásuno*, whose editor was willing to publish material we submitted about the Buendía case that he considered politically risky solely because we were Americans and it could be presented as an informed view from abroad. "It's like the bullfight," Becerra Acosta once remarked to us. "You never know when you will be gored."

The present account proceeds on three distinct planes: narrative, contextual, and analytical. Its overarching purpose is to shed fuller light on a seminal chapter of late Cold War history, which, having been recorded for the most part episodically, tends to suffer from the common historiographic "forest-for-the-trees" malady. More subjectively, it seeks to render justice to the memory of Manuel Buendía, a fallen champion of the democratic ideals many of us still hold, and thus to deny guilty parties who evaded indictment in a court of law identical impunity before the bar of history.

The Buendía assassination was one of numerous episodes marking that dark period, but one that opens a window on the broader panorama of the time in ways that no other single event does. Our narrative, therefore, threads its way serpent-like through several seemingly disparate yet contextually interconnected events: Mexican authorities' handling of the Buendía case; the Kiki Camarena affair; the 1986 slaying of former Yucatán governor and independent-minded newspaperman Carlos Loret de Mola; two high-profile Camarena-related federal trials in Los Angeles, California; a DEA sting in La Jolla, California; illicit Nicaraguan *contra* support operations in Mena, Arkansas, and Guadalajara, Mexico; the Christic Institute's *contra*-related lawsuit in U.S. Federal Court in Miami, Florida; the muzzling of a disillusioned former CIA spy, Lawrence Victor Harrison, who spoke to us about Manuel Buendía in violation of agency secrecy oaths and suffered severe personal consequences for doing so.

If at times Buendía himself seems to fade into the background, it is only because we need to provide the reader with essential information about these various contextual elements that helps locate him in the circumstances that led to his death. We allot ample space here to our discussion of Lawrence Victor Harrison, who is at once the single most important source we have developed for the present inquiry and also the most problematic, given his professional training in the art and techniques of deception, as well as the many pressures he was under not to reveal official secrets learned in the course of his clandestine work in Mexico. His testimony is crucial for a resolution of the Manuel Buendía case and must be tested as rigorously as possible for its veracity, which requires an extended account of the life path that led him into the CIA, his agency service, his eventual disaffection and ultimate repatriation as a coerced government witness, and finally his eleven-year relationship with the authors. We provide that account in chapters 13 through 16.

While each of these episodes is significant in its own right, together they comprise a context that explains the Buendía slaying. In crimes of state, as the Buendía homicide assuredly was, rarely if ever do investigators recover the proverbial "smoking gun" in the form of irrefutable documentary evidence. Orders to assassinate are never issued in writing. Context, therefore, is critical, both as circumstantial evidence and as a reference for evaluating other kinds of evidence, especially informant testimony. As a device to help the reader consider the evidence presented here, we also recount the context and course of our own investigation, which is the narrative thread that ties the book's seventeen chapters together.

I

Knight Errant

One could hardly have chosen a better target than Buendía to inject into Mexican society the feeling of fear, disorder, and ominous change in public life.

—Héctor Aguilar Camín, *Nexos* (June 1984)

MANUEL BUENDÍA (1926–1984) was the third of five siblings raised in Zitácuaro, Michoacán, in a modest middle-class home of traditionally conservative values. He received most of his formal schooling at Catholic institutions, including three years of seminary and a fourth at the Jesuit Instituto Patrio in Mexico City, after which he briefly studied law before devoting himself to a career in journalism. His personality, always outgoing and open to the world around him, was tempered along the way by a number of family tragedies: the diabetes-induced death of his eldest brother José when Manuel was thirteen; his mother's death two years later; then his younger brother Roberto's death in a motorcycle accident; and finally, when he was nineteen, the fatal mugging of his father, at which point he assumed responsibility as paterfamilias for his sister, Gloria, and younger brother Ángel.

Buendía made his first foray into journalism while still a seminarian, when he began to write for the conservative National Action Party's magazine *La Nación*. After a hiatus of interruptions occasioned by family demands and his studies, he returned to *La Nación* at age twenty-three as a full-time reporter. While there he met and courted his future wife, Dolores Ábalos Lebrija, the magazine's secretary. He remained at *La Nación* for four years, then landed a job with the Mexico City daily *La Prensa*, where he honed his investigative skills as a crime reporter. His assignments at *La Prensa* afforded him access to the key secretariats of Government and Foreign Relations, as well as the opportunity to cover the activities of President Adolfo Ruiz Cortines (1952–1958).

Buendía's agile mind, quick wit, and natural reportorial talent assured his emergence as a prominent media personality and influential figure in the sphere of public opinion. While gaining experience as a reporter, he also took an active part in the paper's administrative affairs, serving at one point as president of its board of directors, then as editor, a position he held from 1960 until mid-1963. During his years at *La Prensa* he transitioned from reporting to commentary, debuting his signal "Private Network" (Red Privada) column in 1958. In subsequent decades, he would write a variety of columns for different publications, with politics a distinctive thread throughout. "For Your Control" (Para Control de Usted) and "Political Concert" (Concierto

Político), two that he published in the Mexico City paper *El Día*, are suggestive. Then, in 1976, he resurrected Red Privada, with its implied and frequent insider information, which he published five days a week for the last eight years of his life, first in *El Sol*, a chain of twenty-three daily newspapers; then in the Mexico City daily *El Universal*; and finally in *Excélsior*, at the time Mexico's "paper of record," with national syndication by the AMI.

In the course of this experience, Buendía began to formulate a view of journalism as an integral part of good government that, ideally, should foster ongoing dialogue between those who govern and the governed. This led him at midcareer to occupy several official positions in charge of press affairs and public relations, where he endeavored to implement his concepts of democratic information flow. By all accounts, his most notable achievements in this regard came during a three-year stint as press and public relations director of Mexico's National Council of Science and Technology (CONACYT by its Spanish acronym), where he oversaw the publication of ten books and more than one hundred pamphlets on topics of science and technology, as well as editing the council's technical journals. Simultaneously, he promoted one of the country's first science and technology sections in the newspaper *El Día*.

Buendía's conceptualization of journalism as a reciprocal instrument of democratic governance evolved out of his own life experience into a guiding principle that defined him both professionally and as a man. While he sought to put theory into practice as a government press official, he propagated that theory both in his columns and as a teacher. He was a full-time faculty member from 1952 to 1967 at the Carlos Septién García School of Journalism in Mexico City, then gave seminars and weekly lectures until 1973, when he was offered a faculty position in the School of Political and Social Sciences at the National Autonomous University of Mexico (UNAM), where for the last eleven years of his life he taught courses on editing and press office management.

Buendía brought to his practice of journalism a unique combination of experience and personal qualities that early set him apart from other media professionals. His readiness to confront malefactors and defend lofty ideals, including the national integrity of Mexico, can be traced to his upbringing and expressed itself, by force of his personality, in thoroughly distinctive ways. He was combative and given to manly diversions, yet sensitive and deferential where appropriate. He was familiar with firearms and an accomplished marksman. Since his days as a crime reporter for *La Prensa*, he had made a point of cultivating key figures in the police and national security apparatus, including senior commandants and heads of the DFS. For many years, the latter provided him with a courtesy DFS identification badge (*charola*) that allowed him to carry a concealed weapon, which he often did. "If any of my enemies try to take me out," he once famously quipped, "they'd better shoot me in the back, because otherwise I'll take some of them with me." Which is exactly how it happened: four shots, point-blank, from behind.

When Buendía was brazenly slain on 30 May 1984, public opinion promptly concluded that he had been felled either by agents of his own government or by the CIA. He had been a fierce defender of Mexican sovereignty and a relentless antagonist of the CIA. He could not abide what he perceived to be the subversion of Mexico's internal affairs by his country's omnipresent northern neighbor. Nor would he spare those he considered to be domestic enemies, whom he regularly exposed and censured in his widely read Private Network column. Manuel Buendía was an unreconstructed nationalist, more in the nineteenth-century mold than the twentieth, and could easily have been targeted by globalized interests on either side of the U.S.-Mexico border.[1]

There are striking parallels between the May 1984 slaying of Manuel Buendía and the May 1948 murder of CBS News correspondent George Polk, an early Cold War victim whose corpse, bound hand and foot, a bullet hole in the head, was found floating in Greece's Salonika Bay.[2] Like Buendía, Polk had held to a sense of professionalism rendered unfashionable by the political imperatives of the day, for which both journalists paid with their lives. George Polk's transgression had been to reveal the West's betrayal of democratic ideals in the cradle of democracy and the virtual colonization of postwar Greece by the United States and its allies. Buendía's was to have uncovered a covert American assault on the integrity of Mexico, facilitated by the treachery of influential Mexican nationals and U.S. government collusion with international crime figures.

In both cases, there were massive cover-ups that ultimately failed to conceal signs of American involvement. In the case of George Polk, a convenient scapegoat was found in the person of Gregory Staktopoulos, a reporter for the Salonika daily *Makedonia*, who, together with two communist partisans tried in absentia, was convicted of Polk's murder in a carefully staged show trial and sentenced to a life term in prison. Behind the scenes damage control fell to a former Office of Strategic Services (OSS) chief, retired general William J. Donovan, whose main operative in Greece was Col. James Kellis, himself a former OSS officer and, subsequently, an agent of the CIA. The sole objective of U.S. and Greek officials in the Polk affair, Kellis acknowledged many years later, was "to cover up the facts." That was the objective of Staktopoulos's trial, he stated. As a judicial exercise, "it was a shambles."[3]

The cover-up of the Buendía assassination was more convoluted and of longer duration, but it reflects many of the same elements. Here, too, scapegoats were found and convicted in carefully choreographed legal proceedings designed to dissipate public skepticism. In contrast to Gregory Staktopoulos, who was eventually exonerated and released from prison, the Mexican scapegoats were not without guilt. The purpose of their incarceration, however, was to conceal the involvement of more prominent conspirators rather than to punish duly convicted assassins. Manuel Buendía, the evidence suggests, was also the victim of a Cold War conspiracy, but one that still cannot tolerate the light of day.

Accusations of U.S. complicity in the Buendía killing have been adamantly denied from the outset by American and Mexican officials alike. Popular suspicions that the CIA had retaliated for Buendía's repeated exposure of Agency operatives and operations, prominently summarized in his then recently published book *La CIA en México*,[4] reflected widely held assumptions about U.S. behavior abroad but do not stand up to scrutiny. Buendía himself understood the institutional nature of the CIA and would not have accused it of seeking revenge. He was not sanguine, however, about the agency's readiness to kill in pursuit of specific operational objectives. "To date," he observed, "every political killing committed by the CIA has been 'preventive' in nature.

That is, its objective has been to remove individuals who represented serious obstacles to particular plans of the United States or who were damaging those plans directly."[5]

Both the Polk and Buendía affairs are instructive in this last regard. As Kati Marton has written in reference to the Polk case, they reveal something important about ourselves. They are cautionary tales "about us, our government, our media, and our icons." They remind us "that we Americans have very little cause for either smugness or complacency regarding our own behavior during the Cold War."[6]

George Polk, Marton concludes, was killed by a cabal of military, police, and intelligence operatives in the name of national security and the containment of Soviet-inspired communism. So, too, it appears, was Manuel Buendía. In both instances, the operative particulars of U.S. involvement may never be fully documented. What ultimately matters, however, is to establish the fact of that involvement, together with the complicity of local nationals, and to draw the appropriate conclusions.

Manuel Buendía was gunned down during the evening rush hour on the day of an annular solar eclipse. Forty minutes later, recalcitrant Nicaraguan *contra* leader Edén Pastora was the target of an assassin's bomb at a guerrilla camp press conference in southern Nicaragua.[7] That same night Javier Juárez Vázquez, editor of the Coatzcoalcos weekly *Primera Plana*, was shot in the back of the head and left by the side of the road, his mouth sewn shut with baling wire.[8] Three journalists were killed and another eighteen injured in the attempted assassination of Edén Pastora, a blood toll the perpetrators must have anticipated and thus exacted with calculated intent.[9] The grotesque spectacle of Javier Juárez Vázquez's wire-sealed lips, in turn, conveyed an unmistakable warning to local media professionals, while the effrontery with which Manuel Buendía was slain in full public view placed journalists on notice more broadly that caution should be exercised in seeking to expose corruption and political skullduggery.

Whether by design or happenstance, these seemingly disparate acts of violence were related in their common geopolitical context. Taken together, they constituted an intimidating assault on the media in one of the world's most volatile arenas of political contention—an assault quite as important as the individual targets themselves. The Buendía killing, like that of Juárez Vázquez and the simultaneous attempt on Pastora's life, occurred in the larger context of regional power struggles during the 1980s, in which the mass media became a critical factor for the principal contenders. Manuel Buendía was an influential voice of opposition to the foreign policy objectives of the United States throughout the Mesoamerican region, as well as an effective critic of media and publicly visible personages who fostered those objectives. He presented U.S. national security ideologues with what CIA director William Casey euphemistically called "an informational challenge" and, together with other media critics of American policy initiatives south of the border, himself became a target for neutralization.[10]

From the inception of irregular warfare strategies in the early Cold War period, media manipulation has been a standard instrument for the projection of power beyond national frontiers.[11] Successive U.S. administrations have sought to ensure compliant media both domestically and abroad, an objective they have pursued with particular vigor in the strategic neighboring nations of Mesoamerica and the Caribbean basin.[12] In Mexico the number of journalists who met violent deaths in the final decades of the last century soared to levels greater even than those in violence-rent Colombia and Guatemala, reaching almost one hundred in the combined de la Madrid and Salinas six-year presidential terms (*sexenios*) alone.[13]

While few of these deaths had any direct connection to power politics, their coincidence with increased international tensions in the region and the redefinition of geopolitical stakes by Republican administrations in Washington unavoidably imbued them with political significance. Coupled with the strains of a deepening economic crisis in which thousands of media personnel lost their jobs and both print and electronic outlets were forced to retrench, this dramatic increase in violence effectively emasculated much of the Mexican press as a guardian of civil virtue and national integrity. It amounted to a de facto instrument of destabilization that served the narrower interests of power.[14]

Manuel Buendía was not the first journalist to perish in the maelstrom of renewed challenges to U.S. hegemony emanating from Central America during the 1980s, nor was his the only voice of opposition that concerned neo–cold warriors in Washington. Political exiles from various Latin American countries, many of them experienced professionals, joined together in the late 1970s and early 1980s to forge viable alternatives to the region's established foreign-dominated media—alternatives, in the words of a Costa Rica–based news broadcaster, committed to the struggle for peace, justice, and respect for human rights. Radio Noticias del Continente (RNC), an independent shortwave radio station established in 1979 in the little mountain town of Grecia, Costa Rica, was one such alternative, which, because of its censure of authoritarian regimes allied with the United States, provoked the enmity of American national security strategists, who in turn engineered its closure less than two years after it went on the air. "Having broadcast a message of hope, as well as accurate and objective news," the station's director told listeners in a final broadcast, "we necessarily challenged the dictatorial governments of Argentina, El Salvador, Guatemala, Chile, Uruguay, and Paraguay, among others. And of that we are proud."[15]

More to the point, RNC had challenged the new administration of President Ronald Reagan, whose aggressive commitment to reasserting U.S. hegemony in the region opened the sluices of unrestrained violence that would poison the entire decade. The instrument of RNC's demise was a bomb detonated on New Year's Day, 1981, at its Grecia studio, which served as a pretext for Costa Rican president Rodrigo Carazo Odio to shut the station down. The bomb had been placed by Nicaraguan *contras* with ties to the security apparatuses of Argentina and Israel, as well, presumably, to those of the CIA.[16]

Members of the RNC relocated to Mexico City, where they embarked on a still more ambitious venture: the creation of an independent news service devoted to engaged journalism in the spirit of Mexican publicist Ricardo Flores Magón (1873–1922) and Peruvian essayist José Carlos Mariátegui (1895–1930). This new organization came to life under the acronym SIPE, for Sistema de Información y Promoción Editorial (News and Editorial Support System). Three months after the demise of RNC, it already boasted more than thirty correspondents in over twenty countries and was distributing weekly packets of news and commentary to influential media on both sides of the Atlantic. Among its contributors were some of Latin America's most distinguished writers and journalists, including Gabriel García Márquez, Leopoldo Zea, Gregorio Selser, Luis Suárez, and Miguel Ángel Granados Chapa.[17]

The Sistema de Información posed a more serious challenge to White House policy makers than had RNC, for it threatened to reduce U.S. influence over that region's media and thus to undermine public opinion in ways prejudicial to Washington's national security agenda. Its subversive character was confirmed for the Reagan administration when, in April 1981, it took prominent part in an international media event in Managua, Nicaragua, convened to address distorted news coverage of that country's Government of National Reconstruction.[18] Indeed, SIPE promised to serve as an effective resonator for the most articulate voices of Latin American dissent and from the outset enjoyed ready access to mainstream media routinely denied the region's only other alternative news agency, the Havana-based Prensa Latina.

The organization was largely the inspiration of Argentine journalist Valentín Ferrat, who served as its international coordinator and was its driving force. While on a working trip to Guatemala in December 1981, Ferrat was slain by presumed agents of the hemisphere's U.S.-backed national security network. As a consequence, SIPE collapsed, its overly optimistic life shorter by half than that of its ill-fated predecessor, RNC.[19]

Manuel Buendía was not directly associated with SIPE (although his close colleague Miguel Ángel Granados Chapa was), but nonetheless he shared its commitment to progressive causes and, from his privileged position on *Excélsior*'s front page, contributed significantly to the common effort to redefine societal priorities throughout the region. Buendía was, in effect, a weight-bearing pillar in an imposing new edifice of dissenting Latin American opinion that by the 1980s had interrupted the region's political horizon—an edifice, moreover, whose foundations rested on Mexican soil, where its architects enjoyed a degree of mobility and free expression denied them elsewhere in Latin America. It was a structure that Reagan cold warriors could not allow to stand.

Mexico, declared U.S. Southern Command chief Gen. Paul Gorman just three weeks before Buendía was slain, threatened to become "the number one security problem for the United States in the next decade." Mexico, Gorman noted ominously, had become "the hub of subversion for all of Central America."[20] An essential component of that subversion, he and others in the Reagan administration had concluded, were several organs of the Mexican press (e.g., the daily *unomásuno* and the weekly *Proceso*); certain members of the Mexican press corps (first among them Manuel Buendía); and the independent Federation of Latin American Journalists (FELAP by its Spanish acronym), which gave voice to the region's progressive media professionals and was itself affiliated with the Prague-based International Organization of Journalists, considered by U.S. policy makers to be a Soviet bloc front organization and therefore an instrument of communist subversion.

The Reagan administration, according to *Progressive* magazine associate editor Matthew Rothschild, viewed Manuel Buendía "as an enemy of the U.S. government." American officials considered him "a press agent for the Salvadoran rebels and a paid Cuban agent."[21] Buendía's columns did, in fact, reflect sympathy for the Central American insurgencies of the day, and he had once assured a Nicaraguan confidante that he would personally fight alongside the Sandinistas should Nicaragua be invaded by U.S. forces.[22] "I am, and always will be, so long as I have a voice, decidedly in favor of those who risk everything in the struggle to liberate their homeland," Buendía once told former DFS chief Miguel Nazar Haro, referring to Salvadoran and other Latin American political refugees then being harassed by Mexican authorities. "I admire profoundly," he stressed, "those who are willing to bear such terrible witness to their ideas and feelings."[23] Nazar Haro, as we now know, was one of the CIA's most important Mexican assets and a primary conduit for intelligence related to Mexico and Central America.[24]

In many respects, Buendía was an anomaly on the cusp of a geopolitical sea change that would ultimately sweep him away. His sense of solidarity with the national liberation struggles of the 1970s and '80s—which for a time portended an end to neocolonial dependency and a qualitative advance toward more just social arrangements— derived not from an embrace of Marxism but rather from his sense of identity as a product of Mexico's own history. He had an abiding faith in the virtue of popular self-determination within the framework of the nation-state and readily identified with all who shared that faith, irrespective of their nationality. Mexican journalists, he insisted, must remain faithful "to the juridical system that configures the life of the [Mexican] nation and to the social ideas—in a general, not partisan sense—that lead to the democratic governance of our society."[25] This was Buendía's personal and professional credo, a nationalist creed honorably professed in a time and place where national frontiers were already in an advanced state of historical decay, but one, nonetheless, that continued to resonate deeply in the popular psyche and to which policy makers necessarily paid close attention.

Buendía understood evil, corruption, and injustice. He understood oppression. And he abhorred them all, even as he daily moved in their midst. He was not a Marxist in any acceptable sense of the term and did not require ideological dogma in order to distinguish just from unjust. In his eyes, the excruciating oppression against which Argentine youths had rebelled with revolutionary violence fully warranted their armed response; the historic injustice of Central America's exploitative social order more than justified that region's armed insurgencies; and Cuba's solitary struggle to defend its revolutionary experiment from destruction by an imperial neighbor—the same imperial neighbor that, historically, had compromised Mexico's sovereignty—likewise merited his unwavering support.

What set Manuel Buendía apart from his fellow journalists was his vision of journalism as a socially responsible profession governed not by market forces but by the moral requirements of a particular, historically determined society. In a positive, creative way, he believed, media professionals should actively participate in the governance process, not as manipulative instruments of self-perpetuating bureaucracies and alien interests but rather as vehicles of collective enlightenment and informed democratic practice. Some people, Buendía lamented, saw him as an "avenging angel" devoted to denouncing and exposing corrupt officials and evil institutions. But that was not who or what he was, nor, in his view, was it the proper function of professional journalists.

Journalism, as Buendía conceived it, performed a public service, and journalists, especially a columnist like himself, had an ethical obligation to serve and promote society's "highest interest," which he defined as democratic governance. His professional perspective was not, nor could it properly be, partisan. Rather it was "societal," in the sense that as an active social being immersed in a particular societal context, he felt called upon to rise above that context, above the prevailing "social passivity" of others, to comport himself as a "social guide." It was a delicate and demanding role, he cautioned, one that required him to keep his feet firmly planted in reality and to studiously avoid the trap of believing that he (the journalist) was the creator of that reality. Appearances to the contrary, he once told an interviewer, the truly professional practitioner of journalism "is a profoundly humble man," whose basic humility "puts him in touch with the sufferings, opinions, controversies and all those passions, feelings, thoughts, and impulses that are the driving force of our Mexican society, as well as of human society in general."[26]

"Social communication," as Buendía termed it, was as much the responsibility of government as it was of the Fourth Estate, because in a democracy government had a perpetual obligation to conduct a dialogue with its citizenry. He expended a great deal of energy trying to persuade successive Mexican administrations to implement creative public communications policies. Such was his influence and the professional authority with which he spoke that he could, and did, address presidents of Mexico directly on matters of mass communication. One of the most distressing aspects of Mexico's mounting political crisis, he wrote President Miguel de la Madrid early in the latter's administration, was "the government's inability to engage public opinion with a coherent strategy of collective communication." The most serious problem in this regard was "a tiny handful of capitalists" who owned some of the country's leading newspapers, magazines, radio stations, and television channels and who, from a position of influence out of all proportion to their paltry numbers, "confront, oppose, refute, and even negate actions and basic positions of the Mexican State."[27]

Mexico's press and television barons, Buendía opined, "have reached extremes hardly tolerable in a country where the Presidency enforces the laws, protects society at large, and guarantees national security." And no media organization, he observed, was guiltier than the television giant Televisa, which "for many years [had] gravely compromised the sovereignty of the State." It was simply unacceptable, he expressed to de la Madrid, that any group, no matter how powerful or influential, should be allowed to place itself above the laws that govern society. To do so was not only profoundly undemocratic but also "the beginning of fascism." As things then stood, he lamented in remarkably frank language, "we can already see a debilitated State, a do-nothing government, and a President who no longer embodies national leadership."[28]

Central to Buendía's concept of social communication was the defense of Mexican mores, traditions, and identity against the onslaught of a homogenizing transnational market culture propagated most threateningly by Mexico's colossal northern neighbor. What was required, he suggested, was a press corps of skilled professionals imbued with "patriotism, revolutionary mystique, a spirit of public service, and loyalty to the Mexican State." While many would consider such concepts anachronistic, he recognized, "woe are we as a people if we fail to reaffirm them in their original lofty sense!"[29] It was an enlightened view predicated on a basic belief in free will and humankind's ability to make rational choices, one that struck a resonant chord within Mexican society more broadly and whose premises were shared as well by the insurrectionary movements of neighboring Central America.

In promoting these concepts of social communication, Buendía was advancing a potentially effective program of ideological resistance to denationalization and American hegemony. For this reason alone, he constituted an obstacle to the Reagan administration's policy agenda in the region, an obstacle likely viewed with heightened concern when, during the presidency of Miguel de la Madrid, he carried his nationalist message to Mexico's armed forces. It was axiomatic, he told a Secretariat of Defense audience less than a week before his death, that a power vacuum in the nation's government would quickly be filled "by those who serve alien agendas contrary to the proper interests of the State." Mexico, he pointedly observed, had reached a historic crossroads of "external dangers and internal risks" that could only be confronted by preserving unity among a majority of the country's citizens. And nothing threatened that unity more than "being subjected to the constant bombardment of adverse propaganda from media that serve ends contrary to our national interest."[30]

Seventy percent of the international news carried in the Mexican press, Buendía informed his audience of military brass, originated with four foreign press agencies, and a majority of that came from two American agencies, the Associated Press and United Press International. Those agencies, in turn, served political agendas "generally alien to the national interests of Mexico." In the prevailing circumstances of superpower confrontation, Mexico found itself in a part of the globe "dominated by the propaganda of the United States." Recalling the old adage that in war the first casualty is truth, Buendía urged the assembled senior officers to ponder the country's media dependency as a matter of Mexico's national security.[31]

Buendía had developed these same themes on previous occasions before military audiences. Addressing cadets at the National Defense College ten days after the Reagan administration invaded the tiny island nation of Grenada in October 1983, for example, he declared that "such cowardice and insanity required a brutal suppression of the news" and it would be "professional journalists who exposed to the world this latest exploit of Mr. Reagan." Moreover, he added with biting sarcasm, it mattered not a whit who presided over the empire, for "whether Reagan, Bush, or Mondale, they were but different masks—as on Halloween—of the same immutable personality: our beloved Uncle Sam." So long as Mexico was unable to relocate to some other point in the universe, Buendía told the cadets, "we shall remain one of the highest priorities in the plans for propaganda, disinformation, penetration, espionage, manipulation, and appropriation devised by Washington's civilian and military experts." With the exception of a military blockade or direct invasion, he declared, "there is no greater threat to the security of our nation."[32]

In articulating a program of nationalist priorities to Mexico's military leadership, Buendía entered fully into the maw of the national security beast. Appealing to shared cultural references, he sought to persuade the Mexican officer corps to defend national rather than alien interests and reject the notion that national security as defined by American neo–cold warriors had anything to do with the legitimate concerns of Mexico's constitutional guarantors. In effect, he challenged the core assumptions of the prevailing national security ideology propounded by Washington the world over and did so on the United States' own doorstep, where it mattered most.

Moreover, he challenged those assumptions among a coterie of political actors viewed by U.S. strategists as decisive for the implementation of their national security agenda. That he should have access to the upper echelons of Mexico's military establishment must have concerned the Reagan administration even more than his ability to generate a public following from the front page of *Excélsior*. Indeed, Buendía engaged his country's officer corps in ideological dialogue at a critical historical juncture where the military's role in Mexican society was showing signs of political engagement until then precluded by the institutional primacy of civilian rule.

Mexico's twentieth-century military leadership emerged from the Revolution of 1910 with the mission of defending a new constitutional order against internal and external enemies, a narrowly nationalist mission imbued with historic mistrust of the United States. Three generations later Mexican officers were beginning to rethink their role in a dramatically changed and polarized world where, in Buendía's words, Mexicans were subjected to a U.S. propaganda campaign "like caged laboratory animals."[33] In the case of the military, traditional concerns were altered through ideological indoctrination imparted by U.S. instructors in greatly expanded training programs for Latin American officers and special forces.[34] By the time Miguel de la Madrid took office in 1982, more than three hundred Mexican army officers had received training at the U.S. Army's School of the Americas at Fork Gulick, Panama.[35] And that did not include personnel from other branches of the armed forces or from law enforcement, who also were drawn inexorably into the national security mold.

While military and civilians alike publicly dissociated themselves from the institutionalized repression of other hemispheric national security states, and despite the fact that much effort was made to persuade public opinion of the armed forces' unwavering loyalty to civilian authority and the rule of law, it was difficult to ignore the growing readiness of the Mexican military to coerce domestic conformity in an increasingly transnational society. Civilian politicians, for their part, were playing a parallel role in the gradual transnationalization of Mexico, one that gained momentum during de la Madrid's presidency and has continued apace into the twenty-first century. The North American Free Trade Agreement (NAFTA), promoted and ushered past a deeply ambivalent Mexican public by Harvard alumnus Carlos Salinas de Gortari, and most recently the Enrique Peña Nieto administration's successful opening of the long-protected petroleum industry to foreign investment constitute the most striking manifestations of that historic process.[36]

The tensions inherent in so radical a transformation of Mexico's national priorities were especially apparent within the country's governing Institutional Revolutionary Party (PRI), whose hegemonic institutional apparatus had mediated political power in the country for more than six decades. Already in 1980, Mexico City regent and PRI eminence Carlos Hank González remarked to Manuel Buendía that Miguel de la Madrid would be the last president "to assume power peacefully, [because] the existing political system [had] become inflexible." If Mexico failed to devise a more viable political system, Hank had opined, the country would experience domestic upheaval "and perhaps even foreign intervention"—by the United States, he intimated.[37]

Hank's perceptions of political reality proved prescient, as dramatized by the PRI's near loss of the presidency in 1988, the assassination of its presidential candidate Luis Donaldo Colosio in 1994, the Zapatista uprising in Chiapas less than a year later, and the National Action Party's uncontested victory in the presidential election of 2000.[38] There has, of course, been no direct U.S. military intervention in Mexico, although Pentagon planners certainly have contemplated such a contingency, and expectations of intervention in the event of revolutionary upheavals provoked by the conflicts in Central America were not unreasonable. The popular Mexican adage "Before there can be revolution in Mexico, there must be a revolution in the United States" captures well the geopolitical reality of the day. No U.S. administration, then or since, could allow a radical restructuring of power on the United States' southern frontier.

A key component of U.S. hegemonic sway over Mexico was, and remains, the homogenization of Mexican cultural cues within a globalized, emulation-driven value system of Veblenian conspicuous consumption, whose ultimate objective is to constrain our doorstep neighbors in an economic straightjacket. Central to this process of cultural transformation, wrote veteran CIA analyst Brian Latell two years after Buendía's assassination, were "the constant transfusions of alluring images and information from the United States." Mexican television, which imported its programming and advertising primarily from the United States, was "elevating aspirations that for most can probably never be satisfied." According to one survey cited by Latell, schoolchildren in the Federal District knew more about Superman than they did about Mexican national hero Emiliano Zapata. "In an assimilative culture where American football and baseball compete with soccer, Latell observed, "the irony is surely not overlooked by Mexican nationalists—who indulge bitter memories of the secession of Texas and the fight at the Alamo—that the Dallas Cowboys are the favorite team of football fans in the capital."[39]

This approach began to work its Faustian magic among the more affluent of Mexico's swelling middle class in the 1960s and, over the following decades, brought about corresponding changes in the ways, means, and agents of national governance. A new generation of political elites with advanced degrees from U.S. and other "First World" universities gradually replaced traditional old guard politicians in what has come to be called Mexico's "technocratic revolution." President Miguel de la Madrid and his two predecessors, writes Latell, "all rose through the ranks of the federal bureaucracy without ever having been elected to office, working any length of time in the provinces, or acquiring grass roots political experience. Most of the key members of their administrations [were] similarly parochial. In fact," Latell summarizes, "a large percentage of top government and [PRI] officials since 1970 have been graduates of the same exclusive prep schools and public universities, residents of the same plush neighborhoods, and members of the same clubs and social circles in Mexico City. Typically," he concludes, "they are from middle-and upper-middle-class backgrounds, studied at the national university in Mexico City, completed higher studies at prestigious universities abroad, and then immediately found middle or high level positions in the Mexican bureaucracy."[40]

The elevation of Miguel de la Madrid to the presidency of Mexico in 1982 marked the consummation of this "technocratic revolution." It also marked the consolidation of a new civilian power bloc (*camarilla*, or more colloquially, *familia*) within the country's political class, which sparked a bitter, at times violent, factional struggle within the PRI that would end the party's primacy in Mexican politics and radically alter the country's political landscape. Meanwhile, the inauguration of a new National Defense College, the modernization of Mexico's armed forces, and a refocusing of defense planning toward the oil-rich states bordering Central America, together with explicit demands for increased participation in shaping the nation's future, reflected a parallel globalization of ideological perspectives among the Mexican military.[41]

The principal vehicle of ideological globalization, in turn, was private sector mass media, especially the electronic media, which, as CIA analyst Latell clearly implies, unabashedly promoted the interests of transnational capital, often in direct opposition to nationalist policies of the very administrations that licensed them. The television giant Televisa was the salient example, constituting what one critic aptly described as "a vast project of mass stupidification and transnational indoctrination."[42] Manuel Buendía, for his part, considered Televisa a "corporate Frankenstein devoid of societal responsibility" whose "ideological metropolis" lay outside Mexico's national territory. It and other organs of the Mexican press, he told listeners at the National Defense College, formed part of the arsenal available to foreign interests "who threaten our national security by seeking to block our development as a sovereign and independent nation." There was no better proof, he declared, than the "ominous spectacle of Televisa openly applauding the U.S. invasion of Grenada" in what amounted to "a frontal attack on Mexico's foreign policy."[43]

Just weeks before he was slain, Buendía returned to this theme in his Red Privada column, where he argued that failure to regulate Televisa amounted to bad government. Two events occasioned the typically acerbic column: the adoption by commercial sponsors of a mustachioed chili pepper as the emblem of Mexico's national soccer team, and Televisa's prime-time broadcast of a two-part interview with Nicaraguan *contra* leader Edén Pastora. Both events, Buendía wrote, demonstrated the government's inability to fulfill its basic responsibility as guardian of the "culture, traditions, self-respect, and political values that have allowed [Mexico] to survive as an independent and sovereign nation." The government, he protested, "had the legal and moral obligation to veto an emblem that insults and humiliates our country," although in point of fact "the shabby chili with a mustache" would do little more than make Mexicans "once again look foolish abroad." The Pastora interview, in contrast, was a matter of genuine gravity that could lead to "increased domestic tensions and the upsetting of the precarious balance on which rests [Mexico's] position in Central America."[44]

To abet the Nicaraguan counterrevolution from Mexican soil, as the Pastora interview did, was "a suicidal act," suicidal, that is, on the part of the Mexican government, which failed to prevent the interview's broadcast, for it was in reality an offensive act perpetrated by domestic *contras* intent on "undermining Mexico's foreign policy, destabilizing the government, and compromising the country's national security." Televisa, in effect, had "aligned itself with Washington" in a military strategy that was "costing thousands of human lives" and threatening to engulf other countries as well, "including our own." "One can only wonder," Buendía continued, "how a television network can be allowed to assault our national security by exalting Edén Pastora and everything he represents." Pastora's strongest supporters, it seemed, were Televisa and the CIA.[45] The Mexican government, Buendía reiterated, was itself under assault by domestic contras, who, "allied with the government's natural adversaries abroad," sought to destabilize it.[46]

The Mexican state was "fighting in reverse," he told *Excélsior* interviewer Carlos Landeros soon after Miguel de la Madrid won the 1982 presidential election. And, although it was hackneyed to say so, he stressed that whoever fights in reverse "always loses ground to the enemy. That is why the Mexican state now finds itself defenseless against the entrepreneurs, the dollar thieves [*sacadólares*] and the Far Right, because it has already lost stature, already become ineffective, and little by little its adversary makes greater and greater demands, until its only option is to surrender. This is what it's all about, nothing more, nothing less. That is the purpose of the counterrevolution in this country."

Mexico's political system had departed from its original purpose, Buendía believed, having made a fatal compromise with "the grand political hypotheses of the present." Consequently, it had devolved into a system whose sole objective was survival, which it pursued by constantly seeking to cede as few of its vital interests as possible. It was an inherently flawed strategy that could perhaps prolong the system over a period of six or seven decades but in ever deteriorating conditions that would ultimately lead to its demise, as was abundantly apparent in view of its present precarious state. Even within the system, Buendía thought, there was a general consensus that this was the case. Only by returning to the original lofty ideals of the Revolution of 1910, as expressed in Mexico's Constitution of 1917, might it be possible to salvage the country's institutional structure, but that, he predicted, would never happen.

"Personally," Buendía told Landeros, "I am hopelessly worried, more so than ever before. Never have I feared so much for the country's future as I do now, not even in the worst moments of '68; not even in the crisis of '76–'77.[47] In many aspects, we have seen nothing like it for easily a half century." And what most worried him was his perception that the newly elected president, Miguel de la Madrid, would be unable to follow through on his campaign promise to address some of the system's root problems because "objective conditions" would not allow him to do so. Objectively, Buendía observed, de la Madrid would not be able to make even a dent in the country's systemic corruption, nor could he begin to remedy its economic woes "because all the most detrimental features of the economy elude remedy thanks to the plunder, rapaciousness, incredible immorality, and voracity of our commercial sectors." The downward spiral was hastened, he noted, by "an internal dissolution of the state apparatus," whereby economic policy conformed to International Monetary Fund criteria because

Mexico's economic experts "wouldn't dream of fiscal reform to solve the country's need for social justice, as they don't want to upset the rich, who threaten to take their capital abroad and bankrupt the country."

Mexico had been shaken to its very foundations, Buendía warned, and now found itself in a terribly dangerous moment. "I am not generally a pessimist, simply a realist," he remarked to Landeros. Mexicans themselves needed to accept responsibility for the country's troubles rather than looking for excuses elsewhere. "We've gone through an unfortunate period in which we have failed the essential task of planning for the future. We have squandered our resources. There has been a lack of skill and capacity in how the country has been governed, as well as a lack of patriotism on the part of some officials. We've gone from one deception to the next, which I consider the most dangerous offense of all."[48]

Buendía's use of the "*contra*" metaphor to describe the source of Mexico's societal crisis, with its implied links to the larger geopolitical context that had produced similar crises in Nicaragua and elsewhere in the region, was as apt as it is revealing, for in his own voice it establishes him as an active player in that historic conflict. The coincidence of his assassination and the attempt on *contra* rebel Edén Pastora's life occasioned comment at the time and has been remarked on since by those who have chronicled the Buendía case. Whether or not the simultaneity of those two violent acts was in fact coincidental, there are simply too many elements linking Buendía to Central America not to suspect a connection.[49]

2

Under the Carpet

What's clear to me is that it was a professional job [and] that it was done for political reasons, broadly speaking. It was for something that Buendía wrote. It wasn't a crime of passion. It has all the earmarks of a professional, calculated job. It seems obvious that it came from people, or groups of people, who were threatened by what Buendía was writing. That quickly boils the groups down, I think, to four: it was either the CIA, the drug traffickers, the petroleum union, or the Far Right. To my mind, the two most probable are the traffickers and the CIA. It's possible that they worked together or there was some collaboration.

 —Matthew Rothschild, interview with authors, Madison, Wisconsin
 (19 March 1985)

As if mocking Buendía to the grave, yet also ratifying his concerns about foreign control of the media, news of his assassination was disseminated by the major wire services, with a majority of Latin America's newspapers reproducing accounts of his death from United Press International, the Associated Press, and the French wire service Agence France Presse. The significance of Buendía's murder was immediately appreciated by newspaper editors from Bogotá and Lima to La Paz, São Paulo, Buenos Aires, and Santiago. Based on the wire reports, they informed their readers about the Mexican columnist's violent demise with the usual muddle of facts: the victim's age given as fifty-eight or fifty-four; five gunshots were reported, or four; there were two assailants, or one. Quoting from an editorial published in *Excélsior* (Mexico City) the day after the killing, however, most of the region's editors were quick to make this essential point: "The bullets that felled Buendía were aimed not at the man but at freedom of expression."[1]

News of Buendía's killing was reported on page 3 of the *New York Times* in an article by Richard Meislin filed from Mexico City. Meislin got the basic facts of the event right, then in a dozen well-crafted paragraphs contextualizing the columnist's death suggested revenge as the likely motive. "Mr. Buendía's columns made enemies of dozens of powerful people," he wrote. "He received frequent death threats during his career, and he took them seriously." Most recently he had alleged corruption in the Sindicato de Trabajadores Petroleros de la República Mexicana (STPRM), the powerful petroleum workers union, and illegal acts on the part of the former director of the national oil company, Jorge Díaz Serrano, as well as by former Mexico City police chief Arturo Durazo Moreno. "Mr. Buendía also sparred frequently with the United

States Embassy and the Central Intelligence Agency station here," Meislin reported, "charging them with efforts to manipulate the country." He had written a book called *La CIA en México*, "listing the names of a number of purported operatives in the region," and was particularly critical of U.S. ambassador John Gavin for "the extensive amount of time" he spent away from his post.

Buendía's "Private Network" column, Meislin noted, "was 'must' reading for politicians and other people of power in Mexico. He frequently used it to bring to light corruption and wrongdoing in the upper echelons of Mexican Government, labor and business." While Buendía was viewed by some as too often shooting from the hip, "his feisty, acerbic column was generally respected for its ability to break news" not found elsewhere. "His access to top officials was extensive, and his columns often gave reliable clues to the Government's thinking on a current situation, or even one ministry's thoughts about another—something Mexican officials seldom reveal publicly." Buendía's final column, published the day following his death, Meislin concluded, "was a discussion of alcoholism and social deterioration in Mexico. It was titled 'Sick Society.'"[2]

News of the Buendía assassination was also reported in Europe, where *The Guardian Weekly* (London) offered English speakers the first on-the-ground account by the prominent French journalist Jean-Claude Buhrer.

MANUEL BUENDIA: A MAN WHO KNEW TOO MUCH
By Jean-Claude Buhrer

May 30, 1984; at dusk—about 6:30 pm—the neon signs begin to blaze in the celebrated and noisy cosmopolitan zona rosa in the centre of Mexico City. The many hotels in this district—where London street crosses Genoa, Hamburg, Nice and Rome—are full of harassed tourists. Traffic piles up in the narrow roads converging on the Paseo de la Reforma and the Insurgentes boulevard.

In a nearby car-park, a man walked towards his car which was close to his office. Another man approached him from behind and grabbed him by his raincoat. There was the sound of shots and the first man collapsed. The other moved away quickly but without hurrying. Some distance away, a motorcycle got off to a racing start and was lost in the maze of streets. It all happened so fast that the few witnesses to the incident had no time to react. At first sight, it was a murder like so many others in big modern cities. A routine settling of scores?

Yet, once the alarm was sounded, and the first help and policemen arrived, a name burst like a thunderclap and the news spread like wildfire: Manuel Buendia had been assassinated.

Reference to "a man who knew too much" in the title of Buhrer's article suggested a motive other than revenge: Buendía was killed not for what he had written but rather for what he might yet write.[3]

We had spent the first four months of 1984 in San Luis Potosí directing a foreign study program run by the University of Wisconsin. The main publishing event while we were there was José G. González's sensationalist exposé of former Mexico City police chief Arturo "El Negro" Durazo, released the preceding fall and still prominently displayed at kiosks and bookstores throughout the country.[4] Durazo, a childhood friend and protégé of President José López Portillo (1976–1982), participated in the 1970s repression of political activists, then amassed a colossal fortune as chief of the capital's metropolitan and traffic police. He had not escaped the attention of Manuel Buendía and was an early, albeit doubtful, suspect in the Buendía murder.

Buendía's book on the CIA in Mexico was also something of a sensation that winter and spring, and we read it with much interest.[5] We read as well his daily columns in *Excélsior*, including the 3 May column about the mustachioed chili pepper and Televisa's two-part interview with Edén Pastora discussed in chapter 1. The latter was of particular interest to us, as we had watched the Televisa broadcasts ourselves and, like Buendía, were surprised they had actually aired. We left San Luis Potosí for Mexico City the day after this column appeared, continued on to Nicaragua for two weeks' work for *unomásuno*, then returned home to northern California a week prior to the assassination. We learned of Buendía's death nine days later from one of our semester-in-Mexico students, who paid us an unexpected visit while vacationing with his grandparents on the West Coast.

Russell immediately sat down to write an article about Buendía, one with a slant that experience told us would not be acceptable in mainstream media outlets but one he nonetheless thought might offer some insight into the crime's broader ramifications. He submitted it to *People's World*, a progressive West Coast weekly published by the northern California section of the Communist Party USA. *People's World*'s pages were not restricted to party members, and its editorial policy was refreshingly open, which was the same reason Russell had chosen to write for *unomásuno*. Compared to the mainstream U.S. press, these were more nuanced and informative newspapers.

The Buendía homicide was the latest in a series of ominous developments reflecting "the irreversible internal crisis arising from Mexico's dependent relationship with the United States," Russell wrote. Buendía was a maverick who, for over thirty years, had "relentlessly exposed corruption, malfeasance in public office and other assaults on the integrity and well-being of his fellow citizens." While he readily made enemies among the rich and powerful of Mexico, however, enemies who more than once had threatened his life, he was best known "for his implacable campaign against the U.S. Central Intelligence Agency (CIA) and its ubiquitous meddling in Mexico's internal affairs." Buendía had defended his country's independence and national integrity with total commitment and was silenced by enemies of that independence. That there was a CIA connection to his death, Russell ventured, could be doubted "only in defiance of elementary logic."[6]

Managua, 9 May 1984. Wednesday—We are advised by the government press office to be at Sandino International Airport by 1:30 pm. The Honduran government is sending a plane to retrieve the bodies of eight Hondurans killed when their U.S.-supplied helicopter was downed by anti-aircraft fire near the Nicaraguan town of Potosí, on the Gulf of Fonseca. At 2 pm a large blue and white four-engine Honduran aircraft lands with an official delegation which includes Honduran ambassador Isidro Tapia Martínez, Col. Carlos Aguirre Corrales and Lt. Col. Marco Antonio López, chief of the Honduran Air Force. They are met on the tarmac by the chief of Sandinista anti-aircraft defenses, Maj. Raúl Venerio.

Cover of Manuel Buendía's collected writings on the CIA, published six months prior to his assassination.

Foreign press covering this event in sultry 90-degree heat includes NBC, ABC and Canadian television crews, together with print media reporters from Spain, Italy, Belgium, the Middle East and elsewhere. The NBC cameraman flaunts a baseball cap with the insignia of the U.S. 82nd Airborne Division and the inscription: GRENADA WAR GAMES, 1983.

The Honduran delegation enters the airport's protocol lounge to sign release papers. When they return, the transfer of the coffins is effected with dispatch by means of a hydraulic lift aligned with the cargo bay at the rear of the plane. Two covered army trucks containing the remains of the dead Hondurans back up to the lift. Sandinista troops place the gray coffins—orange crosses on their sides—onto the cargo belt. Honduran personnel stow them in the plane's interior. As soon as the coffins are loaded, the Hondurans—faces grim, anger in their movements—slam the doors shut and fly off in hurried retreat.

—S. E. Bartley, journal entry

We accompanied the *People's World* article about the Buendía assassination with a photograph Sylvia had taken of NBC cameraman John Kechele at Sandino International Airport, wearing his GRENADA WAR GAMES baseball cap. It captured well the bias of U.S. corporate media coverage of that tragic conflict. It also reflected the national hubris that allowed American officials to demand in all seriousness, "What gives Manuel Buendía the right to expose CIA agents in Mexico?"[7]

Russell's professional life in these years was governed by the rhythms and demands of an academic career. He was a senior faculty member at the University of Wisconsin's Milwaukee campus and, by training, a specialist in the modern history of Latin America. This circumstance afforded him the opportunity for extensive travel and made possible his journalistic relationship with *unomásuno*, which he had begun in 1980 and would continue until the paper's integrity was compromised a decade later by government intervention. By the time Manuel Buendía met his violent end, our personal and professional contacts in the region were numerous, a circumstance that would greatly facilitate our investigation of his killing.

We commenced our investigation by creating files of available print sources, both crime-specific and contextual. Then, in March 1985, we traveled to Mexico City to conduct our first in-country inquiry into the killing. While there we made several visits to *unomásuno*, meeting with the paper's editor and colleagues in the newsroom to glean their thoughts about the case, above all about how the government was handling its official investigation. Upon our return to Milwaukee we discovered among our accumulated mail the April issue of *The Progressive* magazine, with a cover story about the slaying of Manuel Buendía. Founded in 1906 by the legendary Wisconsin populist politician Robert M. La Follette Sr., this venerable weekly had sent associate editor Matthew Rothschild and a freelance photographer to Mexico City to investigate the Buendía story. Rothschild's report ("Who Killed Manuel Buendía?") was a paradigm of investigative journalism, all the more remarkable for having been conducted in unfamiliar territory under time constraints measured in weeks. Rothschild had sufficient mastery of Spanish to read print sources in the original and to communicate adequately in conversation. He prepared diligently before traveling to Mexico, a country he had not previously visited, then drew on experience and his professional instincts to surmount the cultural and practical obstacles that littered his way.

"May 30, 1984, Mexico City. The moon passed between the Earth and the Sun. It was the day of a solar eclipse," reads the colorful opening of Rothschild's account. "At 6:30 P.M., fifty-eight-year-old Manuel Buendía, Mexico's preeminent journalist, walked down the six flights of stairs from his office, which he jokingly called the Mexican Intelligence Agency. He met his assistant Juan Manuel Bautista Ortiz in the lobby, turned out on Insurgentes Avenue, one of Mexico's busiest streets, and headed toward his gray 1982 Ford Mustang in the parking lot some twenty paces away. He never reached the car."

Buendía's assailant, "a tall young man wearing a black jacket, blue jeans, tennis shoes, and a baseball cap," approached him from behind and fired four bullets from a .38 Super into his back, then "ran down the block, turned the corner, and vanished." Twenty minutes later, "José Antonio Zorrilla Pérez, head of Mexico's Dirección Federal de Seguridad (roughly equivalent to the FBI), arrived to question witnesses and supervise the initial investigation." At Buendía's funeral the following day, "some 2,000 journalists, students, workers, and politicians gathered to pay their respects. Mexican President Miguel de la Madrid and most of his cabinet attended, and the president ordered 'the most thorough investigation' of the crime." Mexican society "was in mourning," Rothschild wrote. "The Permanent Commission of the Congress observed a minute of silence, and the newspapers brimmed with eulogies."

Buendía was more than just a successful columnist, Rothschild observed. In the words of one close associate, he was "an institution of civil society" and "the most influential journalist in the country," comparable to U.S. muckrakers of the stature of Upton Sinclair and Lincoln Steffens. Another friend and colleague likened him to Walter Lippmann. A third described Buendía's assassination as "historic." Nine months after the event, Rothschild noted, the case remained unsolved. "Mexico's leading journalist was rubbed out, and the culprit has not been found."

Rothschild's *Progressive* article made several important contributions to an eventual resolution of the Buendía killing. While much information had already been brought to light by Mexican colleagues, he was the first journalist to synthesize the case in its multiple facets, from the crime's context and form of commission to the unfolding investigations (official and extraofficial), the responses of interested parties, and the most likely hypotheses. His article also announced serious interest in the Buendía case outside Mexico, itself a factor in how Mexican authorities subsequently handled the case. Press freedom had always been a defining concern of the *Progressive* magazine, and the slaying of Manuel Buendía struck Rothschild as an emblematic assault on that freedom. The more he learned about Buendía, he later told us, the more apparent it became that this was a major story and that people in the United States should know about it.

Meanwhile, it was apparent to us that people in Mexico should know about Matthew Rothschild. Twelve days after our return from Mexico City we recorded a ninety-minute interview with him at the magazine's editorial offices in Madison, Wisconsin.[8] We then translated our interview into Spanish, edited it into a logical Q&A sequence, and six weeks later hand delivered it to *unomásuno* back in Mexico City. It appeared

Matthew Rothschild, associate editor of the *Progressive* magazine, Madison, Wisconsin, 1985. (Sylvia E. Bartley)

April 1985 issue of the *Progressive* containing Matthew Rothschild's investigative account of the Manuel Buendía assassination. (Sylvia E. Bartley)

the *Progressive*

APRIL 1985 / $2.50

Who Killed Manuel Buendía?

A MEXICAN MYSTERY
BY MATTHEW ROTHSCHILD

KEENEN PECK:

ADAM CORNFORD:

WILLIAM STEIF:

eleven days shy of the first anniversary of Buendía's death as the lead feature in the paper's Sunday political supplement, *páginauno*. Rothschild's article, we wrote in a brief introductory note, had offered U.S. readers the first serious account of both the facts and political significance of the assassination. The mere fact of calling public attention to the Buendía case in the United States revealed "a clear awareness beyond Mexico's borders of the crime's real transcendence and again underscored the importance of clarifying once and for all what so far has been covered up."[9]

Rothschild managed to interview an impressive array of informants while in Mexico, from Buendía's widow, several of his closest associates, his office assistant Luis Soto, and the parking lot operator who witnessed the shooting to U.S. ambassador John Gavin and a number of Mexican officials familiar with the case, including a veteran intelligence chief and the Federal District's deputy attorney general. Space constraints had not allowed him to comment extensively about these sources in his article, but in our interview with him he offered additional insights that contributed substantively to the growing body of evidence in the case. As important, perhaps, as the sources he talked to were the ones who refused to meet with him, most notably District Attorney General Victoria Adato Green, the person in charge of the official Buendía investigation; DFS director José Antonio Zorrilla Pérez; and Regino Díaz Redondo, editor of *Excélsior*, the paper for which Buendía was writing his front-page Private Network column at the time of his death.

These were not pro forma denials by busy personalities round-filing written requests or not accepting telephone queries. They were obstinate denials of a reporter's equally insistent requests. Rothschild made an especially determined effort to interview Zorrilla. "I tried and tried and tried to talk with him," he told us. "I must have called Zorrilla's office thirty or forty times! I went over there three times and never got past the lobby." Every day, he recounted, "I would call in the morning and then call in the afternoon and try to talk to one of Zorrilla's aides. I would alternate trying to get one of them to give me an entrée. But he wouldn't talk." Rothschild even attempted to arrange an interview with Zorrilla through the Secretariat of Government, which exercised administrative authority over the DFS. There, too, he was thwarted.

It was virtually the same story at the Federal District attorney general's office. Rothschild called "upwards of forty times," trying to get an appointment with Victoria Adato and was turned down flat. No one of authority would talk to him. Two days before he was to return to Wisconsin he called the presidential press office and complained that no one would grant him an interview in Attorney General Adato's office. He had to write the Buendía story, he said, and wouldn't it be in the government's best interest to let him speak with someone there? Within an hour he had an appointment for the following day with Adato's deputy, René Paz Horta. All he got from Paz Horta, however, was the party line: "The investigation continues. We think we'll be able to solve the crime. It's a difficult crime. There are a lot of possible motives. We're narrowing them down." It was the pat, uninformative response to inquiring media representatives repeated monotonously by the authorities over the previous eight months.

More puzzling was the refusal of *Excélsior*'s editor, Díaz Redondo, to meet with Rothschild. "I tried to get through to him on the phone," Rothschild told us, "and it didn't work." Since the *Excélsior* building was not far from his hotel, he walked there one evening and planted himself in Díaz Redondo's outer office for forty-five minutes, trying to get the editor to meet with him. Eventually, the receptionist emerged from the editor's inner office and informed him that Díaz Redondo would not grant an interview. Rothschild had already talked to the paper's chief foreign correspondent, Raymundo Riva Palacio, she remarked, and "he spoke for the paper."

At issue seemed to be the delicate matter of government pressure on the media to exercise restraint in covering the Buendía case. Immediately following the assassination, Díaz Redondo had assigned a small group of experienced *Excélsior* reporters, including Riva Palacio, to conduct an extraofficial investigation of their colleague's death. It was short-lived, and by the time Rothschild traveled to Mexico, Díaz Redondo had terminated the effort, reassigning the group's members to their regular reportorial duties. "There was a lot of pressure," Rothschild quoted Riva Palacio. "The editor was extremely nervous. He told us to be extremely careful. He had been informed that the police had been ordered to follow us." Rothschild had wanted that kind of confirmation from the paper's editor. "I wanted to get the perspective he had both on the killing and also on what pressure was brought to bear on *Excélsior* after the murder," he told us. That the police had been tailing reporters, however, was easily confirmed, as Rothschild and his photographer were themselves followed while pursuing this story.[10]

The issue of government pressure on the media had been made additionally sensitive by accusations in the U.S. press. *Washington Post* columnist Jack Anderson in particular had written about the difficulties confronting Buendía's colleagues. "The Mexican government doesn't hesitate to use its official powers to discourage dissent in the press," Anderson wrote around the time Díaz Redondo was reining in *Excélsior's* Buendía investigators. "One method is to reward favorite newspapers with the lucrative official advertising—and to withdraw or withhold it from papers that step out of line. Another effective control technique is simply to shut off an offending newspaper's imports of newsprint." As for individual reporters, many depended on various forms of government largesse to supplement their meager salaries. "Buendía's murder was a rarity," Anderson noted, "but only because few Mexican journalists are willing to take the risks he did by criticizing the establishment."[11]

Of the Mexican government personages with whom Rothschild was able to discuss the Buendía case, the most interesting was then director general of roads and bridges Fernando Gutiérrez Barrios. Rothschild had been directed to Gutiérrez Barrios by a number of sources who had assured him that if anyone knew anything about the Buendía assassination, it would be either him or his longtime cohort, Miguel Nazar Haro, a former DFS director and key CIA asset who lurked in the shadows of the Buendía case. Nazar Haro was unavailable, ostensibly "out of the country" at the time, but Gutiérrez Barrios consented to speak with Rothschild about Buendía "off the record."

Fernando Gutiérrez Barrios was the gray eminence of Mexico's national security apparatus. A 1947 graduate of the army's prestigious Heroic Military College, he joined the DFS a year or two later, rising rapidly from inspector to deputy director and, by 1968, director. Subsequently he served for a dozen years as undersecretary of government, from which post he continued to oversee DFS operations. "No one in the entire history of [Mexico's] intelligence services," wrote one local authority on the subject, "has ever maintained such absolute control of those services for such a long time as Fernando Gutiérrez Barrios, whose name became synonymous with the Federal Security Directorate."[12]

A relevant and oft-remarked episode in Gutiérrez Barrios's intelligence career entails the 1957 detention of Fidel Castro and some of his 26 of July Movement comrades in Mexico, where they were preparing to return to Cuba to initiate the armed insurgency against the dictatorial regime of Fulgencio Batista. The Cubans' arrest constituted a national security matter and was therefore handled by the DFS. In a notable twist of history, it fell to Gutiérrez Barrios to oversee their brief incarceration—notable, above all, because Gutiérrez Barrios and Castro appear to have taken an immediate liking to each other, with the young Mexican intelligence officer expressing sympathy for the Cubans' cause. He soon had them released, then facilitated their departure from Mexico aboard the now famous yacht *Granma* for its historic voyage to Cuba.[13]

Although over the years Gutiérrez Barrios would work closely with the CIA to monitor Soviet bloc agents, as well as in combating Mexico's own domestic revolutionary organizations, he was knowledgeable about Marxist and socialist theory and appears to have empathized with some of the region's revolutionary figures. He and Castro developed a lasting friendship that the Cuban leader publicly acknowledged at the time of Gutiérrez Barrios's death in October 2000. When Rothschild asked him about allegations that Manuel Buendía had been a paid Cuban asset, allegations emanating from the American embassy and prompted by Buendía's personal association with Castro, the Mexican flatly denied them. It was an informed denial not easily dismissed.

Gutiérrez Barrios's unqualified endorsement of Buendía's good character in the Rothschild interview was also significant, inasmuch as a strong undercurrent of malicious rumor and innuendo swirled around the Buendía case in that first year. Attorney General Adato made a concerted effort to portray Buendía's murder as a crime of passion stemming from either an extramarital liaison or a homosexual imbroglio. It was not a political killing, she declared at a press conference three months after the event. Even while admitting "the great variety of potential suspects, of every type and every sort," she insisted it was not a political killing. "And I state that categorically," she underscored. "Based on what we have seen thus far, it is not of that nature."[14] The sordid rumors about Buendía's sex life, according to Rothschild, also appeared to emanate from the American embassy.

Rothschild included the embassy in his investigative rounds, and what he learned there was equally enlightening, for our own investigation as well as for readers of our *páginauno* interview with him. What most struck Rothschild was the vehemence of the embassy's animosity toward Buendía, from Ambassador John Gavin down. "They really hated the guy!" he told us. The moment he mentioned Buendía to an assistant press attaché on his first visit, he was informed of the embassy's displeasure over press coverage portraying Buendía in heroic terms. "He was no hero," the man averred. "He was a muckraker in the worst sense of the word." (In her grief, Buendía's widow had remarked bitterly that the only place people celebrated her husband's death was at the

U.S. embassy.) In subsequent conversation with press attaché Lee Johnson, Rothschild was informed that Ambassador Gavin despised Buendía, in part because he had himself been the object of Buendía's acerbic commentary.

What rankled most, however, was Buendía's signature practice of identifying U.S. intelligence operatives, typically with addresses and telephone numbers. On the one hand, American officials dismissed him as a shoot-from-the-hip muckraker who had his facts all wrong, while on the other they excoriated him for endangering agents' lives. It was an imperious attitude reflective of a historically skewed power relationship, as though a Mexican national had some ethical obligation to protect the identities of American spies and covert operatives inside Mexico.

"We as an embassy and I as an individual don't look favorably on the elimination or assassination of any human being, whether he be in or out of the press," Gavin remarked to Rothschild. "But you have to understand that Mr. Buendía was patently a man who was hostile to the United States and had many enemies." It was an odd double non sequitur that by itself opened the door to speculation about U.S. complicity in the Buendía assassination. Rothschild had intended to ask the ambassador about the CIA, but Gavin raised the issue unprompted. In answer to a general question about who Buendía's killers might have been, he offered that there had also been allegations of CIA involvement, then dismissed them out of hand. The suggestion that Buendía posed a threat to agency operatives and operations and had been eliminated by the CIA, he insisted, was "patently absurd" and "did not merit a response."[15] Most likely, he said, Buendía had been felled by drug traffickers.[16]

Based on his investigation, Rothschild offered readers four tenable hypotheses as to who might have killed Manuel Buendía: (1) leaders of the STPRM, whom Buendía had accused of massive corruption; (2) the Far Right, concentrated in Guadalajara and also a frequent target of Buendía's "Private Network" column; (3) drug traffickers, whom Buendía had recently denounced as a national security threat; and (4) the CIA, a regular object of Buendía's ridicule and denunciation. As Rothschild readily acknowledged, these hypotheses did not originate with him but rather were shared by virtually all his Mexican informants. They were new to the U.S. public, however, and had the additional merit of being presented for the first time as coherent elements of a clearly explicated criminal inquiry.

One Mexican columnist remarked that, unlike so many who had written about the Buendía case, Rothschild had the great virtue of respecting his reader, whom he invited "to think rather than oversimplify." Within its obvious limits, this writer suggested, our Rothschild interview nonetheless provided "more objective clues and more significant information than hundreds of square meters of biased newsprint." No less interesting, he added, were Rothschild's unreturned telephone calls, which "revealed an entire social context of unanswerable authority."[17]

Rothschild was reluctant to speculate which of the four hypotheses might be the correct one. To do so would be irresponsible, since he had no more facts than what he had included in his article, although most people close to Buendía, he said, thought it was probably the drug traffickers. He had no doubt that the assassination was a calculated professional job and had been carried out for political reasons, broadly speaking.

It was not, he assured us, a crime of passion. All the evidence suggested "that it came from people, or groups of people, who were threatened by what Buendía was writing."

To Rothschild's mind, the odds were weighted in favor of the drug traffickers or the CIA, there being pragmatic political reasons for excluding the Far Right and the STPRM. In a prescient moment, he even considered the possibility that the traffickers and the CIA might have collaborated. Moreover, he remarked, the murder of foreign nationals was hardly beneath the CIA, as the agency "had done things much worse than kill a leading journalist." (Veteran CIA dandy E. Howard Hunt relates in his autobiography how, in 1972, he and G. Gordon Liddy had conspired to assassinate Nixon nemesis Jack Anderson, desisting only when the operation was aborted by Attorney General John Mitchell.[18]) "That doesn't mean they did it," Rothschild observed, "but it is certainly within the realm of the plausible."

Pursuing a theory first proposed by Mexican journalist and historian Héctor Aguilar Camín under the rubric "Ides of May,"[19] Rothschild suggested a possible variant of the CIA hypothesis that would have had as its object "to bring Mexico into line on U.S. Central America policy." Mexico's support of Nicaragua and sympathy for the Salvadoran rebels had "infuriated the Reagan administration," he noted. The Mexican government had "pursued a policy of accommodation with not only their own leftist elements but with international leftist elements," U.S. Southern Command chief Gen. Paul F. Gorman had alleged in congressional testimony. "They have opened their doors to the guerrilla groups in El Salvador, and Mexico City is now becoming the center for subversion throughout Central America." Manuel Buendía openly embraced the Sandinistas, Rothschild wrote, and "kept a sharp eye on the Mexican government's foreign policy, criticizing it whenever it seemed to buckle under U.S. pressure." May 1984 was a month of unprecedented turmoil in Mexico, with multiple U.S. pressures and provocations. He cited Aguilar Camín, who argued that "the assassination was another element in making very clear to the Mexican government its weaknesses and vulnerability."[20]

By the first anniversary of Buendía's death, the broad parameters of the assassination had been established. While much of the groundwork had been prepared by Mexican journalists, it was Matthew Rothschild who most clearly identified the key elements of the case, and it was his preliminary investigation that oriented our own. Unbeknownst to any of us at the time, his speculation about possible linkages among drugs, geopolitics, and the CIA was sound and would eventually provide the motive for much of that era's Mexican mayhem, including the murder of Manuel Buendía.

A final detail in Rothschild's account that had a significant bearing on the case was a passing reference in his *Progressive* article to "a secret, special commission to investigate Buendía's murder" that had been appointed by President de la Madrid and was headed by presidential aide Samuel del Villar. Rothschild learned of this executive investigative group from an anonymous source and tried to follow up on it, but del Villar would not talk to him. "I called his office so often that his secretaries would abruptly cut off the conversation," he told us. At first he had concealed his real purpose by saying that he wished to speak with del Villar about corruption and the president's ongoing "moral renovation" campaign. Unable to get a foot in the door that way, he told the aide's secretary straight out that he wanted to discuss Buendía's murder and del Villar's role in investigating it. "Well, how do you know about that?" she demanded, then cut him off. Rothschild even tried calling del Villar at his home but failed to reach him there as well. When he met with Deputy District Attorney General René Paz Horta on his final day in Mexico, he asked about the president's secret commission and Paz Horta denied there was any such group. Investigation of the Buendía case, he assured Rothschild, was the exclusive domain of the district attorney general's office.

When Rothschild's article appeared with explicit mention of del Villar's secret investigative group, however, including statements that Buendía had met twice with DFS chief Zorrilla the week before his murder to discuss the names of government officials allegedly involved in drug trafficking and, moreover, that the presidential investigators had actually identified the triggerman, Victoria Adato was livid. Even before the April issue of *The Progressive* reached U.S. magazine racks (obviously, she had received an advance copy), her office issued a blistering news release to the press denying that any of the guilty parties in the Buendía killing had been identified. What *The Progressive* had published about the case was "irresponsible yellow journalism," fumed an official spokesman for Adato. Its purported facts were "totally false and without foundation." In a transparently hollow threat, Adato's office promised to take "appropriate steps" to make sure that the purveyors of such spurious information were appropriately penalized.[21]

Unwittingly, Rothschild had touched a sensitive nerve among Mexican authorities responsible for the Buendía case. At issue was a multiplicity of often competing investigations about which the public knew little or nothing—investigations that in effect served to cover up rather than solve Buendía's murder. As we shall recount in greater detail below, one of those investigations was taking place inside Adato's own shop under the direction of CIA asset and old Gutiérrez Barrios associate Miguel Nazar Haro, separately and apart from what then passed for the "official" investigation. That Adato's office responded to Rothschild's article at all is as surprising as it was clumsy, for it only called attention to what clearly was meant to be concealed. In passing that way, Rothschild had inadvertently kicked back one corner of the authorities' soiled carpet, and what he revealed beneath it could not be swept away.

3

Legwork

I must say that it makes me proud to be one of the few Third World reporters who have hunted down one or another of these [CIA] spies. And the method for trapping them is simple: You have to read, make notes, keep files and have patience. Soon a fact emerges that sheds new light on others that seemed disconnected, and then the profile of a subversive espionage agent appears before the reporter's eyes. It's like completing a puzzle. There is always one piece that gives meaning to the rest.

—Manuel Buendía, *La CIA en* México (1984)

So far from God and so close to the United States, goes the popular Mexican lament. It alludes, of course, to the inherent power imbalance between the two nations and the historic depredations of the United States against Mexico. But its deeper import lies in the opening allusion to God's absence, a barbed reference to Mexican nationals complicit in their own subjugation—Faustian *malinchistas* who, like Cortés's Indian mistress Malinche, willingly sell themselves to their imperial masters. The psychology of these cultural collaborators is complex. Its earliest manifestation was in the statuary of Mexico's colonial churches, exquisite representations of Christian apostles and saints coerced from Indian artisans who artfully concealed sculpted likenesses of their own deities within the venerated statues' hollow interiors. At Mass the subjugated and their subjugators appeared to worship the same heavenly hosts, yet the truth was never quite as it seemed.

Over time the mestizo issue of the Spanish conquerors and their Indian concubines transformed the old Viceroyalty of New Spain into the national mosaic that is now Mexico. They were the products of force and violation, of *la chingada*, that cultural, as well as physical, rape whose psychological injury propagated itself throughout the populace down the centuries. It reveals itself today in the language, in the country's customs and mores, in the social masks people wear to conceal their inherited vulnerabilities. It is reflected as well in distinctively Mexican attitudes toward authority, sex, family, and death, all deeply rooted in the formative experiences of medieval Castile and pre-Columbian Mesoamerica violently fused at the outset of the modern era.

In this cultural fusion parallel habits and patterns were reinforced, most notably ritualism, corporate privilege, administrative centralism, and ready recourse to force. Beliefs and practices alien to the conquering Castilians were directly suppressed, often brutally, but never entirely eradicated. As miscegenation subsumed virtually the entire populace, mental boundaries blurred with relict elements of Amerindian thought finding subtle expression even in the dominant classes of Mexican society. The bronze-skinned

Virgin of Guadalupe may be the most ubiquitous reflection of this composite mental universe, but she is only one and not necessarily the most transcendent.

Beneath the telltale complexion of the skin, no matter its occasional whitening, Mexicans carry a collective memory of pre-Columbian grandeur that continues to infuse their sense of self in a world today ruled by new imperial masters. In the core metropolis of their nation, Mexico City, they move among an architectural maze of colonial edifices, European-inspired public buildings and private mansions, futuristic cubes and towers, congested boulevards, reclusive plazas, and ever-metastasizing slums, all overlying the earlier Aztec metropolis of Tenochtitlán, which Spain's Catholic kings sought but failed to obliterate. Over the years architectural remnants of the original city have resurfaced at construction sites and in the excavation of the Federal District's sprawling subway system. They are now carefully preserved as public archaeological monuments both above and below ground, some even incorporated into underground Metro stations.

Like other twentieth-century visitors from abroad, we would access this urban crazy quilt through Benito Juárez International Airport on the Federal District's northeastern edge. Avoiding the transportation hawkers in the arrivals hall, we would hail a curbside taxi for the twenty-minute drive to a discreet hotel on Calle Guerrero. The Hotel Mónaco faced the Plaza de San Fernando, a small square with stone fountains, a faux Roman pergola, and pollution-blighted flora just a short walk from the central Alameda. Benito Juárez's remains reposed in a parish pantheon at the north end of the plaza, while an immense painted likeness of the national icon's Zapotec countenance gazed out over the immediate environs from the windowless rear wall of an adjacent building.

The Mónaco was an unassuming seven-floor hostelry run by Spaniards and frequented by Petróleos Mexicanos (PEMEX) employees. It was not a hotel that attracted First World travelers, with the occasional exception of budget-conscious youths from the United States and Europe. The rooms were small but clean with tiled bathrooms, televisions, and rotary dial phones. Those facing the street were noisy. Interior rooms had a window that opened onto an air shaft, which offered a different cacophony of nocturnal sounds. Large tippable water jugs sat on stairway landings, for city water was not considered potable, as no one knew precisely where it came from or why it still flowed from faucets and shower heads, portions of the historic mains through which it ran dating back a century or more. There was a diminutive but serviceable elevator, adjacent parking garage, and, to one side of the hotel entrance, a small lounge with upholstered easy chairs, a television set, and a large window that looked out on Guerrero Street.

Russell had first been introduced to the Mónaco in 1978 by a travel-savvy colleague from the University of Wisconsin, found it convenient, and would put up there whenever he was in the Federal District. There were eateries, bookstores, and newspaper kiosks within easy walking distance, as well as the Hidalgo Metro station a half block away. The Metro defined the outer limits of our daily universe within the larger galactic expanse of that improbable megalopolis. The Hidalgo station gave us access to Línea 2, operating between Cuatro Caminos on the Federal District's western edge and Tasqueña in the city's south-central quarter, as well as to the north-south Línea 3, which ran from Indios Verdes to Universidad, at the edge of the National Autonomous University's massive Ciudad Universitaria campus. The editorial offices of *unomásuno* were located three miles south of Chapultapec Park in the Noche Buena–Mixcoac district, which we accessed via Lines 2 and 6. From Línea 2 we would transfer at Tacuba (two stops before Cuatro Caminos) to the north-south Línea 6, operating between El Rosario (Rosary) and Barranca del Muerto (Dead Man's Gulch).

San Antonio, two stops before the end of the line at Barranca del Muerto, was the closest Metro station to *unomásuno*. We would walk east along San Antonio Avenue, then south one block on Revolución and east again for several blocks along the quieter Calle Tintoreto until it met Rodin, a north-south street bordering the mammoth Plaza México bullring. From there it was another two blocks south on Rodin, right two short blocks on Holbein, then left down Correggio, a dead-end street of upscale residences, glass-shard-topped walls, bougainvillea, and barking guard dogs. At midblock a no parking sign warned belligerently "Se Ponchan Llantas Gratis" (Tires Flattened Free of Charge).

Correggio made an *L* to the left before it reached its dead end. The *unomásuno* offices were tucked into a nondescript split-level structure on the short leg of the *L*, what Mexican postal authorities and city planners call a *retorno*. The paper's official address was Primer retorno de Correggio, 12—although so far as we could ever determine there was no second *retorno*. Like the rest of the neighborhood, the building was enclosed behind a protective wall, minus the embedded glass shards, and we would have to present our distinctive, leather-encased ID badges (*charolas*) at the security booth before entering. Typically, we would arrive in the evening to meet with the paper's editor, Manuel Becerra Acosta, who preferred working late while the next day's edition was being put to bed. Evenings were generally the best time to see our reporter colleagues as well, as they wrapped up articles for the next day's paper.

Frequently we would have supper at El Potro Argentino, a nearby Argentine restaurant, before going on to *unomásuno*. Their *parrillada* was authentic and for Russell a pleasant connection to a country where he has deep personal ties. El Potro also reflected the large Argentine exile presence in Mexico, swelled by Argentina's "dirty war" waged by its military from 1976 to 1983, during which thousands of civilians suffered the excesses of state terrorism under successive military regimes. As noted in chapter 1, some of those exiles exerted a palpable influence on the Mexican press, and they were very much in evidence at *unomásuno*. Becerra Acosta's private secretary, Angélica, had fled Argentina when her husband was detained and disappeared by the country's repressive security apparatus. The paper's international editor would return to Buenos Aires after the military was ousted and civilian rule restored to become a founder of the daily newspaper *Página/12*, a new genre of publication clearly influenced by *unomásuno*, in format as well as philosophical outlook.

Both papers sought to engage their readers in a sober, fact-based consideration of current events, and both elevated journalistic standards in their respective countries to new heights. The essence of their shared approach to the news was conveyed by *unomásuno*'s novel name: *one* (the reader) plus *one* (the paper) equals public enlightenment, a variation on Manuel Buendía's notion of government-media dialogue as an essential component of democratic governance. Paper and reader, *unomásuno*'s founders proclaimed, must be equal participants in the public quest for informed views, hence the lowercase, boldface *unomásuno*.[1] The same journalistic criteria informed *Página/12*, albeit without the ideogrammic flourish.

The dirty war that produced this cross-fertilization of Mexican and Argentine journalism also touched Manuel Buendía. In early 1978, he exposed the presence in Mexico of a team of assassins sent by Argentina's military junta to liquidate exiled opponents. In mid-January of that year, he reported that Mexican authorities had detained three Argentine subjects who, in the course of eight days of "exhaustive interrogation" by "discourteous and rude Aztec cops," revealed the full details of their mission. As Buendía sardonically expressed it, "they sang better than Carlitos Gardel," Argentina's most renowned tango artist.[2]

The López Portillo administration chose not to make a diplomatic incident of the affair and refrained from any public comment, preferring instead to let Buendía expose the Argentine generals, which he did with gusto in his own inimitable style. "The Argentine military junta now knows with certainty," he wrote, "that Mexico is not a hospitable country for foreign agents sent to murder or kidnap exiles." Those "discourteous and rude Aztec cops" who had conducted the "exhaustive interrogations" of the junta's assassins meant to give the three detainees a taste of the treatment routinely lavished on prisoners in Argentina. Presumably, Buendía suggested, Gen. Leopoldo Galtieri's position as commander of military operations against Argentina's armed insurgents had been weakened by this incident, since no operation in that country's ongoing civil war had been "more stupidly conceived or carried out." While Mexico would treat the entire affair as a minor police matter, he cautioned, Argentine authorities should keep in mind that it had produced a fat file of confessions, photographs, and other evidentiary material, which could be used against Argentina in the future.[3]

Unomásuno had published the first partial reports of the incident twelve days earlier based on information leaked from government sources and an impromptu telephone conversation with a Galtieri subordinate ingeniously schemed by four of the paper's reporters. Buendía's role was to verify the sources and give full exposure to the violation of Mexican sovereignty. To accomplish this, he conducted a clandestine interview with Tulio Valenzuela, an exiled leader of the Argentine insurgency and presumably a target of the detained assassins. Buendía went to that interview holding a Browning 9 mm pistol between his legs all the while he was being driven to the prearranged location, returning it to his waistband only after reassuring himself of his surroundings once he'd arrived. He grilled Valenzuela hard until he was persuaded of the man's veracity, then, together with information obtained from his DFS and other official sources, he wrote the column that sorely displeased the Argentine generals.[4]

Buendía's involvement in this affair introduced a larger contextual element to the puzzle of his own assassination six years later, as well as a new set of potential players. The dirty war was part of a continentwide campaign to eradicate radical challenges to the established order, challenges attributed to the Cuban Revolution, which numerous insurrectionary movements were inspired to emulate, and by extension to the Soviet

Union, at the time a superpower guarantor of socialist regimes and movements world-wide. The campaign had begun in the mid-1960s with a military takeover in Brazil, then spread successively through the 1970s and early 1980s to Bolivia, Chile, Argentina, Central America, and Mexico. Its ideological and material mentor was the United States, which sought to reconfigure the hemisphere's geopolitical map in accord with its own superpower imperatives.[5]

In the early stages of the U.S.-managed *contra* war against Nicaragua's Sandinista government, the Argentine military provided advisers to train counterrevolutionary combatants at the same time as it was an active participant in the Chilean-engineered Operation Condor, a collaborative arrangement among South American state security apparatuses to pursue opposition political activists across national frontiers. The Condor network also interfaced with the CIA, as well as with the security apparatuses of other nonmember governments, including Mexico and Israel.[6] Manuel Buendía, we realized, could have been killed by operatives from any quarter of this nefarious cabal, even Argentina, whose discredited dirty warriors might have relished the opportunity to administer payback for Buendía's 1978 disparagement of their military leadership.

In the 1980s, *unomásuno*'s editorial plant was a pre-computer-age operation illuminated by creative thinking and an architecturally innovative edifice. The building was an extended warren, only a few areas of which we ever accessed. We could hear the rotary presses working on a lower level somewhere off to our left as we entered, and, on the few occasions when we were there during daylight hours, we observed huge rolls of newsprint being delivered to the same end of the building. The cashier's window where we collected modest pay for our submissions was to one side of the hardwood-floored foyer, while opposite the entrance stairs led to the upper levels. The newsroom, with its clutter of reporters' desks and clacking manual typewriters, occupied a first-floor wing (second floor by American count). Becerra's office suite was on the level above.

Whenever we'd arrive from the United States Russell would bring in typescripts ready for publication. On other occasions, when returning from reporting trips to Central or South America, he would type our articles there in the newsroom while Sylvia had her rolls of Tri-X film processed by the paper's photo department. Although we were something of a curiosity by virtue of our nationality, our reception at *unomásuno* was always collegial and without a hint of the dismissive chauvinism expressed toward us by government officials or an occasional member of the local press whose personal agenda we seemed to challenge. One piece that Russell wrote under the heading "Gringo no soy" struck an especially felicitous note among our *unomásuno* colleagues. "Not all Americans are gringos," he expressed, "nor do all gringos speak English." It was attitude and outlook, not nationality, that inspired the derisive epithet, and there were Mexican gringos, too.

Sylvia's images were likewise well received, for both their quality and the evidence of our ability to move successfully in difficult, even dangerous, situations. Her photos illustrated many of our submissions and were used for other stories as well. One image, a particularly dramatic shot of crumpled fuel storage tanks destroyed by CIA sappers in Nicaragua's Corinto Harbor, was used in a 1986 book on Nicaragua by *unomásuno*'s German correspondent, Heinz Dieterich.[7]

Most of our time in the Federal District was spent in a central zone marked by Chapultepec Park on the west, the Zócalo on the east, Plaza de las Tres Culturas on the north, and the Fundación Manuel Buendía near the Cuauhtémoc Metro station on the south. The key institutional bodies concerned with the Buendía case were located within that six-square-mile area: the Federal District Attorney General's Office, the Federal District Judicial Police (PJDF), the Federal Judicial Police (PJF), INTERPOL, the DFS, the Secretariat of Government, the president's official residence (Los Pinos) and offices (Palacio Nacional), and the U.S. embassy. So, too, were the editorial offices of *Excélsior*, *La Jornada*, and the weekly current affairs magazine *Siempre!* (The news weekly *Proceso* was produced at a more secluded address in the Del Valle district, not far from *unomásuno*.) Also within these core perimeters were Buendía's office, the assassination site, the Zona Rosa, and the AMI building, which housed the Fundación Manuel Buendía and two or three foreign press bureaus.

Our investigative routine in Mexico City combined specific tasks (interviews, pursuit of leads, acquisition of documentary evidence, comparing notes with local colleagues, etc.) with a focused street-level scrutiny of current Mexican affairs. We would typically begin our days at the Café París, a popular neighborhood eatery across the plaza from our hotel where we developed a particularly pleasant relationship with one of the waitstaff, an older man by the name of Jacobo, with whom we shared regular banter and repartee about everything from the state of the world to health, family, and human foibles. It was Jacobo who first alerted us to the presence of plainclothes police at nearby tables.

We never knew for certain which government entity the agents were with, but their appearance and demeanor suggested state security. They were well dressed in neatly pressed slacks, polished boots, and tailored leather jackets and carried briefcases. After we had been at the Buendía investigation for a while, one or another of them would make a point of greeting us on their way out—"Buenos días, señores"—a thin smile spreading beneath an equally thin mustache. Jacobo was not amused and repeatedly warned us to be careful in Mexico. Former CIA dissident Philip Agee once put it more colorfully, warning us to "Be careful they don't take you for a ride to Toluca," which in the local argot meant a one-way drive in the night.[8]

The Café París was almost equidistant between the Interpol offices at 81 Soto Street, several blocks northeast of the Plaza de San Fernando, and DFS headquarters a few blocks to the southwest. The man in charge of the Soto Street address was Florentino Ventura Gutiérrez, a larger-than-life veteran of Mexican law enforcement who began his career in 1948 as an agent of the newly created DFS, rose to become head of the Federal Judicial Police, then was placed in charge of a special investigative group for national security and other major cases directly under the attorney general of the republic. He worked closely with the CIA in the antisubversive campaign of the 1970s and 1980s and was considered by some to be the toughest cop in Mexico.[9] We would interview Ventura about the Buendía case in November 1987. Ten months later he was dead, apparently by his own violent hand, although rumors persisted that his suicide had been staged by powerful but unnamed figures about whom he possessed compromising information.[10]

DFS headquarters occupied a blocky four-story edifice on the southeast corner of Ignacio Ramírez and Avenida de La República, where it looked out on Republic Square diagonally across from the massive domed Monument to the Revolution of 1910, which some wits said had been built to entomb that historic event. It was easy enough to view both structures as symbolic of a moribund system in the throes of sweeping change. Six months after our May 1985 trip to Mexico City the DFS had ceased to exist, the victim of its own rampant corruption and lack of effective institutional control. Its head, José Antonio Zorrilla, had been eased out following the February 1985 abduction of American Drug Enforcement Administration (DEA) agent Enrique Camarena because of manifest DFS collusion with the Guadalajara drug traffickers. Initially, Zorrilla had been given the opportunity to run as a PRI candidate from the state of Hidalgo to the national Chamber of Deputies, but so many DFS irregularities came to light that within a month his candidacy was withdrawn and he was allowed to go into exile in Spain. His strongest defender had been Government Secretary Manuel Bartlett Díaz, but even Bartlett, whose own political ambitions included the presidency, could not ignore Zorrilla's multiple liabilities.[11]

President Miguel de la Madrid, for his part, had long expressed an interest in modernizing and professionalizing Mexico's intelligence and national security services and expressly asked the man he appointed as Bartlett's undersecretary, Jorge Carrillo Olea, to determine what would be required to achieve that goal. Normally, the undersecretary of government would have exercised direct oversight of the DFS, but Bartlett Díaz explicitly retained that function for himself. Carrillo Olea did what he could under the circumstances. When the DFS house of cards finally collapsed, it was Carrillo Olea who oversaw the process with Bartlett's ready consent. Ironically, the collapse was both figurative and physical, inasmuch as the directorate's headquarters building had been rendered uninhabitable by the magnitude 8.1 Mexico City earthquake of 19 September 1985, just ten weeks before the institution's official abolition.

The DFS was replaced by presidential order with a Directorate of Investigation and National Security (DISEN), which would in turn become the Center of Investigation and National Security (CISEN) during the administration of Carlos Salinas de Gortari, both entities having been conceived as intelligence organizations without enforcement authority. To symbolize the break with the old DFS and emphasize the new sense of elevated purpose, DISEN's founding director, Pedro Vázquez Colmenares, had a statue of Benito Juárez cast from recalled DFS badges.[12] The transition was not entirely smooth, however, with frictions arising from the distinct mentalities of personnel drawn from the DFS, on the one hand, and the Secretariat of Government's Political and Social Investigations Directorate (IPS) on the other. Such tensions occurred in the CIA as well and invariably arose when the divergent purposes of intelligence and covert action were folded into the same organization. (When William Casey became Ronald Reagan's director of central intelligence, analogous frictions developed within the CIA's covert operations branch, where experienced professionals balked at the often rash, bend-the-rules operational style resurrected from Casey's World War II experience in the OSS.[13]) As already noted, the CIA had been closely associated with the DFS from the latter's inception and would remain so with DISEN and CISEN, whose organizational charts were developed from those of the CIA and Israel's Mossad. The Israelis, for their part, played a direct advisory role in the creation of CISEN, a detail of interest for the present account given Israel's regionwide involvements in the 1970s and 1980s and Mossad's shadowy appearance now and then over the course of our Buendía investigation.[14]

By the time of our first investigative trip to Mexico City in March 1985, ex-DFS director Zorrilla Pérez had already left the country for Spain and the directorate was in the final throes of institutional dissolution. It still existed when we submitted our Rothschild interview to *unomásuno* the following May, but on all our subsequent visits state security matters were being handled first by DISEN, then by CISEN. Since these post-DFS agencies had been relocated to a sixteen-acre campus complex on the Federal District's southwestern edge, it seems unlikely that any of their operatives would have been taking breakfast regularly at the Café París, unless, of course, they were on assignment in that part of the city. More probably the plainclothes officers we observed were with Florentino Ventura's special unit of *federales* out of the Soto Street office or perhaps Federal District *judiciales* from downtown.[15] Whoever they were, police surveillance of journalists pursuing the Buendía case had never been tasked exclusively to the DFS and continued unabated following the directorate's demise. It was especially intense during the mid to later 1980s, but we were aware of it even after the government officially closed the case in 1989.

> Mexico City, 14/V/85. Martes—A night of broken sleep . . . TV blaring until the station goes off the air, an old Jimmy Stewart movie . . . a man coughing his guts out into the air well . . . occasional rolling thunder in the hot, still night. Dozing under a sheet fitfully as neighbors shower, answer phones. . . . At 8:30 our phone rings. It's Luis Suárez, well-known journalist and author. He can meet with us briefly at 12:15 near the Monument to the Revolution. He is preparing a TV program and has little time. But we will meet one another and hopefully next time will be less hectic.
>
> We breakfast at Café París. Huevos revueltos a la mexicana—the green chile chopped into the eggs bites back relentlessly. Then *café con leche* with the morning papers: *Excélsior* and *unomásuno*. And frequently others: *El Día, Así Es, La Jornada, Punto, Proceso, Nexos.*
>
> Back in the hotel, phone calls to line up the day. Then on to Librería Reforma across the street from the *Excélsior* building, the original edifice now sinking into the ancient Texcoco lake bed at a pronounced angle. Heavy traffic streams by on Reforma, buses belching black clouds of diesel, swarms of taxis and *peseros*, compact cars of all descriptions and colors of the rainbow. They roll the daytime thunder, which stops with the red lights, then rolls again with the green. Our table near the large windows of the bookstore's café offers plenty of light to read and write. It is a good staging area for us, with books floor to ceiling and an interesting clientele of students, poets and businessmen.
>
> —S. E. Bartley, journal entry

Our daily routine in Mexico City was like that. On the surface much of what we did every day seemed unrelated to our primary investigative tasks, and yet the opposite was actually the case. Context was everything—the context of Buendía's killing, of course, but also the context of all that followed. We scoured the press for clues and news while generally ignoring the electronic media, where chances of encountering anything of substance were minimal. Buendía had been a devotee of the printed word, and it was in the print media that his professional associates were most likely to provide relevant information.

This extended to books, which led an elusive life all their own. We searched for them relentlessly in the left-wing bookshops on Avenida Juárez and along Calle Independencia, in the upscale outlets of the Zona Rosa and the Sanborns department store chain, in used-book stalls, and even among the offerings of floating street vendors, where every now and then a relevant volume would appear. We did this throughout our Buendía investigation—from Mexico City and Milwaukee to Moscow, Havana, Santa Barbara, and Berkeley, even in the magazine and paperback aisles of supermarkets and pharmacy chains across the United States, as well as in airport concourses. Also in the digital ether of the web. It was total alertness to the serendipity of evidence and information, which in cases like this often emerge in the most improbable places and when one least expects.

The Centro Cultural Librería Reforma, a combination café and book mart located on the north side of Paseo de La Reforma in the long block between the National Lottery building and Cristóbal Colón Circle, was an especially propitious venue from which to take the pulse of post-Buendía Mexico. It was a large, open gallery space similar in concept to, but without the cultural pretentions of, the middlebrow bookshop cafés then beginning to appear in tony neighborhoods of U.S. cities, or the Borders and Barnes & Noble mega book marts that would become hallmarks of American malls. The Centro Cultural was a more cerebral space, where people came in pursuit of mental stimulation and enlightenment—alone with a book or in search of a book; in twos and threes for conversation over coffee, beer, and perhaps a light meal; or in small groups for an afternoon of dialogue about the pressing issues of the day.

Two-thirds of the space was taken up by books, tens of thousands of books, some displayed flat on table surfaces, most organized on ground-floor and balcony shelving. Subject matter was broad and eclectic, with an excellent selection of current affairs titles relevant to our investigation. The remaining third of the locale was occupied by the café, which served as our primary work space, since our quarters at the Mónaco were too Spartan for such use. We spent time there almost every day, reading, writing, prioritizing investigative tasks, strategizing interviews, and evaluating informants. We left from there for our interview with Luis Suárez.

The *Siempre!* offices, where we had agreed to meet, were on a quiet street just off Plaza de la República, an easy walk from the Centro Cultural. Luis Suárez was an imposing presence in Mexican media circles, a refugee from the Spanish Civil War who, like more recent refugees from Argentina's dirty war, had elevated the standards of news reportage in his adopted country. He wrote for the periodical press, produced nonfiction books, and covered current affairs on television. He had access to prominent figures of the day, both in Mexico and abroad, and was an experienced foreign correspondent. One of his most notable accomplishments was a 1980 reporting trip to Afghanistan during the Soviet occupation, which resulted in an insightful little volume published in 1983 under the title *La otra cara de Afganistán* (The Other Face of Afghanistan).[16]

Suárez was active in FELAP and shared Manuel Buendía's commitment to socially responsible journalism. He had written for *unomásuno* until December 1983, when he joined fifty other staff members in resigning as a consequence of an internal dispute with the paper's editor, Becerra Acosta, whom they accused of abandoning *unomásuno's* original lofty purpose. The dispute would give birth to a new daily newspaper, *La Jornada*, for which Suárez also wrote. For our part, as foreigners we had opted not to involve ourselves in *unomásuno's* internal fray and continued to write for the paper, which Suárez seemed to respect. Our affiliation was never an issue in meeting with him or in conducting the interview. He was much more interested in the matter at hand: Manuel Buendía.[17]

We discussed the case for about an hour. There had, Suárez noted, been two assaults on Buendía: the physical attack that killed him, followed by a clumsy attempt to assassinate his character. The malicious rumors about Buendía's personal life only confirmed the political nature of the crime, he insisted, which could not be separated from its political context. The assassination's immediate purpose was to intimidate Mexican journalists, an objective, he felt, it had failed to achieve. Having said that, Suárez preferred not to comment on Zorrilla Pérez, recently departed into Spanish exile. By way of analogy, he ridiculed Ronald Reagan's Hollywood sheriff tendency to divide the world into "good guys" and "bad guys," then added, in an apparent allusion to Zorrilla, that "the bad guys do exist, which complicates matters." The DFS, while institutionally wounded, remained functional and dangerous, and the physical presence of its headquarters bunker just a few blocks away seemed to give Suárez pause in what he was willing to say for attribution.

As for possible CIA involvement in the Buendía killing, who could say? The American embassy and U.S. intelligence operated with such sophistication in Mexico, Suárez observed, that it was impossible to prove what many people suspected. There was not a single, monolithic CIA, but rather "sub-CIAs," whose cellular structure effectively isolated any given operational group from the agency itself. Was there any substance to warnings we had received not to probe too deeply into the Buendía assassination? Yes, he thought there probably was. The authorities would not be happy, he said, about foreign investigators looking into the case on Mexican soil. Mexican journalists, for their part, would in the main not allow themselves to be intimidated and would actively continue to pressure the government for a transparent resolution of the Buendía killing, as, he predicted, we could see for ourselves a few days hence on the first anniversary of Buendía's death.

The previous evening we had met with Héctor Aguilar Camín, editor of the monthly magazine *Nexos*, founding director of *La Jornada*, and a former associate of Luis Suárez at *unomásuno*. Aguilar had been in Manuel Buendía's inner circle and a week after the assassination formulated his Ides of May scenario as the context in which Buendía's death could best be explained.

> For the general public the weeks of May 1984 were a roller coaster ride of surprises and uncertainty; for public officials they were treacherous ground littered with insecurity and political pitfalls; for society at large they were a zone of fear and renewed doubts about the integrity of their government. Buendía's execution added an ominous note to

the terrible political logic of those weeks, because it was that climate of tension, that atmosphere of deepening crisis, that made it possible. Whoever the assassins may be, there can be no doubt that roiled waters determined the timing of Buendía's death, then transformed it into a defining political event within the conspiratorial logic and destabilization that has taken possession of both Mexico's defenseless society and its immobile government.[18]

Aguilar Camín here refers to an extraordinary sequence of domestic and foreign events that negatively impacted Mexico over the month of May 1984, which some observers at the time thought had likely been coordinated by the Reagan administration as a strategy for inducing the Mexican government to modify its policies in accordance with U.S. wishes, especially with regard to Central America. Matthew Rothschild had conversed at length with Aguilar Camín and included the Ides of May hypothesis in his April 1985 *Progressive* article about the Buendía case.

Aguilar Camín shared Luis Suárez's view that, while the slaying of Manuel Buendía may have sought to intimidate Mexican media, it had largely failed to do so. The local press, he felt, was no more inclined to self-censorship now than it had always been, and if it seemed that reporters were not challenging the authorities the way Buendía did, it was simply because there were no investigative journalists of his caliber. Buendía's death had occasioned a major gap among Mexican media professionals. As for the crime itself, Aguilar Camín thought that his Ides of May scenario still offered the best framework in which to contextualize Buendía's slaying. As a police matter, however, drug traffickers struck him as the most likely perpetrators because of the way the homicide had been carried out. Its style, he said, was typical of Colombian traffickers, not of traditional Mexican political actors like the government or the army. He seemed not to consider the possibility of a cabal of interests implicit in his Ides of May analysis, as had Matthew Rothschild, nor did he take into account the fact that significant numbers of Mexicans had been trained by foreign instructors in the black arts of unconventional warfare, including assassination.

Mexico City, 15/V/85. Miércoles—The air today was incredibly bad . . . thick, foul, burning our eyes. We took a taxi out to unomásuno for an appointment with Becerra Acosta regarding our latest submissions: an anniversary interview with The Progressive's associate editor, Matthew Rothschild, about the killing of Manuel Buendía; a commentary piece on the significance of Buendía's murder; and an interview with Nicaraguan Minister of Culture, Fr. Ernesto Cardenal, conducted by an American friend and poet, Kent Johnson, and edited with an introduction by Russ, plus several of my photos. Becerra thought the material timely and important; said the Buendía material was dangerous but they would publish it anyway.

We walked along Reforma to check a couple of addresses once used as cover by the CIA, but the building had been torn down. Passing by the U.S. Embassy we noticed workmen erecting thick, waist-high, cement barricades all along the sidewalk facing Reforma. The fortress mentality of the embattled power structure is becoming more visible every day. The Mexican power structure is just as nervous, but not so patently obvious for all the world to see.

—S. E. Bartley, journal entry

The American embassy in Mexico City is a square six-story fortress occupying the block bounded by the capital's principal boulevard, Paseo de la Reforma, on which it fronts, and the river-named streets Danubio, Papaloapan, and Sena. It sits a half block from the monument to Mexican independence, whose effective realization the embassy's tenants labor assiduously to frustrate. The building bristles with rooftop antennae and satellite dishes and is devoid of any redeeming aesthetic features. By the 1960s it housed the largest CIA station in the Western Hemisphere and the second largest in the world, surpassed only by the Vienna station, which had been given primary responsibility for Soviet bloc operations.

The web of ties that bound the two nations together in the second half of the twentieth century was both social and institutional and had been woven out of mutual self-interest. At the top of the political pyramid was an established relationship between the Mexican presidency and the in-country head of American intelligence—a personal relationship that extended operationally downward through the Secretariat of Government to the DFS. Not coincidentally, both organizations were formed in 1947 and had as a primary objective the eradication of "communist" influence. By the mid-1950s, the CIA's legendary Mexico City station chief, Winston Scott, had enlisted Mexico's president, Adolfo Ruiz Cortines (1952–1958), as a witting agency asset, a role played as well by Ruiz Cortines's immediate successors, Adolfo López Mateos (1958–1964) and Gustavo Díaz Ordaz (1964–1970). So close was Scott's personal relationship with López Mateos that when Scott remarried in 1962 the Mexican president stood as his official witness.[19]

By the time Scott retired in 1969, the agency's Mexico City station numbered approximately fifty individuals, including some fifteen operations officers under diplomatic cover and another dozen officers outside the embassy under a variety of nondiplomatic covers, plus a support staff of communications officers, technicians, assistants, clerks, and secretaries. According to Philip Agee, who had served under Scott and resigned in disillusionment the same year Scott retired, the CIA ran "a complicated series of operational support programs to the various Mexican civilian security forces for the purpose of intelligence exchange, joint operations and constant upgrading of Mexican internal intelligence collection and public security functions." Day-to-day contact with senior security officials in the Secretariat of Government were handled by two case officers under USAID cover. The CIA's Mexico City station was much better than the local services, Agee wrote, "and is thus of great assistance to [Mexican] authorities in planning for raids, arrests and other repressive action."[20]

The station prepared a daily intelligence briefing for Mexico's president, as well as frequent single-subject reports containing information gathered by "unilateral penetration agents with due camouflaging to protect the identity of the sources." (Lawrence Harrison was such a "unilateral penetration agent," commencing his undercover work in Mexico in 1968 and serving in that capacity for more than a decade. See chapters 13 and 14 of this volume.) These subject-specific reports were shared with both the president and the country's top security officials, including the secretary of government, who in 1968 was future president Luis Echeverría Álvarez (1970–1976). The CIA was also assisting with the development of a secret communications network that would link the president's office to the country's principal cities. "Other joint operations with

Philip Agee (1935–2008), a former CIA
case officer who served in Ecuador, Uruguay,
and Mexico and then, disillusioned, became
the agency's single most damaging public
dissident. He generously shared his insights
and advice with the authors in the course
of their Buendía investigation.
(Sylvia E. Bartley)

the Mexican security services," Agee records, "include travel control, telephone tapping and repressive action."[21]

By the early 1960s, CIA's Mexico City station had laid a surveillance web over the Federal District through which few individuals of interest passed undetected. Flight manifests from all international airlines serving Benito Juárez International Airport were routinely copied, reviewed, and filed in the agency's embassy offices. Passengers boarding or arriving on flights to and from destinations of particular interest were surreptitiously photographed. Phone lines to the Cuban and Soviet bloc embassies were tapped, and all persons entering or leaving those embassies were photographed from nearby observation posts. The movements and contacts of intelligence targets were closely monitored around the clock and throughout the country.[22]

Agents of the DFS were an integral component of the CIA's intelligence network and conducted both photographic and electronic, as well as physical, surveillance on the agency's behalf. During Winston Scott's tenure as station chief, secretaries of government were paid CIA assets, as were key subordinates, including Fernando Gutiérrez Barrios and Miguel Nazar Haro. As Scott biographer Jefferson Morley has put it, "To say that Win had the ruling class of Mexico in his pocket was little exaggeration. He was America's proconsul."[23] Just how this collusive relationship played out following Scott's retirement we cannot say, but there is no reason to think that it did not continue in its overall configuration. It is unlikely that Luis Echeverría Álvarez severed his agency ties when he became president in 1970, and we know as a matter of public record that Nazar Haro remained a key CIA asset at least into the 1980s. We presume that Gutiérrez Barrios did the same. What, if any, personal communications presidents López Portillo, de la Madrid, and Salinas de Gortari may have had with the Mexico City CIA station is unknown, although, given the documented history of such relationships in the past, their possibility during the years of the Buendía affair is not a speculative stretch.

This web of sub-rosa relationships reflects a striking political ambivalence on the Mexican side that mirrors the country's cultural ambivalence over its historical origins in the Spanish conquest. Sentiments of national pride are vulnerable to the temptations of imperial power, and for many citizens loyalty to the Mexican nation is not an absolute virtue. The psychology of Malinche, it would appear, operates across the social spectrum, even, or perhaps especially, within Mexico's political class. Above all, frequently held assumptions about the patriotic integrity of senior government officials vaporize in light of the historical record. Even the president of the republic is capable of collusion with Mexico's imperial neighbor against the professed interests of his own government and citizenry.

The physical and cultural space in which these collusive relationships play out mirrors and reinforces their peculiarly disjunctive quality. It is an ambivalent space, neither wholly Mexican nor fully foreign, yet distinctly imitative of Euro-American "High Life," as proclaimed in neon from the side of one centrally situated edifice in the Federal District's Zona Rosa. The U.S. embassy's location adjacent to the Pink Zone seems appropriately symbolic, as that fortresslike redoubt of diplomats and spies visibly projects an overriding American presence in this mongrel cultural mix. At times, wrote Manuel Buendía in one of his more sardonic moments, the Pink Zone's restaurants are packed with CIA spies, "who only add to the capital's worsening environmental pollution."[24]

If American diplomats and intelligence officers are most comfortable in this culturally hybridized milieu, Mexican officials and elites likewise frequent its distinctive haunts. An iconic venue for discreet meetings is the Sanborns chain of U.S.-style department store restaurants, where in the course of our investigation we met with several Mexican sources. The chain was founded in 1903 by Walter and Frank Sanborn, brothers who emigrated from California and opened Mexico's first American-style soda fountain near the main post office in downtown Mexico City. Branch establishments soon followed, several of which were located within easy reach of our hotel. At the time of the Buendía slaying, the chain was owned by Walgreens. Subsequently it was acquired by the Carso Group, whose CEO and majority stockholder was multibillionaire Carlos Slim Helú, said to be the wealthiest man in Mexico. In their décor, the Sanborns department stores recalled U.S. emporiums we had known in our youth. They exhibited no distinctively Mexican features beyond Spanish-language signage.

FÁBULA DE MAYO

By Eduardo Valle

The blue buzzard had given a bad pecking to the lion, king of the pine forest. The fox told the king that it was the squirrel who had exposed his royal flank, and for days on end the king roared in anger at the squirrel. The skunk paid some wolves to destroy the noisome little animal. When they killed him, almost all of the squirrel's brothers and sisters were grief stricken. The king attended the funeral and promised to investigate: "The guilty parties will fall," he said, "no matter who they may be." Some recalled how the king's predecessors always did the same thing in such cases, so as to buy time and wait for the public to forget. But this time it didn't happen that way. At every

Iconic four-story wall mural of Mexican national paragon Benito Juárez (1806–1872), Plaza de San Fernando, Mexico City. A symbol of Mexico's highest political ideals and, in the muralist's rendition, an allusion to their ultimate betrayal as dramatized by the 1984 murder of Manuel Buendía. (Sylvia E. Bartley)

U.S. embassy building, Mexico City. (Sylvia E. Bartley)

Mexico City's pretentious Zona Rosa (Pink Zone) near the U.S. embassy. (Sylvia E. Bartley)

opportunity the squirrel's brothers and sisters reminded people of his death. They demanded that the murder be solved and the guilty parties punished.

The squirrel had been dead for many months. The skunk had fled to foreign places. The fox was nervous and uncertain about his future. It was said that he would be sent to govern one of the provinces, but nothing came of it. Madam coyote, charged with discrediting or destroying all leads, had successfully accomplished her task. She was promoted and now served as one of the supreme justices of the jungle. Don coyote, wise and humane, hid his head in the sand like an ostrich: "It's not my jurisdiction!" he shouted whenever someone reminded him of the case. The lion, king of the pine forest, observed how all the animals were growing desperate, even those at the court, who concerned themselves more with his well-being than that of the kingdom, pillaged and plundered by voracious natives and even more voracious foreigners. Sorrow and misery spread throughout the jungle. The kingdom was hopelessly adrift.

The revered one, the omnipotent and all-knowing one, the superior one, he whose name must not be uttered and who can only be mentioned with all due respect as El Señor, watched his time slip away. No one said a thing to him about it. To do so would be insanely disrespectful and the mere thought of it terrified his courtiers, who now pampered him to the extreme of confining him to the tremendous solitude of his office. No one told him, but he knew that the unstoppable, impeccable river of time, of his time, continued to flow by. No one told him, but he knew and despaired at the terrible impotence he showed day after day while the blue buzzard soared over the jungle.

From time to time the lion remembered the squirrel and lamented his absence. He had never really liked the little animal and much less so at the time of the royal succession, when the squirrel had invaded territory restricted exclusively to members of the royal family. As members of that family did not suffer violations of privilege gracefully, the squirrel had earned the anointed sovereign's eternal enmity by entering the prohibited grounds.

But now the lion missed the squirrel, at least for his good humor and agile mind. The squirrel's brethren, for their part, did not forget him and now and then would mention him to remind the king of his unfulfilled promise. The lion's time was passing, running out, while a sense of hopelessness spread throughout the realm. Although the time remaining seemed insignificant, the blue buzzard constantly circled overhead looking for any opportunity. It was still possible that despair would turn into desperation and that those who ruminated on their discontent might rebel. Then the jungle would burn to the savage chants of war.

In any case, the squirrel would no longer be present. He had been dead now many months. His brothers and sisters remembered him and remarked how the lion, king of the pine forest, had failed to keep his promise. Whenever the animals of the jungle remembered the squirrel, they looked in despair and sadness toward the forest of pines, where they saw that the lion not only had failed to keep his promise, but also did nothing to end their despair. México, 2 December 1988 [sic].[25]

The date attached to the "May Fable" appears itself to be an intentionally opaque element of Eduardo Valle's political allegory, which was published in the Mexico City daily *El Universal* on 30 May 1985, the first anniversary of Manuel Buendía's assassination. The second of December, 1988, would be the day following the inauguration of President de la Madrid's successor, expected by many in 1985 to be Secretary of Government

Manuel Bartlett Díaz, the "fox" of the fable. Whatever Valle's intended innuendo here, of far greater import was his unmistakable indictment of the United States and collusive Mexican officials as the responsible parties behind the Buendía slaying. In two other commentaries published around the time of the first anniversary, one on 29 May, the other on 15 June, both in *El Universal Gráfico*, Valle linked Buendía's murder to Zorrilla, the DFS, and the drug traffickers.[26]

Together, these three pieces unambiguously inserted the Buendía assassination into an international political context and assigned blame to the principal government actors: the President of the Republic Miguel de la Madrid (the "lion king"), Secretary of Government Manuel Bartlett Díaz (the "fox"), DFS chief José Antonio Zorrilla Pérez (the "skunk"), Federal District Attorney General Victoria Adato ("Madam coyote"), and Attorney General of the Republic Sergio García Ramírez ("Don coyote"). The crime was instigated by the United States (the "blue buzzard") and coordinated from Los Pinos, the Mexican president's official residence (the "forest of pines"). Manuel Buendía (the "squirrel") had compromised official secrets ("invaded prohibited territory") and was murdered by paid assassins ("wolves" hired by the "skunk"). Buendía's colleagues (the squirrel's "brothers and sisters"), however, would not be silenced and insistently called attention to President de la Madrid's failure to keep his promise to bring Buendía's killers to justice.

It was as far as anyone could go in the periodical press of the day, for which "El Buho" ("The Owl," as Valle was popularly known) had something of a reputation. Zorrilla had already been mentioned by name as a suspect in the Buendía killing, and Adato had been accused of impeding the official investigation. No one, however, dared name either the president or his secretary of government as parties to official impropriety, much less murder. Government Secretary Manuel Bartlett Díaz was especially thin-skinned about accusations that impugned his personal integrity or otherwise prejudiced his political ambitions. We ourselves recall an occasion when, discussing the Buendía case with *unomásuno* editor Becerra Acosta, we started to say something about Bartlett Díaz and Becerra immediately cut us off, gesturing emphatically toward an implied listening device in a ceiling light fixture above his desk. "El Buho," in turn, had taken due care in his allegory not to have the "fox" order the "skunk" to hire the "wolves" to murder the "squirrel." Given the chain of government authority, however, it was difficult to suppose that Zorrilla had acted independently of Bartlett, nor did it seem likely that Bartlett would have acted independently of the president.

4

Coordinates of Power

We have about 50 percent of the world's wealth but only 6.3 percent of its population. Our real task in the coming period is to devise a pattern of relationships which will permit us to maintain this position of disparity without positive detriment to our national security. To do so, we will have to dispense with all sentimentality and day-dreaming. . . . We should dispense with the aspiration to "be liked" or be regarded as the repository of a high-minded international altruism. . . . The day is not far off when we are going to have to deal in straight power concepts. The less we are then hampered by idealistic slogans, the better.

   —George F. Kennan, "Review of Current Trends, U.S. Foreign Policy"
   (24 February 1948)

It is now clear that we are facing an implacable enemy whose avowed objective is world domination by whatever means and at whatever cost. There are no rules in such a game. Hitherto acceptable norms of human conduct do not apply. If the United States is to survive, long-standing American concepts of "fair play" must be reconsidered. We must develop effective espionage and counterespionage services and must learn to subvert, sabotage and destroy our enemies by more clever, more sophisticated and more effective methods than those used against us. It may become necessary that the American people be made acquainted with, understand and support this fundamentally repugnant philosophy.

   —Lt. Gen. James R. Doolittle, "Doolittle Report" (26 July 1954)

GOVERNMENTS EXERCISE POWER through a multiplicity of arrangements, some open and acknowledged, others covert, frequently outside established legal and ethical norms. In the 1980s, the U.S. administrations of Ronald Reagan and George H. W. Bush contrived an intricate web of relations with the clandestine services of other countries, private arms merchants, and elements of the criminal underworld as part of a grand strategy to combat their primary contender on the world stage: the Soviet Union and its socialist bloc allies. Their ultimate objective was the age-old dream of global preeminence, pursued by American policy makers with unrelenting determination in the decades following World War II down to the present. In the neighboring Latin American and Caribbean countries, the United States resorted to a variety of covert relationships with international drug traffickers, paramilitary groups, local police, intelligence and national security officials, and even the highest authorities of certain regional governments. In Mexico these collusive relationships proved especially complex, with key roles being played by the CIA, the DFS, and Israel's Mossad, all against a backdrop of highly fluid power struggles throughout the region and across the globe.

At the heart of U.S. foreign policy concerns in those years was Cuba, whose influence in global geopolitics far exceeded the island nation's small population and minimal resources. Key to understanding Cuba's critical international role in the later half of the twentieth century is its geographic proximity to the United States and the history of U.S. interference in its internal affairs, first as a militarily occupied territory, then as an object of neocolonial domination. When in January 1959 an armed rebellion succeeded in ousting the island's subservient strongman, Fulgencio Batista, it did so in a historic moment marked by anticolonial struggles around the world. In the aftermath of the world war, the far-flung empires of England, France, Belgium, the Netherlands, and Portugal had begun to disintegrate into a plethora of new, ostensibly independent countries, soon to be known in the geopolitical discourse of their former masters as the "Third World." The "First" and "Second" worlds in this conceptual scheme were, on the one hand, the developed capitalist economies of the North Atlantic (the so-called industrial democracies) and, on the other, the Soviet-dominated socialist bloc, each with its own ideological mantra by means of which it sought to entice the newly emergent nations into its orbit.

Mexico's place in this global power contest was at once central and elusive. Half of its national territory had been seized in the later 1840s by an aggressively expansionist United States, a historic humiliation still recalled some seven generations after the fact. The country's independence from Spain in 1821 had been formalized by the most conservative elements of the former colonial elite as a strategy to preserve their vested interests against popular rebellion, unleashed a decade earlier by Enlightenment era clergy, then temporarily suppressed after a five-year civil war. Liberal constitutionalist precepts emanating from Europe and the United States clashed throughout the nineteenth century with this entrenched ideology of corporate and class privilege inherited from more than three hundred years of Spanish colonial rule. Fueling Mexico's political struggles in the post-independence era were deep, unresolved issues of class conflict rooted in a long history of economic exploitation of the country's Indian population and landless peasantry. The reformist Constitution of 1857 marked the high point of Mexican liberalism, immortalized in the figure of its Zapotec patron, President Benito Juárez, and thereafter falsely celebrated as an enduring testament of Mexico's ideological commitment to social justice.

La Reforma, as the Juárezian reform program came to be known, suffered from inherent flaws that failed to address the structural causes of concentrated wealth and social inequity. As a consequence, it prepared the ground for future social upheavals that would shape the course of Mexican history in the twentieth century. In the meantime, it precipitated an armed invasion of Mexico by France in 1862, ostensibly for the collection of suspended debt payments but in fact to place a European royal, Austrian Archduke Ferdinand Maximilian of Hapsburg, at the head of a Mexican monarchy. Juárez loyalists fought the French occupiers and eventually prevailed, albeit in a

favorable international context that ultimately obliged France to withdraw its occupation forces. Their victory galvanized Mexicans' patriotic sensibilities and became a core
element of their national ethos, but the whole costly episode exhausted the Juárez
government and opened the country to new challenges from abroad.

The transformation of Mexico from an inchoate, socially conflicted, economically
backward postcolonial society into a modern nation of influence beyond its own borders occurred during the thirty-four-year rule of Porfirio Díaz (1876–1910), a reform era
general who had distinguished himself in the campaign against the French. Surrounding himself with a circle of prominent intellectuals and businessmen influenced by
the positivism of Auguste Comte and the social Darwinism of Herbert Spencer, Díaz
determined to rationalize the governance of society and management of the national
economy under the positivist formula of "order and progress," which translated into
centralized rule by force in a dictatorial regime dubbed the Porfiriato after its authoritarian progenitor. Under that regime Mexico made notable advances in economic
infrastructure, education, urban development, industrialization, and the exploitation
of natural resources. Investment capital flowed in from abroad with a corresponding
increase in foreign influence, especially in mining and the fledgling petroleum industry and in the construction of Mexico's national rail network.

But the Porfirian approach to nation building, like the liberal reformist approach
before it, failed to resolve the long-festering inequities of the countryside, where
entrenched and nouveau land barons continued to hold an impoverished peasantry
in virtual feudal bondage. At the same time, and as a consequence of the country's
industrialization and associated economic development, the Porfiriato brought into
being new social elements who, in furtherance of their own class interests, would play
correspondingly new political roles in a now rapidly changing society. Prominent
among them was a growing industrial proletariat whose ranks were augmented by
increasingly numerous transportation, construction, service workers and an array of
unskilled laborers, many of them desperate rural migrants drawn to the burgeoning
cities by the promise of employment. The Porfiriato produced a new, formally edu-
cated professional, business, and bureaucratic class as well, which likewise would alter
the dynamics of national politics. Unable to control these developing trends, or even
understand the systemic contradictions that set them in motion, the Porfirian regime
was finally consumed in a momentous societal upheaval that historians refer to as the
Mexican Revolution of 1910.

Like all historic revolutions, this was not a discrete chronological event measured
in weeks or months but rather an exceedingly complex process that began to unfold
prior to 1910 and went on for many years thereafter. It coincided with the Russian
Revolution, a parallel process half a world away that included the tumultuous events
of 1905, the February and October uprisings of 1917, the civil war between Reds
and Whites, and the Bolshevik rout of foreign expeditionary forces following World
War I. Distinct in their particulars and with different historical origins, these two
geographically distant revolutions nonetheless responded to analogous societal ills
and together determined some of the political imperatives that shaped the twentieth
century. They also generated in Russia and Mexico a mutual fascination with each

other's revolutionary history that found expression in cultural, as well as political and policy, circles and which on occasion would further complicate Mexico's relations with the United States.[1]

A fundamental difference between the Mexican and Russian revolutions was the absence in Mexico of an ideologically coherent vanguard organization capable of directing the overthrow of the old order and ushering in the new. There were multiple rebellions within the Mexican Revolution, each with its own social dynamic and each vying for primacy among its particular geographic or sectoral constituency. In the end it was a coalition of the new agents of modernization engendered by the Porfiriato that seized control of the revolution and channeled it into a national project of capitalist development that subsumed militant labor and the iconic rural rebellions of Emiliano Zapata and Pancho Villa. The victors gradually institutionalized the revolution through a political party founded in 1929, then transformed it into a well-oiled machine of the country's evolving political oligarchy, which dominated Mexican politics for the next half century, first as the National Revolutionary Party (1938–1946) and subsequently as the Institutional Revolutionary Party (PRI). As an instrument of societal control, the PRI might be compared to the Communist Party apparatus of the former Soviet Union. So striking were the seeming parallels that when in the 1980s Mikhail Gorbachev began calling for *perestroika* (transformation) of the Soviet system, Mexican pundits called for *pristroika* of Mexico's political institutions.

In contrast to the Russian Bolsheviks, who elaborated their revolutionary strategies on the basis of a theory of historical process in which industrial workers were the prime agents of social advancement and communist revolutionaries their natural leaders, the triumphant leaders of the Mexican Revolution had no such overarching revolutionary theory. Instead, they proceeded with cunning and craft to devise a pragmatically flexible system of governance that would effectively serve their vested interests over the long term. Central to that system was the portrayal of the Revolution of 1910 as an epic struggle for social justice and national integrity and identification of the PRI as the historic guardian of the revolution's legacy. Rather than espousing the rhetoric of class struggle, the PRI corporatized Mexico's disenfranchised classes into party-controlled peasant, labor, and popular confederations, which purported to defend their respective constituencies' vital interests but in actuality served as effective mechanisms of social control. Similarly, while extolling the virtues of democratic pluralism and multiparty electoral politics enshrined in the Mexican Constitution of 1917, the PRI allowed the oligarchy to maintain an iron grip on the presidency, the national legislature, and state governorships into the closing decades of the twentieth century.

Despite their ideological and sociocultural dissimilarities, the PRI and Communist Party of the Soviet Union followed similar bureaucratic trajectories, with self-serving party elites increasingly divorced from their respective citizenries as well as their own rank and file. The Soviet system collapsed first, but the PRI was only a decade behind, finally losing the presidency to the conservative National Action Party in July 2000. In both instances the failure of long-established political regimes occurred in a larger international context, which, while not the immediate cause, nonetheless significantly influenced those historic events.

The first real sign of change in the PRI came with the presidential accession of José López Portillo (1976–1982), who as the former treasury secretary marked a historic break with the established practice of selecting the party's official candidates for the presidency from the Secretariat of Government. The reality of that change was confirmed by López Portillo's choice of his programming and budget secretary, Miguel de la Madrid, as the party's presidential candidate in 1982—a definitive choice that signaled the ascendency of technocrats with advanced degrees from foreign universities in economics, business administration, and public policy over traditional PRI apparatchiks typically linked to the state security apparatus. The protracted struggle unleashed in 1982 between the PRI-affiliated "dinosaurs" and the "technocrats," which would eventually destroy the party's monopoly hold on government, was initially reflected by de la Madrid and his principal rival for the presidency, the PRI Executive Committee president and national security heavyweight Javier García Paniagua.

With Miguel de la Madrid's accession to the presidency, there followed in rapid succession the Buendía assassination (we would uncover evidence of García Paniagua's involvement in that signal event); the abduction, torture, and murder of U.S. DEA agent Enrique Camarena Salazar; the discrediting, dissolution, and reorganization of Mexico's national security apparatus; the widely rumored implication of prominent PRI figures in drug trafficking and other high crimes, including the Buendía and Camarena killings; failure of the de la Madrid government to manage even minimally the 1985 Mexico City earthquake disaster; soaring inflation and unmanageable indebtedness to usurious international lending organizations; and then, in 1987, the defection of PRI eminence Cuauhtémoc Cárdenas, son of former president Lázaro Cárdenas (1934–1940), an epic figure who had implemented a massive land reform program and, most dramatically, nationalized the U.S.-and British-controlled petroleum industry.

Cuauhtémoc Cárdenas challenged the PRI in the 1988 presidential campaign as the candidate of the National Democratic Front, a coalition of opposition parties from which emerged the new Party of the Democratic Revolution (PRD), its name alluding pointedly to the absence of democratic practice within Mexico's faux multiparty electoral system and thus challenging the PRI's credentials as guarantor of the country's revolutionary ideals. Cárdenas apparently polled more votes than PRI candidate Carlos Salinas de Gortari but was barred from the presidency by a last-minute manipulation of the Federal Election Commission's computer bank, which gave Salinas a hair-thin majority. The official responsible for overseeing the conduct of Mexico's 1988 presidential election was Secretary of Government Manuel Bartlett Díaz.

We focused our inquiry into the Buendía assassination on the soaring "blue buzzard" of Eduardo Valle's first anniversary "May Fable." By 1984 the *zopilote azul* was circling widely over the Western Hemisphere's middle latitudes, as no carrion-producing event was ultimately divorced from any other. Virtually all of the region's growing violence stemmed from U.S. efforts to reassert its historical hegemony over the countries of Mesoamerica and the Caribbean. Local elites actively colluded with the Americans to preserve their privileged positions in societies long integrated into transnational structures of dependency and now threatened by a post–Vietnam era groundswell of popular rebellion.

Stung by defeat in Southeast Asia and determined to overcome the "Vietnam Syndrome," which had rendered the American public unsupportive of aggressive power projection abroad, the most adamant voices of U.S. preeminence had begun actively to redefine the country's foreign policy discourse as early as the presidency of Jimmy Carter (1977–1981). The signal document of the period for Latin America was a set of regional policy premises and recommendations, articulated by an ad hoc group of foreign affairs ideologues constituted as the "Committee of Santa Fe," published during the 1980 presidential campaign by the hawkish Washington-based Council for Inter-American Security under the title *A New Inter-American Policy for the Eighties*. The Santa Fe document was produced as a talking paper for the presumed incoming Republican administration of Ronald Reagan, and, in fact, it set the tone for U.S. policy toward Latin America over the next decade.

"The Americas are under attack," it proclaimed. "Latin America . . . is being penetrated by Soviet power. The Caribbean rim and basin are spotted with Soviet surrogates and ringed with socialist states. . . . The United States is being shoved aside in the Caribbean and Central America by a sophisticated, but brutal extracontinental super power manipulating client states. . . . The Soviet Union is now ensconced in force in the Western Hemisphere," the Santa Fe group insisted, "and the United States must remedy the situation." Mexico was one of three countries requiring priority attention if the perceived Soviet threat to American vital interests was to be overcome. The other two were Brazil and Cuba—Brazil because of its size, Cuba because of its client relationship with the Soviet Union.[2]

The July 1979 ouster from power of longtime Nicaraguan dictator Anastasio Somoza Debayle by an armed popular insurrection was the decisive episode that unleashed the hard-line reaction to what were seen as the ineffectual regional policies of the Carter administration. "The Nicaraguan base on the American continent," argued the Committee of Santa Fe, "will now facilitate a repeat of the new Nicaraguan revolutionary model. Already U.S. arms previously sold to Nicaragua have been sent to guerrillas in Guatemala. Guatemala is the strategic prize of Central America, adjoining as it does the vast Mexican oil fields."[3] Taking his cue from the Santa Fe document, Senator Jesse Helms inserted the committee's views on the region into the Republican Party's 1980 platform. Following the election, several committee members were brought into key positions in the Reagan administration where they could influence the implementation of their updated Monroe Doctrine.

The CIA's subversion of post-Somoza Nicaragua commenced in the final months of the Carter administration and grew exponentially following the inauguration of Ronald Reagan on 20 January 1981.[4] We had observed Somoza's July 1979 overthrow from Cuba and witnessed the arrival in Havana of an official Sandinista delegation one week later to take part in Cuba's 26th of July national holiday celebration, dedicated that year to Nicaragua's successful uprising against the long-entrenched, U.S.-supported Somoza dictatorship. Anticipating accusations of Cuban subversive influence, Fidel Castro declared that, to the contrary, it was Cuban teachers and doctors doing humanitarian work in Nicaragua who would be influenced by the Sandinistas. And that, he emphasized, "could only be good for Cuba." While there were similarities between the

Cuban and Nicaraguan revolutions, he added, it was important to understand that "every country has its own path to follow, its own problems, its own style, its own goals." Revolutions, in sum, could not be exported, and the Cubans were not responsible for what had happened in Nicaragua.[5]

Three months after Reagan assumed the presidency in Washington, Nicaragua's Government of National Reconstruction sponsored two simultaneous international media events to address the issue of manipulated reportage on regional events by the wire services and mainstream news outlets. Organized by the International Organization of Journalists and the FELAP, together with the Nicaraguan Journalists Union, the events were billed respectively as a "World Assembly of Journalists" and "Operation Nicaragua Today." The World Assembly sought to analyze the role of the wire services and multinationals in shaping public opinion about Nicaragua and its neighbors, while the second event afforded some two hundred foreign media professionals an unrestricted opportunity to speak with whomever and see whatever they wished so as to gain a more objective understanding of what was actually transpiring on the ground.

We attended the World Assembly of Journalists and were struck by the organizers' conviction so early in President Reagan's first term that the United States would intervene in the region militarily. The assembly's final "Declaration of Managua" urged the media and journalists of all countries "to denounce the impending aggression against Central America" and to expose tendentious news coverage "by reporting the truth about Nicaragua and the popular struggles in El Salvador, Guatemala, and the other countries of the area." For the White House to attribute regional upheavals to agents of an alien ideology was "sheer naiveté and political folly," the assembly declared. Indeed, it was alarming "that a world power like the United States should base its international behavior on such simplistic assumptions."[6]

> Managua, 9/V/1984. Miércoles, 6 pm—We join the press corps at a local dance school, the assigned assembly point from which we will be transported to the government convention center for the opening session of a meeting of Non-Aligned Movement labor ministers. Sitting among odd pieces of furniture and piles of lumber waiting for our equipment to be checked by security, we watch a full moon rising in a cloudless tropical sky as the imperious voice of Ronald Reagan, addressing a joint session of Congress on Central America and the "Nicaraguan menace," floats eerily through the gathering dusk on the short wave frequencies of the VOA [Voice of America]. Reagan's praise of the *contras* and his calumnies against the Sandinistas are surreal in this setting: not the remotest connection with reality as we daily witness and experience it in this war-torn country. Salvador Dalí's famous drooping and distorted timepieces, his ants crawling from the wounds of a man's leg, drift through my mind as the president drones on, palm fronds rustling in the evening breeze, a zenate's clarion-like call to its mate piercing the mendacious words from afar.
>
> —S. E. Bartley, journal entry

Mexican media were well represented at the World Assembly of Journalists, and we all came away from that event with a fuller appreciation of the grave issues then in play. Over the next year we would return twice more to work on a television documentary about the post-Somoza transformation of Nicaragua,[7] a circumstance that afforded us privileged access to the country, including to key leadership figures in the Sandinista government. We produced a steady stream of material for *unomásuno*, as well as articles on the deepening regional crisis for the Managua dailies *Barricada* and *El Nuevo Diario* and, back in Wisconsin, for the *Milwaukee Journal*. Already at that early date it was apparent to virtually everyone in the international press corps that the Reagan administration was committed to regime change in Nicaragua and that it was determined to pursue a military resolution of the Central American crisis more broadly. All of us interpreted the October 1983 invasion of Grenada as a dress rehearsal for direct U.S. military intervention against the Sandinistas, which in the first six months of 1984 seemed imminent.

The helicopter downing recounted in chapter 2 was especially ominous, as it had the appearance of an incident contrived to precipitate a Honduran military response that would in turn serve as a pretext for U.S. intervention. Honduras expelled Nicaragua's ambassador from Tegucigalpa, while in Managua a rumor began to circulate that American embassy personnel were destroying classified files in anticipation of an invasion. We attended briefings on the situation at the Ministries of Defense and Foreign Relations and managed to interview Nicaragua's foreign minister, Fr. Miguel d'Escoto, then telexed an account to *unomásuno*. D'Escoto, we reported, tended to think that the purported destruction of classified embassy files was a psychological warfare ruse since that kind of information could only come to light intentionally. As for Honduras, it was "merely a pawn in the United States' regional game of political chess." In any event, d'Escoto emphasized, the situation was becoming more dangerous because the Reagan administration had concluded "that its plan to overthrow the Sandinista government with CIA mercenaries would fail."[8]

Just a week and a half earlier, on the same day that *Excélsior* carried Manuel Buendía's column excoriating the Mexican government for allowing Televisa to broadcast a two-part interview with CIA-supported Nicaraguan counterrevolutionary Edén Pastora, *unomásuno* published a commentary Russell had written about Costa Rican complicity with Pastora's southern front *contras*, the so-called Democratic Revolutionary Alliance, or ARDE. The main point of that commentary was to highlight readily available evidence of covert CIA operations directed against Nicaragua from Costa Rican territory and to expose the active collusion of Costa Rica's president, Luis Alberto Monge, with the Reagan administration in its proxy war against the Sandinistas. It was an important point, since something similar appeared to be happening in Mexico, and Manuel Buendía clearly intuited as much.

While Buendía denounced Mexico's largest commercial television network for effectively aligning itself with the Reagan administration in a militarist strategy that was costing thousands of Nicaraguan lives and threatened to engulf other countries of the region, including Mexico, it was, he implied, the Mexican government itself that permitted Televisa to air such detrimental programming. It was simply intolerable, he insisted, that a private television enterprise should be permitted to compromise national security by exalting Edén Pastora and everything he represented—all the more so given the fact that Mexican mass media were closely monitored and regulated by the

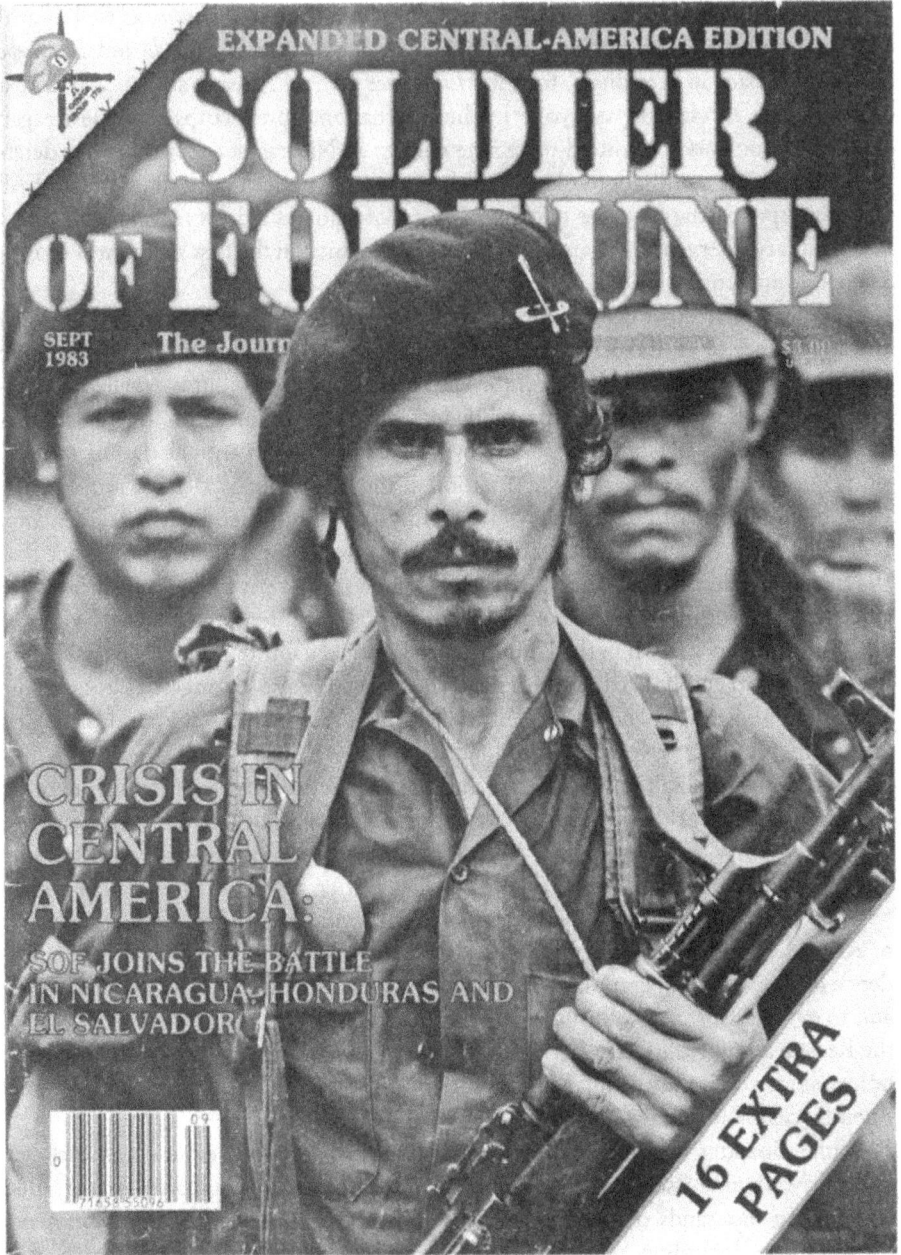

Nicaraguan *contras* on the cover of *Soldier of Fortune*, September 1983. This expanded issue was devoted to the U.S. proxy counterinsurgency campaigns in Central America.

Fuel storage tanks in Corinto Harbor, Nicaragua, destroyed in a predawn attack on 11 October 1983 by CIA paramilitary operatives. (Sylvia E. Bartley)

Sandinista National Liberation Front founder and Nicaraguan interior minister Tomás Borge Martínez being photographed by Sylvia E. Bartley at a 1984 May Day celebration in Chinandega, Nicaragua. (Russell H. Bartley)

Mainstream media bias. The October 1983 U.S. invasion of the Caribbean island nation of Grenada was widely viewed as a dress rehearsal for an invasion of Nicaragua. Here NBC news cameraman John Kechele, wearing a blue and white baseball cap emblazoned with the U.S. Eighty-Second Airborne insignia and the words "Grenada War Games 1983," covers the 9 May 1984 transfer of eight Honduran servicemen killed in the downing of their helicopter over Nicaraguan territory to the custody of a Honduran air force delegation at Sandino International Airport in Managua. The Reagan administration's invasion of Grenada, Manuel Buendía caustically remarked to a National Defense College audience ten days after the event, was "a valiant feat of cowardice in which the world's most powerful army attacked a country whose entire population could fit inside [Mexico City's] Aztec stadium!" (Sylvia E. Bartley)

Secretariat of Government. That could only happen with presidential acquiescence, which implied that the sitting president of Mexico "no longer embodies national leadership." Miguel de la Madrid, it would appear, walked in virtual lockstep with his Costa Rican counterpart, Luis Alberto Monge.[9]

Managua-Miami, 2/III/1986. Domingo—TACA, scheduled to leave at 7:10 am. Didn't arrive until 7:35, but we soon were on board and on our way to El Salvador. Met David McMichael in the waiting area, ex-CIA analyst who went public to expose the falsification of information regarding alleged Nicaraguan aid to Salvadoran rebels. He was leaving from his ninth fact-finding visit to Nicaragua prior to testifying before Congress. Sat with him on the flight to San Salvador. A genuine character. Totally blows my stereotypes of CIA people. He's smart, very personable, full of stories and anecdotes, facts and figures; an effective communicator. He generally agrees with me, taking only occasional exception, such as not thinking that a U.S. invasion of Nicaragua would

necessarily spread beyond Nicaraguan borders. Rather he is convinced it would destroy
U.S. credibility in Latin America (what's left of it) and prove a disaster for Nicaraguan
and U.S. troops.

—S. E. Bartley, journal entry

While it was true, as Buendía averred, that the de la Madrid administration was being
assailed by "domestic *contras*" allied with Mexico's "natural adversaries," de la Madrid's
personal role in the unfolding of events was far from transparent. As with the sixteenth-
century Nahua converts who professed Christianity in the colonial temples of their
Catholic masters, little on the political landscape of late twentieth-century Mexico was
what it seemed. When de la Madrid took office on 1 December 1982, observed veteran
New York Times Latin American correspondent Alan Riding, "his political options
were defined by the economy and his economic options were defined abroad."[10] Major
new petroleum reserves discovered by PEMEX in the 1970s had led to an excessively
optimistic vision of the country's economic future and an accompanying orgy of bor-
rowing, which, together with an unanticipated drop in the price of crude oil a decade
later, inflation of the dollar, and a deep recession in the United States, plunged Mexico
into a financial crisis that sent tremors through the international banking system.

Mexico's increasingly unmanageable economic woes impacted the conduct of Mexican foreign policy, which was the flip side of the distinctive PRI mode of governance.
Because the Revolution of 1910 was what historians describe as a "bourgeois revolution," that is, a mass revolt against the old order dominated and defined by an entre-
preneurial class rather than the exploited laboring classes of a "socialist" revolution
from below, it engendered a dualistic political system of centralized "bourgeois" rule
at home and at least rhetorical support for "radical" movements and regimes abroad.
It was a hypocritical charade imposed on Mexico's postrevolutionary political elites by
the global historical moment, in which Karl Marx provided the prevailing paradigm
for revolution, while their own institutional legitimacy depended on the appearance of
addressing the societal ills that inspired the Marxist paradigm.

This peculiar circumstance would often put Mexico at odds with the United States,
whose political leadership was hypersensitive to politics of class struggle and could not
abide the intrusion of such politics into the arena of Mexican foreign policy. Mexico's
recognition and maintenance of relations with governments repudiated by Washington, in turn, was a way of reaffirming Mexican sovereignty in the face of a historically
aggressive northern neighbor and became a recurring pattern in twentieth-century
Mexican diplomacy. It began in 1924 when the administration of Álvaro Obregón
(1920–1924) established formal diplomatic ties with the Soviet Union, the first country
in the Western Hemisphere to do so, in defiance of American efforts to isolate the new
state. Challenges to Mexican sovereignty by the Moscow-based Communist International (Comintern), combined with relentless anti-Soviet pressure from Washington,
led Mexico to sever its diplomatic ties with the Soviet Union in 1930. Formal relations
between the two governments were reestablished thirteen years later during the wartime alliance against the Axis powers and remained unbroken through the height of the
Cold War, even as several other Latin American countries were again induced to sever
their ties with Moscow.

Successive PRI governments played both sides of the Mexican-Soviet relationship, using it to enhance Mexico's diplomatic independence while at the same time serving U.S. intelligence objectives, as well as Washington's anticommunist agenda more broadly. (E.g., in October 1951 Mexican agents seized U.S. Communist Party fugitive Gus Hall and, in coordination with the Federal Bureau of Investigation (FBI), summarily deported him back to the United States.[11]) A similar situation occurred with Cuba following the 1959 triumph of the Cuban Revolution and the rapid deterioration of relations between Washington and Havana. Despite intense U.S. pressure, Mexico refused to interrupt its relations with Cuba's revolutionary regime and throughout the difficult decades of the 1960s and 1970s remained the island nation's one open channel to Latin America. As in the Soviet case, the PRI sought propagandistic advantage from what it portrayed as shared revolutionary values but now enhanced by a common history of struggle against American domination.

As had occurred with the Soviet Union in the 1920s, however, historic differences between the Cuban and Mexican revolutions confronted the PRI with domestic political challenges that induced successive Mexican administrations to collaborate with U.S. intelligence in countering Cuban influence both within Mexico and throughout the neighboring region. This dichotomy of institutional purpose was played out in a clash of agendas pursued on the one hand by the liberal-minded Secretariat of Foreign Relations and, on the other, by the traditionally conservative Secretariat of Government.[12] The popular insurrection against the Somoza dictatorship in Nicaragua brought these contradictory elements into play during the López Portillo (1976–1982) and de la Madrid (1982–1988) administrations in a manner that, combined with the debt crisis and related social unrest, compromised the viability of the PRI's political machine and ultimately led to its historic demise. Manuel Buendía, for his part, stirred this boiling cauldron and was fatally scalded by its pestilent brew.

President López Portillo had been an outspoken supporter of the anti-Somoza insurgency and a staunch defender of Cuba's revolutionary government, to the decided annoyance of the political establishment in the United States. The Somoza-engineered murder of respected opposition newspaper editor Pedro Joaquín Chamorro in January 1978 sparked the first signs of official Mexican interest in Nicaragua's developing revolution. Venezuela and Panama had already provided material assistance to the Sandinista National Liberation Front (FSLN), and Costa Rica was allowing FSLN combatants to use its territory as a southern front staging area for attacks against Somoza's Guardia Nacional. When the Organization of American States (OAS) dispatched a mediation team to Nicaragua in the fall of 1978, Mexico refused to participate, viewing the OAS effort as a U.S.-inspired maneuver to salvage the discredited Somoza regime.

By then Mexico's embassy in Managua was providing diplomatic refuge to hundreds of anti-Somoza fugitives, while President López Portillo had become personally supportive of the Sandinista struggle. Early in 1979, he entered into secret conversations with FSLN commanders about how best to support their final offensive. The PRI had already provided money to the FSLN, and the Sandinistas were being allowed to conduct their propaganda campaign from Mexico City. And when the OAS mediation effort had failed the previous fall, Mexico had given temporary asylum to seven of the FSLN's prominent civilian spokesmen. In mid-May López Portillo discussed the Nicaraguan situation with Fidel Castro during the Cuban leader's first visit to Mexico since coming to power twenty years earlier, then met with Costa Rican president Rodrigo Carazo Odio, whose account of events inside Nicaragua moved the Mexican president to sever Mexico's diplomatic ties with the Somoza regime. When the following month U.S. secretary of state Cyrus Vance attempted to persuade a meeting of OAS foreign ministers to send an Inter-American Peace Force to Nicaragua, López Portillo had his secretary of foreign relations, Jorge Castañeda, block the proposal as a maneuver by the Carter administration to exclude the Sandinistas from power. In the final weeks of the Nicaraguan insurgency, Mexico sent weapons and ammunition to the FSLN and took the symbolically significant step of naming an ambassador to the newly formed Sandinista government in exile. After Somoza fled and the National Guard had been routed, López Portillo dispatched his presidential airplane, *Quetzalcóatl I*, to transport the new regime's government in exile back to Managua.

Mexico followed up with food, medicine, and other material aid to Nicaragua in the difficult postinsurrection period and increased its political support for the Government of National Reconstruction when other regional governments began to express concern over a perceived radicalization of the Sandinista regime. López Portillo made an official visit to Nicaragua in February 1980, where he declared that, while the Mexican Revolution had brought freedom and the Cuban Revolution had brought justice, the Sandinista Revolution offered hope that "freedom, justice, equality and security could be combined to create a new option for the future"—words that rankled and raised red flags in the Carter administration, but more important in the context of the Buendía assassination, did so as well among the neo–cold warriors who would shape and implement subsequent U.S. policy toward the region during the Reagan administration.[13]

When Miguel de la Madrid assumed power in December 1982, he brought none of López Portillo's professed empathy for Central America's popular insurgencies to the presidency. Instead, he would govern Mexico with calculated pragmatism clothed in the disarming attire of civility and "moral renovation." As a practical matter, de la Madrid understood that Mexican sovereignty could best be assured by defending the principles of nonintervention and the peaceful resolution of international conflict. And like López Portillo, he also understood that the greatest threat to the region's vital interests would be a military invasion of Nicaragua by the United States. As succinctly expressed by Spanish journalist Luis Méndez Asensio, Mexico's shared border with the United States "obliges Mexican diplomacy to validate its sovereignty by explicitly supporting the sovereignty of other governments, especially those whose ideological essence automatically makes them opponents of U.S. regional hegemony and thus circumstantial allies of Mexico."[14] So it was that, in the rapidly deteriorating circumstances of Central America, Miguel de la Madrid engaged in a multilateral diplomatic offensive to achieve a peaceful resolution of the region's contentious political differences, joining with his counterparts from Panama, Colombia, and Venezuela in what came to be known as the Contadora Initiative.

The name Contadora refers to the small Panamanian resort island in the Perlas Archipelago where the foreign ministers of the four participating governments first

met in January 1983, and it quickly became synonymous with the peace initiative itself.
While at the time, and since, it has been identified with Central America, the Contadora Group had significant historical antecedents that made it additionally unpalatable to American neo–cold warriors. An earlier Contadora Group comprised of
Mexico, Colombia, Venezuela, and Costa Rica had been convened in 1976 by the head
of Panama's governing junta, Gen. Omar Torrijos, to provide regional diplomatic support for Panamanian efforts to negotiate a new Panama Canal Treaty with the United
States. Torrijos adroitly guided the difficult negotiations with the Carter administration to a successful conclusion in which sovereignty over the Panama Canal Zone would
be returned to Panama by the year 2000. A not insignificant corollary of the Panama
Canal Treaty that greatly exercised American foreign policy ideologues required the
removal of U.S. military bases from the Canal Zone, which had long been the primary
training ground for American counterinsurgency and jungle warfare forces, as well as
military and national security personnel from other countries supportive of U.S. global
objectives. Torrijos was himself a graduate of the U.S. School of the Americas, then
based in the Canal Zone, and on occasion he would flaunt his counterinsurgency skills
by slipping past American military security to demonstrate the canal's inherent vulnerability to saboteurs.

Torrijos's growing influence as a regional political figure, together with his active
support of the nationalist struggles in Central America, made him a natural target of
U.S. hardliners. When a bomb brought down the Twin Otter in which he was flying
on the last day of July 1981, the prevailing suspicion was that his death had been engineered by the CIA.[15] Just two months earlier, Ecuador's dynamic nationalist-minded
president, Jaime Roldós Aguilera, had suffered a virtually identical fate. Because they
could not be persuaded to accommodate American strategic interests, writes a now
repentant corporate shill who had offered each of them lavish amounts of multinational largesse, both men perished in "CIA-orchestrated assassinations."[16]

Torrijos's successor, Manuel Noriega, proved equally problematic for American
policy strategists, as he continued to defend Panamanian sovereignty over the Canal
Zone and refused to permit a return of the School of the Americas, all the while serving as a paid CIA asset who apparently traded drugs and intelligence secrets on both
sides of the street. Indeed, Noriega appears to have so compromised long-range U.S.
objectives in the region that the agency's onetime director, President George H. W.
Bush, would launch an all-out military invasion of Panama to remove his former asset
from power and neutralize the lingering Torrijos legacy. So criminal was that wanton
act of armed force and so hideous its civilian toll that any doubts about the readiness
of the U.S. government to eliminate strategic individuals like Roldós, Torrijos, or
Manuel Buendía dissipate like so many wisps of fog in the midday sun.

Omar Torrijos had reconvened the original Contadora Group in June 1979 to discuss the worsening situation in Nicaragua and petition the OAS to encourage Somoza
to leave power, which events obliged him to do one month later. As relations between
Nicaragua's new Government of National Reconstruction and the Reagan administration became increasingly strained, Torrijos convened the Contadora countries yet a
third time to consider ways to defuse the escalating confrontation. His death later that

same year not only removed a key player from the conflicted Mesoamerican scene, but it had the additional effect of passing Contadora's leadership to Mexican president José López Portillo, who continued to approach regional affairs in the spirit of his combative predecessor.[17]

López Portillo turned a deaf ear to Reagan administration arguments about Soviet expansionism and communist bloc subversion, insisting to a succession of U.S. envoys that Central America's armed insurrections were a consequence not of "imported subversion" but rather of social injustice and political repression, of disintegrating "neo-feudal social systems" no longer capable of assuring political tranquility. And the single greatest obstacle to a viable resolution of the region's conflicts, he averred, was "direct or covert U.S. intervention," not Havana and Moscow.[18]

To bolster López Portillo's stance against U.S. interventionism, in 1979 the PRI formed the Permanent Conference of Latin American Political Parties (COPPPAL by its Spanish acronym) as a public forum for the region's left-of-center partisan voices, many of them in exile. The group was suggestive of the Havana-based Organization of Solidarity with the Peoples of Asia, Africa and Latin America (OSPAAAL), founded in 1966 by the Cuban-hosted First Tricontinental Conference for the purpose of "uniting, coordinating and advancing the struggle . . . against imperialism, colonialism and neocolonialism, headed by U.S. imperialism."[19] More in the spirit of social democracy than revolutionary Marxism, COPPPAL nonetheless added a significant element of ideological opposition to U.S. objectives in the region and was one of the factors that moved U.S. Southern Command chief Gen. Paul Gorman to describe Mexico City as "the hub of subversion for all of Central America."[20]

López Portillo underscored his dissenting geopolitical view by pointedly reasserting Mexico's historic relationship with Cuba, highlighted by an official presidential visit to Havana in July 1980 at the height of the Mariel boatlift, where he infuriated the Carter administration by declaring that his government would never be a party to reprisals against the island nation because any injury inflicted on Cuba was an injury suffered by Mexico. The following year López Portillo further angered U.S. officials by persuading French president François Mitterand to join him in a joint Franco-Mexican declaration calling for negotiations between the U.S.-backed government of El Salvador and the insurgent Farabundo Martí National Liberation Front (FMLN), a move that gave the Salvadoran guerrillas international standing and, in effect, legitimated them as "a politically representative force" at a time when the United States sought to portray the FMLN as an illegitimate organization of radical terrorists. These diplomatic moves on López Portillo's part had the further effect of making Mexico a recognized player in a diplomatic arena hitherto considered the preeminent domain of the United States.[21]

When Miguel de la Madrid assumed leadership of the Contadora Group in the final days of 1982, he associated his government with a cohort of regional actors whose purposes were both suspect and unwelcome within the Reagan administration, which viewed Contadora not so much as a Mexican initiative as the personal legacy of Omar Torrijos. At de la Madrid's call, the Contadora foreign ministers met again in January 1983 to continue their search for a peaceful resolution of the Central American situation.

Then, in July of that year, the four Contadora heads of state gathered in Cancún, Mexico, to give the peace process additional impetus and visibility. Costa Rica had by then withdrawn from the group following the inauguration of President Luis Alberto Monge, who was openly hostile to the Sandinistas and generally supportive of U.S. policy toward Nicaragua. Its place was taken by Panama, which until then had only provided a venue for the Contadora meetings and limited its formal participation to protocolary expressions of encouragement.

Panama's membership in the Contadora Group ratified what for American policy makers was its single most onerous antecedent: support of Panamanian sovereignty over the Panama Canal Zone. Torrijos's indelible stamp on the group as an effective device for combatting American hegemony, plus López Portillo's prior embrace of that purpose, rendered the Contadora initiative unacceptable to the Reagan White House under any guise. Both sides would continue this intricate dance for another three years, with the Contadora Group achieving some notable diplomatic successes, including a draft peace treaty tentatively accepted by the governments of Honduras, El Salvador, Guatemala, and Costa Rica, while the United States outflanked the diplomats politically and militarily on the ground.

In hindsight it is clear that by the time Miguel de la Madrid came into office the Reagan administration had decided it would accept no Central American settlement that left the Sandinistas in power. The longer Mexico insisted on the post-Somoza status quo as the point of departure for negotiating a binding peace accord, the greater was the pressure from Washington to abandon that position. Matters were made increasingly difficult for de la Madrid by the mounting financial crisis, which gave the United States powerful leverage over every facet of Mexican policy making. A further complicating factor was Mexico's business elites, who traditionally had left the conduct of diplomacy to the country's diplomats and foreign affairs specialists but now, in the later 1970s and 1980s, began to advocate foreign policy positions more responsive to their own vested interests.

Growing opposition to Contadora from inside Mexico, observed former foreign relations secretary Jorge Castañeda, "emanated essentially from the business community, and from those sectors of the bureaucracy most directly in touch with the private sector." By late 1981, Castañeda records, "it became apparent that [Mexico's] private sector and the United States government were at least in tacit agreement on the need for Mexico to keep its distance from Cuba, the Sandinistas, and the Salvadoran insurgents." From that point on, the Mexican business community would actively oppose their government's support of the region's insurgencies and revolutionary regimes, in part for ideological reasons but mainly because they felt strongly that geopolitical disagreements with the United States should not be allowed to disrupt bilateral relations on such critical matters as debt, trade, and investment.[22] These were the influential Mexicans Manuel Buendía would label "domestic *contras*."

To locate the Buendía assassination in this multilayered political matrix, it is necessary to take into account inherent ideological differences within Mexico's governmental bureaucracy. As noted earlier, the Secretariats of Government and Foreign Relations tended to view the world from opposing ends of the political spectrum. Gobernación,

Castañeda notes, had always been "a guardian of good relations with the United States" and had its own reasons for disagreeing with the Central American policy inherited from the López Portillo administration. Likewise, the Secretariats of Finance and Programming and Budget, whose respective bureaucracies interfaced with the private sector, opposed compromising Mexico's economic interests in a foreign policy confrontation with the United States. Much the same could be said of Mexico's military establishment, albeit for geopolitical views peculiar to the armed forces, as noted in chapter I. Mexico, argued these segments of the bureaucracy, ought not to pick fights with the United States on issues that affected its vital national interests and therefore should accede to American wishes in Central America.

Miguel de la Madrid proved sensitive to these arguments, observed Castañeda. What ultimately mattered was "debt, trade, support for the Mexican political system, and the image of friendly relations between [Mexico and the United States]."[23] How this appreciation of the historic relationship between the two nations played out in the privacy of de la Madrid's presidential chambers can only be speculated, but there is ample basis to suppose that the Mexican president's public stance on the affairs of state did not always coincide with the pragmatic measures he set in motion behind the scenes. Eduardo Valle, for instance, once assured us that it was not the drug traffickers who had co-opted the DFS in the 1980s, rather President de la Madrid, who had authorized the directorate to systematize and oversee the traffickers' operations as a major revenue source that could help cover the country's foreign debt.[24]

Harvard historian John Womack, on the other hand, disagrees. In his estimation, Mexican presidents are not the omnipotent rulers Valle portrays in his allegory of the "lion" and the "squirrel," but rather instruments of powerful factions within Mexico's political class who exert their influence through various government secretariats and other extrapresidential channels, including the country's national security apparatus. As a consequence of low pay exacerbated by inflation, DFS officers were easy marks for drug traffickers and anyone else with large sums of money to purchase their services, including the CIA. President de la Madrid, Womack suggests, almost certainly knew about this practice but was powerless to do anything about it.[25]

> On the night of July 16, [1984], Adolfo Aguilar Zinser, an economics researcher and journalist critical of the [Mexican] Government, was abducted at his home by armed men in civilian dress. He was blindfolded and taken to an unidentified location, where he was questioned for 14 hours before being released. . . . Mr. Aguilar Zinser had recently criticized the Mexican policy toward Guatemalan refugees, whom the Government is making an effort to move from the border to new camps in the interior.
>
> —*New York Times*, 23 September 1984

The kidnapping occurred in Mexico City six weeks after the Buendía assassination. The victim was a thirty-four-year-old professor of international relations and public administration at UNAM, an editorial adviser and weekly columnist for *unomásuno* (1978–1988), and a future public figure from a prominent family whose abduction caused an immediate sensation. In early February 1988, we discussed the incident and its possible connection to the Buendía case with him during a visit to Milwaukee.

Aguilar Zínser was seized when he opened the door to his apartment and was taken blindfolded to a clandestine detention center, presumably at the infamous Military Camp No. 1 on the western outskirts of the Federal District. His abductors turned him over to military interrogators, who roughed him up but did not subject him to serious physical abuse, as had clearly been the experience of other prisoners with whom he was confined. Aguilar's father, a prominent Mexico City attorney, intervened directly with President de la Madrid, while *unomásuno*'s editor, Becerra Acosta, did the same with Secretary of Government Manuel Bartlett Díaz. The victim was released within twenty-four hours, a stroke of good fortune rarely granted political detainees. As he was being placed into the vehicle that would transport him to the release point, one of his captors informed him of the furor his abduction had caused and remarked darkly, "So, you've turned into a little Buendía." A short while later he was set free on a quiet residential street, wrapped in a blanket and still blindfolded, the allusive death threat echoing in his ears.[26]

Aguilar Zínser's kidnapping was roundly denounced in the local periodical press, then reported in the *New York Times*, which angered the Mexican government. Sometime later he traveled to New York to give a talk and at one point neglected to take his passport and personal papers with him when he left the hotel. Upon his return he discovered that his room had been searched and his travel documents and other papers, including detailed notes about the kidnapping, taken. Replacing his Mexican passport was a simple enough procedure, but his permanent U.S. visa allowing unlimited entries proved to be another matter. When not long afterward he was again invited to speak in the United States, officials at the U.S. consulate in Mexico City initially refused to reissue his permanent visa, because, they intimated, his name now appeared on the "excludables" list. He threatened to denounce the American authorities publicly for having rescinded his U.S. visa by means of theft, an accusation that prompted the hasty intervention of Ambassador John Gavin, who ordered consular personnel to issue Aguilar a new visa immediately.[27]

It was a bizarre sequence of events that opens another small window onto the inner workings of U.S.-Mexico relations at the governmental level. It had, we concluded, all the earmarks of a joint intelligence operation to prevent Aguilar from publicizing a criminal act of intimidation authorized at the highest levels of the Mexican government and related to sensitive covert activities conducted jointly on Mexican territory by the Reagan and de la Madrid administrations. Mention of Manuel Buendía as part of that intimidation effort both implied official complicity in the Buendía assassination and ratified Aguilar Zínser's own stature as a journalist.

Official interest in Adolfo Aguilar Zínser was well warranted, as he would go on to play a unique role in the political transformation of Mexico through the turn of the century. He had begun his public life in the mid-1970s as a protégé of PRI stalwart Luis Echeverría, would join Cuauhtémoc Cárdenas's breakaway movement of PRI dissidents a decade later, and then would support the successful Partido de Acción Nacional (PAN) challenge to the PRI political machine in the presidential election of 2000. He was never a partisan ideologue and exercised his political talents wherever he thought they might most effectively contribute to Mexico's legitimate national interests, a posture he shared with Manuel Buendía. In the 1990s, he served as an independent legislator in the national Chamber of Deputies (1994–1997), then the Senate (1997–2000), where he concerned himself primarily with foreign affairs, border issues, mass media, and corruption.

In the first ever PAN government of Vicente Fox Quesada (2000–2006), Aguilar was appointed national security adviser, a newly created position in which he took tentative but symbolically significant steps to institute a Mexican version of the U.S. Freedom of Information and Privacy Act. He attained his greatest notoriety, however, as Mexico's permanent representative to the United Nations, a position he held from January 2002 until November 2003. His UN appointment coincided with the beginning of Mexico's two-year term as a nonpermanent member of the Security Council, which provided him with a privileged forum from which to influence international, and especially Third World, opinion against American preparations for war in Iraq. His effectiveness as an opponent of the Iraq war sorely exercised the administration of George W. Bush, whose secretary of state, Colin Powell, finally prevailed on President Fox to replace him. In an oft-cited speech that Buendía would have applauded but that apparently was the final straw for the White House, Aguilar averred that what Washington really sought was "a relationship of convenience and subordination" and that it continued to view Mexico not as a partner but as its "backyard."[28]

Aguilar Zínser perished in a traffic accident on 5 June 2005 while returning to the Federal District from his country home in Tepoztlán. Had circumstantial evidence to the contrary not been so persuasive, one might be allowed to wonder if that accident had possibly been induced, for the victim had powerful enemies, some of whom he had shared with Manuel Buendía. Although his personal style differed from Buendía's, the two men also had a similar sense of Mexican nationalism and purpose, which led to direct contact between them—even, perhaps, what one Buendía associate has described as a "close relationship."[29] In the final months of his life, Buendía asked Aguilar to arrange a meeting for him with the distinguished Mexican sociologist and migrant labor specialist Jorge A. Bustamante, which he did. The three of them met at Sanborns in the Zona Rosa, where they discussed various aspects of U.S.-Mexico relations, including possible linkages between the drug trade and border state politics. At one point in the conversation, Bustamante later recalled, Buendía expressed his strong conviction that the Reagan administration was launching a destabilization campaign against Mexico.

Bustamante had no doubt after that initial meeting that Buendía was actively investigating U.S. efforts to strong-arm the Mexican government. There appears to have been a follow-up meeting with Bustamante, as well as two or three phone conversations on the same general topic. Aguilar Zínser, for his part, held views virtually identical to those of Buendía. The United States, he had concluded, sought "to dismember the PRI-dominated state in order to undermine traditional Mexican nationalism, which constituted an obstacle to the realization of Washington's foreign policy objectives in the neighboring region." It was a prescient view of what came to pass over the next decade and a half.[30]

Manuel Buendía struck his full journalistic stride during the presidency of José López Portillo. His "Private Network" column began to appear in *Excélsior* the first week of December 1978, initially on page 4, then by the following summer on the front page. At least one of his columns appeared in English translation as an op-ed piece in the *New York Times*, where he wrote, "Mexico serves as a sort of crossroad for international espionage traffic. There are spies here of every imaginable nationality: Soviets, Arabs, Israelis, Germans (from both sides), British, etc. I suspect that even Portugal and Italy are represented."[31] And, of course, there was the American CIA, which was the op-ed piece's main focus. "Some of these agents," Buendía noted, "are not actually spies. They are weapons experts and salesmen working for their respective governments. . . . For example, the representatives of Israeli and Spanish manufacturers; in both cases they are supported by their governments, and have been able to establish close working relationships with countries all through South and Central America."[32]

Here again Israel appears on Mexico's geopolitical landscape. Already the year before, Buendía had called attention to an Israeli arms firm that had recently opened an office in the Federal District's tony Polanco district under the name Industrias Aeronáuticas de Israel (IAI) and posed the rhetorical question, "Was it morally proper to have permitted Israel to open an agency in Mexico that sold armaments to Somoza, Pinochet, Videla, and other [repressive] Latin American regimes?" Two of IAI's employees, Buendía noted, were listed as "civilian attachés" at Israel's Mexico City embassy. Their business cards identified the Polanco office as the firm's "Permanent Mission for Latin America," leaving little doubt that it was an arm of the Israeli government. "In fact," Buendía concluded, "numerous qualified observers now think that Israel and Spain are the 'black hand' of the United States, supplying arms to governments with whom Washington would prefer not to deal directly in such matters so as not to soil Mr. Carter's public image as a defender of human rights."[33]

Buendía expressed his personal view of regional affairs in vintage fashion midway into the López Portillo presidency. "Out of an antiquated and pretentious sense of nationalism," he wrote, "some of us still resist 'the American way of life,' which, with its moral qualities and plastic beauty, has already sapped the vitality of other Mexicans, who are even moved to purchase homes in Coronado or open bank accounts in Los Angeles." But, he quipped,

> whatever aversion the few of us remaining anti-Yankees in Mexico may have will immediately be assuaged upon reading a U.S. magazine that only costs two dollars. It's called *Soldier of Fortune* and bills itself simply as "The Journal of Professional Adventurers." Inside you can find a small personal ad that reads:
>
>> Vietnam vet offers his services to anyone who can pay for them, inside or outside the U.S. Expert at killing Asian communists. Would very much like to take part in hunting down communists in the jungles of Central America. Please write to . . . specifying conditions of employment.
>
> On another page a glitzy color ad offers a large batch of light machine guns and automatic assault rifles sufficient to equip "any number of fighters." Classified ads and editorials tell readers when, where and at what price they can acquire anything from dozens of bazookas to a pair of helicopter gunships.

Soldier of Fortune magazine, Buendía wrote, was "pure ideology," part of an elaborate ideological system that spouts pathetic statements about human rights at the same time as it auctions off "half-wasted human beings" together with used machine guns and assault rifles, because it must constantly replace them with new soldiers and new weapons "to persuade public opinion of their system's economic, social and political worth." (*Soldier of Fortune* [SOF] was, we would agree, an artifact of the prevailing predatory culture that supported the end-of-century American imperial project, a culture marked by the camo clothing fad in civilian dress, the proliferation of weekend paintball warriors, pervasive violence in popular entertainment, and the manufacture, hype, and sale of General Motors' Hummer, a civilian version of the U.S. military's signature replacement for its previously iconic Jeep.) It was "pure American dream," Buendía lamented, which tragically appealed to the many tired, gullible souls who were fed up with the shortcomings of this "little country called Mexico." One typical SOF image that struck him was a photograph of Omar Torrijos with the caption "Re-elect Carter, the best president Panama ever had."[34]

Buendía traveled to Panama at the end of September 1979 to cover the formal transfer of sovereignty over the Canal Zone from the United States to Panama. It was one of the rare occasions when he reported events from the scene. President López Portillo was one of the participating foreign dignitaries, and Buendía quoted him with evident political intent. Whether he actually accompanied the president or made the trip on his own account is unclear, but, whatever the case, it is apparent that the two men shared similar views on the historic significance of the Panama Canal transfer and that they were developing a symbiotic relationship in opposition to U.S. regional objectives. Readers would perhaps find his observations of interest, he wrote, because, "as President López Portillo expressed," they recalled historic episodes "that we in Mexico have been obliged to suffer from the same cause: American imperialism."

Buendía began his account with a description of the U.S. cultural presence in Panama. The night before the historic transfer ceremony, he wrote, the only programs on local television "were two comedies in English and an American movie about the sufferings of U.S. soldiers in the First World War." When he placed an international telephone call to Mexico, the hotel operator, a native Panamanian, understood his Spanish but answered him in English. The morning of the ceremony, 1 October 1979, when he would have expected to find the country's leading news anchors on location, broadcasting live well before the actual event, the only programming he could find on his hotel room TV was Liz Taylor in the Hollywood movie *Cleopatra* and cartoons, all in English. On that historic day, he marveled, three-quarters of Panamanian television consisted of American movies without Spanish subtitles.

A single channel broadcast the formalities, Buendía noted incredulously, and it did not commence its coverage until the very last minute. Much to his relief, by midday a quarter million celebratory Panamanians had entered the U.S. air base at Albrook Field to hear speeches and witness the raising of the Panamanian flag atop the Canal Zone's Ancón Hill. "And when President López Portillo spoke out so sharply against U.S. imperialism; when he vindicated the merit of the Panamanian people, of their civilian heroes and martyrs; when he moved the multitude by evoking the triumph of

Nicaragua's revolution, at that moment," Buendía exulted, "it was possible to believe that in Panama colonialism would one day be banished even from the hearts and minds of the most wretched."

Buendía compared the twenty-eight Panamanian students killed by U.S. troops in the January 1964 "flag riot" to Mexico's "Niños Héroes," the young military cadets who in 1848 made a last stand at Chapultepec Castle against the invading U.S. army of Gen. Winfield Scott. As part of the canal ceremony, Panama's president, Arístides Royo, read out the names of the fallen flag riot youths, the crowd responding in unison to each one with a thunderous *¡Presente!* "And," Buendía concluded, "when the mother of one of those young men felled by Yankee bullets handed President Royo the Panamanian flag and it began slowly to ascend, then waved gently and gracefully from the very top of the pole, I was one of the many who wept."[35]

When Omar Torrijos's aircraft went down a year and nine months later, Manuel Buendía devoted two extensive columns to the possibility of CIA involvement. A week after that fatal crash, Fidel Castro and López Portillo met for a second time in Cozumel, Mexico, where, Buendía reported, they discussed the implications of Torrijos's death but could offer no information that would allow them to refute the official version of an accident. The Soviet news agency TASS, on the other hand, implied that Torrijos had been slain by the CIA as a reprisal for the Panama Canal Treaty. But Buendía rejected such speculation out of hand, noting that, while it would not be the first time a foreign leader had been assassinated "by the long arm of the U.S. government," for such an accusation to stand it had to rest either on direct evidence that the plane had been sabotaged or on a demonstrable motive "equal to the gravity of the crime." Reprisal, he stressed, was not part of the CIA's modus operandi.[36]

Circumstantial evidence, while insufficient in itself, may add weight to a plausible hypothesis, and Buendía elaborated a persuasive motive for CIA complicity in Torrijos's untimely demise against a backdrop of other recent deaths. Quoting the celebrated Colombian writer Gabriel García Márquez, who had written an op-ed piece about Torrijos's death in the Spanish newspaper *El País*, he observed that, while the victim "afforded equal opportunity to fate and his enemies [and] either one could have caused his death," it was impossible not to relate this incident to several others that had occurred over the previous fourteen months. "In June 1980," recalled García Márquez,

> the plane in which the Bolivian vice president elect, Jaime Paz Zamora, was flying plummeted to the ground in flames. It was thought at the time, though never proven, that someone had put sugar in the fuel tank. Afterward came the tragedy of Ecuador's president, Jaime Roldós; then that of Gen. Luis Hoyos Rubio, chief of Peru's General Staff; and now that of Gen. Omar Torrijos, the providential and irreplaceable Panamanian. Four progressive figures, whose disappearance could only favor the hemisphere's darkest tendencies. It is not easy to believe that so many disasters in a row have been coincidental, because the index finger of death is not so selective and even coincidences have their own inexorable laws.

García Márquez was a close personal friend of Omar Torrijos and had flown with him that July in the same Twin Otter aircraft that, just a week later, would fatefully crash in circumstances that "did not seem entirely accidental."[37]

Buendía cited the distinguished educator and former rector of the University of El Salvador, Fabio Castillo Figueroa, to the same effect. Jaime Roldós and Omar Torrijos shared a progressive outlook and may have been slain "by the same criminal hand," Castillo opined. The chances that two heads of state would perish in similar accidents within four months of each other were statistically remote, he added, "which suggests the same culprit in both cases." More interestingly, Castillo went on to report that Torrijos was personally involved in working out an "independent solution" to the Central American conflict, "one that differed significantly from the U.S. approach." Here, Buendía intimated, was the kernel of a possible motive for state-sponsored assassination.

But there was more. A "thoroughly credible" diplomatic source informed Buendía that Torrijos had been engaged in an effort to unify the various guerrilla factions fighting against the U.S.-supported Salvadoran government. Moreover, according to this source, he had been seeking support from sympathetic regional governments, including Mexico. ("I dealt with [Torrijos] in the final critical moments of his exemplary struggle," Buendía quoted López Portillo as saying. "He was a man who still had many contributions to make to the struggle against the colonial regime that characterizes our history.") Had Torrijos's efforts succeeded, Buendía believed, "it would have been totally impossible for the United States to contain the popular rebellion in El Salvador." And that, he concluded, was an "adequate motive" to assassinate an influential figure like Omar Torrijos.[38]

This Red Privada column appeared on a Friday. Over that weekend, Buendía consulted further with his diplomatic and intelligence sources, "including a counterintelligence expert who can be found in Mexico City" (we suspect either then DFS chief Miguel Nazar Haro or Secretary of Government Fernando Gutiérrez Barrios), then the following Tuesday he developed more fully what he saw as the likely motive behind Torrijos's death. Torrijos, he wrote, "was involved in two projects that could have blown U.S. strategy in Central America to bits." One of them entailed the infiltration into the Guatemalan insurgency of Dr. Hugo Spadafora, a Panamanian medical doctor and renowned guerrilla fighter whom the CIA at the time compared to "Che" Guevara. The other project, to which Buendía had alluded in his previous column, was a double-faceted effort to mediate the unification of El Salvador's insurgent groups and then to arrange for their recognition by a coalition of international political movements and foreign governments as belligerents in a civil war.

Spadafora was a wild card in the region's geopolitical deck. He had fought together with Amílcar Cabral in Guinea Bissau's anticolonial war against Portugal; had met with Palestinian leader Yassir Arafat in Libya; had formed the international Simón Bolívar Brigade, which fought alongside Edén Pastora's southern front forces against Somoza's Israeli-supplied Guardia Nacional; was now thought to be contemplating a similar involvement in Guatemala and perhaps El Salvador; and subsequently would collaborate with Pastora's *contra* forces against the Sandinistas. And he, too, was destined to perish in the regional struggles of that historical moment—significantly, for our investigation, in circumstances that further help contextualize the Buendía assassination.

Three weeks before Torrijos's death, Spadafora issued a call in the Mexican press for volunteers to form an international force that would join the popular insurgencies in

Central America. The CIA, Buendía wrote, "had confirmed the existence of a close but secret tie between Spadafora and Gen. Omar Torrijos, who, with his unlimited influence in the Panamanian National Guard, had agreed to provision Spadafora's force and give him political and logistical support." If one combined the implications of Torrijos's activities, which impacted the most sensitive aspects of Washington's Central American strategy, with explicit statements by the U.S. president, his secretary of state, and his UN ambassador that the United States would prevent "by whatever means necessary" any further advance of "communism" in the region, then, Buendía suggested, "all the required elements were in place to order a political assassination." This was the motive behind Torrijos's murder, he concluded, "and it points in only one direction."[39]

For the neo–cold warriors of the Reagan White House, the López Portillo administration was the geopolitical measure of Mexico throughout the 1980s. Accordingly, Washington's Caribbean basin strategizing in that era viewed its southern neighbor as an obstacle to the achievement of U.S. objectives and sought to neutralize Mexican opposition both overtly and covertly. Manuel Buendía, for his part, had by then become a highly visible actor in Mexico's opposition to American regional interests, a visibility that increased markedly in the López Portillo *sexenio* as a consequence of his identification with the United States' principal hemispheric adversaries. He was an outspoken defender not only of Panamanian sovereignty and the Central American insurgencies but also of Cuban sovereignty, as well as a personal acquaintance of Fidel Castro.

We are uncertain when Buendía first met the Cuban leader, but it could have been at the time of Castro's 1979 meeting with López Portillo in Cozumel, or perhaps during López Portillo's official visit to Cuba the following year. We know that he and *Siempre!* editorial writer Francisco Martínez de la Vega met with Castro in Havana in March 1982, and that Buendía had traveled to Cuba once before that. Reading between the lines of Buendía's 21 August 1981 column, which opens with the statement "Fidel Castro and López Portillo talked in Cozumel about the death of Torrijos and its consequences," we think it likely that he was present to cover the talks and may well have spoken with Castro on that occasion.[40] What even some of Buendía's professional associates did not know (but U.S. and Mexican intelligence surely did) was that in 1984 he and his family had been invited to Cuba as guests of the Cuban government to attend that year's 26th of July celebration, the national holiday marking the opening battle of the Cuban Revolution. Buendía had informed his wife, María Dolores, that in Cuba she and their three children would have a car and driver at their disposal to take them wherever they wished to go, while he "would be with Fidel" and other officials discussing certain unspecified matters. A short while after Buendía's assassination, his widow told us, Cuba's ambassador to Mexico informed her that the invitation for her and her children to visit the island was still open and that they were welcome to remain in Cuba for as long as they wished. She was not emotionally ready to make the trip so close to her husband's passing, however, and when at last she did express an interest in going, the Cubans deemed the moment inopportune.[41]

The combination of these prominent associations and Buendía's own combative engagement in the regional contentions of the day projected what American intelligence analysts would perceive as a hostile political profile. On one occasion, the widow recalled, Buendía had been invited to accompany Mexico's secretary of mines on an official visit to the United States, and the U.S. embassy had summarily refused to issue him an entry visa because, she said, "he was already on their list of 'undesirables.'"[42] In a predictably futile yet revealing exercise, we subsequently sought to obtain a copy of the political profile that the CIA would routinely prepare for a subject of interest like Manuel Buendía. In response to our Freedom of Information Act (FOIA) request for Buendía's profile, we were advised with risible agency circumlocution that "in all such requests as [ours], the CIA can neither confirm nor deny the existence or nonexistence of any CIA records responsive to [that] request. The fact of the existence or nonexistence of records containing such information—unless, of course, it has been officially acknowledged—would be classified for reasons of national security under Section 1.3 (a) (5) (foreign relations) of Executive Order 12356." In a follow-up paragraph, CIA's information and privacy coordinator underscored, "By this action, we are neither confirming nor denying the existence or nonexistence of such records."[43]

At the time we submitted our FOIA request we possessed documentary evidence that the agency maintained an active file on Manuel Buendía, and subsequently we would obtain firsthand testimony confirming as much. It was thoroughly improbable, moreover, that U.S. intelligence would not pay close attention to a Mexican media personality of Buendía's stature who was in personal communication with Cuban premier Fidel Castro and whose influential column appeared on the front page of Mexico's leading daily newspaper. We early concluded that Buendía's Cuban link needed to be investigated further, and eventually we would travel to Havana for that purpose.

5

Ballet Folklórico, Act I

What if a crime could be created in which as soon as one false scenario was rebutted, another one was ready to take its place? There would always be one more thing like *this* that could be made to seem as if it must have had something to do with *that*.
—Francisco Goldman, *The Art of Political Murder* (2008)

TWELVE HOURS AFTER HIS ASSASSINATION, Manuel Buendía lay in state at the prestigious Gayosso mortuary on Félix Cuevas Street in the capital's Del Valle district. At 8:30 on the morning of 31 May, President Miguel de la Madrid arrived to pay his respects, accompanied by Secretary of Government Manuel Bartlett Díaz, Secretary of Foreign Relations Bernardo Sepúlveda, and Presidential Press Secretary Manuel Alonso. As he approached Buendía's casket, an impertinent hand thrust suddenly against de la Madrid's chest brought him up short. Stunned by the improbable affront, the president found himself face-to-face with the distraught younger brother of the deceased.

"You're in charge of this country's institutions!" Ángel Buendía blurted out. "It's your responsibility to see that justice is done in this crime! Otherwise you will be suspect and will have shown us yourself what kind of country we live in!" Flustered, de la Madrid replied hastily that Don Ángel "had every right to demand justice" and promised him that the government would not stop until his brother's murder had been solved and the guilty parties brought to justice, "no matter who they might turn out to be." Buendía's anguished brother then stepped aside, allowing the presidential party to take up positions on either side of the open (glass-covered) sarcophagus, de la Madrid and Bartlett Díaz at the casket's head, Sepúlveda and Alonso at its foot. The weight of the moment, heightened by Ángel Buendía's unexpected challenge, was evident in the president's furrowed brow, which contrasted noticeably with the blank faces of his government and foreign relations secretaries.[1]

De la Madrid did not speak to Don Ángel again, although subsequently Bartlett Díaz was to have extensive contact with him. After years of persistent efforts to unravel his brother's murder, Ángel Buendía would become convinced that no major decision concerning the official handling of the case could have been taken without the express approval of the president. It could have been solved quickly, he concluded, but was not because Miguel de la Madrid intervened to prevent it. He was an accomplice "by virtue of cover-up and by the high office he occupied at the time."[2]

Manuel Buendía's younger
brother Ángel. (Sylvia E. Bartley)

Ángel Buendía played a key role in the elaborate dance between the Mexican government and the media around the search for a credible resolution of the Buendía case. Initially he was paralyzed by grief and depression, a precarious emotional state from which he gradually emerged as a result of subsequent conversations with friends and sympathetic members of the press, who persuaded him to channel his anguish toward avenging his brother's death. He did not seek biblical eye-for-an-eye vengeance, where the offended sibling finds and kills his brother's killer, but rather a broader retribution that would "unmask all participants in the crime and cause them to rot in prison." From the outset Don Ángel assumed that the assassination had been a political killing, which greatly complicated matters but also promised greater satisfaction should he and his associates manage to unravel the case, because along with the gunman, highly placed accomplices would be brought down as well.[3]

Don Ángel's active involvement in the Buendía case developed gradually over the better part of three years, during which he mustered courage and found his own voice. He was not a journalist or trained investigator, nor had he moved in the same elevated circles of power and influence as had his brother Manuel. He had made a career as a tour guide, however, and was accustomed to dealing with a wide variety of people and personalities, which, combined with personal integrity and fortitude, allowed him to play a decisive role in exposing official complicity in his brother's assassination.

From the outset his closest supporters and confidants were Miguel Ángel Sánchez de Armas, founding director of the Fundación Manuel Buendía, and Rogelio Hernández López and Jorge Meléndez Preciado, both key figures behind the *Excélsior* investigative team. Sánchez de Armas had a personal and professional relationship with Buendía, whom he considered his master teacher, and would devote the next several years to propagating Buendía's journalistic legacy. Hernández and Meléndez were not personal associates of the victim, yet they fully appreciated that Manuel Buendía was Mexico's most important and influential journalist and for that reason alone felt that resolution of his murder demanded their professional commitment. Whereas they would remain steadfast in their support and encouragement of Ángel Buendía and contribute commentary to his eventual book about the case, there came a moment when Sánchez de Armas broke with his fallen *maestro*'s younger brother. It was a sudden break, jarringly out of character, one that raises additional questions about the handling of the case that we will address in the course of our narrative.

As months became years, Don Ángel followed the tortuous, frequently bifurcating course of the official investigations with growing disillusionment. Muddying the waters from the start was the irregular intervention of the DFS, which lacked jurisdiction but by virtue of its national security role was able to throw its weight around in disruptive, self-serving ways. As Rogelio Hernández expressed it, "The DFS was diverting information and obstructing the official investigation. . . . [It] was first on the scene, took charge of witnesses, seized evidence, distorted facts with misinformation, and even tried to erase [the perpetrators'] tracks."[4] Mexico City attorney general Victoria Adato Green,[5] meanwhile, focused the official investigation into Manuel Buendía's private life, intimating that his assassination had been a crime of passion rather than one related to his Red Privada columns. Buendía's death, she declared just four months after the event, was not political. It was a categorical assertion that persuaded none of the victim's professional colleagues and dumbfounded Ángel Buendía for its sheer improbability.

It further transpired that within two weeks following the assassination, Adato ordered a separate, extrajudicial investigation within her own office conducted by former DFS chief and key CIA asset Miguel Nazar Haro. Nazar had been brought in as a special adviser to Adato. His unofficial investigative role in the Buendía case was far from transparent and to this day has not been clarified beyond his reported supervision of police sketches, the creation of a life-sized wax mannequin based on witness descriptions of the gunman, and a filmed reenactment of the crime.[6] Then, at the end of January 1985, Deputy Prosecutor René Paz Horta announced that the Buendía case was "80 percent complete," that the authorities had a "95 percent profile of the killer," that law enforcement "had the criminal surrounded," and that the remaining 20 percent of the case "entailed his pursuit and capture."[7]

The Mexico City earthquake of 19 September 1985 collapsed the edifice that housed the district attorney general's offices and in the process destroyed a portion of the Buendía case files. Only the head of Nazar Haro's wax mannequin survived, while the clothes Buendía had been wearing when he was shot conveniently vanished. Inconveniently for the authorities, the ruptured structure revealed basement cells containing the bodies of physically abused prisoners, which produced a scandal requiring cosmetic changes of personnel. Victoria Adato was appointed to the Supreme Court, which afforded her immunity from prosecution and was widely viewed as prima facie evidence of official malfeasance, including her handling of the Buendía case.

Adato's replacement as federal district attorney general was system minion Renato Sales Gasque, a humorless, balding lawyer who would stage-manage damage control of the Buendía case for the next two years. On 27 February 1986, just two months after assuming the position of attorney general, Sales Gasque informed representatives of the influential Democratic Journalists Union (UPD by its Spanish acronym) that the authorities had not yet developed a viable hypothesis, nor was there any reason to expect a prompt resolution of the case. Paz Horta's statement of a year earlier that the Buendía investigation had been approaching completion was plainly false. Moreover, Sales Gasque told the reporters, the passage of so much time had the unfortunate effect of obscuring leads and allowing the culprits' trail to grow cold. Twenty-one months after the event, it was now necessary to begin the investigation again, with new personnel devoted to redeveloping evidence and discovering new leads.[8]

Ángel Buendía observed this course of events with mounting frustration from his home in Guadalajara. Following the second anniversary of his brother's assassination, he noted a sharp drop-off in media coverage of the case, which became a virtual silence during the second half of 1986. Moreover, he had personally witnessed the incompetence of the police investigators ostensibly assigned to pursue leads in Guadalajara, as well as that of their superiors in Mexico City. Convinced that something dramatic would be required to exert renewed pressure on the government, he took advantage of a chance encounter at the beginning of January 1987 with a television reporter from Guadalajara's Channel 4 to do a taped interview. In response to the reporter's question about the official investigation, Don Ángel reminded President de la Madrid of his promise to resolve the Buendía case and emphasized that should the president fail to keep his word, then for Don Ángel "the name of Manuel Buendía's assassin could only be Miguel de la Madrid Hurtado."[9]

He had doubts about whether the Guadalajara TV station would actually air the interview, and when it did not, he contacted Felipe Cobián, a local correspondent for the Mexico City daily *La Jornada*, whom he knew well and trusted. Cobián told Ángel that if it was his intention to have his words reach the president, then he, Cobián, would be happy to conduct his own interview with him. Don Ángel agreed and repeated the same pointed assertions he had made to the reporter from Channel 4. *La Jornada* carried the interview in its Sunday edition of 4 January 1987. Two days later Ángel Buendía received a telephone call from attorney Rubén Guerrero, Manuel Bartlett Díaz's personal secretary, inviting him to meet with Bartlett in Mexico City.[10]

UNSOLVED SLAYING AN ISSUE IN MEXICO CAMPAIGN

Los Angeles Times, 21 May 1987

By Dan Williams, Times Staff Writer

Mexico City—Who killed Manuel Buendía, Mexico's most influential newspaper columnist?

Almost three years after Buendía was gunned down in a Mexico City parking lot, the question is still unanswered. It is being raised again because May 30 will be the third anniversary of his death—and because the lack of progress in finding his killer has become an issue in Mexico's presidential campaign.

. . .

The investigation into his killing has gone virtually nowhere. He was shot four times at close range, witnesses said, by a tall, mustachioed man who fled on foot through Mexico City's entertainment district, the so-called Pink Zone.

TWO CANDIDATES

Two men who are now candidates for the presidential nomination have had responsibility for solving the Buendía mystery: Manuel Bartlett Díaz, secretary of the interior, who is considered a strong candidate for the nomination, and federal Atty. Gen. Sergio García Ramírez, who is ranked among the second-tier candidates.

The nominee, who will run under the banner of the ruling Institutional Revolutionary Party (PRI), will be designated this fall by President Miguel de la Madrid. The president's choice is regarded as certain to be elected, given the PRI's dominance of electoral politics in Mexico. Election Day itself is not until next year.

Any mention of the Buendía case in the press is considered an indirect criticism of the candidacies of Bartlett and García. Sometimes the criticism is direct.

Manuel Moreno, a former PRI leader in the Senate, said in an interview with the magazine *Proceso*: "I exclude, among the aspirants, all those who have to do with repression. I concede no chance to Bartlett while the question of who killed Manuel Buendía is not resolved. The same goes for Sergio García Ramírez."

The two candidates avoid the subject. They generally limit their remarks to praise for De la Madrid or to their records as public officials.

Nor do other candidates mention the Buendía case, although some encourage their journalist friends to bring it up.

Publicly, the government has given high priority to the Buendía investigation. After the shooting, De la Madrid told the attorney general's office to put all its "effort and resources" into finding the killer. It soon became a ritual of incoming police chiefs, Mexico City attorneys general and other law enforcement officials to promise a quick solution.

January 1987 through June 1989 marked the Mexican government's theatrical resolution of the Buendía case. It was an elaborate folkloric ballet in two presidential acts and several scenes, replete with acrobatic leaps, pirouettes, practiced poses *en pointe*, and a thoroughly improbable corps of nimble-footed dancers. Act I was President de la Madrid's choreography of damage control, in which he attempted to recover credibility lost in the first two and a half years of transparently deceptive efforts to resolve the Buendía assassination. Its lead performers were District Attorney General Renato Sales Gasque and, in scene 2, independent Special Prosecutor Miguel Ángel García Domínguez, with counterpoint provided by the elusive former DFS chief José Antonio Zorrilla Pérez and Zorrilla's former superior and PRI presidential hopeful Secretary of Government (Gobernación) Manuel Bartlett Díaz.

Act II was President Carlos Salinas de Gortari's choreography of the official Buendía case finale. The star performers were again Special Prosecutor García Domínguez, Sales Gasque's successor as district attorney general, Ignacio Morales Lechuga, and alleged assassination mastermind Zorrilla Pérez, with supporting roles played by a foursome of former DFS officers straight out of central casting—a mustachioed soap opera idol fingered as the gunman and three directorate accomplices, one of them female. Both acts played out against a backdrop of insistent media challenges, conflictive geopolitics, and Mexico's defining bilateral relationship with the United States.

When Ángel Buendía stepped unexpectedly onstage in act I, scene 1, he introduced a pulse of syncopated dissonance into the official choreography that would continue to reverberate long after the final curtain dropped. As recounted in *Mi testimonio*, he accepted Bartlett Díaz's invitation to meet with trepidation, and, against the advice of friends who feared for his life, determined to risk everything in the interest of exposing his brother's killers and gambling that the government could not afford the murder of a second Buendía. He was surprised by Bartlett's civility, having formed a prior image of him based on press accounts as despotic and aloof. He had expected the secretary to reprimand him for having suggested that de la Madrid might have been responsible for his brother's death, but instead he encountered a most solicitous Bartlett, who reassured him that neither he nor the president had had anything to do with the killing, that Ángel had every right to demand justice for his brother, and that the government had an obligation to satisfy that demand. Bartlett promised to keep him fully apprised of developments in the official investigation, as well as to cover all expenses for Don Ángel's case-related travel between Guadalajara and the Federal District.

As a first step, Bartlett promised to arrange for the new district attorney general, Sales Gasque, to brief him on the case. The meeting was scheduled for 21 January 1987, a Wednesday. The preceding Monday, Don Ángel met with a group of media confidants to strategize, and it was decided that he should not meet with Sales Gasque alone so as to avoid the risk of being manipulated. Informed of Ángel's intention to bring several journalists with him to the briefing, Bartlett strenuously objected but was unable to dissuade him from doing so, finally agreeing that "however Don Ángel wished to proceed was how it would be done." At 9:00 a.m. on the twenty-first, Ángel Buendía arrived at Sales Gasque's office accompanied by *La Jornada* columnist Miguel Ángel Granados Chapa, Manuel Buendía Foundation director Miguel Ángel Sánchez de Armas, and *Excélsior* reporter Rogelio Hernández López.[11]

No doubt forewarned by Bartlett, Sales Gasque received them with the false courtesy typical of senior government officials. He spoke briefly and unconvincingly about several purported lines of investigation that his interlocutors believed had not actually been pursued, then turned them over to his immediate subordinate, Deputy Prosecutor Miguel Ángel García Domínguez, a prominent jurist from Guanajuato who at the time was the official directly responsible for overseeing the Buendía case. As the individual most familiar with the details of the case, Sales Gasque informed them, García Domínguez would conduct their briefing. Don Ángel described the district attorney general's deputy as a "cold, calculating, suspicious man with the fixed gaze of an old-time studio photograph," which conformed well with our own impressions of García Domínguez when we interviewed him on two subsequent occasions.

García Domínguez's briefing that day went on for more than two hours in what afterward Don Ángel dismissed as "crinoline tactics," an expression coined by his brother Manuel to describe official explanations that "beat around the bush," as the English expression goes, but never touch on the heart of the matter. It was what less colorfully but more precisely we would call "quantification tactics," a procedure employed from the outset in the Buendía case whereby the public, via periodic news conferences, was provided with a litany of statistics that purposely confused activity with direction and investigative motions with substance: x numbers of files created; y numbers of hypotheses formulated or discarded; and z numbers of witnesses and suspects interrogated.

García Domínguez read endlessly from file after file that offered nothing Ángel and his three media associates did not already know. When he finished, Rogelio Hernández asked pointedly, "Are we to conclude from this that nothing has been done and we will have to wait for the next administration to see progress in the Buendía case?" The question infuriated García Domínguez, but before he could recover his composure, the others followed suit with a barrage of pointed questions he was unable to answer. "Why," demanded Don Ángel, "had the Public Ministry not yet received the former DFS Buendía files if, as García Domíngez had just acknowledged, former directorate chief José Antonio Zorrilla Pérez was a primary suspect?" This was a key issue in the Buendía case, one that threatened to expose far graver matters than the celebrity murder of a prominent newspaper columnist and one that García Domínguez could address neither then nor later in his role as independent special prosecutor. When Ángel Buendía reported back to Bartlett Díaz on the outcome of the meeting with Sales Gasque and García Domínguez, Bartlett performed a fleet step *en arrière* to dissociate himself from Sales Gasque's slowness in producing satisfactory results, promising Don Ángel that "on orders from the president" he, Manuel Bartlett, would now personally assume responsibility for moving the official investigation forward.[12]

EXCERPTS FROM PRESS CONFERENCE CONVENED BY DISTRICT ATTORNEY GENERAL SALES GASQUE, MEXICO CITY, 25 JANUARY 1988

Q: Señor Procurador, what can you tell us in regard to the articles by Bartley that say the Buendía homicide is a national security matter and that related CIA documents have been mutilated?

A: We have gathered all the information collected by the former Federal Security Directorate and it contains absolutely nothing that allows us to affirm the involvement of foreign intelligence agencies. Everything that the Federal Security Directorate had in this regard we now have and we have reviewed it and will continue to do so.

. . .

Q: Señor Procurador, in a recently published report [by Russell H. Bartley] it is suggested that foreign services, concretely the CIA, may possess better information [on the Buendía case] than our own Mexican authorities. How do you respond?

A: Well, we have corroborated the evidence, the supposed evidence, presented by this person, as well as by others in the media, and it is not evidence of any such thing.[13]

The articles that so exercised Sales Gasque were a five-part series published by *unomásuno* about U.S. State Department cable traffic concerning Manuel Buendía in the years 1978–1984, copies of which had been routed to the CIA.[14] The series was based on fifteen cables from the U.S. embassy in Mexico City released to Matthew Rothschild in response to an FOIA request submitted three years earlier when Rothschild was commencing his Buendía investigation for *The Progressive* magazine. No longer working on the case when he finally received the redacted cables in the fall of 1987, he made photocopies for us and invited us to use them as we wished.

Despite the repeated denials of complicity in the Buendía assassination by U.S. government spokespersons and the continuing insistence of Mexican authorities that it had not been a "political" killing, this modest handful of "restricted," "confidential," and "secret" diplomatic cables lent documentary weight to continuing questions about possible foreign involvement in Buendía's dramatic demise. Of particular interest, we suggested, was the way these official documents had become public through an invariably drawn-out legal process perfectly susceptible to government manipulation. Just as improbable as the CIA's assertion to us that two newspaper clippings comprised its only record of the Buendía assassination, or the National Security Council's contention that it possessed no documentation at all relating to the case, was the State Department's assertion to Rothschild that these fewer than two dozen cables constituted the full extent of its retrievable records on Buendía.

An internal analysis of the cables, Russell wrote, revealed that the U.S. State Department had been monitoring Buendía since well before 12 October 1978, the date of the first in the series released to Matthew Rothschild. In that heavily redacted cable, which reported Buendía's allegation in the Mexico City daily *El Universal* of the same date that Lawrence Sternfield was the local CIA station chief, embassy personnel described Buendía as "a left-wing columnist" and referred to previous columns he had written. Given this manifest interest in Buendía, the absence among the FOIA-released documents of similar cables concerning other provocative "Private Network" columns strongly suggests the conscious omission of extant documents—most likely, we suspect, to conceal the actual extent of the State Department's Buendía files. "These few documents that now come to light, as well as those still hidden from public view," Russell noted, "reveal the degree to which Manuel Buendía concerned those responsible for U.S. policy in Mexico and the neighboring countries of the region." They also documented official U.S. antipathy toward Buendía personally.[15]

We were back in Mexico City that fall with a full schedule of interviews, including three with the head of Mexico's INTERPOL office, Florentino Ventura Gutiérrez; PJDF chief Jesús Miyazawa Álvarez; and Ministerio Público deputy prosecutor Alejandro Sosa Ortiz, the official then in charge of the Buendía case. These interviews had been arranged by *unomásuno* editor Manuel Becerra Acosta, and the first two came off without a hitch. When we arrived at the district attorney general's Avenida Coyoacán offices for our meeting with Sosa Ortiz, however, things soured quickly. It was the day after the first of my five articles on the State Department cables about Manuel Buendía had appeared in *unomásuno* and late enough in the morning for Ministerio Público staff to have read the second in that series. Sosa was standing in the hallway outside his office conversing with a colleague as we approached and, after we introduced ourselves, immediately wanted to know what ground we proposed to cover. At our mention of foreign intelligence, he summarily canceled the interview, dismissed us with an ill-tempered wave of the hand, and slammed his office door in our faces. Possible U.S.

complicity in the Buendía assassination was not a subject to which Mexican authorities would grant even hypothetical credence.

By the close of 1987, the studied aversion on the part of Sales Gasque and his subordinates to any consideration of possible outside involvement in Buendía's killing, coupled with the mounting political imperative to offer the public a plausible resolution of the case, had led them into a conundrum of their own making. The initial false step was taken half a year earlier when, on the eve of the third anniversary of the assassination, Sales Gasque had choreographed the unveiling of a colorful prime suspect: international arms dealer and decorated Third Reich war hero Gerhard Georg Mertins. Pressured personally by the secretary of government to assuage public opinion with a credible suspect, Sales Gasque had utilized the third anniversary date to full histrionic advantage.

Three days before the anniversary, which fell on a Saturday that year, the district attorney general had met with reporters to announce that the Ministerio Público would soon release an official summary of the Buendía investigation to the media, implying that it would contain new information about probable suspects. He made a point of lauding the active collaboration given his office and the PJDF by Federal Attorney General Sergio García Ramírez and Secretary of Government Manuel Bartlett Díaz, while in response to a reporter's suggestion that the Buendía case was still not being taken seriously by the authorities, Sales Gasque insisted that both for his office and for the national government it was in fact the single most important criminal case then being investigated. "We are," he expressed in what now seems an understatement, "most anxious to resolve this case." Pressed by a reporter who wanted to know why the attorney general thought the Buendía matter so important, Sales Gasque replied with vintage official boilerplate. "Because," came his straight-faced reply, "freedom of opinion and criticism is fundamental to a free society and when a representative of that freedom is affected, the democratic basis of the rule of law is affected. It affects our social order, which is based on full respect for human liberty in the pursuit of social justice."[16]

On Friday, 29 May 1987, Sales Gasque held the announced press conference, at which he distributed a six-page document titled "Información sobre el caso Buendía" (Information on the Buendía Case), together with a list of twenty-four individuals who had been investigated as possible suspects. First and second on the list were Buendía's assistants, Juan Manuel Bautista and Luis Soto. Also on the list was Susana Fisher, wife of the popular caricaturist and illustrator "Ekko" (Héctor de la Garza Batorzki) and alleged paramour of the victim. (Buendía was said by close associates to have been on his way to see Fisher the evening he was killed.) Notably absent from the list was Mertins, the authorities' just unveiled prime suspect in the case. "Of the different probable intellectual authors of the homicide of Manuel Buendía," announced Sales Gasque, "Gerhard Georg Mertins stands out prominently," given that he had a clear motive and had made death threats against Buendía. Also present at the press conference was Deputy Prosecutor Alejandro Sosa, who noted that Mertins owned a silver mine in the state of Durango valued at some eight million dollars and had been connected with arms traffic from the United States and Europe to Central America. Mertins was, allegedly, "the number one trafficker in arms to Central America."[17]

RED PRIVADA: TRAFICANTE PROTEGIDO

Excélsior (Mexico City)—Miércoles, 29 February 1984
Manuel Buendía

In mid-March chancellor Bernardo Sepúlveda will visit Germany, but his stay there may not be very pleasant. People in the Bonn government are preparing to demand that Mexico reconsider its expulsion of German citizen Gerhard Mertins, which occurred March 16, 1983.

[. . .]

Gerhard Mertins was expelled from Mexico fourteen days after Red Privada said a few things about him following a long investigation. Mertins had established himself in Durango as the owner of a silver mine, but in reality had created a base for ex-Nazi immigrants from the refuge they built after the war south of Santiago, Chile, a site called Colonia Dignidad.

Mertins had also established his arms business to Central and South America through offices in Mexico and was seeking authorization from the government to set up a factory here for the manufacture of military hardware. We also reported that Mertins's Mexican operation was probably backed by the CIA, which for years had been an old associate of his in various countries.

An energetic government functionary took Mertins and his son and put them on a plane to Germany the same night that Germany's new ambassador to Mexico arrived in our capital. They practically crossed paths at the airport.

In a still naive society like ours, this may all seem like the stuff of fiction, but not to experienced foreign correspondents or to intelligence services. Gerhard Mertins is a real personality who could never have imagined the humiliation of being declared persona non grata by so folkloric and inoffensive a country as Mexico.

As an example of the constant interest Mertins generates in the German media, one major interview with him was 27 pages long. The author, Bruno Bandulet, recalls that since the Second World War 35 million people have died in approximately 130 limited wars and uprisings.

This uncontrollable slaughter occurs in "an irrational, bizarre world where cannons and rockets are sold like kitchen pots and pans. . . ."

"Private arms traffickers seek only and exclusively personal gain," says Bandulet, "and Mr. Gerhard Mertins, the head of Merex, A.G., is considered one of the most influential men in the arms business."

President de la Madrid might find it interesting to learn more about Mr. Mertins, Buendía concluded suggestively. Sales Gasque, for his part, soon learned more about Mertins than he likely cared to know. Indeed, if the German arms dealer turned Durango silver miner served the authorities' immediate purpose of persuading public opinion that the government was at last making serious progress in the Buendía investigation, they would quickly discover that Mertins led them straight into the mire of foreign covert operations they so wished to avoid.

Gerhard Mertins had not been one of Hitler's senior people nor was he a prosecutable war criminal, but neither was he an ordinary Nazi veteran struggling to make his way in a post-Holocaust, antifascist world. As a Wehrmacht paratrooper who distinguished himself in the Balkans, on Crete, and at the Eastern Front, then on the Western Front following the Normandy invasion, he was wounded several times, attained the rank of major, and received Nazi Germany's highest military decoration, the Ritterkreuz (Knight's Cross). Following the war, he worked briefly for Volkswagen, then operated a bus company serving Bremen and Berlin. He maintained a close association with wartime comrades and by 1951 formed part of a German advisory group sent to Cairo to train Egyptian troops, a mission supported by the fledgling CIA. His particular assignment on that occasion was to supervise the training of an elite parachute regiment, a task he subsequently performed for another German advisory group dispatched to Syria. He would do the same in Saudi Arabia some years later.[18]

Mertins's associates on these postwar military missions included numerous prominent Nazis who not only avoided Allied prosecution but actively served as agents and assets of the United States and other western governments in their Cold War offensive against the Soviet Union, among them former naval captain Theodor von Mauchenhein, Panzer general Oskar Munzel, Wehrmacht general Wilhelm Fahrmbacher, Wehrmacht captain Gerhard Bauch, Schutzstaffel (SS) commando Otto Skorzeny, and Hermann Goering's wartime industrial works manager Wilhelm Voss. His association with Skorzeny would extend over the decades to the latter's exile in South America, where Mertins would also have dealings with Fritz Schwend, a wartime purchasing agent for the SS and Wehrmacht, and former Gestapo chief Klaus Barbie, the "Butcher of Lyon," who was eventually extradited to France and imprisoned for war crimes.

These German military missions to the Middle East were part of a larger postwar program in which the United States covertly consorted with its former enemy to counter the growing projection of Soviet power and influence. As has now been well documented, even certifiable Nazi war criminals were spirited out of Europe into anonymous foreign exile in return for their assistance in the global anti-Soviet campaign. Perhaps the most notable Nazi official to receive such protection was Gestapo general Reinhard Gehlen, Hitler's chief of Eastern Front intelligence throughout World War II.

Gehlen parlayed his carefully preserved intelligence files and intact Eastern European agent network into professional immunity, first as head of a new German intelligence organization overseen by the Americans and known informally as the "Gehlen Org," then as chief of West Germany's Bundesnachrichtendienst (Federal Intelligence Service, BND), which he ran until his retirement in 1968. "Among his senior staff in the BND were the same officers who had served with him under Hitler," writes one historian of the times. "And the instruments for this remarkable metamorphosis were agencies of Gehlen's former enemy: U.S. Army Intelligence, which acquired Gehlen and the core of his unit immediately after the war and nurtured them in deepest secrecy; and later the CIA."[19]

"I don't know if [Gehlen]'s a rascal," CIA director Allen Dulles is once said to have quipped. "There are few archbishops in espionage. . . . Besides, one needn't ask him to one's club. He's on our side and that's all that matters."[20]

The Gehlen Org, and later the BND, utilized the German military advisers in the Middle East for their own (and American) intelligence purposes. With a nod from

Allen Dulles, Gehlen recruited Otto Skorzeny in 1952 to train the security forces of Gamal Abdel Nasser's new government in Egypt. Skorzeny, perhaps best known for having rescued Benito Mussolini from his Allied captors in 1943, had himself escaped from a U.S. prison camp in Germany in 1948 and made his way to Spain, where he worked for a time as the representative of several Spanish and German arms manufacturers. His fugitive status notwithstanding, American intelligence operatives established a cordial relationship with him, and when he was given the Nasser assignment, it was CIA money that paid for his handpicked group of approximately one hundred trainers, all of them German veterans sympathetic to the neo-Nazi movements in which Skorzeny himself was active. Mertins first appears on the scene as an arms trafficker in conjunction with the training of Nasser's security forces, when, according to U.S. Army Intelligence, he was contacted by Skorzeny on behalf of the Spanish weapons manufacturer ALFA to help consummate an arms deal with the Egyptians.[21]

Mertins took advantage of his military training missions to the Middle East to broker a wide variety of export deals for German companies, from Mercedes-Benz automobiles to parachutes and steel helmets. Then, in 1963, he incorporated his own export firm, Merex, which he had initially intended to operate as a general exporter but, at the urging of BND chief Reinhard Gehlen, developed instead into a major player on the international arms market, West Germany's unofficial weapons dealer, and a convenient cutout for American covert ops. Within five years Merex was selling everything from sidearms to aircraft, one of its most notable transactions being the 1966 sale of ninety F-86 Saber jets to Pakistan, followed by several dozen Seahawk fighter-bombers to India, at a time when both countries were under a North Atlantic Treaty Organization (NATO) arms embargo.

That same year Mertins established an American branch of Merex in Bethesda, Maryland, where he could more easily conduct relations with the Pentagon's Defense Intelligence Agency (DIA), as well as with the CIA. He brought in former Wehrmacht captain and Gehlen Org operative Gerhard Bauch to oversee the subsidiary's operations and, in 1970, hired recently retired U.S. Army Intelligence officer Col. Richard Amity to serve as the company's president. Both Bauch and Amity attested many years later to the large sums of money Mertins received from his American handlers. According to Bauch, whenever Mertins came to Washington he would meet with people at the DIA and they would pay him in cash. "He'd come back [to the Bethesda offices of Merex] and hand out $500 to whoever happened to be around." Added Amity, "Mertins always came back from the DIA with money to spread around."[22]

Mertins developed a lucrative array of business and intelligence relationships in Latin America out of his Merex offices in Bethesda. By the time Manuel Buendía first wrote about him in March 1983, he was serving as a convenient conduit for military hardware and security technology to the anticommunist authoritarian regimes of the region's Southern Cone while at the same time funneling arms to U.S. proxies in Central America through Mexican territory via his corporate holdings in Durango. As elsewhere in the world, Mertins accomplished these covert transactions with the assistance of veteran Gehlen Org operatives and members of the broader Nazi diaspora, as well as with DIA and CIA support. Klaus Barbie, Fritz Schwend, Hans Ulrich-Rudel, and Otto Skorzeny, all high-ranking officers of the Third Reich, facilitated his dealings with official clients in Peru, Bolivia, Paraguay, and Chile.

Mertins developed a particularly close relationship with Chilean dictator Augusto Pinochet, with whom he already had business dealings prior to the military coup of 11 September 1973, which overthrew the democratically elected government of Salvador Allende Gossens, in which Pinochet had served as chief purchasing officer for the Chilean Army. General Pinochet was "a great patriot," and most Chileans were glad to see an end to the "Allende-Castro show," he declared at the height of the region's "dirty wars" against Cuban-inspired popular insurgencies. Mertins was a frequent visitor to Chile during the dictatorship and an active supporter of that country's pro-Nazi German agricultural community, Colonia Dignidad, where he occasionally stayed and on whose behalf he raised money in Germany.[23]

Mexico broke diplomatic relations with Chile following the 1973 coup and did not reestablish official ties again until 1990, when formal democracy was reinstituted and Pinochet was replaced with an elected civilian president. Mertins's known sympathy for the Pinochet regime may have put him at odds with elements of the Mexican government, especially the foreign relations establishment, and thus complicated his ability to operate effectively in Mexico as a Cold War arms merchant. Nonetheless, by the later 1970s he had managed to negotiate the labyrinthine political maze of the PRI-dominated state skillfully enough to acquire property in Durango and form a joint mining venture called Minera Romer, S.A. The official who eased Mertins into the country was Director of Immigration Diana Torres, a combative anticommunist who appears to have run her department with little interference from then government secretary Jesús Reyes Heroles.

Mertins's principal partner was Enrique Rosales Moreno, a Durango businessman with dual U.S.-Mexican citizenship whom he met through an American identified by Buendía as "an old ex-CIA agent," Jerome Wiesnewsky. The company name, Romer, was a combination of the first syllable of the principal partners' respective surnames: Rosales and Mertins. Mertins was the majority shareholder, with an additional block of shares above the 49 percent he was allowed as a foreigner registered in the names of several proxies. Moreover, he had physical possession of Rosales's shares, which represented a one-third interest and were held as collateral.

Mertins invested some five million dollars in his Durango holdings, which included two mines, an airstrip capable of handling small jets, a ranch, and a mansion said to have been previously owned by former U.S. secretary of defense and World Bank president Robert McNamara. Earnings from Romer's mining operations amounted to several hundred thousand dollars and never came close to justifying the original investment, lending credence to the widely held view that silver mining was merely a cover for much more profitable illicit transactions. "The company's business lies elsewhere," stated a Mexican mining engineer employed at a neighboring mine. "Around here we all know that Mertins is more interested in selling arms than ore."[24]

Mertins, Buendía wrote at the beginning of March 1983, "has established offices in Mexico, and from here, according to his own words, conducts operations in Central America 'to combat communism.'" Deputy Prosecutor Alejandro Sosa emphasized this point in the press conference held by Renato Sales Gasque on the eve of the third anniversary of Buendía's death. In his column of early March 1983, Sosa reiterated, Buendía had referred to Mertins's mining company as a cover for his arms business, "preferably via Central America." Sosa's use here of "via" in place of Buendía's "in" is significant, since the inescapable implication of the columnist's formulation was that Mertins was supplying arms to the Nicaraguan *contras* and other U.S. proxies in Central America, which in turn opened a Pandora's box of possible motives for the Buendía killing that Mexican authorities did not wish to consider.[25]

The Mertins hypothesis presented by Sosa and Sales Gasque was that, by influencing the Mexican government to deport Mertins, Buendía had so prejudiced the German's business interests that Mertins had him murdered. While it had a certain plausibility, it also presented serious weaknesses, highlighted by the particulars of the assassination's timing and commission, which we will consider later in our account. Its primary flaw from the authorities' point of view, however, as they no doubt quickly appreciated, was that it linked a known foreign intelligence and covert ops asset to the flow of arms through Mexican territory to the Nicaraguan *contras* and other regional proxies of American hegemony. Behind Mertins's Mexican enterprise, wrote Buendía, "was probably the CIA, which for years had been an old associate of his in various countries." Indeed, confirms investigative journalist Ken Silverstein, Mertins "had a four-decade-long relationship with American intelligence and sometimes worked in conjunction with government operations . . . including a controversial deal Oliver North's Enterprise arranged for the *contras*." A retired intelligence officer who spoke with Silverstein about Mertins's role as an American asset stated, "You were either so high up that you didn't say anything about him or too low to know."[26]

CASO BUENDÍA: NO DESCARTAN VÍNCULOS ENTRE TECOS, MERTINS Y EX AGENTES DE LA DFS

La Jornada (México City)—Miércoles, 21 October 1987
Rafael Croda

The possible connection between German arms dealer Gerhard Mertins, the ultra-right-wing Tecos group and the former Federal Security Directorate in the assassination of Manuel Buendía "is being analyzed" by investigators from the Mexico City Attorney General's office, but thus far "that connection has not been found."

"We remain interested" in the possibility of proving such a theory and therefore "we continue investigating it," states deputy prosecutor Alejandro Sosa Ortiz in an interview with this newspaper. . . .

[Sosa], who took over the case in November 1986, clarifies that an actual plot between the three groups to assassinate the columnist "has not yet been considered a hypothesis in the investigations," but "could become one at any moment, because the *Tecos*, Mertins and ex-DFS agents continue to be investigated."

On a related matter, Sosa Ortiz reiterates that since the first of last June an order has been in effect "to locate" former DFS chief José Antonio Zorrilla Pérez. . . . Most immediately, "it's a matter of having the Judicial Police confirm what is *vox populi*: that [Zorrilla] is perhaps not in the country, then tell us where it is he may be."

Later in the interview, Sosa Ortiz refers to the primary motive for seeking to depose José Antonio Zorrilla: "What we have been able to document is that he arrived on the scene very, very quickly after the crime was committed and that he was the one who first examined the archive and files that Manuel Buendía had in his office: that's what we want to clarify."

. . .

The interview with Alejandro Sosa Ortiz takes place in his small office on Coyoacán Avenue. On his desk are various Buendía case files, which he uses selectively to document his remarks. One folder containing newspaper clippings remains open the whole time. There, underlined in red, is a reference to the Mertins-Tecos-DFS connection.

On 5 August 1987, Ángel Buendía unexpectedly encountered Miguel Ángel García Domínguez at a tourism security meeting in Guadalajara. In response to Don Ángel's query about the status of the Buendía case, García Domínguez offered to provide him with copies of the weekly summaries of investigation sent to President de la Madrid, to which Don Ángel replied dismissively that he had seen various of those reports; that they were all the same, a farce in fact; and that there was no real investigation. To his great surprise, García Domínguez acknowledged that he was right and concluded their conversation with the provocative advice: "Goad them from a different angle."[27]

After consulting with friends and associates who had been advising him over the previous three-plus years, Ángel Buendía decided to risk everything by insinuating his brother's case into the politics of the presidential succession. He made an appointment with Bartlett Díaz for 6:00 p.m. on 25 August 1987, then arranged for his journalist supporters to call a press conference that same evening. He had not told Bartlett what it was he wished to discuss and when, after the usual polite greetings, the government secretary asked what was on Don Ángel's mind, he vented his pent-up frustration with the government's manifest failure to conduct a serious investigation of his brother's murder. Despite all of Bartlett's previous assurances, he said, no effort had been made to solve the crime. Adding insult to injury, the responsible authorities were making fools of the victim's family and friends, as well as the general public. His patience had run out, he told Bartlett, and when he left their meeting he was going straight to a prearranged press conference to inform the public of the whole sordid charade. He was meeting with the secretary beforehand, he explained, because he wanted to keep his gentlemen's agreement not to speak to the media without informing him first.

By Ángel Buendía's account, Bartlett was stunned to the point of panic. He protested that Don Ángel's planned statements to the media would doom his own presidential aspirations and pleaded with him to hold off for another month, by which time the president would have designated the PRI's candidate in the party's ritualistic unveiling (*destape*) of the individual virtually certain to succeed him. Framing his plea in personal rather than institutional terms, he gave Don Ángel his "word as a man" that, as either the presidential candidate or secretary of government, he would personally see to it that the Buendía case was solved. Don Ángel allowed as how, having already waited more than forty months for the wheels of justice to turn, one more month hardly mattered and therefore he would agree to the secretary's request. Abandoning

all semblance of official formality, Bartlett gave him an emotional embrace of gratitude, then promised that whatever the outcome they would meet again the day after
the *destape* to decide how best to remedy the stalled investigation.

Bartlett kept his word. On Monday, 5 October 1987, the day after it was announced
that de la Madrid's secretary of programming and budget, Carlos Salinas de Gortari,
would be the PRI's candidate, he met with Don Ángel in his Secretariat of Government office. When Ángel arrived for the noon meeting, he was startled to find an
unshaven, dispirited Manuel Bartlett in shirtsleeves, hair uncombed, and in need of
sleep. After venting his dismay and frustration over the president's choice of a successor, he turned to the Buendía case. Reiterating his promise to bring it to a transparent
resolution, he needed a few days, he said, to discuss it with Sales Gasque. To which
Don Ángel retorted, "We want nothing to do with that *hijo de la chingada*! We want
my brother's case taken out of his hands and made a federal case."[28]

A week after returning home to Guadalajara, Ángel Buendía received a phone call
from the head of Gobernación's legal affairs office, Salvador Rocha Díaz, who asked
to meet with him as soon as possible to continue discussing strategy. At their initial
meeting in mid-October, Rocha made another effort to have Don Ángel read Sales
Gasque's latest weekly case reports to the president, only to receive the same dismissive
response Ángel had given Rocha's boss. Rocha then broached the possibility of appointing an independent prosecutor, citing the Swedish example of slain prime minister
Olof Palme, who had been felled on an Oslo sidewalk in February 1986 by a lone gunman in circumstances not unlike those surrounding the slaying of Manuel Buendía.

Such a prosecutor, Rocha explained, would be answerable directly and solely to the
president of the republic, completely independent of the secretaries of government
and national defense, as well as of the federal and Mexico City attorneys general.
Immediately below the special prosecutor in the organizational chart that Rocha
sketched for Don Ángel was the journalists' oversight group. Under it were "however
many Public Ministry agents and investigators the special prosecutor might require."
Asked who would name the special prosecutor, to Ángel's astonishment Rocha replied
that Don Ángel himself, together with his journalist associates, would make that determination. They should look for a hard-nosed attorney attracted by the challenge, he
said, and should understand that whatever that person required by way of compensation was no obstacle. There were no limits to available financial support, Rocha emphasized, inasmuch as the president himself had guaranteed "all the political, material, and
human backing the special prosecutor might need" to carry out his charge.[29]

A close reading of Ángel Buendía's firsthand account suggests that this entire course
of action had been carefully planned at the highest levels of the Mexican government,
right down to the persistent attempts to persuade Don Ángel to leave the Buendía case
in the hands of Sales Gasque. It is even possible, we suppose, that his chance encounter with García Domínguez in Guadalajara was not coincidental, but rather a calculated opportunity to learn his thinking about the case three years on. However it may
have been, the de la Madrid administration seems to have considered Ángel Buendía's
threat to denounce the official investigation publicly serious enough to warrant a dramatic diversion. When Rocha Díaz met with him eleven days after the *destape*, he was

authorized to propose a historic departure from established institutional practice in the handling of criminal investigations, which he could not have done on his own authority.

Rocha's proposal set in motion a train of events that culminated three and a half months later in the presidential appointment of Dr. Miguel Ángel García Domínguez as special prosecutor for the Manuel Buendía case. It was the first such appointment in the modern history of Mexico, perhaps vaguely reminiscent of the colonial era *visitador* periodically dispatched by the Spanish crown to investigate malfeasance in its overseas possessions. García Domínguez's name had been proposed by Miguel Ángel Sánchez de Armas after several weeks of frustrating attempts to identify viable candidates for the special prosecutor post. Informed of his pending appointment, García Domínguez declared that it would be political suicide to accept such an appointment and that he was no "kamikaze." For him even to consider accepting it, he would have to have the president's personal assurance of complete institutional autonomy and the federal government's unrestricted operational support. This was granted on 29 January 1988, when President de la Madrid received him at Los Pinos and personally agreed to his various demands, including the authority to hire personnel from outside the Ministerio Público. When asked by the president why this was necessary, García Domínguez replied matter-of-factly, "Because the [Federal District's *judiciales*] are the most corrupt police force in the country."[30]

6

Ballet Folklórico, Act II

If drug traffickers were involved in the assassination of Manuel Buendía, it will not have had anything to do with drug trafficking, rather with the traffickers' ties to other interested parties.

> —Jesús Blancornelas, comments made at the Autonomous University of Baja California (22 October 1988)

The drug trafficking world, where the Buendía case appears to take us, is formed by impenetrable design. Personalities and products fall continuously, but there are always more where they came from. The "kingpins" divide up specific areas and merchandise. Agreements are broken by violations of territory, conflicts erupt, and the media are utilized to take down offending "business associates" for purposes of reprisal and ensuring control. And, above all, to silence the truth and remove the pointing finger of the serious critic and honest reporter.

> —Luis Suárez, "Buendía: Credibilidad recuperada" (15 June 1989)

MIGUEL ÁNGEL GARCÍA DOMÍNGUEZ assumed the position of special prosecutor for the Manuel Buendía case on Friday, 29 January 1988, immediately following his in-person ratification by President Miguel de la Madrid. As an unprecedented appointment coming almost four years after the event, assignment of the Buendía investigation to an independent judicial authority answerable solely to Mexico's president predictably ruffled bureaucratic feathers and was not a seamless process. The official most likely to obstruct the special prosecutor was García Domínguez's ministerial superior, Renato Sales Gasque, for whom the appointment represented both a personal and a professional affront. Doctor of Jurisprudence García Domínguez, after all, enjoyed a more distinguished legal reputation than did the Federal District's attorney general.

While Secretary of Government Manuel Bartlett Díaz could impose the special prosecutor on the capital's chief judicial officer, in order to preserve the integrity of extant Buendía case files, which might purposely be compromised by an overly resentful Sales Gasque, Bartlett decided that the most politic way to proceed was for Ángel Buendía and his media oversight group to petition the district attorney general to appoint his own deputy prosecutor to the interim special prosecutor post. The point, Don Ángel later recounted, was to avoid making Sales Gasque look like what he in fact was—"inept, a liar, and even an accomplice"—because otherwise he might react negatively in such a way as to hinder further progress in the Buendía investigation.[1]

Don Ángel requested that Bartlett have his own Gobernación staff draft the petition, which he and his media associates would then have published in the press prior to their meeting with the district attorney general. The draft was reviewed by the oversight group, which deemed it too bland and rewrote it. Ángel passed the revision back to Bartlett, who, for appearances' sake, showed it to Sales Gasque. The district attorney general thought the wording excessively harsh, in light of which Bartlett suggested a few stylistic changes that were accepted by Ángel and his media supporters. The open letter to Sales Gasque requesting the appointment of an independent prosecutor for the Buendía case was published on Tuesday, 19 January 1988. The next day Ángel and the oversight group met with Sales Gasque, who informed them that, in response to their petition, he was assigning "his best man, Dr. Miguel Ángel García Domínguez," to head up the special prosecutor's office.[2]

The following Monday, 25 January, Sales Gasque held a news conference to announce the appointment and, above all, to defend his own handling of the Buendía case. (This was the same news conference where reporters questioned him about our *unomásuno* series on U.S. diplomatic cable traffic regarding Manuel Buendía.) He categorically rejected the widely held view that virtually nothing had been accomplished by official investigators in the forty-four months since Buendía's assassination, insisting that, to the contrary, his office had diligently pursued the case, as had Victoria Adato and her staff before him. He likewise defended Jesús Miyazawa Álvarez, chief of the PJDF, for his active role in the Buendía investigation.

Most revealingly, however, Sales Gasque issued a thinly veiled challenge to García Domínguez's operational autonomy: the newly appointed special prosecutor, he declared, "obviously cannot have direct and exclusive responsibility for this investigation, because that responsibility continues to reside in the chief officer of this institution; that is, he cannot relieve me personally of responsibility for a basic function of the Ministerio Público, over which I preside as Attorney General of the Federal District."[3] By this he meant, in effect, "I'm still in charge!" or more fully, "You wanted a special prosecutor for the Buendía case, so now you've got one. You asked for García Domínguez, and there you have him. But I'm still the boss!"[4]

As detailed in *Mi testimonio*, when two days later Ángel Buendía learned of Sales Gasque's statement from local press reports, he was livid and called his own press conference in Guadalajara, where he urged García Domínguez not to accept the appointment as special prosecutor if, in fact, Sales Gasque was to continue exercising ultimate jurisdiction over the Buendía case. That was not the arrangement the federal government had promised, he declared, and he remained adamant that the case be completely removed from the district attorney general's hands. When Manuel Bartlett Díaz arrived at his office that final Friday morning in January 1988 and read news reports about Don Ángel's Guadalajara press conference, he immediately called Miguel de la Madrid, informed him that Ángel was making potentially damaging statements to the media, and insisted it was urgent that the president personally ratify his appointment of the special prosecutor. Within the hour Sales Gasque and García Domínguez were summoned to Los Pinos, where President de la Madrid accepted García Domínguez's conditions of absolute bureaucratic autonomy and officially relieved Sales Gasque of further administrative authority over the investigation.[5]

With less than eleven months remaining in the *sexenio*, the Mexican government now launched a tightly choreographed effort to achieve closure in the Buendía case before de la Madrid left office. A week after his presidential confirmation, García Domínguez met with Ángel Buendía and the oversight group to outline the steps he would take to get the special prosecutor's office up and running. First on his agenda, he told them, was to find adequate quarters separate from the Ministerio Público, hardly a simple task, yet one he would seem to accomplish—paperwork, repairs, furnishings, and all—in only three weeks. A two-story neocolonial *caserón* with a tiled roof, white exterior, and enclosed private parking would be leased to accommodate the special prosecutor and his staff, who occupied the premises in late February. Set among the drab high-rise buildings of Mexico City's Hipódromo-Condesa district, the requisitioned manse stood out as strikingly as did its distinguished white-haired tenant.

García Domínguez was going to the United States, he informed the oversight group, to purchase computer and polygraph equipment. On the way back, he would be stopping in Monterrey to recruit criminology graduates from the Autonomous University of Nuevo León, who, together with recent law graduates to be recruited from UNAM, would comprise the special prosecutor's investigative staff. He also was drafting a detailed work plan to be submitted for presidential approval. The plan envisioned a thoroughly professional effort employing the latest investigative and analytical techniques, including computerized control of evidentiary data and consultation with foreign police establishments experienced in the conduct of high-profile homicide investigations.

Miguel Ángel García Domínguez, special prosecutor for the Manuel Buendía case. (Sylvia E. Bartley)

Headquarters of the Buendía case special prosecutor, Hipódromo-Condesa district, Mexico City. (Sylvia E. Bartley)

Following this briefing of the oversight group, García Domínguez concluded real estate arrangements for the exclusive Hipódromo-Condesa property, purchased polygraphs and up-to-date computer hardware and software in the United States, recruited his proposed investigative team of recently graduated lawyers and criminologists, then submitted his operational plan to President de la Madrid, who approved it on 23 February—all like virtual clockwork. On Wednesday the twenty-fourth, he held a press conference at the Special Prosecutor's new quarters, where he summarized what had been accomplished in the first month since his appointment, outlined procedures and priority tasks, and answered reporters' questions.

He and the initial members of his staff had reviewed the Buendía case files and analyzed all of Buendía's Red Privada columns from 1981 through the date of the columnist's assassination, an effort, he told reporters, that had produced 130 suspects and forty possible motives, including three related to the victim's private life. In an apparent rejoinder to Sales Gasque, García Domínguez declared that the PJDF had been "useless" in the Buendía investigation. For more than a year under the command of Jesús Miyazawa, he insisted, they had "done nothing at all to move the case forward." Consequently, the PJDF would be "totally excluded" from the special prosecutor's investigation. Asked by a reporter if that was due to PJDF negligence in its earlier handling of the case, García Domínguez replied tersely, "Negligence or something more serious." Actual physical evidence had disappeared, he said, including the victim's clothes, two bullets recovered at the scene, and possibly some of Buendía's files.

The special prosecutor's administrative team was comprised of Public Ministry officials, underscoring the unbroken institutional link to the district attorney general's office. Operational autonomy on the Buendía case notwithstanding, García Domínguez retained his position as deputy prosecutor under Sales Gasque, and as such he theoretically remained Sales Gasque's subordinate. Within this anomalous scheme, García Dominguez's immediate subordinate—his deputy director—was Alejandro Sosa Ortiz, whose previous aversion to hypotheses of international political intrigue now appeared to be shared by the special prosecutor. Asked by a reporter at the 24 February news conference about possible political motives behind the Buendía killing, García Domínguez replied evasively, "I don't know what you have in mind. We are working intensely [on this case], and thus far the evidence has not pointed in that direction."[6]

Nevertheless, Gerhard Mertins remained a prime suspect, and the special prosecutor said he would endeavor either to depose Mertins in Germany or to secure his written responses to a lengthy questionnaire. The defunct DFS, for its part, was also a prime object of investigative interest, and García Domínguez now spoke openly of the imperative need to depose its former chief, José Antonio Zorrilla Pérez. The manner in which he referred to Zorrilla suggested that the authorities did not know his actual whereabouts. "I take this occasion," the special prosecutor declared, "to ask the news media to publish our exhortation to Licenciado Zorrilla to appear before us to give his version of events and tell us what he knows. If he fails to do so, then we can only conclude that he was somehow involved and is therefore a suspect, in which case we will request through diplomatic channels in the countries where he may be that local police find him and bring him before the appropriate judicial authorities."

Among other steps being taken, García Domínguez continued, was the offer of an unprecedented five-hundred-million-peso reward, roughly equivalent to twenty-two million U.S. dollars at the 1988 rate of exchange. It had been personally authorized by President de la Madrid, who, although the practice was rarely if ever used in Mexico, nonetheless considered this case important enough "for the Mexican State to make every possible effort to clarify the [Buendía] homicide." The reward was for anyone who provided "sufficient evidence to identify and convict the victim's killers." The informant's identity would be kept secret.[7]

The special prosecutor was also seeking technical assistance abroad. He was arranging for new ballistics analyses of the two remaining bullets to determine the type, caliber, brand, and provenance of the murder weapon and cartridges used. (This, he subsequently told us, was done at an FBI crime lab in the United States.) Arrangements were also being made, he said, to consult with the Swedish police about the techniques and methodology used in the Olof Palme investigation.

Finally, he emphasized, everyone should keep in mind the time factor. Almost four years after the event, potentially critical evidence had been lost or compromised; now, with just ten months remaining in the president's term, it was necessary to restart a full-scale, inherently complex investigation in a country that lacked adequately trained police investigators. The scope of the problem could be appreciated, he suggested, if one took as a starting point the hypothesis that whoever ordered the killing was someone who had been affected, or feared being affected, by Manuel Buendía's Red Privada column in the twenty-four months prior to the assassination, a reasonable assumption that right away presented the special prosecutor with more than one hundred suspects. For all these reasons, García Domínguez cautioned, it was imperative to abandon the notion of a prompt and decisive resolution of the Buendía case. The only viable approach was "rigorous planning and organization, tireless work, constant self-criticism, honesty, and autonomy with respect to what has been done to date and still needs to be done. And probably," he concluded, "a little bit of luck."[8]

Immediately following the 24 February press conference, García Domínguez and his staff began to move into their new Hipódromo-Condesa quarters at the corner of Aguascalientes (no. 170) and Chilpancingo Streets, a task that occupied the remainder of that week. The Buendía case files, "comprising 13,231 pages in ninety-nine folders and standing 1.40 meters high," were transferred to the special prosecutor's Aguascalientes offices from the main investigations section of the Federal District's Ministerio Público. García Domínguez was fully operational by the following week, and he and his staff commenced a normal work routine on Tuesday, the first day of March 1988.[9]

That same Tuesday, *Excélsior* published a lengthy paid statement by José Antonio Zorrilla Pérez, the original of which had been sent to García Domínguez the preceding Friday. It contained twelve numbered paragraphs in legalistic style, which described the DFS's role and Zorrilla's own actions as director in the Buendía case. It was an exculpatory document addressed "To public opinion," and it sought to refute the most damaging charges leveled against Zorrilla in the media, which he dismissed as "absurd," "twisted," "insidious," "fallacious," and "without merit"—all examples of "yellow journalism." Zorrilla specifically rejected media assertions that he had been summoned "various times" to testify but failed to appear. "I have never been formally subpoenaed," he wrote. "Had I been, I would have appeared on the appointed day and time to state what I know about the facts of this case." He was now making these statements "under oath and for the legal purposes they may serve" and would "ratify each and every one" whenever the special prosecutor wished to subpoena him. He gave his residence as Apt. 201, Bldg. 1, Avenida Universidad 1953, Colonia Copilco Universidad, Distrito Federal.[10]

One week to the day after García Domínguez and his staff had moved into the Aguascalientes house and just nine days since the special prosecutor had suggested to reporters that the authorities did not know Zorrilla's whereabouts or even if he was in the country, the former DFS chief appeared for a deposition accompanied by his attorneys Javier Hernández Cervantes and Guillermo Cuata Domínguez. Zorrilla was deposed over a sixteen-hour period from 12:20 p.m. Friday to 4:20 a.m. Saturday, 4–5 March 1988. He responded to 193 questions concerning diverse aspects of the Buendía investigation, many of which focused on the DFS and his own actions at the crime scene, as well as the subsequent handling of evidence and witnesses. Cuata Domínguez was also deposed in a separate proceeding lasting just under three hours. Cuata had served as head of the directorate's Legal Affairs Department and was one of the officials Zorrilla had ordered to conduct a search of Buendía's office immediately following the assassination. He had also paid for Zorrilla's *Excélsior* statement of 1 March.[11]

¿Intereses políticos internacionales en el asesinato de Buendía?

Páginauno, suplemento político de *unomásuno*—Domingo, 17 April 1988

Russell H. Bartley

Any halfway informed observer has to be struck by the strange and irregular manner in which the supposedly priority investigations of the still unresolved murder of columnist Manuel Buendía Tellezgirón have been unfolding. Even more noteworthy are the most recent turns the case has taken as a result of last January's appointment of a special prosecutor.

While the columnist's killing most immediately impacted the Mexican political arena, it had repercussions beyond the country's borders as well, since whoever took Buendía's life not only assaulted press freedom in Mexico, but did so throughout the entire hemisphere. Moreover, there are sound reasons to admit the possible involvement of outside interests. That, in turn, explains the interest shown in the case by a number of foreign observers.

. . .

What strikes us above all is the quality of spectacle the Buendía case is now acquiring after almost four years of fruitless and mismanaged investigations in which, despite a presidential commitment . . . to spare neither effort nor resources to track down the responsible parties, the political will to resolve this homicide has not, in fact, existed. Nor does it now, we suspect, for what the outside observer perceives from a prudent distance is a great deal of theatricality surrounding the case; theater directed at public opinion so as to distract it, no doubt, from the case's deeper questions and issues. . . .

. . .

While one might interpret such lavish resources as evidence of seriousness on the part of the country's highest authorities in their reiterated commitment to determine the facts and impart justice, both the circumstances in which these resources have materialized and the manner in which they are being utilized cause us lingering doubt. The waters, we fear, are deep and turbid.

. . .

A sensational element [of this latest effort] that we cannot help but view as an intricate piece of political choreography is the sudden appearance at the end of this past February of the man who served as chief of the former Federal Security Directorate and is one of the main suspects in the Buendía affair, José Antonio Zorrilla Pérez. . . . Had the authorities really wanted to find him, a Mexican colleague recently remarked, "they'd have brought him in, forced him to talk, and afterward his body would have turned up on an Alaskan ice pack."

In other words, it is impossible not to consider the curious chronological coincidence that inevitably links the dramatic reappearance of Zorrilla, his paid tract in *Excélsior*, and [his] subsequent interrogation to the theatrical creation of a special prosecutor for the Buendía case. Indeed, Zorrilla did not make himself available for a formal deposition out of simple goodwill and a readiness to fulfill his obligations as a citizen, but rather under judicial protection and prior arrangements to guarantee his personal security. According to sources close to the case, once deposed—his deposition has not yet been released to the public—Zorrilla again absented the country.

We arrived in Mexico City the week after Zorrilla's deposition and promptly asked *unomásuno* editor Becerra Acosta to see if he could get us an interview with García Domínguez. Disinclined to give exclusive interviews at that early stage of his assignment, the special prosecutor nonetheless granted our request and agreed to meet with us on Thursday, 17 March, at 10:00 a.m. In the meantime, we had a full agenda and spent the preceding five days pursuing other aspects of our investigation: a luncheon meeting with Soviet correspondent Anatoly Borovkov, reviewing and photocopying files at the Fundación Manuel Buendía, a conversation with *Arizona Republic* bureau chief Peter Katel, and strategizing with local press colleagues.

Russell first met Borovkov in October 1980 at the University of Pittsburgh, where they had both traveled as members of official delegations to negotiate a bilateral exchange agreement between U.S. and Soviet scholarly organizations concerned with Latin American affairs. Russell had known the head of Borovkov's delegation, Viktor Volsky, and numerous other Soviet Latin American area specialists since the later 1960s in connection with his own academic work on the history of Russo–Latin American relations.[12] We saw both men again in June 1981 at an academic symposium in the Soviet Union. When Borovkov was subsequently assigned to Mexico City as a correspondent for the Soviet Academy of Science's monthly Latin American studies journal *Latinskaya Amerika*, we made it a point to see him whenever we visited the Federal District. Among the topics of mutual interest we discussed on this occasion was Manuel Buendía, one of whose posthumous books had been published in Russian translation by the Soviet publishing house Progress Publishers.[13]

Our encounter with Peter Katel, in contrast, had not been planned, but rather came about on the impulse of Fundación Manuel Buendía director Miguel Ángel Sánchez de Armas, who thought we might find it useful to meet an informed "fellow American." The *Arizona Republic*'s Mexico City bureau was located in the same building, on the same floor as, and adjacent to, the Fundación, a detail we thought curious but resisted attributing to anything more than happenstance. Katel, for his part, exhibited a hard edge, and our brief conversation with him was strained. At one point, Sylvia inquired about his name; she said it struck her as unusual and asked what it meant, to which he curtly replied, "It means 'killer' in Hebrew." (It does not, a rabbi later assured us.) Peter "Killer" wanted to know what we thought and had learned about the Buendía case while offering no substantive thoughts of his own. Afterward we wondered if he might not be an Israeli agent, a suspicion later confirmed by ex-CIA operative Lawrence Harrison, who claimed to have known Katel at the time.

The day before our appointment with García Domínguez, we met with Rogelio Hernández at the Zona Rosa Sanborns to discuss interview strategy. As one of the prime movers behind the Buendía case oversight group, Hernández had interacted with García Domínguez on several occasions and offered us helpful insights into the special prosecutor's professional modus operandi. The next morning, García Domínguez received us in his spacious second-floor Aguascalientes office. We had accessed the building through a side entrance on Calle Chilpancingo and were struck as we entered with its expansive, understated elegance. There were other people present that day, but they seemed to be few in number and for the most part remained out of view.

In person the special prosecutor was every bit the urbane, self-possessed personality portrayed in the press and described to us by our Mexican colleagues. He had not yet formulated a strategy for dealing with the media, he informed us, because "no one was satisfied with how the Buendía case had been handled thus far and he was now everyone's target," which, he explained, was why he did not wish to grant exclusive interviews. We surmised that his willingness to meet with us stemmed from the articles we had published in *unomásuno* and his wish to learn more about us. He acknowledged as much during our interview.

Becerra Acosta had had *unomásuno*'s well-connected police reporter Fernando Ramírez de Aguilar make the original request on behalf of the paper. According to García Domínguez, Ramírez had pitched it not so much as an interview as an informal conversation in which the special prosecutor would have the opportunity to interview us. Seeing that this had been neither our understanding nor intention, García Domínguez dismissed the apparent deception as a reporter's "trick of the trade" and agreed to answer a few questions provided we avoided "delicate points" and he could avoid "compromising answers." We discussed the Buendía case for the next hour.

What he most feared, García Domínguez began, was making a fool of himself. "Lo que más temo es hacer el ridículo" were his precise words. He had not wanted to serve as special prosecutor and had hoped that the president would not ratify his appointment because it was a thankless job that would cause him nothing but grief. No one would be satisfied with what he did, while everyone would make him the target of their criticism. Moreover, he thought it unlikely that the Buendía case would actually be solved.

In the well-practiced judicial manner that had become so familiar to us, he then proceeded to quantify the status of operations in his newly opened office: staff of forty-six, including a deputy director, a supervisor, five unit heads, five unit secretaries, thirty detectives and four psychologists; fifteen telephones; fifteen vehicles; two hundred million pesos in salaries; fifty-seven million pesos in computers and lie detectors, including a trip to San Diego for their purchase. He repeated the same litany of investigative hypotheses he had given reporters at his press conference the month before and confirmed that he was in communication with the FBI about ballistics analyses. Zorrilla was one of the "delicate points" to be avoided. Nor did we ask about Mertins. The single new item of information was that two days hence he would be traveling to Stockholm to consult with Swedish authorities on their handling of the Olof Palme investigation. He allowed Sylvia to take a couple of photographs, made some final small talk, then bid us *adiós*.

Late the following evening we met again with Rogelio Hernández to review and evaluate our interview with the special prosecutor. Also present was another member of the Buendía case oversight group, Octavio González, whom Rogelio introduced to us as a close friend from years before when both had been active in the Mexican Communist Party. He would subsequently describe González in his book about DFS chief Zorrilla as an "ex-agent of the Federal Security Directorate with nationalistic political views and a strong belief in the need to cleanse the country's police." González's primary task in the oversight group, Hernández wrote, was to glean information from established informants within law enforcement.[14]

More directly, he was to spy on García Domínguez. The oversight group had informants inside the special prosecutor's office, Ángel Buendía later told us—there and everywhere else, even among the police. "The main reason for having Octavio there," he explained, "was to monitor and check what García Domínguez was doing, to verify what García Domínguez was telling us. Octavio was the individual we assigned to do that because of his contacts in law enforcement."[15] That being the case, it was logical that he would wish to learn what the special prosecutor had stated to us.

We assumed that González was evaluating us as well. That evening's conversation, also at Sanborns, lasted more than two hours, beginning with our García Domínguez interview, then ranging over the full scope of the Buendía case. Afterward González and Hernández insisted on driving us back to our hotel, saying it was too dangerous to walk at that hour of night, as had been our intention. González drove a late model Chrysler, whose rear doors, we immediately noted, could not be opened from the inside. As we passed through dimly lit back streets, he suddenly pulled into a well-lighted underground parking area, apologized for the momentary stop, got out, and disappeared into what we supposed were security offices of some kind. Rogelio offered no explanation from the front passenger seat. González soon returned, also without explanation, and we continued on our way. Back at the Mónaco he opened the rear doors for us and we took our leave, thanking them for the lift. It was, we concluded, a bit of theatricality contrived either to warn us off or as a chauvinistic message to the effect that we gringos were in over our heads and had little if anything useful to contribute.

García Domínguez arrived in Stockholm three days later and spent the week of 20 March meeting with Swedish judicial and law enforcement authorities. He met first with the deputy director of the Swedish National Police and three of his subordinates for a briefing on police entities and operations in Sweden, institutional relations between police and the Swedish attorney general's office, and specifically the Olof Palme case. He then met with the head of the Stockholm Interpol office, who informed him about international police cooperation in the Palme case; with the National Police chief, deputy chief, and other officials of the Criminal Investigations Department and that department's homicide section; with Sweden's deputy attorney general and various of his subordinates; and, finally, with the director of the Swedish National Police Academy.

García Domínguez came away from these meetings with a good deal of information, including a two-volume interim report on the Palme case and a number of instructional texts utilized by the National Police Academy. The one practical benefit of this otherwise extravagant trip were several suggested refinements of the special prosecutor's computer database. Aside from that, his week in Stockholm served primarily García Domínguez's preoccupation with his own professional image, as well as the overriding agenda of the de la Madrid administration to contain the Buendía case within politically acceptable bounds. While his weeklong consultation with Swedish authorities received relatively little media coverage, on his return to Mexico he did prepare a detailed written summary of his trip and made it available to interested reporters.[16] Of particular interest for the special prosecutor's purposes was the fact that the official Swedish investigation of the high-profile Palme assassination had undergone four reorganizations within an initial two-year period, compared to three reorganizations of Mexico's Buendía investigation in not quite four years. For all of their First World sophistication, the Swedes had experienced some of the same internecine institutional clashes that had plagued the official Mexican inquiry, especially between the police and the judiciary. What the Swedes were unable to achieve in the Palme case, García Domínguez inferred, should not be expected of the Mexicans in the Buendía case. The Swedish experience, moreover, fully validated his conception of the special prosecutor's office and the implementation of his presidentially mandated investigation.[17]

During the week García Domínguez was in Stockholm, two Mexico City newsweeklies kept the Buendía case prominently before the public. *Proceso* appeared on newsstands that Monday, 21 March 1988, with a major investigative story about Gerhard Mertins and his relationship to the case. Based on interviews with Mertins's former business associates in Durango and other sources, it offered readers a more detailed account of the German arms dealer's activities in Mexico than had Mexican authorities and, in effect, corroborated the scathing exposé previously published by Buendía.[18]

Of perhaps greater concern to the authorities, and certainly more annoying, was a three-column sidebar pointing out that almost four years had elapsed since Manuel Buendía was slain, yet only at this late date was the country's Secretariat of Government attempting to demonstrate serious interest in the case. It was a thinly veiled indictment of Manuel Bartlett Díaz, passed over as PRI presidential candidate but still a powerful political figure whose role in the Buendía affair reflected on the de la Madrid administration generally. The official investigation of the journalist's murder, wrote *Proceso* columnist Carlos Marín, had thus far been characterized "not by positive results so much as by a string of illegalities, inefficiencies, negligence, and false expectations." Especially disturbing had been the secretariat's silence around the case, given that its responsibility for national security had led to a variety of agreements and understandings with foreign governments, including "the presence of U.S. narcotics police and operational freedom for Central Intelligence agents [within Mexico]." Gerhard Mertins, noted Marín, had been connected to Oliver North and other associates involved in the Iran-Contra scandal, again raising the delicate matter of possible foreign links to the Buendía assassination. Almost four years on, however, exposure of such involvement seemed increasingly unlikely. "As time passes," holds a Mexican police maxim, "truth slips away" (El tiempo que pasa es una verdad que se aleja).[19]

That same Monday the newsweekly *Quehacer Político* appeared with a cover story about ex-DFS chief José Antonio Zorrilla Pérez in which Manuel Buendía's widow was reported to have expressed the belief that Zorrilla was innocent of complicity in her husband's assassination. Coming two weeks after Zorrilla's paid statement in *Excélsior* and subsequent deposition by the special prosecutor and his staff, it was a journalistic scoop with distinctly sensational appeal. The reporter, Tizoc Arista Jiménez, had interviewed Dolores Ábalos de Buendía in the Lindavista home she had shared with her husband and their three children, quoting her at length on the nature of her spouse's relationship with Zorrilla and Zorrilla's comportment with her following the murder. "Personally," she told Arista Jiménez, "I am convinced that he had nothing to do with it. Because of the friendship the two of them shared and the courtesies he showed me the day of the crime, I truly want him to come away from this untainted." Zorrilla's account of events in his published *Excélsior* statement, she added, was "absolutely factual and without distortion."

There was a note of uncertainty in the widow's defense of Zorrilla, however. "I've said all along," she continued, "that I hoped [Zorrilla] had nothing to do with it. Perhaps he knows something. I imagine he does, because he was head of the Federal Security Directorate and knew many things. Besides, he studied the case from the very first moment." Yet it was her fervent wish, she insisted, that Zorrilla not prove to have been "directly involved" in her husband's slaying. It was clear from this hedged formulation and other reported comments that her knowledge of Buendía's relationship with the former DFS chief was impressionistic rather than firsthand and that, as we ourselves were aware and would later confirm in personal interviews with her, there was much in her husband's professional life she simply did not know. He made a point of not bringing his work home in order to shield his family from the inherent dangers of authoring a politically influential newspaper column like Red Privada. In this sense, Doña Dolores readily acknowledged, she was never Manuel's *compañera*, only his spouse and *ama de casa* (homemaker). As for the veracity of Zorrilla's testimony about DFS and the Buendía assassination, observed Arista Jiménez, "there were a number of contradictions."[20]

Coverage of the Buendía case in the 21 March 1988 issue of *Quehacer Político* was a continuation of reporting and commentary from the previous week's issue, in which Tizoc Arista Jiménez had published a feature article arguing that, rather than imbuing the official investigation with greater transparency, creation of a special prosecutor's office under the direction of Miguel Ángel García Domínguez instead was making the case more opaque.[21] Based on anonymous police sources, Arista presented an elaborate hypothesis in which Manuel Buendía was the victim of competing international drug mafias and their government patrons on either side of the U.S.-Mexico border. It was a flawed hypothesis, yet one that linked real transnational players who would eventually be shown to have had a hand in Buendía's slaying, albeit for other motives. It also had a ring of plausibility in Mexican public opinion, already deeply cynical about rampant corruption in government.

In essence Arista proposed that behind the Buendía case there was an all-out struggle between the Italo-American and Mexican drug mafias for control of the illicit narcotics market in the United States and that the U.S. and Mexican governments were in league with their respective national crime syndicates as practical vehicles for the generation of revenue and projection of geopolitical influence. The Americans' key asset in this scenario was former Mexico City police chief Arturo "El Negro" Durazo, while the primary facilitator of Mexican drug cartel interests was said to be DFS chief José Antonio Zorrilla Pérez. Manuel Buendía, in turn, supposedly served as Zorrilla's agent of influence and was eliminated on behalf of the Italo-American mafia as a blunt message to the de la Madrid administration and its local cartel associates.

Arista Jiménez's hypothesis did not hold together but was nonetheless interesting for the allusions it made to actual operative relationships and institutional motives that were never meant for public disclosure. According to former Federal Judicial Police commandant Armando Pavón Reyes and other Mexican police informants, wrote Arista, the CIA used the DEA as a cover for its operations in Mexico. Agency operatives in the guise of DEA agents could move unimpeded throughout the country and were themselves involved with the traffickers. The February 1985 kidnapping and murder of DEA special agent Enrique Camarena Salazar, Arista's police informants had assured him, were ordered by the Americans in order to prevent Camarena from exposing CIA methods and operations. It was an explosive allegation whose veracity was rumored for many years thereafter and one that former U.S. intelligence sources would eventually confirm to us.

The main inconsistency in Tizoc Arista's hypothesis lies in his framing of the Buendía and Camarena killings as by-products of a struggle between an established Italo-American crime syndicate and a rising Mexican narcotics mafia, each with government support, while at the same time suggesting that the primary objective on the U.S. side was to pressure Mexico "to change its foreign policy, principally toward Central America." Geopolitics in fact determined the nature of this contest, and bilateral political imperatives were always the decisive factor, with the Central American insurgencies foremost among the regional concerns of U.S. foreign policy strategists. Whether Arista had not fully developed his hypothesis or perhaps purposely confused its elements in order to veil the implications of what he was reporting is unclear. Whatever the case, he here introduces for the first time in a public venue pivotal facts that authorities on both sides of the U.S.-Mexico border felt compelled to conceal: (1) the Buendía and Camarena slayings were linked, (2) both slayings had to do with the geopolitics of Central America, and (3) both men were killed on orders from the United States.

¿INTERESES POLÍTICOS INTERNACIONALES EN EL ASESINATO DE BUENDÍA?

Páginauno, suplemento político de *unomásuno*—Domingo, 17 April 1988

Russell H. Bartley

There can be no doubt that from the outset the Buendía case has been considered an affaire of State. How else to explain the aggressive investigative presence of the organs of national security? How else to explain the repeated efforts to depoliticize a case that is so eminently political? How other than an affaire of State to explain that it was deemed necessary to surveil—all but openly—this paper's correspondent during a recent visit to the Federal District to pursue our own investigation of the Manuel Buendía assassination?

. . .

But, why an affaire of State? Either because the Buendía case is viewed as a political factor at a moment when the hegemonic authority of the ruling party is being increasingly questioned or because the case contains some imponderable that, if revealed, would impact national interests. Or perhaps some combination of elements related to these two priority concerns of Gobernación.

. . .

Indeed, few aspects of this case strike us so forcefully as the bullheadedness with which from the beginning the authorities have sought to depoliticize it. How do they wish us to understand the repeatedly censured qualifier "political"? By rejecting it, do they seek a priori to preclude the possible complicity of high government officials? Of the PRI? Of some other political group? It goes without saying that the very principles of criminal investigation make such criteria inadmissible.

But the Buendía murder could also be considered political in a broader context, which includes the current international situation. We have alluded to this on various occasions, as have our Mexican colleagues. And with the same reticence the responsible authorities have sought to evade any such suggestion, which likewise fails to accord with the requirements of disciplined investigation.

In our own investigation of the Buendía case it is precisely this official reticence to consider possible foreign involvement in the crime that most attracts our attention. Nor, it seems to us, is it a matter of having formulated the corresponding hypotheses, duly investigated them, and then rejected them on the basis of gathered evidence, but rather that they have not even been formulated.

The week in which these latest issues of *Proceso* and *Quehacer Político* were on Mexican newsstands and while the special prosecutor was meeting with Swedish officials in Stockholm, we drafted a four-thousand-word article describing the special prosecutor's office as an elaborately choreographed piece of political theater contrived to achieve closure of the Buendía case once and for all. Initially, we had envisioned a six-part series to appear on successive days over the course of a week, but when *unomásuno*'s editor saw our material, he decided to run it as a lead feature in the paper's Sunday political supplement *páginauno*. Illustrated with two of Sylvia's photos, it appeared on *páginauno*'s front page one month to the day following our interview with García Domínguez, whom it predictably angered, so much so that for several weeks thereafter he would have nothing to do with *unomásuno*.[22]

The elaborate measures approved by President de la Madrid to establish a special prosecutor for the Buendía case so late in the president's term, we wrote, raised doubts about the real purpose of those measures. The leasing of an ostentatious building physically apart from the Federal District's Public Ministry, ostensibly to assure operational independence from potential interference on the part of the district attorney general, for example, seemed designed more for public consumption than to address a genuine bureaucratic problem, which presidential authority could have obviated within established institutional structures had the political will to do so in fact existed. Likewise, García Domínguez's ballyhooed trip to Sweden seemed more about appearance than substance. While it was logical for there to be consultation between Mexican and Swedish investigators on the Olof Palme and Manuel Buendía cases, that should have occurred on a working level out of public view and over an extended period, not in five short days.

At that late date, moreover, we found it difficult to believe that Mexican investigators had anything to learn from the Swedes or anyone else. "On the contrary," we suggested, "it [was] not a matter of professionalism, [but] rather of resolve on the part of the authorities who say they want to solve the case." But, we added, a more portentous, surely calculated effect of the special prosecutor's visit to Stockholm was its subliminal linking in public opinion of the two high-profile Palme and Buendía cases and the implied message that "if the Swedish police—among the most advanced in the world—had been unable to clarify the murder of so distinguished a figure as Olof Palme, then one could hardly expect the Mexican police, as experienced as they might be, to solve the equally complex murder of Manuel Buendía."

The sudden reappearance of former DFS chief José Antonio Zorrilla and his sixteen-hour deposition by García Domínguez also struck us as "a curious chronological coincidence . . . obviously related to the theatrical creation of a Special Prosecutor's office."[23] Zorrilla had been considered a suspect virtually from the outset, yet Mexican officialdom had endeavored for more than three years to keep him out of the case. Now, it would appear, the authorities were utilizing Zorrilla to give the special prosecutor added credibility and thereby persuade the public that the de la Madrid administration was serious about actually solving the Buendía slaying. (The only information released to the media about the Zorrilla deposition was a typed three-and-a-half-page double-spaced report paraphrasing Zorrilla's responses to a dozen or so questions out of a total of 193, with no contextualization or further commentary.[24]) Having officially brought Zorrilla into play as a suspect, however, García Domínguez was now drawn inexorably into a mire of contradictions from which neither he nor the Mexican government would be able to extricate themselves.

By calling into question Zorrilla's role in the Buendía affair, the special prosecutor was in effect questioning as well the role of the former DFS, which, as the institutional interface with and operational partner of the CIA, necessarily raised the hypothesis of possible agency collusion. That, we wrote, had to be one of García Domínguez's forty "priority" hypotheses as to who might have masterminded Buendía's assassination. We recalled for *unomásuno*'s readers the earlier case of former DFS chief Miguel Nazar Haro, who had been arrested in San Diego, California, and charged by the U.S. Justice Department with operating an international car theft ring but was allowed to avoid prosecution because the CIA protested that he was the agency's "most important source for Mexico and Central America" and exposing him in an American courtroom "would compromise delicate relations of international cooperation in intelligence matters."

When viewed against the backdrop of U.S. policy toward Central America during the first Reagan administration, we suggested, the CIA hypothesis seemed all the more plausible, for Mexico was the pivotal piece in U.S. regional planning and Manuel Buendía represented a challenge to the achievement of those plans. While over the years Buendía had exposed CIA operatives and assets, his most damaging impact on U.S. clandestine operations in Mexico was Red Privada's ongoing exposure of agency methods—"its sophisticated and widespread spying on the citizenry, its ability to insert disinformation into the country's mass media, its use of local criminal elements and Cuban exiles to perpetrate acts of political violence in blatant violation of the nation's sovereignty, and even its penetration of Mexico's national security organs." Of all these recurrent themes in Buendía's column, we proposed, the most delicate was the CIA-Mexican national security relationship, because it called into question the loyalty of high government officials.

It was, we wrote, "an unequal relationship characterized by a distinctly anti-Mexican national security ideology," since it was U.S. rather than Mexican interests that were being served. In order for that to happen, key officials in the de la Madrid administration had to be complicit with the Reagan administration in the pursuit of U.S. regional objectives, which opened them to charges of hypocrisy, *malinchismo*, and even outright treason. Having "no hair on his tongue," as the popular Spanish expression goes, Manuel Buendía could be expected to denounce such turncoats and the covert policies they facilitated. Neither government, in turn, could tolerate such foreseeable public exposure.

The unavoidable hypothesis suggested by these circumstances, then, was that Buendía had been slain to prevent him from revealing the White House/Los Pinos/*contras*/drug and arms traffickers nexus in support of U.S. efforts to overthrow Nicaragua's Sandinista government. It was a reasonable, straightforward hypothesis, we emphasized, yet one that Mexican authorities appeared not even to have formulated, much less prioritized—a remarkable circumstance that in and of itself would seem to give that hypothesis greater weight than most of the other forty or so theories cited by the special prosecutor. We were in no way suggesting that other hypotheses should be discounted, we clarified, but rather that the possibility of a political killing of the nature and for the motive we had described be investigated as thoroughly as any others, since "only on the basis of unimpeachable empirical evidence would it be possible to dispel the fog that continue[d] to envelop the guilty parties."[25]

Act II, scene 2 of this grand folkloric performance opened with the 6 July 1988 presidential election of Carlos Salinas de Gortari and the anticipated failure of the now lame duck de la Madrid administration to solve the Buendía case. Doubts proliferated about the special prosecutor's prospects beyond de la Madrid's departure from office. Then, barely a month before Salinas's inauguration, García Domínguez confirmed his intention to close the special prosecutor's office. At the end of October 1988, he summoned Ángel Buendía to Mexico City and informed him that in two weeks' time he would be shutting down operations. He could not do otherwise, he explained, as he was answerable directly to the president and his mandate had ended at the conclusion of de la Madrid's presidential term.

There being no valid counterargument, Ángel Buendía responded with a hypothetical question: what if he were to secure the same assurances of autonomy and material support from Carlos Salinas that had been granted the special prosecutor by Miguel de la Madrid? "That," García Domínguez replied, "would be another matter altogether." Don Ángel had prefaced his question with an appeal to the special prosecutor's notable ego. "How can a man with your distinguished career and spotless record just drop everything and leave without completing perhaps the most important undertaking of your life?" he asked. "That would amount to having failed, and failure is not part of your résumé."[26]

By García Domínguez's calculation, he had taken on the Buendía assignment unwillingly, accomplished more in nine months than the government's various law enforcement agencies had done in three and a half years, established an impeccable record of investigative professionalism, and would now leave having achieved more than could reasonably have been expected of him in the impossibly truncated time frame of his mandate. His image would remain untarnished, his ego intact. Moreover, he had little reason to believe that Ángel Buendía would be able to prevail upon Carlos Salinas as he had managed to do with Miguel de la Madrid. He gave Don Ángel until 15 November, two weeks hence, to speak with the president elect and promised not to announce the cessation of the special prosecutor's activities prior to that date.

Within a matter of days Don Ángel managed to obtain Salinas's agreement to meet with him and was instructed to work out the details with the president elect's appointments secretary. That proved to be an exercise in frustration and obstruction likely contrived to dissuade Don Ángel from his intended purpose, but it so angered him that Salinas's inner circle apparently thought it best to placate him rather than risk his making inconvenient statements to the media, as he had done before. With histrionic flare, it was arranged for Salinas and Ángel Buendía to meet on Tuesday, 15 November, the very day on which García Domínguez was scheduled to close the special prosecutor's office.

Carlos Salinas had studiously avoided the matter of Manuel Buendía throughout the presidential campaign and in the months immediately following his election. The prevailing wisdom was that he preferred to distance himself from the controversial case, letting it recede into the past as a legacy of the previous administration, and that he was therefore disinclined to reappoint García Domínguez. His opening question to Don Ángel at their 15 November meeting seemed to confirm as much. "Why," he asked, "do you want to continue with the same prosecutor now in charge of your brother's case?" "Because," Don Ángel replied, "after three years of being lied to, mocked, and misled, he is the first government official to take us seriously, to conduct himself as a responsible civil servant, and to devote himself fully to my brother's case."[27]

"But what about García Domínguez's health?" Salinas queried, in reference to what we would soon learn was throat cancer. What ailed García Domínguez, Don Ángel insisted, was exhaustion from the personal effort he was making to resolve the Buendía case, but he had no health concerns that would move him to seek relief from his investigative responsibilities. The reason he had indicated that he would not continue as special prosecutor under the next administration, Ángel explained, was his belief that President Salinas would not extend to him the same essential guarantees of material support and operational independence that he had enjoyed under Miguel de la Madrid.

Salinas appeared to make his decision on the spot. "Don Ángel," he replied, "rest assured that I will speak personally with Dr. García Domínguez to persuade him to stay on as special prosecutor for the Manuel Buendía case and to reassure him that he will have the full backing of my government." Ecstatic at the president elect's positive response to his petition, Ángel Buendía went straight from their meeting to the special prosecutor's office. Upon learning of Salinas's decision to meet his terms and conditions, García Domínguez slumped back in his chair and commented wearily, "Ya me fregó usted, ni modo" (Now you've screwed me; I've no way out). His professional image, he seemed to imply, was back on the line, with no guarantee that he could salvage it intact.[28]

El asesinato de Buendía, visto por extranjeros

Novedades de Baja California (Mexicali, BC)—Domingo, 21 October 1988

Sergio García Domínguez

Almost four and a half years after "the most transcendent political crime in recent Mexican history, at least since the events of October 1968 in Tlatelolco Square," the assassination of Manuel Buendía was examined yesterday at the Autonomous University of Baja California by two foreign journalists and two Mexican intellectuals, who all agreed that, like the subsequent 34 murders of media professionals in our country, the Buendía killing was a criminal act committed with impunity.

In the university's Graduate Studies building, where the annual meeting of the Pacific Coast Council on Latin American Studies (PCCLAS) is taking place, this was one of the topics discussed by Russell H. Bartley (University of Wisconsin), Matthew Rothschild (editor of the *Progressive* magazine), Miguel Ángel Sánchez (director of the Fundación Buendía), and Enrique Semo (University of San Diego).

For the first of these commentators, "The foreign investigator is drawn to this case because a resolution of the Buendía killing may well reveal a degree of involvement and treachery that reach far beyond the columnist himself and which affect us all, regardless of our nationality."

[Bartley] offered a view of the case from abroad, noting among other things, the unprofessional way in which, at least during the first three years, the crime was investigated. He cited in this regard jurisdictional conflicts between investigating authorities, blatant attempts to fabricate guilty parties, improper behavior on the part of ex-attorney general Victoria Adato, the creation of a mysterious investigative group directed by a former director of the secret police with ties to the CIA, the intimidation of journalists trying to investigate the case, and even the inexplicable disappearance of material evidence, including two of the bullets recovered from the victim and the clothes he was wearing when he was shot.

The U.S. professor commented that, "despite repeated presidential promises to spare neither effort nor resources to solve the Buendía murder and bring the guilty parties to justice, the will to do so has been lacking."

. . .

The editor of *The Progressive* magazine, for his part, stated that Buendía was "a thorn in the side of the CIA and the U.S. embassy" and added that embassy personnel despised Buendía, whom they branded "a liar." Matthew Rothschild even recalled how ex-ambassador John Gavin had once told him that "Buendía was hostile to the United States."

As part of the panel held before dozens of local and foreign attendees, [Rothschild] described how, through the Freedom of Information Act, he had obtained seventeen State Department documents that dealt with Buendía as "a leftist journalist," one of which discussed the possibility of suing him for defamation based on an article he had published accusing an embassy employee of being an expert in torture techniques."

The presenter noted that, based on the State Department documents, it would appear that the embassy had been surveilling the murdered journalist. "In the context of Reagan administration aggression [in the region], the motive for CIA involvement becomes more plausible. Buendía was one of the most outspoken and strongest critics [of the United States] in Latin America, and he was not afraid to expose the clandestine activities of the U.S. government. He was assassinated just as the CIA and Oliver North were expanding their illegal activities in Central America."

By the time Ángel Buendía informed Miguel Ángel García Domínguez of the president elect's decision, the special prosecutor had boxed all the Buendía case files and laid off staff, whose contractual period ended that same day. The following week, just three days shy of the end of President de la Madrid's term in office, he released what was to have been his final report as special prosecutor but now contained a concluding statement that the investigation "remained open to be continued by the new administration." The report was another litany of quantified data documenting its author's uncommon level of professionalism: 304 files containing 49,349 pages, which if stacked would exceed 50 feet in height; 230 individuals deposed plus 79 follow-up sessions, occupying a total of 588 hours; 2,138 memos and 364 subpoenas issued; 50 investigative and judicial files and 801 reports reviewed; 202 lab requests filed; 429 firearms examined, 80 sent for ballistics tests; 376 active and 2,500 inactive police personnel files reviewed; over 900 Buendía columns analyzed, resulting in 22 potential assassination masterminds and 54 hypothetical assassins. The special prosecutor and his staff had conducted a methodical analysis of all available facts, García Domínguez reported, and based on that analysis had formulated logical hypotheses, "no matter how delicate or dangerous they may have been." Many were subsequently discarded, while the rest continued to be investigated. The special prosecutor's overall investigative plan was now 87 percent complete, the report concluded, with 13 percent still unfinished.[29]

Carlos Salinas formally reappointed García Domínguez as special prosecutor for the Buendía case on Tuesday, 3 January 1989, one month after his own inauguration as president. He reassured the public that his administration would give new impetus to the special prosecutor's investigation. With the new president, however, came a new cast of players and a profoundly altered political panorama in which, for the first time in six decades, the future of the PRI political machine had been placed in doubt. Presidential cabinet appointments most directly concerned with García Domínguez's renewed mandate were national security veteran Fernando Gutiérrez Barrios as secretary of government, former Jalisco governor Enrique Álvarez del Castillo as the nation's attorney general, and Ignacio Morales Lechuga as Federal District attorney general. Former secretary of government Manuel Bartlett Díaz was the one holdover from the previous administration, now with the portfolio of public education secretary, a consolation appointment, perhaps, for having been passed over as the PRI's presidential candidate, as well as a reward for having plucked Salinas's precarious election victory from the digital ether when the Federal Election Commission's computer bank mysteriously crashed in the midst of vote counting. Two other Salinas cabinet appointees with personal political agendas related to the Buendía case were Mexico City regent Manuel Camacho Solís and Federal District police chief (secretary of public safety and traffic) and former DFS head Javier García Paniagua. Both Camacho Solís and García Paniagua were political heavyweights, each having held leadership positions on the PRI's National Executive Committee.

The Salinas administration entered office politically battered and with a reactionary sexennial agenda that predictably made itself felt in the special prosecutor's domain. Foremost among its programmatic priorities was a PRI face-lift after a nearly fatal electoral challenge by former party stalwart Cuauhtémoc Cárdenas. The new administration's declared goals began with a list of boilerplate policies few took seriously: opening up Mexican democracy, improvement of election procedures, standardization of political norms and practices, respect for pluralism and effective participation in the political process, renovation of PRI practices and procedures, and the strengthening of party principles. Salinas's overriding unstated policies were retaliation against Cárdenas's newly formed Party of the Democratic Revolution (PRD by its Spanish acronym) and preparation of the groundwork for Mexico's incorporation into NAFTA.

On the morning of 10 January 1989, Salinas made the first of what would be a series of dramatic political moves by dispatching army troops to arrest the powerful head of the oil workers' union, PRI veteran Joaquín "La Quina" Hernández Galicia, at his Gulf Coast home in Ciudad Madero just north of Tampico. Hernández was charged with fraud and corruption in his management of union affairs, although the actual reason appears to have been his readiness to draw on union resources for political purposes and, most immediately, as payback for having urged the oil workers to support opposition candidate Cuauhtémoc Cárdenas. An omen of hidden agendas accompanied La Quina's arrest in the form of a presidential press release suggesting that he had masterminded the assassination of Manuel Buendía. When Ángel Buendía saw the press release barely two hours after La Quina had been taken into custody, he immediately called García Domínguez to ask about it, then, at the special prosecutor's request, flew to Mexico City that same afternoon to discuss it in person.[30]

It was not true, García Domínguez assured Don Ángel, that Joaquín Hernández Galicia had anything at all to do with his brother's homicide. He did not. But it was also true, García Domínguez added, that someone "very high up" in the Salinas administration—whom he preferred not to name—had insinuated that the special prosecutor should pin the Buendía assassination on La Quina. By his own account, he had replied indignantly that he would not fabricate scapegoats and no one should think for a moment that he would be party to such a crude machination. The matter was dropped, he told Don Ángel, and no further effort was made to have him frame a culprit. In light of how the Buendía case was then unfolding and ultimately would play out, however, this seemed a clear ploy to save ex-DFS chief José Antonio Zorrilla Pérez from prosecution.

The Salinas administration was no more transparent in its handling of the Buendía case than had been the previous administration. Despite the new president's reappointment of the special prosecutor and his publicly expressed promise of full political and material support for García Domínguez's investigation, by the time of La Quina's arrest the special prosecutor's ability to function had been effectively compromised by the Salinas administration's failure to reinstate personnel and resources terminated at the close of de la Madrid's presidential term. More than half the vehicles, furnishings, and equipment assigned to García Domínguez had been returned to the Federal District's

Public Ministry, now presided over by District Attorney General Ignacio Morales Lechuga. Over half of the special prosecutor's staff, some twenty-six persons, had been dismissed or reassigned to their original jobs, while those who remained were hobbled by embargoed fiscal resources. It amounted to a dismantling of the special prosecutor's office by default and was perceived as such by the journalistic community, which through the Union of Democratic Journalists (UPD) now launched a campaign calling the administration to account.[31]

A delegation of journalists led by UPD president Eduardo "El Buho" Valle arranged a meeting with Secretary of Government Fernando Gutiérrez Barrios, to whom they repeated their insistent demands for government action on the thirty-one unresolved murders of media personnel committed during de la Madrid's presidency, a more proactive attitude on the part of the authorities in the defense of media rights and protection of journalists, and a more effective response by the Secretariat of Government to attacks on reporters. With regard to the Buendía case, the UPD delegation informed Gutiérrez Barrios about what was occurring with the special prosecutor's office and protested that the dismantling of García Domínguez's operation suggested an impending de facto closure of the case without public announcement, this despite the president's protestations of full support for the special prosecutor. Gutiérrez Barrios exerted a little pro forma pressure on Morales Lechuga on behalf of the UPD and created a permanent media rights office within the Secretariat of Government, but he did nothing beyond that to salvage the special prosecutor's stalled Buendía investigation.

A more ominous development was the creation in the first month of the Salinas administration of an Intelligence Directorate (DI) within the Federal District's police force and the appointment of ex-DFS chief and key CIA asset Miguel Nazar Haro as head of the new directorate. As García Domínguez was quick to point out, there was neither an institutional precedent nor a legal basis for the new investigative body. That Nazar Haro should be placed in charge of the DI was an immediate cause for concern, given his reputation as one of Mexico's darker state security enforcers. Concerns were heightened by the assignment of various ex-DFS commandants to the DI, senior agents who had been close to José Antonio Zorrilla and, in concert with Nazar Haro, were now well placed to sabotage the special prosecutor's threatened indictment of him. Within six months, three of these individuals would themselves be charged as coconspirators in the Buendía assassination.

The web of vested political interests was tightly woven. The new district attorney general, Ignacio Morales Lechuga, was an experienced hand in matters of state security, having held senior positions in the government secretariats of Veracruz State and the federal government. Mexico City regent Manuel Camacho Solís was a PRI insider and close associate of Carlos Salinas. He had presidential ambitions of his own and could be expected to impose Salinas's firm grip on the politically crucial Federal District, as reflected in his appointment of García Paniagua to head the capital's Public Safety and Traffic Police (DPV), his creation of the unprecedented DI within the DPV, and García Paniagua's appointment of Nazar Haro to run it. Discounting the brief term of Capt. Pablo González Ruelas, who oversaw the dismantling of the DFS in

1985, the last three DFS directors now occupied center stage in this increasingly intricate political performance, with two of them, Javier García Paniagua (1977–1978) and Miguel Nazar Haro (1978–1982), working to save the hide of the third, José Antonio Zorrilla Pérez (1982–1985), who was "a man of the system," had followed orders, and stood to take the fall for the former president and his secretary of government if the special prosecutor's investigation could not be derailed.

7

Grand Finale

I remember thinking then, when the murder happened, not only that the CIA must have been involved, but also [that] this would probably never come out, because even if the Mexican government nailed the guys behind it, there was no way any Mexican government would point the finger at Washington and say your agents murdered [Buendía]. . . . Nailing Zorrilla Pérez, who everybody political in Mexico knew was then the CIA's main Mexican dispatcher, was all that any government there could do to point a finger, i.e., point at the U.S. reflection or agency in Mexico. It's a sad comment on Mexican sovereignty.

—John Womack Jr., personal communication (14 February 2012)

The closing of the case July 5th was shocking. In García Domínguez's now official scenario, Zorrilla Pérez is the intellectual author and Juan Rafael Moro Ávila Camacho (now appearing in "Days of Violence" on your local screen) is the material triggerman. The motive was to suppress publication of information revealing Zorrilla Pérez's ties to Caro Quintero, Ernesto Fonseca and Miguel Ángel Félix Gallardo. Most everyone I talk to laughs out loud at this solution.

—John Ross, personal communication (26 July 1989)

IT WAS IMPOSSIBLE to anticipate Salinas de Gortari's endgame in his determination to close the Buendía case. Given his strategy of taking down previously untouchable figures identified in public opinion with crime and corruption, it was not inconceivable that he might find it politically advantageous to sacrifice Zorrilla Pérez in a dramatic show of federal housecleaning. But apparent steps to undermine the special prosecutor and divert attention away from Zorrilla sufficiently alarmed journalists that they decided to launch an all-out media campaign pressuring the Salinas administration to let García Domínguez complete his original assignment.

The influential UPD demanded and was granted an audience with District Attorney General Ignacio Morales Lechuga to clarify the status of the special prosecutor's Buendía investigation. In response to the pointed concerns expressed by the UPD delegation, Morales Lechuga emphatically denied that the special prosecutor's ability to pursue his original presidential mandate was being compromised. On the contrary, he informed the journalists, President Salinas had explicitly instructed him to publicize his ratification of the special prosecutor and to make certain everyone understood that, while Miguel Ángel García Domínguez would retain his deputy prosecutor position within the district attorney general's office, as special prosecutor for the Buendía case he would continue to have complete autonomy and could count on "the full material and human support" of the Ministerio Público, as had been the case under the previous administration.

García Domínguez, who had been asked by Morales Lechuga to attend the 31 January 1989 meeting with the UPD representatives, acknowledged the attorney general's pledge of full backing, then informed the assembled reporters that he had been assured by both President Salinas and his secretary of government, Fernando Gutiérrez Barrios, of the new administration's unqualified political support. As for reductions in the special prosecutor's staff, García Domínguez explained that this was a foreseeable consequence of the transition process from one administration to another but that his current staff was adequate for the tasks at hand, given a lightened work load as a result of the advanced stage of the investigation. The large universe of hypotheses they had confronted at the outset had been reduced to seventy, and 60 percent of those had now been eliminated. As a consequence, he announced, the Buendía investigation "would be completed by April" of that year.[1]

This was a remarkable statement by García Domínguez, all the more so in light of the doubts and uncertainties surrounding the Buendía case in the first two months of the Salinas administration—doubts and uncertainties that had been fueled by the special prosecutor himself and had sufficiently alarmed the UPD to insist on this meeting with District Attorney General Morales Lechuga. Just the previous month García Domínguez had told reporters that he could say nothing with certainty, that the case might be resolved the following day or not resolved at all during the Salinas presidency.[2] And now suddenly he was stating on the record that he would have the case solved in three months' time. To anyone paying close attention, this might have suggested the existence of a script for how the Buendía case was to play out.

> Mexico City, 16/III/89. Jueves—We take the metro to *unomásuno*, where we find parts of the building under reconstruction and Manuel Becerra Acosta gone, to live and write books in Spain. The new editor, Luis Gutiérrez Rodríguez, reassures us of our continued importance as contributors and authorizes a telex credit card in our name. Afterward we meet with our colleague, police reporter Fernando Ramírez de Aguilar. He is worried about the paper's future, and his own. Fernando recently interviewed García Domínguez, who told him the Buendía case "will be wrapped up in June." Does this mean there's now a Salinas administration choreography to end the case?
>
> —S. E. Bartley, journal entry

Manuel Becerra Acosta, who had encouraged and facilitated our association with *unomásuno* over the previous nine years, was now a victim of President Salinas's reprisal campaign against all those who had supported the candidacy of Cuauhtémoc Cárdenas. There likely were other factors as well, both editorial and personal, that piqued Salinas's ire, including publication of our articles on the Buendía case. In any event, Becerra was unceremoniously told to take a one-million-dollar buyout and go into foreign exile for the remainder of the Salinas presidency or face imprisonment. His replacement as senior editor was the paper's general manager, Luis Gutiérrez Rodríguez, a longtime associate of Becerra but also a personal friend of Carlos Salinas.[3] The change had occurred on 3 March 1989, not quite two weeks prior to our arrival in the Federal District.

While we had no illusions about there being any transparency around Becerra Acosta's sudden departure and immediately foresaw the possibility of having to terminate our own association with *unomásuno*, we decided for the time being to accept Gutiérrez's assurances of the paper's continued independence and his readiness to publish our material. Over the next months, we would experience no change in our ability to get articles into the paper but soon enough detected clear signs of editorial alignment with the new Salinas agenda. Despite initial assertions that Gutiérrez had been Manuel Becerra's personal choice to succeed him as the paper's editor, by year's end the break between Gutiérrez and Becerra had come out in the open and Salinas's co-optation of *unomásuno* could no longer be concealed.[4] At that point, we severed our ties to the paper.

Meanwhile, UPD columnists and reporters joined the public outcry against Nazar Haro and the capital city's newly formed police intelligence unit. The ensuing media exposé of Nazar's sordid police curriculum obliged him to resign as DI director after only two months on the job, thereby eliminating an experienced covert operative thoroughly familiar with the Buendía case from his early collaboration with District Attorney General Victoria Adato, an operative quite capable of derailing the special prosecutor's investigation should the president choose to do so.[5] Salinas, for his part, seemed unperturbed by Nazar's forced departure, portraying it after the fact as simply one more instance of overdue housecleaning. Indeed, it may actually have been Salinas himself who contrived Nazar Haro's public discrediting as part of the new president's offensive against the PRI's old guard. García Paniagua would be another *dinosaurio* targeted by Salinas.[6]

> Mexico City, 25/III/89. Sábado—10 am appointment at Sanborns facing the Monument to Independence with Felipe Victoria Zepeda, ex-attorney in the Ministerio Público, now a reporter for *El Sol de México*, columnist for the weekly *Quehacer Político*, and author of a new book that purports to solve the unsolved murder of Manuel Buendía. Victoria invited us to breakfast by phone last night; insisted on speaking to Russ in nearly unintelligible English, saying there were "problems with the phones," yet seemed perfectly at ease meeting with us at Sanborns just a block from the U.S. Embassy. He offered dirt on every name we mentioned, except Nazar Haro and Bartlett Díaz. Much of his "information" contradicted what we already knew of the case or simply didn't jibe. He avoided answering certain questions without seeming to do so; responded with ambiguous gestures and suggestive facial expressions. Victoria paid for our breakfast; left us with more questions than answers. He did not inspire confidence. We debriefed at El Centro Cultural over notepads and cappuccinos.
>
> —S. E. Bartley, journal entry

As the calendar approached the fifth anniversary of the Buendía assassination, the Federal District press corps unleashed a barrage of articles and columns recapping the government's failure to clarify Buendía's death and demanding a final resolution of the case. The influential newsweekly *Proceso* led off two weeks before the anniversary with a double salvo of featured pieces: an exclusive interview with García Domínguez headlined "It's Very Likely the Mastermind behind Buendía's Death Is a Political Figure"; and an accompanying boxed article about key police officials who had compromised the homicide investigation, two of whom, José Antonio Zorrilla Pérez and former PJDF chief José Trinidad Gutiérrez Sánchez, would soon enjoy protection from potential obstruction of justice charges under a five-year statute of limitations.[7]

Gone was the caution with which reporters had previously covered the high-profile Buendía case, with *Proceso*'s Raúl Monge and Ignacio Ramírez now accusing former senior officials by name of cover-up and obstruction of justice. Their primary source was the special prosecutor, who had decided to use *Proceso* in a tactical maneuver to prevent Carlos Salinas from terminating his mandate before he could hand down indictments. Although Salinas had officially extended the special prosecutor's presidential mandate, his intentions in the matter were far from transparent. The president had dealt only minimally with García Domínguez, yet was fully apprised of the latest developments in his Buendía investigation, including García Domínguez's ongoing battle with throat cancer.[8]

At the end of April 1989, García Domínguez began a thirty-day course of daily radiation treatments at Mexico City's Centro Médico and within two weeks had become so debilitated that he began to doubt his capacity to carry the Buendía investigation through to its approaching conclusion. Faced with that possibility, he summoned Ángel Buendía to Mexico City to strategize on how to proceed in the event that he should in fact be unable to continue. Sensing the urgency in García Domínguez's voice, Don Ángel asked Fundación Manuel Buendía director Miguel Ángel Sánchez de Armas to accompany him to the meeting.

At that meeting on the morning of 10 May, García Domínguez told the two men that if it became physically impossible for him to see his mandate through, they should petition the president for a judicial review of the special prosecutor's Buendía case files, which he would leave organized in such a manner that any prosecutor assigned to the task could easily pick up where he had left off and take the investigation to its logical conclusion. He was himself almost there, he said, but for the moment could not share the details. He was optimistic that he could successfully accomplish what at the outset had seemed an impossible undertaking and did not want his effort to be in vain.[9]

The plot thickened, and the drama spiked when, six days later, *Excélsior* reporter Rogelio Hernández López received a phone call from García Domínguez's assistant secretary, Victor Manuel Pastor, who urgently asked to meet with him on behalf of the special prosecutor. Hernández was just then putting the final touches on a sixty-nine-page report on the status of the Buendía case for circulation among key UPD members and other interested parties. When the two met later that day, Pastor informed Hernández that the special prosecutor, "who was recovering from a serious throat ailment," wished him to insert a brief article in the next day's edition of *Excélsior* that "gave a little push" (*un empujoncito*) to the special prosecutor's Buendía agenda. What García Domínguez wanted, Pastor explained, was for President Salinas to learn through the press that he had completed his investigation, was ready to hand down indictments, and only awaited the president's authorization to proceed.

Asked why García Domínguez did not inform the president directly or, alternatively, convene a press conference, Pastor replied that from the beginning the special prosecutor had not had the president's ear and that his access to Salinas was being blocked by those above him—this despite the fact that García Domínguez theoretically answered solely to the president. As for a press conference, in light of his isolation from the president he thought it would be viewed as a personal challenge to Salinas and thus counterproductive. The best strategy, he had concluded, was to filter the information through Hernández, the reporter generally recognized as most conversant with developments in the Buendía case, and not to be seen himself as the instigator of the news report.

On page 4 of the following morning's paper, the article Hernández had finally agreed to write appeared under the headline "Special Prosecutor Apparently Locates Mastermind of Buendía Slaying: A Personage Linked to Public Office and Police Agencies." The crux of the piece read, "According to information obtained by *Excélsior*, a few hours from now President Salinas de Gortari will hear the special prosecutor's main report and may then authorize the use of all available means to wrap up the case and make the necessary arrests, including use of the military."[10] Ex-DFS chief Zorrilla Pérez was the unmistakable suspect, and the president's hand was being called to force his arrest.

For its part, the UPD had involved opposition party members from the Federal District's Representative Assembly and the national Congress in the rising clamor for a definitive resolution of the Buendía case. On the same May morning that Rogelio Hernández's planted article appeared in *Excélsior*, a congressman from Cuahutémoc Cárdenas's PRD and two District Assembly members, one each from the PRD and the conservative PAN, attended a strategy session with UPD representatives at the iconic Café de Tacuba in Mexico City's historic downtown quarter. After discussing the morning's *Excélsior* piece and the sixty-nine-page UPD report drafted by Hernández, it was agreed to bring the case before the local Representative Assembly and the Congress for wider public ventilation and perhaps legislative action. Most significant, it was agreed that the UPD would file suit with District Attorney General Morales Lechuga against key former officials for obstruction of justice and abuse of power in the Buendía case, including Zorrilla Pérez, and that the legislators would support that suit.[11]

After the Café de Tacuba meeting, "El Buho" Valle informed the *Proceso* reporters who had been covering the Buendía case of the special prosecutor's intentions and gave them a copy of the UPD report. The following Monday, 22 May, *Proceso* appeared on the newsstands with a four-page feature article headlined "Every Trail in the Buendía Case Leads to Zorrilla and His Men: Official Inaction Appears to Have Been for His Protection." The article's opening paragraphs announced that the next day the UPD would file charges with the Federal District attorney general's office and the Congress against former district attorney general Victoria Adato,[12] ex-DFS chief José Antonio Zorrilla Pérez, and former PJDF chief José Trinidad Gutiérrez Sánchez for obstruction of justice in the Buendía case. The action was intended to prevent the three former officials from obtaining immunity against prosecution when the statute of limitations on obstruction of justice ran out one week hence. The suit, Valle informed *Proceso*, would be extended to other former officials who may have been involved in hindering the investigation, "including ex-government secretary Manuel Bartlett Díaz and ex-president Miguel de la Madrid."[13]

The PRD and PAN District Assembly representatives persuaded their colleagues to have García Domínguez update them for the record on the status of his Buendía investigation. Apprised of this action on the part of the capital's legislators, District Attorney General Morales Lechuga contrived to have the special prosecutor make his report behind closed doors at the Public Ministry rather than in the assembly's chambers, which García Domínguez did on 24 May. The day before, however, Morales Lechuga had summoned several PAN and PRD assemblymen to his office, where he repeated assertions that he had been filtering to the media to the effect that the special prosecutor's Buendía investigation would be shut down "without positive results" and the case returned to the Federal District's Public Ministry "with a new strategy." A great deal of money was being spent unnecessarily to sustain the special prosecutor's investigation, Morales Lechuga told the opposition legislators, and García Domínguez "no longer wished to continue." Moreover, he added suggestively, García Domínguez's throat cancer "might induce him to do something imprudent." When, in Morales Lechuga's presence, García Domínguez gave his report to local assembly representatives the next day, he provided a quantified summary of tasks performed and results obtained but carefully avoided giving any hint of his intentions with regard to Zorrilla Pérez. In what can only be interpreted as a tactical smoke screen, García Domínguez assured the assembly members that in his sixteen months as special prosecutor he had encountered no political obstacles and under no circumstances would the Buendía case be closed prematurely.[14]

On that same day, Wednesday the twenty-fourth, the Permanent Commission of the Congress resolved to have the Senate and Chamber of Deputies justice committees consider a proposal introduced by PRD deputy Jesús Ortega that they be informed directly by the special prosecutor on the status of his investigation and that they subpoena testimony from previous investigators involved in the Buendía case. Ortega had participated in the Café de Tacuba strategy session with the UPD leadership and District Assembly representatives. He was now joined in his call for congressional action on the matter by PAN deputy Gerardo Medina Valdés, himself a founding member of the UPD, who, while unable to attend the previous week's Café de Tacuba meeting, had conveyed his full support of the group and its efforts to force a transparent resolution of the case.

Both deputies pointed to Zorrilla as the prime suspect in the Buendía slaying, suggesting that at the very least he must know who was behind it. Ortega caused a stir in the Chamber by asserting that there had been disagreements among senior officials that prevented Zorrilla's arrest and kept Buendía's murder from being solved. Almost five years after the event, Ortega declared, the public still did not know who the guilty parties were and, it was to be supposed, would not soon find out, "because prominent government politicians are implicated."[15] While the presumed complicity of prominent personages in the Mexican government remained the primary issue in the still unresolved Buendía case, an inescapable subtext was now the rising political challenge to PRI preeminence. Hence the calculated intervention of the PRD and PAN, the PRI's two principal contenders.

Carlos Salinas's dilemma was how to salvage a modicum of benefit from a high-profile criminal investigation that threatened further damage to the ruling political machine no matter how it was resolved. By the eve of the fifth anniversary of Manuel Buendía's death, to prevent the special prosecutor from making his case and handing down indictments would invite widespread derision and public repudiation. Charging Zorrilla, the prime suspect and a key establishment figure, on the other hand, would amount to an indictment of the country's national security apparatus, and with it the governing PRI. Jesús Ortega's pointed endorsement of Miguel Ángel García Domínguez from the podium of the Permanent Commission of the Congress was a partisan challenge Salinas could not very well ignore.

EVIDENCIAS DE UN POSIBLE INVOLUCRAMIENTO DE INTERESES FORÁNEOS EN EL ASESINATO DE MB: EL CASO VISTO DESDE EL EXTERIOR

Revista mexicana de comunicación—May–June 1989

Russell H. Bartley

The assassination of Manuel Buendía Tellezgirón five years ago is perhaps the most transcendent political crime in the recent history of Mexico, at least since the fatal Tlatelolco Square events of 2 October 1968. This is because of the place the victim occupied in national political discourse and the grave assault his murder signified on the country's political integrity, as well as the presence of circumstances suggestive of possible foreign involvement. It is, above all, the latter possibility that moves this investigator to pursue the case, for clarification of Manuel Buendía's death may reveal meddling and treachery whose implications extend beyond the man himself and injure us all, regardless of our nationality.

. . .

"The trail has turned cold," a Mexican colleague recently lamented. "Too much time has gone by without identifying the culprits. This case won't ever be solved." We have heard people close to the official investigations express the same thing, to their evident relief. Special prosecutor Miguel Ángel García Domínguez himself has said this to us.

In other words, for the criminal investigator the mere passage of time tends to thwart the investigative process, whereas for the historian the time factor furthers it. As events recede into the past, they lose immediacy in the minds of those who focus on the present. It's a psychological phenomenon, which the perpetrators of political crimes—as the Buendía slaying clearly seems to be—take into account.

For the investigator who looks beyond the present moment, however, time contextualizes, reveals relationships, uncovers evidence. Tongues loosen, be it out of carelessness or any number of other factors. Documents surface. Political circumstances change, and with them those who benefit from the crime or its cover-up. . . .

. . .

While already the day after May 30, 1984, people were pointing to the Central Intelligence Agency (CIA) as the culprit behind Don Manuel's death, above all because of the mordant columns he had devoted to that omnipresent and subversive U.S. spy organization, we dismissed the idea that the CIA would have taken part in the assassination as an act of simple reprisal. As much as the columnist's exposure of CIA agents and operations in Mexico may have bothered the Americans, it is implausible that U.S. intelligence should have fallen into the puerile trap of seeking vengeance, for as we have already noted, vengeance for vengeance's sake only harms the interests of those who perpetrate it. And the CIA, needless to say, is concerned exclusively with the interests of the U.S. political elite, however those interests may be defined at any given moment.

However, that the CIA may have had motives other than reprisal for involving itself in the assassination of Manuel Buendía is quite another matter. Indeed, various hypotheses are valid here. At the same time, one must always keep in mind that the CIA is not the United States' sole instrument of foreign intervention. In addition to such other government bodies as the National Security Council, the Pentagon, and the Drug Enforcement Administration (DEA), there are numerous private-sector entities devoted to subversion and political terrorism that can perfectly well serve State interests. Take, for example, the case of the so-called Enterprise, which in the tangled Iran-Contra affair carried out the covert policy of the Reagan administration in the Middle East and Central America.

One should also take into account the clandestine services of other nations, like those of Israel, Chile, and Argentina, to cite just three that are active in the region and which in recent years have worked closely with Washington. It is worth recalling here that in February 1978 Don Manuel himself frustrated an operation of Argentina's military junta to assassinate exiled opponents on Mexican territory and that subsequently these same special services from the River Plate, together with Israel's Mossad and local forces of repression—including, no doubt, those in Mexico—worked to advance the violent designs of the White House in Central America, designs tenaciously opposed by Manuel Buendía.

In September 1988, a cadre of journalists and media analysts affiliated with the Fundación Manuel Buendía launched Mexico's first professional mass communications journal, the semimonthly *Revista mexicana de comunicación*, edited by Buendía protégé Miguel Ángel Sánchez de Armas. That October Sánchez de Armas traveled to Mexicali to participate in a panel session on the Buendía case at the thirty-fourth annual meeting of the Pacific Coast Council on Latin American Studies. The following May, as the Salinas administration was bringing the official Buendía inquiry to its uncertain conclusion, he featured Russell's and Matthew Rothschild's Mexicali presentations in the journal's fifth issue. Both pieces posed the possibility of CIA involvement in Buendía's death.[16]

As media clamor for a definitive resolution of the Buendía case crescendoed in the weeks leading up to the fifth anniversary of the assassination, the CIA remained the elephant in the room. Newspaper reportage and opinion pieces focused on Zorrilla, the special prosecutor, and an imminent denouement of the case, with only passing, albeit pointed, reference to possible foreign involvement. Ángel Buendía was quoted as having expressed optimism that his brother Manuel's homicide would at last be resolved, at the same time as he called for criminal investigations of former district attorneys general Victoria Adato and Renato Sales Gasque, together with former police officials José Antonio Zorrilla, José Trinidad Gutiérrez, and Jesús Miyazawa.[17]

Four days later, on the actual eve of the anniversary, *Proceso* reporters Raúl Monge and Ignacio Ramírez published a feature article based on transcripts of two separate interrogation sessions totaling twenty-two hours of testimony before the special prosecutor in which Zorrilla "had lied and contradicted himself in an effort to clear himself of any responsibility for [Buendía's] murder." There had come a moment, Monge and Ramírez reported, when Zorrilla's interrogators suspected that he was baldly putting them on. Asked about the former DFS's relationships with the American DEA and CIA, Zorrilla had replied with a straight face that the DFS had no ties to those agencies. All he knew about the DEA, he had stated, "was what he read in the press." As for the CIA, "he knew only what he saw in the movies."[18]

These were striking statements and virtually the sole public confirmation that the special prosecutor had actually included U.S. complicity in Buendía's death among the cluster of hypotheses guiding his investigation. It was also significant that Monge and Ramírez chose to conclude their exclusive feature with this revelation, contained in two short paragraphs set off from the preceding fifty-odd paragraphs by asterisks. This had the effect of a suspended interrogatory demanding an answer, which may have been what the special prosecutor and *Proceso* intended.

Allowing the two reporters to examine Zorrilla's depositions while the case was still officially open constituted a clear violation of investigative protocols but seems to have been a calculated move on García Domínguez's part to prevent the Salinas administration from aborting his Buendía inquiry short of its logical conclusion. Reference to American intelligence agencies intimated potentially compromising information whose continued concealment might provide the basis for a mutually acceptable resolution of political agenda conflicts, whereby García Domínguez would come away with his professional image intact while Salinas took credit for yet another blow against the "untouchables" of systemic crime and corruption. (In a follow-up interview ten months later, García Domínguez would acknowledge to us that the hypothesis of a U.S. intelligence connection to the Buendía homicide was not one he could realistically pursue.[19]) However it may have been, through the influential medium of the newsweekly *Proceso*, the special prosecutor himself legitimated the notion of possible CIA complicity. By giving Matthew Rothschild and Russell featured space in its May–June 1989 issue, the *Revista mexicana de comunicación* provided additional substance to that hypothesis.

As May drew to a close, the local press was filled with commentary about the Buendía case. *El Día* ran a front-page interview with renowned author and Ateneo de Angangueo regular Elena Poniatowska, who had written the prologue to Buendía's 1984 book *La CIA en México*. It was necessary, Poniatowska insisted, "to expose the feral cat" responsible for the cover-up of Buendía's killers. It was a political crime, she averred, with many interested parties involved, which explained why five years after the event none of the culprits had been arrested.[20]

Another Buendía associate and Ateneo member, Manú Dornbierer, weighed in with an op-ed piece in *Excélsior* attacking the special prosecutor as an institutional opportunist seeking personal gain. "Tomorrow, May thirtieth," Dornbierer wrote, "is the fifth anniversary of Manuel's assassination, and we can now say, with justified sadness, that his death has served above all to permit the expenditure of much money and the travel of police agents 'in search of facts.'" And no one had benefited more, she opined, than Miguel Ángel García Domínguez, "who traveled to various European countries and the United States without bringing back a scintilla of relevant information, not even as a 'souvenir.'" The prevailing view among those most informed about the case was that when García Domínguez agreed to accept the appointment as special prosecutor, he understood perfectly well that he "was doing the government a great favor" by making it appear that the Buendía case was finally receiving the attention it deserved, when in actual fact "there was not the slightest interest in solving it." The assassination of Manuel Buendía had not been solved, Dornbierer emphasized, "because it was not convenient."[21]

That same day our *unomásuno* colleague Fernando Ramírez de Aguilar published the first of a two-part series highlighting the persistent uncertainty about how the special prosecutor's Buendía inquiry would actually play out. All indications were, he wrote, that the case would not be solved in the short or even medium term. García Domínguez himself acknowledged that "90 percent of his investigative agenda had been completed without yet having determined who had masterminded and carried out the assassination of Manuel Buendía." The reason, according to García Domínguez, was because there were still "many, many suspects." The special prosecutor had also indicated, Fernando reported, that the individual behind Buendía's homicide "might be a high or former high public official." To date the case had involved three district attorneys general, four PJDF chiefs, four Public Safety and Traffic secretaries, and two DFS directors, plus more than a hundred police officers, technicians, and Public Ministry agents, as well as the special prosecutor. Nonetheless, and despite the fact that "there is no perfect crime," repeated García Domínguez, the authorities were still unable to identify the guilty parties. "All the efforts to date, and they are substantial," ratified District Attorney General Morales Lechuga, "do not suffice for us to reach serious conclusions [in the case]."[22]

Notable for its absence on the eve of the fifth anniversary of Manuel Buendía's death was any official statement from the district attorney general's office, which in the final days of May each of the previous four years had issued a status report on the investigation and reiterated the government's intention to bring the guilty parties to justice. For those of us paying close attention, however, there were clear hints of impending developments. In a lead article on page 4 of *Excélsior* on Monday, 29 May, the same edition that carried Manú Dornbierer's caustic op-ed column about the special prosecutor, Rogelio Hernández announced that the Buendía case "had now entered its defining stage." Within the next forty-eight hours, Hernández ventured, José Antonio Zorrilla Pérez would be officially identified as "the principal subject of interest" for a resolution of the case. "According to information obtained by *Excélsior*," he wrote, "over the weekend Zorrilla Pérez was the focus of intense activity . . . in the district attorney general's office, the special prosecutor's office, the presidency of the republic, the Assembly of Representatives, the Chamber of Deputies, and those organizations and media outlets most concerned with the case."[23]

On Tuesday the thirtieth, the anniversary proper, there were memorial gatherings throughout the country to mark the date and vent recriminations against the government for its failure to solve Buendía's slaying. In the press that day, additional pointed commentary was directed at the authorities for their continued failure to act decisively. With the mass dismissal of officials in positions of authority at the time of the crime, Manú Dornbierer noted in a second *Excélsior* column, those who replaced them were handicapped from the outset by diminished familiarity with the details and nuances of the Buendía case, "even supposing they came to it in good faith," which she did not. It was all too easy for these relief players to muddy the waters, especially, Dornbierer suggested, "if they were under orders not to clarify anything." And nothing had really changed, she concluded. Five years on, it still wasn't "convenient."[24]

It was not convenient, Fernando Ramírez de Aguilar suggested in the second of his two-part series in *unomásuno*, because Buendía's murder appeared to be a political killing. The special prosecutor himself had acknowledged as much. "I really don't know on what basis [former attorneys general Victoria Adato and Renato Sales Gasque] dismissed the hypothesis of a political crime," Ramírez de Aguilar quoted García Domínguez as saying. "Nor do I know how each of them understood the term 'political crime.' . . . As for the victim's journalism, however, we do know that his column was eminently political and affected many people in politics, so it is quite probable that this was a political crime."[25]

By way of editorial comment, the Mexico City daily *El Día* published a brief chronology of the official inquiries into the Buendía homicide. "Today, at 6:39 p.m., marks five years since the assassination of Manuel Buendía and the crime still has not been clarified," began the chronology's introductory statement. There followed eighteen chronological entries from the day following Buendía's murder to the eve of the fifth anniversary, each with notable highlights of case history. The final entry, dated 29 May 1989, conveyed the paper's editorial summation: "Neither the special prosecutor's office nor the Federal District attorney general's office has provided the public with any information at all about the case."[26]

Well out of public view, the Salinas administration debated its options in the face of the concerted media and partisan challenge to render some semblance of closure in the Buendía case. The president's main strategists were Federal District regent Manuel Camacho Solís and District Attorney General Ignacio Morales Lechuga, plus Special Prosecutor Miguel Ángel García Domínguez, who, as a holdover from the previous administration and by virtue of his de facto centrality in the case, could not feasibly be marginalized from related decision making. As journalists and press freedom activists around the country gathered to mark the fifth anniversary of Buendía's violent demise, the three officials met for several hours to consider the government's best options. García Domínguez insisted on arrests and a full-press law enforcement operation to carry them out.

Noteworthy here was the low profile of Secretary of Government Fernando Gutiérrez Barrios, who in striking contrast to his predecessor, Manuel Bartlett Díaz, appears to have preferred not to involve himself in the politically volatile Buendía case. Zorrilla Pérez, for his part, was kept fully apprised of developments by his own inside sources, as well as the media. He now began to have doubts about how the Buendía affair would play out and in the final days of May sought to meet with his former superior, Gutiérrez Barrios, to learn where matters actually stood. But Don Fernando chose to absent himself from his Gobernación office during those critical days so as to avoid the eventuality of such a meeting. Zorrilla's concerns spiked with the publication of Rogelio Hernández's *Excélsior* article of 29 May, in which Hernández intimated that the ex-DFS chief would soon be the object of some dramatic government action. That same day Zorrilla conveyed a personal threat to Hernández, which the UPD denounced in a complaint lodged directly with President Salinas, as well as in the press. Zorrilla also filtered veiled threats to the media against *Proceso* editor Julio Scherer García and UPD president Eduardo Valle.[27]

As the fifth anniversary of the Buendía assassination passed without official comment, expectations turned to the annual 7 June Press Freedom banquet, where national journalism awards would be given to select recipients and the president would address a representative gathering of editors, columnists, and reporters on administration media policy and the state of the Mexican press. Three days earlier, *unomásuno* had published a special twenty-four-page edition of its Sunday political supplement, *páginauno*, featuring two interviews and an article of ours under the collective heading "Between the Press and Power: The Limits of Freedom." The interviews were with Spanish mass communications specialist Vicente Romano and Mexican political historian Lorenzo Meyer. Featured separately in this same issue was an interview with Cuauhtémoc Cárdenas titled "The Government Has Not Called on Us to Dialogue." The Meyer and Cárdenas interviews, as well as our highlighted article on Buendía and the CIA, were announced on the paper's front page.[28]

EL AFFAIRE BUENDÍA: ¿LA CIA INVOLUCRADA?

Páginauno, suplemento político y económico de unomásuno—
Domingo, 4 June 1989
Russell H. Bartley

Milwaukee, Wisconsin—An obligatory topic for this time of year is the still unsolved slaying of Manuel Buendía Tellezgirón. Now on the fifth anniversary of that notorious crime our Mexican colleagues assure us that once again the authorities are expressing their regrets that, even under the new administration, "insurmountable obstacles" will preclude a definitive resolution of the Buendía case.

And why doubt it? Fierce is the caged cat, as the saying goes. Foul are the hidden agendas and powerful those who conceal them. Despite the fact that President Carlos Salinas de Gortari has seen fit to reconfirm the special prosecutor for the Buendía case, Dr. Miguel Ángel García Domínguez, rumors persist that the special prosecutor's days are numbered. In fact, the current government, like its predecessor, is incapable of publicly elucidating the true motives behind the murder of Manuel Buendía.

While the Buendía case exhibits its own peculiarities, which distinguish it from other attacks on those who have challenged established power, it nonetheless fits into an international context where every day more and more media professionals lose their lives. In the six-year term of Miguel de la Madrid alone, historian Enrique Semo recently observed, more journalists died in Mexico than in Nicaragua or El Salvador, more than in the Mexican Revolution itself. Even during the rule of Porfirio Díaz, stresses Semo, a Filomeno Mata is jailed thirty-three times in nine years but is always released to be jailed again, an opportunity not once afforded Manuel Buendía.

This means, in the view of some observers of Mexican politics, that there has been a qualitative change in the historic relationship between political power and the press. While Mexican journalists have always been exposed to the violence of provincial bosses, the assassination of Manuel Buendía appears to have established a new and ominous norm for Mexican media, where vested power interests resort directly to force to defend themselves against combative journalism. Another example of the many we could cite is Tijuana columnist Héctor *El Gato* Félix Miranda, felled with a shotgun a little more than a year ago by suspects known to all.

With regard to Manuel Buendía, Félix's combative comrade, Jesús Blancornelas, argued not long ago that we must reject any hypothesis of personal grievance as a viable murder motive. As for drugs, Blancornelas adds, "if drug traffickers were involved in the assassination of Manuel Buendía, it won't have had anything to do with drug trafficking, rather with other interests altogether."

We recall, in this connection, past arrangements between the White House and the Italo-American mafia that sought the physical elimination of Fidel Castro and other leaders of the Cuban Revolution.

Indeed, there is also room for the hypothesis that involved in the murder of Red Privada's author was the long arm of the Central Intelligence Agency (CIA). As noted by Matthew Rothschild, editor of the respected U.S. magazine *The Progressive*, there exists documentary evidence that the CIA kept Buendía under surveillance and that in Washington the assassination of the celebrated columnist is considered "a matter of national security."

Buendía, Rothschild reminds us, "was one of the most vociferous and influential critics of U.S. policy in Latin America. He was not afraid to expose the clandestine activities of the United States government. He was assassinated just as the CIA and Oliver North were pursuing their illegal activities throughout the Central American region. We know," emphasized Rothschild, "that the CIA is perfectly capable of perpetrating a crime of this nature."

In any case, we should not expect clarification from those who hide in the dark. If one day we manage to identify one or another of the pieces put into play that ill-fated 30th of May 1984, it will be as a consequence of the implacable efforts of professional journalists and those of us in and outside of Mexico who have committed ourselves to a free and critical journalism in service to the public. Despite the troglodytes and bad Mexicans who sought to silence a voice that exposed them day after day before public opinion, Manuel Buendía's worthy legacy survives intact and, by its own force, transcends time and national boundaries.

Páginauno accompanied our article with a dramatically suggestive illustration by one of the paper's political cartoonists depicting a wild-eyed CIA agent wrapped in the American flag at the base of a flagpole. The symbolism was as clear as the illustration was offensive: the flag unceremoniously lowered by an unworthy subject unable to conceal himself behind the stars and stripes of the U.S. national banner. It was enhanced by bold shading with the flagpole dividing the allotted space vertically, the article's heading and first four paragraphs rendered as a column of white type against the illustration's black to dark gray background. In overall effect, the article's presentation was very much in the spirit of Manuel Buendía.

The following day *Proceso* appeared on the newsstands with an article by Miguel Cabildo and Raúl Monge highlighting public disillusionment with the government's mishandling of the Buendía case. The two reporters had interviewed Buendía's widow, Dolores Ábalos, who during the previous four years had lived "in the hope that justice would be done." She had believed the promises made to her by the authorities, especially President de la Madrid's promise that the case would be solved and the perpetrators punished. But her attitude had now changed, Cabildo and Monge wrote. She was speaking out against those who had been in charge of the case, including the special prosecutor. "When the police want to clarify something," she observed, "they can do it. In this case, they haven't wanted to. That's what I see after five years. As far as I'm concerned, they haven't done a thing. They've deceived me."

On a personal level, Buendía's widow had been slighted by several of the principal officials concerned with the investigation of her husband's homicide, from District Attorney General Victoria Adato to Miguel Ángel García Domínguez. She was particularly offended by the incivility of Jesús Miyazawa Álvarez and Rosalino Ramírez Faz, chief and second in command of the PJDF under Attorney General Renato Sales Gasque. Both men were Lindavista neighbors who had been on friendly terms with Manuel Buendía and often visited with him at his home. Following Buendía's assassination, Miyazawa in particular reassured her that he would do everything in his power to solve her husband's murder yet within months was giving her the cold shoulder and never spoke to her again. It was the same with Ramírez Faz. Victoria Adato had met with Doña Dolores once at the Public Ministry and assured her that Manuel's murder would be solved but had no further contact with her. García Domínguez, in turn, paid her a single visit, offered nothing, and did not speak with her again. They had all ignored her, she told *Proceso*, and resolved nothing.

The two *Proceso* reporters reinforced the widow's disillusioned indictment of the Mexican authorities by repeating, and in effect publicizing, the more damning indictment made on the fifth anniversary by UPD president "El Buho" Valle. None of the investigators assigned to the Buendía case had done anything more than destroy evidence and deceive the public, Valle had expressed to a crowd of demonstrators gathered before a Mexico City monument to the liberal nineteenth-century newspaperman Francisco Zarco. "That happened," Valle declaimed, "at the sufferance of Miguel de la Madrid, who bears political responsibility for the crime." As a matter of fact, he asserted, "the subordinates of De la Madrid and Manuel Bartlett intervened to obstruct justice and the assassins therefore remain unpunished."[29]

Two days later, the Press Freedom event took place in the main ballroom of Mexico City's uptown Hotel Camino Real. As captured by investigative journalist Jorge Fernández Menéndez, the gala affair reflected perfectly the socioeconomic crazy quilt of media-state relations in Mexico. A long, U-shaped head table on a raised platform was reserved for President Salinas, members of his cabinet, and other guests of honor, including the awards panel and their selected honorees. Tables on the main floor revealed a distinct class division: those closest to the head table were occupied by representatives of the Newspaper and Magazine Publishers Association, together with influential friends willing to pay the peso equivalent of eight thousand dollars a plate for the privilege of posturing and being seen in such rarified company. These particular attendees had come to applaud the long-established power imbalance between press and state, an outright contradiction of the occasion. Virtually absent from their number were working journalists, those who labored day and night to gather, report, and get out the news. Distinguishable by their dress, demeanor, and palpable disdain for the Fourth Estate's managerial collaborators with established power, reporters and other representatives of the media work force had been relegated to the rear of the hall.[30]

There were two distinct, overlapping events in the Camino Real's main ballroom that evening: one a celebration of business as usual by the publishers, their high-rolling guests, and a handful of kept press personalities; the other a demand from the rear of the hall for abolition of the co-optive status quo. The continued furor over the government's failure to achieve a transparent resolution of the Buendía case, together with increasingly vehement demands for press freedom and official protection of journalists against physical assault or other profession-related reprisals, had an impact on the Salinas administration. The president's calculated response included several changes in the formalities of Press Freedom Day.

Whereas in previous years the national journalism awards ceremony had been held earlier in the day at the national palace, in 1989 it was combined with the presidential banquet. Also contrary to established custom, both the recipients of awards and members of the awards committee were permitted to address the gathering, thereby assuring the expression of discordant views. Carlos Salinas himself made an unprecedented entrance, breaking all previous security protocols as he walked slowly through the ballroom smiling, greeting people, and stopping to exchange a few words, studiously eschewing the formality of his office.

The featured speaker of the evening on behalf of the Mexican press corps was Héctor Aguilar Camín, editor of the monthly cultural and public affairs magazine *Nexos*. Framing his remarks within the conceptual scheme of "modernization" invoked by President Salinas as the solution to Mexico's troubled economy, Aguilar Camín skillfully deconstructed the corporate straightjacket that restricted the practice of independent journalism, then called for a structural modernization of the country's media that would allow journalists to exercise their profession unfettered by systemic constraints. "The commercial and political relations of the press with the government and other centers of power and influence in Mexican society lack transparency," he emphasized, "to the media's detriment and that of the reading public." While there had been some improvement in reporters' pay, insufficient remuneration remained "the primary source of corruption and lack of professionalism" among Mexican journalists. Indeed, he reproved, financially sound and profitable organs of the press kept their professional staffs in such precarious economic straits that, pathetically, there were still instances in which veteran reporters went to their grave "with one hand out in front and the other extended behind."

Aguilar Camín addressed his closing remarks directly to Carlos Salinas. "Señor Presidente," he began, "the challenges of modernization aside, we journalists have various unresolved issues at present. First among them, of course, is the memory of Manuel Buendía, whose unsolved death casts a recurrent shadow of mourning over our profession. Adding to that sorrow is a distressing list of journalists killed for unclear reasons, not related in every case to their work but which nonetheless set off alarm bells of concern and fear among us." He believed that he was expressing the sense of the country's journalistic profession, he concluded, by taking the occasion to once again request that those pending investigations be resolved and the public informed of their results.[31]

The two audiences in the hall received Aguilar Camín's words in accordance with their respective outlooks: resounding applause from the rear and mixed surprise, consternation, and disapproval closer to the head table. The president himself listened attentively but revealed no particular reaction. When, following the meal and presentation of awards, it was his turn to speak, Salinas delivered a predictable address of platitudes and programmatic boilerplate with something for both areas of the hall. "Society proposes that the media modernize so as to be more socially responsive and thus better serve the country," he intoned, for the media were "coparticipants" in a grand modernization project to achieve sustained national development that was "healthy," "free," and "just," a development that preserved Mexico's historic "essence, traditions, and lifestyles." He called on the media "to exercise to the fullest" their freedom of expression, to speak out on behalf of society's legitimate demands, and "to continue promoting debate and reflection." He exhorted them "to join in the great challenge of modernizing Mexico" by defending the nation's sovereignty and promoting the expansion of Mexican democracy.

Two-thirds into his address, Salinas referred to the Buendía case. "Freedom of expression," he remarked, "begins with the physical and personal security of those who exercise this right; demands for respect of the integrity and security of journalists are just and will be met. We will assure maximum security to those who express their thoughts—or the thoughts of others—and will punish with the full force of the law those who assault them." The Salinas administration, he stated, would not close any pending investigation of crimes against the press, "particularly the case of the assassination of the distinguished journalist Manuel Buendía." That very week, Salinas announced, the district attorney general and the special prosecutor for the Buendía case would present a public summary of their investigation.[32]

Ex-Chief of Mexico Police Group Accused as Mastermind of '84 Killing of Journalist

Los Angeles Times—Wednesday, 13 June 1989

Marjorie Miller, Times Staff Writer

Mexico City—Five years after Mexico's most influential newspaper columnist, Manuel Buendia, was shot in the back and killed in a downtown parking lot here, the government has accused a former police chief in the administration of President Miguel de la Madrid of masterminding the killing.

The Mexico City attorney general's office announced late Sunday that Jose Antonio Zorrilla, who headed the now defunct Federal Security Directorate, was "presumed responsible" for the May 30, 1984, murder.

Police officers went to Zorrilla's house in the Pedregal neighborhood of southern Mexico City on Sunday afternoon to arrest him, but the former chief was not there.

. . .

SEARCH CONTINUES

Officials said they have asked Interpol, the international police network, to help locate Zorrilla. Octavio Campos, spokesman for the Mexico City attorney general's office, said police were still searching for Zorrilla late Monday.

Journalists and political observers criticized the police failure to capture Zorrilla, noting that when the government decided to arrest oil union chief Joaquín Hernández Galicia earlier this year, it did so swiftly in a secret operation with the army. They said they doubted the government's sincerity in prosecuting the Buendia case.

"The government wanted to have its cake and eat it too," said Adolfo Aguilar Zinser, a columnist in the newspaper Excelsior. "They wanted Zorrilla responsible and wanted him free."

Teresa Gil, a spokeswoman for the Union of Democratic Journalists, which launched its own investigation of the case, said: "They say that Zorrilla has been their prime suspect for the last 12 months, and yet they didn't have any surveillance on him. That's absurd. We have to presume he was tipped off that he was going to be arrested."

Buendia was known for his exposés of government corruption that appeared in Excelsior, Mexico City's largest daily newspaper, and he had many powerful enemies. He routinely wrote about the activities of the CIA in Mexico, corruption in the vast Oil Workers Union and violence committed by extreme right-wing groups. He reportedly was about to publicize government ties to drug traffickers when he was gunned down near his office in the Zona Rosa section of the capital.

JOURNALISTS ANGERED

His murder outraged journalists and intellectuals, who viewed it as an attack on freedom of expression.

According to local press reports, Zorrilla arrived on the scene within minutes of the slaying and proceeded immediately to Buendia's office, where he allegedly removed documents.

. . .

While journalists have long accused Zorrilla of involvement in the killing and a subsequent coverup, they were skeptical that the police chief would decide on his own to kill Buendia.

"The question that many Mexicans will necessarily ask now is if Zorrilla, as head of the Federal Security Directorate under Interior Secretary Manuel Bartlett in the administration of Miguel de la Madrid, acted on his own or on orders of some of his superiors," columnist Francisco Cardenas Cruz wrote in Monday's issue of the newspaper El Universal.

EDUCATION SECRETARY

Bartlett is secretary of education in the Cabinet of President Carlos Salinas de Gortari. As interior secretary he oversaw the Federal Security Directorate, or DFS, an investigative agency similar to the FBI.

Last month the Union of Democratic Journalists filed a complaint with the federal attorney general's office accusing Bartlett and other officials of negligence in pursuing the case. Union spokeswoman Gil said they have received no response from the government.

The final act of the Mexican government's Buendía performance played out with implausible choreographic license. In the early evening of Sunday, 11 June 1989, four days after President Salinas's Press Freedom Day promise to provide the public with a summary of the official investigation, District Attorney General Morales Lechuga and Special Prosecutor García Domínguez held a press conference to announce that former DFS chief José Antonio Zorrilla Pérez was being indicted as the mastermind behind the homicide of Manuel Buendía Tellezgirón and that a warrant had been issued for his arrest. Earlier that same day PJDF officers had been dispatched to Zorrilla's Jardines del Pedregal residence just west of UNAM's University City, but, the object of their operation being absent, had failed to make the arrest. Zorrilla was declared a fugitive, at which point the authorities requested the assistance of INTERPOL, Immigration Services, the Federal Judicial Police, and DISEN, as well as auxiliary airport security units to close off potential escape routes out of the country.[33]

As was no doubt anticipated, these sensational developments were front-page news in the Monday morning papers. The histrionics of Zorrilla's alleged flight from justice were blatant even at the time. *Excélsior*'s Rogelio Hernández, for example, had been in telephone contact with the ex-DFS chief and thought to meet with him for an interview but was brusquely warned off by District Attorney General Morales Lechuga. "It's best that you not see him," Morales allowed. "You never know how a cornered animal may react." Nor what his pursuers may have in store for him, he might have added.[34]

When the district attorney general's office dispatched the capital's *judiciales* to Jardines del Pedregal on Sunday the eleventh, ostensibly to arrest Zorrilla, they had to have known beforehand that he was not there. As would soon become public knowledge, Zorrilla owned thirty-one pieces of real estate in the Federal District alone, including several houses, apartments, and condominiums. In addition, he possessed condominiums in Cancún and Morelos, an apartment in Ixtapa, a house in Cuernavaca, another in the State of Mexico, and a ranch in the State of Hidalgo, as well as three houses in the United States: one in La Jolla, California; and one each in Horseshoe Bay and Houston, Texas.[35] All these addresses were known to the Salinas administration, and all would have been surveilled had Zorrilla's whereabouts not yet been determined.

Moreover, it was a simple enough matter to monitor and trace telephone conversations, as would have been done when Rogelio Hernández spoke with Zorrilla six days earlier. It is not plausible that a prominent journalist closely associated with the official inquiry into the Buendía homicide would be in communication with the prime suspect without the authorities getting a fix on the suspect's location. Zorrilla was, in fact, holed up at another of his residences located at 2570 Paseo de la Reforma, near the intersection with Constituyentes Avenue, in the upscale Lomas de Chapultepec district five miles to the northwest of Jardines del Pedregal.

Tuesday, 13 June, was José Antonio Zorrilla Pérez's saint's day (St. Anthony of Padua) and the occasion of his sacrifice as official scapegoat for the assassination of Manuel Buendía.[36] It was a command performance that would occupy news analysts and pundits for days and weeks to come. In the early afternoon, some two hundred PJDF officers secured the immediate vicinity and took up discreet positions around the Lomas residence. They were under orders from Morales Lechuga not to precipitate a blood-bath with collateral casualties among local residents. Zorrilla was known to be armed and accompanied by four armed bodyguards. When several officers made an initial attempt to enter the building, they were met with gunfire. At least two of them were wounded, one seriously. Reporting to Morales Lechuga, the commander of the *judiciales* was instructed to take no further action until the attorney general himself arrived on the scene. Morales had apparently been in phone contact with Zorrilla and convinced him to discuss the situation face-to-face.

What followed was unprecedented. Unarmed and unescorted, the chief judicial authority of Mexico's Federal District entered the premises of an emotionally agitated Zorrilla Pérez, who reportedly kept a gun trained on him and had made it known that he would not be taken by force. The two men remained ensconced together for more than an hour—several hours by some accounts—negotiating a mutually acceptable end to the standoff. Until just a few days earlier, Zorrilla had apparently believed that he was still a system untouchable and would not be prosecuted for involvement in the Buendía slaying. But as he came to realize that this was no longer the case and he had no viable options for escape, he plunged into a volatile state of belligerent depression in which he could as easily open fire on the authorities come to detain him as turn his weapon on himself.

While there is no reason to suppose that Zorrilla could or would have survived a police assault that day, it was not in the Salinas administration's interest to have him removed in a body bag, which would only have exposed it to further charges of cover-up. Instead, Morales Lechuga used all his powers of persuasion to convince Zorrilla that even while serving a lengthy prison sentence there could be benefits for him and his family. At some point during the late afternoon, Mexico City regent Manuel Camacho Solís was brought into the conversation via telephone to guarantee Zorrilla's physical integrity and that of his immediate family. Finally, as dusk fell, the heavily armed police units were ordered to withdraw, and Morales Lechuga led a compliant, uncuffed Zorrilla from his residence to the district attorney general's waiting car.[37]

Contrary to established procedure as mandated by the language of his arrest warrant, Zorrilla was not immediately turned over to the issuing magistrate but was taken first to the district attorney general's offices and held there incommunicado for twenty-five hours of interrogation, as well, presumably, as discussion of the terms of his now inevitable incarceration. He was interrogated by Morales Lechuga and Rutilio Solís Alonso, a Public Ministry official assigned to the special prosecutor's office. The morning after Zorrilla's detention, capital regent Manuel Camacho Solís paid an unexplained visit to Morales Lechuga, followed in succession through the rest of the day by federal narcotics prosecutor Javier Coello Trejo, presiding judge Roberto Hernández Martínez, Zorrilla's attorneys, several former DFS agents, and, finally, Francisco Durán Juárez, director of Mexico City's North Side Penitentiary (Reclusorio Norte), who informed Morales that preparations had been completed to accommodate their high-profile prisoner.

As some details of what had transpired behind closed doors during that twenty-five-hour period filtered out to the media, reporters were struck by the kid gloves with which the authorities had handled the ex-DFS chief. The deference shown Zorrilla was unprecedented and included meals, time to sleep, and the opportunity to bathe, as well as the luxury of responding to interrogators' questions in the comfort of the district attorney general's private conference room instead of the customary prison interrogation cell. In contrast, no deference at all was extended to members of the press, who after a long vigil outside the building were handed a minimalist boilerplate bulletin stating, "In compliance with Article 107, Section XVIII, Paragraph 3, of the Political Constitution of the United States of Mexico, the Attorney General's Office of the Federal District has today placed Señor José Antonio Zorrilla Pérez at the disposition of penal law judge 34, Licenciado Roberto Hernández Martínez. The investigation continues." A previously scheduled press conference with Morales Lechuga was canceled without explanation, and the ministry's public affairs director, Octavio Campos, imperiously informed the waiting reporters that they were free to seek a meeting with "Nacho" Morales on their own but that he, Campos, "was nobody's errand boy" and would not convey their request to the attorney general. When they tried, they found the building's entrances had been closed to the public and placed under tight police guard.

That evening, Wednesday, 14 June, Zorrilla was transferred to the Reclusorio Norte in a three-vehicle caravan escorted by a Mexico City motorcycle cop. Several reporters were injured by the caravan's aggressive exit from the Public Ministry's enclosed parking area, others by guards who brooked no challenge from angered journalists protesting the gratuitous assault. The entire episode, many concluded, was but a continuation of the past five years of cover-up and intimidation that had characterized the authorities' handling of the Manuel Buendía case. "The abuse, blows, insults, and threats hurled by Judicial Police agents at the journalists who had waited all those many hours outside the Attorney General's building," summarized *unomásuno* columnist Rigoberto López, "give some idea of the officers' abuse of authority and how, under the pretext of following orders, they themselves can turn into journalist killers."[38]

Common Law Justice Court 34 was attached to the capital's North Side Penitentiary, where indicted detainees participated in their trial proceedings from a recessed cell that opened onto the courtroom. Zorrilla's first appearance before Judge Roberto Hernández Martínez took place the morning of 15 June and was witnessed by numerous representatives of the media. By Friday the sixteenth, photographs of a clean-shaven, neatly combed Zorrilla wearing regulation khakis and looking out through prison bars commanded the public's attention from virtually every kiosk and newsstand throughout the country. Even *Time* magazine would publish a jailhouse image of Zorrilla in its 26 June issue. "Solving the [Buendía] crime," concludes the brief note accompanying the *Time* photo, "would be a breakthrough for President Carlos Salinas de Gortari, who is refurbishing his image by going after people thought to be untouchable."[39]

The remaining elements of the grand finale followed flawlessly in train. On Saturday, 17 June, front-page headlines announced that Buendía's assistant, Juan Manuel Bautista, had seen the gunman at DFS headquarters several days after the assassination. Bautista told Judge Roberto Hernández Martínez that he had not informed Zorrilla at the time "because he was afraid" but had described the sighting when he was deposed by Special Prosecutor García Domínguez. Attorney General Morales Lechuga, in turn, confirmed that "the assassin of Manuel Buendía [was] indeed alive," alluding to an earlier suspect, "El Chocorrol," who had been killed by DFS agents not long after Buendía's death and was now officially dismissed as the gunman. It was further reported that various efforts had been made over the previous two days to arrest the latest suspect but had proven unsuccessful, in part because the individual was familiar with police procedures. "We are so close," Morales Lechuga ventured, "that last Thursday we were a half hour away from apprehending him, but he managed to escape."[40]

Sunday's papers were filled with commentary on Zorrilla's detention as part of the Salinas administration's strategy to recover waning political legitimacy through a dramatic assault on prominent symbols of lawlessness and corruption. On Monday the nineteenth, *Proceso* appeared with a smiling Zorrilla in suit and tie on its cover next to the words "Zorrilla no se deja" (Zorrilla not cooperating). Inside, eleven pages were devoted to the Buendía affair. The ex-DFS director, wrote the three reporters assigned to cover the case, "had enjoyed five years of impunity, as had other public officials, police chiefs, military officers, magistrates, cops, and drug traffickers, who in the matter of drugs had directly or indirectly implicated the entire previous administration."[41] The magazine detailed the various statutory violations committed by the Ministerio Público in its handling of Zorrilla's arrest and reported that the defendant's adamant denial of guilt in all the charges against him promised to create "a real imbroglio for the authorities."[42] (Mexico City regent Camacho Solís's reported statement to the media that "Zorrilla had been in danger of losing his life" the day of his arrest could be interpreted more than one way—an opaque allusion, perhaps, to some quid pro quo in which Zorrilla's survival was contingent on his cooperation.[43]) Meanwhile, *Proceso* further informed readers that an arrest warrant had been issued for the gunman in the Buendía killing and that the suspect may have been a former DFS agent.

Playing to public expectations with a calculated heightening of dramatic tension, the authorities filtered a steady stream of new details to the media. On Tuesday, the press reported that four ex-DFS officers had been detained in connection with the Buendía slaying. The former Zorrilla subordinates were Juventino Prado Hurtado, Raúl Pérez Carmona, Sofía Marysia Naya Suárez, and Esteben Guzmán, until their arrest all active duty officers in the Mexico City police department's recently created DI. Tuesday's papers also reported that four hundred agents from five different police bodies were engaged in the search for the gunman who had fired the fatal shots. Unnamed PJDF commanders told *unomásuno* reporters that, once again, the suspect had "inexplicably escaped" just as they were about to nab him, leading them to suspect that someone on the inside was warning him. The suspect, these sources added, "was a skilled motorcyclist who had participated in various competitive events."[44]

That same day, the daily *El Nacional* headlined a front-page story, "Capture of Manuel Buendía's Killer a Matter of Hours," which it accompanied with a sensational description of the suspect. "According to reports provided this paper," read the unsigned article, "he is a young, highly experienced policeman who, together with other officers, was sent to various countries of Europe and Asia for training." With his good looks, the paper was informed, he had even played roles in television soap operas (*telenovelas*) and was a rakish figure in the Mexican cinema world. He was said to be an inveterate ladies' man, often seen in the company of movie actresses, and a cocaine addict "given to inhaling angels' dust provided by José Antonio Zorrilla Pérez." He had worked as a motorcycle stuntman and several times demonstrated highly dangerous maneuvers "on five cycles owned by Zorrilla Pérez." Because of his military training and other experience, he was considered "an extremely dangerous criminal" who could be expected to defend himself with "high-powered weapons" and, if cornered, "might choose to commit suicide." In a desperate situation, the suspect's pursuers were authorized to shoot to kill. The authorities were confident, however, that their quarry would be taken alive within hours, "so that he might explain in detail how he had executed Manuel Buendía."[45]

Around two o'clock that same afternoon, a dozen Federal Judicial Police officers under the command of Director Nicolás Suárez Valenzuela arrested Juan Rafael Moro Ávila Camacho on a street corner in the Roma district, barely ten blocks from the site on Avenida Insurgentes where Buendía had been slain five years before. This was the highlight of the next day's headlines, predictably enhanced with a sinister, droopy-eyed mug shot of the accused assassin. Moro's capture, averred an *unomásuno* editorial, was the "touchstone" that would finally allow the authorities to declare the Buendía case solved—an achievement of District Attorney General Ignacio Morales Lechuga and President Carlos Salinas de Gortari "not to be belittled," the paper editorialized.[46]

Over the remaining week and a half of June, headlines and accompanying articles supplied a steady flow of titillating details that added dramatic color to the government's resolution of the case, at the same time as they complicated analysis of the evidence. In further declarations before Judge Hernández Martínez, Zorrilla insisted that he "was not autonomous"; that he "always kept [his] superiors informed"; that he "periodically informed [his] chief, Bartlett";[47] and that there had been "two or more triggermen" in the shooting of Manuel Buendía.[48] Moro Ávila Camacho, for his part, declared that ex-DFS asset José Luis Ochoa Alonso, aka "El Chocorrol," was Buendía's assassin, then admitted "to having helped" Ochoa escape after the shooting, implausibly "unaware" that he was participating in a murder. "I didn't really know what the operation was all about," he told jailhouse reporters, "because they didn't have the decency to tell me."[49]

The press also reported that in the course of Moro's sordid police career he had received narcotics training from the U.S. DEA, as well as "antiterrorism" training in Israel, and that he had been a bodyguard for former government secretary Manuel Bartlett Díaz. It likewise came to public light that Moro had served in the infamous Mexico City Division of Investigations for the Prevention of Delinquency (DIPD) during the tenure of the capital's incomparably corrupt police chief, Arturo "El Negro" Durazo, and that when the DIPD was disbanded at the beginning of the de la Madrid administration he was integrated into the DFS on the recommendation of former chief Javier García Paniagua, who at the time of Moro's arrest for the Buendía killing was himself serving as the Federal District's chief of police.[50]

The final week of June began with a torrent of sensational headlines about the Buendía case: "Tortured by the Judicial Police, says Juventino Prado"; "Prado Sinks Zorrilla"; "Plan to Disappear Buendía Revealed by Prado"; "Chocorrol Case Files Missing";

"Naya Suárez, Ex-DFS Agent, Tortured"; "Those Implicated in Buendía Case Unlikely to be Absolved." Juventino Prado Hurtado, commander of the DFS's "Special Brigade" at the time of Buendía's slaying, testified that Zorrilla had planned the assassination and that he, Prado, had brought in Moro Ávila Camacho and Ochoa Alonso to carry it out. The disappearance of the "Chocorrol" files was immediately suspicious because it made confirmation of Prado's and Moro's accounts virtually impossible.

The further fact that Prado and his fellow ex-DFS defendants Pérez Carmona and Naya Suárez had, until their arrests, been senior Mexico City police commandants under García Paniagua and that they had been turned over to District Attorney General Morales Lechuga by García Paniagua was noteworthy in light of García Paniagua's own antecedents in the netherworld of state security. (We would eventually learn that he, too, had apparently had a hand in the Buendía killing.) A dissonant note in the closing choreography of the government's Buendía spectacle was the reported disintegration of the Federal District DI as a consequence of the Prado Hurtado, Pérez Carmona, and Naya Suárez indictments. Some 350 DI officers were said to have deserted. Sixty agents under the direct command of Prado and Pérez Carmona had abandoned ship immediately on learning of their superiors' detention. The rest of the DI's command structure apparently decamped with them, leaving the institution leaderless. The few remaining intelligence personnel had been ordered to remain silent about the directorate's internal crisis. Violation of that order, one of them assured our *unomásuno* colleague Fernando Ramírez de Aguilar, "would cost them their job or even their life."[51]

Proceso interrupted the official performance with an unwelcome flourish of discordant counterpoint in its issue of 26 June 1989. With Manuel Buendía on its cover demanding eye contact, the combative newsweekly invited readers to turn to that week's feature: "The Buendía thriller: Negligence, cover-ups, false trails, witnesses for all occasions, loose ends, intrigue." Inside, thirteen pages dissected government mismanagement of the case from beginning to end. Despite the impression left by Morales Lechuga and García Domínguez that it had finally been resolved, the authorities' latest actions had given rise to "innumerable doubts, irregularities, negligence, cover-ups, false witnesses, concealment of information, conspiracies, false trails, loose ends, intrigues, and deception." The record, wrote Ignacio Ramírez, "established the previous government's lack of political will to resolve the [Buendía] affair and its protection of José Antonio Zorrilla Pérez, as well as an endless list of public servants, police, and security agents who obstructed the investigation." And now the present administration was "bending the law and supplying carefully proportioned bits of information as though the case were a novel."[52]

The novelesque character and theatricality of the government's handling of the Buendía case was widely noted. "All the recent developments in the Buendía case," opined a Federal District assemblyman, "are part of a public relations program within the country as well as abroad." The whole affair had unfolded "as in a movie thriller one has watched many times," wrote one columnist. It was all "a game of mirrors." It was like a theatrical performance, Ángel Buendía would conclude, a performance "masterfully executed by then District Attorney General Ignacio Morales Lechuga."[53]

The curtain dropped on the last day of June 1989, a Friday, when Special Prosecutor Miguel Ángel García Domínguez made public his final report and declared his investigation concluded. The mastermind ("intellectual author") behind the assassination of Manuel Buendía Tellezgirón was former DFS chief José Antonio Zorrilla Pérez. Zorrilla's coconspirators as intellectual authors were former DFS officers Juventino Prado Hurtado, Raúl Pérez Carmona, and Sofía Naya Suárez. The gunman who fired the fatal shots was former DFS operative Juan Rafael Moro Ávila Camacho. García Domínguez read his thirty-four-page report aloud in a final press conference, thanked presidents Miguel de la Madrid and Carlos Salinas de Gortari and former government secretary Manuel Bartlett Díaz for their support, apologized for not having concluded his investigation by the end of the previous administration, and then slipped away for a weekend out of public view. Officially, the Buendía case was now closed.[54]

8

After the Curtain

The way the Buendía case has been handled offends one's intelligence. It is impossible to accept what they now offer as the resolution of this historic crime, for in reality they have resolved nothing. By charging Zorrilla and four of his ex-DFS subordinates with the killing, the special prosecutor guarantees that from this point forward the case will be contained within the narrow limits of judicial procedure, thus removing any further possibility of raising inconvenient questions. With an elegant sleight of hand, the key issues and mysteries have been swept from the table, reducing the entire case to the guilt or innocence of the five defendants.

—R. H. Bartley, "El caso Buendía" (November–December 1993)

MORE THAN TWO DECADES ELAPSED between the Mexican government's official conclusion of the Buendía case and the writing of these remaining chapters. While we had chronicled the case from its initial stages, and even been participants in its fitful unfolding, the nature and scope of our inquiry required much additional effort. Above all, we required time to develop sources previously unavailable to us or whose personal knowledge gained added relevance in light of how the Buendía affair had been officially resolved.

On the ground, we continued to consult with our Mexican contacts and to interview key sources. We also pursued a number of time-consuming leads that led us to dead ends. Increasingly, we focused our attention on the trials of the alleged coconspirators in the 1985 abduction and torture slaying of DEA special agent Enrique Camarena Salazar, which were held in U.S. District Court in Los Angeles, California, during 1990–1992. The defendant of primary interest to us in those trials was Rubén Zuno Arce, a prominent Mexican businessman and brother-in-law of former president Luís Echeverría Álvarez. Zuno Arce's prosecution by the U.S. Department of Justice established a connection between the Buendía and Camarena cases and opened up a whole new arena of investigation for us. Following the trials, we contacted and subsequently developed a collaborative relationship with Zuno's lead defense attorney, Edward M. Medvene, who at the time was with the Los Angeles law firm Mitchell, Silberberg, and Knupp. Over the next several years, we would consult with Medvene and other members of Zuno's defense team as they appealed their client's conviction all the way to the U.S. Supreme Court.

In addition to our many conversations with him and his associates, Medvene opened his Zuno case files to us, which provided additional documentary evidence of

U.S. government interest in the Buendía case. It also put us on the trail of two witnesses who would prove central to our own inquiry: Héctor G. Berréllez, the DEA group supervisor in charge of Operation Leyenda, the official Camarena investigation; and Lawrence Victor Harrison, a former CIA agent who had served in Mexico and been brought back to the United States as a government witness for the Zuno Arce prosecution. Together with a third intelligence source we had developed independently, veteran DEA undercover agent Michael Levine, these three informants would lead us to tie both the Buendía and Camarena slayings to American covert operations in Mexico and Central America.

La muerte de Buendía, una investigación policiaca inconclusa

El Financiero—Lunes, 10 July 1989

Carlos Ramírez

Notwithstanding the special prosecutor's final report and the letter of gratitude from the Buendía case oversight commission—friends, brother, and Foundation bearing his name—for the "success achieved" in the investigation, Manuel Buendía's death has still not been solved. . . .

One of the most complicated and difficult cases of police investigation, having consumed five years of rationalizations, complicity, false leads, and much deception, it has now been solved in less than two weeks. The authorities' intent was to limit indictments to a group of ex-cops involved in drug trafficking who could conveniently be blamed for Buendía's death. Special prosecutor Miguel Ángel García Domínguez's final indictment appears to be a well-honed product of juridical inefficacy but elevated political efficiency: avoiding the involvement of Manuel Bartlett Díaz and ex-president Miguel de la Madrid. . . .

One need not be a cop, private investigator or special prosecutor to understand the hoax of García Domínguez's final report. It is, we should say, a document that Manuel Buendía, with all his cunning, distrust, and analytical ability, would have torn to shreds, since it attempts to fill a water barrel with a sieve.

It was clear to all of us who had followed the case closely that it had not in fact been solved, only concluded in a formalistic manner that let the government pretend to have met its legal obligations, to pretend that justice had been served and the matter was now closed. While former DFS chief José Antonio Zorrilla Pérez was ultimately convicted of masterminding the Buendía assassination and Juan Rafael Moro Ávila Camacho was convicted as Buendía's executioner, their trials, amply reported by the local press, only raised further doubts about the integrity of the government's case. Both Zorrilla and Moro quickly muddied the waters with conflicting and inconsistent, as well as suggestive, statements about their own actions and the actions of others around the Buendía assassination.

"I was not autonomous," Zorrilla stated to the court one week after his arrest. "I regularly reported to my chief, Manuel Bartlett, on how the investigations of Manuel Buendía's murder were progressing. How is it possible," he asked, "that now, five years on, the district attorney general's office proposes to blame me for its mistakes and to charge me with obstructing the investigations?"

Zorrilla affirmed that he had also kept Assistant District Attorney General René Paz Horta and PJDF chief José Trinidad Gutiérrez Sánchez apprised of the DFS inquiry into Buendía's homicide. "I was a government official," he reiterated, "and as long as I was involved in the [Buendía] investigations I kept my superiors informed, as I did Attorney General Adato and the assistant attorney general."[1]

Zorrilla also stated that Manuel Buendía had been felled by "two or more gunmen." Moro, for his part, insisted that Buendía's assassin was a DFS *madrina* by the name of José Luis Ochoa Alonso, alias "El Chocorrol" (Chocolate Roll), in reference to his dark complexion. (In Mexico *madrinas* are street thug initiates who, after a probationary period spent carrying out extralegal assignments for the police, are themselves admitted into an agency as regular officers. Ochoa had an established history as a DFS operative and was on the verge of becoming an active duty agent at the time of Buendía's murder.) Six weeks after the assassination, Ochoa was himself shot to death by DFS agents, ostensibly in reprisal for attempting to shake down a wealthy business associate of former DFS chief Miguel Nazar Haro.[2]

Moro gave inconsistent accounts of his presence at the crime scene but stuck to the improbable assertion that he had been "an unwitting participant" in the homicide. In an unusual prearraignment press conference called on 20 June 1989 by Deputy District Prosecutor Abraham Polo Uscanga, Moro told reporters that as the officer in charge of a DFS motorcycle unit he had been ordered around 6:00 p.m. on the day of the crime to take two subordinates and await further instructions at the corner of Hamburgo and Insurgentes, a half block from Buendía's office.[3] Once there, he stated, he had been ordered to proceed on his motorcycle to the corner of Havre and Liverpool and, "no matter what happened, to wait there for a person." Minutes later he heard

Former Federal Security Directorate head (1982–1985) and convicted Buendía assassination mastermind José Antonio Zorrilla Pérez. (CISEN, Mexico City)

gunshots, he said, and "within seconds" an individual he recognized as "El Chocorrol" jumped on his bike and, "in a clearly agitated state," yelled, "Ya está. ¡Vámonos!" (That's it. Let's go!). Several blocks farther on, according to this account, "El Chocorrol" had Moro let him off and continued running. Moro added that two other individuals had climbed onto his subordinates' bikes and escaped in the same way. While he was unable to see who they were, he subsequently concluded that they were DFS officers assigned to cover the assassin's escape.[4]

At his arraignment the next day, Moro altered his account. Actually, he stated, he had not heard the shots because Buendía was already down when he and the other two officers arrived at Hamburgo and Insurgentes. At that point, he said, they were ordered "to comb" the area for a subject wearing "a baseball hat, jeans, and tennis shoes." As he was restarting his motorcycle, Moro now claimed, a man in blue jeans and tennis shoes approached him out of a cluster of people at the adjacent bus stop and said, "I'm going with you, *comandante*." Recognizing the fellow as "El Chocorrol," having seen him on various occasions at DFS headquarters, Moro agreed to let him ride along. "But I never imagined that he was the assassin," he protested. Four streets farther on, "El Chocorrol" supposedly asked him to stop briefly. "Thinking he had seen something suspicious, or had seen the criminal," Moro told the court, "I let him off, then circled the block. When I didn't see him, I went around again, and again, and once again. Not finding him, I decided to go back to the scene of the crime."[5]

Moro further stated to the court that on the night of the assassination he had seen papers from Buendía's office on Zorrilla's desk at DFS headquarters. Zorrilla had summoned him for a debriefing, he said, after which he had placed Moro on indefinite leave and ordered him "to keep his mouth shut." It was during that debriefing, he claimed, that he had observed Buendía's papers on the desk, together with some cardboard cartons from the columnist's office "that also contained important documentation." Moro, reported the lead sentence of a front-page article in *Excélsior*, had even discerned that the papers from Buendía's office "referred to the [DFS] director's relationship with the drug traffickers."[6] This last assertion was implausible on its face and clearly suggests coached testimony.

Arraignment proceedings against Manuel Buendía's accused killers continued through the weekend. On Sunday, 25 June, former DFS Special Brigade commander Juventino Prado Hurtado was charged, along with fellow ex-DFS officer Raúl Pérez Carmona, alias "El Diablo." Both Prado Hurtado and Pérez Carmona told presiding judge Roberto Hernández Martínez that they had been physically abused while in custody and that their latest statements of record regarding the Buendía homicide had been coerced. They exhibited multiple contusions on their abdomens and backs, and defense counsel asked the judge to order medical examinations by a court-appointed physician to determine the cause and extent of their injuries. Pérez Carmona, in particular, seemed debilitated and requested the judge's permission to remain seated during the proceedings because of his weakened condition and severe back pain.[7]

Of particular interest to us was Raúl Pérez Carmona's account of his, Prado's, and their ex-DFS associate (not in court that day) Sofía Naya Suárez's shared custody between federal and district authorities. All three subjects, at the time senior officers in the Mexico City police department's controversial DI, had been made available to District Attorney General Ignacio Morales Lechuga by the Federal District's police chief, Javier García Paniagua. In effect, they had turned themselves in "voluntarily" to the Ministerio Público for additional questioning, each having previously given testimony to Special Prosecutor Miguel Ángel García Domínguez. According to Pérez Carmona, the district authorities turned them over to the federal attorney general's office, where they were immediately handcuffed and blindfolded.

"They threw us on the floor of a room and began kicking us," Pérez stated. "I could hear my companions moaning but didn't know who was kicking us, because we were blindfolded." He said he was kicked unconscious and then they were transported to another location where the beatings continued for several more days, after which they were returned to the custody of the district authorities. Again they were subjected to physical abuse. At one point, Pérez testified, he could hear the moans of Juventino Prado. He himself, he said, had been blindfolded and tied to a chair, then "had a hot object applied to my neck, which produced the sensation of dislocating my arms." After giving this account of their evident mistreatment by federal and district authorities, Pérez Carmona refused to answer any further questions, claiming that he was too weak to continue. "I feel very weak," he insisted. "I can barely stand the pain in my back from the blows."[8]

Prado Hurtado, for his part, denied the Public Ministry's charge of coconspiracy in the Buendía homicide and refused to ratify before Judge Hernández the statement prosecutors represented as his. It had been extracted from him "during twelve days of severe beatings by the Federal Judicial Police," he asserted, and was not his true version of events. That version, Prado insisted, was contained in earlier depositions he had given to Special Prosecutor García Domínguez in 1987 and 1988, which he now reaffirmed. District prosecutors dismissed this assertion, arguing that Prado had lied to the special prosecutor, "both in 1987 and in 1988," to cover up "for himself, for Zorrilla, and for others in the former DFS."[9]

We note here that the special prosecutor's office for the Buendía case did not exist in 1987 and only began to function on the first day of March 1988. If Prado indeed gave a deposition in 1987, it would have to have been under District Attorney General Sales Gasque's authority with possible participation of then Deputy Prosecutor García Domínguez and/or Deputy Prosecutor Alejandro Sosa Ortiz. In light of how the Buendía case evolved subsequently, that strikes us as improbable. While it is possible, we think this was more likely a lapse of institutional memory in the haste of manufacturing a plausible case for public consumption.

The statement officially attributed to Juventino Prado and presented to Judge Hernández Martínez as having been freely given by Prado alleged Zorrilla and Moro's complicity in the Buendía assassination. It also incriminated Raúl Pérez, Sofía Naya, and himself as coconspirators. By this account, in midafternoon on the day of the assassination Prado Hurtado was instructed by the DFS chief to place the directorate's Special Brigade on alert, then to meet with the director at his headquarters office, where Zorrilla informed him that it had become necessary to eliminate Buendía and he needed someone who was absolutely reliable to carry out that task. Prado proposed

Moro Ávila Camacho, who was a member of the directorate's Special Brigade and, as ordered, was at that moment standing by awaiting further orders.

Prado brought Moro to Zorrilla's office and purportedly witnessed the subsequent exchange between the two men. As recorded in the Ministerio Público's version of Prado's statement, Zorrilla explained to Moro that the matter at hand was "a delicate and dangerous one that required much discretion." What he needed Moro to do, he said, was "whack" the newspaperman Manuel Buendía, "Se trata de darle en la madre al periodista Manuel Buendía," as Zorrilla allegedly expressed it. He wanted Moro to take an accomplice who also "knew how to shoot" and in whom he had complete confidence and go to 58 South Insurgentes Avenue. They were to wait there for Buendía to exit the building sometime around seven o'clock that evening, then kill him and make their escape on Moro's motorcycle. Moro, according to Prado's alleged statement, accepted the assignment and informed Zorrilla that his accomplice would be "El Chocorrol." Later, after Buendía had been shot, Prado accompanied Zorrilla and assistant DFS director Alberto Estrella to the crime scene, where he imposed DFS control over Buendía's office and oversaw the directorate's gathering of evidence.[10]

Ex-DFS *comandante* Sofía Marysia Naya Suárez, in turn, was arraigned on Monday, 26 June 1989. She essentially reiterated the testimony given the day before by Prado Hurtado and Pérez Carmona, adding that, "inexplicably," within three weeks of Buendía's slaying the DFS had ceased all efforts to investigate the case. (Prado testified that his instructions as lead DFS investigator of the Buendía assassination were to simulate a serious investigation but that his actual assignment was to purge compromising evidence.) Naya Suárez also recounted how the three of them had been turned over to the Mexican attorney general's office and physically abused for more than a week by members of the Federal Judicial Police (PJF), who attempted to exact confessions from them. In addition to the beatings and many other abuses, she testified, late at night they would strip her, tie her to a board and immerse her in a tank of cold water. Federal Attorney General Enrique Álvarez del Castillo, for his part, issued a statement denying that Naya Suárez, Prado Hurtado, and Pérez Carmona had been tortured by the PJF. It was, he said, "nothing more than rumor."

When she, Prado, and Pérez Carmona were returned to the district attorney general's office, Naya Suárez stated, they continued to be tortured in an effort to secure confessions of guilt in the Buendía slaying. "After I don't know how many days, since I'd lost all sense of time, they took us to sign some papers they said were our statements. Obviously they'd been falsified, so we did not want to sign them. Later a man, apparently an agent from the Ministerio Público, arrived accompanied by a typist and began to interrogate us. Based on that we were sent here last Saturday," she told the court, "accused, I've just learned, of taking part in the Buendía assassination, when in reality I had nothing to do with it." Moreover, she added, the day Buendía was killed she and a group of DFS officers led by Raúl Pérez Carmona had been pursuing suspected kidnappers when Pérez stumbled in a drainage ditch and injured his knee. "We took Comandante Pérez Carmona to the office of Dr. Rafael [*sic*] Portilla, who ordered several days' rest," Naya recounted, "so it is impossible that he or I, or anyone in our group, could have been present at the time Manuel Buendía was slain."[11]

The following day Dr. Juan Antonio Portilla Valencia testified on behalf of Pérez Carmona, offering an account that differed in its particulars from Naya Suárez's version of events but essentially corroborated her testimony to the effect that Raúl Pérez Carmona could not have taken part in the Buendía assassination because he had been injured. Dr. Portilla stated that on 30 May 1984, around five o'clock in the afternoon, he had received a phone call from Pérez Carmona's wife asking him to come to their residence to attend to her husband's injured knee. He had arrived an hour later to find Pérez Carmona lying on his bed with a painfully inflamed right knee due to a ruptured synovial capsule and escaped fluid. He gave Pérez a cortisone injection, which caused the injured DFS agent to fall sleep. It was not likely, Dr. Portilla testified, that Pérez had gone anywhere that night.[12]

REPORT OF DEPUTY ATTORNEY GENERAL DR. MIGUEL ÁNGEL GARCÍA DOMÍNGUEZ, SPECIAL PROSECUTOR FOR THE CLARIFICATION OF THE HOMICIDE OF MANUEL BUENDÍA TELLEZGIRÓN

Procuraduría General de Justicia del Distrito Federal—30 June 1989 [excerpts]

Manuel Buendía Tellezgirón was assassinated in this city on 30 May 1984.

As is well known, he was a prominent journalist who also collaborated with the federal government in various areas of social communication and who steadfastly denounced corruption, misdeeds, and irregularities of every kind in the life of our country. His criticism basically sought to move influential figures whose activities affected the public to rectify and correct their detrimental behavior.

. . .

The motive for taking the life of Manuel Buendía . . . was [his] knowledge of José Antonio Zorrilla Pérez's ties to the drug traffic.

Coconspirators in Manuel Buendía's homicide were Juventino Prado Hurtado, Raúl Pérez Carmona, and Sofía Naya Suárez.

Juan Rafael Moro Ávila was the gunman who shot Manuel Buendía.

. . .

The [Buendía] case file includes the following evidentiary items:

1. Statements made on 29 June 1989 by Juan Manuel Bautista Ortiz and Rosa Elvia Chávez, in which before the special prosecutor they identify Juan Rafael Moro Ávila as the person who shot Manuel Buendía on 30 May 1984.
2. Statement by Juan Rafael Moro Ávila, in which he affirms that he was ordered to take part in "Operation News" for the purpose of "silencing a person," and in which he acknowledges having been present at the site of the events.
3. Statement by Jacaranda Alfaro on 15 June 1989 that mentions textually: that Juan Rafael Moro Ávila said to her, "They're going to get me because they're after Zorrilla. They're going to get me for killing Manuel Buendía." Jacaranda Alfaro maintained that Juan Rafael Moro Ávila commented to her that Licenciado Zorrilla had called him into his office specifically to talk about the Buendía matter. On that occasion, Moro told Zorrilla that if he ever turned him in, then he would expose Zorrilla as the mastermind [behind Buendía's assassination].
4. Statement by Juventino Prado Hurtado on 24 June 1989 in which he textually establishes that Zorrilla called him on the day of the events and said to him, "Look, I need a person I can trust. Do you have anybody?" He answers "yes," and Zorrilla

goes on to tell him that they're going to assassinate the journalist Manuel Buendía. He asks Prado about the individual he recommends, and Prado replies that the man is Juan Rafael Moro Ávila. Afterward he introduces Moro to Zorrilla, who tells Moro what is required. Moro accepts the assignment.

5. Juan Rafael Moro Ávila and Juventino Prado Hurtado acknowledge their participation in the operation, along with Raúl Pérez Carmona and Sofía Naya Suárez.

This is an astonishing document. Intended to be a persuasive rendering of evidence that credibly resolved Manuel Buendía's murder and removed it once and for all from the public agenda, the special prosecutor's final report proved, in fact, to be a slipshod, poorly written exposition unworthy of a first-year law student let alone a distinguished doctor of jurisprudence and future Supreme Court justice. The original document is a thirty-six-page typescript,[13] just under half of which narrates the history of García Domínguez's tenure as special prosecutor for the Buendía case. Six pages, under the rubric of "Results" (El Resultado), lay out the indictments of Zorrilla, Moro Ávila Camacho, Prado Hurtado, Pérez Carmona, and Naya Suárez, as well as former DFS deputy director Alberto Estrella for the related homicide of Gobernación investigator José Luis Esqueda Gutiérrez, committed nine months after Buendía's death. Barely three pages are devoted to the Buendía homicide indictments, and the evidence presented in support of those indictments is unpersuasive.[14]

Most remarkable, in this regard, is the timing of key witness statements, which were said to have been obtained in the two weeks preceding completion of the special prosecutor's final report. The "decisive" elements of proof offered in support of the murder indictments against Zorrilla, Moro, Prado, Pérez Carmona, and Naya Suárez are Jacaranda Alfaro's 15 June statement to the effect that Moro had told her "they were going to get him for killing Buendía" (which following the report's release she denied having made); Prado Hurtado's 24 June statement that, on the day of the murder, Zorrilla had asked him to find an assassin and Moro was that individual; statements on 29 June by eyewitnesses Juan Manuel Bautista and Rosa Elvia Chávez Almanza identifying Moro as the gunman; and, finally, statements allegedly made by Moro and Prado acknowledging their participation in the assassination plot together with Pérez Carmona and Naya Suárez. We say "allegedly" because Moro and Prado made contradictory statements both in court and to the media.

For purposes of the case against these defendants, Prado Hurtado's statement that "on the day of the events" Zorrilla had tasked him with procuring an assassin, that he had proposed Moro Ávila Camacho for the job, and that Moro had agreed to carry it out was pivotal. It also is implausible and, in our estimation, the place where the government's case falls apart. The political stakes were simply too high for Manuel Buendía to have been assassinated in such an allegedly haphazard, spur-of-the-moment manner. Moreover, the timing, circumstances, and particulars of the homicide all point to careful prior planning, a fact we would eventually have confirmed by ex-CIA operative Lawrence Victor Harrison, who at the time of Buendía's slaying was embedded in the DFS and knew of the planned assassination weeks in advance.[15]

A particularly questionable piece of evidence said to be in the special prosecutor's Buendía case files and cited by García Domínguez as proof of Buendía's intention to expose Zorrilla's links to narcotics traffickers, and thus proof of the motive adduced by the government for the journalist's homicide, was two telephone conversations of unspecified date said to have been recorded by Buendía in which he supposedly discussed with Zorrilla what he had learned about the DFS chief's involvement with the traffickers. After the assassination, according to the special prosecutor, Zorrilla retrieved the two audiocassettes on which the conversations ostensibly had been recorded from Buendía's Insurgentes Avenue office. No member of the press ever saw those cassettes, however. No independent audio specialist was allowed to examine them, nor was any purported transcript of their alleged contents ever made available for public scrutiny. Their existence, in sum, has never been established.

As *El Financiero* columnist Carlos Ramírez observed at the time, García Domínguez's version of the tape-recorded telephone conversations made Buendía "look like a naïf or a blackmailer, and he was neither." Are we really to believe, Ramírez asked, that Manuel Buendía "was going to reveal his cards *on the telephone*, when he knew that his phone had been tapped by at least three different agencies?" Nor is it reasonable to suppose that the DFS chief would have broached such sensitive matters over an open phone line.

In light of these glaring evidentiary weaknesses, it is noteworthy that a full sixteen of the twenty pages of the special prosecutor's final report devoted to charges and evidence have nothing whatsoever to do with the slaying of Manuel Buendía. Four of those pages concern the Esqueda Gutiérrez homicide. The remaining dozen pages, comprising almost a third of the entire report and three-quarters of its "Results" section, focus on collateral charges against Zorrilla essentially unrelated to the Buendía case: illicit possession of firearms; illicit enrichment; and illicit association with drug traffickers, this last being cited as substantiation of the adduced motive for Buendía's murder. Among the Mexican journalists who followed the Buendía case, most of whom remarked on the contradictions and weaknesses of the special prosecutor's report, Carlos Ramírez was the only one to actually deconstruct the report and correctly assess its broader implications. The report's central contradiction, Ramírez notes, is that on the one hand García Domínguez claimed to have resolved the case "in the first ten days of June" (having indicated to the media as recently as 30 May that he still "had no leads" on Buendía's real killers), while the indictments that would assure a long prison sentence for Zorrilla, the necessary high-profile defendant who could credibly take the fall for higher-ups, was based on evidence that had been in the authorities' hands since 1985.

Any moderately competent criminal lawyer could make shreds of García Domínguez's "overwhelming" evidence against the accused killers of Manuel Buendía, Ramírez observed. Indeed, judicial authorities blatantly ignored the empirical fact that at least three of the defendants had been seriously beaten while in custody and that statements entered into the evidentiary record had in all likelihood been made under duress, as the defendants themselves claimed. But the official handling of the Buendía case, Ramírez insisted, had always been about covering for senior Mexican officials. And when it finally became necessary to appease the public with a credible culprit, it was reluctantly decided to sacrifice the former DFS chief. Hence the judicial tour de force of corollary indictments to ensure Zorrilla's incarceration, which in a public relations sleight of hand could then be passed off as punishment for masterminding the Buendía homicide.[16]

A particularly murky aspect of the official conclusion to the Buendía case was the alleged gunman. Only eight days before García Domínguez presented his final report indicting Moro Ávila Camacho as the lone killer, the district attorney general's office had issued a press release naming "El Chocorrol" as Buendía's assailant. "José Luis Ochoa Alonso, alias 'El Chocorrol' or 'El Negro,' material author of the homicide of Manuel Buendía," it read, "was murdered at 10 p.m. on 11 July 1984." Ochoa was described as being thirty-four years old at the time of his death, an electrician, separated from his wife (with whom he had fathered five children), and living with another woman by the name of Patricia Patlán. According to family members, Ochoa's wife, and Patricia Patlán, "El Chocorrol" was "an aggressive, violent and irritable person who generally wore jeans, a shirt, hat, tennis shoes, and a leather jacket," clothing that seemed to coincide with eyewitness descriptions of the gunman.[17]

Moro, in turn, did not exhibit all of the physical features initially described by eyewitnesses and subsequently rendered by police artists in sketches and wax mannequins. Nor did his features correspond precisely to those portrayed in an eight-minute filmed reenactment of the assassination produced by the special prosecutor's staff and broadcast on Mexican television during the month of June 1988. The two key eyewitnesses, Buendía's assistant Juan Manuel Bautista and a pedestrian, Rosa Elvia Chávez Almanza, coincided in describing the gunman as being of moderate height (1.70 meters), slim with a dark complexion typical of the Gulf Coast, straight hair cut short "military style" (first reported as chestnut, later changed to black), full eyebrows, straight nose, thick mustache, thin lips, and a prominent chin. While Moro was within the height range and possessed the general facial features reported by eyewitnesses, he had a more muscular build and a much lighter complexion than the Gulf Coast type they described. Five years after the event, he wore his hair long, but no determination appears to have been made as to how he wore it in the spring of 1984. "El Chocorrol," on the other hand, was darker skinned and in photos from those years wears his hair short. His lips were full, however, and he lacked a mustache. Neither man matched witness descriptions perfectly, yet the day before the special prosecutor presented his final report, Bautista and Chávez Almanza both identified Moro Ávila Camacho as Manuel Buendía's assassin. Sufficient time had elapsed to impair their recollection of such physical details, and they likely were pressured as well to confirm the authorities' identification of Moro as the killer.[18]

In yet a further twist of the absurd, less than a week before García Domínguez officially charged Juan Rafael Moro Ávila Camacho as the sole gunman, it was reported that the district attorney general's office had lost its case file for the 11 July 1985 slaying of José Luis Ochoa Alonso, "El Chocorrol," which could not be located in the special prosecutor's sixty linear feet of Buendía case files and was said to have also disappeared from the archives of the Federal District's Forensic Medicine Service.[19] The key document in the missing file was a detailed progress report on the PJDF investigation of the Manuel Buendía homicide being conducted by Commandant Luis Aranda Zorrivas and submitted by him on 31 July 1985 to then chief José Trinidad Gutiérrez Sánchez. A copy of that report was published in its entirety by the newsweekly *Proceso* the day after it was reported missing by the district attorney general's office.

Aranda Zorrivas and his team of investigating officers had been comparing police sketches of the Buendía assassin with agents and ex-agents of various law enforcement agencies, including the DFS, when they came across a DIPD file photo of "El Chocorrol" and were struck by the way a number of Ochoa's features coincided with eyewitness descriptions of Buendía's assailant. They immediately attempted to locate Ochoa, only to learn from his widow that he had been shot to death by DFS agents on 11 July 1984. Aranda Zorrivas recounts at great length each and every interview he and his fellow officers conducted with relatives, friends, and associates about Ochoa's activities up to the moment he was killed. He notes that all interviewees remarked on Ochoa's preference for "baseball caps, denim or corduroy 'cowboy' pants, and both cloth and leather sports jackets in different colors and styles." That was his habitual way of dressing, Aranda Zorrivas emphasized, "as no one ever saw him dress any other way." This was significant, Aranda implied, because that is how eyewitnesses to the Buendía homicide described the killer.[20]

Proceso's reporters Miguel Cabildo and Raúl Monge were able to produce the Aranda Zorrivas report that District Attorney General Ignacio Morales Lechuga claimed had vanished from the Public Ministry's files because one of their colleagues at the Mexico City daily *Ovaciones*, police reporter Mario Munguía, had obtained a copy three years earlier, kept it for possible future use when his editors would not allow him to draw on it to implicate Zorrilla Pérez or the DFS, and now made it available to his colleagues at *Proceso* to utilize in their ongoing exposé of the government's mishandling of the Buendía case. "The problem," Munguía said, "was that Zorrilla and his people were everywhere. And 'El Güero' ['Whitey,' as the blond, fair-complexioned Zorrilla was popularly known] was clever. He would win people over, including newspaper editors. He'd talk with them frequently, invite them to go shooting with him. If they had a problem, he'd take care of it. He would place the DFS helicopter and airplane at their disposal. So, no one wanted Zorrilla touched."

Munguía's editors at *Ovaciones* subsequently assigned the Buendía story to his colleague, Sergio von Nowaffen, who conducted a seven-month investigation of his own, then published a three-part series in which he concluded that "El Chocorrol" was the gunman in the Buendía homicide and had been murdered by DFS agents as part of a cover-up to conceal official complicity. "The mystery surrounding [Ochoa's] death, the suppression of information, and the disappearance of all evidence about him," von Nowaffen told the *Proceso* reporters, "led me to conclude that 'El Chocorrol' was the murderer." As with Munguía, *Ovaciones* editors excised mention of Zorrilla from the von Nowaffen series.

Munguía shared information he had developed about the Buendía case with von Nowaffen but not the Aranda Zorrivas report, which now in very different circumstances he was allowing other colleagues to bring to light in another venue where it would have the greatest impact. All the key government people knew about the report, he assured *Proceso*. "Doña Victoria [Adato] knew about it. Trinidad [Gutiérrez Sán-chez] knew about it. They all must have known about it, but they kept it under wraps. They smoothed it over and gave us four years of theater. President De la Madrid him-self knew about it. What does that tell us? That they were all involved in a conspiracy to keep this matter quiet. Just imagine," Munguía suggested, "the housecleaning they could have given the system! It would have been a gigantic housecleaning if, a year and a half after Buendía's death, they had only released this report."

Munguía did not know what to make of the government's supposed resolution of the Buendía case and had even come to wonder whether "El Chocorrol" had had any direct involvement at all in the Buendía assassination. The problem, he lamented, "is that here they fabricate everything. . . . And they don't let you speak with the people they've arrested, who are told what to say in court. Just look at Moro's statements. He learned his lines well." Von Nowaffen generally shared Munguía's view of the case, emphasizing to the *Proceso* reporters that it was still far from resolved. "The fat chickens remain at large," he expressed, namely, "de la Madrid, Bartlett, and [Secretary of Defense Juan] Arévalo Gardoqui."[21]

From behind bars, Zorrilla and Moro continued to make conflicting statements, which kept the government's version of events shrouded in doubt. "It was not Moro who killed Buendía, I can assure you of that," Zorrilla told the court on 2 July 1989. "It wasn't 'El Chocorrol' either, since neither one of them exhibit the appearance of the individual who shot the journalist."[22] Four months later Moro departed completely from his earlier statements to the court, suddenly claiming that the "real" assassins of Manuel Buendía were three members of the DFS's Special Brigade: Luis Sayas, Pedro Alba Rincón, and Alba Rincón's brother, Samuel, none of whose names had come up previously in connection with the Buendía homicide. By this account, Samuel Alba was the DFS officer in charge of the operation, while the other two men carried it out, arriving at the South Insurgentes Avenue location on motorcycles just over an hour before the shooting. Luis Sayas was the assassin, Moro now claimed, and subsequently was himself killed as part of a plan to cover up DFS complicity in the crime. Nothing further came of this story, and Moro was sentenced to prison as the material assassin of Manuel Buendía.[23]

Moro, the late John Ross wrote in an article submitted to the *San Francisco Exam-iner*, would make the sensationalist hall of fame: he was "a movie stunt man and motorcycle daredevil currently appearing on local screens jumping through rings of fire in a potboiler entitled *Days of Violence*" and appeared regularly on nighttime *tele-novelas*, or soap operas. Moro was also the grandson of former Mexican president Manuel Ávila Camacho (1940–1946) and the nephew of newspaper magnate Rómulo O'Farrell. "His starring role in the Buendía affair," Ross commented, "has cast a little glamour over what until now seemed a murky, sexless conspiracy to silence the colum-nist. One of Moro's alibi witnesses [was] Jacaranda Alfaro, a starlet about to film a Grade B'er named 'The Narco Satánicos.'"

"Pinning the triggerman tag on Moro has not impressed police beat vets like [Sergio] Von Nowaffen, who, two years ago, scooped the pack with a two-part exposé identify-ing Zorrilla and the DFS as the authors of the Buendía assassination," Ross recalled, "a revelation not taken seriously at the time because a highly edited version was spot-lighted in the afternoon *Ovaciones*, a journal not noted for accuracy in reporting. 'Moro is such a bad shot that he could have killed his partner by mistake,' Von Nowaffen sneers at the government's resolution of the case." Von Nowaffen claimed to have proof of two hit men, "one 'El Chocorrol' (literally 'The Chocolate Roll,' a darkskinned DFS agent killed by his co-conspirators 41 days after Buendía) and the other, an army officer never previously connected to the case before."[24]

Following Zorrilla's arrest, the *San Francisco Bay Guardian* ran a feature by Ross about the Buendía case and endemic violence perpetrated against Mexican journal-ists.[25] We contacted Ross, informing him about our own investigation and expressing our wish to discuss with him some of the people and points he had mentioned in his article. Another five and a half years would pass before we finally managed to do that at one of his favorite haunts in San Francisco's Mission District, but he replied imme-diately to our initial inquiry with a lengthy typewritten missive from Mexico City. "So much sewage has flowed under the bridge since the Zorrilla bust," he wrote us, that it was difficult to sort it all out.

Ross expressed the view of many close observers when he characterized the special prosecutor's closing of the case as "shocking." García Domínguez had taken out paid ads "in all the papers, even *Proceso*," announcing his resolution of the Buendía assas-sination, and then was nominated to serve on the supreme court. In his now official scenario, Ross marveled, "Zorrilla Pérez is the intellectual author and Juan Rafael Moro Ávila Camacho . . . is the material triggerman. The motive was to suppress publication of information revealing Zorrilla Pérez's ties to [Mexican drug lords Rafael] Caro Quintero, Ernesto Fonseca, and Miguel Ángel Félix Gallardo. Most everyone I talk to," Ross remarked, "laughs out loud at this solution. . . . According to García Domínguez's script, Zorrilla asks Juventino Prado for a man that can be entrusted to murder Manuel Buendía on the very day Buendía is offed. Not believable that Moro would be chosen." Nor, we insist, is it believable that a political crime of that magnitude would have been perpetrated in such an impromptu manner.

According to Sergio von Nowaffen, Ross wrote us, Buendía's clothes were seized by the DFS "because they revealed powder burns," and powder burns "revealed two gun-men." Von Nowaffen named Col. Jesús Rodríguez Santillán as the second shooter. "This," Ross noted, "points to an army connection, possibly [Defense Secretary Juan] Arévalo Gardoqui—who, it was rumoured, just spent several weeks under house arrest. The investigation, now closed, would have had to step up to first Bartlett Díaz, then perhaps Arévalo Gardoqui, eventually to De la Madrid."

Ross went on to note what to us seemed obvious: "Zorrilla (and Nazar Haro) (and Florentino Ventura) (and Miguel Aldana) were all CIA contacts [in Mexico]. You didn't read that in Buendía however. The question I ask is what did Buendía do for them? If Zorrilla is the director of this operation, the CIA has a major stake in the assassination (closing down Buendía means keeping its real agents covert while its narco allies con-tinue to generate funds for the Contras). Sorry that this is so encoded," John offered by way of an apology we would hear more than once over the course of our investigation, "but speculation is the norm here, rumours fly, even the relatively clear is obscure."[26]

Through all the smoke and mirrors deployed to secure a semblance of closure in the Buendía case, the actual or manufactured guilt of the convicted defendants was beside the point, that point being—as John Ross and others suggested—the evident complicity of more powerful figures and interests. In their follow-up to the indictments handed down by the special prosecutor, several reporters revisited the matter of Gerhard Mertins, the German arms dealer who in the final two years of the de la Madrid administration had been identified as a primary suspect, then was allowed to slip quietly away into the smoke. Initially, García Domínguez had considered traveling to Germany to take a formal deposition from Mertins, but when that proved unworkable he opted instead to forward through diplomatic channels a list of 772 questions for Mertins to answer in writing.[27] The special prosecutor reported nothing further about the questionnaire and made no reference to Mertins in his final report.

Subsequently, in response to a reporter's question during an interview granted to *Excélsior*, District Attorney General Ignacio Morales Lechuga stated that Mertins had been cleared of any involvement in the Buendía assassination. Morales Lechuga assured *Excélsior* that the special prosecutor had conducted "a profound investigation" of the German arms dealer and had "even sent him a questionnaire to answer," although, implausibly, Morales claimed not to know whether Mertins had in fact answered the special prosecutor's questions or what his responses might have been. Then, as trial proceedings continued into the fall of 1989, a dozen witnesses testified before Judge Hernández Martínez about Mertins's activities in Mexico. The former attorney for his Durango-based Compañía Minera Romer, Samuel García Cuéllar, established that Mertins had maintained a close relationship with Zorrilla Pérez, a fact bearing, perhaps, on Zorrilla's legal defense strategy but of greater interest to us as further evidence of a CIA presence in the Buendía affair, as well as a possible link to events in Central America. It also transpired that, despite the ostensible refusal of Mexican immigration authorities to grant Mertins permission to reenter Mexico for the purpose of wrapping up his business affairs in Durango, he apparently managed to do so, "not once, but several times."[28]

In mid-August 1989, Luis Suárez wrote a lengthy column in *Excélsior* again raising the possibility of a connection between the La Penca bombing attempt on the life of Nicaraguan *contra* commander Edén Pastora and the assassination of Manuel Buendía in Mexico City, both events having occurred on the same day within an hour of each other. Suárez based his column, titled "Assaults against Buendía and Pastora More Than Mere Coincidence," on an interview with Costa Rican journalist Roberto Cruz Sandoval, who had lost a leg and an eye and sustained other severe injuries in the La Penca bombing. "Mexican police were involved [in the Buendía assassination]," Suárez quoted Cruz Sandoval as saying, "but the initial decision [to carry it out] came from outside, from far away, from very high-ranking foreigners, as also happened in the La Penca bombing in Costa Rica."

The secret services of the two countries had a hand in these crimes, Cruz averred. In Costa Rica, it was the Intelligence and Security Directorate (DISCR, by its Spanish acronym), in Mexico the DFS, both "associated with and manipulated by the CIA." In Cruz's reading of events, the attempted assassination of Edén Pastora and simultaneous slaying of Manuel Buendía both occurred as elements of the Reagan administration's scheme to circumvent congressional limits on its ability to foment the overthrow of Nicaragua's revolutionary government. The CIA and President Reagan's National Security Council, with Pentagon and State Department backing, had created an elaborate covert network of official and "plausibly deniable" extraofficial operatives to finance and conduct the illegal offensive against Nicaragua. Key to that effort, Cruz suggested, was a link to Colombia's Medellín drug cartel and its exorbitantly profitable cocaine traffic as a convenient way to fund the United States' proxy army of Nicaraguan *contras*. Dirty money from this source was also used to pay off key civil and military authorities throughout the region, Cruz added, "which allowed them to act with impunity and, later on, to blackmail and subvert local governments into alignment with U.S. interests and objectives." As for Mexico, a large portion of the cocaine smuggled into the United States from Colombia transited that country, "which establishes the Mexican traffickers' link to the Medellín Cartel" and, by implication, to the CIA.

The objective of the La Penca bombing, Cruz concluded, was threefold: first, to blame Pastora's anticipated death on Nicaragua's Sandinista government with a view to swaying U.S. congressional opinion in favor of direct intervention; second, to eliminate a rogue CIA asset; and, third, to distract attention from the Buendía assassination in Mexico. Buendía's death, in turn, served to prevent exposure of covert Reagan administration efforts to overthrow the Nicaraguan government, including, or perhaps especially, CIA ties to Mexican drug traffickers.

Through this Costa Rican colleague, Luis Suárez entered prohibited territory and spoke the unspeakable. Mexican authorities, he clearly suggested, "had deceived the public, created a myth, and prosecuted lower-level scapegoats" in order to protect the real perpetrators of Manuel Buendía's assassination. It was a striking example of reporting the informed views of a foreign source to make points Mexican editors considered politically too delicate for their own reporters and columnists to express. The official resolution of the Buendía case, Suárez was saying, in effect, had failed to touch the actual plotters and did not reveal the true motive behind the slaying.[29]

From our perspective, Luis Suárez's interview with Roberto Cruz Sandoval had the additional virtue of introducing a new piece of the puzzle that would shed light on aspects of the Buendía case not publicly examined by Mexican authorities: a civil lawsuit filed on 29 May 1986 in U.S. District Court for the Southern District of Florida against twenty-nine defendants accused of complicity in an elaborate scheme to supply and support the Reagan administration's proxy war against Nicaragua. The suit had been filed by the Christic Institute, a Washington, DC, public interest law firm, on behalf of Tony Avirgan and Martha Honey, American freelance journalists based in Costa Rica. Avirgan had attended Edén Pastora's La Penca press conference and himself been injured in the bombing. Among the defendants in the Christic Institute case were Medellín cartel kingpins Pablo Escobar and Jorge Ochoa.

Although only passing reference was made to one of Mexico's drug kingpins (Rafael Caro Quintero) and Christic attorneys concentrated their attention on Central America,[30] these legal proceedings in Miami nonetheless produced early evidence of CIA and National Security Council collusion with regional drug traffickers in support of the Nicaraguan *contras*, collusion that would subsequently be shown to have extended to the Guadalajara cartel. As we will examine more closely in later chapters, widespread rumors and allegations of CIA ties to cocaine trafficking as a funding source for congressionally prohibited covert operations in Central America presented the Reagan administration with an increasingly serious challenge to plausibly deny these clearly impeachable and prosecutable offenses.[31]

¿VÍNCULOS MEXICANOS CON LOS CONTRAS?
CARO QUINTERO NO FUE

unomásuno—Martes, 17 March 1987

Russell H. Bartley

In the March 9–15 issue of the capital city's newsweekly *Punto*, Hernán Casares Cámara asserts that the infamous Mexican drug trafficker Rafael Caro Quintero "supplied arms to the Nicaraguan Contras."

Based on a Spanish translation of a legal document obtained in the United States and passed on to him by an anonymous Mexican official, Casares claims that Caro Quintero was tasked by the Central Intelligence Agency (CIA) to organize a fictitious company to supply arms to the Nicaraguan *contras*; that a company was created in Miami under the name Orca Supply; and that from Florida, "as well, presumably, as from Mexico," Caro transferred "guns, ammunition, explosives, and other military equipment to the *contras* based in Honduras."

The alleged involvement of this Mexican drug lord in arms trafficking to Central America relates to the tangled efforts of the Reagan administration to circumvent obstacles to the supply of lethal matériel to the Nicaraguan counterrevolutionaries imposed by the United States Congress, efforts that have recently resulted in the so-called Iran-Contra scandal.

Various implications jump out from Casares's report about supposed links between Mexican drug trafficking and the White House's interventionist policy in the Central American region. In the first place, the individual in question is not the Mexican, Rafael Caro Quintero, but rather the Cuban American, Rafael *Chi Chi* Quintero, who in the 1960s took an active part in the CIA's *secret war* against the revolutionary government of Fidel Castro and subsequently worked as a professional killer for the well-known arms dealer and rumored rogue CIA agent Edwin Wilson. This incorrect identity is apparently a mistake of the translator, who inexplicably changed the name *Rafael "Chi Chi" Quintero*, which appears in the original document, to *Rafael Caro Quintero* in the Spanish version.

We wrote the above article in response to a report by Hernán Casares Cámara in the Mexico City newsweekly, *Punto*. We were thoroughly familiar with the Christic Institute's lawsuit and found Casares's linkage of that case to Mexico based on a conflation of two key players with similar names more than a little puzzling. Casares himself told us that he had had serious doubts about the information but that his source, a veteran Federal Judicial Police officer, had vouched for its authenticity. At the time, we were about to fly from Mexico to South America, and Casares said he would run our questions by his source while we were traveling, then meet with us when we returned.

Our primary interest in what Casares had reported was how it might bear on the Buendía case. As we have noted, various reporters and investigators have suggested a possible connection between the Buendía assassination and the La Penca bombing attempt against Edén Pastora. We repeated that suggestion elsewhere in our *unomá-suno* commentary on Casares's *Punto* article. "It may have been simple coincidence," we wrote. "Or perhaps something more." Of course, we added, the coincidence of two or more events does not in itself establish causal relationships, but it does justify the hypothesis that La Penca and Buendía's death both had to do with the Reagan administration–*contra*–drug trafficker nexus. According to Christic Institute attorneys, "Chi Chi" Quintero was directly involved in obtaining and transferring to Costa Rica the C-4 explosive used in the La Penca bombing, while by Casares's account Caro Quintero, the man alleged to have arranged the abduction, interrogation, and murder of DEA special agent Enrique Camarena Salazar, was able to flee Mexico to Costa Rica as a result of CIA and DEA collusion with Mexican drug traffickers. The main question posed by the Casares article, we suggested, was why this distorted version of events had been leaked to *Punto* in the first place.[32]

It would take us another twenty-plus years to venture a likely answer, but already upon our return to Mexico City from South America we began to discover key elements of that answer. Our *unomásuno* article, Casares informed us, had annoyed both the PJDF and Mexico's attorney general, Sergio García Ramírez. Casares's PJDF source blamed the identity confusion on a "bad translator" and lamented that not having handled it more competently reflected poorly on the force. But that "bad translation" of the Christic brief had also come directly across the attorney general's desk, the source told Casares, and García Ramírez had immediately recognized that the individual identified as "Rafael Caro Quintero" could not be the Mexican drug trafficker, a fact he quickly confirmed after obtaining a copy of the original English text. Asked by Casares why the *judiciales* themselves had not realized the document's error, his informant replied that they had taken it for granted that there was a link between the traffickers and the *contras* and found nothing at all remarkable about the allegation that Caro Quintero was involved.[33]

Casares Cámara, for his part, had done considerably more in his article than we appreciated at the time. While we focused on Casares having confused Caro Quintero for "Chi Chi" Quintero, our colleague had actually exposed Caro Quintero's links to the *contra* support network, as well as pointed to the existence of narco-related *contra* supply routes through Mexico. Caro, according to Casares, had become involved in supplying the *contras* shortly after the overthrow of Nicaraguan dictator Anastasio Somoza Debayle in 1979, to which end he began spending time in Costa Rica. He had business dealings there with two Mexican associates from Guadalajara, Javier and Eduardo Cordero Staufer, who in turn were in a business partnership with a brother-in-law of then Costa Rican president Luis Alberto Monge. He was so well connected by then, Casares reported, that he had no difficulty securing necessary immigration documents and even managed to obtain a set of diplomatic license plates, which allowed him to move around the country unmolested.[34]

The question remains why this tangled information had been leaked to the press. In hindsight we now conclude that the Casares piece was almost certainly a coded message between key players in the regional imbroglio that took the lives of Kiki Camarena and Manuel Buendía. Years later Lawrence Harrison would assure us that the reason the bodies of Camarena and his Mexican pilot were found not where they had originally been buried but rather on a ranch in the neighboring state of Michoacán was to send just such a message to the Americans. That ranch in Michoacán, Harrison told us, "had to do with guns, not drugs." It was, he said, a way point on one of the covert transit routes for arms being sent to the *contras* from the United States. In that instance, the coded message was apparently a veiled threat from Mexican authorities to expose the Americans' illegal *contra* supply operation if they did not stop using the Camarena affair to strong-arm Mexico into line with Washington's interventionist policy in Central America.[35] Now, two years later, a similar message appeared to have been sent again. "Caro Quintero Supplied Arms to the *Contras*," trumpeted the headline of Casares's *Punto* article, and "The Mexican Trafficker Had the Blessing of the DEA and the CIA."

Confusion over who was who in the Christic brief notwithstanding, the assertions contained in these headlines were true: Rafael Caro Quintero, together with the other two primary Guadalajara-based drug capos, Ernesto Fonseca Carrillo and Miguel Ángel Félix Gallardo, was supplying arms to the Nicaraguan *contras*. And all three were doing so in coordination with American intelligence. Reference to the DEA here would seem to imply its complicity in the murder of its own agent, Kiki Camarena, a potentially even more explosive allegation than the threatened exposure of CIA collaboration with Mexican traffickers.

> A short wiry man with a touch of Napoleonic arrogance not entirely unjustified, Ed Heath was one of the best-informed and hardest-working men in the embassy. He spoke fluent Spanish, had wide experience of Latin America, and had made it his business to win the trust and confidence of Mexico's Primer Comandante. That trust was one of Heath's most formidable tools, for the Primer Comandante was Florentino Ventura . . . said by some to be the most powerful police official in Latin America.[36]

> The tension between Mexico City and the Guadalajara office worsened after Ed Heath was named DEA attaché in Mexico City in mid-1983. . . . Heath made friends of officials in the Mexican Attorney General's Office and MFJP [Mexican Federal Judicial Police] headquarters, particularly MFJP director Manuel Ibarra. His slow, solicitous approach to his prickly counterparts gratified Ambassador John Gavin and many U.S. embassy political officers but ensured clashes with [James] Kuykendall and other field men.[37]

DEA country attaché Edward Heath met with reporters at the American embassy in Mexico City on 29 June 1989, two weeks and two days after the arrest of José Antonio Zorrilla Pérez for allegedly masterminding the assassination of Manuel Buendía and ten days after the arrest of Juan Rafael Moro Ávila Camacho as Buendía's alleged killer. It was his farewell encounter with members of the press at the conclusion of a six-year assignment in Mexico. Interestingly, he spoke on that occasion about Manuel Buendía, dismissing as "apocryphal" a document implicating senior Mexican officials in drug trafficking that had been attributed to the DEA and reportedly leaked to Buendía. None of the information in the DEA's possession, he told the reporters, led him to think that Buendía's assassination had anything to do with drugs.[38]

Yet the DEA had shown a decided interest in the Buendía case at least since 1986 and would continue to do so following Heath's return to the United States. In April 1986, DEA operative Antonio Gárate Bustamante approached Buendía case oversight group investigator Octavio González with the offer of what he described as the "DEA's Buendía file" in exchange for information about a purportedly planned prison escape by Rafael Caro Quintero, at the time incarcerated for the murder of Kiki Camarena. The mastermind behind Buendía's assassination, Gárate assured González, was Secretary of Government Manuel Bartlett Díaz, and the documentary proof was in the proffered DEA file. González's associate Rogelio Hernández, he intimated, should publish that information in *Excélsior* around the time of the second anniversary of the assassination.[39]

We were puzzled by this DEA approach to *Excélsior* from the moment we learned of it, as it had no apparent bearing on the Camarena case but rather suggested a covert operation intended to influence political events in Mexico by compromising Bartlett Díaz's viability as a potential PRI presidential candidate. That is how Hernández and *Excélsior* editor Regino Díaz Redondo interpreted it, which led them to turn down Gárate's offer.[40] When years later we had the opportunity to ask Héctor Berréllez about Gárate's 1986 approach to *Excélsior*, he acknowledged it but avoided a direct explanation of its purpose. Asked why the DEA had shown any interest at all in the Buendía case, Berréllez told us it was because Camarena had apparently met with Buendía on one occasion and that Buendía's murder, "like Camarena's," was related to what he had learned about the CIA–drug trafficker connection.[41]

Gárate made the approach to *Excélsior* during Ed Heath's tenure as country attaché and presumably would have done so only on his instructions, or at the very least with his personal knowledge and authorization. Indeed, Heath seems to cast a long shadow over both the Buendía and the Camarena cases. He had served in Mexico in the 1970s and was reassigned there as the DEA's senior in-country officer the year before Buendía's assassination. He oversaw the initial responses to Kiki Camarena's abduction and remained in Mexico until Washington's focus on the Camarena case shifted from field investigations to indictments and prosecutions in Los Angeles, where Heath reappeared in the early 1990s as part of a team controlling former CIA illegal Lawrence Harrison, who had been extricated from Mexico to serve as a government witness against Rubén Zuno Arce.

That the DEA had been penetrated and used as a cover by the CIA became increasingly apparent in the course of the 1980s, and Ed Heath's role in handling this particular witness raises questions about his own agency affiliation. Years later Harrison intimated to us that Heath was himself a CIA officer, while a retired DEA acquaintance of Charles Bowden familiar with Heath believed that to be the case as well. "In DEA," he told Bowden, "we had at least four enemies: (1) State Department, (2) CIA,

(3) FBI, (4) the cartels plus corrupt government officials north and south."[42] Octavio González's prior affiliation with the DFS raises a further question about possible CIA involvement in this apparent attempt to taint Bartlett Díaz.

Should the allegations of Heath's CIA ties prove true, that might explain his distinctive operational style and the tensions it caused with DEA agents under his command, particularly those assigned to the Guadalajara field office. Investigative journalist Elaine Shannon has remarked at some length on his independent modus operandi.[43] Whereas Heath's counterparts in Colombia and Thailand, she notes, regularly communicated their operational needs and concerns to headquarters, especially when DEA objectives ran counter to CIA or State Department priorities, Heath, apparently, did not, preferring instead to carry out his intelligence tasks autonomously through a carefully cultivated network of personal relationships with key Mexican officials. Such an approach would have allowed him to prioritize CIA purposes over DEA objectives, were that in fact his assignment.

The quality of Heath's relationship with Florentino Ventura, as described by James Mills, for example, reveals a degree of mutual professional respect between two veteran intelligence operatives that we think improbable had Heath been a mere badge-on-the-vest lawman. Ventura had taken down major drug traffickers in his career (including Caro Quintero, whom he personally brought back to Mexico following Caro's flight to Costa Rica in February 1985) and could be expected to meet with American antinarcotics agents in the course of his official duties, but he was much more than a Mexican lawman and would be unlikely to carouse with a foreign officer he did not consider to be his equal.[44] We were afforded an opportunity to appraise this aspect of Ventura's personality when we interviewed him in November 1987, an interview arranged through *unomásuno* late one evening for 11:00 a.m. the following morning, an unheard-of turnaround time for such a request that surprised our colleagues at the paper, since Ventura did not readily grant interviews to the press. It was a sign, we concluded, that he wanted to evaluate us.[45]

Ventura's Soto Street office reflected his personality. At the opposite end of the room as one entered was a large hardwood desk covered with a clutter of papers and sundry personal articles. Behind the desk sat a carved, wooden, high-backed, leather-padded chair more appropriate for a magistrate or ecclesiastical hierarch than a police official. To one side stood the Mexican flag, and on the wall behind it there hung the obligatory presidential portrait of Miguel de la Madrid Hurtado. As with other visitors, Ventura received us at a round faux-wood-veneer table next to the main entrance, just barely inside his private office. On the wall behind us hung a violent oil painting of three Goth warriors locked in mortal combat with bloody broadswords and a battle-ax. Hanging beneath it were two smaller oils depicting aspects of the bullfight. Against this same wall stood bookshelves, on which were prominently displayed a deluxe edition of James Mills's *The Underground Empire* (1986) and next to it a Spanish-language edition of *New York Times* correspondent Alan Riding's recently published *Distant Neighbors* (1986). On the sidewall to the right as one entered hung several framed photographs related to the American gangster Al Capone, among them a "portrait" of a Thompson submachine gun.

It quickly became apparent that Ventura was not going to discuss any aspect of the Buendía case with us. Alluding to its political ramifications, he remarked that "it was not the place of police professionals to concern themselves with politics." We had begun our interview by observing that it was precisely his exceptional record as a law enforcement professional that had moved us to seek his thoughts about the Buendía case, but he deflected that approach to a discussion of ongoing efforts to modernize Mexico's various police agencies, especially the Federal Judicial Police, with which he had been most closely associated. He obviously viewed himself as the epitome of law enforcement professionalism. Indeed, "thirty-seven years of professionalism" had made him the *Primer Comandante* Mills describes in his book, a description that clearly pleased Ventura. He wanted us to know that his top-cop reputation derived in part from training he had undergone abroad, particularly in the United States, where he had received specialized instruction from "all the major agencies, [including] the FBI, Customs, Border Patrol, CIA, and DEA." Moreover, he had traveled "excessively" (*demasiado mucho*) to all the Latin American countries and most of Europe, "as well as to other continents," virtually all of that travel undertaken in conjunction with his police work. Ventura acknowledged that he had also been involved in national security matters, but hastened to define *national security* as "the defense of society against delinquency."[46]

Another of Ed Heath's DEA colleagues who, like Heath, was much more than a simple badge-on-the-vest lawman and had worked closely with Florentino Ventura is Patrick Gregory, a former CIA agent whose fellow DEA officers doubted he had ever really left the agency. Gregory was still in the CIA when he and Ventura first collaborated operationally. That was back in the 1970s during Mexico's scorched earth campaign against domestic "subversives," when Gregory assisted Ventura with the capture of antigovernment political activists in the Tijuana–San Diego area. Subsequently, Gregory worked with Ventura on the high-profile Alberto Sicilia Falcón case, which was enmeshed in an intricate web of criminal, political, and foreign intelligence interests analogous to the one enveloping the Kiki Camarena case a decade later. Sicilia Falcón was a legendary Cuban exile, a narcotics trafficker based in Mexico, whose money "had been secreted around the world in the banks of a half-dozen nations" and whose influence "reached into the intelligence services of many nations, among them Mexico, Cuba, and almost certainly the United States." Sicilia's private security force, according to Mills, had "fought battles, pirated boats, murdered, robbed—and done it all with the knowledge and protection of the Mexican government."[47]

Ventura had headed the Mexican investigation of Sicilia Falcón and would also be placed in charge of the Camarena case. He was one of twenty-two founding officers of the DFS under its first director, Lt. Col. Marcelino Inurreta de la Fuente (1947–1952). By the time Sicilia Falcón established the first trans-Mexico cocaine route in the early 1970s between Colombian suppliers and U.S. consumers, Ventura had risen through Mexican law enforcement to a position of authority only once removed from the president. During the Echeverría *sexenio* (1970–1976), he commanded a special unit of fifty detectives directly under the federal attorney general who worked national security and other major cases that the administration wanted handled with maximum discretion and efficacy. Ventura attained his unique position of power, Patrick Gregory told

Mills, "by being able to take care of problems that other people couldn't take care of."
To work with him "was like going to Washington and working with the director of the
FBI." As a matter of fact, Gregory averred, "Ventura's got more power than the FBI
chief ever thought of having. The man is a legend."[48]

Ventura, by Gregory's account, was a man who understood power, who had been
given a position of power, including the power of life and death, and who had no
qualms about using it. He was, Gregory said, "the most brutal man I have ever met.
And efficient. Efficiently brutal." He was an experienced interrogator who readily
resorted to torture but left the actual administration of physical abuse to subordinates,
timing his own entrances and exits for maximum psychological effect in eliciting the
prisoner responses he sought. "I think he's probably one of the finest guys I've ever
worked with," Gregory told Mills, "along with probably the cruelest human being that
I personally know." Gregory's relationship with Ventura, like Heath's, appears to have
been one of professional camaraderie that extended well beyond the formalities of
bilateral interagency accords. "I don't have any problems with Ventura," he expressed
to Mills. "He's always been a gentleman, he's always been willing to discuss with me
things that aren't normally discussed between policemen in different countries."[49] Ten
months after we interviewed Ventura he was dead, an apparent suicide following a
violent altercation in which he shot to death his Federal Judicial Police officer wife
and one of her close friends.[50]

We dwell on these details of individual character and personal relationships here
because they offer a small window into the comportment of real actors in the geopolitical netherworld where Manuel Buendía, Enrique Camarena, and countless others lost
their lives. As we gradually discover links between the Buendía and Camarena murders,
Ed Heath and Florentino Ventura emerge as apparent actors in both cases. Through
them we begin to attach recognizable faces to the covert actions of the U.S. and Mexican governments that abetted these sensational homicides, then covered them up.

It was Ed Heath, for example, who first publicly linked José Antonio Zorrilla Pérez
to the Guadalajara drug traffickers, who in turn abducted, tortured, and murdered
Kiki Camarena.[51] When it later developed that Camarena's interrogation under torture
had been tape-recorded, it was Florentino Ventura who, at the request of Attorney
General Sergio García Ramírez, produced two tape cassettes containing Camarena's
voice. Drug Enforcement Agency administrator John C. Lawn had learned about the
existence of what he initially thought was a single tape through the CIA's Mexico City
station and demanded that García Ramírez turn it over to him. García at first refused,
saying the matter was too sensitive, but he finally agreed that Lawn could listen to the
tape, then make a formal request for a copy through official channels.[52]

Initially, Lawn was only allowed to listen to a single recording in the attorney general's offices. On that tape, he was struck by the presence of a patient, methodical
questioner who exhibited all the traits of an experienced police interrogator and who
Camarena addressed as "Comandante."[53] While it is unlikely that we will ever obtain
proof positive and at this juncture can only speculate, we must wonder if Camarena's
interrogator might possibly have been Comandante Ventura himself. There are, of
course, other possible candidates, and Ventura is said to have shared with the DEA the

view that his own government had engineered the Camarena abduction.[54] Yet the question remains: How did Ventura obtain the tapes of Camarena's interrogation so soon after the American agent's abduction? And how did the CIA already know about them in those initial weeks?

Then there is the larger question: Why was Camarena's interrogation recorded in the first place? And, for whom? Lawrence Harrison, who was himself a specialist in electronic espionage and, while embedded in the Mexican secret police, had performed communications and other services for the principal Guadalajara narcotics traffickers, scoffed at the notion that they would have recorded Camarena. More than once he remarked to us that the traffickers were "electronic illiterates" and "wouldn't even have known how to turn on a tape recorder" much less record a prolonged interrogation.[55] Elaine Shannon implies as much in her book. Camarena's abduction, she writes, was not the impetuous act of "illiterate dope peddlers." To the contrary, the recovered interrogation tapes reveal "a great degree of advance planning and considerable sophistication," including the use of "experienced interrogators and electronic equipment."[56]

As in the Buendía case, there are official fingerprints all over the Camarena affair, both Mexican and American. Héctor Berréllez, for example, who supervised the DEA's investigation of the Camarena murder, assured us that Manuel Buendía and Kiki Camarena were both killed for what they had learned about the CIA's involvement with the Guadalajara cartel and the Nicaraguan *contras*. Moreover, Berréllez told us, longtime CIA operative and *contra* supply coordinator Félix Rodríguez was present during Camarena's interrogation and personally participated in the questioning.[57]

As telling as the Camarena tapes themselves is the way they surfaced. As noted, it was the CIA that first brought their existence to the attention of the DEA. Initially, Jack Lawn thought there was a single tape, but he was soon made aware of a second by Mexican attorney general García Ramírez. When Mexican authorities finally turned over copies of the tapes to DEA country attaché Ed Heath, there were four of them. After filtering and enhancement by FBI lab technicians, analysis of the tapes revealed tampering. Voices were interrupted and segments excised, so questions and answers did not always follow. Subsequently, the CIA provided the DEA with a transcript of a fifth tape, but not the tape itself. The transcript appeared to be part of the Camarena interrogation, yet it differed in content from the others and ended abruptly when the interrogator's questioning turned to the alleged complicity of Mexican defense secretary Juan Arévalo Gardoqui with the Guadalajara cartel.[58]

Manuel Buendía and Enrique Camarena . . . Caro Quintero and "Chi Chi" Quintero . . . Florentino Ventura, Edward Heath, Zorrilla Pérez, Nazar Haro . . . Bartlett Díaz . . . García Ramírez, García Paniagua, García Domínguez . . . and how many others? They were all scrambled pieces of a devilish puzzle. "In Mexico," Florentino Ventura assured us, "there is no link between guerrilla fighters and drug traffickers." The Buendía assassination, Ed Heath publicly opined, "had nothing to do with drugs."[59]

9

Back on the Pavement

A handful of columnists have also emerged as important leftist spokesmen, although in recent years few have exercised as much influence as Manuel Buendía in *Excélsior*. He avoided identification with any party and in fact maintained good relations with many officials, but he also campaigned daily against ultra-rightist factions, corruption in powerful sectors of the government and U.S. policy toward Central America.

—Alan Riding, *Distant Neighbors* (1986)

Mexico City, 7 March 1990. Wednesday—A friend drives us from Milwaukee to O'Hare International Airport. It's partly cloudy, 22°F, a foot of snow blankets everything. We trade the glazed ground for whipped cream-like clouds rolling in endless patterns, shrouding the planet below. Where continent and Gulf meet, the clouds boil up into an alien fantasyscape of towering pinnacles through which we fly at 37,000 feet, immersed in our own world. We descend with the setting sun gilding volcanic crags and glinting off a sea of windows in the newly washed city of twenty million souls below.

Daytime temperatures hover between 75°–80°F. Air quality is marginal to bad. Newspaper headlines record the state of the nation: "82% of people in the capital suffer from malnutrition," "One million children ages 6–14 work every day to survive," "Border maquiladoras becoming Mexican Hong Kong," "Mexican police robbing migrant workers returning from U.S.," "Shoot-outs between Federal District and Federal Judicial Police," "84 drug traffickers arrested in Matamoros."

Strange night at the Mónaco lying in bed listening to the sounds from the hotel's air shaft. Around 2:00 a.m. we hear banging on the pipes. Then a rising, shrill whistle. In Room 308 next to ours a deep male voice announces, "Tengo que irme." Within seconds the door clicks shut and the man disappears down the carpeted hallway. A sleepy female converses briefly with a male companion. Toilets flush. Then, from down the shaft comes strangled coughing, hawking and spitting, nose blowing from one end and remarkable flatulence from the other. Probably a heavy smoker, aggravated by the sundry contaminants of the world's largest city. At last the coughing and farting stop, followed by more toilet flushing. Then, tentatively, a pair of crickets chirping at the bottom of the shaft.

After breakfast at the Café París, we walk to a money-changing house on Reforma so we can pay our first week's hotel bill. Then we sit for a while in the Librería Reforma, writing and preparing for today's interview with Manuel Buendía's widow. She took a day to decide whether or not to meet with us; probably reread what we have published on the case in *unomásuno* and *Revista mexicana de comunicación*. Yesterday she agreed. We will see her at 4:00 o'clock this afternoon.

—S. E. Bartley, journal entry

The official denouement of the Manuel Buendía case left us with many unanswered questions and a seemingly endless list of investigative tasks yet to accomplish. We returned to the Federal District on the last day of February 1990 to commence what would prove to be the most protracted part of our investigation, now reframed in light of the way the case had been closed by the Mexican authorities. On this trip our first priority was to interview Buendía's widow, María Dolores Ábalos Lebrija. She had spoken to the media on numerous occasions over the five years it took the government to conduct its various investigations and finally name perpetrators. We had taken careful note of her various public statements but felt no immediate need to speak with her ourselves. We observed her attitude change from initial optimism that the authorities would spare no effort to find and punish her husband's killers to growing frustration over their lack of progress and, ultimately, complete disillusionment with how they concluded the case, accompanied by a nagging suspicion that the government itself had had a hand in Don Manuel's death. "There's been no political will to solve my husband's murder," she bitterly expressed to *Proceso* on the fifth anniversary of the assassination.[1] For our purposes, the widow's views and reminiscences in the light of all that had transpired since 30 May 1984 now promised additional insights beyond what she had shared with reporters to date. It had become imperative that we discuss the case with her in person.

We met twice with Doña Dolores at her Lindavista home, first on Wednesday, 7 March, from 4:00 to 6:00 p.m., and again on Friday the ninth, from 4:30 to 7:00 p.m. We clarified for her that our purpose was to contextualize her husband's murder as part of a long-term investigation, which at some future date would result in a book, and not to fish for new quotable statements we could insert into a current news article. We no longer wrote for *unomásuno*, we explained, and were only interested in pursuing the politically delicate lines of inquiry the official investigations had sought to block. She appreciated the explanation and received us most graciously.[2]

The Buendía residence was an unpretentious three-story, flat-roofed house on the corner of Casma and Otavalo streets in a quiet neighborhood of sidewalk plantings and vining bougainvillea. The ground level was windowless and contained a two-car garage, as well as Manuel Buendía's personal study. The living quarters occupied the first and second floors (second and third by American count). They were spacious, with large plate glass windows and heavy curtains that could be drawn for privacy or opened for light, as desired. The house was conservatively furnished with a traditional sense of refinement and no hint of ostentation. A vigilant ceramic cherub peered down from a ledge above the garage door.

We commenced our interview by inquiring about Manuel Buendía's work habits. Doña Dolores elaborated on what we understood to have been Buendía's practice of not mixing his professional and family lives. He did this, she told us, so as not to endanger his family or expose it to possible problems as a consequence of what he might write in his newspaper columns. Such was this barrier between work and family, she had remarked to an earlier interviewer, that she had never considered herself to be her husband's *compañera* (confidante), "only his wife and homemaker." She was still an *ama de casa*, she insisted.[3]

Buendía's separation of work and home was not 100 percent, however. His Linda-vista office, which Doña Dolores took us downstairs to see, was a windowless study where the columnist could ponder and write, secure from unwelcome intrusions. It had been constructed in such a way, she said, that nothing her husband did there could be heard on the floors above. Buendía would transcribe recorded interviews and write lectures in that office. He occasionally wrote columns there as well, especially those that appeared on Mondays, which he prepared over the weekend. Now and then, she recounted, he would awake during the night, have an idea for a column, and, unable to sleep, go down to his study to write it up. Sometimes he would leave a draft column on his desk, and she would read it, though rarely would she comment on it, because he did not like her reading his unpolished drafts. On the few occasions when she did, he would chide her good-naturedly, then consider what she had to say.

Buendía was fastidious, however, about not bringing potentially compromising material home. He made no notes in his pocket calendar books other than appoint-ments, committing sensitive information to memory. Although he called himself for-getful, Doña Dolores remarked, her husband in fact had an exceptional memory. When occasionally he did jot down some delicate piece of information, she told us, he would tear it up or burn it as soon as he had made use of it. The proof that he kept nothing sensitive at home, she noted, was that following his assassination neither the DFS nor any other police agency searched, or even asked to search, their Lindavista residence.

The main question on our minds was Buendía's relationship with Zorrilla Pérez. *Excélsior* reporter Rogelio Hernández, who had coordinated the independent Buendía case oversight group and chronicled Zorrilla's role in the case, described their relation-ship as a close, thirteen-year friendship in which they would meet periodically for meals, go hunting, talk firearms and practice target shooting together, discuss national secu-rity issues, and exchange information. When Buendía misplaced the DFS credential that Zorrilla's predecessor, Miguel Nazar Haro, had provided him, Zorrilla replaced it. (The credential allowed Buendía to carry a handgun.) To document their closeness, Hernández reproduces a letter that Buendía wrote to Zorrilla in April 1983 commend-ing the DFS chief for the way he had handled a kidnapping case, which opens with "My very dear friend," is written in the familiar second person voice, and ends with an em-brace: "Te abrazo: Manuel Buendía." "I feel proud to be your friend," wrote Buendía, "and desire nothing more than to continue this friendship of mutual respect."[4]

Collating available testimonial and documentary evidence, it seems clear that the relationship between Manuel Buendía and José Antonio Zorrilla Pérez was one of mutual utility rather than personal affinity. "They respected each other," Buendía's widow emphasized, "but were always very proper." Whenever he spoke to her about the DFS chief, she said, her husband always referred to him as "Zorrilla," never "José Antonio" or "El Güero" (Whitey). Buendía's familiar form of address in the letter cited by Rogelio Hernández did not alter Doña Dolores's assessment of their relationship, for within their cultural context it actually remains consistent with the customary formality she described. Buendía was more than half a generation older than Zorrilla and in congratulating the younger man on his felicitous handling of an emotionally

moving crime (the kidnapping of an infant girl), he drew on his own paternal sentiments to express more forcefully his gratitude of the moment. His closing embrace was
offered as an elder to someone not as far along life's path. He reasserted the formality
of their relationship, however, with his signature, a very formal *Manuel Buendía*.

Hernández seeks to reinforce the implication that Buendía and Zorrilla were genuine
cuates (pals) by placing Zorrilla in Buendía's private Lindavista study in early February
1984, where, according to Hernández, they had a heated argument over whether or not
Buendía was going to accept round-the-clock DFS protection, ostensibly in response
to threats resulting from his recent columns in *Excélsior*. Hernández attributes this
account to Buendía's widow, who, he writes, overheard the argument as she was about
to enter her husband's downstairs office with a tray of coffee for the two men.[5]

Not so, the widow informed us. To the contrary, she insisted, Zorrilla had never
been in their home. Not once. She had made this same statement to the press even
before Hernández completed his book about Zorrilla and the Buendía case.[6] Her husband, she told us, only entertained at their Lindavista residence once a year, on his
saint's day, when he would host a party for close friends and a few journalism students.
But Zorrilla never came to those gatherings, nor was he ever invited. He was not a
family friend, Doña Dolores explained. She knew who he was, she said, but did not
actually meet him until the night of her husband's assassination.

The matter of Zorrilla having placed Buendía under DFS protection is a significant contextual datum in the sequence of events leading up to the columnist's homicide. From the second week in February through mid-May 1984, DFS agents watched
Buendía's house and immediate neighborhood and tailed the columnist wherever he
went. Buendía complained more than once to Zorrilla about this unwelcome violation
of his privacy, but to no avail. Doña Dolores, for her part, not knowing what to make
of this sudden DFS intrusion into their lives, remained courteous in her interactions
with the agents posted outside their home. She would bring them coffee and provided
a power outlet for an electric light they had set up on the sidewalk, but she did not
allow them inside the house.

The purpose of this DFS vigilance has never been clarified. While Zorrilla insisted
that it was in response to heightened threats against Buendía occasioned by recent
columns, no single topic stands out from what Buendía had been writing all along that
might suddenly warrant police protection. As Rogelio Hernández perceptively notes,
however, rather than any particular topic or column, the real threat to Manuel Buendía
was the thread of connections linking seemingly disparate national security matters
that ran through his Red Privada columns: "the CIA, the planting of disinformation,
arms trafficking, paramilitary groups like *Los Tecos*, drugs, the activities of State security agents, and even the smuggling of contraband goods through the Gulf ports of
Veracruz with the complicity of the oil workers' union." Few of Buendía's readers
noticed that thread, Hernández observed, but to those in the know it was apparent
that Buendía was connecting the dots.[7]

In this light, Zorrilla's imposition of DFS protection would appear to have been a
warning rather than a practical measure to safeguard the columnist's personal security.
And Buendía no doubt understood it as such. Under the guise of personal protection,

the DFS also surveilled his every move, which, in view of Buendía's assassination barely three weeks after the operation ended, was likely Zorrilla's primary purpose. Hernández refers to DFS agent reports that record Buendía's daily routine, as well as all his contacts during the three and a half months he was under DFS surveillance and even advance notice of forthcoming Red Privada columns. The surveillance group's final report was apparently submitted on 10 May 1984. Unfortunately, Hernández provides no information as to how he gained access to these reports or anything else about them.[8]

Hernández's version of the argument between Zorrilla and Buendía regarding DFS protection, supposedly overheard by the widow, brings us back to the murky matter of the two alleged phone conversations about Zorrilla's links to drug traffickers discussed in chapter 8. There was indeed a heated conversation between Buendía and the DFS chief overheard by the widow, but it was not the one Hernández describes in his book. Rather it was a telephone call from Zorrilla one night toward the end of 1983. Doña Dolores could not recall the exact date but said it was sometime between November of that year, "when her husband had surgery [to remove his appendix]," and May 1984.

The call came after they had gone to bed, and she remembered it distinctly, she told us, because of her husband's uncustomarily strong language. Manuel made a point of not using profanity in her presence, she explained, but on that occasion he responded to Zorrilla with a torrent of expletives she had not heard him utter before. She also recalled that he did not simply hang up the phone that night but rather had angrily slammed it back on the receiver. When she asked him what had happened, he replied opaquely that Zorrilla was "involved in drugs," then dismissed the call, urging her to go back to sleep.

Doña Dolores may have recounted this incident to Rogelio Hernández as well. Whether he then transformed her account into an argument between Zorrilla and Buendía in Buendía's downstairs study we do not know, but we think that is probably the case. In any event, Hernández clearly took excessive literary license in reporting a purportedly verbatim exchange between the two men, since Buendía's widow denied it ever happened and therefore could not have given him even the gist of such a conversation. At the same time, her assertion to us that her husband had intimated Zorrilla was "involved in drugs" lends some credence to the special prosecutor's contention that Buendía and Zorrilla had referred to that involvement over the phone. Contrary to what the special prosecutor averred in his final report on the Buendía case, however, the circumstances of the nighttime call Doña Dolores described to us, as well as her husband's violent reaction to it, diminish the likelihood that Buendía was prepared to tape-record that, or any other, telephone conversation with the DFS chief on so delicate a subject.

There were also imprecisions in Hernández's account of Buendía's murder that Doña Dolores wished to clarify. Her husband, she told us, was carrying his own handgun when he was killed, not the one Zorrilla had given him. It was a 9 mm semiautomatic with the gold initials "MB" inlaid in the grip. Zorrilla returned it to her a few days later, she said, along with Buendía's vehicle, personal effects, and documents, but not his DFS credential, which had allowed him to carry the gun. (Zorrilla could have recovered Buendía's personal weapon from the columnist's 58 South Insurgentes office rather than from his body.) A few items had been returned to the widow that same evening shortly after she arrived at the crime scene, including the fountain pen that had been partially severed by one of the assassin's bullets. She used the pen one last time to sign the autopsy authorization, then had it mounted in an oval frame for permanent display.

Doña Dolores was puzzled as well by Hernández's reconstruction of the actual shooting. The killer could not have tugged on Manuel's trench coat, she noted, because her husband had thrown it over his shoulders like a cape; his arms were not in the sleeves, so together with his own reflexive movement, any tug from behind would have pulled the coat off. Yet when she arrived on the scene a short while after the shooting, she found her husband lying on his back on the sidewalk, "presumably where he had fallen," with the trench coat still over his shoulders and no sign of it having been pulled askew. Moreover, she said, the initial reports indicated that the gunman had fired the fatal shots without laying a hand on his victim. Then there were other reports of the body having been manhandled and moved by DFS agents searching Buendía's clothes.[9] Who could know, for certain, what had transpired in the first minutes following Manuel Buendía's demise?

As for the official resolution of the Buendía case, Doña Dolores said simply, "My husband's murder was too well planned to have been as simple as the authorities now present it. The business about drugs [being the motive], I just don't believe it." During a personal conversation with Federal District regent Manuel Camacho Solís sometime after Zorrilla's arrest, she recounted, Camacho had asked her if she believed Zorrilla to be the mastermind behind Don Manuel's homicide. "Am I speaking with the head of the Federal District," she inquired, "or am I speaking with attorney Camacho Solís?" "With attorney Camacho Solís," he replied. "Then how," she asked, "am I to believe it

María Dolores Ábalos Lebrija,
widow of Manuel Buendía.
(Sylvia E. Bartley)

was Zorrilla when much more powerful interests were so obviously involved?" To this, she assured us, Camacho did not offer the slightest objection.

We decided that a follow-up session with Buendía's widow would be helpful, and she agreed to meet with us again two days later. This time we met in Buendía's downstairs study, where Matt Rothschild had also interviewed her five years earlier. The family had kept the study more or less as Buendía left it, preserving it, in effect, as a home museum of the columnist's legacy, now used by their twenty-three-year-old daughter Gabriela, who was herself studying journalism with the intention of perpetuating that legacy. After viewing the study during our initial visit, it occurred to us that a complete catalog of Buendía's books would provide useful insights into his mental universe, and we proposed to Doña Dolores that we undertake that task.

She replied that the study library was no longer the same as when her husband was alive. Moreover, he never used it as a reference library. Books related to his work, she explained, he kept at his Insurgentes Avenue office. There were many of them there, she added: dictionaries and specialized reference volumes; journalism texts; books about spies, the mafia, and organized crime; police novels; and even literary works and books on music and the arts. After his death, she brought some of those books home and gave the rest to the newly created Fundación Manuel Buendía. Consequently, she did not feel that the disorganized selection of volumes then occupying Buendía's study bookshelves really reflected her husband's intellectual world.

We thought a representative selection of titles could yet be recovered and that the idea still had merit but did not press our proposal. We spent the next hour and a half discussing further aspects of the assassination. Doña Dolores detailed for us her movements on the night of the slaying. She expressed revulsion at Zorrilla's utter hypocrisy in his feigned sympathy and remorse over her husband's death. She also spoke to us at some length about Buendía's trips to Cuba and recounted how the whole family had been invited by the Cuban government to visit the island that July. (On a bookshelf just to the right of Buendía's desk were three photographs of Don Manuel together with Fidel Castro.) We allowed as how her husband's personal association with Castro was not an insignificant detail in the tangled web of interests surrounding his murder and that we would make an effort to pursue it directly with the Cubans.

We could not know as we took our leave of Buendía's widow that afternoon that she would not live out the year. She succumbed nine months later. Remarkably, Carlos Salinas de Gortari had presidential condolences inserted in the government's daily newspaper, *El Nacional*, in an official obituary that read more like a defense of the government's case against José Antonio Zorrilla than an expression of sympathy for Doña Dolores's survivors.

El Nacional—Viernes, 21 December 1990

Salinas de Gortari Expresses His Condolences

MARÍA DOLORES ÁBALOS, WIDOW OF MANUEL BUENDÍA DIES

   * Survived by her three children
     J. Manuel, Gabriela, and J. Carlos

* Her death does not interfere with
Zorrilla's trial: Morales L.

ARIEL VELÁZQUEZ

President Carlos Salinas de Gortari expressed his deepest sorrow for the death of María Dolores Ábalos Lebrija, wife of who in life was one of the country's most distinguished journalists, Manuel Buendía Téllezgirón.

In a note of condolence, the Executive-in-Chief has joined the Buendía Ábalos family in their grief. News of her death has caused great dismay in official, political, and media circles around the nation.

Victim of a liver ailment, she succumbed in the early hours of yesterday. Following the wake in chapel 32 of a funeral agency on Sullivan street, her body was cremated in the Spanish Pantheon.

Personalities from diverse spheres visited the funeral chapel to express their condolences to the Buendía children: José Manuel, Gabriela, and Juan Carlos, ages 28, 23, and 18, respectively.

On behalf of her brothers and herself, Gabriela Buendía Ábalos (daughter) expressed gratitude for the expressions of support they had received.

She also said that their mother was hospitalized the day before yesterday around four o'clock in the afternoon at Guadalupe Tepeyac Hospital, located on the corner of Insurgentes and Ticomán, in the Lindavista district, where she succumbed a short while later.

It represented a great responsibility for them, Gabriela expressed, to be the children of a man who in life was one of the most widely read journalists, and of their mother, who in the family sphere always motivated and loved them.

Federal District attorney general Ignacio Morales Lechuga, for his part, assured those present that the death of Señora Ábalos de Buendía would in no way hinder the criminal prosecution of ex-federal security director José Antonio Zorrilla for masterminding the murder of the journalist Manuel Buendía, inasmuch as she has already testified and the evidence she provided has been duly recorded.

As is known, Buendía's widow overheard some conversations between Zorrilla Pérez and her husband, which is why she has been considered a key piece in the case.

Buendía's widow, of course, could only have overheard her husband's end of any such conversation, since by her own insistent testimony Zorrilla was never in their home and, as she never accompanied her husband on work-related matters, she would only have chanced to overhear him speaking with the former DFS chief on the telephone. Now the Salinas administration was taking the cynical opportunity of the widow's demise to assert through published presidential condolences that Doña Dolores had overheard multiple conversations (*algunas charlas*) incriminating Zorrilla as the mastermind behind her husband's homicide. Special Prosecutor García Domínguez claimed that Buendía had tape-recorded two of those conversations, although, as noted in chapter 8, it was most improbable that either man would have discussed such matters over an open phone line and the government never established that the alleged tapes actually existed. The widow, for her part, stated clearly to us that there had been a single phone call from Zorrilla to her husband and that she had testified solely about that one call, whose actual content she did not know beyond her husband's opaque comment that the DFS chief "was involved in drugs."

We met several times during our March 1990 sojourn in the Federal District with Miguel Ángel Sánchez de Armas, cofounder of the Fundación Manuel Buendía and founding editor of the professional media journal *Revista mexicana de comunicación*. At our initial meeting shortly after arriving in Mexico City, he suggested that we do a follow-up interview with the now former special prosecutor for the Buendía case, Miguel Ángel García Domínguez. We were incredulous. In light of García Domínguez's anger over the feature we had published about him two years before, as well as our continuing criticism of the way the Mexican authorities had handled the Buendía case, we thought it unlikely that he would wish to meet with us a second time. But Sánchez de Armas insisted that "El Doctor" held no grudge and would in fact be willing to talk to us. The two of them had obviously discussed the matter previously, and our colleague, it seemed, was not idly tossing out the idea of a second interview. When I reached García Domínguez by phone later that day, he was quite affable, indicated to me that he would indeed be pleased to meet with us, and invited us to his home a few days later.

García Domínguez's Mexico City residence was an unpretentious home of understated elegance on a quiet street in the capital's Churubusco district. We arrived a little before 10:30 a.m. on Monday, 13 March, and, after salutations and small talk, spent the next three and a half hours discussing the Buendía case. García Domínguez appeared to have recovered from his bout with throat cancer. His voice had the same raspy quality we had noted two years earlier, but he spoke easily and generally seemed to be in good health. It was also apparent that having us there served some private agenda, no doubt related to his pending appointment to Mexico's Supreme Court and, above all, defense of his professional image as the judicial authority primarily responsible for resolving the most celebrated crime in recent Mexican history.

We initiated the interview by observing that the motive adduced for the assassination of Manuel Buendía ("the victim's knowledge of Zorrilla's ties to the drug trade") seemed inconsistent with the manner in which the homicide had been perpetrated. If the object of the slaying was simply "to keep the rooster from singing," we reasoned, then it seemed unlikely that the assassins would have exposed the gunman to the unnecessary risk of assaulting his victim in plain view of so many potential witnesses. There were many other, more convenient places where the killing could have been accomplished had the very brazenness of the act itself not been a calculated part of the crime.

That is what we see in the related homicide of Gobernación investigator José Luis Esqueda Gutiérrez, for which Zorrilla was also charged and convicted. The motive adduced for Esqueda's murder was the same as in the Buendía case, yet Esqueda was shot in the back of the head, at 4:30 a.m., on a quiet residential street.[10] In contrast, we implied, the brazenly visible Buendía killing would appear to have been both an execution and a message—a cautionary message to members of the media, as well as to key actors in Mexico's political establishment. Manuel Buendía had public stature. José Luis Esqueda did not.

García Dominguez responded with a discourse on the nature and exercise of power in Mexico. Presidential power, he explained, is broad but not deep (*es omnímodo, pero no es profundo*), whereas police power is narrow but also deep.[11] Consequently, within their own realm, Mexican police agencies often wield greater effective power than the president of the republic. And if power corrupts, he emphasized, in Mexico police power corrupts totally, especially at the senior command level. Agency directors like Zorrilla typically see themselves as untouchable and therefore act with complete abandon. It would not even occur to Zorrilla, he averred, to view a crowded public space as posing potential risks to a DFS assassin.

Our mistake, García Domínguez stated, was not having taken into account the Mexican cultural milieu in which the Buendía assassination had occurred. To draw conclusions from the particulars of how that crime was committed was to impose culturally biased criteria of analysis on a societal milieu where they did not apply. The manner of commission, he insisted, was irrelevant. That Buendía was slain in full public view, while Esqueda was killed on an empty street late at night, both ostensibly for the same motive, had no material bearing on either homicide. In Mexico, he wished us to believe, police assassins target their victims as readily on a congested rush-hour avenue as on an empty back street at 4:30 in the morning. Their only concern is where they can most easily approach the target. All other factors are extraneous to the task at hand and can be managed.

We thought it a specious argument reflective of García Domínguez's own cultural hubris in his appraisal of us. (Lest anyone doubt that Mexican assassins, like assassins everywhere, carefully plan their hits, we direct readers' attention to the stunning first-hand testimony of a veteran drug cartel hit man published in 2011 by Nation Books under the title *El Sicario: The Autobiography of a Mexican Assassin*.[12]) It was our perception that García Domínguez's opening discourse on the culture and social psychology of Mexican law enforcement sought to dissuade us from pursuing a line of reasoning that called into question his own, now official resolution of the Buendía case and to do so by suggesting that, as foreigners, we did not really understand the cultural subtleties of criminal behavior in Mexico. His attempt to dismiss us as American naïfs, however, was belied by the evident fact that he felt a need to revisit the case with us and to do so in the privacy of his own home.

Before proceeding further, García Domínguez insisted on establishing ground rules for our interview. He had no political ambitions, he explained, at least not in the narrow sense, but was expecting to be appointed to an important post (justice of Mexico's Supreme Court) and did not wish to jeopardize that appointment by having inconvenient statements he might make to us about the still sensitive Buendía case appear in the press. Unless he indicated otherwise, we were free to use whatever information he gave us as long as we did not attribute it to him until after he had been confirmed in his new position. If we agreed to honor this request, as we assured him we would, he promised to answer our questions fully and candidly.

Once agreed on the terms of our interview, we proceeded to discuss the special prosecutor's investigation for the next two-plus hours, in the course of which García Domínguez did, in fact, speak with notable candor, sharing various pieces of information not reported previously. In the end, he told us, he had made the case that was possible within the judicial and political constraints of contemporary Mexico: a mastermind, three accomplices, and a material killer. The conviction of Zorrilla, Prado Hurtado, Pérez Carmona, Naya Suárez, and Moro Ávila Camacho, he acknowledged, did not preclude the possible involvement of other individuals and interests opportunistically associated with the drug traffickers in furtherance of their own agendas. But, as a practical matter, he had no hope of establishing the truth or falsity of such hypotheses and had therefore made no effort to do so beyond a few tentative inquiries.

Like other key people in Mexican judicial, law enforcement, military, and government circles, García Domínguez had developed a professional relationship with U.S. officials. Even before his appointment as special prosecutor, he told us, he had asked established contacts in the American embassy for whatever information they might have about the Buendía assassination. Those contacts were convinced, he said, that Zorrilla was behind the killing but could provide no evidence that would stand up in court. Subsequently, after he had completed his investigation and those charged had been arrested, he met again at the U.S. embassy with senior American officials (*altos oficiales*) to formally request any evidence in U.S. possession that would strengthen the case against Zorrilla and his codefendants. Within a few days, he recounted, the Americans had informed him that neither in Washington nor at the embassy was there any documentation responsive to his request—a reply, he acknowledged, that could be interpreted more than one way.

Midway into the interview we dropped the name Hans Klaus, derived from an ostensibly fictitious character (Hansen Klaus) in a pulp novel purporting to resolve the Buendía case, whose publication had suspiciously been timed to coincide with the 1988 presidential election and the rapidly approaching end of the special prosecutor's mandate. The book's author, Felipe Victoria Zepeda, a former Ministerio Público investigator turned journalist, presents "Klaus" as a CIA operative with direct access to Ambassador John Gavin (Joseph Garden), as well as to the American columnist Jack Anderson (Frank Sanderson), implying that Klaus had played a role in the Buendía assassination.[13] We had interviewed Victoria the year before and concluded that he was one of various disinformation agents then actively endeavoring to muddy the waters around the case. His publisher even attempted to persuade the Fundación Manuel Buendía to promote the book, which, had the approach succeeded, would have served the dual purpose of boosting sales and discrediting the foundation.

Victoria told us that Hans Klaus was the CIA station chief, that he knew Klaus personally and saw him with some frequency, and that the two of them had developed a mutually respectful relationship. "Hemos aprendido a tener cierta amistad" is the way Victoria expressed it. He also wanted us to know that he traveled frequently to Southern California, implying that those trips had something to do with the Americans.[14] When many years later we learned that Felipe Victoria had served as one of Héctor Berréllez's Operation Leyenda informants, the circle of our suspicions that he had been compromised by American intelligence closed.[15]

Had the name Hans Klaus come up in the special prosecutor's Buendía investigation?, we now asked García Domínguez. Instantly, the whole tenor of the interview changed. Until that moment, "El Doctor" had been sitting back comfortably on a couch, facing us and seemingly in control of the conversation. But on hearing the name Hans Klaus he visibly tensed, slid forward to the edge of the couch, folded his hands around his knees, and fixed us in a strangely intense gaze. We had crossed some invisible line into prohibited territory, his body language conveyed, where agreed-upon ground rules of discretion on our part, frankness on his, no longer applied. "Yes," he said softly, "that person was in Mexico at the time of the Buendía assassination. But, predictably, no cooperation was forthcoming from that quarter."

As special prosecutor for the Buendía case, García Domínguez had subpoenaed Victoria Zepeda to testify but did not consider him a reliable witness. A background check had found no evidence that Victoria had ever completed his law studies, despite his habit of using the professional title *licenciado*, and García Domínguez thought he exhibited the compensatory psychological profile of a wannabe attorney who had failed to make the academic grade. He thought, too, that Victoria's journalistic endeavors were part of that psychological compensation, that he had also failed to earn peer acceptance as a media professional, and that he had sought to overcome that failure by inserting himself into a major news story with a thinly veiled fictional potboiler.

García Domínguez's psychologizing aside, it was apparent to us from our own contact with Victoria that he was a viable candidate for recruitment as an intelligence asset. His boast to us of a personal association with the CIA station chief may have been self-serving blather, or not, but his concerted efforts to indict the character and motives of Manuel Buendía generally, and to sway us in particular, at the very least made him a serendipitous agency asset. Whatever the case, his introduction of Hans Klaus into the mix of characters surrounding the Buendía affair appears to have been a matter of some import, although we have not been able to determine precisely why.

Felipe Victoria had played us for a couple of gringo naïfs, warning us off the Buendía case, then feeding us a full plate of horse pucky about the victim and the circumstances of his death. What we were doing, he insisted, was dangerous, and we should be very careful. He himself had been severely beaten the year before as a consequence of his own involvement in the case, ostensibly to prevent him from participating in the special prosecutor's interrogation of Zorrilla Pérez. He was, he wanted us to know, a ten-year veteran investigator with the Public Ministry and was working out of its central office when the Buendía assassination occurred, which is how he had come to be so well informed about the case. What he gave us, however, was bald disinformation.

"Manuel Buendía had been a CIA agent," by Victoria's preposterous account, and his widow now received monthly "pension" payments from the U.S. embassy. Victoria also lived in the Buenavista district, he told us, and had personally seen the official envelopes with the embassy seal addressed to the widow. He even claimed to have persuaded a mailman to allow him to photocopy one of the checks before delivering it. Only a feverish mind, we thought at the time, could imagine that such payments would ever be made in this manner, or that even a couple of "gringo" investigators would give credence to such a preposterous scenario.

The CIA itself had provided Buendía with the apocryphal list of Mexican officials involved in the drug trade, Victoria further alleged, and had given a copy of the same list to Jack Anderson. Among the names on that list, he said, was José Antonio Zorrilla Pérez, whom Buendía then tried to blackmail, which was the real motive behind his murder. There had been no larger conspiracy, Victoria wanted us to believe, just a blackmail attempt gone sour. It was a disjointed, hopelessly flawed account, whose obvious inconsistencies he could not resolve, nor had he anticipated, apparently, that we might know enough to point them out. He had no answer at all, for example, when we asked him who had been protecting Zorrilla from prosecution all those years since Buendía's murder.

García Domínguez, for his part, dismissed as totally baseless Victoria's allegations that Buendía had used knowledge of Zorrilla's ties to drug traffickers to blackmail the DFS chief, that Buendía had been suborned by Secretary of Government Manuel Bartlett Díaz, or that he had ever collaborated with the CIA. He likewise dismissed Victoria Adato's earlier hypotheses of a possible crime of passion. Manuel Buendía was neither gay nor a skirt chaser, the evidence had persuaded him. Buendía kept no mistress and did not actively pursue women, but rather was himself occasionally pursued by media professionals of the opposite gender with whom he regularly associated. In those instances when he may have accepted such advances, García Domínguez concluded, it almost certainly was by way of completing a shared intellectual relationship rather than satisfying the primal sex drive. The special prosecutor's investigators had confirmed that Buendía did not expend personal resources of any consequence on female friends.

Of potentially greater relevance for an eventual resolution of the case was testimonial evidence obtained by the special prosecutor from several sources indicating that Buendía indeed intended to continue writing about drug trafficking as a national security issue. Significantly, the first person to confirm this intention on Buendía's part was "a certain well-known general," as García Domínguez referred to him, presumably Secretary of Defense Gen. Juan Arévalo Gardoqui. In a casual conversation supposedly unrelated to the special prosecutor's investigation, García Domínguez told us, "the general" had recounted how, following Buendía's 25 May 1984 lecture to an audience of cadets at the Secretariat of Defense, he and another senior officer had met with the columnist in an adjacent office, where Buendía had discussed more fully with them his intention to continue treating the topic of drugs and national security in his Red Privada column. Buendía had recognized the danger of delving into that topic, according to Arévalo, but he considered the threat to Mexico's national security too great for him not to bring it to public attention.

García Domínguez also provided us with additional insights into the conduct of the special prosecutor's investigation. He was furious with himself, he said, for not having realized until after the case was closed that Octavio González was an ex-DFS agent, all the more so because González "exhibited all the classic traits" of a federal security operative. He felt deceived by Rogelio Hernández, who had introduced González to him as "an Excélsior colleague"; by Miguel Ángel Sánchez de Armas, who had not alerted him to González's background; and, above all, by Ángel Buendía, who as front man of the journalists' oversight group was the direct link to the administration and the person who submitted the oversight group's expense invoices to Secretary of Government

Manuel Bartlett Díaz. While he was constantly having to fight for the release of approved funds to cover the operating expenses of the special prosecutor's office, he recalled acidly, Gobernación was expending significant sums to support an independent oversight group, with a major part of that group's expenses being generated by an ex-DFS agent whose assignment was to spy on the special prosecutor. The web of intrigue, we would eventually learn, was even more intricate than García Domínguez had imagined. At the same time as Octavio González was spying on the special prosecutor, Gobernación had tasked Lawrence Harrison to spy on the oversight group.[16] What García Domínguez most feared, he repeated to us during this second interview, was not a professional hit or some reprisal against his family but simply making a fool of himself.

PLAZA PÚBLICA: LA MUERTE DE MIGUEL NOCHEBUENA
La Jornada—Viernes, 16 June 1989
Miguel Ángel Granados Chapa

On 15 June 1988 a sleazy book appeared with the title *The Case of the Slain Journalist*, subtitled "A sure trail to the capture of his killers." Its author is a lawyer and ex-Ministerio Público agent by the name of Felipe Victoria Zepeda. The book is wrapped in ambiguity, as on both the front and back covers and in a preliminary editorial note explicit reference is made to the murder of Don Manuel Buendía, while the author invents a character with the grossly allusive name of Miguel Nochebuena who is killed on the same date as Don Manuel. To make clear the play on names, the president of the Republic of Nova Hispania, where the plot unfolds, is called Manuel de Sevilla.

Pulp literature of this sort does not warrant notice in the pages of a respectable newspaper like this one. That is why we gave it no notice when it first came out, as well as because it took the liberty of slandering the fictitious Nochebuena, i.e., Buendía, who is depicted as a corrupt journalist "not adverse to earning thousands of pesos by not exposing people on whom he had gathered dirt." Indeed, the author implies that this practice constitutes the cause of his protagonist's death.

But now the book's publisher, Octavio Colmenares, in the prologue to a new book by Victoria Zepeda (episodes from his time as a Ministerio Público agent), makes explicit what had only been crudely implied. Which now changes how we view it. The general manager of EDAMEX, the firm that publishes both books, says that Victoria Zepeda "revealed on the basis of hard evidence that the crime's mastermind is the man who served as head of the Federal Security Directorate at the beginning of the De la Madrid administration." Then, lamenting that so much effort and money had been expended on Special Prosecutor Miguel Ángel García Domínguez's inquiry, Colmenares concludes, "It would have been so easy to resolve this matter, had they only availed themselves of the reliable information revealed by Licenciado Victoria Zepeda!"

It would have been simple indeed had it not been for the lame effort to disguise the protagonists of the case with obvious pseudonyms and the fact that, despite the novel's subtitle, no explicit charges are actually made.

Earlier on the day of our second interview with Manuel Buendía's widow we had paid an unannounced visit to the editorial offices of EDAMEX, Felipe Victoria's publisher. We told the doorman that we wished to see Licenciado Octavio Colmenares. He had us sign the registry, then said we would find the *licenciado* on the third floor. We

The Case of the Slain Journalist: A Sure Trail to the Capture of His Killers (1988), by Felipe Victoria Zepeda, a character assassination of Manuel Buendía that spuriously attributes the victim's murder to attempted blackmail of DFS chief Zorrilla Pérez. Ironically, the opening paragraphs of Buendía's 14 May 1984 Red Privada column superimposed on the book's cover do point to his true assassins.

handed the general manager's receptionist an *unomásuno* business card and explained our wish to see Colmenares. He was preparing to leave when we arrived but, on learning the purpose of our visit, invited us into his office. He was a pleasant man, probably in his fifties, well groomed, with a bit of gray in his otherwise wavy black hair, of medium stature, dressed in a blue suit and white silk shirt with a red silk tie. His office was spacious, well lighted, and furnished in generic executive modern.[17]

Colmenares told us that Felipe Victoria's fictionalized account of the Buendía assassination had not been much of an editorial success. The first edition had numbered three thousand copies, he said, and when Zorrilla was arrested they had published an additional three thousand, of which one thousand remained. The book would have been more successful, Colmenares thought, if Victoria had used the real names, but he was unwilling to do so because he had been attacked and severely beaten the year before, ostensibly in connection with the Buendía case, and was afraid to name people explicitly. Colmenares added that EDAMEX would not have been averse to publishing the actual names and that during the previous administrations of Luis Echeverría and José López Portillo it had published much more controversial titles, which had occasioned audits of its financial records, as well as a failed attempt on his life and another on one of his authors.

Colmenares shared Felipe's thesis (he constantly referred to Victoria by his first name) that Manuel Buendía was far from upright, that Buendía had demanded payoffs, and that this was the reason he was killed. Colmenares had heard directly "from persons of influence," he told us, that they had been blackmailed by Buendía. And no, he replied to our direct question, Felipe's book had not been subsidized by outside parties. That, he averred, would have exposed EDAMEX to potentially serious problems. They had simply paid Felipe the standard author's fees, he stated, and handled the book as any other commercial publication. Nor had EDAMEX had any communication with the special prosecutor's office, although Colmenares said he did not know whether Felipe might have been subpoenaed.

In response to our observation about *unomásuno* editor Manuel Becerra Acosta's allusion to the risk of publishing our 1985 interview with Matthew Rothschild regarding the Buendía case, Colmenares remarked—"with our forgiveness"—that for Becerra Acosta it might indeed have been risky "because he definitely was extracting large payoffs from the government." Becerra's successor, Luís Gutiérrez Rodríguez, for his part, had assured us six months earlier that no doubt the Mexican government itself had underwritten Felipe Victoria's *Case of the Slain Journalist*.[18] That afternoon, following our impromptu conversation with Octavio Colmenares, we brought a copy of Victoria's book to Buendía's widow. She knew about it, Doña Dolores had told us during our first interview, and, its slanderous content notwithstanding, she wished to have a copy to complete her collection of writings about the case.

Las lecciones del caso Zorrilla

unomásuno—Miércoles, 21 June 1989 (editorial)

With the capture of Manuel Buendía's material killer, we are about to learn the details of a case that has understandably attracted national attention. Even when the Federal

District's attorney general had revealed the motive for the homicide (none other than the dark interests of the drug trade), the touchstone of the case remained to be put in place so as not to leave the crime unpunished: the capture of Juan Rafael Moro Ávila Camacho, the man who shot the famous journalist in the back.

Now that the shadows have been removed, there is no longer any basis for continuing suspicions. Zorrilla ordered Buendía killed because, presumably, Buendía intended to expose the federal security director's ties to narcotics trafficking. There were no political motives, aside from the fact (impossible to ignore) that Zorrilla, a senior government official, colluded with the drug lords. (José Antonio Zorrilla Pérez also ordered the murder of the agent who passed Buendía the information about the link between drug trafficking and the Federal Security Directorate.)

. . .

The crime against Manuel Buendía has been clarified, and we ought not dispute the merit of District Attorney General Ignacio Morales Lechuga or fail to recognize the political resolution of President Carlos Salinas de Gortari. They have demonstrated that when there is the will to follow through on investigations, even the most difficult cases will be solved.

When we first read this editorial in post–Becerra Acosta *unomásuno*, we were appalled by what struck us as sycophantic deference to the Salinas administration and an uncritical readiness to accept its version of events in the Buendía case. The shadows long obscuring Buendía's death certainly had not been removed, and there was perhaps even more reason now to suspect that the actual motive and players remained carefully concealed in a shroud of deception. We were also put off by the inflated credit given Salinas and Morales Lechuga, when so many others had labored determinedly over the previous half decade to bring Buendía's assassins to justice. We decided then and there that our association with the paper had come to an end.

As these things often work out, the occasion to formalize our break with *unomásuno* seemed to come serendipitously in the fall of 1989, when the paper's new editor traveled to Milwaukee to participate on a public panel titled "Journalism and Politics in Mexico" at the local University of Wisconsin campus. As the University of Wisconsin–Milwaukee Department of History's Latin America specialist and because of his own connection to *unomásuno*, it fell to Russell to chair that panel, in anticipation of which he prepared a two-and-a-half-page statement explaining our nine-year association with the paper and the reason why we now felt compelled to terminate that relationship. Before delivering this statement, however, we met with Luis Gutiérrez over lunch at Milwaukee's Phister Hotel, where he managed to dissuade us from breaking with the paper during the program later that afternoon.

He had met Manuel Buendía, admired his exceptional talent as an investigative journalist, and had steadfastly supported demands for a transparent resolution of his murder, Gutiérrez insisted. He had also dealt personally with Zorrilla Pérez and Bartlett Díaz. Buendía's assassination, he said, went higher than Zorrilla. When on one occasion in 1985 he had asked Bartlett why Zorrilla had been forced to abandon his candidacy for representative from Hidalgo to the national Chamber of Deputies, Bartlett had replied suggestively that it was because "Zorrilla had failed both him and the president." When we now showed Gutiérrez a copy of the *unomásuno* editorial about Zorrilla and the Buendía case that had so exercised us, he professed not to have seen it, saying that it had to have been written either in his absence or by some other staff-person to whom he had assigned that space. On reading it in our presence, he exclaimed, "Bartlett has to have been behind this!" He offered no explanation for how that might have happened with Bartlett Díaz now serving as education secretary in the new Salinas administration.

Gutiérrez acknowledged that he was a personal friend of the president, that Salinas had facilitated a credit arrangement that allowed Gutiérrez and several associates to purchase *unomásuno*, and that presidential press secretary Otto Granados Roldán had in fact exerted considerable editorial pressure on him, although Gutiérrez claimed that he had brushed it aside. The paper clearly remained vulnerable, however, inasmuch as its new owners had assumed a heavy debt and would be given no further financial assistance beyond the paid government advertisements that kept all of Mexico's daily newspapers afloat. Gutiérrez's upbeat assurance that he intended to bring a broader spectrum of views to the paper and adhere to its original lofty purpose was not persuasive. Salinas had a coherent program, he insisted. But the problem for the country's—and the paper's—future, he added presciently, was that the PRI showed no signs of making the political adjustments required by the president's program. The implication, we understood, was that *unomásuno* would have to adjust, too, almost certainly in ways that we would find unpalatable. The final article we would write for the paper had in fact already appeared four weeks earlier, the last in a three-part series on alleged Cuban links to the international drug trade.[19]

Mexico City, 15 March 1990. Thursday—Returning from the Centro Cultural around 8:00 p.m., we find a message at the Mónaco from Anatoly Borovkov: "Call right away." He answers immediately: "Can you meet us in an hour at the Hotel Premier?"

"Of course!"

We change our clothes and set out walking west along Reforma. Anatoly is coming by taxi, as Wednesday is his day of the week not to drive—part of a new program to lower smog levels in the Federal District. (Anatoly, we recall from previous visits, drives a red Mercury Topaz with Texas plates.) The Premier is on a side street a block south of Reforma. Anatoly calls out to us from across the street: *"¡Rassel! ¡Por aquí!"* We cross to hugs, kisses, and back slaps. He recognizes us on a dark street in the midst of a city of over 20 million. We last saw one another five months ago, in October.

Viktor comes right down and we take a table in the hotel restaurant to talk. At 70, he looks fit. We last saw him a year ago, ran into each other quite by accident at El Hórreo, a restaurant specializing in Spanish cuisine just off the Alameda. As we banter and catch up, I am struck by the four of us: two Soviets and two Americans meeting in a third country, communicating in Spanish. Hardly the old stereotype of bushy-browed Russians in baggy pants skulking around with ridiculous accents!

—S. E. Bartley, journal entry

Having known Anatoly Borovkov for a number of years and interacted with him in both the Soviet Union and Mexico, as well as in the United States, we assumed that he was at the very least a Soviet intelligence asset and perhaps an active Committee for State Security (KGB) agent. (Some years later Sergo Mikoyan, former editor of the Soviet Latin American studies journal *Latinskaia Amerika* and son of veteran Soviet Politburo member Anastas I. Mikoyan, would confirm as much to us.[20]) Viktor Volsky, in turn, as director of the Soviet Union's primary academic institution for the study of contemporary Latin America, was in regular contact with Soviet intelligence personnel and, some twenty years earlier, had actually attempted to involve Russell in an information-gathering project whose purpose was transparently not academic. We took for granted that both the Soviets and the Cubans had developed intelligence on the Buendía assassination, and we intended to probe our contacts in both countries for any information they might be willing to share. This was our opportunity to approach the Soviets.

We had discussed our Buendía investigation with Borovkov previously, and now he and Volsky asked for an update. Where were we headed with it? After listening to our summary and considering the hypothesis that Buendía had been killed because of what he had learned about the U.S.-Mexico connection in the proxy *contra* war against Sandinista Nicaragua, Volsky wanted to know how we expected to prove it. It reminded him, he said, of the Kennedy assassination, where twenty years afterward books were

The authors with Viktor Volsky in Moscow, June 1981. (Courtesy of the Institute of Latin America of the USSR Academy of Sciences)

still appearing with new hypotheses. How was it possible, after all, to establish CIA involvement in Buendía's death? He then recounted how three years earlier he had been interviewed about the Buendía murder by *Excélsior*'s Moscow correspondent and that, when asked who he thought was behind it, had suggested "the logical suspects" based on a consideration of who had most benefited from the killing.[21] With that in mind, Volsky wondered, were we not concerned for our own safety? Yes, we replied, but given the transcendence of the case we would not allow ourselves to be immobilized by such concerns.

Borovkov wanted to know what we thought of Zorrilla. Was he or was he not the mastermind behind the assassination? To our reply that we believed the ex-DFS chief had been sacrificed to cover for higher-ups, he agreed that was likely the case. We then asked him what he could tell us about some Soviet journalists whom we understood had been looking into the Buendía assassination and had recently visited the murder site accompanied by the victim's widow. He said he had not heard anything about them and knew nothing of their interest in Buendía. We subsequently learned from Miguel Ángel Sánchez de Armas that it was a crew of Soviet filmmakers working on a documentary about media repression in Latin America that had selected the Buendía case to illustrate the situation in Mexico. Whether that project ever came to fruition we do not know.

At this point in our conversation, I brought up the ethereal "Hans Klaus" and floated the possibility of their helping us determine whether or not he had in fact had anything to do with the Buendía homicide. All we were asking them to obtain for us, we emphasized, were yes or no answers to two questions. First, was this person in fact the man we had been told he was, that is, CIA station chief in Mexico? And, second, was he present in Mexico City on 30 May 1984? Both men studied us intently as we formulated this request but offered no direct reply, immediately turning the conversation to other, unrelated topics. It was clear to us both that they had comprehended perfectly what we were asking and it was probably within their ability to get those answers for us. They never did, which, in light of the historic collapse of the Soviet state that same year, was hardly surprising. We would not see or hear from either of them again.[22]

The following morning we spent an hour and a half at the Café París conversing with Miguel Ángel Sánchez de Armas about his personal recollections of Manuel Buendía and the events of 30 May 1984.[23] On the night of the assassination, Sánchez de Armas recounted, he did not arrive at the crime scene until after Buendía's corpse had been removed. He went unimpeded up to the victim's sixth-floor office, where he found Buendía's two assistants, Luis Soto and Juan Manuel Bautista, "at least one reporter," and several other persons he did not know. Zorrilla, he recalled, was no longer present.

The whole episode had been so emotionally trying for him, he told us, that his recollections had been reduced to disconnected slices of memory, "which explained why they had never subpoenaed him to testify." This was a curious and potentially significant detail, given that Sánchez de Armas had been a close associate of Manuel Buendía, considered Buendía his mentor, and was the one person most responsible for promoting Buendía's professional legacy following the assassination. Per standard investigative protocol, he should have been deposed by the district attorney general's staff and again by the special prosecutor. Asked over two decades later to confirm that he had, in fact, not been deposed by Victoria Adato, Renato Sales Gasque, or Miguel Ángel García Domínguez, nor questioned by DFS investigators, Sánchez de Armas replied that he had had "a cordial conversation over coffee" with Adato and her deputy, René Paz Horta, in Adato's private office. Insofar as he could tell, they had not recorded his remarks, nor had he signed any statement. That, he assured us, was the full extent of the authorities' interest in what he could tell them about the victim.[24]

Although the DFS had occupied Buendía's Insurgentes Avenue office just minutes after the shooting and would exert total control over that space for several weeks thereafter, by his own account Sánchez de Armas was given free access to the office, as were Buendía's two assistants. Soto and Bautista, for their part, were both interrogated over a period of weeks by DFS personnel, while Sánchez de Armas seems not to have been questioned at all. Nor, apparently, were any of Buendía's closest professional associates ever summoned to testify, which implies that a priori parameters had been established for an eventual resolution of the Buendía case and that investigative hypotheses arising from the potential testimony of those most familiar with the victim's work were not to be allowed on the table.[25]

Two days later we again sat down with Sánchez de Armas at the Café París, where he recorded a lengthy interview with Russell for the *Revista mexicana de comunicación*.[26] Afterward we picked up the thread of our previous conversation with a question about the integrity of the independent oversight group headed by Manuel Buendía's younger brother Ángel. It was true, he recalled, that the oversight group's expenses were paid by the Gobernación and that the largest portion of those expenses had been generated by Octavio González, the former DFS agent brought into the group as a private investigator by Rogelio Hernández. While he could appreciate Bartlett's wish to be seen as facilitating a transparent resolution of the Buendía case, and thus as having nothing to hide personally, Sánchez de Armas said he never could understand why the members of the oversight group had agreed to such an arrangement, as it compromised their operational integrity and placed in doubt the legitimacy of their purpose.

Revisiting the matter of Manuel Buendía's relations with women, which District Attorney General Victoria Adato had attempted to weave into a motive for murder and García Domínguez had dismissed as immaterial, we asked Sánchez de Armas about Buendía's alleged dalliances. In response, he essentially endorsed García Domínguez's characterization of those associations as primarily friendships rather than testosterone-driven liaisons. While there were no mistresses in Buendía's life, he does appear to have maintained a long-term relationship with a woman he had met in the early 1970s while working for CONACYT, Susana Fisher. According to Sánchez de Armas, when Buendía left his office the fateful evening of 30 May 1984, he was on his way to see her.

Susana Fisher was married to the mordantly erotic caricaturist Eko (Héctor Estanislao de la Garza Batorski), whose stunningly executed illustrations regularly appeared in *unomásuno*.[27] Eko and Fisher had separated but not formally terminated their marriage and apparently remained on amicable terms. There were even occasions, Sánchez de Armas told us, when Manuel Buendía was at Fisher's residence and Eko would drop by to chat. Following Buendía's assassination, Fisher feared that the authorities were going to implicate her in the homicide and initially ignored subpoenas to testify, but eventually she had to submit to questioning by Federal District prosecutors. Afterward she took temporary refuge in Spain, then returned to Mexico. As with Buendía's home, there was no police search of Fisher's residence, in part, perhaps, because of her close friendship with Sánchez de Armas and his ability to expose any fabricated crime-of-passion scenario involving her.[28]

We concluded that day's conversation with Sánchez de Armas by asking him about a heated exchange he had had the year before with *El Financiero* reporter Carlos Ramírez, who in an article questioning the official resolution of the Buendía case (excerpted in chapter 8) had harshly criticized the journalists' oversight group for publicly endorsing the special prosecutor's final report, which he described as a political whitewash. That report, Ramírez had protested, amounted to "the death certificate for a second slaying of Manuel Buendía," this one of his character. Given the innumerable questions raised by García Domínguez's summation of the case, he wrote, "the oversight group appears not to have overseen anything. They failed as a group, because they accepted the official version of events as valid. Despite the flimsiness of the prosecutor's charge, they endorse the official investigation and thus become accomplices to the cover-up." Ramírez concluded his otherwise justified excoriation of the government's case with a gratuitous slam at the Manuel Buendía Foundation. "What kind of professional and moral respectability can the Fundación Manuel Buendía have," he asked rhetorically, "if it has failed to promote a proper investigation of the murder of the journalist whose example it claims to respect?"[29]

Understandably, Sánchez de Armas took umbrage at Ramírez's critique of the special prosecutor's performance and of the posture adopted by the oversight group with regard to the results of García Domínguez's investigation. He responded a week later with an emotionally charged rebuttal that revealed personal doubts and insecurity about his own role in the Buendía affair, doubts and insecurity that we ourselves have perceived in our subsequent interactions with him. He was especially exercised by Ramírez's unwarranted salvo at the Buendía Foundation and replied with atypical ad hominem vehemence to what for Ramírez had been little more than a rhetorical afterthought. Of considerably greater significance from our perspective was Sánchez de Armas's explicit recognition of the possibility that the oversight group, and he personally, "had chanced to propose a public official [García Domínguez] to serve as special prosecutor who was already involved in a cover-up plot."[30]

Now, eight months later, Sánchez de Armas remarked to us that he was annoyed with himself for having allowed his emotions to dictate his response to Carlos Ramírez, above all because he considered himself a close friend of the Ramírez family. Carlos, he said, had developed into an exceptionally talented journalist but had a tendency to make extreme statements, as exemplified by what he had written about the Buendía Foundation. As the foundation's president, Sánchez de Armas had made a conscious effort to keep its activities separate from the work of the oversight group. Ramírez's readiness to defend Buendía against posthumous slights and offenses, he explained, stemmed from the fact that Carlos's father and Manuel Buendía had been fast friends, *cuates* who went hunting together in the mountains of Oaxaca and had often taken young Carlos along. Quite apart from these subjective factors, however, was the understandable offense Ramírez took at the oversight group's rush to endorse the official resolution of the Buendía assassination. It was the very same dismay we had felt over *unomásuno*'s editorial of 21 June 1989 proclaiming the Buendía case solved and the reason we had terminated our relationship with that paper.

IO

SECRET, NOFORN

As one of Mexico's most renowned investigative journalists, Manuel Buendía had stepped on a lot of toes by the time he was gunned down in May 1984. . . . It now appears Buendía, known by some as Mexico's Jack Anderson, was slain in a sweeping coverup of an international drug-dealing network that had the complicity of the Mexican government and had even looped in the CIA. The intrepid Buendía had tread uncomfortably close to illegal drug operations protected by Mexico's one-time version of the FBI, and used by the CIA to ship arms to contra guerrillas in Nicaragua.

—Jack Anderson and Dale van Atta, "A Mexican Journalist's Fatal Scoop" (21 August 1990)

In mid-March 1990, *unomásuno* police reporter Fernando Ramírez de Aguilar informed us that there would soon be an important revelation about the Buendía case in Los Angeles, California, and that we should watch for it. This information, he said, had come from "Hector Berreyes" (Berréllez), who was in charge of the DEA's investigation of the Enrique Camarena case, code named Operation Leyenda. Berréllez had given this heads-up to one of Fernando's colleagues, who in turn passed it on to him. Fernando also listed for us what he anticipated would prove to be the key linkages in the Buendía case: Manuel Buendía → "Kiki" Camarena → Miguel Aldana Ibarra → Gen. Juan Poblano Silva → Gen. Juan Arévalo Gardoqui → Veracruz.

Aldana Ibarra was head of the Mexican Federal Judicial Police, Poblano Silva was Arévalo Gardoqui's brother-in-law and commander of the Puebla military district, and Arévalo was Mexico's secretary of defense. The Veracruz link referred to an alleged CIA-run training camp for Nicaraguan *contras*, as well as the covert transshipment of arms to Central America in collusion with PEMEX, Mexico's national petroleum monopoly. President Salinas had ordered an investigation of Poblano Silva and Arévalo Gardoqui, Ramírez told us, which likely would be the next political bombshell of the new administration.[1]

Unbeknownst to us at the time, the previous September a mysterious government witness by the name of Lawrence Victor Harrison had given testimony before a federal grand jury in Los Angeles against Rubén Zuno Arce, brother-in-law of former Mexican president Luis Echeverría Álvarez. Harrison had been questioned by Assistant U.S. Attorney Manuel A. "Manny" Medrano, who elicited for the record the first pieces of a shadowy personal history in order to establish the witness's bona fides: law studies at the University of California, Berkeley; fluency in Spanish, French, and German; long-term residency in Mexico; work for the Mexican Secretariat of Government as an electronics and communications specialist; contact with top figures of the Guadalajara drug cartel; and a personal association with Zuno Arce dating back to the early 1970s. Medrano had taken Harrison through a line of questioning that placed Zuno at a saint's day party given by the Guadalajara cartel for Rafael Caro Quintero. That testimony then became the basis for indicting Zuno as a coconspirator in the February 1985 abduction, torture, interrogation, and murder of DEA special agent Enrique Camarena Salazar.[2]

While Harrison's grand jury testimony was relatively brief, it introduced more than enough information for any juror who considered it to wonder about the witness and what he had been doing in Mexico. When, for example, Medrano asked Harrison how he came to be in the house of drug boss Ernesto Fonseca Carrillo, Harrison testified, "I was at that house because I had been assigned to Mr. Fonseca. . . . I maintained various radio systems which were shared by him and the Federal Security Directorate and the Institute for Political and Social Investigations, which are units of the Mexican government, roughly equivalent to the CIA and FBI here. I had been assigned to his house, assigned to him personally to carry out the electronic duties that he gave me to do." Yet only one juror asked a question of the witness, and it had nothing to do with how he had come to be moving in such dubious circles. Was he a radio operator himself, the juror wanted to know? "I'm an amateur radio operator and I've been interested in electronics since I was 12 years old," Harrison replied.[3]

How Rubén Zuno Arce came to be detained in the United States, how he was subsequently charged, tried, convicted, and imprisoned as a coconspirator in the Camarena killing, and how Lawrence Harrison came to be the witness who set that process in motion are issues that place in doubt the integrity of the government's case against Zuno and raise serious questions about the ulterior purposes of his prosecution. When, as the case unfolded, it became evident that the Camarena and Buendía homicides were somehow related and that Harrison was a link between them, those questions urgently demanded answers, yet they were never directly addressed by either defense counsel or the media.

Zuno was first detained on 9 August 1989 at the San Antonio, Texas, airport on a previously issued DEA "hold" order. He had arrived in the United States on a regular commercial flight under his own name, as he had done on numerous other occasions during the four and a half years since the Camarena abduction. Notified of his detention by the Immigration and Naturalization Service (INS), the DEA asked the U.S. Attorney's Office in Los Angeles to obtain a material witness warrant, which was issued the following day by District Judge Edward Rafeedie. Zuno was immediately taken into custody by DEA agents, transferred to Los Angeles, and brought before a grand jury then considering indictments in the Camarena case.

Zuno answered all questions put to him by the grand jury, and on 5 September 1989 Judge Rafeedie ordered his release from custody. Despite the court order, however, Zuno was not released. Rather, at the DEA's request, INS officers transported him back to San Antonio, ostensibly for a hearing to determine whether or not he should be deported to Mexico. However, that hearing never materialized and the whole maneuver appears to have been a ruse to buy time for the U.S. Attorney's Office to bring in Lawrence Harrison as a government witness who could implicate Zuno in a prosecutable violation of the law. Two days later Harrison appeared before the empaneled grand jury and, based solely on his testimony, Zuno was indicted that same day for perjury, it being alleged that he had testified falsely when he denied knowing either Rafael Caro Quintero or Ernesto Fonseca Carrillo. No charges of involvement in the Camarena abduction were lodged against him at that time.

While Zuno's perjury trial was pending, he was freed on bail of two hundred thousand dollars and allowed to return to Mexico. He abided by the conditions of his release, even returning to Los Angeles on two occasions for pretrial hearings. Meanwhile, the Justice Department made a concerted effort to find a witness who could link Zuno to the Camarena kidnapping. In the later part of November 1989, DEA agents persuaded one Héctor Cervantes Santos to testify that he had seen Zuno at a meeting in early February 1985 where the kidnapping had been planned. Cervantes claimed to have worked as a handyman and bodyguard for Javier Barba Hernández, another of the principal figures in the Guadalajara drug cartel. The DEA essentially bought Cervantes's testimony against Zuno with a thirty-five-hundred-dollar advance and the promise of regular payments of three thousand dollars per month, plus relocation to the United States for him and his family. Based on Cervantes's testimony, the grand jury issued an indictment on 6 December 1989 charging Rubén Zuno Arce with participating in the planning of Camarena's abduction.

Two days later Zuno and his wife flew back to Los Angeles so that he could attend pretrial proceedings on the perjury charge. He had been warned by defense counsel that upon reentering the United States he might be arrested on a new charge of complicity in the Camarena abduction, but he brushed that warning aside, saying there was no basis for the charge and he had nothing to fear from the U.S. justice system. Zuno's determination to defend himself in a U.S. court weights the circumstantial evidence in his favor, since he could perfectly well have avoided prosecution and possible conviction by opting to remain in Mexico, as did several other prominent Mexican officials who were charged in the Camarena case. There was no bilateral accord providing for the extradition of a citizen of one country to the jurisdiction of the other. On his arrival in Los Angeles, Zuno was in fact arrested on the new charge. He sought to proceed with the original perjury trial, but in mid-March 1990 the U.S. government dismissed that case and moved ahead with the far more serious Camarena-related prosecution. The case went to trial in May of that year and concluded two months later with Zuno's conviction.[4]

DEA-6

Report of Investigation

Date prepared
February 13, 1990

SECRET

NOFORN

SYNOPSIS:

On February 9, 1990, Special Agent Wayne Schmidt and G/S Hector Berrellez [sic] debriefed [Lawrence Victor Harrison] concerning intelligence information related to the

murder of Manuel BUENDIA-TELLESGIRON [*sic*] an investigative reporter;
narcotics trafficking information relating to Ruben ZUNO-Arce; arms trafficking by
GERHARDT MERTINS; and other related intelligence concerning corrupt Mexican
Police Officers and elected Mexican officials.

DETAILS:

1. [Harrison] reported the following intelligence information with regard to the
   murder of Manuel BUENDIA-TELLESGIRON:
2. Manuel BUENDIA-TELLESGIRON was an investigative reporter who supported
   candidate (FNU) DELMASO [*sic*], PRI party member who aspired to be the
   President of Mexico.[5] BUENDIA conducted an investigation into the collusion that
   existed between Manuel BARTLETT-DIAZ, former secretary of the Interior, Miguel
   ALDANA-Ibarra former head of the Mexican anti-drug program and Manuel
   IBARRA-Herrera, former head of the Directorate of Federal Security (DFS) [*sic*]
   who were acting in consort [*sic*] with narcotic traffickers.[6]
3. Between 1981 to 1984 BUENDIA received information from another reporter (FNU)
   VELASCO [Javier Juárez Vázquez], in Vera Cruz [Coatzacoalcos], that Guatemalan
   Guerrillas were training at a ranch owned by Rafael CARO-Quintero in Vera Cruz.

The operations/training at the camp were conducted by the American CIA, using
the DFS as a cover, in the event any questions were raised as to who was running the
training operation.

4. [Harrison] reported that representatives of the DFS which was the front for the
   training camp were in fact acting in consort [*sic*] with major drug overlords to insure
   a flow of narcotics through Mexico into the United States.
. . .
6. BUENDIA had allegedly also gathered information on CIA arms smuggling activity
   and the relationship the CIA had with known narcotic traffickers in Vera Cruz area.

BUENDIA allegedly contacted Jose Antonio ZORRILLA-Perez in 1985 [*sic*] and
reported the information BUENDIA had developed and asked for ZORRILLA's advice
on how to proceed. ZORRILLA allegedly told BUENDIA that the CIA, Narcotic
trafficker situation was very delicate (not to be spoken about).

ZORRILLA sent a contingent of DFS agents to ostensibly provide security and
protection for BUENDIA and his family. The security detail surrounded the
BUENDIA residence.

7. Approximately 41 days later BUENDIA was murdered by elements of the DFS
   security detail. One hour later [Javier Juárez Vázquez], BUENDIA's initial source of
   information in Vera Cruz, was murdered in Vera Cruz. The murder was carried out
   on the orders of BARTLETT-Diaz, currently the Secretary of Education.
. . .
11. Colleagues of BUENDIA who worked for the Newspaper EXCELSIOR identified as
    Rogelio HERNANDEZ and Froylan M. LOPEZ formed a committee to push the
    murder investigation of BUENDIA.
12. It was later learned by the colleagues that BUENDIA had allegedly obtained infor-
    mation that would expose high ranking members of the PRI political party who
    were assisting the CIA with arms smuggling and knew of the CIA link to narcotics
    traffickers.

...

14. [Harrison] allegedly was told by the colleagues of BUENDIA that they had been approached by DEA agents sent by Country Attache Edward Heath (DEA).

The agents allegedly physically handed over a principal file, taken from the BUENDIA office, by the DFS after the murder, and allowed it to be viewed by the colleagues.

15. There was no explanation given by the DEA agents as to how they obtained the file. The colleagues however recognized the file and most of its contents. They indicated that the file was genuine. However, the colleagues also observed that information had been apparently added to the file to implicate BARTLETT-Diaz in CIA arms smuggling and a connection to narcotics traffickers.

16. In exchange for the information in the file, the agents wanted information on DFS credentials signed by Jose Antonio ZORRILLA-Perez and Manuel IBARRA-Herrera which were in possession of various narcotics traffickers at the time of their arrests.

...

23. [Harrison] had learned that the reporter from Vera Cruz [Javier Juárez Vázquez] before his death (1985) [sic] was allegedly developing information that, using the DFS as cover, the CIA established and maintained clandestine airfields to refuel aircraft loaded with weapons which were destined for Honduras and Nicaragua.

24. Pilots of these aircraft would allegedly load up with cocaine in Barranquilla Colombia and in route to Miami, Florida, refuel in Mexico at Narcotic trafficker operated and CIA maintained airstrips.

25. [Harrison] reported that the Cubans were working a similar type of refuel operations, picking up cocaine in Medellin, Colombia and flying it thru Cuba into Miami.

26. [Harrison] speculates that Ruben ZUNO-Arce not only had a hand in trafficking in Mexico but from other information developed, tends to believe was associated with the Cubans.

27. This may be true in that unknown to [Harrison] a passport seized from Ruben ZUNO-Arce at the time of his arrest bore an official Cuban Immigration Stamp which gave ZUNO-Arce unlimited immigration access into Cuba.

SECRET

DEA sensitive

DRUG ENFORCEMENT ADMINISTRATION

This report is the property of the Drug Enforcement Administration.
Neither it nor its contents may be disseminated outside the Agency to which loaned.

The DEA's "Report of Investigation" from which the preceding paragraphs have been excerpted first came to full public light, and to our attention, when it was published in its entirety in Spanish translation on 16 July 1990 by the Mexican newsweekly *Proceso*.[7] It had been improperly withheld from Zuno Arce's defense attorneys by government prosecutors, then in midtrial was leaked to the *Los Angeles Times* and the Spanish-language Los Angeles daily *La Opinión*, at which point Zuno's defense team demanded, and Judge Rafeedie ordered, its release.

At the time, we were seeking to obtain copies of DEA files related to the Buendía case. In September 1988, we had filed a Freedom of Information Act (FOIA) request for "all documents retrievable" pertaining to Manuel Buendía, including documents "offered to the Mexico City daily *Excélsior* in May 1987 by two DEA agents . . . which purportedly implicated former Mexican security chief José Antonio Zorrilla Pérez and interior minister Manuel Bartlett Díaz in the Buendía killing."[8] The following April we received a blanket denial of our request pursuant to six subsections of the FOIA, of which the most interesting to us were "(b)(1) Information which is currently and properly classified . . . in the interest of the national defense or foreign policy; and (b)(7) Investigatory records compiled for law enforcement purposes, the disclosure of which would: (A) interfere with law enforcement proceedings, including pending investigations, (D) reveal the identity of an individual who has furnished information to DEA under confidential circumstances or reveal information furnished only by such a person and not apparently known to the public or otherwise accessible to DEA by overt means; and (F) endanger the life or physical safety of law enforcement personnel."

That denial issued by John H. Langer, chief of DEA's Freedom of Information Section, confirmed for us that the DEA had been, and remained, actively engaged in an investigation of the Manuel Buendía assassination; that the Buendía case had a sensitive bearing on some aspect of U.S. foreign relations; that the Buendía case was linked to the Camarena case; and that the DEA in fact possessed records of probable relevance for our inquiry into the Buendía killing. We immediately appealed Langer's denial to the Justice Department's Office of Legal Policy on the grounds that a blanket denial of our request violated the FOIA requirement that "any reasonably segregable portion of a record shall be provided . . . after deletion of the portions which are exempt." We also called attention to the documents DEA agents had attempted to leak to *Excélsior* in May 1986 and challenged the Justice Department's refusal to provide copies of those documents to a U.S. citizen who lawfully sought their release under the FOIA when they had previously been offered to a major foreign newspaper. Finally, in the event it should choose to continue withholding some or all of the requested material, we asked that the Justice Department provide us with an index of those documents together with a specific justification for denial of each item withheld. This last request was a chimerical attempt on our part to quantify the DEA's Buendía files.[9]

We were promptly notified by paralegal specialist Carolyn D. Poindexter that our appeal had been placed in queue behind a substantial backlog of pending appeals and would be adjudicated as expeditiously as possible. That turned out to be a full two and a half years later, over the course of which we periodically requested clarification of our appeal's status, protested the inordinate delay, and then sought redress through political and legal channels. We initiated conversations with the Center for Constitutional Rights about filing suit against the DEA to force release of its Buendía files, or at least segregable portions of those files, together with an inventory of all withheld material and the corresponding FOIA justifications. We also informed Democratic congressman Ron Dellums (Eighth District, California) of our inability to obtain an appropriate response to our FOIA appeal and asked him to intervene on our behalf.[10]

Having learned from *Proceso* that the 13 February 1990 DEA-6 report of Lawrence Harrison's debriefing by agents Schmidt and Berréllez had been released to Zuno Arce's defense attorneys, and having since obtained an incomplete photocopy of that report from a private investigator working on another aspect of the *contra* affair for the Christic Institute's public interest law group,[11] we specifically identified that document in a follow-up communication with Carolyn Poindexter as one of the items whose release we sought. Meanwhile, we were advised by the Center for Constitutional Rights that our case against the DEA would be strengthened if we could obtain copies of material released to defense attorneys in the Los Angeles trial, to which end we contacted Zuno Arce's lead counsel, Edward M. Medvene, then with the Los Angeles law firm Mitchell, Silberberg and Knupp. After two letters and a follow-up phone conversation, in early April 1993 Medvene sent us photocopies of the 13 February 1990 DEA-6 report, plus three earlier DEA-6 reports on Lawrence Victor Harrison, a fifty-nine-page transcription of a recorded debriefing of Harrison, a set of handwritten debriefing notes by Special Agent Wayne Schmidt, and court transcripts of Harrison's testimony before the Camarena case federal grand jury and in the two subsequent Zuno Arce prosecutions.[12]

Meanwhile, our pending appeal of the DEA's continuing refusal to release any of its Buendía-related files to us had again been denied. In early October 1991, we had complained to the assistant attorney general about Ms. Poindexter's failure to answer, or even acknowledge receipt of, our latest inquiries as to the status of our appeal. A month later we received an official denial of our appeal from Richard L. Huff, codirector of the Justice Department's Office of Information and Privacy. Material that had been withheld under Subsection (b)(1) of the FOIA as classified in the interest of national defense or foreign policy, Huff informed us, would be submitted for internal review and reconsideration of its classification. Should a decision be made to declassify any of that material, we would be notified. All other items, he wrote, had been properly denied and would continue to be withheld.

Our request for itemization of withheld material, with a justification in each instance, was also denied as "unreasonably burdensome" at that stage of our appeals. Huff advised us that judicial review of his action was available to us in U.S. District Court either in the judicial district where we resided or in the District of Columbia, "which is where the records you seek are located." In other words, "Sue us!" We would have pursued that option with the Center for Constitutional Rights had we not obtained copies of the DEA-6 reports and related material from Ed Medvene. With those materials now in hand, such action was pointless, and we let the matter drop.[13]

This initial contact with Ed Medvene would develop into a collaborative association of many years' duration. After a first reading of the DEA documents and Harrison's court testimony, we offered Medvene our preliminary assessment of the government's special witness. In a previous phone conversation, Ed had described Harrison as "a strange duck," and at that point we could only agree. More important, there were major gaps and inconsistencies in Harrison's testimony that almost certainly identified him as a U.S. intelligence operative. His background story struck us as implausible and seemed contrived to create a cover for some long-term agenda, most likely a deep-cover assignment in Mexico. His ability to earn a living in Mexico without having obtained a work permit, as Medvene had established during cross-examination in court, suggested a prior arrangement with Mexican authorities.

Moreover, it was inconceivable that a U.S. citizen could have served as an agent of Mexico's Secretariat of Government, as Harrison testified he had, without an explicit understanding between the appropriate officials of both countries. "In sum," we wrote, "Harrison's alleged involvement with Mexico's national security apparatus, particularly at the levels he indicates, is credible only if he were a U.S. agent working in concert with Mexican counterparts." Likewise, we noted, his claim to have conducted an investigation of the Buendía assassination "on his own initiative and for no one else" was simply not believable.[14]

> The hour-long meeting went incredibly well. The three Mexicans addressed me as though I were visiting royalty. It was exactly as I had predicted—they wanted to please me. [Colonel Jorge Carranza Peniche] had brought his military-school yearbook and pointed out the photos of officers who would "work" with my organization. It seemed that the whole Mexican army was for sale. The colonel spoke freely, making it very clear that he was not on his own; his boss was General Poblano Silva.
>
> Three feet in front of a camera disguised as a lamp, the colonel and I laid out maps and photos of landing sites where my cocaine-laden plane would land. Meanwhile, four feet above our heads, in the attic, video and sound recorders whirred softly. He pointed out where his troops would be and how they would protect and refuel the plane. We went on to discuss future, much larger cocaine shipments.
>
> The little colonel and I really got on well. Within a short time he was speaking freely on almost any subject I probed, and volunteering information I had not asked or bargained for. He even pointed out an area on the maps, stating that they were bases for the training of [Nicaraguan] Contras.[15]

At the same time that the DEA's Los Angeles office was attempting to engage Lawrence Harrison as an in-place asset who could link Mexican officials to narcotics trafficking and the murder of Kiki Camarena, its San Diego office was running an audacious covert operation, which, if successful, promised to disrupt the by then torrential flow of cocaine from South America into the United States by taking down key drug kingpins in Bolivia, Panama, and Mexico. It was also linked to our inquiry. Dubbed Operation Trifecta by its principal operative, veteran federal undercover agent Michael Levine, the plan was for Levine, in the role of a New York Italo–Puerto Rican mafia capo by the name of Luis García López, to purchase an initial thousand kilos of cocaine from Bolivian dealers for five million dollars cash, on the understanding that an additional fourteen thousand kilos would follow once this first transaction had been successfully concluded.

That Levine had succeeded in persuading the Bolivians to proceed with the deal was especially significant not only for its size but above all because it was the first time they had dealt directly with American "traffickers." The Bolivians were the primary producers of cocaine but did not deliver their product to buyers outside their own national borders. As a consequence, Colombian traffickers had become the principal wholesalers of cocaine, with a fleet of aircraft regularly transporting it over the vast expanses of the western Amazon Basin from Bolivia to Colombia, where it was reconsigned by myriad routes to customers in North America and, increasingly, Europe. Now representatives of a shadowy association of Bolivian cocaine producers known among traffickers as La Corporación (previously unknown to American authorities) were seeking to break the Colombian marketing monopoly on their product.

What most intrigued us about Operation Trifecta was that it had originated in Mexico and implicated some of the same actors who had been linked to the Camarena and Buendía cases: Attorney General Sergio García Ramírez, Defense Secretary Gen. Juan Arévalo Gardoqui, Gen. Juan Poblano Silva, and Col. Jorge Carranza Peniche. Carranza was of immediate interest to us, because he was our first credible source to establish direct Mexican support for the Nicaraguan *contras*. Parenthetically, we would eventually learn that during the 1970s he had also worked closely with CIA operative Lawrence Harrison, who once told us that Carranza, a grandson of Constitutionalist army chief and former president Venustiano Carranza, "had taught him Mexican history."[16]

Trifecta got its improbable start when an individual by the name of David Laird Wheeler, facing serious jail time in Oklahoma for possession and sale of eight hundred grams of cocaine, claimed to have firsthand knowledge of narcotics trafficking in Mexico, as well as high-level contacts among corrupt Mexican officials, and offered to serve as an informant in exchange for leniency. Initially rejected by the Oklahoma City DEA office as an unreliable prospect, Wheeler was subsequently employed by U.S. Customs as an asset in its offensive under Commissioner William von Raab against corrupt Mexican officials engaged in cross-border contraband. He was flown to Southern California, given an expensive wardrobe, which included high-end alligator shoes and a Rolex watch, set up in a luxury beachfront home, and instructed to cultivate his corrupt contacts across the border.

Ironically, the only contact that showed any promise was a Federal Judicial Police officer and former DFS agent by the name of Pablo Girón, with whom Wheeler had supposedly trafficked narcotics in the past. Wheeler now tried to interest Girón in various illicit schemes that fell under exclusive Customs jurisdiction, but Girón only wanted to discuss drugs, insisting that he had "the biggest cocaine connection in the world" and wanted Wheeler to find a suitable customer. At that point, by law primary responsibility for the case reverted to the DEA, with Customs relegated to a supporting role.[17]

The DEA's San Diego office then brought in Mike Levine, aka *Luis*, as the "suitable customer," set him up in an appropriate oceanside home in La Jolla where *Don Luis* could credibly negotiate a prosecutable transaction, and instructed Wheeler to entice Girón and his associates to come to California to explore a possible deal. In late September 1987, as Ángel Buendía was pressuring Secretary of Government Manuel Bartlett Díaz to take decisive steps in the official investigation of his brother's assassination, Pablo Girón and two Mexican associates were met at the Tijuana border crossing by Wheeler and undercover Customs agent George Urquijo, both "employees" of El Mero Mero (The Big Guy). Wheeler and Urquijo first treated the Mexicans to an unhurried alcoholic lunch, then drove them to the undercover house for their introductory meeting with *Don Luis* himself. The two men accompanying Girón were Efrén Méndez Dueñas, a Mexican representative of the Bolivian Corporación, and Héctor Álvarez, ostensibly a member of the security detail of PRI presidential candidate Carlos Salinas de Gortari.[18]

Méndez was the key member of the trio, and by the end of the La Jolla meeting he and *Luis* had agreed in principle to do a deal. It remained to arrange a face-to-face discussion between *Luis* and his Bolivian counterpart, Jorge Román Salas, which subsequently took place in Panama over a two-day period in mid-November 1987. Román invited *Luis* to visit Bolivia and personally inspect their massive operation, an offer *Luis* declined but agreed to send one of his people, together with the pilot who would be flying the initial thousand-kilo load back to the United States once the deal was finalized.

From this point on, Trifecta unfolded in a frightful tangle of conflicting agendas, woeful tradecraft, and interagency turf challenges that recklessly endangered undercover operatives and, but for a fluke of fate, should have aborted the entire operation. To Levine it began to feel like a replay of an earlier sting he had run out of Argentina against the godfather of Bolivia's cocaine producers, Roberto Suárez, which had been sabotaged by the CIA in support of a conflicting executive branch geopolitical agenda. The result of that subterfuge was the July 1980 military coup, which prevented Bolivia's newly elected president, the widely respected Hernán Siles Suazo, from assuming office and, in his stead, imposed an army general, Luis García Meza Tejada, who oversaw a brutally corrupt regime underwritten by Roberto Suárez and his trafficker associates. Dubbed "the cocaine revolution," it was probably the first time in history that an entire government had been bought by drug dealers. And it could not have been done, in Michael Levine's view, "without the tacit help of DEA and the active, covert help of the CIA." Anyone who has spent any time in the intelligence community, Levine told an interviewer in 1990, "knows without any doubt that there are no changes of government in this hemisphere without the CIA being involved."[19]

By the time Operation Trifecta dispatched operatives to Panama in the fall of 1987, the CIA was already casting a shadow on the scheme to disrupt Bolivian cocaine production. It is axiomatic that in nation-state governance foreign policy takes precedence over law enforcement, and whenever these two spheres conflict, law enforcement will be compromised. At the upper administrative levels of government there tends to be a greater cohesiveness of strategic purpose than one finds farther down departmental bureaucratic ladders or among field and street-level operatives, which explains how the CIA was able to penetrate the DEA, as well as, presumably, the Customs Service, and bend those federal agencies to its own purposes. In the case of Trifecta, matters were further complicated by the fact that Customs was technically the lead agency while the DEA had primary operational responsibility, which added a disruptive overlay of institutional turf issues.

From the outset, senior DEA administrators ("suits" in the parlance of operations personnel) seemed determined to keep Trifecta from succeeding, even as the involvement of Customs obliged them to give the appearance of moving it forward. For starters, they transferred a Southeast Asia operative from Bangkok to serve as Trifecta's group supervisor, a post that ought to have been assigned to an agent with Latin American experience. Then there was a striking lack of cooperation from the DEA's country attaché in Panama, who failed to provide appropriate cover and backup for the San

Diego office's undercover team when it arrived to negotiate with representatives of La Corporación, nearly compromising the entire operation by having them put up at Panama City's Airport Marriott, known in the trafficking underworld as the U.S. government's preferred lodging for its narcotics agents.

When Levine, alias Luis García López, nonetheless persuaded the Bolivians to proceed with their deal and it became necessary to send a couple of *Don Luis*'s "employees" to inspect the Corporation's operations, an experienced contract pilot by the name of Jake Sales, who had previously flown missions for both the CIA and the DEA, was brought in to accompany David Wheeler on the preliminary reconnaissance. And when it then appeared that Trifecta was actually going to proceed to the stage of dispatching an aircraft to retrieve the first thousand kilos of cocaine negotiated by *Luis* and Jorge Román, an additional CIA pilot was assigned to fly the mission together with Sales. By Levine's account, this second pilot had come straight from central casting wearing "a green one-piece flight suit . . ., a silk scarf tied around his neck, an Australian bush hat, and an exotically curled pipe stuck in his mouth."[20]

Levine's proposed sequence of events for Operation Trifecta was, first, to actually spend the five million dollars for the purchase of the initial thousand kilos of cocaine, so as to give *Don Luis* sufficient credibility to arrange a follow-up meeting in Panama with top representatives of the Bolivian Corporación and senior Mexican officials, who, with Mexico's presidential election now past, were believed ready—for a price—to facilitate the passage of *Don Luis*'s cocaine shipments through Mexican territory. Phase one of Trifecta would end with the arrest of that meeting's Bolivian and Mexican attendees, including the Corporation's Panama-based money launderer. Phase two would entail an armed assault against the traffickers' jungle labs, storage facilities, and landing strips, with DEA agents and Bolivian troops arriving on the aircraft supposedly sent to pick up *Don Luis*'s multi-ton load of cocaine.

The Washington suits were not on the same page, however, and in the end events did not play out as Levine had briefly allowed himself to hope. A second rendezvous in Panama during December 1987 between *Luis* and Corporation representatives encountered unforeseen snags, which again nearly scuttled Trifecta but which Levine adroitly managed to avert, with the Bolivians finally accepting blame for the hang-up. *Don Luis* had told the Bolivians that his "organization" in New York had arranged with Customs agents in Miami to allow the initial thousand-kilo shipment into the United States on Christmas Day, when airport operations were much reduced and there were fewer agents on duty. That date had passed, however, and *Luis* persuaded the Bolivians that it was now necessary to reroute that flight through Mexico, which would require yet another meeting to work out terms and logistics, this time back at *Luis*'s oceanside residence in La Jolla, California.

The revised Trifecta plan was now for Efrén Méndez, the Mexican liaison with the Bolivian Corporación, together with Bolivian traffickers Jorge Román and Mario Vargas and a Corporación pilot, to travel to San Diego to collect the five-million-dollar cash payment for the initial thousand kilos of cocaine, after which Vargas and the Bolivian pilot supposedly would accompany *Don Luis*'s plane back to the jungle strip in the

Bolivian Amazon to retrieve the purchased product. It had been agreed that Méndez and Román would remain in La Jolla as *Luis*'s "guests" until the cocaine shipment was actually delivered.

Héctor Álvarez and Pablo Girón had arranged with General Poblano Silva for Mexican soldiers to seal off a stretch of roadway in the State of Puebla where *Luis*'s plane supposedly would land, refuel, then take off again on its return flight from Bolivia to San Diego. They, too, would attend the La Jolla meeting, accompanied—at *Luis*'s insistence—by "a senior Mexican army official," to confirm refueling logistics and receive six hundred thousand dollars as partial payment for Poblano's cooperation. The total fee for Mexican army assistance was one million dollars, the remaining four hundred thousand to be paid to the general's bagman, Col. Jorge Carranza, upon the cocaine-laden plane's safe arrival in Southern California.

Once the Bolivians' and Mexicans' participation in a conspiracy to import cocaine into the United States had been duly documented by the surveillance cameras and recording devices in the La Jolla undercover house, they would be jailed, indicted, and held for trial. In what Levine envisioned as a tightly coordinated sequence of events, Bolivian army units would immediately strike the clandestine airstrips and production sites identified by Wheeler and Sales, while he and George Urquijo would fly to Panama to arrest the Bolivian Corporation's money man, Remberto Rodríguez, whom they had met on their initial trip to Panama two months earlier. At that point, U.S. Customs could grandstand a sucker punch against corrupt high-level Mexican officials while the DEA could finally claim a serious blow to cocaine production at its source. As Levine had feared all along, however, events did not, in the end, play out as planned.

Key to the success of Levine's plan was to obtain recordings of telephone conversations between the principal Mexican and Bolivian players confirming final arrangements for the thousand-kilo transaction, namely, between Jorge Carranza and General Poblano Silva in Mexico and between Jorge Román and Pato Pizarro, reputed head of La Corporación, in Bolivia. But for some obscure reason there was resistance from up the chain of command to those calls being placed, much less recorded. This was especially evident in the case of General Poblano Silva, with informant David Wheeler and his Customs handlers offering the stiffest opposition to having Colonel Carranza engage the general in a compromising conversation. They were backed by the U.S. Attorney's Office, which, inexplicably from a law enforcement perspective, refused to authorize the phone taps.

When it was finally agreed that Levine could legally record a call to Poblano provided he was listening to the conversation on an extension with Carranza's knowledge, Trifecta's operational overseers contrived to keep the three Mexicans otherwise occupied until the only opportunity for Carranza to phone Poblano was at a time when they knew the general would not be available to take the call. In the end, Carranza spoke to a man he identified as the general's disabled brother, who confirmed that all arrangements were in place for the drug plane's refueling but whose identity could not subsequently be established as evidence for the prosecution. Matters were further complicated by Attorney General Edwin Meese, who informed his Mexican counterpart and potential PRI presidential contender, Sergio García Ramírez, of the impending

Trifecta arrests, which allowed the de la Madrid administration to take preemptive steps to cover for General Poblano Silva and other senior officials at risk of being implicated in the DEA/Customs sting.[21]

In what appeared to be a grotesque publicity ploy contrived by senior Customs Service administrators with total disregard for the security of their own and DEA undercover agents still on assignment in the field, arrangements were made for full media coverage of the arrests on Thursday, 14 January 1988—first, around midday, of General Poblano Silva's representatives, Col. Jorge Carranza, Pablo Girón, and Héctor Álvarez, then, later that afternoon, of Bolivian Corporation representatives Efrén Méndez, Jorge Román, and Mario Vargas, together with their pilot Rolando Ayala. This phase of Operation Trifecta was supposed to have been kept completely under wraps for at least forty-eight hours so as not to alert Corporation money launderer Remberto Rodríguez in Panama until Levine and Customs agent George Urquijo had arrested him, supposedly with in-country support from the DEA's Panama country attaché, Alfredo Duncan, and cooperating Panamanian police. By the time Levine and Urquijo landed in Panama the following day, however, news of the Trifecta arrests had spread throughout the region and Remberto Rodríguez was nowhere to be found.

Levine was later told by Customs informant David Wheeler that Rodríguez had been spirited out of Panama City by the CIA and taken to Contadora Island, where the agency kept him under round-the-clock guard until the Trifecta threat had passed. Rodríguez was by all indications a key player in the hemisphere's drug trade, handling billions of dollars for the Bolivian Corporación, the Colombian cartels, and perhaps the Mexican traffickers as well. No one could operate on that scale in Panama without being linked to Panamanian strongman Manuel Noriega, himself soon to be indicted in the United States for drug trafficking even as he remained on a CIA retainer. Rodríguez, according to Wheeler, was in fact tied to both Noriega and the CIA through secret Panamanian bank accounts. Had Levine and Urquijo managed to locate Rodríguez following the La Jolla arrests, Wheeler assured Levine, they both would have been killed."[22]

Levine never could sort out to his own satisfaction Wheeler's role in Operation Trifecta. While inclined to dismiss him as a con artist possessed of uncommon chutzpah, he could not explain how it was that Wheeler the informant seemed to be making operational decisions and was even allowed to carry a firearm despite a felony drug conviction. Wheeler had, on occasion, claimed to have ties to the CIA and, difficult though it was for Levine to believe it, he could not entirely dismiss that possibility. The CIA's fingerprints were all over everything having to do with hemispheric geopolitics, especially the Nicaraguan *contras*. Soon after Operation Trifecta was launched, Levine has written, "frantic DEA and Customs upper management personnel" informed him that the CIA "was closely monitoring [the Trifecta] team's every move." Then the operation "was sabotaged by top-level suits in Customs, DEA, [the] Department of State and [the] Justice Department." Only the four Mexicans and three Bolivians arrested in La Jolla were allowed to be prosecuted. None of the major figures in Mexico, Panama, or Bolivia was ever implicated by the U.S. government.[23]

Intrigued by Levine's account of Colonel Carranza having been recorded by surveillance cameras as he pointed out *contra* training camps on a map of Mexico at the

La Jolla undercover house, we arranged to meet with Mike and his wife, Laura Kava-
nau, to discuss our Buendía investigation in light of the Trifecta case. They invited us
to stay with them at their home near Kingston, New York, where we talked at length
over the weekend of 20–21 May 1995. Mike reiterated his view that the so-called war
on drugs was a colossal sham cynically employed to advance U.S. geopolitical interests,
as well as the careers of senior government bureaucrats. By the early 1990s, drug trafficking had infused over two trillion dollars into the global economy, and, he predicted,
if illicit drugs were ever eliminated "the world's banks would collapse." The CIA, he
insisted, was massively involved with narcotics and arms traffickers, citing Alfred W.
McCoy and Peter Dale Scott as two academics who had amply documented what he
himself knew firsthand from his years as an undercover agent in Southeast Asia, Latin
America, and the United States.[24]

Levine is emblematic of distinctly American personality types that become involved
in police or intelligence work fully persuaded that they are serving venerable government institutions on behalf of the citizenry, only to discover that they are in fact being
used to further amoral political agendas contrary to the vaunted values and beliefs of
our national mythology. He is the inevitable product of the Faustian compromise
propounded by Cold War architects George Kennan and James R. Doolittle in the late
1940s and early 1950s, whereby traditional national ideals and norms of human conduct were to be set aside in favor of a "fundamentally repugnant," no-holds-barred
strategy for the projection of American power. The inevitable result was a growing
number of disillusioned secret agents and national security personnel who, from the
Vietnam era down to the present, have felt compelled to tear away the veil of deceit
that envelops American intelligence and covert action operations around the world.
Daniel Ellsberg (Pentagon/Rand Corporation), Victor Marchetti (CIA), John D. Marks
(State Department), Philip Agee (CIA), John Stockwell (CIA), William Blum (State
Department), and Edward Snowden (National Security Agency) are some of the more
familiar names.[25]

Investigative journalist Charles Bowden, who has written extensively on Mexico's
role in the "war on drugs," once remarked to us that "no one can honestly and decently
serve our government in an undercover capacity without taking serious personal damage and becoming disillusioned." Anyone who is intelligent and serves undercover
"eventually thinks they have wasted their life."[26] Mike Levine conforms perfectly to
this profile. "It is both sobering and painful," he wrote in an author's note at the beginning of *Deep Cover*, "to realize, after twenty-five years of undercover work . . . that my
career was meaningless and [has] had absolutely no effect whatsoever in the so-called
war on drugs. The war itself is a fraud."[27]

Like other disaffected American agents, Levine's only remedy for the realization that
he had devoted the prime of his life to a fraudulent cause has been to expose the deceit
of that cause, which is why he was talking to us. Our Buendía investigation encom-
passed the Camarena case as well, and the fate of Enrique "Kiki" Camarena epitomized
the cynicism with which U.S. officialdom sacrificed its own people. *Deep Cover* was
dedicated to the memory of Camarena and to all other American agents "whose lives
have been, and are being, sacrificed for this war of lies, hypocrisy, and self-interest."[28]

Veteran DEA undercover agent Michael Levine with his wife, Laura Kavanau-Levine, May 1995. (Sylvia E. Bartley)

Just as there are disaffected members of the American intelligence, military, diplomatic, and law enforcement establishments, not all Justice Department attorneys have been willing to take political cues from the attorney general.[29] A salient example bearing on our investigation is the case of U.S. Attorney William H. Kennedy, who in 1982 was blocked from indicting former DFS chief Miguel Nazar Haro for involvement in a cross-border car theft ring, then revealed the CIA's intervention on Nazar's behalf, and was fired for doing so.[30] In a similar vein, the government's case against Jorge Román Salas, Efrén Méndez Dueñas, Jorge Carranza Peniche, and others was prosecuted by Assistant U.S. Attorney Stephen G. Nelson in the same San Diego courthouse where Kennedy had been sacked for exposing CIA obstruction of a federal indictment. Nelson, described by CIA turned DEA agent Pat Gregory as "very dynamic, intelligent, [with] an extremely large set of gonads," was not what one might call an ideological dissident, but rather a determined federal prosecutor who brooked no interference from other government agencies.[31] Although their motives differed, he and Mike Levine joined forces to counter an executive branch cover-up of trial evidence pointing to official Mexican collusion with Bolivian cocaine traffickers.

At issue were the alleged collusive roles in Trifecta's bogus thousand-kilo cocaine deal of Mexican army officers Gen. Juan Poblano Silva, Col. Salvador de la Vega, and Col. Jorge Carranza Peniche, as well as National Defense Secretary Gen. Juan Arévalo Gardoqui, without whose personal authorization the proposed refueling of *Don Luis*'s drug-laden aircraft on an embargoed Puebla highway could never happen. (Colonel de la Vega was Poblano Silva's immediate subordinate and the officer ostensibly assigned to command the military units that would carry out the clandestine refueling operation.) Nelson requested that the DEA's Mexico City station conduct a background investigation of the implicated military figures but was stonewalled by drug enforcement's Mexico country attaché Edward Heath. Heath, it developed, had dealt with Col. Jorge Carranza in the past, and Carranza, upon his arrest on 14 January 1988, claimed to be a personal friend of the veteran DEA officer. Heath's home address and phone number were found in Carranza's pocket address book.

Carranza, for his part, was key to the prosecution of the Trifecta case because his status as a Mexican army officer, and thus his alleged access to General Poblano Silva, had been placed in doubt by both the de la Madrid and Salinas administrations, which claimed that Carranza had been discharged from the military in 1971 and was therefore in no position to interact with an officer of Poblano Silva's rank. That assertion was echoed by U.S. ambassador to Mexico Charles Pilliod, who would not likely have done so without first consulting the embassy's senior DEA officer, Ed Heath. In light of Carranza's long-standing reputation as a legendary covert operative, described as early as 1969 in *Sports Illustrated* as "Mexico's James Bond,"[32] the logical explanation for the official Mexican response, Levine observed, was that Carranza "had been assigned to the kind of sensitive duties that would require him to dissociate himself from the army." Given his repeated references to having been involved in the training of Nicaraguan *contras*, a "secret association with our government" would go a long way toward explaining the Mexican government's disavowal of Carranza, as well as White House reluctance to be forthcoming with Nelson.[33]

While we did not know it at the time, our ex-CIA source, Lawrence Harrison, had dealt with Carranza in the early 1970s and has since mentioned him to us on several occasions. By his account, Carranza worked for Mexican "G-2," army intelligence, and in the period immediately following Carranza's supposed discharge from the army, Harrison was reporting to him in Cuernavaca—all of which lends credence to Levine's suspicion of a "secret association" with the U.S. government.[34] It would also explain Carranza's rank of colonel and his apparent ability to communicate with senior active-duty military officers.

Exasperated by Ed Heath's failure to obtain and provide him with case-related information from Mexico, in January 1989 Assistant U.S. Attorney Nelson addressed a five-page memorandum to Charles Hill, the special agent in charge of the DEA's San Diego office, detailing the various items he had sought unsuccessfully to have Heath's Mexico City office investigate. While Nelson's memo did not explicitly accuse Heath and the DEA of a cover-up, Levine noted, "it certainly put the ball in their court" to prove otherwise.[35] Invoking the defense attorneys' clear intention to embarrass the DEA by claiming that no effort had been made to verify the status and backgrounds of their Mexican defendants, Nelson asked Hill to have the Mexico City office document the scope of their investigation of the matters he had requested, the individuals who carried out the investigation, the approximate time spent on the investigation, the individuals contacted, and the sources accessed. Mexican officials who were themselves the subjects of the Trifecta-related grand jury investigation, Nelson concluded, "are not considered reliable and should not be contacted"—a pointed reference to Ed Heath's allegedly having contacted Arévalo Gardoqui to verify Carranza's military status. Against the possibility that the DEA might not act on his memo, Nelson gave a copy to Levine. "If they don't answer it," he said, "you put it in your book and let the people know."[36]

Steve Nelson's memorandum produced some interesting results. Within two weeks Ed Heath replied with a memo of his own, albeit responsive only to Nelson's questions regarding Jorge Carranza. Heath stated that he had been in personal contact with Carranza on several occasions in 1981, 1983, and 1987 and that during that period Carranza had had a relationship with Mexican military intelligence. Of particular interest to us was a meeting Heath described in May 1987 at which, together with Carranza, PJDF deputy director of operations José "Pepe" Tort, and Col. Mario Arturo Acosta Chaparro, he discussed the establishment of a "discreet method of communication between himself and Mexican Military Intelligence." At that meeting, Acosta Chaparro had urged Heath "to brief the Army's chief of staff on the seriousness of drug trafficking in Mexico, with the aim of getting the Mexican military more involved in the fight against drugs." Heath had not pursued the matter, he told Nelson, because it was not "politically convenient" for the DEA to do so.[37]

Colonel Acosta Chaparro, subsequently promoted to the rank of general, had been one of the principal figures in Mexico's 1960s and '70s scorched-earth campaign against radical antigovernment groups.[38] He and Carranza were fellow officers in that campaign, which lends additional weight to Lawrence Harrison's assertion that Carranza was "G-2," just as Harrison's association with Carranza suggests a presumed link between Mexican military intelligence and the CIA. Likewise, the fact that Mexican military intelligence was interested in establishing secure back-channel communications with Ed Heath is consistent with Harrison's intimation to us that Heath was himself CIA, notwithstanding his official post as DEA's Mexico country attaché.

It further transpired that Acosta Chaparro's name appeared in the DEA's Narcotics and Dangerous Drugs Information System (NADDIS) database as an individual who "associates with and provides protection for narcotics traffickers," and that he had met on at least two occasions with fugitive Guadalajara cartel capo Miguel Ángel Félix Gallardo—once in May 1987, the same month he met with Heath, Carranza, and Tort, and again in May 1988, eleven months before Félix Gallardo's arrest on orders of the new Salinas administration. (Shortly after Félix Gallardo's arrest, Ed Heath was allowed to question him about the Camarena case, in which Félix denied having taken part.)[39] In April 1989, Heath testified as a defense witness in the San Diego trial of Pablo Girón Ortiz, Héctor Manuel Brumel Álvarez, Jorge Carranza Peniche, and others, but under cross-examination by Assistant U.S. Attorney Nelson he acknowledged that Carranza did, in fact, have access to Mexican army brass and had been in a position to provide military protection for Levine's cocaine-laden airplane as it transited Mexican territory. Questioned about his having stonewalled Nelson for the better part of a year, Heath stated that he had been trying to obtain the information requested by Nelson but the Mexican government had not been cooperative. He had, he implausibly averred, been "snookered" by Mexican authorities.[40]

During our May 1995 visit with Levine and his wife, Mike expanded on his *Deep Cover* account of Operation Trifecta, as well as offering helpful thoughts about our own Buendía investigation. The CIA's involvement with drug and arms traffickers, he repeated, had been massive. Gen. Juan Poblano Silva was a CIA asset, he told us. Gen. Mario Acosta Chaparro was Poblano's front man and dealt as well with Guadalajara cartel capo Miguel Ángel Félix Gallardo, which completed the CIA–Mexican military–drug-trafficker circle. Ed Heath was in contact with Poblano, Acosta, and Carranza, Mike added, but denied in court that Carranza had had anything to do with Félix Gallardo. Heath perjured himself, Mike said, to cover up Mexican army links to the drug traffickers, which reached all the way up to former defense secretary Gen. Juan Arévalo Gardoqui.[41]

Mike also talked to us about Celerino "Cele" Castillo, a disillusioned former DEA agent who had been stationed in Central America from late 1985 through early 1990, where he documented CIA-protected links between the Nicaraguan *contras* and South American drug traffickers, abetted by high-level DEA acquiescence. Mike had written a foreword to Castillo's 1994 exposé, *Powderburns*, in which he describes Castillo as a "consummate investigator who documents every one of his claims." When Levine wrote *Deep Cover* four years earlier, he observed, he possessed only circumstantial evidence of U.S. government links to narcotics trafficking and the *contras*, whereas Cele Castillo had provided "the smoking gun."[42] Mike thought Castillo might be helpful and gave us his contact information in McAllen, Texas.

He also told us about another potential source, an American by the name of Michael Keith Hooks, who had been a major marijuana smuggler for the Caro Quintero clan in Mexico and was then serving time at the Terminal Island federal prison in San Pedro, California. At the height of his smuggling career, Hooks was overseeing cultivation of the Caro Quintero cannabis plantations in Sonora and Chihuahua, as well as operating a personal fleet of twenty-eight aircraft, which ferried industrial quantities of marijuana below the radar into the United States.[43] Because of his personal association with Rafael Caro Quintero, subsequently imprisoned in Mexico for the murder of Kiki Camarena, Mike thought it possible that Hooks might know something about the Buendía assassination and offered to write him on our behalf.

But the single most significant piece of evidence that Mike shared with us during our May 1995 visit was video surveillance footage taken at the La Jolla undercover house of Col. Jorge Carranza Peniche pointing out locations on a map of Mexico that he identified as *contra* training sites, as well as identifying Mexican army officers who could be enlisted to facilitate the movement of drugs through Mexican territory, including General Arévalo Gardoqui. We had read Levine's account of that meeting with Carranza,[44] but sitting on our king-sized bed that Saturday evening in Mike and Laura's guest room viewing a two-hour segment of DEA surveillance footage that Mike had managed to retain following his retirement, we were able to witness for ourselves what he had described in his book. Mike loaned us that videocassette, which allowed us to scrutinize it more closely back in California.[45]

As promised, he also wrote to Hooks and, without providing any specifics, asked him if he knew anything about "the murder of a Mexican journalist." Hooks's reply, while hardly case breaking, was nonetheless interesting for what it revealed about how details of the Buendía assassination had spread in Mexican trafficker circles. "The only one I know of," Hooks replied, "would be Buendía. [He] was murdered in Mexico City in 1983–84. He was shot by someone on a motorcycle. It was said that the murder was [an] order from the higher DFS echelon. I know Comandante Durruti," Hooks wrote. "He was the one who shot and killed the one who killed Buendía. The whole business was a setup."[46] Hooks here refers to the DFS *madrina* José Luis Ochoa Alonso, aka "El Chocorrol," initially identified as the gunman who had felled Manuel Buendía, who was himself shot to death six weeks later by three DFS agents, among them Fernando Durruty Castillo.

That Hooks could respond to Levine with these details and connections more than a decade after the event, and do so without Levine having mentioned Buendía by name, suggests that the matter of Buendía's assassination had been a topic of more than passing interest among the Mexican drug kingpins with whom Hooks was involved. That he should have known Fernando Durruty and known that Durruty had been implicated in the Buendía case further confirms the DFS-trafficker nexus, as well as the readiness of DFS agents to share information about current directorate operations with their narco-trafficker associates. During the two and a half years (1983–1985) that Hooks was a partner of Rafael and Miguel Caro Quintero, he had a DFS agent assigned to him full time as his personal bodyguard and facilitator for dealing with Mexican law enforcement.

Hooks thought the U.S. government more than likely knew about the Caro Quintero cannabis plantations in Sonora and Chihuahua. It was not unusual, he told investigative journalist Peter Gorman, to see U.S. AWACS (Airborne Warning and Control System) aircraft overflying the area, planes with which he would have been familiar from his previous military service as a Marine Corps radar specialist assigned to the California–Mexico border, where he had tracked incoming drug flights with newly developed portable radar units as part of a marijuana interdiction operation dubbed Grasshopper. (It was Hooks's knowledge of all the blind spots along the border where planes could cross undetected that made him such a successful smuggler.) But the Caro Quintero people were so well protected, he told Gorman, that prior to the abduction and murder of Kiki Camarena they were virtually untouchable. "There was always a DFS agent with me," he said. "Everybody knew who I was. We were the good guys down there, the people bringing in U.S. dollars."[47]

Although Hooks spent most of his time in the northern states of Sonora and Chihuahua, he did travel on occasion to Jalisco, where he met other key figures in the Guadalajara cartel, including Miguel Ángel Félix Gallardo, Juan "El Azul" Esparragoza Moreno, Joaquín "El Chapo" Guzmán Loera, Emilio Quintero Payán, and Juan José Quintero Payán.[48] Another element behind the official protection enjoyed by the Caro Quintero organization, he told Gorman, was the fact that the Nicaraguan *contras* were receiving CIA-directed training at one of Rafael Caro Quintero's ranches near Guadalajara. "I knew about it," Hooks recounted. "Hell, everybody did. But that was way over on another ranch, and not one most of us would ever go to, because it was a secret operation by the U.S. government. But that certainly helped play a role in how protected [we] were."

This statement was supported by the testimony of former DEA agent Cele Castillo. "I was working in Guatemala at the time," Castillo told Gorman. "We had word that the *contras* were training [in Mexico] at a Caro Quintero ranch." Camarena had been trying to get the U.S. government to pressure Mexican authorities to take down the industrial-size marijuana plantations in Sonora and Chihuahua [*sic*], Castillo said, but the Reagan administration was reluctant to do so because it was protecting Rafael Caro Quintero in return for his support of the *contras*.[49]

> The next thing I knew, three Mexican Interpol henchmen, led by the First Comandante Florentino Ventura Gutiérrez, had knocked me to the floor and were thrashing me about the ribs and stomach with their riot sticks and their pointed cowboy boots. They made real sure they didn't hit me in the face and arms though, that would leave marks and the U.S. Embassy representative might see them. Of course, I was reminded that if I complained about my treatment to anyone, I would be beaten much worse than I already had been. . . .
>
> [Ventura] Gutiérrez seemed to know everything about me. He knew about Jesse Lee Bishop and Jesse Livingston Barnes, my aliases that I had managed to hide from law enforcement for so long. He knew about the planes and the luggage, and most importantly, he knew about Rafael Caro Quintero, my supplier and partner. They wanted to know about my association with Quintero and the kidnapping and murder of DEA agent Enrique "Kiki" Camarena. . . . They knew just about everything there was to know about my personal and business relationships, including my connection with the Búfalo Ranch in Chihuahua. . . .
>
> Señor Gutiérrez spoke to me with the quietest of voices. "Tell me your life story Jesse, from the beginning, from the very beginning. That's the only way to stop this. You've brought this on yourself Jesse, so start at the beginning and do not leave anything out. And believe me Jesse, we'll know if you do," he stated ever so calmly.
>
> "From the very beginning?" I asked.
>
> "Yes Jesse, from the very beginning. Are you comfortable? What do you need to begin?" the Comandante whispered.
>
> I recalled images, places, faces and names floating inside my mind. Thirteen years of drug smuggling; so many people, so many places, so many drugs. But as the Comandante's men approached me with their riot sticks for the last time, these floating images began to take shape, and for the first time in 8 days, the pain seemed to leave my body with the first words that came out of my lips.[50]

Because of his association with Rafael Caro Quintero, Hooks became a priority target of the DEA. Several months after the Camarena killing, he was arrested by the Mexican Federal Judicial Police in Cancún, where he had gone to lie low until the storm over the Camarena affair had abated. Drug enforcement agents participated in the manhunt and were standing by to repatriate him to the United States for prosecution. Facing a prison sentence of twenty to one hundred years for outstanding charges against him in the United States, however, he preferred to be jailed in Mexico on a lesser possession charge, which he managed to engineer with local authorities. When several years into a sixteen-year Mexican prison sentence he learned that Miguel Caro Quintero had appropriated some of his real estate holdings, he got word to the DEA that he would now assist in its pursuit of his former trafficking partner in return for repatriation and leniency. Arrangements were subsequently made with Mexican judicial authorities for Hooks's transfer to American custody, and, in the argot of the traffickers, he became a DEA snitch—with the attendant threat of a permanent contract put out on his life by the Caro Quintero clan.

Following up on Mike Levine's initial inquiry on our behalf, we contacted Hooks by mail, explained briefly the scope of our investigation and what information we hoped he could provide us, and indicated that we would need to know the specifics of his experience in Mexico, as well as the circumstances of his indictment, arrest, and conviction. He replied two months later, apologizing for the delay, which he attributed to time he had been putting in on an "outline for a perspective [*sic*] Book/Movie Deal." He said he would be happy to answer whatever questions we might have about his knowledge of "the people and events surrounding the 1984 assassination of Manuel Buendía" and that we should let him know when he could call us collect to discuss it further.

We wrote back, saying that we were reluctant to discuss any aspect of our investigation on the phone and would prefer to meet with him in person. We asked Hooks to let us know what we needed to do to arrange such a meeting and, if possible, to provide us with a copy of his indictment. We had indicated to him in our initial letter that we were particularly interested to learn if he had encountered other Americans or foreign nationals who were involved with the Mexican traffickers and, in that connection, did the names Hans Klaus or Lorenzo Harrison mean anything to him? He replied promptly, instructing us to contact Warden Michael Benov to arrange an in-person meeting. Hooks said he had spoken with the assistant warden about our wish to meet and that he did not foresee any problems provided we were not writing about the prison. As for Lorenzo Harrison and Hans Klaus, he wrote, "I really can't help you with any first hand information about them," a reply that we thought could be interpreted at least two ways but which we took to imply that he knew nothing about them.[51]

Along with his second letter, Hooks included photocopies of a thirty-three-page indictment of Rafael and Miguel Caro Quintero, himself, and twenty-four codefendants; his forty-five-page book/movie synopsis; an article about Tijuana's La Mesa penitentiary (from which he had escaped in 1978); six sheets of poorly reproduced photographs from his Caro Quintero years, including three photocopied images of Kiki Camarena; and a detailed organizational chart of the "Hooks-Brown-Markham

Cocaine and Mexican Marijuana Trafficking Organization Based in Arizona and Sonora, Mexico," dated February 1988 and marked "DEA Sensitive." Although we did not know at the time that Hooks had become a DEA informant, this last item, together with his access to photocopiers and ready ability to provide us with such abundant documentary material while serving a federal prison sentence, immediately put us on alert. We thought it unlikely, for example, that he could have sent us the Hooks-Brown-Markham organizational chart without prior DEA authorization, which would suggest some ulterior purpose on its part probably not in the best interest of our investigation. Accordingly, we decided not to proceed with our proposed meeting and had no further communication with Michael Hooks.

Nonetheless, we found Hooks's account of his trafficking career persuasive and attached significance to information he gave us that bears on the Buendía case. His personality is a recognizable psychological type, and there is internal consistency to the tale he tells. Moreover, some of what he recounts is confirmed by the federal indictments against him, while other investigators have confirmed additional parts of his story from other testimonial and documentary sources. "Current and retired U.S. Drug Enforcement Administration agents attest privately to his honesty," *Albuquerque Journal* investigative reporter Mike Gallagher wrote, for example. "There are government letters and contracts that support his story, as do federal court records and DEA files reviewed by the Journal."[52] Mike Levine, for his part, had put us onto Hooks because he considered him a reliable source.

That Hooks had turned DEA informant was perfectly comprehensible in light of his difficult confinement in a Mexican prison and therefore was not in itself of concern to us. He had not turned on his former trafficking associates, he insisted, until they betrayed him. Our concern was rather that, in his present situation, he might be pressured by the DEA to obtain information from us about the status and direction of our investigation, which would make it all but impossible for us to have a frank conversation with him. It seemed best to leave matters where they stood.

II

Attorneys in Wonderland

During World War II, [U.S. District Judge Edward Rafeedie] traveled the carnival circuit with a portable electric horse-race game called Derby. . . . Later in life, he described himself as the only carny to ever get to the federal courts.

    —Obituary, *Los Angeles Times* (30 March 2008)

I was instructed to sit up there [on the witness stand] and act like a clown! They told me to lie.

    —Lawrence Victor Harrison, telephone conversation with Russell H. Bartley
    (25 April 2005)

The U.S. Government in the midst of its self-proclaimed War on Drugs, was using its own powers of law enforcement and justice to protect known drug traffickers. . . . It would be reassuring to think that the cover-up of the Contra-drug connection was a passing anomaly. . . . Unfortunately, the Kerry sub-committee found such official U.S. collaboration with corrupt governments, and official U.S. cover-ups of drug trafficking, to be more the rule than the exception.

    —Peter Dale Scott and Jonathan Marshall, *Cocaine Politics* (1998)

BY THE TIME Lawrence Victor Harrison took the witness stand on 6 June 1990 in *United States of America v. Juan Ramón Matta Ballesteros del Pozo, Rubén Zuno Arce, Juan José Bernabé Ramírez, and Javier Vásquez Velasco*, the CIA, Justice Department, and White House were fully engaged in a concerted, ongoing campaign of damage control to discredit repeated allegations of executive branch collusion with international narcotics traffickers in support of the Nicaraguan *contras*. That campaign has spanned three decades, commencing with a lawsuit filed in Costa Rica in 1985 against American journalists Martha Honey and Tony Avirgan for having implicated a CIA asset in *contra* drug trafficking and continues as we write.[1] As recounted in chapter 16, Harrison has since seen his life virtually destroyed for talking to us about his CIA undercover work in Mexico, while attempts have been made to intimidate us as well. "Be absolutely sure of your facts and thorough in your documentation," Harrison has warned us more than once, "because they will come after you and do all they can to discredit your book."

    The executive branch's full-press campaign to conceal the true nature and scope of its covert proxy war against Nicaragua's Sandinista government was triggered by media

fallout from the 30 May 1984 La Penca bombing attempt on the life of southern front
contra commander Edén Pastora. Among the twenty-one journalists injured in the explosion at Pastora's jungle camp that night was Tony Avirgan, who, together with his
then wife Martha Honey, would conduct an independent investigation into the La
Penca bombing, then write and publish a report that implicated the CIA and an American with dual U.S.–Costa Rican citizenship by the name of John Hull, whom Honey
and Avirgan identified as a CIA asset with extensive landholdings in northwestern
Costa Rica.[2] When Honey and Avirgan issued their La Penca report in October 1985,
Hull filed a libel suit against them in the First Penal Court of San José, Costa Rica, for
injuries, falsehood, and defamation of character, denying their allegations that he
(1) worked for the CIA and was a conduit of National Security Council funds; (2) had
played a role in providing Cuban exile military trainers for Edén Pastora's southern
front *contras*; (3) had been involved in the La Penca bombing, as well as a second plot
to assassinate Pastora; and (4) had been under investigation for complicity in *contra*-
related drug trafficking. Honey and Avirgan also stated in their La Penca report that
John Hull had been involved in a subsequent terrorist plot to bomb the American
embassy in San José and kill U.S. ambassador Lewis Tambs, blaming the attack on the
Sandinistas and using the incident as an excuse for direct U.S. intervention in Nicaragua. Curiously, Hull did not challenge that allegation in his libel complaint.[3]

Hull's legal strategy, apparently based on erroneous assumptions about Honey and
Avirgan's ability to find witnesses willing to testify against him, was designed to hobble
their journalistic work and prevent them from pursuing their exposé of CIA links to
the *contras*. (Thirteen years later, the agency's own inspector general, Frederick P. Hitz,
would publicly acknowledge that Hull had been a CIA asset.[4]) Inasmuch as in Costa
Rica libel cases involving the media are heard by the country's three-judge Supreme
Court, Hull filed suit against Honey and Avirgan not as journalists but as private individuals, thus assuring that it would be heard in a lower court by a single judge, apparently thought to be more susceptible to pressure and influence than a trio of Supreme
Court justices. At the trial the only evidence he presented was the defendants' La Penca
report. He called just one witness, an American mercenary whose testimony contributed nothing of substance to his case, then opted not to testify on his own behalf.

The defendants, in turn, presented nine witnesses, testified on their own behalf,
and were acquitted. Hull appealed the verdict to Costa Rica's Supreme Court and lost
again. He then used a local CIA-funded *contra* support organization called the Asocia-
ción Democrática Costarricense (ADC) to file a six-hundred-page criminal complaint
against Honey and Avirgan, accusing them of espionage and demanding that they be
expelled from the country. The Costa Rican judiciary dismissed that complaint, too,
as meritless, in February 1988.

Hull himself had become a target of Costa Rican law enforcement beginning two
months before the La Penca bombing, when a local resident brought suit against him
for his involvement with the *contras*. The country's Rural Guard conducted several
raids on his property, but he was always forewarned and managed to conceal compromising evidence. Then, following dismissal of his ADC criminal complaint against
Honey and Avirgan, he was formally indicted for "hostile acts" (including cocaine

trafficking) and murder in the La Penca bombing. Throughout this period, the U.S. embassy in San José intervened on Hull's behalf to frustrate local efforts to prosecute him. When he was finally arrested in early 1989, U.S. representatives David Dreier, Lee Hamilton, and seventeen of their congressional colleagues addressed a letter directly to President Oscar Arias threatening a deterioration in U.S.–Costa Rica relations if local authorities did not cease harassing Hull, to which Arias replied angrily, "Mr. John Hull is accused of serious crimes, among them that of participating in the illegal traffic of drugs to the United States. It pains me that you insinuate that the exemplary relation between your country and mine could deteriorate because our legal system is fighting against drug trafficking, no matter how powerful the people who participate in it."[5] Five months later Hull jumped bail and, in a joint DEA-CIA operation, was secretly flown to the United States on a flight arranged by a DEA agent on the ground in Costa Rica.[6]

The overall strategy for Honey and Avirgan's defense in their San José trial was provided by Daniel Sheehan and Fr. Bill Davis of the Christic Institute, a public interest law firm based in Washington, DC. It was basically a reverse strategy of having the defendants go on the offensive against the plaintiff, in this case putting John Hull and the CIA on trial for criminal acts against the sovereign states of Nicaragua and Costa Rica. Sheehan, a Harvard Law School graduate and crusading defender of victims of state and corporate power, was best known at the time for his defense of Vietnam War protesters Daniel and Philip Berrigan and his successful litigation of the Karen Silkwood suit against the Kerr-McGee Corporation. One week after Honey and Avirgan's acquittal in Hull's San José libel suit, the Christic Institute filed a civil suit on their behalf against Hull and twenty-eight other *contra*-related defendants in U.S. District Court for the Southern District of Florida (Miami).

Avirgan and Honey v. Hull et al. became a cause célèbre among a wide spectrum of politically engaged Americans opposed to U.S. intervention in Central America, as well as a major challenge to the Reagan and Bush Sr. administrations. Sheehan, with his signature curly hair, imposing presence, and bring-on-the-bad-guys attitude, quickly became the poster boy for the Christic's counteroffensive against the Reagan administration's covert efforts to bring down Nicaragua's Sandinista government. He spoke about the case before innumerable audiences around the country, including at major fund-raising events with big-name performers, which netted the Christic impressive sums of money with which to pursue pretrial preparations, including depositions of more than seventy persons—among them Eugene Hasenfus, a CIA contract flight crew member captured by Sandinista soldiers when his plane was shot down in early October 1986 and whose 8 April 1988 deposition taken on the Oneida Indian reservation outside Green Bay, Wisconsin, we attended.

The Christic Institute filed its civil suit against Hull et al. four months prior to Hasenfus's capture and revelation of CIA/National Security Council (NSC) involvement in *contra* operations. Then, in November 1986, a month after Hasenfus was captured, the U.S.-Iran arms-for-hostages deal and related diversion of funds to the Nicaraguan *contras* also came to light as a consequence of leaks in Beirut and Teheran. Up to that point, CIA/NSC damage control had been focused on maintaining plausible deniability of any direct involvement in the *contra* affair, which included a concerted effort to discredit Honey and Avirgan's ongoing inquiry into the U.S.-*contra* connection. Now, however, matters suddenly turned dire, with Director of Central Intelligence William Casey concluding that the covert anti-Sandinista program was about to unravel. Immediately after the Hasenfus shootdown, Casey ordered Oliver North "to shut down the entire Central American operation." When the Iran-*contra* connection was revealed soon after, he advised North to hire an attorney and instructed him "to clean up his files." The operational mistake, North would subsequently aver, was not the proxy *contra* war itself, but rather the crossing of two covert operations, Iran and Nicaragua, with the same overseers, namely, himself and retired Air Force general Richard V. Secord.[7]

The issue for the executive branch had never been the "rightness" of Iran-Contra, but rather how best to insulate the two interrelated covert operations from unmanageable political and judicial challenge. For the CIA as an executive branch agency, the immediate issue was to obfuscate its role in Iran-Contra, but its overarching concern was to shroud its operational methods and assets from public view. Especially delicate was the question of CIA collusion with drug traffickers, which would occupy agency damage controllers into the new century and bears centrally on our account of the Manuel Buendía case. As veteran investigative reporter Robert Parry, who broke many of the Iran-Contra stories, expressed it, "The notion that the U.S. government would sanction the drug trade was more than could be tolerated."[8] The result was an all-out counteroffensive by the White House, the intelligence community, the Justice Department, and politically sympathetic members of Congress to discredit anyone offering evidence of covert government involvement with drug-trafficking assets.

The extraordinary feature of Iran-Contra, Independent Counsel Lawrence Walsh concluded, was that "a cover-up engineered in the White House of one President and completed by his successor prevented the rule of law from being applied to the perpetrators of criminal activity of constitutional dimension."[9] In point of fact, the cover-up of *contra*-related criminal activity by U.S. agents and assets was relentless through the administrations of four presidents and has continued down to the present. The Christic Institute's Racketeer Influenced and Corrupt Organizations Act (RICO) lawsuit against John Hull et al. in Miami, the Trifecta prosecution in San Diego, and the three Camarena trials in Los Angeles, as well as the takedown of *San Jose Mercury News* investigative reporter Gary Webb for his 1996 "Dark Alliance" exposé of CIA links to *contra* cocaine traffickers, all occurred against this backdrop of a concerted executive branch cover-up.

Administration efforts to derail, neutralize, or otherwise thwart congressional inquiries, media investigations, and judicial proceedings that threatened to expose the criminal underside of the proxy *contra* war against Sandinista Nicaragua included the full gamut of active measures, from public denials, perjured testimony, and manipulation of the media to intimidation and homicide. Honey and Avirgan were aggressively surveilled, their Costa Rican residence was broken into multiple times and their files rifled, their sources were threatened, one was murdered, and another was forced to flee the country with his family. Oliver North is reported to have personally ordered surveillance and countermeasures against Honey, Avirgan, and the Christic Institute. And in the end their U.S. District Court case against John Hull et al. was dismissed by Judge James Lawrence King as "frivolous," while levied court costs and defendants' legal fees amounting to almost two million dollars effectively destroyed the Christic Institute's ability to challenge vested political and economic interests on behalf of the public.[10]

In Los Angeles, meanwhile, a grand jury had returned indictments against three Mexicans then in U.S. custody: René Verdugo Urquídez and Raúl López Álvarez for the murders of Enrique Camarena and his Mexican pilot Alfredo Zavala Avelar; and Jesús Félix Gutiérrez as an accessory to the killings. The trial of the three commenced on 28 July 1988 in Federal District Court for the Central District of California, Judge Edward Rafeedie presiding. In the course of the eight-week trial, defense attorneys argued that their clients were essentially scapegoats for Guadalajara cartel boss Miguel Ángel Félix Gallardo, who, they asserted, was also implicated in the Camarena murder but had not been indicted because of his support for the Nicaraguan *contras*. Based on undisclosed supporting evidence submitted to the court, they filed a motion for dismissal with Judge Rafeedie, who rejected it on the basis that, whatever Félix Gallardo's relationship with the *contras* was, it had no bearing on the trial issues at hand. Assistant U.S. Attorney Roel Campos described the attempt to implicate the U.S. government in the trafficker-*contra* relationship as a "sideshow" and "irresponsible leap into fantasy" and the motion for dismissal as "one of the most outrageous that has been filed in a criminal proceeding in recent years."[11] Allegations of executive branch complicity with narcotics traffickers in its proxy war against the Sandinistas would be repeated over the next several years in Los Angeles Federal District Court, but Judge Rafeedie consistently dismissed them as meritless and prevented counsel from presenting evidence to the contrary.

Rafeedie, for his part, was an interesting personality. One of the defense attorneys in the second Camarena trial (*United States v. Matta Ballesteros, Zuno Arce, Bernabé Ramírez, and Vásquez Velasco*, 1990) described him to us offhandedly as an "ex-carnival barker." As a young man, he had operated rides at the old Pacific Ocean Park in Santa Monica, California, then traveled the carnival circuit with a portable electric racehorse game called Derby. In later years, he would describe himself as "the only carny" ever to become a federal judge.

Rafeedie was born in Orange, New Jersey, to Palestinian immigrant parents, who subsequently went back to Palestine for a period before returning permanently to the United States. He could recall as a boy throwing rocks at British occupation forces and likely would have traveled a very different life path had his parents not decided to resettle in Southern California. Following service in the U.S. Army during the Korean War, he completed undergraduate studies at the University of Southern California, then earned a law degree from its School of Law. After a decade in private practice, two years as a Santa Monica Municipal Court judge, and eleven years as a California Superior Court judge, Rafeedie was appointed to the federal bench in 1982 by then president Ronald Reagan. He was, according to his *Los Angeles Times* obituary, one of thirteen "Reagan judges" who formed a conservative majority at the U.S. Federal District Courthouse in Los Angeles.[12]

UNITED STATES DISTRICT COURT FOR THE
CENTRAL DISTRICT OF CALIFORNIA

Los Angeles, California, Wednesday, 6 June 1990

Direct examination of Lawrence Victor Harrison by Assistant U.S. Attorney John L. Carlton per court recorder's Transcript of Proceedings, Case No. CR 87-422(F)-ER, vol. 13, 75–83.

Q: Mr. Harrison, is the name you just gave the name you were born with?
A: No, it isn't.
Q: At some point in your life, did you adopt that as the name you would use?
A: Yes, I did.
Q: How long ago did you do that?
A: Approximately 25 years ago.
Q: Have you used it continuously ever since?
A: Yes, I have.
Q: You've used it in all your dealings?
A: Yes, I have.
Q: Now, are you an American citizen, Mr. Harrison?
A: Yes, I am.
Q: Have you . . . did you study at any colleges and universities in the United States?
A: I attended classes at Berkeley—University of California at Berkeley—in the 1960s. And I also attended classes at the Boalt Hall School of Law.
The Court: You say you attended classes. Did you graduate?
The Witness: I did not graduate. I was auditing classes. I was an unregistered student during the '60s.
By Mr. Carlton:
Q: All right. During what time did you attend these classes?
A: I began in 1965 and I ended in 1971.
Q: Now, at some point, did you move to Mexico?
A: Yes, I did.
Q: When was that?
A: I first moved to Mexico in 1968. I lived there off and on. I came back for classes until 1971. I was there on spring breaks, summer vacations.
Q: Did you eventually move to Mexico on a permanent basis?
A: Yes, I did, in 1971.
Q: And how long did you then live in Mexico?
A: I lived in Mexico until the first part of this year.
Q: Now, during the time that you lived in Mexico, did you obtain some employment there?
A: Well, I began as a law clerk for a Mexican attorney in 1971. That actually began in 1968, but on a very tenuous basis, because I had to come back to the United States. From 1971 on, I worked for him full time as a law clerk. It wasn't employment at that time. It eventually became employment. . . .
Q: How long did you work as a law clerk for this individual?
A: Until 1976.
Q: And where did you work? What city?
A: In Guadalajara.

Q: And during the period that you lived in Mexico, did you live in Guadalajara that entire time?

A: Yes. I lived in Guadalajara most of the time that I lived in Mexico.

Q: Did you obtain other employment in 1976?

A: In 1976, I left the employ of the attorney I worked for as a law clerk and began doing work for C.N.O.P. [Confederación Nacional de Organizaciones Populares], which is an organism [*sic*] of the PRI political party in Mexico.

. . .

Q: Now, during the period that you worked as an attorney for the C.N.O.P., were you a licensed attorney in Mexico?

A: There was no licensing procedure in Mexico at that time. Even today, more than 80 percent of the attorneys in Mexico are not yet licensed.

Q: And during the period that you worked in the social service law office for the C.N.O.P., did you also have your own personal clients?

A: Yes. Later on, after I settled in at the law office there, I began to have my own private clients, together with the social service practice I was doing then.

Q: Now, at some point, did you leave your law practice?

A: I left my law practice in the latter part of 1979 and I moved to Acapulco.

. . .

Q: When did you return to Guadalajara?

A: In the . . . it was sometime during 1980, probably about the middle part of 1980, the early part of 1980.

. . .

Q: And at this time, then, did you decide to take up another line of work?

A: Well, I needed another line of work. I was interested in electronics. I've always been interested in electronics. I had installed a two-meter VHF [very high frequency] communication system in the city of Guadalajara, just for my own purposes, my own use. Some attorneys and members of the police organizations saw this system, they saw that it worked, and they became interested in it. That led me to offer my services to them as an electronics technician, a communications technician.

Q: Now, how did you offer your services?

A: Well, I initially made up a resume listing what I'd done in Mexico since I'd come and listing what I could do with the communications systems, and I circulated it among police agencies in Guadalajara. . . .

. . .

Q: What agencies did you circulate the resume to?

A: Well, generally I circulated the resume with all the agencies: the State Judicial Police, the Federal Judicial Police, the DFS. At the end, I was given employment by a high official of the State Judicial . . . the State Police Department . . . the State Department of Public Security. And I was also given employment by one of the commandants of the DFS.

Jury selection for *United States v. Matta Ballesteros, Zuno Arce, Bernabé Ramírez, and Vásquez Velasco* was completed on Friday morning, 11 May 1990. The panel was sworn in and its members instructed not to read, hear, or listen to news reports about the case or to otherwise discuss the case with anyone for the duration of the trial. Proceedings commenced immediately and ran for the next nine weeks, followed by three weeks of jury deliberations resulting in convictions of all four defendants. In opening arguments, Assistant U.S. Attorney John L. Carlton framed the government's case as a reprisal killing for economic damages inflicted on the Guadalajara narcotics cartel by agents of the DEA. It was, he told the jurors, part of a campaign "to intimidate the DEA" following major American-instigated marijuana raids on cartel cannabis plantations during 1984.[13] It was a straightforward scenario with a plausible motive, but—as government prosecutors had to know—one that did not correspond to fact.

The four defendants sat at separate tables in the courtroom and were tried individually beginning with Matta Ballesteros, followed by Bernabé Ramírez, Zuno Arce, and Vásquez Velasco. Zuno Arce's case was argued midway into the proceedings, at which point Assistant U.S. Attorney Carlton first called the government's star witness, Lawrence Victor Harrison. Carlton spent much of the morning and afternoon of 6 June establishing Harrison's bona fides as a credible witness able to confirm Zuno's personal association with the perpetrators of the Camarena and Zavala homicides. The testimony that Carlton elicited from Harrison that Wednesday was a veritable tale from wonderland, whose coded subtext—plainly evident yet obfuscated by government prosecutors and the court—was the evasive narrative of an American intelligence agent.

UNITED STATES DISTRICT COURT FOR THE
CENTRAL DISTRICT OF CALIFORNIA

Los Angeles, California, Wednesday, 6 June 1990

Continued direct examination of Lawrence Victor Harrison by Assistant U.S. Attorney John L. Carlton, Case No. CR 87-422(F)-ER, vol. 13, pp. 85–87, 92–95, 98, 113, 121–126.

. . .

Q: And during what period of time did you perform this piecemeal electronics work for law enforcement agencies?

A: Between the first part of 1981 and the latter part of 1983. I continued working for one specific commandant until 1984, September of 1984.

Q: Now, during that period, was there a particular agency for which you performed most of your work?

A: From 1983 until 1984, I was the chief of communications for the IPS office—that's Investigaciones Políticas y Sociales; that's Political and Social Investigations of the Ministry of Interior of Mexico and the local commandant's office of Guadalajara— from the middle of 1983 until the end of 1984.

. . .

Q: Now, during the period that you performed this electronics work for these various agencies, were you issued any kind of credentials?

A: Well, I was given what is known as an *oficio de comisión*. An *oficio de comisión* is a letter made up on the letterhead of the local commandant's office, signed by the local commandant. It has a picture on it with a seal over the picture, a seal underneath the name of the commandant. It's normally wrapped in plastic and reduced in size and put inside a badge case.

. . .

Q: Did you obtain more than one of those?

A: Well, in all, during the period from 1981 until 1984, I held three *oficios de comisión*.

Q: Can you describe those?

A: Well, they're letters written on the letterhead of the local commandant's office describing the work that you've been assigned, in my case, communications work. I was the communications technician for the office.

Q: And were all of those *oficios* DFS *oficios*?

A: No. Two were DFS and one was IPS.

Carlton methodically substantiated the unique abilities and experience that allowed Harrison to testify knowledgeably about the inner workings of the Guadalajara drug cartel and its extensive ties to Mexican officialdom. He established for the record that Harrison was an American citizen who had resided in Mexico for almost two decades, had performed technical services for various Mexican police and intelligence agencies, had been issued official credentials identifying him as an agent with the DFS and IPS (both attached to Mexico's Secretariat of Government), and had been assigned by an IPS superior to perform certain technical services for Ernesto Fonseca, one of the principal figures in the Guadalajara cartel. Carlton further established that Harrison personally knew and had interacted with the principal bosses of the Guadalajara cartel, photographs of whom he easily identified for the court and the jury.

Resumed direct examination of Lawrence Victor Harrison by Assistant U.S. Attorney John L. Carlton following the noon recess:

Q: Mr. Harrison, I believe when we left off, you testified that at some point you came to live in Ernesto Fonseca's residence. Now, when did that occur?

A: That occurred in July of 1983.

Q: How did that come about?

A: I was invited by a member of his entourage to join the group around him at the same time the commandant of the IPS office in Guadalajara told me that I would be assigned to help [him] and his people establish a communications system in the city of Guadalajara.

Q: Who was the IPS commandant who told you that?

A: That was Sergio Espino Verdín. He hadn't really taken office at that time, but he had been appointed and he was in Guadalajara organizing the *comandancia*.

Q: Had you known Sergio Espino Verdín prior to that time?

A: Yes, I had.

Q: When did you first meet him?

A: I met him sometime in 1982 in Matamoros. He was with a group of agents around Quintero Benítez, who was a DFS commandant in Matamoros. At that time, I went up and did some work for them. . . .

    . . .

Q: All right. So when you moved into Fonseca's house, you began working on a communications system for him?

A: Yes.

Q: Was this to be a communications system that was different from the one you had previously been maintaining for him?

A: Yes, it was different. It was a new one.

Q: And did you in fact design a system for Ernesto Fonseca?

A: Yes, I did.

Q: Did you then have occasion to create this system for him?

A: Yes, I did.

Q: And during what period of time did it take you to create this radio communications system?

A: I did the preliminary mathematics and the plots and the equations and everything in July. And that same month, they sent me up to the United States to purchase components.

Q: Did you in fact purchase the components in the United States?

A: Yes, I did.

Q: And did you take them back to Mexico?

A: Yes, I did.

Q: And did you then put this system together?

A: Yes.

Q: Could you, in a general fashion, describe the system that you put together for Ernesto Fonseca, the radio communications system?

A: It was a VHF communications system, very high frequency. It had a 74 megahertz offset. It was situated in channels that are property in Mexico of the Social Security Office, but they're not used. That was to insure that they would not be interfered with by other people and that they wouldn't have anybody else on the frequencies. The separation of the frequencies was so that anybody who would be listening to the frequencies would not be able to hear who was talking—the separation between transmission and reception. It consisted of four repeaters and, initially, some 50 radios.
. . .

Q: . . . Well, how long did it take you to set this thing up and get it in operation?

A: It took me approximately two and a half weeks to build the first repeater. I brought it in pieces and built it myself in the kitchen of [Fonseca's] house and then I installed the entire system.

Q: And when was it relatively complete?

A: It was complete by the latter part of September [1983].

Q: After the system was completed, did you have some continuing duties with regard to it?

A: Well, I had a group of people who were assigned to aid me in maintaining it and repairing the radios. There were a number of repeater sites that had to be . . . they were maintained by batteries. We had to go and charge the batteries and align the repeaters and check the antennas daily.

Q: Did you, in the course of your work, in maintaining this system, have occasion to make frequent checks on how well the system was performing?

A: As the system engineer, I listened to the system and had full control of it 24 hours a day during the entire time that it was installed and operated.

Carlton elicited further details from Harrison about the capabilities of the radio communications system he had created for Ernesto Fonseca and Fonseca's cartel associates. He established that Harrison had performed other tasks for Fonseca as well, including armed escort of drug shipments transiting the Guadalajara area; that he would do whatever Fonseca ordered because Fonseca possessed IPS credentials accrediting him as a Gobernación officer of superior rank; and, above all, that he had been part of the overlapping inner circles of Mexican narcotics traffickers, law enforcement, and national security in the critical years of the early 1980s. Finally, Carlton directed Harrison's testimony to what we conclude was the government's primary objective in this trial: to establish the existence of a close working relationship between defendant Zuno Arce and the perpetrators of the Camarena murder.

Continuation of direct examination of Lawrence Victor Harrison by Assistant U.S. Attorney John L. Carlton, the afternoon of 6 June 1990:

Q: Did you ever hear Ernesto Fonseca refer to Caro as his partner?
A: Yes, I did.
Q: And vice versa?
A: Yes.
Q: Now, did you know Miguel Ángel Félix Gallardo?
A: Yes.
Q: How did you come to meet him?
A: I met him through Ernesto Fonseca and Rafael Caro Quintero.
Q: Was this during the period that you were living with Fonseca?
A: I had met him before that.
Q: How many times after that did you meet him?
A: In total, 20 or 25.
Q: Were you on a first-name basis with him?
A: Well, we had to say "Don," "Don Miguel." It wasn't exactly a first name.
. . .
Q: Do you know an individual named Rubén Zuno Arce?
A: Yes, I do.
Q: How long have you known him?
A: I've known of him and seen him frequently since the 1970s.
Q: How did you come to first meet him?
A: When I started studying law in Guadalajara, I was assisted by his father, Don Guadalupe. . . . From that time on, I knew him, his brothers, from many contacts in the legal scene, in the political scene in Guadalajara—I also worked for the political party [PRI]—and I saw him many times.
Q: When was the last time that you saw him?
A: The last time I saw Mr. Zuno was at a *quinceañero* [coming-out] party for Alicia Sánchez Flores in 1989.
. . .
Q: Now, drawing your attention, Mr. Harrison, to the month of November in 1983, did you have occasion at that time to attend a party in Guadalajara?
A: Yes, I did.
Q: And where did this party take place?
A: The party took place at the house in Las Fuentes on Circunvalación Sur, 113.
Q: Now, is this the house you previously described as being the first house you went to when you began working for Mr. Fonseca?
A: Yes. I installed the security system at that house, four times.
Q: Do you recall when this party occurred?
A: It occurred in the latter part of 1983.
Q: And what was the occasion?
A: I understood that it was a birthday party for Rafael Caro Quintero.
. . .
Q: Well, what was your function at this party?

A: . . . I was sent by Mr. Fonseca in the early afternoon to check on the security system, install some communication sets, take some beer, cases of beer, and supplies for the party, and in general make myself helpful.

Q: Did you remain there then until the party began?

A: I remained there until about 12 o'clock midnight.

Q: And when did the party begin?

A: It began around 3 o'clock in the afternoon.

Q: Do you recall how many people arrived at that party?

A: There were probably 175, 200, maybe 250 people.

Q: Did you see Rafael Caro Quintero there?

A: Yes, I did.

Q: Ernesto Fonseca?

A: Yes.

Q: Miguel Félix?

A: Yes.

Q: Were there any law enforcement officers there?

A: Well, almost all of our office, IPS, was there. There were 20 or 30 State Judicial Police agents; a number of Federal Judicial Police agents; two people from the Army, in uniform; people that were normally at these types of affairs.

Q: Did you see Mr. Zuno there?

A: I saw Don Rubén greet Mr. Caro at the party.

Q: Now, what was Caro doing at that time?

A: Mr. Caro was on top of a horse. He was making a horse dance. They had purchased some horses that had been taught to dance . . . and they were dancing these horses to music. Mr. Caro was smoking a base cigarette and seated on top of the horse making it dance. When Mr. Zuno appeared, he walked over to him, Mr. Caro got down off the horse, and they embraced each other in an *abrazo*, which is a way of greeting. And that's what I saw.

Q: Do you recall any clothing that Mr. Zuno was wearing at that time?

A: I remember that I was surprised to see Don Rubén there. He was dressed like a cowboy, in a casual outfit, and he had on a kind of a cowboy hat.

. . .

Q: Now, did you ever see Mr. Zuno at Mr. Fonseca's residence?

A I saw Don Rubén come there one time. He was led into the gate, the gate that was in the garage. He was taken directly to Mr. Fonseca's office. They were there together 45 minutes, perhaps an hour, and then Mr. Zuno left.

Q: Do you recall when that occurred?

A: It was sometime after November of 1983. I would assume that it was somewhere in the first part of December.

In response to Carlton's further questioning, Harrison testified about his personal familiarity with the address in Guadalajara where Enrique Camarena was interrogated and killed (Lope de Vega, 881); about one time having overheard Rafael Caro Quintero communicating by radio from that address; about friction between himself and Ernesto Fonseca over the inordinate amount of time Fonseca required of him, which interfered with his communications work for the DFS and IPS; about being severely wounded and almost killed in a Jalisco State Judicial Police ambush on 11 September 1984; about his subsequent convalescence and six-month incarceration in the Jalisco State Prison;

and about having handled the ground communications for two aircraft from Colombia in the summer of 1985, then accompanied unloaded cargo to a ranch in the State of Durango.

These last tasks, Harrison testified, had been carried out at the request of Antonio Gárate Bustamante, a Jalisco Judicial Police Special Weapons and Tactics (SWAT) officer for whom Harrison had previously done electronics work. At the time, Gárate also appears to have been a DEA undercover operative. He would subsequently be exposed and have to take refuge in the United States, where he and Harrison would maintain a friendly association until Gárate's demise in Nogales, Arizona, in 2009.

Carlton drew his direct examination to a conclusion with several questions about Harrison's employment history. Had he been employed prior to returning to the United States? Yes, he had. What was his employment? Harrison stated that he had been the owner and chief executive of his own communications consulting firm since the fall of 1988, a company called Comunicación Arboledas. He had, he testified, done contract work for the Jalisco gubernatorial campaign committee, the Jalisco State secretaries of finance and urban renewal, and the Jalisco highway patrol, as well as for a number of Guadalajara businessmen. And prior to that? Carlton asked. He had been the vice president, communications officer, operating officer, and attorney "of a large housing development company with nine housing developments."[14]

What Harrison neglected to state in response to this last question, and what Carlton may not have known, was that the real estate company for which he had worked was owned by Javier García Paniagua and that some of the large properties it managed belonged to the drug bosses then serving prison sentences in Mexico for the Camarena and Zavala killings. García Paniagua, a former DFS director and, at the time of the Camarena trials, Mexico City police chief, was accused by attorneys Medrano and Carlton of having participated in the planning of the Camarena abduction, while Harrison told us that García Paniagua had actually been present during Camarena's interrogation. He further assured us that García Paniagua had also played a role in the Manuel Buendía assassination.[15]

Cross-examination of Lawrence Victor Harrison by lead Zuno defense attorney Edward M. Medvene, afternoon of 6 June 1990, per court reporter's Transcript of Proceedings, Case No. CR 87-422(F)-ER, vol. 13, pp. 144–145.

Q: Now, what name were you given at birth, Sir?

A: George Marshall Leyvas [sic].

Q: And in the course of your lifetime, how many different names have you used?

A: Two.

Q: And what are they, Sir?

A: The one I just told you and Lawrence Victor Harrison.

Q: Haven't you also used, Sir, Harrison Cumens, C U M E N S? You've used that name, haven't you, Sir?

A: No, I have not; not in the way that you're trying to state, Counsel, no.

Q: You've used it . . . I'm asking you if you ever used it. I'm not asking what way you used it. My question, Sir, is: Have you on occasion used the name Harrison Cumens? Yes or no Sir, please.

A: I have used the name Lawrence Victor Harrison Cumens [*sic*].
Q: Have you used the name, Sir, George Marshall Davis?
A: Yes, I have.
Q: So when you just told us you used two names, and only two, that was a lie. Is that right?
A: No, Sir. That is not a lie.
Q: You've used the name George Harrison Lawrence also, have you not, Sir?
A: No, I have not.

The preceding excerpt from the court recorder's transcript encapsulates well the textbook trial strategy employed by Rubén Zuno Arce's defense team to impugn the veracity of prosecution witnesses. More important, it reveals linguistic and cultural impediments to an accurate understanding of witness testimony and thus to an impartial determination of guilt or innocence. Attorney Medvene's attempt to demonstrate that Harrison had not been truthful when he stated that he had only used two names in his life, for example, was based on errors in the official trial transcript, as well as a lack of understanding of how family names are used in Spanish-speaking societies.

When Harrison gave his birth name as George Marshall Davis, the court recorder apparently heard "Leyvas," a familiar Hispanic surname, and so transcribed his birth name as "George Marshall Leyvas," which Medvene then seized on to suggest an untruthful response by the witness. Having only recently returned to the United States from many years' residence in Mexico, Harrison was a fluent Spanish speaker and fully acculturated to Mexican society, as a consequence of which Spanish frequently interfered with his use of English. It is easy to see how his pronunciation of the *D* in Davis could have been interpreted as an *L*, hence the recording of Leyvas. Harrison, of course, would not know how the court recorder had rendered his name, nor would Medvene's ear have detected the phonetic nuance.

Similarly, when Medvene established that in the past Harrison had also given his name as Lawrence Victor Harrison Cumens, suggesting that this was yet a fourth name he had used and thus another instance of untruthful testimony, he did so evidently without any comprehension of the Mexican custom of combining paternal and maternal surnames. Cumens is a misrendering of Cummings, which was Harrison's mother's maiden name. When Harrison denied that he had used the name Cumens in the deceptive way Medvene sought to imply, he was, in fact, being truthful. It was simply an instance of carrying over a customary Mexican practice into a U.S. cultural setting where it was misinterpreted. It was another instance, as well, of linguistically impaired hearing.

More broadly, Zuno's defense team appeared not to grasp who Lawrence Victor Harrison really was, namely, a U.S. intelligence operative, and so framed its defense strategy around the bizarre persona portrayed by the government, which in the end served the government's ulterior purposes well: Zuno Arce would be convicted, while Harrison's testimony regarding CIA involvement with Mexican narcotics traffickers and Nicaraguan *contras* would be dismissed as "incompetent," nothing more than rumor and hearsay. Had Ed Medvene and his associates fully processed the evident fact that Harrison was an American agent, we think it likely they would have pursued a different courtroom strategy, one that might have resulted in a dismissal of the case on national security grounds.

Instead, they accepted the prosecution's version of Harrison's extraordinary past and determined to show a pattern of falsehoods and inaccuracies in his testimony about that past so as to vitiate his testimony regarding their client, Rubén Zuno Arce. Several months prior to trial, defense counsel learned from routine paperwork filed with the court that, since Zuno's initial indictment for perjury in August 1989, government prosecutors had made numerous in camera filings with Judge Rafeedie of classified documents whose contents had been withheld from Zuno's attorneys, among them the DEA-6 reports described in chapter 10. In early February 1990, Medvene and his associates formally requested that Rafeedie either release those documents to defense counsel or remove himself from the case. Rafeedie opted to release the documents, including tapes of the 25 September 1989 interview of Harrison.[16]

Brian M. Colligan, a junior attorney working for the Zuno defense team, listened to the tapes, then prepared a memo outlining their key points, the most important of which was Harrison's suggestion that the CIA was complicit in Mexican drug trafficking and that the agency had been behind the recorded interrogation of Enrique Camarena. "Harrison says that it was the Americans who controlled the entire drug trade down in Mexico," Colligan noted. "Fonseca and Caro planned and orchestrated the Camarena incident for others higher up in Mexico City, possibly the CIA, and it was that faction that wanted the interrogation tape recorded." It was Harrison's understanding, Colligan concluded, "that the CIA was involved with the interrogation tapes."[17]

Ed Medvene, as Zuno's lead defense attorney, chose not to introduce the matter of possible CIA involvement in the Camarena affair into his cross-examination of Harrison, preferring instead to conduct a focused attack on Harrison's credibility as a witness. Counsel for defendant Bernabé Ramírez, however, did attempt to question Harrison about alleged ties between the CIA and drug traffickers. Attorney Mary Kelley had been questioning Harrison about DFS commandant Sergio Espino Verdín. When Harrison stated that Espino had reported to DFS chief Miguel Nazar Haro, Kelly asked if Nazar was connected to the CIA but was cut off by Judge Rafeedie, who sustained a government objection that such questions were irrelevant to the case at hand. A month later, however, Rafeedie reversed himself in response to defense counsel insistence that the classified DEA debriefings were indeed germane to the Camarena case and ordered Harrison to return to court to testify in a special voir dire hearing about his statements to DEA debriefers concerning alleged CIA collusion with Mexican narcotics traffickers.[18]

Voir dire examination of plaintiff's witness Lawrence Victor Harrison (jury not present), per court reporter's Transcript of Proceedings, 6 July 1990, Case No. CR 87-422(F)-ER, vol. 26, pp. 54–55.

By Assistant U.S. Attorney John L. Carlton:

. . .

Q: And were these discussions by you with Agent Schmidt on February 9th based upon anything that you personally knew to be true through personal involvement?

A : There are one or two instances in there that were based on personal knowledge. The
majority of it was based on a reconstruction of rumors then prevalent in Mexico that
were prevalent among the Mexican intelligence community and the Mexican police
departments, which led them to believe that the United States was not being entirely
forthcoming in depicting the relationship between them and the Mexicans.

Q : During your interview with Agent Schmidt, did you make any representation based
upon your own personal knowledge that the CIA was involved with narcotics
traffickers in Mexico?

A : No, I did not.

Q : Did you make any representation to Agent Schmidt on that date based upon your own
personal knowledge concerning events surrounding the death of Manuel Buendía?

A : No, I did not.

Q : So, basically, you were providing to Agent Schmidt information you had obtained
from other individuals in Mexico?

A : I was providing to Mr. Schmidt an intelligence report on what the prevailing ideas
were among the Mexican intelligence community and the Mexican police
departments on the true relation of events that had transpired in 1983, '84, '85 in
Mexico. I was giving evidence as to beliefs, opinions.

The procedural purpose of Harrison's voir dire testimony was to determine the extent
to which he possessed personal knowledge of the events he had recounted in the
DEA-6 debriefing reports of September 1989 and February 1990. By holding this hearing, vigorously opposed by attorneys Carlton and Medrano, Rafeedie was opening up
the explosive matter of alleged CIA involvement with Mexican drug traffickers in support of the Nicaraguan *contras*, a subject he had not allowed to be pursued in trial but
now proceeded to broach in a carefully staged public session outside the presence of
the jury that satisfied defense counsel demands at the same time that it would serve the
ulterior executive branch agenda of discrediting Harrison's testimony about CIA activities in Mexico. From the government's perspective it was a delicate maneuver that
threatened to confirm as much as it might cover up. And in light of prosecution objec-
tions, it would appear to have been Rafeedie's decision rather than a fully concerted
government scheme.

Inasmuch as a voir dire hearing is solely for the purpose of determining specific
information pertinent to ongoing trial proceedings, it is limited to direct questioning
of a witness and is not a venue for cross-examination. In this instance, it was counsel
for defendants Matta Ballesteros (Martin R. Stolar), Bernabé Ramírez (Mary Kelley),
and Vásquez Velasco (Gregory Nicolaysen) who questioned Harrison most extensively
about his knowledge of CIA involvement in Mexico. Martin R. Stolar began the probe.

Voir dire examination of Lawrence Victor Harrison by Martin R. Stolar, 6 July 1990,
Case No. CR 87-422(F)-ER, Reporter's Transcript of Proceedings, vol. 26, pp. 62–64.

Q : Now, what personal knowledge, if any, do you have of any American intelligence
agency working with or using the DFS as a cover?

A : That I could definitely identify these Americans as being from an American
intelligence agency, none, Sir. . . . I was told by Mr. Fonseca Carrillo and Mr. Caro

Quintero, by Javier Barba Hernández, by Sergio Espino Verdín, by Federico Castel del Oro, and by other members of the Federal Security Directorate that these activities did, in fact, occur, and [I] met with two Americans at Mr. Fonseca's house in 1983 who referred to themselves as trainers for the Contras. . . . They told me that they were working with the Contras, that they were somehow together with the American government. They did not pull out any credentials or identify themselves as being CIA agents or agents of any other agency of the U.S. government.
. . .

Q: What was it that Fonseca, Caro, Ibarra, Espino, Castel del Oro told you about their relations with any American intelligence agency?

A: They indicated to me that they had some type of a relationship with the American government; that they had no reason to fear any reprisals from the American government; that somehow or another they were in some type of a political conflagration with the American government; and that I shouldn't ask about it or get involved in it, that it was political.

At this point in the voir dire hearing, Harrison turned Stolar's attention to his debriefing five months earlier about the assassination of Manuel Buendía. Stolar had asked him about paragraph 6 of Special Agent Wayne Schmidt's 13 February 1990 DEA-6 report, in which Schmidt notes that, according to Harrison, Buendía had been gathering "information on CIA arms smuggling activity and the relationship the CIA had with known narcotic traffickers." Stolar was focusing on what Harrison knew personally about CIA activities in Mexico and had not indicated any particular interest in the Buendía case. Neither had the government prosecutors. Harrison, however, for his own opaque reasons wanted to insert Buendía into the official court record and took the opening now provided by Stolar to do so.

Continued voir dire questioning of Lawrence Victor Harrison by Martin R. Stolar, Case No. CR 87-2(F)-ER, vol. 26, pp. 66–71.

Q: If you would look at paragraph 6, you provided information that there was some information gathered on CIA arms smuggling activities and the relationship the CIA had with known narcotics traffickers in the Veracruz area.

A: Yes.

Q: Is that also a condensation of a more expanded version of what you described?

A: That is a condensation of the results of an investigation I made, yes.

Q: You made an investigation?

A: Yes, I did.

Q: Could you tell us what the conclusions were of your investigation and then tell us how you went about it?

A: I went about it by conducting interviews with friends of a group of Mexican newspaper reporters who had formed themselves into an informal group to investigate and push forward the police investigation into the assassination of Manuel Buendía. Part of the investigation was talking to people. The other part was the reading of books that they published, newspaper articles that they published— that were published in Mexico and then withdrawn from publication after a very short amount of time.

Q: Under unusual circumstances?

A: Yes, under unusual circumstances, with some of the pages missing in the original publication when it was originally published.

Q: And were there any indications that you or the group you were working with learned that it was American intelligence officials or Mexican intelligence officials that might have had a hand in that?

A: There was a strong suspicion of that.

Q: American CIA?

A: There was a strong suspicion of that; yes, Sir.

Q: Okay, go ahead.

A: Mr. Buendía had investigated primarily the relationship with the CIA in Mexico. That was his primary focus in the books that he published. He jokingly called his newspaper office the MIA, the Mexican Intelligence Agency. He kept a plaque on the door that said MIA. The facts stated in the newspapers in Mexico did not support the contention that his assassination was carried out because of the [DFS] credentials, because the credentials that were picked up from the narcotics traffickers were immediately published in the newspapers. And had he, in fact, been killed for that reason, they would not have been published so quickly. The conclusion was that there was another reason. What that reason was has not been brought to light. . . .

. . .

Q: You indicated that it was learned by certain colleagues that Mr. Buendía had obtained information on certain members of the PRI who were assisting the CIA with arms smuggling and knew of the CIA link to narcotics traffickers. That is what is reported here.

A: Yes, Sir.

Q: Is that an accurate statement of what you told the agents?

A: Yes, that is an accurate statement of what I described to the agent.

Q: Could you tell us where you learned that information?

A: Also as part of the investigation that I told you I had made. I was relating to the agent the facts that I had uncovered, or the suppositions or the rumors that I uncovered, in support of this hypothesis only.

Q: Did you speak to any members of the American intelligence community in connection with your investigation?

A: I don't know if I did or not.

Q: So you may have?

A: Anything is possible, Sir.

Q: Have you ever had any formal relationship with any American intelligence agency in Mexico?

A: Formal relationship? No, I haven't.

Q: How about an informal relationship?

A: I don't think so.

Q: Do you know where the CIA office was in Guadalajara, for example?

A: I have no idea. I don't know if there was an office there.

Stolar went on to question Harrison about his contacts with the DEA and CIA. Harrison acknowledged that one of his jobs had been to tap into the DEA's radio communications system. To whom had he reported the information he obtained from monitoring the DEA's radio communications? He had reported to the head of the Guadalajara DFS office, Sergio Espino Verdín. "Not to the CIA or any chief of station in Guadalajara or Mexico City?" "Not that I know of," Harrison replied. Stolar then questioned Harrison at length about a meeting he had had in 1987 with a man from the U.S. embassy by the name of Dale, who had intimated—and Harrison believed— he was with the CIA. The meeting had been arranged through the Guadalajara DEA office, and Harrison was taken there by DEA agents, who themselves were not permitted to be present during the meeting.

In response to Stolar's questioning, Harrison confirmed what he had reported to S/A Schmidt about his conversation with Dale; that Dale had asked him what he knew about CIA operations in Mexico and what he had told the DEA about the CIA; that in response he had told Dale that Mexican intelligence knew the CIA was working with local drug traffickers, which, he said, Dale had acknowledged with an affirmative nod of his head; that CIA operatives had stayed at Ernesto Fonseca's Guadalajara residence, which Dale also acknowledged with an affirmative nod; and that Dale had then offered to get him a job "any place in the world" if he agreed to leave Mexico.

Martin R. Stolar's continued voir dire examination of Lawrence Victor Harrison, 6 July 1990, Case No. CR 87-422(F)-ER, vol. 26, p. 79.

Q: What kind of work were you supposed to be doing for [Dale]?
A: We didn't get that far. I turned him down.
Q: Was it your understanding that he was offering Company work for you? CIA work?
A: That crossed my mind.
Q: It more than crossed your mind. That's what you understood, is that right?
A: The thought came to my mind, Sir. Yes.
Q: You told Dale—or it's reported, anyway, that you told Dale that you didn't trust the U.S. government and that if the CIA involvement didn't bother Dale, it didn't bother you. What is the basis for Agent Schmidt telling us that in his report?
A: I had already gone through an assassination attempt by the Mexican police at the behest of the narcotics lords. I didn't want to get in trouble with other—I didn't need any more enemies at that point, Sir.
Q: And the other enemies you were thinking about were possible CIA enemies, is that right?
A: Yes, Sir. At the time these statements were being made, this was sensitive knowledge.

"Dale" was subsequently identified as Dale L. Stinson. He actually testified at the 1990 Camarena trial as a government witness, but not about his 1987 Guadalajara meeting with Lawrence Harrison. Indeed, he testified on 7 June of that year, the same day that Harrison completed his testimony before the jury. Harrison was the day's first witness, Stinson its last. Stinson was called to the stand by Assistant U.S. Attorney Medrano, who established in the course of his direct examination that "Dale" had served as a DEA agent for the previous seven years; that he was currently the acting DEA group supervisor in Phoenix, Arizona; that he had been assigned to Mexico from March 1986 to March 1988; that from 1973 to 1983 he had served as a special Justice Department agent with the Border Patrol; and that earlier he had served as a voice recognition specialist with U.S. Naval Intelligence. It was a public resume that could easily have served as a CIA cover, as Harrison suspected. The focus of Stinson's testimony for the prosecution was the role he had played in identifying voices on the recovered tape recordings of Camarena's interrogation.

The Alice in Wonderland quality of Dale Stinson's participation in these trial proceedings derives from the seeming disconnect between his June presence on the witness stand and Harrison's July voir dire testimony about him. In July it was as if no one in the courtroom had ever heard of Stinson beyond the opaque references to "Dale" in S/A Wayne Schmidt's DEA-6 report of 18 September 1989. Defense attorney Martin Stolar in particular questioned Harrison about "Dale" during the voir dire hearing, seemingly oblivious to the fact that he had himself cross-examined Stinson just four weeks earlier. All of the lead defense attorneys had been present during Stinson's June testimony, and three of them had cross-examined him. We would think that at least one of them might have made an effort to question Harrison about his conclusion that "Dale" was CIA in light of what Stinson had told the court about his own government employment record. Yet none did. It would seem all had understood that the CIA was substantively out of bounds.[19]

During the voir dire hearing, Stolar asked Harrison about his reported statement to S/A Schmidt that the German arms dealer Gerhard Mertins had a relationship with the CIA. Harrison replied that Schmidt's version was incorrect and what he had actually said was that Mertins had a relationship with the Israelis in the matter of arms trafficking. In response to a direct question by Stolar, Harrison stated that he had never met Mertins (although he later told us that he had[20]), then said that what he had learned about Mertins had been in connection with his Buendía investigation, which led Stolar to inquire if he had been asked to conduct that investigation by some intelligence agency and whether or not he had been compensated for his work. Harrison claimed, improbably, that he had looked into the Buendía assassination solely out of personal interest, that he had not been paid, and that he had reported the results of his investigation only to Schmidt. (He told us that he had been assigned by the Mexican Secretariat of Government, i.e., by Manuel Bartlett Díaz, to monitor the activities of the independent journalists' oversight group for the Buendía case.[21]) Stolar concluded his voir dire examination of Harrison with a few questions about narcotics boss Miguel Ángel Félix Gallardo.

Final voir dire questions for L. V. Harrison by Martin R. Stolar, 6 July 1990, Case No. CR 87-422(F)-ER, vol. 26, pp. 86–89.

Q: Now, you know or you met a gentleman by the name of Miguel Ángel Félix Gallardo, is that right?

A: Yes, Sir, that's true.

Q: Do you know that he was a very strong supporter of the Contras, the Nicaragua Contras?

A: He told me that.

Q: Under what circumstances did he tell you that?

A: General conversation.

Q: Face to face?

A: Yes, Sir.

Q: Did he describe to you what kind of support he was involved with?

A: No, Sir, he did not.

Q: Was he, to your knowledge, in the business of supplying arms to the Contras?

Mr. Carlton: Object to this as being hearsay, Your Honor.

The Court: Well, it is hearsay, but I'll permit it for the purpose of this hearing.

The witness: He gave me to understand that he was. Yes, Sir.

By Mr. Stolar:

Q: Was he also giving you to understand that he was supplying money to the Contras?

A: He gave me to understand that he had caused money to be supplied to them.

Q: Did he give you any indications or understandings that the CIA or any other intelligence agency was aware of these activities with respect to the Contras?

A: Every time I spoke to him or any other person they always said the Americans, but they never specified any agency of the United States government.

Q: But they said the Americans knew what they were doing, is that right?

A: Yes, they did, Sir.

Q: Did Mr. Gallardo, Félix Gallardo, make any comments to you with respect to the sources of the funds for supplying arms to the Contras?

A: No, Sir. He didn't.

Q: Was it your understanding that he was involved in narcotics trafficking?

A: Yes, Sir, it was.

Q: Did he give you any indication or did anybody who was associated with him give you any indication that the funds derived from narcotics trafficking were the funds being used to help the Contras?

Mr. Carlton: This calls for speculation, Your Honor.

The Court: Sustained.

By Mr. Stolar:

Q: Did he tell you that's what happened?

A: Yes, Sir, he did.

Q: Did he give you any indication that his money raising operation, that is, narcotics trafficking, was thereby safe from intervention by the Americans because of what he was doing?

Mr. Carlton: Again, speculation and hearsay, Your Honor.

The Court: Overruled.

The witness: He did say that to me.

The Court: Did or didn't?

The witness: He did, Sir.

Mr. Stolar: Thank you. I'm going to quit while I'm ahead.

Defendant Bernabé Ramírez's lead defense counsel, Mary Kelley, questioned Harrison further about his knowledge of CIA ties to the Guadalajara cartel and the Nicaraguan *contras*, focusing on two American pilots he had seen at Ernesto Fonseca's residence, an arms shipment he had inspected, a 1983 meeting between Fonseca and individuals Harrison identified as "Cuban nationals," and conversations he had had with Félix Gallardo and other Mexican traffickers about their support of the Nicaraguan *contras*. Lead Zuno attorney Ed Medvene concluded the voir dire hearing with questions about Harrison's contacts with the DEA, the handling of his DEA debriefings, and his monitoring of trafficker radio communications for the DEA between October 1989 and February 1990, when he and his family were permanently relocated to the United States. In contrast to the other defense attorneys, Medvene showed little interest in what Harrison knew about CIA activities in Mexico and appeared rather to be using the voir dire session to further a defense strategy of discrediting witnesses and challenging the prosecution on technicalities.

As Medvene concluded his questioning of Harrison and Judge Rafeedie was about to excuse the witness, Martin Stolar interrupted with a request that the court take steps to determine the identity of "Dale" and a second man, by the name of "Benny," who had met with Harrison in Guadalajara in 1987; both of them had been observed in the courthouse during the trial. Stolar's request sparked a heated exchange between himself and the judge that captured perfectly the judicial wonderland in which law befogs truth.

> MR. STOLAR: With respect to the [voir dire] hearing, I believe that at a bare minimum the government, or perhaps the court, should call as a court's witness somebody from the CIA or National Security Agency, particularly with respect to the narcotics operation being run by Mr. Félix Gallardo. It is clear that the only Americans who are involved with Contras—and this is general knowledge throughout, and the court might even take judicial notice of various congressional hearings—are the CIA. Those are the Americans. That is who's running the Contras. That's clear. If Félix Gallardo is involved in his narcotics business and made admissions to this gentleman that his narcotics business is protected by the CIA because he's doing Contra work, then I think we have an obligation to at least call somebody who has knowledge of that and have that person from the CIA or NSA called in to find out if what Félix Gallardo told this gentleman is true. . . .
>
> JUDGE RAFEEDIE: I'm not going to call anybody from the CIA or anybody else, because I haven't heard one word of competent evidence of any CIA involvement. This witness's testimony is based entirely on hearsay, supposition, rumors, gossip, speculation. People with no names. That is hardly the basis for continuing an inquiry or calling witnesses by the court. It's clear to the court this witness had no personal knowledge of what he reported. He was simply reporting what was in the air and what was being said and discussed and what he heard from various people. To use that as a basis for me to call anyone or to permit it would be simply to extend this fishing expedition, which it was when it started and it still is, and that has not changed. So the request is denied. I'm not inviting argument. I'm simply telling you that your request is denied.[22]

At this point, Medrano requested that Rafeedie instruct defense counsel to make no comments to the press about "this whole issue of the CIA" because when it first broke it had been "front-page news in virtually every major paper in the country" and the government did not want the jury to be tainted by "this innuendo and hearsay" as a consequence of "courthouse step interviews with the press." He agreed that the media had a right to report what they saw and heard in the courtroom, but he did not want what they reported to be shaded by defense attorney spin. "Well," Rafeedie replied, "the press are generally fairly objective and they will report that the court has declared this evidence to be incompetent." He denied Medrano's request to place a gag on defense counsel.[23]

The following day, as Rafeedie had anticipated, the press reported his determination not to admit Harrison's testimony into evidence because it was based solely on rumor and hearsay and was therefore "incompetent." Indeed, Harrison himself had provided Rafeedie with the language that permitted the judge to dismiss his testimony about CIA collusion with the Mexican traffickers and had done so, he would tell us years later, on instructions from his government handlers. "I was instructed to sit up there [on the witness stand] and act like a clown!" he exclaimed over the phone one day in the spring of 2005. "They laid a mine field for me and I didn't want to step on any mines. They told me to lie!" His entire voir dire testimony had been scripted, he later reiterated, so as to give Rafeedie the verbiage he needed to dismiss it.[24]

During the voir dire hearing, government attorney Carlton had elicited from Harrison that most of what he reported to his DEA debriefers was based on "rumors," "beliefs," and "opinions." Harrison repeated to defense attorney Stolar that he had reported "suppositions" and "rumors" and had little firsthand knowledge of CIA involvement with the Guadalajara drug cartel. And when, in response to the objection quoted above as to whether Harrison knew that Miguel Ángel Félix Gallardo "was in the business of supplying arms to the Contras," Rafeedie acknowledged that the witness's response would constitute hearsay but decided, "for the purpose of this hearing," that he was going to allow it anyway, his response seemed as much an allusion to the government's purpose of discrediting Harrison's revelations about the CIA as to the procedural purpose of determining how much of what the witness had recounted to DEA debriefers was firsthand knowledge. When we later asked Harrison if he thought Rafeedie was witting in the government's effort to discredit his testimony concerning CIA activities in Mexico, he said there could be little doubt. The judge "had to be witting."[25]

While newspapers across the country reported Rafeedie's characterization of the Harrison testimony about the CIA as without merit, media coverage of that testimony was not as dismissive as the government might have liked. "Witness Says Drug Lord Told of Contra Arms," read the next day's Los Angeles Times headline of a lengthy article by staff writer Henry Weinstein. Weinstein dutifully quoted Rafeedie's dismissal of Harrison's voir dire statements as "hearsay, gossip and speculation," but he did not lead off with the judge's opinion, focusing instead on what Harrison said Mexican drug lords had told him about their support of the Nicaraguan contras. Weinstein clearly found what Harrison had to say about the alleged trafficker/contra/CIA nexus more significant than Rafeedie's characterization of the witness's testimony as "incompetent," and he conveyed that implied assessment to his readers. Other news outlets picked up Weinstein's coverage of the Camarena trial and disseminated it across the country.[26]

Of more serious concern to executive branch spin strategists was a front-page, four-column, 2,600-word illustrated feature article that appeared in the Washington Post the day Judge Rafeedie turned the trial over to the jury for deliberation. Written by Post foreign service reporter William Branigin and datelined Mexico City, the article focused on friction between the DEA and CIA around the Camarena case and, in effect, lent credence to Harrison's testimony about CIA collusion with Mexican narcotics traffickers. "The trial in Los Angeles of four men accused of involvement in the 1985 murder of a U.S. narcotics agent," read Branigin's lead paragraph, "has brought to the surface years of resentment by Drug Enforcement Administration officials of the Central Intelligence Agency's long collaboration with a former Mexican secret police unit [DFS] that was heavily involved in drug trafficking."[27]

Behind the Camarena case, wrote Branigin, lay "a tangled web of allegations about the CIA's special relationship with an increasingly corrupt and brutal DFS, clandestine aid for Nicaragua's contra rebels, gunrunning through Mexico and the involvement of shadowy Americans in the Guadalajara drug cartel." Branigin provided an extensive summary of Harrison's testimony, with only passing mention of Rafeedie's criticisms in a brief paragraph more than halfway through his article, essentially using it to suggest that there was substance to the "hearsay, gossip and speculation" about agency collusion with corrupt Mexican officials, the Guadalajara cartel, and Nicaraguan *contras* that Rafeedie would not allow the jury to consider. He further bolstered this view by quoting defense counsel Gregory Nicolaysen, who concluded that, embellishments aside, Harrison "does have a fair amount of credibility." Branigin also used Nicolaysen to imply what seemed obvious but no one would state explicitly in court, namely, that Harrison was himself a CIA agent. Basically, averred Nicolaysen, Harrison "was the liaison between the agency and the cartel." "The CIA obviously was cultivating a very powerful and efficient arms network through the cartel," he asserted, "and they didn't want DEA screwing it up."[28] The explosive inference of this last statement was that S/A Enrique Camarena threatened to do precisely that and, by extension, had been killed to prevent him from doing so—just, we conclude, as was Manuel Buendía.

On 31 July 1990, the jury returned guilty verdicts against Zuno Arce on three counts of conspiracy in the abduction and torture-murder of Enrique Camarena. While all four defendants in the 1990 Camarena trial were convicted, Zuno appears to have been the one the government most wished to convict, due, we suspect, to his social prominence and political connections in Mexico. We have no illusions about Zuno's personal virtues, the transparency of his business enterprises, or the company he kept, but the charges against him in the Camarena case seem contrived and the evidence in their support unpersuasive.

When we asked Harrison years later what the Zuno prosecution was really all about, he replied matter-of-factly that Zuno had been "our guy," meaning a CIA asset, as had his brother-in-law Luis Echeverría, first as secretary of government, then as president of the republic. "Zuno was our guy in the '70s and '80s," Harrison told us. "We dumped him in the '90s to make us look clean. It was a cleansing ritual."[29] Zuno allegedly had a history of mercury, heroin, and marijuana smuggling, but no compelling evidence has surfaced to mark him as a principal figure in the Guadalajara drug cartel. Harrison's reference to a "cleansing ritual," therefore, likely signifies a CIA break with former assets in the Echeverría faction of Mexico's political elites.

A subsequent conversation we had with Ed Medvene and Zuno's then attorney, Kenneth M. Miller, lends credence to the view that Zuno was prosecuted for political motives rather than in the interests of criminal justice. Miller recounted to us how, in light of Zuno's age and deteriorated health and his having served more than a decade and a half as a model prisoner, Miller had petitioned to have Zuno paroled, only to have a senior Justice Department official intervene with the parole board to block Zuno's release from prison. Zuno would never be released, Miller concluded, "so long as he refuses to tell all he knows," in other words, to implicate Echeverría and other high Mexican officials in crimes and corrupt practices.[30]

The intrepid Tijuana journalist and founding editor of the combative Baja California weekly *Zeta*, Jesús Blancornelas (1936–2006), had confirmed Miller's account of Zuno's situation three years earlier. Writing in the electronic version of *Zeta*, Blancornelas recounted that he had written to Zuno asking him about his case and Zuno had replied at length, telling him, among other details, that U.S. officials had offered to free him but only if he would accuse former presidents Echeverría, López Portillo, and de la Madrid of involvement in narcotics trafficking, which, understandably, he refused to do. In an effort to coerce him to cooperate with American authorities, Zuno told Blancornelas, prison officials had arranged to have him attacked and beaten by Mexican inmates. Miller would mention this incident to us as well, referring to Zuno's attackers as "Mexican mafia" and citing it as the only negative episode on his prison record. He said nothing to us about the attack having been orchestrated by Zuno's jailers, but there is no compelling reason to doubt Blancornelas's version of the event.[31]

By the time this information came to our attention, Judge Rafeedie had thrown out Zuno's conviction based on prosecution misconduct and ordered a retrial, in which Zuno was again convicted and sentenced to two life terms. Zuno's initial conviction had rested on the dubious testimony of Héctor Cervantes Santos, a former Jalisco Judicial Police officer who had done double duty as a Guadalajara cartel security guard. Cervantes placed Zuno, as well as then government secretary Manuel Bartlett Díaz, at meetings with Guadalajara cartel bosses where ostensibly Camarena's abduction had been planned. For undisclosed reasons of their own, government attorneys Medrano and Carlton decided not to call Cervantes as a prosecution witness in Zuno's retrial, opting instead to rely on the testimony of two new, equally dubious witnesses, René López Romero and Jorge Godoy López, both of whom also had been Jalisco police officers in the employ of the Guadalajara cartel.

Incredibly, López Romero admitted that he had participated in Camarena's abduction and been present when Camarena was tortured, yet he was granted immunity and put on the stand as a key prosecution witness. As an exercise in discerning the truth of the Camarena case, none of the testimony elicited at trial from René López, Jorge Godoy, or Héctor Cervantes warranted credence. Manuel Bartlett's American attorney, Michael J. Lightfoot, retained to challenge the testimony of the DEA's paid Mexican witnesses, summed up the decade-long Camarena investigation and court proceedings by observing that the Justice Department had produced "not one conviction of any of the actual kidnappers or masterminds of the plot." Instead of prosecuting the one person in U.S. custody who admitted playing a role in Camarena's abduction, Justice Department officials determined to use that individual to provide testimony "that served only to ruin the reputation of [potential PRI presidential candidate] Bartlett Díaz."[32] It served as well, of course, to convict Rubén Zuno Arce.

DEA-6

REPORT OF INVESTIGATION

Date prepared
April 9, 1992

Report RE: Debriefing of [René López Romero]:[33] Events at 881 Lope de Vega,
Guadalajara, Jalisco, Mexico: The abduction/interrogation and torture of DEA S/A
Enrique Camarena

SYNOPSIS:

On April 9, 1992 [René López Romero] was debriefed by G/S [Group Supervisor]
Hector Berrellez and S/A Salvador Leyva. It should be noted that [López Romero] was a
personal body guard for Ernesto Fonseca-Carrillo, who was a powerful Guadalajara
Drug Cartel overlord and a primary member of the group which participated in the
kidnap, interrogation, and murder of S/A Enrique Camarena.

[López Romero] reports that he/she was present at 881 Lope de Vega on the morning
of February 7, 1985, when arrangements were made for three teams of enforcers to drive
to the U.S. Consulate in Guadalajara to kidnap S/A Enrique Camarena. [López
Romero] reported that he/she was present during the surveillance at the Consulate and
the actual kidnapping of the DEA agent. [López Romero] was also present at the
residence at 881 Lope de Vega during the time that S/A Camarena was interrogated and
tortured. The following details [are López Romero's] recollections of the events that
took place at 881 Lope de Vega on February 7th and 8th, 1985.

DETAILS:

[Paragraphs 1–13]

14. [López Romero] added that while conversing with Piliado and Ramírez-Razo they
    had been approached by one of Rafael Caro-Quintero's enforcers, who stated that
    Rubén Zuno-Arce requested to know if it had been decided if the agent would be
    killed. The enforcer told Ramírez-Razo and Piliado and [López Romero] that
    Zuno-Arce wanted to know if in fact it had been decided that the agent was going
    to be killed, that he (Rubén Zuno-Arce) and the other important people would
    interrogate the agent themselves. Ramírez-Razo told the enforcer that he did not
    know, and that Rafael Caro-Quintero had to be consulted with regarding [sic] that
    request.

[Paragraphs 15–16]

17. [René López Romero] stated that after he/she and Torres-Lepe ate, they entered the
    dining room area of the residence to empty ashtrays. [López Romero] while in the
    dining room area observed the room to be full of influential political figures to
    include the following:

    Secretary of Interior Manuel Bartlett-Díaz
    Minister of Defense Juan Arévalo-Gardoqui
    Mexican Army General Vinicio Santoya Feria
    Mexican Army Lt. Col. Jorge Garma
    Governor of Jalisco Enrique Álvarez del Castillo
    Rubén Zuno-Arce
    Sergio Espino-Verdín
    MFJP Director Manuel Ibarra Herrera
    Director of Interpol Miguel Aldana-Ibarra

MFJP Agent Alfonso Vásquez-Velasco
MFJP Agent Juan Gilberto Hernández-Parra
Dr. Humberto Álvarez-Macháin
MFJP Comandante Armando Pavón-Reyes

18. [López Romero] stated that also present in the living room were numerous drug lords and their enforcers to include:

Miguel Félix-Gallardo
Rafael Caro-Quintero
Ernesto Fonseca-Carrillo
Javier Barba-Hernández
Manuel Salcido-Zazueta
Sergio Salcido Zazueta
Abelardo Fernández
Ramiro Pérez-Arrellano
Manuel López-Razón
Ernesto Piliado-Garza
Jorge Salazar
Rafael Ruiz-Velasco
José Luis aka "El Russo" [*sic*]

[Paragraphs 19–20]

21. While in the living room [López Romero] noticed Arévalo Gardoqui to be the most worried of the group. [López Romero] reported that he/she overheard Gardoqui instruct those present to be very sure that the two subjects were disposed of, and very well hidden so they could never be found.

22. Bartlett-Díaz assured those present that the problem had been dealt with accordingly and that things should now go in the right direction. Bartlett made numerous other reassuring statements which [López Romero] does not recall. According to [López Romero] Bartlett-Díaz expressed himself in eloquent, sophisticated Spanish, so sophisticated that [López Romero] could see that the traffickers had a difficult time understanding him. [López Romero] heard Caro-Quintero tell Bartlett-Díaz "Don't worry we are going to kill all of them anyway. You are going to make it all the way to the top. We need you at the top."

23. According to [López Romero] the meeting lasted until approximately midnight at which time the politicians and drug lords departed with their enforcers. Fonseca-Carrillo, [López Romero] and Fonseca's immediate group departed at approximately 1:00 AM on February 8, 1985.

24. [López Romero] reported that before and after S/A Camarena was brought to 881 Lope de Vega, security consisting of between 50 and 60 heavily armed military personnel, federal police agents, Jalisco State agents and the personal enforcers of the drug lords were on the grounds of the residence.

[Final paragraph plus index of 53 individuals said by René López Romero to have been present at the 881 Lope de Vega address where Enrique Camarena was interrogated and killed.][34]

As the basis for the testimony that clinched Rubén Zuno Arce's conviction and incarceration for life as an accomplice in the Camarena murder, the preceding document is thoroughly suspect. We note immediately that it conforms perfectly—too perfectly, we think—to the prosecution's agenda, as well as to a broader U.S. foreign policy agenda of expanded hegemony over Mexico. Elements of René López Romero's account of Camarena's abduction and related events at the Lope de Vega address where he was interrogated and killed do not jibe contextually, as, for example, when López Romero recounts how he and another cartel security person entered the dining room "to empty ashtrays" only to discover a houseful of very prominent government, military, and law enforcement officials, among them Jalisco governor Enrique Álvarez del Castillo, Secretary of Government Manuel Bartlett Díaz, and Secretary of Defense Juan Arévalo Gardoqui. All too conveniently, López Romero inserts Guadalajara cartel kingpins Ernesto Fonseca, Rafael Caro Quintero, and Miguel Ángel Félix Gallardo into this celebrity mix of Mexican officials, then completes his improbable scenario by stating that during the Camarena operation the Lope de Vega property had been secured by fifty to sixty heavily armed military personnel and federal and state police officers, together with the traffickers' own security people. If the Camarena abduction were in effect a government-authorized operation, then we can only wonder what possible threat would have required such a conspicuous display of military and police firepower?

This version of events conveniently reinforced Lawrence Harrison's testimony that Mexican government, law enforcement, and the military officials were all corrupt and involved with the country's narcotics traffickers.[35] It also furthered what appears to have been a multiadministration strategy of breaking with previous PRI allies in support of a new cohort of political players more amenable to long-term American regional interests. Zuno Arce, we think, was a victim of the break with the Echeverría clan. The most prominent target of American political perfidy, however, seems to have been Bartlett Díaz, who, through what almost certainly was the purposefully scripted testimony of López Romero, was smeared as having been in league with the Camarena assassins. The 9 April 1992 DEA-6 account of Bartlett's remarks while purportedly at the Lope de Vega residence, and of Caro Quintero's alleged reassurance that Bartlett would be the next president of the republic because the traffickers "needed him at the top," would be risible if it were not so crude.[36]

Even former Reagan ambassador to Mexico John Gavin was appalled at the absurdity of López Romero's allegations. "That high government officials, members of the president's Cabinet, would attend a torture session of an American agent in a drug baron's house at a moment's notice hundreds of miles from Mexico City is preposterous on its face," Gavin observed. He could only conclude that the evidence was spurious. "My record in the war against illegal drugs and the corruption they engender is known," he remarked. "In this instance, however, I am saddened and embarrassed to note that it is officials within the U.S. Justice Department who are dead wrong. It is another example of how drugs corrupt on both sides of the border."[37]

Matters became still murkier when, seven years after his testimony had resulted in guilty verdicts against Zuno Arce and the other three defendants in the 1990 Camarena trial, Héctor Cervantes Santos declared that he had testified falsely at the insistence of lead government prosecutor "Manny" Medrano and DEA group supervisor Héctor Berréllez. Medrano and Berréllez had wanted him to implicate Zuno and Bartlett Díaz in the Camarena murder, he told Bartlett's Los Angeles attorney Michael Lightfoot.

Former Secretary of Government (1982–1988) Manuel Bartlett Díaz accused in a 5 January 2014 *Proceso* newsweekly cover story of having witnessed the torture interrogation of U.S. DEA S/A Enrique Camarena.

"I told Berréllez that I had never seen either Zuno or Bartlett in person in my life," he stated, but Berréllez supposedly insisted that Cervantes "had to have seen them" and just didn't recall it. "They told me that they would give me a few days so that I could remember," Cervantes said. He now claimed that Medrano and Berréllez had actually scripted his court testimony and Medrano had even quipped jokingly that he should sleep with a photograph of Zuno under his pillow "so as not to forget Zuno's face."[38]

Lightfoot had Cervantes submit to an extensive polygraph exam administered by Edward Gelb, a former Los Angeles Police Department lieutenant and experienced polygrapher who had taught polygraphy for the FBI. In the course of the exam, Gelb asked Cervantes three different times if he had seen Zuno and Bartlett in the presence of drug traffickers and whether Assistant U.S. Attorney Medrano and G/S Berréllez had encouraged him to falsely implicate the two men. He concluded that Cervantes had answered truthfully, saying it was highly unlikely that he could have beaten the test three times in a row. Additionally, former DEA chief Terrence Burke interviewed Cervantes for several hours, then stated that the perjury allegations appeared credible and should be looked at more closely. Whether or not Cervantes's recantation was truthful, Burke said, it was troublesome and raised doubts about the prosecution's decision to rely on him so heavily.[39]

In a further, equally bizarre twist, Cervantes recanted his recantation six months later, stating in a videotaped interview conducted in Guadalajara by DEA officials that Bartlett's and Zuno's attorneys had paid him to lie about his handling by government prosecutors, that he had been taken to Puebla to meet with then Governor Bartlett, that Bartlett had had him detained and beaten until he finally agreed to repeat his allegations to a *Los Angeles Times* reporter, and that he had been coached on how to pass the polygraph test. According to the U.S. Attorney's Office, Cervantes then appeared voluntarily on 18 January 1998 at the U.S. consulate in Guadalajara in order to recant his earlier allegations against Medrano and Berréllez.[40]

In the end, nothing that this witness may have said about Zuno Arce's association with members of the Guadalajara cartel warranted belief. The one constant in his contradictory allegations, as well as the subsequent testimony of prosecution witnesses López Romero and Godoy López, was the impugning of Bartlett Díaz. Of particular interest to us here is that this defamatory offensive against Manuel Bartlett, which appears to have been a covert political operation rather than part of a legitimate criminal investigation, links the Camarena case to the Buendía case. Well before Rubén Zuno Arce was indicted and the government's key witnesses sought to sully his and Bartlett's names by tying them to the Camarena murder, the DEA had attempted to portray Bartlett as the mastermind of the Buendía assassination, with the apparent intention of compromising his political viability as a potential PRI presidential candidate.[41]

Why, we keep asking ourselves, was the DEA concerning itself with Manuel Buendía? Why were agents of the U.S. government insistently linking the murders of an influential Mexican newspaper columnist and an American narcotics officer on foreign assignment? Zuno, for his part, remained steadfast in his refusal to implicate former Mexican officials and, as predicted by his attorney Kenneth Miller, would die in a U.S. prison.[42]

12

On Down the Rabbit Hole

Even if we leave aside the question of active CIA complicity, the coincidence between cocaine trafficking and covert operations made the DEA's task of drug interdiction almost impossible. For DEA to determine which light aircraft crossing the Caribbean were CIA, cartel, or both became increasingly difficult. Simply by launching a major covert operation in a strategic drug zone, the CIA contributed, albeit indirectly, to a major expansion of America's cocaine supply.

—Alfred W. McCoy, *The Politics of Heroin* (1991)

FEDERAL DISTRICT JUDGE Edward Rafeedie had a full docket of *contra*-related trials in the summer and fall of 1990. Of particular concern to executive branch damage controllers was a case unrelated to the Camarena murder prosecutions: the trial of seven Los Angeles County sheriff's deputies charged with skimming money confiscated from drug traffickers linked to the Nicaraguan *contras*. Members of the Los Angeles sheriff's major crimes task force had been shaking down crack cocaine dealers in the impoverished, largely black neighborhoods of South Central Los Angeles, where the principal cocaine suppliers were Nicaraguan traffickers Danilo Blandón and Norwin Meneses, both active *contra* supporters.

The seven deputies had been caught in an FBI sting in late 1989 and were indicted early the following year. Among them was Daniel Garner, a seasoned detective who in the mid-1980s had participated in a raid on the Mission Viejo home of Ronald J. Lister, a shadowy associate of Danilo Blandón who claimed to have links to the CIA and appears to have been involved with the *contras* and also the repressive, U.S.-supported regime in El Salvador. The raid recovered no cocaine but did produce a trove of documents, phone records, correspondence, weapons manuals, training films, photographs, and a paper trail of bank deposits totaling almost ten million dollars to U.S. government and offshore Cayman Islands accounts. Garner and his fellow deputies were stunned to discover that these files unambiguously established Lister's association with both the CIA and the Pentagon's DIA, as well as with the Nicaraguan *contras* and the Salvadoran government. As an instinctive precaution, Garner and another officer made photocopies of representative documents for safekeeping. Within a matter of days the seized records had disappeared from the sheriff's evidence locker, apparently removed by federal agents, while all remaining items were subsequently destroyed.[1]

When the indictments of the seven Los Angeles sheriff's deputies were handed down in February 1990, Garner determined to defend himself by using his copies of the seized Lister documents to implicate the federal government in the multimillion-dollar crack cocaine market of South Central Los Angeles. He hired the prominent Los Angeles criminal defense attorney Harland W. Braun, who during cross-examination of an FBI agent involved in the federal sting casually asked the witness if he was aware of seized drug money having been laundered, then diverted to the *contras* by the CIA. Later, in reply to a reporter's question about his opaque reference to the CIA, Braun explained that his client's defense would rest in part on evidence that some of the money the deputies were accused of stealing from South Central drug dealers had actually been laundered by the agency and used to purchase arms for the *contras* and the government of Iran. This assertion produced an instant response from the Justice Department, which demanded that Judge Rafeedie issue a gag order restraining defense counsel from introducing any evidence related to alleged covert government operations in Central America and Iran.

Braun responded with an explosive written objection detailing the materials the deputies had recovered from Ronald Lister's residence and the connections they established between Lister, U.S. intelligence, international drug traffickers, the massive influx of crack cocaine into South Central Los Angeles, and the *contras*. He had asked the Justice Department for an official letter stating that "no drug money was used by the United States government or any United States government agency to purchase weapons for the *contras* or weapons to be traded for hostages from Iran," a request that was denied. Braun told Rafeedie that he interpreted Justice's refusal to go on record in the matter of drugs, guns, and the *contras* as a tacit admission that the allegations were true. "The government," he declared, "obviously fears the exposure of its drug financed Central American operations." Moreover, he added, the accused deputies had been pilloried in the media by Justice Department prosecutors, yet they were not the ones protesting prejudicial media exposure. "The only party that complains about the publicity," Braun wrote in opposition to the government's requested gag order, "is the very party that was arguably using drug money to buy weapons for the *contras*."[2]

The federal prosecutors immediately responded with an insistent request that Rafeedie exclude from the trial proceedings "any questions, testimony, or other evidence relating to any alleged CIA plot to launder drug money to finance Nicaraguan operations or operations in Iran." The intelligence matters to which Braun alluded, Assistant U.S. Attorney Thomas Hagemann argued, fell outside the time frame of the illicit acts for which the deputies were being tried and therefore had no bearing on the legal issues of the trial. In what could be interpreted as a tacit admission of the truth of Braun's allegations, Hagemann emphasized to Rafeedie that there was "no connection of any kind between this scheme involving the CIA" and the case at hand. The evidence introduced by Braun, he concluded, "would do nothing more than confuse the jury and be a waste of time."[3]

Judge Rafeedie agreed and, in contrast to a similar request by federal prosecutors in the Camarena trial three months earlier, now imposed a gag on the defense attorneys, prohibiting them from making any statements outside the courtroom about possible covert CIA operations utilizing drug money in support of the Nicaraguan *contras* or to obtain the release of American hostages in Iran. He gave Braun an unusually harsh dressing down, saying he could not believe that "a lawyer of [Braun's] ability and skill" would ever consider that the *contra*-related evidence he had tried to introduce might somehow be admissible. Because it clearly was not, at least under any theory that he could conceive, the judge fumed, what Braun had in effect done was to introduce this information about Ronald Lister, the CIA, and the laundering of drug money on behalf of the *contras* "simply to ensure that it gets into the public print and perhaps might contaminate this case." That he had done so, Rafeedie fulminated, was a violation of "the American Bar Association model rules of professional conduct" and in itself "the most clear and convincing evidence that [a restraining order] in this case is necessary." When Braun then requested time to gather additional evidence in support of his client's assertions, Rafeedie replied angrily, "We are not trying to determine the Iran-Contra affair. Suppose I accept as true everything you have said. . . . I don't see the relevance."[4]

Braun's client, Daniel Garner, did managed to state during his trial testimony that the government had been conducting illegal activities "in which the guys in the CIA were getting rich." While Judge Rafeedie instructed the jury to ignore Garner's comment, it nonetheless remained in the public record. Garner and other deputies further testified that as part of their job "they sometimes worked with federal agencies on money-laundering cases," where Los Angeles County sheriff's deputies would pose as money launderers, receive large sums of cash from the traffickers, and turn it over to the federal agents, "who would actually launder it" for their own purposes.[5] Garner was convicted of corruption and sentenced to four and a half years in prison. On his release in 1996, he would remark pointedly, "I didn't pump 500 tons of cocaine into the ghetto. I stole American money and spent it in America. The United States government can't say that."[6]

Although Ronald Lister was not mentioned by name in these court proceedings and it would remain for *San Jose Mercury News* reporter Gary Webb to identify him six years later, Lister's links to the CIA, Central America, and the South Central Los Angeles crack cocaine market did surface as a consequence of Harland Braun's court filings. And despite Judge Rafeedie's gag order, public attention was once again drawn to the increasingly evident links between domestic cocaine trafficking and the executive branch's proxy *contra* war in Central America. Rafeedie's rulings on discussion of these matters in the various CIA-related court cases that came before him in the late 1980s and early 1990s, while procedurally defensible, all appear to have had the ulterior purpose of reinforcing plausible deniability of executive branch covert operations in Central America and Mexico. Even his seemingly inconsistent decision in the second Camarena murder trial to actually encourage media coverage of Lawrence Harrison's voir dire testimony about alleged CIA collusion with Mexican narcotics traffickers pursued this end, albeit with mixed results.

Yet a further twist in the DEA's pursuit of S/A Camarena's killers would result in a much-commented-on ruling by Judge Rafeedie that had the collateral effect of legitimating his other decisions in the Camarena prosecutions: the 2 April 1990 kidnapping of Guadalajara physician Humberto Álvarez Machaín and his surreptitious rendition to the United States for prosecution as an accessory to the DEA agent's murder. Álvarez

Macháin was the personal physician of the Rafael Caro Quintero family and was accused of having administered lidocaine to prolong Camarena's life while the agent was being interrogated under torture. Álvarez's rendition was in essence a bounty operation authorized by Operation Leyenda G/S Héctor Berréllez, arranged by DEA asset Antonio Gárate Bustamante, and paid for by the U.S. Justice Department. It was a blatant violation of the U.S.-Mexico extradition treaty then in force and was so ruled by Judge Rafeedie when the U.S. attorney sought to indict Álvarez as a coconspirator.

The U.S. Ninth Circuit Court of Appeals upheld Rafeedie's ruling, but the U.S. Supreme Court reversed it and ordered Álvarez Macháin to stand trial, which put him back in Judge Rafeedie's Los Angeles courtroom. Rafeedie then combined the Álvarez Macháin prosecution with the retrial of Rubén Zuno Arce in the summer and fall of 1992. He ultimately decided that the government's case against the Mexican doctor was too weak to be turned over to the jury, acquitted him, then ordered that Álvarez be released from custody and allowed to return to Mexico. The Justice Department made what the *Los Angeles Times* described as "an extraordinary last-ditch legal battle" to retain Álvarez in U.S. custody while Mexican diplomats fought the effort right down to "a midnight standoff at Los Angeles International Airport," where the American side finally relented and allowed Álvarez to depart the country.[7]

The detention and attempted prosecution of Álvarez Macháin precipitated a serious diplomatic confrontation between Mexico and the United States that threatened to compromise executive branch strategic objectives in the neighboring Mesoamerican region. President Carlos Salinas de Gortari, considered by U.S. foreign policy strategists to be a friend and asset, had vehemently denounced the Álvarez Macháin abduction as "a dark page in international law" and the Camarena trials as "an aberrant situation [in which] the essence of law was set aside." The U.S. government, Salinas charged, was using the Álvarez and Zuno Arce prosecutions to slander Mexican officials. Judge Rafeedie's dismissal of the case against Álvarez Macháin, he declared, was "an honest act [that] allowed for the correction of a violation of law by liberating a Mexican citizen illegally subject to trial in the United States."[8]

The Mexican government had denounced the earlier kidnapping (24 January 1986) of Mexicali-based marijuana trafficker and Caro Quintero associate René Verdugo Urquídez as a violation of Mexico's sovereignty, refused to assist U.S. authorities in their search for evidence implicating Verdugo in the Camarena case, and threatened to discontinue further cooperation in bilateral efforts to combat narcotics trafficking. Inasmuch as Verdugo's abduction had occurred during Miguel de la Madrid's presidential term, incoming President Salinas de Gortari chose not to make a further issue of it. But when Dr. Álvarez Macháin was abducted from a Guadalajara street four years later and rendered to the United States for criminal prosecution, that bald repeat violation of Mexican sovereignty was more than the Salinas administration could tolerate.

After filing a formal diplomatic protest with the U.S. State Department, then forcefully communicating Mexico's unwillingness to let the Álvarez Macháin incident pass during face-to-face meetings between President Salinas, U.S. vice president Dan Quayle, and the two countries' respective attorneys general, the Salinas government retained a prominent District of Columbia law firm and fought the Bush Sr. administration's attempt to prosecute Álvarez all the way to the U.S. Supreme Court. When the Supreme Court ruled against Mexico two years later and Álvarez was returned to Judge Rafeedie's courtroom to stand trial, the Salinas administration responded by imposing severe restrictions on the activities of DEA agents assigned to Mexico. It also lodged an official request for the extradition of Operation Leyenda G/S Héctor Berréllez and his main operative in the Álvarez Macháin abduction, Antonio Gárate Bustamante.

The Salinas administration simultaneously launched a diplomatic campaign to portray as a violation of international law the U.S. Supreme Court ruling that the abduction of foreign nationals outside U.S. borders and their rendition to the United States for criminal prosecution was permissible. Several South American heads of state were persuaded to request an advisory opinion on the Álvarez Macháin kidnapping by the Inter-American Law Committee (IALC) of the Permanent Council of the OAS. With nine votes in favor and one abstention, the IALC issued an opinion stating that the Guadalajara abduction constituted "a transgression of Mexican territorial sovereignty" and "a grave violation of international law," and that the United States was therefore obligated to repatriate Álvarez.

Mexico next took the Álvarez Macháin case to the Second Ibero-American Summit in Madrid, where concern was expressed about any judicial ruling that violated the principle of respect for the right of states to exercise full and exclusive sovereignty over their own national territories. From Madrid the case was taken to the UN General Assembly, which in turn requested an advisory ruling on Álvarez Macháin's abduction from the International Court of Justice in The Hague. What most exercised the Bush Sr. administration, however, was President Salinas's determination to formalize strict rules governing the scope and conduct of DEA operations in Mexico. To do so, the U.S. side protested with unbridled imperial hubris, would set a very bad precedent that other countries might choose to follow as well. Moreover, if DEA activities were subject to formal rules, then other U.S. agencies, too, might find themselves similarly hobbled, including the CIA.

Undeterred, in early July 1992, the Salinas administration went ahead and published the new rules in the government's *Diario Oficial de la Federación*. The DEA would henceforth be limited to a maximum of thirty-nine agents assigned to Mexico. Those agents could only be stationed in a half-dozen cities where the United States maintained consulates, including the Federal District. They could only perform their duties within the area served by the consulate to which they were attached and could not travel outside that area without written authorization from the Mexican government. Agents would not be granted diplomatic immunity and were prohibited from carrying weapons. Finally, any intelligence they developed had to be shared immediately with the appropriate Mexican authorities.

If the Salinas administration insisted on leaving these rules in place, Bush Sr.'s attorney general, William Barr, pointedly informed his Mexican counterpart, Enrique Álvarez del Castillo, it would send the wrong message to the U.S. Congress at the very moment when congressional support was critical for approval of NAFTA. The free trade agreement was a double-edged sword, however, and Salinas appears to have wielded it more skillfully than his American opponents. Mexico's political establishment, he notes in a political memoir of his presidency, was deeply ambivalent over whether or not to form part of what one PRI legislator described as a U.S.-dominated trading bloc that "would devour the Mexican economy."

Even within his own cabinet, not everyone was of the same mind. Foreign Secretary Fernando Solana Morales proposed expelling the DEA or at the very least suspending those agents then assigned to Mexico. Consideration was also given to recalling Mexico's ambassador to the United States for consultations, but Salinas feared that such an action would be tantamount to a break in relations and thus preclude approval of NAFTA, which by his own account he firmly supported. For his part, he avers, he could not understand why the Americans had allowed their own agents to provoke gratuitous tensions in the bilateral relationship "at the very moment when his administration was preparing to implement a strategic change in Mexico's relations with the United States." Salinas seems to write it off as rogue law enforcement interests on both sides of the border having sought to impose their own political agendas. The empirical fact of the matter, in any case, was that the Álvarez Macháin kidnapping threatened to derail the NAFTA negotiations, and neither administration was prepared to let that happen. In the end, the U.S. side backed down and, two years and eight months after his abduction, Caro Quintero's family physician was allowed to return to Mexico.[9]

There was, in fact, more circumstantial evidence against Dr. Álvarez Macháin, who admitted being present at the 881 Lope de Vega address while Camarena was being interrogated, than prosecutors had managed to develop against Zuno Arce or, previously, against René Verdugo Urquídez. Yet Rafeedie freed the Guadalajara doctor, whose possible conviction threatened unacceptable diplomatic repercussions, while showing little judicial restraint in the questionable prosecutions of Zuno and Verdugo. The effect of Rafeedie's action in the Álvarez Macháin case was that he was perceived as an independent judge ready to oppose government prosecutors on points of law but equally disposed to dispense frontier justice to defendants accused of crimes against the United States. It made him, in other words, the perfect foil for executive branch political purposes.

On Wednesday, 29 August 1990, in the middle of my campaign for mayor of Mérida, I received an unexpected phone call:

"This is Antonio Gárate Bustamante, calling from Los Angeles. Do you place me? I'm a member of the DEA's Leyenda group. As you surely know, we are conducting various investigations to unravel the Camarena case."

"And what do I have to do with all that, Señor Gárate?" I asked.

"We are very interested to know more about your reports on DFS personnel involved in the death of your father, the journalist [Carlos] Loret de Mola."

"My statements have all been published. There is nothing further to add."

"Look," he insisted, "we have reason to believe that your father's death may be linked to the deaths of Buendía and Camarena. For starters, they share something in common: the masterminds behind them are the same."

"Who, Señor Gárate?"

"Bartlett, of course. And Arévalo Gardoqui—Juan, ex-secretary of defense. And Cervera Pacheco. Did you know that he controlled the peasants who cultivated the marijuana in the north? And that he promoted the drug traffic in Yucatán during his term as governor? There are dozens of clandestine routes through his state that have only just begun to be discovered."

. . .

"As I understand it, Señor Gárate, you're involved in the kidnapping of Dr. Humberto Álvarez Macháin and cannot enter Mexico because you would be arrested."

"That's right. Which is why we would like you to make a trip to Los Angeles, together with your informant. The Mexican authorities are very sensitive about our detention of Álvarez, who is actually involved up to his neck in the Camarena case. That's why they were unwilling to turn him over to us in the first place."

"Señor Gárate, I can't do that. I'd be incapable of serving as yet another instrument with which to tarnish the image of Mexico."

"We wouldn't ask you to do such a thing. But we can't judge Mexico on the basis of a few corrupt officials. To the contrary, we must unmask the guilty parties, because, you know, this mess goes very high up. Just imagine, if Bartlett figures as one of the principal suspects, then what are we to suppose?"[10]

This telephone conversation between Gárate Bustamante and the outspoken Mexican journalist Rafael Loret de Mola was one of many calls from Gárate and Operation Leyenda G/S Héctor G. Berréllez concerning the death of Loret's father, Carlos Loret de Mola Mediz (1921–1986), and what they insisted was its connection to the Buendía and Camarena homicides. Carlos Loret had perished one year, virtually to the day, after the murder of DEA S/A Enrique Camarena, in what was officially recorded as a single-vehicle accident at kilometer 112.7 on the two-lane Ciudad Altamirano-Zihuatanejo road (National Route 134), in southwestern Guerrero. Ostensibly, Loret's vintage black Mercedes Benz had failed to negotiate a tight descending curve to the left, gone off the road at a point called El Filo Mayor (The Precipice), and plunged into the most precipitous ravine of the entire route.

Loret de Mola Mediz was accompanied on that fateful trip by his secretary, Rosa Elena Jasso Rico, who appears to have been driving when they were stopped around eight o'clock in the evening at the Mexican army's El Güirindalito checkpoint (*retén*), twenty-eight kilometers southwest of Ciudad Altamirano. Six months later the victim's son Rafael was allowed to read, but not copy, the official military report of his father's stop at El Güirindalito, where soldiers had confiscated a .38 caliber revolver the elder Loret normally carried in the glove compartment of his Mercedes but which, on this occasion, was reported to have been retrieved from beneath the passenger seat. According to the report, Carlos Loret and his female driver were allowed to continue their journey after a fifteen-minute delay. The alleged accident occurred forty-five kilometers farther down the road.[11]

Mexican army checkpoints in Guerrero were holdovers from the antiguerrilla campaign of the 1970s, which had been especially intense in the country's mountainous southwestern region. While the army's presence in these remote areas was ostensibly to combat narcotics traffickers and other lawless elements (*pistoleros*), it also served as leverage against Mexico's governing political class. Despite the fact that by the mid-1940s the Mexican military had effectively removed itself from direct involvement in

presidential politics, the army in particular remained sensitive to its institutional interests and, on more than one occasion in the later decades of the last century, floated
rumors of possible revolt or otherwise exerted pressure on the national executive.[12]

We ourselves remember vividly the weekly rituals instituted by the de la Madrid
administration, in which members of the armed forces and representatives of civil
government would jointly raise and lower the national banner as a public protestation
of loyalty to the Mexican state and its constitutional order. For us, as well, we suspect,
as for many of the Mexicans who would stop to observe the martial pomp, these
ceremonial displays were unsettling, since in their ostentation they seemed to reflect
uncertainty about the military's commitment to the existing political order rather than
reassuring onlookers of its enduring subordination to civilian authority. What transpired in Guerrero the first week of February 1986 between El Güirindalito and El Filo
Mayor appears to have occurred within this dense web of competing institutional
interests.

Don Carlos Loret de Mola Mediz, a former national deputy and senator, then governor of the state of Yucatán, as well as a prominent, independent-minded journalist of
nationalist persuasion similar to that of Manuel Buendía, left his Mexico City home for
the Guerrero coast around noon on Wednesday, 5 February 1986. He was on a reporting
assignment for *Excélsior*, the same newspaper that had carried Buendía's front-page Red
Privada column and for which Loret was also an editorial writer. He brought with him
a book manuscript he intended to hone over the three days he expected to be at the
Hotel Camino Real in Ixtapa. He never arrived. And the manuscript, a severely critical
dissection of the de la Madrid administration titled *Que la nación me lo demande* (Let
the Nation Sue Me), vanished from the wreckage of his old Mercedes at El Filo Mayor.[13]

The political transcendence of the victim's death is reflected in the high-level officials and governmental bodies that concerned themselves with the case: the Secretariat
of National Defense, with the direct intervention of Secretary of Defense Gen. Juan
Arévalo Gardoqui and his chief of general staff, Gen. José Ángel García Elizalde; the
Secretariat of Government in the person of Secretary Manuel Bartlett Díaz; the Federal Highway Police (PFC); Guerrero attorney general Nelson Bello Solís and the chief
of the Guerrero State Prosecutor's Department of Preliminary Investigations (Averiguaciones Previas), Antonio Nogueda Carbajal; and President Miguel de la Madrid and
his successor, Carlos Salinas de Gortari. Every effort was made to persuade the younger
Loret that his father had in fact perished in an unfortunate automobile accident. Steadily
accumulating empirical evidence, however, strongly suggested otherwise.

Initial concern over the elder Loret's whereabouts developed when Don Carlos
failed to attend a scheduled *Excélsior* editorial meeting on Sunday afternoon, 9 February. On Monday morning, the tenth, General Arévalo Gardoqui tried several times
to reach him at his home in Mexico City. Informed of the phone calls, Rafael Loret
telephoned the general at the Secretariat of Defense and advised him that his father
was missing. Arévalo professed surprise, then told Rafael that he had his father's .38
caliber revolver from the El Güirindalito military *retén* and had called that morning
to ask Don Carlos for three photos so that he could issue him a permit for the gun. In
response to Rafael's insistent questions about what had transpired at El Güirindalito,

he replied, "Nothing. Nothing at all." Rafael was not to worry. He'd get back to him as soon as he learned anything. As something of a non sequitur, Arévalo added that he and Rafael's father had been (past tense) great friends, going back to their school-days in Mérida, Yucatán. This latest development pained him very much, "But not to worry." He rang off.[14]

Tuesday morning, the eleventh, Arévalo called Rafael with an improbable report that Don Carlos had passed back through the El Güirindalito *retén* the previous Saturday, "happily driving a red sports car in the direction of Ciudad Altamirano, apparently on his way back to the capital." He'd no doubt tarried along the way. Not likely, Rafael replied, given his father's professional habit of keeping appointments, which, in addition to the Sunday meeting at *Excélsior*'s editorial offices, had included a breakfast meeting that very morning with the governor of Nuevo León. "Well, there's always a first time," Arévalo quipped. In any event, his people would continue to look for Don Carlos. Where Carlos Loret de Mola might have acquired a "red sports car," when he was known to be traveling in his vintage Mercedes Benz, was never addressed.

Rafael Loret then phoned Miguel de la Madrid's personal secretary, Emilio Gamboa Patrón, a fellow *yucateco* and old family friend, to ask if the president's inner circle had learned anything and to inform him that *Excélsior* would wait until midday before going to press with a special edition reporting Don Carlos's disappearance. It would be a major scandal, he pointedly observed. Gamboa agreed, saying that he had already informed de la Madrid and would meet with Arévalo over lunch and get back to Rafael later in the day.

Confirmation of Carlos Loret de Mola's death came in the early afternoon while Rafael was at the *Excélsior* editorial offices. It did not come from Gamboa, Gobernación, or the Secretariat of Defense, but rather from a close friend of the victim, Julián Aznar, who reached Rafael by phone with the news. Aznar had been contacted by another close Loret family friend, Luis Barrera González, who had a home in Zihuatanejo and learned from local authorities that the elder Loret's body had been identified.

The circumstances in which the remains of Don Carlos and his secretary, Rosa Elena, were recovered constitute the first unequivocal evidence of foul play. They had been hastily buried as "unknown persons" in a sparsely inhabited locality called Vallecitos de Zaragoza. On 9 February, a local hunter allegedly informed the Vallecitos police chief, Rigoberto Pérez González, that there appeared to be "two more dead persons in the gulch." As the ninth was a Sunday, Pérez had supposedly waited until Monday to investigate, when he claimed to have found the bodies in such a state of advanced decomposition that he summarily ordered them interred rather than transporting them to Zihuatanejo for autopsies as required by law. According to the official account, word of the incident reached the office of the Guerrero state prosecutor, who had the bodies disinterred, transported to Zihuatanejo, and autopsied on Tuesday, 11 February.

As Rafael Loret de Mola has not tired of pointing out, there are immediate problems with this account, highlighted by the results of the official autopsies and conflicting statements made subsequently by the forensic personnel that performed them. The PFC report stated that, according to local residents who heard the crash, the victims had plunged into Filo Mayor gulch three days before Pérez González was informed of their presence, which would have been Thursday, the sixth, one day after Don Carlos and his secretary were reported to have passed through the El Güirindalito military checkpoint. If true, that would mean the bodies had been exposed to the remote area's abundant animal predators over a four-day period, yet the autopsy reports stated explicitly that the two bodies exhibited no post mortem lesions. The logical implication was that the victims had been buried immediately upon their deaths. By whom and why remained to be determined.

Equally puzzling was the fact that the elder Loret had been interred with all his identification, including his passport, yet he was initially reported to have been a person of unknown identity. Along with some personal effects, Guerrero authorities turned over 31,000 pesos in cash to the victim's son, a sum said to have been recovered from Don Carlos's billfold. According to Rafael Loret, his father was carrying 270,000 pesos when he set out on the drive to Ixtapa. Robbery may not have been the motive for Loret de Mola Mediz's violent demise, but a significant amount of cash had nonetheless been stolen from his corpse.

There were material inconsistencies in the autopsy results as well. The initial report stated that the victims had succumbed between Friday and Saturday, 7–8 February 1986, which immediately raised the question of where they had been during the forty-eight hours that had reportedly passed since the military *retén* on Wednesday evening, the fifth. It was an isolated stretch of road between El Güirindalito and El Filo Mayor, completely devoid of roadside establishments or private accommodations where passing travelers might reasonably stop. Subsequently, the forensic specialist who performed the Loret autopsy, Dr. Alejandro Toriz Díaz, revised his report to state that death had occurred "no less than six nor more than seven days, approximately, prior to the date of the [autopsy] on 11 February," which neatly coincided with the 5 February date of their arrival at El Güirindalito as reported by the army.

Post mortem forensic lab work likewise raised serious questions about the circumstances of the victims' demise. Carlos Loret's corpse contained an unusually elevated level of ethyl alcohol, roughly consistent with having consumed eight glasses or more of hard liquor in a short period of time. The obvious implication was that alcohol had caused the driver of Loret's Mercedes Benz to lose control on the Filo Mayor bend. The problem with that scenario, however, was that the military report of the Mercedes' passage through the El Güirindalito *retén* noted no sign of inebriation on the part of either Loret or his secretary; there was no place along the way to purchase alcoholic drinks, had they been so inclined; and no remains of liquor bottles or other alcoholic beverage containers were found in the wreckage. Moreover, Don Carlos could not abide drunkenness, was a moderate drinker himself, and had never been known to drink to excess.

These inconsistencies and improbabilities would continue to mount as authorities insistently strove to explain Loret's death as an accident. Most remarkable, in this regard, is the initial tour de force with which the de la Madrid administration sought to persuade Rafael Loret de Mola that his father had suffered a lamentable accident and not, as he suspected, an assassination. Carlos Loret's body was disinterred from the Vallecitos burial site on 11 February 1986, removed to Zihuatanejo for autopsy, then transported to Mexico City, where on the following day, Wednesday, 12 February, it lay in state in a Federal District mortuary—all in a time lapse of twenty-four hours. Then, while Rafael Loret was accompanying his father's remains at the mortuary, Bartlett, completely insensitive to the man's emotional distress, summoned him to Gobernación for an exposition of the evidence surrounding his father's demise.

Less than twenty-four hours after the elder Loret's remains had been disinterred in the southern Sierra Madre, the secretary of government had assembled a gaggle of state and federal officials at his Bucareli Palace headquarters in Mexico City to make the case that Don Carlos Loret de Mola had perished in a motor vehicle accident. Present when Rafael arrived at Bucareli were Secretary Bartlett, Deputy Secretary Jorge Carrillo Olea, Guerrero attorney general Bello Solís, and every one of the investigators and forensic experts who had conducted the initial inquiry into the Loret de Mola case. Also present were *Excélsior* associate editor Raúl Vieyra Campos and reporter Víctor Payán, who had witnessed the autopsy in Zihuatanejo the day before, as well as Rafael Loret's brother-in-law, Arturo Solís Quintero, and Carlos Capetillo Campo, who had served as Carlos Loret de Mola's chief of public security during the latter's term as governor of Yucatán (1970–1976).

For three hours, Bartlett conducted the assembled investigators and forensic specialists through what Rafael Loret described as a "horrific review" of the physical evidence, which, Bartlett insisted, was cumulatively consistent with deaths resulting from a vehicular accident. Rafael was too emotionally distraught, he later wrote, to challenge the evidence presented that day. At the conclusion of the presentation, Bartlett indicated his wish to issue an official report of their meeting in order to put an end to public speculation about Carlos Loret's demise. Did the younger Loret have any objection? No, Rafael replied, provided that the proposed press release noted his doubts about the case and stated that those doubts would be duly addressed. When later that evening Televisa news personality Jacobo Zabludovsky read the official government statement on the air, it falsely averred that Rafael Loret had accepted the government's version of how his father had died, while omitting any mention of his express reservations about the official account.

The government's case was hopelessly flawed from the outset and quickly unraveled, although federal and state authorities persisted in repeating the falsehood that Rafael Loret de Mola's citing of contradictory evidence was merely his subjective view of the facts and had no bearing on the hard forensic evidence pointing to a driving mishap. Two weeks after attending Secretary Bartlett's command Bucareli performance, Rafael Loret personally examined the Filo Mayor site accompanied by Antonio Nogueda Carbajal, then director of Averiguaciones Previas for the state of Guerrero. Among various details that conflicted with the official version of events, Loret and Nogueda determined that the elder Loret's vehicle had not been traveling at an excessive rate of speed; that, given the location of the wreckage 150 meters down the precipice, it had in all likelihood gone over the edge from a resting position—in other words, been pushed;[15] and that, despite massive impact injuries to the thorax and head of both victims, the steering wheel and column had remained intact, suggesting that there had been no driver behind it at the moment of impact.

Three months later Carlos Márquez Arias, former head of the Guerrero State Judicial Police, approached Rafael Loret in Chilpancingo, where the latter had been subpoenaed to testify about his father. Márquez had known Don Carlos in Mérida during the 1970s, he said, and had been one of the first on the scene of the Filo Mayor incident. A number of details he had observed at the site, he told Rafael, struck him as inconsistent with the official account. Don Carlos's body was lying a few feet to the right of the wreckage, which meant that he could not have been driving as the authorities claimed. Márquez confirmed that the Mercedes had been pushed over the edge of the precipice, noting that steps had been taken to assure there would be no fire: the fuel tank had been emptied and the motor turned off when it plummeted into the gulch.

Several weeks after this exchange, Carlos Márquez Arias was shot to death. Rafael Loret describes the three gunman simply as "ex-agents," without clarifying whether they had been DFS agents or former Guerrero Judicial Police officers previously under Márquez's command. Their institutional affiliation is of some interest, inasmuch as a number of individuals Rafael identifies as "DFS" agents appear to have intervened in the Loret de Mola case after the DFS had been officially disbanded (29 November 1985) and its functions, together with those of the IPS, were being folded into the newly created DISEN.[16] Even Pablo González Ruelas, a thirty-year DFS veteran in charge of telephone tapping and the individual selected to close down directorate operations, concerned himself briefly with the case, which raises the question of operational continuity during the reorganization of Mexico's intelligence organs.[17]

González Ruelas had shown up at Rafael Loret de Mola's residence on 10 February 1986, barely two hours after Loret had informed Manuel Bartlett that Don Carlos was missing. Accompanying González was Juventino Prado, who at the time of the Buendía slaying less than two years before had served as commander of the DFS's Brigada Especial and just over three years later would be indicted as a coconspirator in the Buendía homicide. They had been sent by Deputy Secretary of Government Jorge Carrillo Olea to learn what Rafael could tell them about his father's disappearance. Comandante Prado was Gobernación's "premier expert in solving kidnappings," González Ruelas volunteered in a curious non sequitur. Prado would be in charge of the government's investigation. Based on what Rafael had told them, González remarked, they were no doubt looking at either a kidnapping or an assassination, a conclusion Loret later thought strange in light of official insistence on the one-car accident scenario.

A third ex-DFS operative on the scene as events unfolded in the Carlos Loret de Mola case was Víctor Manuel Gómez, aka "El Gringo," who had been a member of the Brigada Especial under Juventino Prado, was thought to have served as a liaison between the DFS and the CIA, and who, according to Rafael Loret de Mola, was the motorcyclist who extricated Manuel Buendía's assassin from the crime scene on 30 May 1984, although he was never charged as an accessory to the Buendía slaying. Gómez had been observed at the mortuary in Zihuatanejo where the remains of Carlos Loret and Rosa Elena Jasso Rico were autopsied. He'd been assigned to surveil Julio Alberto Pérez Benítez and Arturo Solís, Loret family friends who had been sent to Zihuatanejo to identify the victims and return Don Carlos's remains to Mexico City. While the majority of its personnel had been dismissed when the DFS was dismantled,

Prado and "El Gringo" appear to have transitioned smoothly into the new DISEN under Pedro Vázquez Colmenares, a Bartlett Díaz ally.[18]

While Manuel Buendía and Carlos Loret de Mola may or may not have been slain for the same reason (Lawrence Harrison thinks they were not[19]), links between the two cases steadily multiplied. In addition to the carry-over of DFS personnel from one directorate to the other, Rafael Loret was contacted not long after his father's death by the prominent Mexico City columnist and former member of Manuel Buendía's inner circle Manú Dornbierer, who had received a communication from anonymous witnesses to a violent assault at the El Güirindalito checkpoint on the night of 5 February 1986. The witnesses, a man and wife, had driven up to the *retén* after dark and, as they approached, observed soldiers darting back and forth in a state of general agitation. A second lieutenant, pistol in hand, had curtly instructed them to drive on through, not to stop. As they obeyed his order, they managed to observe soldiers beating an already bloodied person, while two individuals in civilian clothes stood to one side. Nearby, they had noticed an American-made pickup truck with Baja California border plates "like the kind used by the Federal Judicial Police or the Federal Security Directorate." They also reported seeing a Mercedes Benz in one of the parking spaces, "an unusual sight that immediately caught one's attention." After this initial communication with Dornbierer, they were too frightened to have any further contact, but their account of events at El Güirindalito now became part of the evidentiary record.[20]

Three months into the Salinas administration, Rafael Loret de Mola met with Salinas's predecessor, Miguel de la Madrid, at the latter's Coyoacán residence in the Federal District. As with the Buendía case, de la Madrid lamented his failure to achieve closure in the death of Rafael Loret's father.[21] The Secretariat of Government, that is, Bartlett Díaz, had "swaddled" the whole affair, he remarked, "Me las empañaron en Gobernación." In other words, it had been covered up and the facts of the case concealed from the president. "It all transpired at the El Güirindalito *retén*, didn't it?" de la Madrid acknowledged. Yet Bartlett, Arévalo, and Attorney General García Ramírez had all assured him that the victim's son accepted the official version of a highway accident. Hardly, Rafael Loret replied. Contrary to what de la Madrid had been told, Bartlett had placed every possible obstacle in his way to prevent him from clarifying the multiple evidentiary contradictions adduced in his father's violent demise.[22]

Following this conversation with Miguel de la Madrid, Rafael Loret requested a meeting with President Salinas, which was granted and tentatively scheduled for the later part of April. In the meantime, he met on the fourth of that month with Salinas's national defense secretary, Gen. Antonio Riviello Bazán, whom he pointedly informed of his upcoming audience with the president, then proceeded to discuss the evidence he had gathered implicating the army in his father's death. In addition to the army's own internal report establishing that the El Güirindalito military checkpoint was the last place Carlos Loret and his secretary had been seen alive and the anonymous witness account of someone being beaten there by soldiers six days before the two bodies were recovered from the Vallecitos de Zaragoza burial site, Rafael Loret now informed General Riviello that Loret family representatives had personally observed an unusual deployment of military personnel around the rudimentary grave from which the victims' remains were being disinterred and that they had seen army officers actually filming the disinterment.

The area had remained secured by soldiers for several days, Loret told the defense secretary, while the same officers who had filmed the disinterment later seized the autopsy photos and refused to turn them over to judicial authorities. General Riviello claimed to have no knowledge of either the filming or the military presence at Vallecitos. He was disturbed, however, that the army was being implicated in the Loret de Mola affair and said he would make the appropriate internal inquiries. In the meantime, he assured Rafael Loret that he was free to continue his own investigation and the defense secretary would assist him in any way he could.[23]

At one o'clock in the afternoon of 25 April 1986, Rafael met for thirty minutes with President Salinas at Los Pinos. After summarizing the accumulated evidence of foul play in his father's death, he requested that the president instruct Attorney General Enrique Álvarez del Castillo to open a federal inquiry into the Carlos Loret de Mola case. The state of Guerrero, he explained, had thus far exercised sole jurisdiction in the case and was steadfastly refusing to consider evidence that countered the official version of a single-vehicle accident. Professing "profound esteem" for Don Carlos and stating that "his memory of course deserved that justice be done," Salinas gave Rafael Loret his presidential word that there would be federal follow-up.[24]

Eight weeks earlier, meanwhile, *unomásuno* founding editor Manuel Becerra Acosta had been summarily obliged by the Salinas administration to divest himself of his majority interest in that influential newspaper and go into foreign exile, thus "decapitating," Rafael Loret would later recall, "what had until then been an independent daily." Becerra Acosta had been replaced at *unomásuno* by the paper's general manager, Luis Gutiérrez Rodríguez, who, as noted in chapter 7, was a personal friend of the president, as well as, according to Loret, a close associate of Salinas's government secretary, Fernando Gutiérrez Barrios. And like Carlos Loret de Mola, whose book manuscript critical of the de la Madrid administration had vanished from the wreckage of his car at Filo Mayor Gulch, Becerra, too, was assaulted while driving near Andorra in the eastern Pyrenees, where his attackers seized a manuscript exposé of his expulsion from Mexico. (Rafael Loret would himself be briefly expelled from Mexico by the Salinas administration, following in Becerra's footsteps to a village in the eastern Pyrenees, where he spent a three-month exile in 1991.[25]) Meanwhile, as Carlos Salinas was giving Rafael Loret de Mola his personal word that justice would be done in the death of his outspoken journalist father, Buendía homicide special prosecutor Miguel Ángel García Domínguez was commencing radiation treatment for his throat cancer, further fueling doubts about how the Salinas administration intended to resolve that high-profile case.

There appears to have been no immediate presidential follow-up in the Loret de Mola case, due probably to Salinas's preoccupation at the time with staging the grand finale of the Manuel Buendía case. When former DFS chief José Antonio Zorrilla Pérez was indicted and arrested in June 1989, Rafael Loret was moved to write Salinas a congratulatory letter, taking the occasion "to insist, respectfully, on the necessity of reopening [the Carlos Loret de Mola case] and pursuing it wherever it might lead." He had come away from their April meeting, he wrote, persuaded that the president would not leave his father's "barbaric homicide" unsolved and that "reason would triumph over simulation"—a reference more pointed than Loret perhaps realized as the government's final curtain was coming down on the Buendía homicide. "The crude scenography of a highway accident," he emphasized, "no longer holds up."[26]

By the end of the year, Salinas had instructed Secretary of Government Gutiérrez Barrios to arrange for Rafael Loret to meet with Attorney General Álvarez del Castillo about the Loret de Mola case. The meeting took place on Wednesday, 31 January 1990. Among the abundant documentation that Rafael brought with him that day were photographs taken at El Filo Mayor the very day Don Carlos Loret's black Mercedes went off the road and into the gulch below. The images had been sent to him, he explained, "by a friend in the Judicial Police" (federal or state is unclear). What was most extraordinary, he pointed out and the attorney general immediately appreciated, was that one of the photographs clearly captured the vehicle in full descent down the precipice, wheels oriented across and downslope as it cycled through a roll, debris kicking up from the impact.

A second photo showed the wreckage where it came to rest, upright, with the four tires apparently blown out. Five men could be seen on the steep slope around the wreckage, including a uniformed police officer. A third photo featured Carlos Loret's curiously intact license plate positioned on the rear of an otherwise thoroughly mangled vehicle, while a fourth, interior, image showed the intact steering column and relatively undamaged steering wheel. These photographs, reproduced in the 1995 revised edition of Rafael Loret de Mola's *Denuncia: Presidente sin palabra*, eloquently and incontestably document that the elder Loret's vehicle did not accidentally drive off the road and that the physical evidence in Filo Mayor Gulch had been contrived for ulterior purposes.[27]

Other information that had come to Rafael Loret's attention during the almost four years since his father was killed, together with what could now only be described as crime scene photos, left Álvarez del Castillo little option but to go through the motions of opening a federal criminal inquiry into the Loret de Mola case. Early on, for example, Rafael had been contacted by Lilia Arellano, a reporter with the Mexico City daily *Ovaciones*, who informed him that she had learned from one of the forensic specialists who had participated in the autopsies that they had detected bullet traces through what remained of both victims' brain tissue, one bullet in Carlos Loret's case, two in that of his secretary. The head of the autopsy team, Dr. Alejandro Toriz Díaz, denied that forensic examiners had found any indication of gunshot wounds, asserting incongruously that they had taken special pains to look for such evidence, "because they had already heard a rumor to that effect."

When, we can only wonder, and from whom might the Guerrero state forensic specialist have heard such a rumor in the few brief hours between disinterment of the badly decomposed bodies and their subsequent autopsies in Zihuatanejo? According to Rafael Loret's brother-in-law, Arturo Solís Quintero, who witnessed the autopsies, the upper frontal portion of both craniums was missing from the midforehead up, ostensibly smashed open by the impact of the vehicle as it plummeted into Filo Mayor Gulch. The immediate problem with that explanation, however, is that such an injury would have caused profuse bleeding, yet there were no traces of blood in the wreckage. Cranial damage of that nature, on the other hand, would be consistent with an upwardly angled shot to the base of the skull from a large-caliber handgun. That both corpses should exhibit similar head trauma was likewise problematic, since they would have been positioned differently in the vehicle and sustained correspondingly different impacts.

Rafael Loret also possessed pertinent information concerning the individuals who had crafted the official account of the Filo Mayor incident. According to Lilia Arellano's eyewitness source, the initial draft of the autopsy report took due note of the coup-de-grâce-like bullet traces, but all reference to them had been excised from the final official version. Moreover, she said, de la Madrid's secretary of health, Dr. Guillermo Soberón, was aware of the excision. Asked by Loret how she knew that, Arellano replied that, again according to her firsthand forensic source, Soberón had sent then deputy health secretary José Francisco Ruiz Massieu to Zihuatanejo as his representative, Ruiz Massieu had been present during the autopsies, and presumably he had had a hand in approving the final wording of the official autopsy report. Having revealed these details to Arellano in the confidentiality of two lifelong friends, then realizing the gravity of what he had told her, Arellano's source refused to say anything further about it and, frightened, went into hiding. The federal authorities' inability to locate him would in time become a convenient excuse for allowing the Loret de Mola case to languish unresolved.[28]

The appearance of José Francisco Ruiz Massieu at the critical juncture of the Zihuatanejo autopsies brings us to what is perhaps the contextual crux of not only the Loret de Mola killing but also the Manuel Buendía and Enrique Camarena homicides, namely, the deep politics of Mexico's increasingly challenged governing party, the PRI. Ruiz Massieu was neither a health care professional nor a trained forensic specialist, but rather attended the Carlos Loret de Mola and Rosa Elena Jasso Rico autopsies in a political capacity as an institutional representative of the federal government. He was, in fact, one of the emerging political players who within the next decade would attain dubious notoriety as another prominent assassination victim belonging to a terminally conflicted, violence-riven PRI.[29] At the time of his killing in late September 1994, he was general secretary of the PRI and had been directly involved in formulating policy for the Salinas administration. Ruiz Massieu, Lilia Arellano insisted, knew what the forensic specialists had learned from the victims' remains and almost certainly had intervened to excise from the autopsy report any reference to bullet traces in the head of a politically troublesome PRI veteran. "The country's orographically sinuous political terrain," Rafael Loret writes in this connection, "can just as easily lead to clumsily staged [automobile] 'accidents' as to brutal power disputes among supposedly kindred groups."[30]

On examining the Filo Mayor photographs that Rafael Loret brought to their 31 January 1990 meeting, Attorney General Álvarez del Castillo had enthused that he would use them to "teach the Federal District prosecutors a lesson." District Attorney General Ignacio Morales Lechuga and his people had sought to impress President Salinas with the arrest of José Antonio Zorrilla Pérez and their supposed resolution of the Buendía case, he remarked dismissively, "but they've done so based on pure falsehoods."

Now, however, he would show them that "at least the federal attorney general could solve the murder of a journalist!"[31]

It was indeed a propitious opportunity, Loret had replied with just a hint of sarcasm. But, he warned, the attorney general would confront a major obstacle should he determine to pursue the case to its logical conclusion. Two prime suspects were sitting members of President Salinas's cabinet: Secretary of Agricultural Reform Víctor Cervera Pacheco and Secretary of Education Manuel Bartlett Díaz. Cervera Pacheco was a former governor of Yucatán, willing instrument of PRI centrist interests, and confirmed enemy of Carlos Loret de Mola; Bartlett had controlled the state security apparatus at the time of both slayings and was the possessor of Mexico's darkest political secrets. Yes, Álvarez agreed, the Loret de Mola case "had very dangerous ramifications."[32]

At the other end of the line were two DEA agents, Héctor Berréllez and Antonio Gárate Bustamante, each one on an extension.

"The bigwigs met to figure out what to do with you, Rafael. There were five of them. The heavyweights, you understand."

"Was the president among them?"

"Maybe yes, maybe no. We have a recording, and you can hear very clearly what they are saying about you. 'Do we kill him or not?' they ask. 'No, that's not a very viable option.' They thought of everything. One of them proposed offering you money, but they discarded that idea, because they know you too well. Another proposed having you beaten up as a warning, but then you could denounce them. And when they considered the ultimate solution, they were afraid of making you a martyr."

"So, they pardoned me?"

"They're going to leave you alone. No one's to talk about you or support you. Insofar as possible, your books are to be given no exposure. They intend to wear you down, hassle your family, demoralize you. We're warning you, Rafael, so that you can take your precautions."[33]

We would pursue the links revealed by Rafael Loret de Mola between Manuel Buendía, Carlos Loret de Mola, and Operation Leyenda into the new century, but in the meantime there were other important investigative tasks still demanding our attention. On 11 March 1992, we flew from Chicago to Guadalajara, checked into the Hotel Francés, then met Manuel Buendía's younger brother Ángel, who drove us to his home, where we discussed the case for three and a half hours. Prior to our trip, Russell had drafted a thirteen-page "Síntesis de investigación," which was not a summary of investigation per se but rather a series of pertinent observations and suggested conclusions based on our investigative work to that date and brought together as a way of simultaneously broadening and sharpening our perspectives on the Buendía case. We gave Don Ángel a copy and waited while he read carefully through it. When he had finished, he set it pensively down on the table where we were sitting, collected his thoughts, then said he both agreed and disagreed with it; he thought we would perhaps find it helpful if he recounted for us some of the details of his involvement with the Buendía case oversight group.[34]

The main points of the *síntesis* were: (1) that Buendía was the victim of an international conspiracy, (2) that he had been slain by Mexicans in concert with Americans, (3) that he was killed not for what he had learned about the involvement of government officials with drug traffickers but rather to prevent him from exposing Mexican collusion with the Americans in support of the Nicaraguan *contras*, (4) that DFS chief Zorrilla Pérez would not have acted on his own authority in such a high-profile assassination, (5) that the guilt of the alleged gunman and other DFS coconspirators had not been duly established, and (6) that Special Prosecutor García Domínguez had in effect completed the government's cover-up of the Buendía case. We noted two key unanswered questions. Why, eight years on, was the Manuel Buendía case still considered a national security matter in the United States? And why had the Americans ever considered it a national security matter?

As Don Ángel recounted his experiences as the prime mover in the independent Buendía case oversight group, we were struck by how susceptible he seemed to manipulation by the key officials concerned with the case: the de la Madrid administration's government secretary Manuel Bartlett Díaz and Special Prosecutor Miguel Ángel García Domínguez. While he would eventually modify his views with a measure of skepticism, three years after the government's official resolution of his brother's assassination Don Ángel continued to believe that Bartlett Díaz had been completely sincere in his professed commitment to solving the Buendía homicide and that García Domínguez likewise had been thoroughly transparent in his handling of the case.

The accused, Don Ángel was persuaded, were unquestionably guilty as charged and had all been properly convicted. He acknowledged that, of course, the CIA, DEA, Mexican Far Right (Los Tecos), and drug traffickers were all in cahoots, but how to prove their connection to his brother's killing? García Domínguez had achieved what no one else had managed to accomplish, he insisted, by meticulously assembling hard evidence to convict the material assassin and his immediate overseers, in the process creating a shock wave that was bringing down other criminal elements as well.

Within a year of this first meeting with us, however, Ángel Buendía would accept our thesis of American involvement in the assassination. "I am convinced that it was the CIA that ordered my brother's murder," he told an interviewer for the weekly magazine *Jalisco Hoy* on the eve of the ninth anniversary of Manuel Buendía's violent demise. The motive, he now averred, was to prevent Manuel from exposing the CIA's link to Mexican narcotics traffickers.[35] In a subsequent phone conversation, I commented on his apparent change in thinking about the case. Not with regard to the guilt of Zorrilla and his accomplices, he replied, but on rereading our "Síntesis de investigación" he'd been struck by several details he had not considered before, especially Miguel Nazar Haro's relationship with the CIA, which had convinced him that the agency was behind his brother's slaying. After going through our *síntesis* again, he said, he had asked Bartlett and García Domínguez about Nazar Haro, and they had both confirmed Nazar's role as a key CIA asset. And when on the eve of the new century Don Ángel at last published his own account of the Buendía case, he would take his book's closing paragraph directly from that same early *síntesis*. There was, he wrote, "one final, obligatory, question: Why, at fifteen years' remove, was the Manuel Buendía case still a 'state secret' and national security case in the U.S.?"[36]

Don Ángel shared some interesting Buendía family history during our 11 March visit. His older brother Manuel, he recounted, had set out on his combative journalistic course in 1950 as a direct consequence of their elderly father's fatal stoning by a pair of *marijuanos*. At that point, Manuel had assumed the role of family head for his younger siblings. He later developed a great admiration for Cuba and Fidel Castro, as well as for the Sandinistas. He admired Castro as a man, Ángel told us. "They had a mutual admiration for one another." We had asked Don Ángel about his brother's contacts with Fidel Castro, inasmuch as we were then on our way to Cuba to see if we might learn something further about that significant association.

We flew from Guadalajara to Mexico City on Thursday, 12 March, stopped at the Mexicana counter to reconfirm our Sunday flight to Havana, then took a cab to the Mónaco. That Friday we did some work at the Fundación Manuel Buendía and met with Miguel Ángel Sánchez de Armas, leaving with him a copy of our "Síntesis de investigación," which we agreed to discuss when we returned from Cuba. We spent a leisurely Saturday between bookstores, the Centro Cultural Librería Reforma, and the Café París across the plaza from our hotel. Sunday morning, we took Mexicana's daily 8:00 a.m. flight to Havana and by early afternoon had checked into the Hotel Vedado.

We wanted to appeal directly to Fidel Castro for assistance in clarifying the nature of Manuel Buendía's contacts with Cuban authorities and to do so in such a way as to be reasonably certain that our request would actually reach Castro himself. By 1992 we had dealt with Cuban officials on various occasions regarding journalistic and University of Wisconsin–related matters, so we were known quantities in Havana and not perceived as hostile to the Cuban regime. Our conduit to Castro was the then dean of foreign correspondents in Havana, Lionel Martin, whom we had known since 1981.

Lionel was an American expatriate who had pursued graduate studies in political science and international relations at the University of California, Berkeley, in the 1950s, got caught up in the university loyalty oath controversy of those years, and concluded that it would not be feasible for him to complete his doctoral degree. He then worked for a while as a news commentator and correspondent for KPFA Radio in Berkeley, reporting from the UN in New York and from Cuba, where he arrived one month before the April 1961 Bay of Pigs invasion. He covered the U.S.-supported assault from the defenders' forward positions, then decided to remain in Cuba.

Over the next thirty-eight years, Lionel worked as a correspondent for the ABC, BBC, and CBC broadcast networks, the British news agency Reuters, and the *Washington Post*. He wrote an insightful book about Fidel Castro's ideological formation and became the point man for high-profile U.S. media personalities seeking interviews with Castro. As he himself recounts:

> I've trekked along behind Fidel Castro on visits to farms, schools, and the mountain locales of his guerrilla exploits. I watched him as he interrogated the prisoners after the Bay of Pigs invasion, and I sat in a small television studio-theater as he painfully told the Cuban people of [Che Guevara's] death in Bolivia. I've seen and listened to him in hotel lobbies, at diplomatic receptions, at the inaugurations of new towns, and before the multitude in Revolution Square. I've stood on the edge of the tarmac at José Martí airport dozens of times as Fidel welcomed important world leaders. I've participated in I don't know how many impromptu news conferences with him. I've written about him for newspapers and fed voice reports about him to ABC and CBC.[37]

Cuban leader Fidel Castro, 1986, admired
by Manuel Buendía and with whom
Buendía was in personal contact.
(Sylvia E. Bartley)

Fidel Castro with Mexican columnists Francisco Martínez de la Vega (*left*) and Manuel
Buendía (*right*) in Havana, 1982. (Courtesy of the Fundación Manuel Buendía)

On Monday the sixteenth we visited with Lionel and his wife Adrienne Hunter at their Calle 18 home in Havana's Miramar district, where we began strategizing our approach to Fidel Castro. We had brought along a copy of our "Síntesis de investigación," together with photocopies of our published articles on the Buendía case, to accompany the formal interview request. Lionel thought our request was both legitimate and reasonable but cautioned us that, aside from the large number of such requests under consideration at any given moment, Cuba's relationship with Mexico was more delicate than most and, for that reason alone, might persuade the Cuban leader to deny us the access we sought. That said, Lionel assured us that he would endorse our request when he submitted it to Castro's aides.

Over the next two days we finished drafting our interview request, typing up the final version at Lionel's place. We outlined the scope of our Buendía investigation, explained our own involvement in the case and the thrust of our proposed book, noted that we had come to Havana for the express purpose of delivering our request directly to him, and concluded with our contact information should he decide to grant us an interview or otherwise wish to communicate with us about the matters we had raised. Lionel delivered our letter and accompanying documentation to Castro's personal aide on Thursday, 19 March, and three days later we caught Mexicana's daily flight back to Mexico City.[38]

We received no reply to our interview request, nor any official assistance in clarifying Manuel Buendía's contact with Cuba. As with our Soviet colleagues, we had mentioned the Buendía case to Cuban officials whom we'd known over the years but never elicited more than personal expressions of interest. We concluded that Lionel Martin's caveat about the delicacy of Cuban-Mexican relations was in fact going to prove an insurmountable obstacle to this line of inquiry and set the entire matter aside.

Three years later, Russell's last before retiring from the University of Wisconsin, we would address a second interview request to Fidel Castro. It was a single-page, three-paragraph letter in which we recalled our earlier request and the reasons for it, again described the book we intended to write, and stressed our wish to learn firsthand from him about Buendía's visits to the island. We sent this follow-up request through the Cuban Interests Section in Washington, DC, but, as previously, we received no response. Years later Lawrence Harrison would assure us that Manuel Buendía's personal association with Fidel Castro and the Cubans had nothing at all to do with his assassination. Harrison, the evidence persuades us, is correct on this count, albeit with the qualification that, viewed from the Reagan White House, Buendía's contact with and sympathy for Cuba made him a convenient target of opportunity beyond the assassins' primary motive of protecting potentially explosive covert operations in Mexico.[39]

On our return from Havana, we laid over one day in Mexico City in order to meet again with Miguel Ángel Sánchez de Armas. The three of us got together late Monday afternoon, 23 March, at the Fundación Manuel Buendía, where we discussed the "Síntesis de investigación" we had left with him a week earlier. Sánchez de Armas found our suggestion that Special Prosecutor García Domínguez had himself been complicit in the Mexican government's cover-up of the Buendía case personally disturbing, inasmuch as he, together with Rogelio Hernández, had been responsible for having

García Domínguez appointed in the first place. As hard as it was for him to believe that García Domínguez could have played such a duplicitous role, he acknowledged that there were in fact elements of the special prosecutor's handling of the Buendía case that were difficult to explain.

For example, just two weeks prior to DFS director Zorrilla Pérez's arrest, he told us, García Domínguez had actually closed his investigation, claiming that he had insufficient evidence to indict Zorrilla, only to suddenly reopen the case and have Zorrilla taken into custody. This was not reported in the press, Sánchez de Armas noted, nor had Rogelio Hernández mentioned it in his book, *Zorrilla: El imperio del crimen* (1989), while García Domínguez, for his part, never offered any explanation for his actions. Although Sánchez de Armas said he did not know what, if any, personal relationship the special prosecutor may have had with President Salinas, he did know that García Domínguez and Secretary of Government Manuel Bartlett Díaz were *cuates*, in other words close friends.

All this now led Sánchez de Armas to wonder if he had been played as the useful fool (*tonto útil*) in a dirty political charade. These disquieting doubts raised by our "Síntesis de investigación," he commented, were heightened by his coincidental viewing that week of the Oliver Stone film *JFK*, about the November 1963 assassination of U.S. president John F. Kennedy. He seemed sobered, even frightened, we thought, by the possible dimensions of the cover-up we were suggesting. We would recall his disquiet that day when, in subsequent years, he evidenced a distinct desire to distance himself from the Buendía affair and eventually even had a falling out with Ángel Buendía, whom he described to us as a fine person but "politically naive" and perfectly susceptible to manipulation by Manuel Bartlett and other figures in positions of power.[40]

El caso Buendía: ¿cerrado sin resolver?

Revista mexicana de comunicación—November–December 1993

Russell H. Bartley

When, on 15 February of last year, Penal Law Judge Roberto Hernández Martínez sentenced the supposed assassins of Manuel Buendía Tellezgirón to thirty-five years in prison, the curtain fell on what can only be described as a major theatrical production.

But there is nothing entertaining about the theater of abuse—abuse of the public and of people's well-being. The way the Buendía case has been handled offends one's intelligence. It is impossible to accept what has been presented as the *solution* of this high-profile crime, because in reality it has not been solved at all. The facts of the case remain as before, hidden from view and buried in formulaic legalisms.

These are the opening sentences of an article submitted to Sánchez de Armas in April 1993 about the way Mexican authorities had closed the official Buendía investigation. When it appeared the following November, we were struck and displeased to note that, in his capacity as editor of the *Revista mexicana de comunicación*, he had inserted a question mark following the article's title. It was not an insignificant detail, inasmuch as it substantively altered the article's thrust from its intended declaratory statement (that Mexican authorities had in fact closed the Buendía case without resolving it) to a hypothetical question of whether or not there might still be loose ends. We recognized that this editorial change perhaps reflected concern on the part of the *Revista*'s parent organization, the Fundación Manuel Buendía, which necessarily functioned within the constraints of the PRI-manipulated political order and thus might have led Sánchez de Armas to soften a contribution he felt pushed too hard against the limits of what was politically permissible. In light of subsequent developments, however, we now conclude that the editorial decision to change the article's title from a declaration to an interrogatory was Sánchez de Armas's alone and that it constituted a first telltale sign that he was being pressured to back away from the Buendía case.[41]

When next we saw Sánchez de Armas three years later, we found him living in a spacious Mexico City apartment seemingly beyond the means of a journalist of his status, as he himself acknowledged to us without further explanation. In the course of our conversation that evening, we remarked to him that he seemed to be losing interest in the Buendía case and that his personal commitment to preserving Buendía's journalistic legacy appeared to be waning. To which he replied matter-of-factly that he wanted to get on with his own career and also needed to be concerned for his daughter's future. "Tengo que preocuparme por el bienestar de mi hija" was how he expressed it, leaving little doubt in our minds that he had been given an ultimatum and took it very seriously.

By the time Ángel Buendía completed his own published account of the Buendía case on the eve of the new millennium, he felt compelled to denounce Sánchez de Armas's changed attitude publicly. It pained him deeply, he wrote in his acknowledgments, that the man he had considered one of his closest friends not only had refused to contribute an afterword to his book but had actually belittled his modest effort to expose the motive and masterminds behind his brother's murder. He'd been naive, he expressed, to have thought that Sánchez de Armas, "who was inside and knew the bowels of power," could allow himself to shed any light on the assassination. That realization finally brought home to Don Ángel that there were no exceptions in such matters. "No one who has been co-opted by the system," he lamented, "is able to speak freely, much less jeopardize the benefits the system has provided them." Perhaps, he suggested bitterly, "Sánchez de Armas does not wish to compromise any of his patrons' friends, past or present."[42]

Don Ángel's hurt was deep and his judgment of Sánchez de Armas harsh. By the same token, Sánchez de Armas's judgment of Don Ángel—that he was naive, politically unsophisticated, a poor writer, *testarudo* (obstinate), and given to unsubstantiated hypotheses—was gratuitously insensitive, of little substance, and, above all, revealed an uncharacteristic inability on Sánchez de Armas's part to maintain a civil relationship with an established friend who was emotionally consumed by his brother's homicide. He could not contribute to Ángel Buendía's book, he told us some years later, because Don Ángel would not allow him to make substantive revisions to his manuscript and he could not endorse some of Don Ángel's undocumented charges.

Rather than accept Ángel Buendía's book for what it was, that is, inherently valuable firsthand testimony about the Buendía case, Sánchez de Armas sought to edit that testimony in conformity with criteria other than the author's. When prohibited from doing so, he abandoned his friend and the friend's book project in an unseemly huff, all of which suggests that Miguel Ángel Sánchez de Armas had indeed been compromised by anonymous parties with a vested interest in the Buendía case, parties predictably sensitive to what Manuel Buendía's younger brother might write about it.

Sánchez de Armas's coerced role on their behalf, we suspect, was to neutralize Don Ángel's testimony before it went to press or, barring that, to discredit the book once it appeared in print. Dismayed though we were to realize that this was probably what had transpired, it was not for us to pass judgment on our colleague's behavior. What mattered was the apparent fact that Sánchez de Armas had been compromised and coerced, not that he opted to accede to the demands of those who pressured him. For him the personal stakes were unacceptably high, and no one can legitimately insist that he should have acted differently.

13

By Mutual Consent

The man who must depend upon research and investigation inevitably falls victim to the many pitfalls of the secret world and of the "cover story" world with its lies and counter-lies. . . . Those career professionals who have devoted their lives to this cause and who have totally lived the party line just cannot bring themselves to see some things as they appear to others, and then admit it even if they should. There is much about a life in the Agency that is like a religious order or a secret fraternity.

—Col. L. Fletcher Prouty, *The Secret Team* (2008)

BY THE FALL OF 1992, as Rubén Zuno Arce's retrial approached what from hindsight appears to have been its foregone conclusion, it had become apparent to us that prosecution witness Lawrence Victor Harrison was an essential source for our investigation if we were ever to move beyond the realm of circumstantial evidence and conjecture. As recounted in chapter 10, it was Zuno's lead defense attorney, Ed Medvene, who first provided us with key documentation about Harrison.

Law Offices
Mitchell, Silberberg & Knupp
11377 W. Olympic Boulevard
Los Angeles, California 90064-1683
file number 22958-1-8
ZAV6CBHI54

MEMORANDUM	Date: (Amended on 5/22/90)

Dictated but not Read

To: Zuno Team

cc: Zuno File
Witness Files: Lorenzo Harrison (aka George Marshall Davis), Enrique Placentia, Cesar Garcia-Bueno, Manuel Crespin, Hector Cervantes-Santos, Jesse Najar-Zuno, Eugene Hollestelle, Antonio Garate-Bustamante, Frederico Castel Del-Oro, David Dieter

From: Jim Blancarte

Subject: Zuno Trial (telephone interviews on 5/22/90 with Government Witnesses)

LORENZO HARRISON (aka George Marshall Davis)

At approximately 10:05 A.M. on Monday, May 21, 1990, I received a call from Lorenzo Harrison. Lorenzo Harrison said he did not want to speak to me or any other defense counsel for "security reasons." I assured him there was no security problem in speaking with me. I asked him for his full true name and he confirmed that the name the government gave us is his full true name. I asked him if he knew Mr. Zuno personally and he said he did. I asked him if Mr. Zuno knew him and he said yes. He would not confirm under what name Mr. Zuno knows him but he assured me "that Don Ruben knows very well who I am." I asked Mr. Harrison to at least give me how he knew Mr. Zuno and how long he knew Mr. Zuno. Lorenzo Harrison again told me he did not want to speak to me or to any other defense counsel for security reasons. I asked Mr. Harrison to at least give me some basic information in order to refresh Mr. Zuno's memory as to how Mr. Harrison and Mr. Zuno knew each other. Mr. Harrison refused to give me any details and simply said tell Don Ruben "I still respect him as long as he respects me and tell him that I still appreciate everything his father did for me and I still respect him (Zuno's father), his brothers and his family."

I then asked Mr. Harrison when he first learned that he would be making this phone call to me? Mr. Harrison said that he was told about the phone call just prior to contacting me by telephone. He would not tell me anything further and that ended our conversation.

In early April 1993, Medvene sent us a packet of photocopied documents related to Harrison, including the DEA-6 debriefing reports we had unsuccessfully been seeking from the DEA and key court transcripts of Harrison's testimony in the recently concluded Zuno trials. After reading this material, we shared our initial thoughts about Harrison with Medvene.

(1) Harrison was indeed "a strange duck," as Medvene had described him in a previous phone conversation; his lack of a paper trail while at the University of California, Berkeley, suggested activities in preparation for "a deep-cover career in Mexico."

(2) The year 1968 was a significant one for Harrison to begin his involvement in Mexico, given the global wave of student protests and the challenge Mexican students posed to that country's government.

(3) The Autonomous University of Guadalajara (UAG) played an influential role in Mexican politics, and Harrison's association with that institution was probably not coincidental.

(4) Cross-examination of Harrison during the Zuno trials regarding his testimony that he had not possessed a Mexican work permit while performing legal services for the PRI and, subsequently, while working as an electronics specialist, "was very much to the point."

(5) It was inconceivable that, as a U.S. citizen, Harrison could have served as an agent of Mexico's Interior Ministry "without an explicit understanding between the appropriate officials of both countries." His involvement with Mexico's national security apparatus, especially at the levels he indicated, was credible "only if he were a U.S. agent working in concert with Mexican counterparts."

(6) Harrison's electronics expertise and apparent familiarity with military weapons likewise pointed to an intelligence background.

(7) Harrison's assertion that he conducted his investigation of the Buendía killing on his own initiative and for no one else was "simply not believable."

We enclosed a copy of the Buendía article that Russell had just submitted to Miguel Ángel Sánchez de Armas for publication in the *Revista mexicana de comunicación*, together with photocopies of articles from a recent issue of *Proceso* concerning the Camarena case, and suggested that Medvene might wish to have a member of his staff take a look at them. In the event that there was yet another trial, in which Medvene would have an opportunity to cross-examine Harrison, we indicated our willingness to work with him on refining a line of questioning to probe Harrison's credibility further. It might be helpful in this regard (and certainly would be for our investigation), we added, "to pin Harrison down on times and places of his personal contacts with senior Interior Ministry (Secretaría de Gobernación) officials, especially José Antonio Zorrilla Pérez (head of DFS, 1982–1985) and Manuel Bartlett Díaz. Did he travel to Mexico City? If so, when? How often? Why?"[1]

At the time, Medvene and his associates James E. Blancarte and Jack R. Luellen were preparing to appeal Zuno's second conviction to the Ninth Circuit Court of Appeals in Pasadena, a process that would continue through the remainder of the decade on its way to the U.S. Supreme Court. Although Harrison was not called to testify again, he remained a subject of interest to Zuno's attorneys, and we would continue to discuss him with them into the new century. For our part, we were struck by how many parties on all sides of the Camarena and Buendía affairs were quick to discredit Harrison. Even the prosecuting assistant U.S. attorneys limited their insistence on his credibility to the narrow issue of Zuno's alleged association with Guadalajara drug lord Rafael Caro Quintero.

While Harrison's credibility was widely questioned in the U.S. press based on Judge Rafeedie's disallowance of his CIA-related testimony, in Mexico it was attacked frontally as yet another offensive element in an increasingly strained bilateral relationship. In the toxic atmosphere generated by the DEA's April 1990 kidnapping of Dr. Humberto Álvarez Macháin and the doctor's pending prosecution in the United States as an alleged accomplice in the torture interrogation of Enrique Camarena, *Excélsior* dispatched reporter Rogelio Hernández López to Los Angeles to interview the admitted masterminds behind the kidnapping, DEA G/S Héctor Berréllez and his Mexican asset, Antonio Gárate Bustamante. Hernández, accompanied by *Excélsior* photographer Antonio Reyes Zurita, arrived in Los Angeles in the later part of July 1990, where, in addition to encounters with Berréllez and Gárate (subsequently embellished in *Excélsior* with an excess of melodrama), he also met with Zuno's defense attorneys, whose jaundiced views of Lawrence Harrison he would repeat back in Mexico.[2]

"The prototype of moral authority among the DEA's operatives and witnesses," Hernández wrote in a feature four-part series in October 1990, "is ex-CIA agent Lawrence Victor Harrison." Repeating verbatim the assertions made in court by Ed Medvene to discredit Harrison as a reliable witness, Hernández stated that Harrison had been charged "with at least eight criminal offenses"; that he claimed to have studied at Berkeley but "could not recall the name of a single professor"; that he further claimed to have studied at the University of California's Boalt Hall School of Law, "falsely implying that he had received a law degree" from that institution; that he had resided in Mexico "as an illegal alien"; and that he had worked for Mexican drug traffickers and "had personally and knowingly escorted narcotics shipments."[3]

Moreover, Hernández assured *Excélsior*'s readers, Harrison had been diagnosed with "mental dispersion" (*dispersión mental*), a disruption of normal thought processes characterized by the unstructured, disorderly flow of thoughts, which in turn compromises one's decision-making ability with corresponding negative impacts on one's behavior. While "mental dispersion" describes a condition that, in greater or lesser degrees of severity, affects many people, it is not widely recognized among the general public as a discrete psychological affliction. Hernández claimed to have learned about Harrison's supposed diagnosis from the Zuno defense team's case files, yet we ourselves have examined those files, as well as discussed Harrison with Zuno's attorneys over a period of several years, and not once have we seen or heard any mention of "mental dispersion" with reference to Lawrence Harrison.[4]

The journalistic sin committed here by Rogelio Hernández was to label Harrison with a vague diagnostic term that effectively implied he was not of sound mind while failing to provide his readers with even minimal insight into Harrison as the singular witness he obviously was. The larger sin, however, was Hernández's underlying chauvinism, which prevented him from scrutinizing Harrison's court testimony for what it revealed or implied about the underside of U.S.-Mexico relations, leading him to opt instead for ad hominem smears of an ex-CIA agent in illusory defense of Mexico's national dignity.[5] Nor was Hernández alone in those chauvinistic sentiments.

Former UPD president Eduardo "El Buho" Valle likewise dismissed Harrison as "an out-of-control liar who went to Mexico to make the Mexicans look ridiculous by performing electronics tasks they supposedly were incapable of doing themselves." Moreover, Valle opined, Harrison "lacked the requisite discipline and discretion of a professional agent, above all when it came to not compromising his superiors." When asked how Harrison could have done the things he claimed to have done in Mexico, El Buho exclaimed, "Now that is interesting, *caramba*!" The only way, he answered, was with a prior agreement between Mexico's DFS and "some agency of the U.S. government," which he could not name "for lack of proof."[6]

Given the nature and history of the DFS, would not that agency have to have been the CIA? we asked. To which he again replied, enigmatically, "only with a prior agreement between the DFS and some agency of the U.S. government I am unable to name." As for Harrison's supposed assertion before a congressional subcommittee that Enrique Camarena had been killed by his own government for having discovered a clandestine Pentagon operation to supply arms to the Nicaraguan *contras*, that, Valle offered dismissively, "was a total fabrication, just one more of the fantastic tales surrounding the Camarena case."[7]

Not all observers, however, were so ready to dismiss Harrison as a cracker and a nut case. While the 1990–1992 Camarena trials were still in progress, French investigative journalists Mylène Sauloy and Yves Le Bonniec concluded that Harrison's court testimony merited closer scrutiny. Harrison, they wrote in a major book about cocaine trafficking, had informed DEA debriefers "that the CIA used ranches belonging to two of the principal drug traffickers of the Guadalajara cartel to train *contra* fighters," that he had identified veteran CIA pilot Theodore Cash as "one of the people who transported drugs and arms for the Guadalajara cartel," and that Cash himself admitted flying for the agency. Until 1985, observed Sauloy and Le Bonniec, "the Guadalajara cartel operated with total impunity." And for good reason, they emphasized, because the traffickers "were in league with the powerful DFS—Mexican state security—with the approval of the CIA."[8]

Sauloy and Le Bonniec accepted as factual Harrison's account of having worked simultaneously for the DFS and Mexican drug kingpins Ernesto Fonseca and Miguel Ángel Félix Gallardo, also that in the early 1980s he had installed radio communications systems and listening devices first for the DFS, then for Fonseca and Félix Gallardo, as well as tapping into DEA communications at their Guadalajara office. Lawrence Harrison, Sauloy and Le Bonniec observed, "had all the profile of either an informant or a CIA agent." Citing defense counsel Gregory Nicolaysen as quoted by *Washington Post* reporter William Branigin, they suspected that Harrison "was the liaison between the CIA and the cartel." The CIA "obviously was cultivating a very powerful and efficient arms network through the cartel, and didn't want DEA screwing it up." Which, they aver, "is precisely what the ill-fated Camarena was about to do."[9]

LETTER [TO THE EDITOR]. THE CIA AND THE CAMARENA CASE

The Washington Post, 18 July 1990

Joseph DeTrani, Director of Public Affairs, Central Intelligence Agency, Washington

A front-page article in The Post ["Trial in Camarena Case Shows DEA Anger at CIA," July 16] contained a number of baseless allegations, and we believe it is necessary and appropriate to set the record straight:

- The Central Intelligence Agency never used Mexico as a training site for the Nicaraguan contras or for Guatemalan guerrillas, nor did it use Mexican drug traffickers or territory as a conduit for support of any type to the contras.
- The CIA supported DEA fully in the Camarena investigation and provided DEA with key information in the case.
- Allegations that the CIA knew about the drug traffickers' monitoring of DEA and did not inform DEA are simply not true.

We want to emphasize once again in the strongest possible terms that the CIA neither engages in nor condones drug trafficking. Nor did the agency participate in any coverup of the Camarena case.

The DEA may have released certain internal documents to federal prosecutors as an expression of institutional discontent vis-à-vis the CIA, Sauloy and Le Bonniec perceptively note, "but the DEA would never expose specific compromises entered into by other agencies of U.S. intelligence. And the Justice Department even less . . . while the presiding judges have obstinately refused to allow any evidence concerning links between the CIA and Félix Gallardo, considered to be the Medellín cartel's main contact in Mexico." And Gallardo was identified as one of the principals behind the

Camarena slaying, which, in Sauloy and Le Bonniec's view, closed the circle by implicating the American government in Camarena's death.

"At the heart of the Mexican government," they summarize, "the DFS was the Guadalajara cartel's 'official' arm. The cocaine traffickers had as their partner and client the CIA, which placed its logistical network at their disposal. When one understands that the DFS has traditionally been a branch of the CIA in Mexico, the three apices of the triangle come together in the triple alliance that channeled cocaine through Mexico into the United States between 1980 and 1985." And embedded at the center of that unholy alliance was Lawrence Victor Harrison.[10]

Mexican journalist Jorge Fernández Menéndez also took Harrison's court testimony seriously, in marked contrast to Rogelio Hernández, who in 1990 had dismissed the improbable gringo as an unbalanced wild man and later, in a lengthy review of the Buendía case included in Ángel Buendía's 1999 book, does not even mention Harrison.[11] Fernández Menéndez took his cue from Sauloy and Le Bonniec, whose study of cocaine trafficking during the 1980s informed his own inquiry into the linkage between narcotics and power politics as it related to Mexico, published the same year as Don Ángel's *Mi testimonio*.[12] Harrison's primary task, as he perceived it, was to monitor DEA communications in Guadalajara so as to prevent its agents from exposing the CIA/DFS/trafficker connection and, above all, "the clandestine scheme conceived by Oliver North to support the [Nicaraguan] *contras*." According to Harrison, Fernández wrote, "Enrique Camarena was murdered because he had discovered the traffickers' link to the CIA and that would expose North's operation, as well as being used by the DEA in its own internal struggle with the CIA." It was also, he added, "the real cause of Manuel Buendía's death."[13]

For our part, after reading the documentation we had obtained from Ed Medvene, we had little doubt that Harrison was potentially a key source for unraveling the Buendía case. Russell again spoke with Medvene by phone in mid-February 1995 and expressed to him our wish to meet with Harrison if there "were any way that might be arranged." We assumed that once Harrison's role as government witness had concluded, he and his family would be placed in the federal witness protection program, making it all but impossible for us to contact him. We hoped, nonetheless, that Zuno's attorneys might still be able to access him and that through them we could as well. Meanwhile, in a follow-up letter to Medvene, we indicated our wish to obtain whatever biographical information he had on Harrison: "age, date and place of birth, name on birth certificate, family background, schooling, etc.," anything that might help "make sense of the inconsistencies in his bio as presented in the court transcripts and other documents" he had sent us previously.[14]

There were further phone conversations with Medvene about Harrison, and also with Medvene's associate Jack Luellen. Luellen described Harrison as "a pathological liar," which, we subsequently concluded, was wide of the mark and one more reflection of how little Zuno's attorneys actually grasped what had transpired during the Zuno trials. At that point, however, we were only beginning to look closely at Harrison and had little understanding ourselves of the pressures he had been under or how his testimony had been choreographed by his federal handlers.

By late winter 1996, we were again ready to take our investigation into the field, first to Los Angeles, then to Guadalajara and Mexico City. In early March, we flew from Milwaukee to Los Angeles, rented a car, and drove to the home of relatives in Santa Monica. At 10:00 a.m. on Tuesday, 5 March, we met Ed Medvene at his Trident Building office in downtown Los Angeles and for the next hour discussed our mutual interests in the Buendía and Camarena cases. Medvene then placed a conference room at our disposal, had an assistant bring us the relevant Zuno case files concerning Lawrence Victor Harrison, and left us to examine them at our leisure.

Over the next five hours, we separated out sixteen documents related to Harrison, eighty-four pages in all, which Medvene's assistant photocopied for us as we identified them. Most were Mitchell, Silberberg & Knupp (MS&K) interoffice memoranda concerning Harrison's background, his debriefing statements to DEA agents, and his pretrial statements to defense counsel. There was also a detailed summary of an October 1992 interview with Harrison conducted by a former MS&K attorney, Mary E. Fulginiti; a photocopied personal information sheet obtained from the Mexican Attorney General's Office (III Circuit, Guadalajara, Jalisco); and a stapled eight-page packet comprising a cover sheet summarizing Harrison's activities in Mexico and the U.S. government's agreements with him following his repatriation, an FBI record of Harrison's fingerprints obtained from the Guadalajara police, an FBI personal data sheet dated 3 August 1992, and four pages recording government payments to Harrison between September 1989 and September 1992.[15]

There were a number of significant details in this documentation. As a general observation, we are struck by the inability of Zuno's defense team to compile a coherent background profile of Harrison, although in hindsight we realize that it took us several years to do so, and then only after gaining his personal confidence, which neither the assistant U.S. attorneys nor Zuno's attorneys would ever be able to do. At one point, an East Coast private investigator and former FBI agent by the name of Bill McCoy appears to have been retained to gather background information on Harrison. McCoy was said to be able to turn around that sort of information "within twenty-four hours or less," but in this instance he seems to have produced little, if anything, of substance. While Ed Medvene and his associates failed to make sense of the inconsistencies in Harrison's name and personal history, there were multiple clues in the documentary record they compiled that identified Harrison as an intelligence agent, which had a material bearing on the Zuno prosecution and suggested a different defense strategy from the one the MS&K attorneys unsuccessfully pursued.

A photocopied page of descriptive and related data from Harrison's FBI file obtained by MS&K incorrectly records his date of birth as 19 September 1940 and his place of birth as Newark, New Jersey, while the personal data form obtained from the Mexican attorney general's Guadalajara office correctly gives his birth date as 19 September 1944 but incorrectly gives his place of birth as Boston. In this latter case, Harrison himself would have provided the information, whereas U.S. government sources would have determined what to record in Justice Department records.

At issue here was Harrison's CIA cover identity, which federal authorities sought to conceal. We have found no indication that Zuno's attorneys ever grasped this not

insignificant detail, which perhaps explains in part the knots they twisted themselves
into trying to persuade a jury that Harrison had lied about his name. He was, in fact,
born George Marshall Davis on 19 September 1944, in Pasadena, a fact easily established by searching the public record under that name. A similar search for the birth
date of Lawrence Victor Harrison, on the other hand, produces no results attributable
to him.

Another noteworthy detail in Harrison's FBI file is the absence of his Social Security
number, which is recorded as "unknown," an unlikely circumstance for anyone with a
normal documentary paper trail and given the ease with which the bureau can access
those records. The issue here, too, would appear to be concealment of the fact that
George Marshall Davis had been given a fictitious identity.

Yet a third item of interest to us in this file was Harrison's address, given as 772 Day
Street, San Francisco, with the year 1971 specified in parentheses. As recounted below,
this was the last year Harrison audited law classes at the University of California, Berkeley, and the year he relocated permanently to Mexico. Previously, he had been living
in Santa Clara County, then in early 1968 suddenly dropped from sight. According to
his sister, he walked away from his apartment one day leaving everything behind—
clothes, appliances, furnishings, personal effects—and disappeared. We assume, from
context and disparate pieces of information acquired subsequently, that he was overseen throughout his agent training by the CIA's San Francisco office and that the Day
Street address reflects that relationship.

Most intriguing among the items recovered from MS&K's Zuno files were several
references to closed-door testimony Harrison had given to an unnamed congressional
oversight committee. In November 1990, MS&K attorneys contacted the office of
Congressman Al McCandless (R-CA) to inquire about "hearings that took place
recently in Washington, D.C. regarding Victor [sic] Lawrence Harrison's statements
about possible CIA involvement with drug trafficking in Mexico." They were informed
that a hearing report would not be written until the committee received information
from the Justice Department "about the testimony and Harrison's background." As
Congress was then in recess, they were told, that report would not be voted out of
committee until February 1991 at the earliest.[16]

Two years later Zuno's attorneys were still trying without success to obtain a copy
of Harrison's congressional testimony. In early September 1992, Ed Medvene circulated
a memo among his Zuno case associates in which he informed them that an unidentified Washington source had provided the writer Paul Goepfert with information about
Harrison's closed-door testimony. According to that source, Medvene wrote, the substance of Harrison's testimony was that DEA S/A Enrique Camarena "had stumbled
upon an infiltration system set up by the Defense Intelligence Agency and that he had
been killed to protect their own cover." The implication, Medvene noted, was that "the
U.S. Government had orchestrated the killing of Camarena."[17]

In Mary Fulginiti's October 1992 memo noted above, she reports that in a follow-up
conversation Harrison confirmed his closed-door congressional testimony but refused
to say anything about it or even identify the committee before which he testified.[18]

Extrapolating from the fact that Zuno's attorneys had approached Congressman McCandless in their unsuccessful attempt to obtain a copy of Harrison's congressional testimony, and that Harrison himself later mentioned to us that Congressman Henry Waxman (D-CA) was one of the key people who took his testimony, we conclude that he must have testified before the intelligence subcommittee of what at the time was called the House Government Operations Committee, on which both McCandless and Waxman sat as senior members. The oversight subcommittee, Harrison has told us, did not believe him when he testified that Camarena had been killed because of what he had learned about the CIA's utilization of Mexican drug traffickers to support the Nicaraguan *contras*.[19]

It was also Harrison's belief, Zuno's attorneys had learned, that the CIA had had something to do with the Camarena interrogation tapes. They apparently learned this from the transcript of his 20 September 1989 recorded DEA debriefing, released to them by order of Judge Rafeedie. Among the MS&K interoffice memoranda we obtained from Ed Medvene's case files was a review of the original tape recordings of Harrison's 20 September debriefing prepared by Zuno defense team member Brian M. Colligan. "Harrison says that it was the Americans who controlled the entire drug trade down in Mexico," Colligan noted, and throughout this recorded interview "Harrison seemed to be very skeptical of the American Government's part in drug trafficking, particularly the CIA."[20]

As for the Camarena interrogation tapes, Colligan reported, it made no sense to Harrison that they would have been made by the traffickers because "Fonseca and the others never recorded their interrogations." Fonseca, according to Harrison, "did not own a tape recorder and certainly would not be able to operate it." It was Harrison's speculation, Colligan wrote, "that Fonseca and Caro [Quintero] planned and orchestrated the Camarena incident for others higher up in Mexico City, possibly the CIA, and it was that faction that wanted the interrogation tape recorded."[21] Many years later, Harrison would repeat that belief to us. The Guadalajara traffickers, he insisted, did not conduct tape-recorded interrogations. They were, in his view, "electronic illiterates who wouldn't even know how to turn on a tape recorder."

DRUG ENFORCEMENT ADMINISTRATION
REPORT OF INVESTIGATION

(Form DEA-6)

By: Manuel R. Martinez, S/A   Date prepared: September 25, 1989
At: Los Angeles, CA
Other Officers: S/A Morales
Report RE: Debriefing of [Lawrence Victor Harrison]

On September 20, 1989, Cooperating Individual (CI) [Lawrence Victor Harrison] was debriefed by S/A's Martinez and Morales while enroute from Los Angeles, California to Nogales, Arizona. This debriefing was recorded and the following is a transcription of the recording.

. . .

. . .

CI [HARRISON]: Somebody had to put the blame on [Camarena]. And somebody had to be able to set it up with [the traffickers], that they would go get him, and they'd UI [unintelligible], but that they could be there and make a tape. These guys never made a tape, ever. In all the years I worked with them, they never ever thought about making a tape in an interrogation. No comandante ever made a tape. . . . Ernesto never made a tape of an interrogation. Think that was the first person they ever killed? I guess the first person they ever tortured or beat up. They never ever made a tape.

MORALES: Well . . .

CI: I'll tell you what, other authorities [were] there during the Camarena interrogation. They had to have said to them, look this is the guy that screwed you on Buffalo. This is the one that wants to put you away. We have to abandon you because these, this is the guy that, that's writing everything down about you. Right? They had to steam 'em up so they'd go do this. And at the same time they had to say, just let us be there please.

M: Why do you think they made a tape?

CI: I think they made a tape for somebody else in Mexico City. I don't think it was necessarily them that made the tape, they wouldn't even know how to turn the tape recorder on.

M: That, that was my next question.

CI: They'd never done that. They didn't work with that kind of equipment. They never ever had done that.

M: Yeah.

CI: And I don't think they were the only ones there either. If they weren't the only ones there, you have to picture them getting these guys to take the blame. Sending their man, taking him to their house, and having their people torture him, while these other people are standing by looking on making tapes. They covered themselves very well. Wasn't any army people in the car that went and picked him up. They didn't take him to any army house. They didn't take him to any regular police house. They took him to their houses and they sent their people and blamed it all on them afterwards. Said okay only them, it's all settled now. Ernesto and Rafa, they did the whole thing. And they didn't do the whole thing. That's not their style. Beating up, torturing, that yes. I don't say no. Alright? I do know one thing, I don't think they'd ever pick somebody up and then take him back. I can't picture in my mind, I can't reconcile it in anything that I've ever known about them and I know them pretty well, to pick somebody up openly without [masks] or anything. In broad daylight, in a public parking lot, and take them away and then bring them back the next day. Okay we tortured you, you can go now. Go and tell your people what we asked you. How could they do that, how could they bring him back?

. . .

M: Well, I'm going to go over it again, okay? All these years that you've known these guys, worked with them, has there been one instance where they've asked you, since you're the electronics expert, to tape any interrogation?

CI: Never.

M: Never.

CI: Never.

M: Never.

CI: They don't do that. They never did that. Never. Why would they do it? So they can play the tape back later and listen to it and laugh? Never. I've heard them talking about many years before. They never ever said anything like that. I don't think they know how to turn a tape recorder on. They didn't have any tape recorders.

. . .

TAPE #2 SIDE 2:

. . .

CI: But I don't think the CIA would've gone directly, they would've sent the Mexicans. The CIA are not so stupid they were gonna go in there themselves. They're gonna send some of their minions in there. One of whom would be Miguel Nazar Haro, who they had been, he'd been on, had been on their payroll for ten years. He was their chief agent. So chief that you can't even arrest him down there. You've got a valid arrest warrant, you've had it since [1982], can't do anything about it. . . .

M: How'd you find that out?

CI: You don't think we know that?

M: Well, that's what I want to know, is how, how you knew that.

CI: How I know that?

M: Yeah.

CI: I would know 'cause he was my commandant.[22]

On Thursday, 7 March, we met for two hours with Ed Medvene's colleague Jack R. Luellen, who by then had left MS&K to form his own law firm in the Watt Towers at 1875 Century Park East, also in downtown Los Angeles. We discussed our Buendía investigation, the places where it overlapped with the Camarena case, and details that Zuno's attorneys wished to clarify concerning Gárate Bustamante, Rafael Loret de Mola, and the Carlos Loret de Mola case. We had already agreed with Ed Medvene to pursue some of this information in Mexico as a pro bono quid pro quo for the assistance he and his associates were providing us. As for Lawrence Harrison, Luellen repeated his view that the man was "a pathological liar."

Two days later we flew to Guadalajara and took a room at the Hotel de Mendoza, where our first evening we met for two and a half hours with Ángel Buendía. We met for another two and a half hours the following afternoon and agreed to meet again in a week on our return from Mexico City. On Monday the eleventh, we took a bus to the Federal District and checked in to the Mónaco. To our dismay, we discovered that our old Centro Cultural Librería Reforma haunt on Paseo de la Reforma had been closed down and sold since our previous visit. We spent a leisurely week, marked by severe air pollution and several minor seismic events, prowling the bookstores in search of volumes bearing on the Buendía case. We found a number of new titles, including two by former Buendía colleagues Francisco Martínez de la Vega and Manú Dornbierer; one each by Julio Scherer, Eduardo Valle, and Felipe Victoria Zepeda; and three by Rafael Loret de Mola.[23] On Wednesday we met for a late breakfast at the Café París with Miguel Ángel Sánchez de Armas, which was when he first mentioned his new Mexico City apartment to us. He invited us to come by and see it that Friday evening, an invitation we accepted and later concluded, as recounted at the end of chapter 12, was his way of informing us that he had been pressured to cease further involvement in the Buendía affair.

We had been attempting without success to contact Rafael Loret de Mola by phone. He finally called us at the Mónaco late Saturday evening and agreed to see us at 9:00 a.m. the following morning, our last day in Mexico City. We arrived at Loret's Colonia Alpes–San Ángel home a little past nine o'clock and discussed our mutual interests for the next hour. The phone conversations with Héctor Berréllez and Antonio Gárate Bustamante had occurred exactly as he described them in his books, Loret assured us. The calls were always initiated by Berréllez or Gárate, he said, and sometimes were conference calls with all three of them on the line at the same time. He confirmed that he had recorded those conversations and expressed to us his willingness to provide dubs of the tapes to Rubén Zuno Arce's defense attorneys if they wished. He had no idea what Berréllez and Gárate's real purpose was in making those calls.

As for the Buendía and Carlos Loret de Mola cases, Rafael Loret said he was persuaded that Secretary of Defense Gen. Juan Arévalo Gardoqui and Secretary of Government Manuel Bartlett Díaz were behind both slayings. The Buendía assassination, he told us, was actually a military operation. By his account, Bartlett had ordered Buendía's murder at the personal request of Arévalo Gardoqui, while Arévalo had ordered the Loret de Mola killing at the request of Bartlett. In the Buendía case, Arévalo had provided the actual assassin. Moro Ávila Camacho, the convicted triggerman, Loret averred, was in fact a scapegoat used to conceal the assassin's military affiliation. Loret was a personal friend of Moro's defense attorney, who, he said, had assured him that Moro was in a restaurant near the Secretariat of Government at the time of the Buendía shooting. Manuel Bartlett, Loret concluded, had allied himself with Arévalo as part of a strategy to secure the presidential *dedazo*, that is, designation as the PRI's candidate for the presidency in the 1988 election.[24]

That same afternoon we flew back to Guadalajara and again checked in at the Hotel de Mendoza. The next morning Ángel Buendía drove us to his home, where we spent another two and a half hours discussing his brother's case. We talked at some length about Octavio González, the ex-DFS agent who served as the Buendía oversight group's private investigator. Don Ángel defended the decision to bring in Octavio González, while we challenged that decision, insisting that González's DFS background necessarily raised questions about whose interests he really served in the government's official resolution of the Buendía case.

Don Ángel replied that Bartlett had objected to including González in the oversight group (as had Sánchez de Armas, he also noted), but that he trusted Rogelio Hernández, accepted Rogelio's endorsement of González, and had persuaded Bartlett to relent in his opposition to González. "The main reason for having Octavio there," he repeated to us, "was to keep an eye on García Domínguez, to check and confirm everything that García Domínguez was doing and saying. Because of all his police contacts, he was the one person who could best keep us apprised of what the special prosecutor was actually doing. He was a kind of spy for us." "And," Don Ángel added, "I'm certain he did not betray us. Not him. Never!"[25]

It is doubtful that anyone will ever be able to sort out all the intrigues surrounding the Manuel Buendía case, especially those involving Secretary of Government Manuel Bartlett Díaz. Whether Bartlett in fact objected to Octavio González's participation in the oversight group, as Ángel Buendía averred, or instead was in league with González we likely will never know. At the time, according to Don Ángel, González was employed by the Secretariat of Communications and Transportation and Bartlett had to intervene to have him released from his job so that he could work with the Buendía oversight group, now as a paid Gobernación operative. This institutional arrangement implies a more nuanced involvement on Bartlett's part than simply acceding to a request that González be allowed to join the oversight group.

On this occasion, Don Ángel also told us about contact he had had with a DFS *comandante* by the name of Ezequiel Navarro Luna immediately following his brother's assassination, an episode he would again recount three years later in his book about the Buendía case.[26] Navarro had been dispatched to Guadalajara in June 1984 by DFS chief José Antonio Zorrilla Pérez with instructions to "place himself at Don Ángel's disposition" while investigating the UAG-based Tecos organization for possible links to Manuel Buendía's killing three weeks earlier. We presume that sending Navarro Luna to Guadalajara was a tactical move by Zorrilla to cover his own tracks and deflect suspicion from himself by giving the appearance of focusing DFS attention on a violent neofascist group often savaged by Buendía in his newspaper columns and openly hostile to him. However, it appears that Navarro took his assignment seriously, without ulterior purpose, and was not an unconditional Zorrilla cohort.

Toward the middle of February 1985, just a week or two prior to the announcement that Zorrilla would be leaving the DFS in order to campaign for a seat in the national Chamber of Deputies, Navarro informed Don Ángel that the DFS chief was pulling him from Guadalajara and reassigning him to the Federal District. The reason, Navarro explained, was he had recently discovered that on 30 May 1984, the day of Manuel Buendía's assassination, a Gobernación aircraft utilized by the DFS had flown three individuals from Guadalajara to Mexico City, including Georg Thomas Mertins, son of the German arms dealer Gerhard Georg Mertins. The other two persons were DFS *comandante* Rogelio Muñoz Ríos and Marco Elías Reyna, a former Colima State Judicial Police officer, then personal secretary and driver for Antonio Leaño, whom Navarro described as the "owner [*propietario*] of the Autonomous University of Guadalajara." Before returning to Mexico City, Luna gave Don Ángel a small sheaf of typed and handwritten investigative notes about possible Guadalajara links to his brother's assassination. Don Ángel, in turn, now gave us a photocopied set of Luna's notes.

The UAG was the first and most influential private university in Mexico. It was founded in 1935, primarily through the efforts of the anti-Marxist Jalisco Student Federation (FEJ) and in opposition to what the FEJ perceived to be the socialist educational project of the national university system. Antonio Leaño Álvarez del Castillo sat on the FEJ's eight-member *mesa directiva* and, together with his older brother Ángel, was one of the UAG's original founders. He was also a leading figure in the UAG-based neo-nazi Tecos organization, an anti-Semitic, anticommunist secret society whose membership was drawn from traditionalist, pro-clerical elements of the university's student body and faculty. The Tecos' creator, Carlos Cuesta Gallardo, had served as president of the FEJ and, together with the Leaño brothers, was another of the UAG's principal founders. He had spent much of World War II in Berlin, was close to the Nazi leadership, and shared the Hitlerian view of a global "Jewish-Freemason-Communist plot to take over the world." He had been groomed to create a nazi fifth column in Mexico and in the postwar years forged the secretive, rigidly disciplined, paramilitary Tecos organization, which maintained contacts with the Nazi diaspora and liaised with neo-nazi groups on both sides of the Atlantic.[27]

The transformation of what for many years had been a struggling, largely shadow institution with neither campus nor status into a fully accredited, multischool university outside, and philosophically opposed to, Mexico's national university system was brought about by the United States in the 1960s and 1970s with massive infusions of money through the U.S. Agency for International Development (USAID) and the Ford, Rockefeller, and Carnegie foundations. The UAG's official ideology, as articulated by the last of its original founders and Rector for Life Antonio Leaño, was the capitalist creed that "only private initiative can satisfy humankind's needs" and "the sophistry of Marxism," with its claim of seeking social justice through the appropriation of the means of production, "leads people into totalitarian slavery." History, Leaño declared, "has demonstrated that Marxist socialism is the system condemned to disappear."[28] By implication, the system destined to survive was capitalism in the U.S. paradigm.

These were the values imparted to the UAG student body, which, through its original anti-Marxist FEJ organization, had brought the university into existence. It was noteworthy, Leaño emphasized, that in the institution's sixty-five-year history "there had not been a single strike, sit-in, or demonstration"; rather, the students had exhibited "a constant attitude of cooperation with administrators and faculty in a shared educational commitment."[29] What Leaño did not say, aside from the fact that student affairs at the UAG were far from tranquil in the politically volatile 1960s and '70s, was that the coercive instrument employed to ensure campus conformity was the secretive Tecos organization in which Leaño himself played a key role.

As revealed by Manuel Buendía less than two months before he was assassinated, Los Tecos constituted "a fascist organization supported economically by businessmen and politicians, as well as U.S. government agencies like the CIA, which totally dominated one of the country's largest universities." As in Orwellian systems many of us have been taught to abhor, "members [were] obliged to renounce parental obedience and denounce their parents should they oppose their son's involvement in the organization." Prospective members were required to complete a lengthy questionnaire, submit to an interview, and agree to a Tecos investigation "of their parents, siblings, half-siblings, friends, teachers, and employers." They promised as well to answer truthfully all questions put to them, agreeing that should they lie or conceal anything they would be considered "a spy and traitor to the association subject to the curse of God and the punishment reserved for traitors." Buendía made these revelations in three successive columns based on a sheaf of internal Tecos documents obtained from a disaffected member. "This secret society of 'Tecos' affects numerous families in Jalisco," he wrote, "but also important aspects of [our] national security."[30]

The Autonomous University of Guadalajara, Buendía had written several years earlier, was "one of the major fascist centers of Latin America and perhaps the world." It received financial support from the U.S. government, as well as from "an excellent part of the Mexican oligarchy." Not all UAG students were Tecos, he noted, but it was the Tecos "who dictated what [students] should think, what they could say, how they should dress, what films they could see, and even who could attend their parties." The life of any student who failed to adhere to the Tecos' code, Buendía assured readers of his column, "could turn into the worst of all nightmares," including physical assaults and even death at the hands of Tecos enforcers. The UAG, he wrote, has trained generations of ultra-rightists "whose purpose is to attack the power structure both from within and from without," some of its graduates having secured "important positions in federal ministries and the legislative chambers, as well as in state and municipal government."[31]

Internal UAG records, Buendía wrote six months prior to his assassination, "prove beyond all doubt the international coordination of extreme-right terrorist groups. It can be shown perfectly well," he averred, "that there is an axis linking Mexican militants to the United States and Europe's Fascist International, which so often has occupied the attention of police in Spain, Italy, Germany, and France. And all these paths cross in Guadalajara."[32] The international umbrella under which the Tecos sheltered with like-minded organizations from around the globe, Buendía noted, was the World Anti-communist League (WACL), which in turn served as a convenient cover for the CIA as it channeled resources and coordinated covert operations throughout the world.[33]

According to investigative reporters Scott and Jon Lee Anderson, a significant portion of the millions of dollars in U.S. financial assistance given to the UAG was laundered through it for use by the Tecos in support of far-reaching political activities, which included furthering their ties to neo-nazi groups in Europe and South America, publication of an anti-Semitic magazine called *Réplica*, and liaising with regional death squads. Much of the death squad activity in Central and South America during the regionwide dirty war years of the 1960s–1980s, the Anderson brothers learned, was coordinated by the Latin American Anti-communist Confederation (CAL by its Spanish acronym), in which the Federación Anticomunista Mexicana (FEMACO) played a decisive role. The FEMACO was the Mexican chapter of the WACL, which had been founded in 1966 in South Korea and would eventually number more than ninety chapters on six continents. The Mexican FEMACO formally affiliated with the WACL in 1972.[34]

A key anticommunist ideologue recruited by Tecos founder Carlos Cuesta Gallardo was Raymundo Guerrero Guerrero, who would eventually assume leadership of the Tecos, as well as occupying influential UAG faculty and administrative posts.[35] Guerrero sat on the executive board of FEMACO, which gave the Tecos major influence within the WACL. "Since they had created the entire Latin network," Scott and Jon Lee Anderson write, "the Tecos naturally assumed leadership of the Latin American Anti-Communist Confederation, . . . [drawing] in their violent brethren from throughout Latin America with little or no review by the [WACL's] Asian godfathers."[36]

In March 1983, a physician at the National Hospital in Tegucigalpa and after-hours member of the Honduran Ejército de Lucha Anticomunista (ELA) death squad described to Jon Lee Anderson how such extrajudicial groups throughout Latin America were linked. "Our movements are coordinated out of Mexico," the doctor told Anderson. "That's where CAL is located," he said, referring to the Confederación Anticomunista Latinoamericana, created and overseen by FEMACO. A Mexican intelligence source subsequently confirmed this account to Anderson, noting that the Confederación was also known as the White Hand, the White Force, and the White Brigade. "It got its name," the anonymous source explained, "because it has the backing of powerful people who erase all evidence surrounding a murder."[37]

Six months before he was shot down outside his Mexico City office building, Manuel Buendía exposed yet another strand in the Guadalajara web of Mexican national security threats that he had been revealing to readers of his Red Privada column: the presence of significant numbers of former Nicaraguan national guardsmen (Guardia) who had fled their country following the July 1979 ouster by an armed popular insurgency of the long-entrenched, U.S.-supported dictator Anastasio Somoza Debayle. These exiled guardsmen, Buendía wrote, had been brought to Guadalajara from Miami, Florida, by one Henry Pérez, a former Somoza government minister who resided in the Jalisco State capital, and who had found work for them there as bodyguards. Pérez himself, Buendía had previously revealed, was employed by the UAG, where he administered "a hefty budget of funds from anonymous donors and agencies of the U.S. government, among others USAID and the CIA itself." Among those who employed these Nicaraguan bodyguards were "the rector of the University of Guadalajara, senior clerics, several industrialists, and leaders of the political Right in Jalisco." Even the papal nuncio, Msgr. Girolamo Prigione, was accompanied on a 1983 visit to Guadalajara by a Somocista bodyguard disguised as a Franciscan monk. "The false monk carried an automatic weapon concealed beneath his habit," Buendía informed his readers, "and not once during the entire visit did he leave the monsignor's side."[38]

But the decisive strand in this sinister web, Buendía made clear, was its tie to Washington's proxy *contra* campaign to overthrow Nicaragua's post-Somoza revolutionary Sandinista government. "At this point," he wrote in early October 1983, "not even the most obtuse of observers can ignore that the U.S. government is the principal manager of the [*contra*] groups attacking the Sandinistas from Costa Rica and Honduras." What until recently had been more or less covert operations were now the subject of daily news reports in the press and on radio and television. "Literally the entire world," he observed, "is familiar with the process of American intervention in Nicaragua."[39]

And the Somocistas exiled in Mexico were "the face and voice of Washington," as well as of a segment of influential Mexicans opposed to the de la Madrid administration's foreign policy. That opposition, Buendía insisted, was becoming increasingly violent and had originated "in the same place as the military supplies provided to the enemies of the Sandinista government." On 30 September 1983, he noted, the main Guardia-dominated *contra* force based in Honduras had threatened to sink Mexican tankers delivering fuel to Nicaragua. Mexico, it had stressed, should take its warning very seriously. And Mexico did, Buendía assured his readers, because the threat had come out of Honduras, which "for all practical purposes was a U.S. military base."[40]

Just three months earlier, he further noted, *contra* southern front commander Edén Pastora had confirmed in a press conference that he had received support not only from the CIA but also "from friends in Mexico." This latter support, Buendía suggestively observed, comprised financial aid and "arms traffic" provided by "Mexican entrepreneurs whose identity could not be unknown to the authorities." In his view, the collusion of all these actors aimed to force a change in the de la Madrid administration's regional foreign policy and therefore constituted a threat to national security. It was time for the government to explain the facts of the matter to the citizenry so as to stimulate popular support for the country's political authorities, who, he added in a curiously opaque remark open to more than one interpretation, "wished, as far as one could tell, to preserve the country's best foreign policy traditions." Indeed, Buendía declared, it was time for those officials charged with ensuring Mexico's national security to reveal how this Mexican fifth column was organized. "We refer, of course," he concluded, "to José Antonio Zorrilla, the competent director of the Federal Security Directorate."[41]

While we had not yet connected these dots when we met with Don Ángel in March 1996, we knew enough about his brother Manuel's UAG enemies to appreciate the potential significance of the DFS documents he was giving us. We were struck then by the Mertins-Leaño-UAG connection and, in light of further investigation, would become even more so. Given Mertins Sr.'s Nazi past and subsequent links to the Pentagon and CIA, his association with WACL-linked circles in Guadalajara seemed yet another piece of a large and expansive whole. Mertins's son Georg Thomas, we knew, had been a student at the UAG. We would later learn from Lawrence Harrison that he was also a close friend of a son of Guadalajara cartel capo Rafael Caro Quintero and that Caro's son had apparently died of a cocaine overdose while partying on one occasion with the younger Mertins. Caro and the Leaño brothers were thick as thieves, Harrison told us, implying that cartel money had helped finance some of the Leaños's ultrarightist, anticommunist causes.[42]

On our return to Milwaukee, Russell called Ed Medvene and gave him a quick summary of what we had learned. With Russell's permission, he recorded the conversation, then asked Russell to provide him with a written report, which he did. The first half of that report detailed what we had learned about Berréllez and Gárate Bustamante and their communications with Rafael Loret de Mola; the second half focused on Lawrence Harrison. "We are persuaded at this point," Russell wrote, "that Harrison was, in fact, a U.S. intelligence operative." He seemed to confirm as much himself when, under cross-examination during the first Zuno trial, he responded tartly to the impugning of his patriotism for having participated in a conspiracy to import narcotics into the United States, stating that "a person who [is] put in place to watch and report, watches and reports. What decisions are taken farther up the line . . . didn't really concern me." At that time, Russell further noted, German arms dealer Gerhard Georg Mertins's son, Georg Thomas Mertins, was enrolled in the UAG, "a center of right-wing politics around which was concentrated a large number of Nicaraguan exiles from the former régime of dictator Anastasio Somoza Debayle." By his own sworn testimony, "Harrison had developed 'informants' among Georg Thomas's UAG friends," unmistakably an intelligence-gathering activity.[43]

Harrison's closed-door congressional testimony that DEA S/A Enrique Camarena "had stumbled on an infiltration system set up by the Defense Intelligence Agency and that he had been killed to protect their own cover," Russell wrote, citing the above-referenced MS&K interoffice memorandum, was intriguing from several angles: (1) such knowledge, if accurate, would identify Harrison as an American agent; (2) the alleged "DIA pipeline" was perfectly compatible with the presence in Mexico of Gerhard Mertins, whom the Mexico City attorney general's office had confirmed was involved in "arms traffic from the United States and Europe to Central America"; and (3) the alleged pipeline also meshed well with subsequent assertions by former CIA asset Terry Reed that in 1985, under orders from *contra* supply coordinator and NSC operative Félix Rodríguez (aka Max Gómez), he had established a shell import-export company at the Guadalajara airport for the purpose of covertly transferring arms to Central America.[44]

"Against the backdrop of regional conflict, cold war power projection and the growing confluence of arms and narco dollars," Russell summed up, "little imagination is required to link Harrison, Gárate, Zorrilla, Fonseca, Caro Quintero et al. to the deaths of Manuel Buendía, Enrique Camarena and who knows how many others." The Camarena case was especially blatant inasmuch as, whatever Camarena's personal merits, his death had been used by successive U.S. administrations for indisputably political ends, that is, the furtherance of foreign policy objectives in Mexico and Central America. We had long wondered about Camarena's status as a national martyr, Russell informed Medvene. Was he perchance the first U.S. undercover agent to perish on foreign soil? Were not law enforcement officers succumbing to drug traffickers' bullets in growing numbers on the streets of our own cities? When, he asked rhetorically, had so much been made of the fate of a single agent? There was, we believed, much more to the Camarena affair than met the eye. "Whether or not U.S. operatives had a hand in the slayings of Enrique Camarena and Manuel Buendía," Russell wrote, "they have indisputably involved themselves *ex post facto* by leaking tainted information about the two crimes to politically influential individuals in Mexico. Hector Berréllez and Antonio Gárate Bustamante have been especially visible in this activity. Nothing these two agents assert with respect to the Camarena/Zuno Arce case, in our opinion, warrants credence."[45]

> The man who has not lived in the secrecy and intelligence environment—really lived in it and fully experienced it—cannot write accurately about it. There is no substitute for the day to day living of a life in which he tells his best friends and acquaintances, his family and his everyday contacts one story while he lives another.
> . . .
> To look at this matter in another way, the man who has lived and experienced this unnatural existence becomes even more a victim of its unreality. He becomes enmeshed beyond all control on the horns of a cruel dilemma. On the one hand, his whole working life has been dedicated to the cause of secrecy and to its protection by means of cover stories (lies). In this pursuit he has given of himself time after time to pledges,

briefings, oaths, and deep personal conviction regarding the significance of that work. Even if he would talk and write, his life has been so interwoven into the fabric of the real and the unreal, the actual and the cover story, that he would be least likely to present the absolutely correct data.

On the other hand, as a professional he would have been subjected to such cellularization and compartmentalization each time he became involved in any real "deep" operation that he would not have known the whole story anyhow.[46]

We very much wished to interview Harrison, but he had dropped from sight following the Zuno prosecutions, and, as recounted in chapter 14, another eight years would elapse before we managed to locate and contact him. Once we did, it quickly became apparent that we needed to gain insight into his youth and family background if we were to make sense of what he had testified in court and what he began to tell us in an ever lengthening series of multilayered conversations. He was, we could see, a complex and conflicted personality of exceptional intellect and multiple private agendas, not the "strange duck," lying buffoon, or self-serving "piece of work" portrayed by the Zuno defense attorneys and parroted in the Mexican press.

Like other aspects of our Buendía investigation, fleshing out Harrison's personal history required several years' time and a variety of approaches. We began by asking him directly about his life story. He gave us a few specifics—for example, born in Pasadena, grew up in Bakersfield, had an older sister (Kathleen) who now lived in Las Vegas—as well as some disconnected anecdotes, but was reluctant to talk about himself in any detail. He did not want our book to be about "him, Hector [Berréllez], and Gárate," he told us early on. Rather it should be about "the larger implications of the Buendía case."[47]

Starting with the few hard facts we were able to glean from court and defense counsel records, as well as from Harrison himself, we conducted a protracted public records search. Eventually, Harrison gave us his sister's contact information, and we got in touch with her. When Russell initially spoke with her by phone, she straight away informed him that her brother's name was not Lawrence Harrison; it was George Davis. "His name is George!" she said. "I should know, I'm his older sister!"

Understandably leery at first, but also anxious to learn all she could about her brother's life during the twenty-plus years since he had mysteriously dropped from sight, Kathleen agreed to talk further with us. Ultimately, we would meet with her in person on four separate occasions and also speak with her periodically by telephone. She provided us with a wealth of information about her own and George's childhood experiences and family history, including family photographs, which has allowed us to expand, correct, and refine Harrison's fragmented version of his youth, as well as to gain deeper insight into the person he became as an adult. It has also helped us to refine and expand our public records search for corroborating documentation in support of the biographical account we offer here.

Harrison was born George Marshall Davis on 19 September 1944 in Pasadena. His sister, Kathleen Anne, was born in Pasadena on the last day of December 1942. Their father, Francis "Frank" Clifford Davis, had also been born in Pasadena (in 1894) and died there in mid-March 1947. Their mother, Eleanor Mary Cummings, was born in 1912 in Yuma County, Colorado, a few miles from the Colorado-Kansas line. She took her own life in Bakersfield on 21 March 1968, the year her son George first traveled to Mexico under his CIA alias, Lawrence Victor Harrison.

Frank Davis owned and managed a used car dealership at 2193 East Colorado Boulevard in Pasadena. The business, called F. C. Davis Auto Sales, advertised "Better Used Cars, Auto Reconditioning, and Painting." Harrison once quipped that during World War II his father would obtain scarce tires and vehicles for friends and associates and that following his father's death he recalled relatives referring to Frank as "a dirty crook." He punctuated this recollection with a hearty laugh, but left us with little doubt that he admired his father deeply. Kathleen has recounted how, one day soon after their father's death, two-and-a-half-year-old George gave family and friends a fright by suddenly disappearing. A frantic search finally located him in a neighbor's basement, where he had gone looking for his missing papa. At all the office and residential locations where we have interviewed Harrison, he has kept a formal photo portrait of Frank Davis close by his desk.[48]

Harrison's mother was the youngest of six Cummings siblings, five girls and a boy, all raised in the prairie ranching country along the South Fork of the Republican River between Hale, Colorado, and St. Francis (Wano Township), Kansas. The Cummings family had been converted by an itinerant Nazarene preacher in the latter 1920s, and that evangelist denomination's Wesleyan holiness doctrine informed the clan's worldview for many decades thereafter. Eleanor Cummings, the baby of the family, chafed at the Nazarenes' corseted social code, according to her daughter Kathleen, and early on decided that she wanted to be more than "a preacher's wife." The Nazarene Church, as Kathleen described it, "was all about getting to heaven," not comporting oneself as a compassionate human being.[49]

By 1930, George and Flora Cummings had relocated their family to Pasadena so that the children could attend Nazarene-affiliated Pasadena College. They purchased two homes near the Bresee Avenue Nazarene Church, living in one while renting the other. Eleanor put herself through Pasadena College by working as a gardener and housecleaner. She was musically talented, had a fine singing voice, and would direct the Bresee Avenue Church choir.

Eleanor Cummings's marriage to Frank Davis appears to have been felicitous. When Kathleen and George came along, the family resided in the Pasadena suburb of Altadena at the foot of the San Gabriel Mountains, just a short drive from the Davis auto dealership. Whatever Eleanor's reservations about church dogma, the Nazarene Church remained central to her world, and when her son was born they named him after his maternal grandfather, George Marshall Cummings, the Nazarene patriarch of the Cummings clan. Harrison would in time embrace Roman Catholicism, but on some intimate level he continued to identify with his family's Nazarene heritage. "My people founded a Nazarene Church," he told us in 2009. "That was their hope." He was not a Nazarene, he said, but he did believe in God and that "we have to expiate sin."[50]

In an emotional e-mail exchange he and Russell had in January 2010 about his deteriorating personal situation, Harrison revealed the depth of his childhood internalization of the family's Nazarene heritage. "You probably don't know about my family," he wrote Russell. "My grandfather gave part of his Colorado ranch for the first Nazarene church in the nation. He then came west to found [*sic*] the Pasadena Nazarene College from which all of my mother's family graduated. . . . The General Administrators, even today, are all my cousins and uncles." As a child, Harrison recounted, "I attended Bresee Avenue Nazarene Church, also founded by my grandfather [*sic*], while my mother began the music program for the church after working for [evangelist] Aimee Semple MacPherson as choirmaster, organist, violinist, pianist, all on the Four-Square Ambassador College Radio Station . . . and at the Ambassador Auditorium." He supposed this would not mean much to someone of "Russell's extraction," but "the music was touching and [is] still remembered by artists today," he wrote. And it meant a great deal to him. He admired his mother's people. "I was so proud," he wanted us to know, "not of their scholarship, but of their simple grit. To have started with so little and built so much."[51]

When Frank Davis died one Monday in March 1947, it plunged his widow and children into trying straits of many years' duration, which left emotional scars on all three. Now Eleanor Davis suddenly found herself a single mother with two toddlers to support. She owned the Altadena house and continued to live there while sorting out her new circumstances, then sold that property and purchased a small apartment building in Pasadena, occupying one of the apartments herself and renting out the others. She also worked as a clerk in the Pasadena City Controller's Office. Although she had extended family in the Pasadena area and some of her relations assisted her in different ways, none could assume the burden of caring for her children while she held down a full-time job, so she arranged to place them in foster care. For the better part of their childhood and early adolescence, Kathleen and George found themselves in a variety of foster care settings, occasionally together but usually apart, seeing their mother and each other only on weekends and holidays. These were not happy arrangements, and both children had to learn to cope, gradually developing survival skills they would utilize throughout their lives.

Whereas Kathleen was inclined to please her foster guardians, George was rebellious and the object of frequent punishment, physical as well as humiliating and occasionally abusive. Once he had to be taken to the hospital for treatment of a nose hemorrhage produced by a slap to the face. On another occasion, a police officer in whose home the boy had been placed intimidated young George with a handgun and made him parade around the front yard with a sign reading "Dirty Davis." At one point, George's contentious behavior became so problematic that he was sent to a boarding school in Los Angeles, from which he proceeded to escape together with another boy. He had fled barefoot and was later found with raw and bleeding feet.

In the early 1950s, Eleanor met and married an insurance adjuster by the name of Benjamin J. Lane. Acceding to her new husband's wishes, she pulled up stakes in Pasadena and relocated to Bakersfield. By Kathleen's bitter account, Lane was "a disbarred New York attorney" and abusive husband who took grievous advantage of their mother and wanted nothing to do with his two stepchildren, making it necessary for them to continue living in foster care settings until their mother at last made the difficult decision to divorce. Harrison preferred not to talk about his stepfather, telling us only that, prior to meeting their mother, he had changed his name from Levine to Lane.

By the time George Davis entered high school, he exhibited a distinctive set of character traits that would mark him for the rest of his life and that, all these many years later, sheds light on his remarkable career as a once committed, now disillusioned American intelligence operative. Whether rooted in his genetic makeup or acquired as a consequence of his difficult childhood, George developed a full kit of survival tools and an abiding determination to wield them against all odds. He was endowed with an agile mind, a large physical frame, and a strong constitution. In school he would challenge his teachers and chafed at the constraints of rote, prepackaged public education, often earning demerits or other disciplinary punishments. So pronounced was his distaste for, and inability to comply with, classroom routines that he was obliged to drop out of high school in his senior year.

George was endlessly curious about the world around him and constantly sought to ground his schoolwork in that world. The rote memorization of German grammar, syntax, and vocabulary, for example, was an abstract exercise that did not begin to satisfy his curiosity about Germanic culture and history, which he proceeded to study on his own. It was the same with math, algebra, and other school subjects, especially history. "George has always been different," his childhood friend and brother-in-law Roy once remarked. "He was so much smarter than the rest of us." Roy's own family, he explained, had been poor and each summer would "go north" as migrant workers to pick fruit. One year, he said, George decided to tag along to see what it was all about and spent the entire summer with them picking fruit.[52]

George also developed a fascination with electronics. He was, in his own words, "an electronics nerd," who as a teenager would repair radios, telephones, and household appliances. By the time he was sixteen, he had secured a part-time job with a local Bakersfield television station as a news cameraman and another as an announcer for KEAR-Radio. In 1960 he was hired by the Spencer-Roberts political management firm as a cameraman for Richard M. Nixon's unsuccessful presidential campaign. The firm hired him again in 1962 for Nixon's also unsuccessful California gubernatorial campaign. In the course of this work for Spencer-Roberts, George likely met politically connected people who later would help facilitate his entrée into the CIA. He has implied as much to us but has not identified anyone by name.

Having been expelled from Bakersfield High School in his senior year, George enrolled in classes at Bakersfield College in order to prepare for the California high school equivalency exam, which he passed easily in 1964. Now in possession of a GED certificate, he left Bakersfield for the San Francisco Bay Area, where his movements blur and remain hopelessly opaque. An entry in the San Jose city directory for 1965 places a George M. Davis at 2041 Lakewood Drive, spouse "Margaret," occupation "technical writer" and "electronics technician." Harrison once told us that he "had been married for six months" to a woman by the name of "Mary Christine Myers," whom he said he had met while working for Spencer-Roberts on one of the Nixon campaigns. At some point in his youth, he also made friends in the Santa Cruz area, with one of whom he would later father, but not raise, a daughter. His sister Kathleen has told us that he had an apartment in San Jose after leaving Bakersfield, and Harrison has confirmed that he lived for a while "in Santa Clara County." We presume, therefore, that the George M. Davis listed in the 1965 San Jose city directory is, in fact, the same George Marshall Davis who would soon transmogrify into Lawrence Victor Harrison.

The precise progression of events that brought young George Davis to the attention of the CIA remains as murky as many other key elements of his intelligence career. He was not recruited by the agency, it appears, but instead approached it, as much out of curiosity as due to any youthful infatuation with spies. He has told us that "friends in Santa Cruz" knew Oregon's then governor Mark O. Hatfield (1959–1967), that he spent a month in Oregon with those friends and met Hatfield, and that the governor subsequently arranged for him to be interviewed by the CIA in San Francisco. However the contact actually came about, it likely unfolded more or less as described by veteran case officer Robert Baer, who followed Harrison into the agency a decade later, also through San Francisco.

A federal switchboard operator gave Baer a telephone number to call in the Los Angeles suburb of Lawndale, where a woman took down Baer's name and address and promised to mail him an application form, together with an admission pass for a written exam to be administered at the Federal Building in San Francisco. The application form included a lengthy personal history questionnaire that probed "every conceivable" aspect of his background and current circumstances. There was also a psychological profile to be filled out. The written examination, Baer recalls, "was a cross between the SAT [Scholastic Aptitude Test] and the Foreign Service exam." A month later he was instructed to report to a San Francisco hotel for an interview. Sometime after that, he was flown to Washington, DC, where in quick succession he went through "a half-dozen interviews and exams; a couple of [Directorate of Operations] case officers, a shrink and a security officer; and a French and German test," all followed by a protracted polygraph exam. Three months later he received his security clearance and was accepted for case officer training.[53]

A second insightful account of CIA affiliation and training has been written by veteran clandestine services officer Henry A. Crumpton, who, like Baer and Davis, approached the agency in his early twenties and applied for employment in the Directorate of Operations (DO), which oversaw all the agency's covert activities. In Crumpton's case, the preliminary evaluation process dragged on for more than a year. His first application at age twenty-two was rejected, with the advice that he pursue graduate studies, learn a foreign language, and gain additional experience abroad. He enrolled in a graduate program at American University but quickly tired of the academic routine, located a CIA recruiting office in Rosslyn, Virginia, and then sat in the waiting room one day until a receptionist summoned an interviewer to hear him out. After nine months of follow-up interviews, tests, and the obligatory polygraph exam, he was finally accepted for training as a case officer.[54]

George Davis presented CIA evaluators with a very different background and personality profile. Unlike Baer and Crumpton, he had no postsecondary degree and no foreign experience, but he did possess an exceptional IQ, had an uncommonly inquisitive mind, showed an interest and ability in foreign languages (German and French), was familiar with electronics, and had practical experience in radio and television. Moreover, he apparently came to the agency with influential political endorsements stemming at least in part from his media work for the Nixon campaigns. He was physically strong and possessed a full set of survival skills honed in the trying foster care experiences of his childhood.

Employees of the CIA operate in multiple institutional settings, Harrison once explained to us, including military, diplomatic, and law enforcement. On foreign assignment, he said, there are two categories of agency people: "legals" and "illegals." The legals are given a legitimate cover, which allows them to reside in another country. Illegals have no such cover, and if they are exposed the agency denies any relationship with them. "Illegals do not exist," as Harrison expressed it. Case officers are considered legals, even though their intelligence-gathering activities violate the laws of the countries to which they are assigned. Should the host country choose to make an issue of a particular case officer's offending activities, he or she will be expelled as a diplomatic persona non grata. Not so the illegal, who will suffer whatever punishment the host country deems appropriate. In contrast to Robert Baer and Henry Crumpton, George Davis would be trained as a CIA illegal.[55]

When exactly that decision was made is not clear, nor has Harrison recounted for us a precise chronology of his training and preparation for insertion into Mexico. What we do know is that it was a seven-year process, the first two years of which, 1965–1967, he spent immersed in the activist student movement at the University of California, Berkeley. Whether he had been instructed to do so by agency handlers or was simply giving free rein to his own youthful curiosity we do not know, but there is little doubt that he was being evaluated in this period and that sometime in 1967 it was decided to give him a fictitious identity. The agency gave him the name Lawrence Harrison, while Victor was his own choice for a second name, "as in *Veni, vidi, vici*," he explained to us with a smile.

"I came, I saw, I conquered," words attributed to Julius Caesar that well reflect both Harrison's combative character and his keen interest in history. Saint George the Dragon Slayer, too, occupies a place in Harrison's personal pantheon of life guides, as does the bronze-skinned people's Virgin of Guadalupe. Another is "keeper of the secrets" Richard Helms, a veteran intelligence professional whose June 1966 appointment as director of central intelligence coincided with George Davis's induction into the CIA. "I wish Richard Helms were alive to arrange my funeral!" Harrison exclaimed while in the throes of a medical crisis more than forty years later. An iconic depiction of Saint George hangs on his wall. Another of the Virgin of Guadalupe keeps his back. Perhaps in a gesture of youthful rebellion against the hypocrisies of his Nazarene relations, Harrison converted to Roman Catholicism while still George Marshall Davis in Bakersfield. He is proud of his Mexican wife's African slave heritage.

When George Davis became Lawrence Harrison, he disappeared overnight. Sometime in late 1967 or early 1968, he simply walked away from his South Bay apartment, leaving all of its contents behind: clothes, appliances, furnishings, and personal effects, even radios he had repaired as a boy, including a handsome Philco floor radio that his sister managed to recover and that, decades later, he would himself preserve as one of his most treasured possessions. Neither his mother nor his sister knew where he was living at the time, but George had informed a Bakersfield friend of his San Jose address. The friend told his own mother about the abandoned apartment, and she informed George's mother. Kathleen Davis then went to San Jose and recovered her brother's belongings.[56]

Up to this point, Harrison says that he had spent his time auditing classes at the University of California, Berkeley, and the Free University of Berkeley, created in 1966 as a counterculture alternative to the establishment university and its overriding agenda of dominant culture indoctrination. He smoked pot, attended free speech movement rallies, and associated with Students for a Democratic Society. "It was Ken Kesey times," he once quipped in reference to the sixties counterculture icon and acclaimed author of *One Flew Over the Cuckoo's Nest.*

Kesey, in fact, seems to occupy a significant place in Harrison's recollection of those years. He even implied that he had tracked Kesey down in Mexico when Ken was on the lam from a marijuana conviction in San Mateo County and a pending possession charge in San Francisco. If there is any truth to this story, it would have to have occurred in 1966, when we might suppose that George Davis was sent to locate Kesey as a CIA evaluation exercise. The agency did have an interest in Kesey, who had volunteered as a subject in its MKULTRA study of LSD and other psychoactive drugs while enrolled in Stanford University's creative writing program in 1959–1960.

Kesey eventually tired of his self-imposed Mexican exile and slipped back into California via Brownsville, Texas, and Salt Lake City. He was arrested on the Bayshore Freeway by the FBI for flight to avoid prosecution, but the federal felony charge against him was ultimately dropped and a San Mateo judge sentenced him to six months on a county work farm for his possession conviction. Two hung juries in the pending San Francisco possession case resulted in a nolo contendere plea to a lesser charge and a ninety-day jail term that he was allowed to serve concurrently with his San Mateo work farm sentence. By the time George Davis morphed into Lawrence Victor Harrison, Ken Kesey had left the Bay Area drug scene and returned to writing on the family farm in Oregon's Willamette Valley.[57]

As described by Baer and Crumpton, CIA clandestine service personnel were put through an extensive training program comprised of both standard and individually tailored courses of professionalization. All inductees receive a basic institutional orientation in the greater District of Columbia area, as well as obligatory tradecraft instruction, and, in most cases, paramilitary training at the "Farm," the agency's Camp Peary base on the York River outside Williamsburg, Virginia. Field exercises were often conducted at appropriate locations off base. In between these de rigeur courses, clandestine trainees (CTs) would pursue individually selected practicum assignments of varying duration, lasting from several weeks to several months.

In Harrison's case, it was decided that he should maintain a presence in the student milieu at the University of California, Berkeley, perhaps with a view to eventual foreign placement in an analogous setting where radicalized students were playing increasingly significant political roles of concern to American policy makers. Arrangements were made for him to audit classes at Berkeley's Boalt Hall School of Law, which would have required the intervention of an agency asset in the university administration. Facebooks containing photographs of each first-year law student were created for the use of teaching faculty, who made a practice of calling on students by name in the classroom. As we suspected, no photo of Harrison appears in the Boalt Hall facebooks for the years he audited classes there, nor is there any record of him in the law school archives. "Illegals," we are reminded, do not exist.[58]

We asked Harrison if Richard Nixon had had anything to do with his being allowed to audit law courses at Boalt Hall. Yes, he replied, but Nixon's influence there was limited. "The president of Rice University had more to do with it," he told us.[59] That would have been Kenneth Pitzer, the distinguished chemist trained at Cal Tech and Berkeley who served as Rice president from 1961 to 1968 and was responsible for transforming that institution into a major university. During World War II, Pitzer undertook classified work for the military at the Maryland Research Laboratory, serving briefly as the lab's technical director. After the war, he spent two years as director of research for the Atomic Energy Commission and in that capacity was instrumental in expanding federally sponsored research from government laboratories to public and private institutions of higher learning.

Pitzer had joined the Berkeley faculty in 1937 on completion of his PhD, rising rapidly through the academic ranks to full professor and occupying the administrative posts of assistant dean and then dean of the College of Chemistry. From Rice University he went to Stanford, where he served as president during three of that institution's most tumultuous Vietnam-era years, after which he rejoined the Berkeley faculty in 1971. In light of this background, it is not implausible that Pitzer could have facilitated Harrison's irregular admission to Boalt Hall. He clearly had the institutional and professional standing to do so.[60]

The decision to have Harrison audit law courses at Boalt seems in hindsight to have been taken with a view to developing a viable cover for him in Mexico, where he would be insinuated into a PRI-affiliated law firm. When the agency first considered the possibility of assigning him to Mexico is not clear, but if he in fact pursued Ken Kesey there in 1966, it could have stemmed from that episode. He first traveled to Mexico as Lawrence Harrison two years later, when he was introduced to a Guadalajara attorney and agency asset by the name of Julio César Montoya, for whom he worked periodically over the next two years as a law clerk and under whom he would apprentice in the practice of law. Harrison's CIA trainers, he has told us, doubted that he could master Spanish well enough to pull off a convincing cover as a Mexican paralegal. Much to his personal satisfaction, he proved them quite wrong.

Harrison's presence in the San Francisco Bay Area was carefully compartmentalized so as to reduce his profile and avoid unwanted notice of periodic absences necessitated by agency assignments. While he had tasks to perform in Berkeley and on the University of California campus, it was decided that he should not reside in the East Bay. When George Davis disappeared from his San Jose area apartment, he reemerged as Lawrence Harrison in San Francisco, from which he commuted to Berkeley in a red Triumph TR3 convertible. As noted above, his FBI master file locates him in 1971 at 772 Day Street in the city's Noe Valley district.[61]

While Harrison was reluctant to discuss his training as a CIA illegal, dates and facts he has provided in court testimony, as well as in our multiple conversations with him, allow us to establish a probable chronology for that training. Based on agency policy and practice as described by Philip Agee, Robert Baer, and Henry Crumpton, the initial vetting process would have taken the better part of a year or more. That would have been followed by an institutional orientation, then time at the Farm for tradecraft and paramilitary training, occupying most of another year. In all probability, he would not have been given a false identity until he had successfully completed this basic training and a decision had been made that he was qualified for deployment as a deep cover operative. Although CIA case officers and other clandestine personnel typically operate under some sort of official cover, most retain their real names. The few who receive false identities are exceptional, requiring fabricated life histories and official government records to support those histories. In Harrison's case, this would seem to imply that he completed his basic agency training sometime prior to 1967, while he was still George Davis.

Camp Peary, where that training is imparted, appears on Virginia road maps as a thirty-plus-square-mile military reservation situated between I-64 and the lower York River, a couple of miles as the crow flies to the northeast of Williamsburg. Until Philip Agee published his 1975 exposé *Inside the Company*, the Farm was a covert operation so sensitive that it was referred to in official communications only by its cryptonym, ISOLATION, and trainees were instructed not to reveal its meaning to anyone, neither spouses nor other agency employees, without a need to know.[62] It would have been the same when George Davis received his operations training there in the mid-1960s. Even forty years later, when a disillusioned Lawrence Harrison revealed to us the kinds of agency training he had received, he could not bring himself to acknowledge explicitly that he took his basic training at Camp Peary.

"Have you ever spent any time on a farm?" we asked him in clear allusion to ISOLATION. "Yes," he answered. "On the East Coast?" we inquired. "Well, I spent some time on George McGhee's farm," he replied evasively. George C. McGhee was a senior Cold War diplomat who appears to have influenced Harrison's career significantly, about which we will have more to say below. What Harrison here calls McGhee's "farm" was a country-estate-cum-farmer ("a dignified, elderly gentleman whom everyone called Mr. Lloyd") located in the exclusive equestrian and fox-hunting country around Middleburg, Virginia, some 50 miles west of Washington, DC, and 150 straight-line miles northwest of Camp Peary.[63]

George Davis may have been an electronics nerd in his youth, but it was at the Farm that he acquired the advanced skills that allowed him to set up and monitor the sophisticated communications systems he described in his Los Angeles court testimony. As recounted by Agee, basic training included long hours in ISOLATION laboratories mastering the techniques of telephone tapping, room bugging, and other audio operations. It also included instruction and practicums in photography, secret writing, and the surreptitious opening of mail ("flaps and seals"), as well as basic tradecraft techniques of surveillance, surveillance avoidance, surreptitious entry, message drops, agent recruitment and communications, and the writing of field reports.[64]

Without once explicitly acknowledging that he had been to Camp Peary, Harrison told us that he had been trained in the elements of spycraft and while in Mexico he had utilized traditional drops, as well as "procedures of his own," to communicate with his superiors. "I was put in place to write reports no one would read," he remarked dismissively, "ended up in places they hadn't expected or thought possible, and became involved in things they didn't control." He was also trained in techniques for withstanding abusive interrogations, including the torments of systematically applied electric shocks. On one occasion, he said, he was detained by Mexican police and tortured for three days, but the names he gave his interrogators "were all members of Teddy Roosevelt's administration," which he had committed to memory for just such an eventuality. Apocryphal or not, the tale is wholly consistent with Harrison's character and personal engagement with the historical record.

On his first agency trip to Mexico in 1968, Harrison further told us, he had been "mapping rebel locations in the mountains of Jalisco" and, while there, had met antisubversive legend Miguel Nazar Haro, at that point, in his estimation, "a low-level gorilla for the PRI."[65] There is no way that Harrison could have been engaged in such activity or would have had contact with Nazar Haro except as a CIA operative and in coordination with Mexico's national security authorities. As with his entire "illegal" presence in Mexico, he was there by mutual consent of both governments.

In a similar vein, when during our initial interview with Harrison we intimated that our conversation was moving inexorably toward the question of his presumed CIA affiliation, he stated matter-of-factly, "You're going to ask me and I'm not going to tell you."[66] It was the same with the question of his having been trained at the Farm. He would not say so directly, but the information he shared with us and the facts of his Mexican experience confirm our assumption.

The same holds for his notable familiarity with firearms, as revealed in his court testimony about military weapons handled by members of the Guadalajara cartel. On our initial reading of the relevant court transcripts and Harrison's DEA-6 debriefing reports, we speculated that he might have obtained this knowledge through military service and that perhaps he had been sent to Mexico by the Pentagon's DIA. Eventually, however, we concluded that this was not the case and Harrison had in fact served in the CIA. This accords with Robert Baer's description of his experience at Camp Peary and the weapons training that he and his agency classmates received there a decade later.

They had begun, Baer writes, by "fieldstripping every assault rifle, machine gun, pistol, and rifle known to man. As soon as we knew our way around an M-16 or an AK-47 or a suppressed Sterling submachine gun, we took it out to the range for target practice." But their firearms training did not end there, he recounts. "We then fieldstripped and cleaned the same gun blindfolded. And to make sure we felt comfortable with it, we then fired it from a moving car, on a pop-up range, and at night. We even practiced on several weapons after forty minutes of physical training, to simulate the heart-thumping excitement of firing a weapon in a real combat situation."[67] When Harrison actually found himself in such a situation years later, he used the agency-learned tactic of keeping a vehicle's engine block between himself and his attackers to avoid being mortally wounded.[68]

Harrison's CIA preparation as a deep cover operative continued for more than three years following his basic training at Camp Peary. In addition to whatever the specific objectives of his time at Boalt Hall may have been, he was given at least two interim assignments of the sort described by Henry Crumpton, which lasted several weeks to several months and were designed to provide future case officers with hands-on experience in the various geographic or functional divisions within the CIA's Directorate of Operations. The rookie officers typically spent these periods serving as "basic office grunts" while receiving "tutorials by real spies who were working at headquarters (HQS), after their operational stints in the field."[69] Although Harrison would be developing and running his own informants ("agents") in the field, as an illegal his role would differ substantially from that of the case officer. So, too, did his training requirements. Rather than assigning him to HQS, with which he would have minimal contact while operational, he was given at least two major field assignments before being sent to Mexico: one in Germany, the other in Southern California.

Closely associated with these field assignments, it appears, was George C. McGhee. McGhee was a major player in U.S. Cold War diplomacy who knew and interacted personally with presidents Truman, Eisenhower, Kennedy, Johnson, and Nixon. He was a trained and notably successful exploration geologist (BS, 1933, University of Oklahoma; PhD, 1937, Oxford University) who accumulated substantial wealth from his involvement in the early development of Gulf Coast offshore oil. He served in Naval Intelligence during World War II, then joined the State Department, where he became one of the principal architects and overseers of American Cold War policy. He served as coordinator of Truman Doctrine aid to Greece and Turkey; negotiated the original Aramco agreement with Saudi Arabia; and served as U.S. ambassador to Turkey (1951–1953), undersecretary of state for political affairs (1961–1963), and U.S. ambassador to the Federal Republic of Germany (1963–1968).[70]

Harrison's six-month assignment in West Germany took place during McGhee's term as U.S. ambassador in Bonn, probably in the later half of 1967 and possibly into early 1968, after he had assumed his new identity. Harrison told us that he had "worked under George McGhee" and had gone to Germany "to babysit 'Mickie' McGhee," the ambassador's "pot-smoking, LSD-tripping" son Michael, whom "he was to keep from selling Nikes and Levis on the East German black market."[71] It was a transparently improbable cover story that he hardly expected us to believe. What he actually did in the Federal Republic we do not know for certain, although in hindsight we can see possible connections to his subsequent undercover work in Mexico, where he had contact with German arms dealer Gerhard Mertins, one of the CIA's cutout suppliers of weapons to the Nicaraguan *contras*.

As McGhee records in his Cold War memoirs, there was a large CIA station attached to the American embassy in Bonn, "with responsibilities going beyond Germany." The embassy's responsibilities extended to Berlin, which, situated 150 kilometers inside the German Democratic Republic, offered a major intelligence window into the Soviet bloc. Its CIA station had no doubt provided support for Operation Gold, the mid-1950s tapping of buried Soviet military landlines via a 78-inch-diameter, 1,476-foot tunnel excavated under the Berlin Wall from the American sector to an intercept point in East Berlin directly beneath the heavily traveled Schoenefelder causeway. The tunnel had been discovered and abandoned a dozen years before Harrison arrived in Germany, but increasingly sophisticated electronic espionage techniques continued to be employed against the Soviet bloc and it is certainly plausible that at least part of his six-month assignment to McGhee's embassy may have been to gain field experience in those techniques.[72]

Precisely how Harrison came to know George McGhee is not clear. In his conversations with us, he has implied that he met McGhee's son Michael in Berkeley, that they had become friends, and that Michael had introduced him to his father. He further implied that he had been invited to Germany by Ambassador McGhee because of his friendship with Michael; in other words, as a family friend. Even on its surface, however, that is an implausible sequence of events. The elder McGhee was thoroughly occupied in Europe in those years and would not have had either the time or the occasion to get to know his son's friend. Harrison, for his part, was not at liberty to make such choices, as all his activities were determined by agency handlers. The more likely scenario is that Harrison was assigned to the Bonn CIA station, that he met and interacted with the ambassador in that capacity, and that any social visits would have taken place following McGhee's return to the United States in 1968.

This connection to George McGhee relates, in a curious, perhaps significant, way, to Harrison's second post-ISOLATION assignment: participation in a survey of the political views and attitudes of Iranian students enrolled in Southern California institutions of higher learning. He would drive in his Triumph TR3 from San Francisco to an address in the Los Angeles suburb of Bel Air, where Iranian students would be brought in from UCLA and other area schools to take the written survey. He would help administer it, then review and evaluate the completed questionnaires. In general, he said, the students were critical of the shah, and already at that early date he concluded that the shah would face serious domestic challenges in the foreseeable future. The Iranian students, he told us with a chuckle, described SAVAK, the shah's security service, as "a salve for the prostate," alluding to the sodomization of political prisoners.[73] We wonder if perhaps some of those same CIA-surveyed students took part in the November 1979 seizure of the American embassy in Tehran.

We have been struck by Harrison's continued interest in Iran even after the Mexican odyssey that has consumed the core of his adult life, to the point where at the slightest suggestion he will launch into a discourse on contemporary Iranian history. We attribute this interest to his association with George McGhee, who was personally involved in the events surrounding the 1953 CIA-engineered overthrow of Prime Minister Mohammed Mossadeq. McGhee met with Mossadeq during the prime minister's 1951 visit to the United States, holding eighty hours of conversations with him in New York, in Washington, and at his Virginia estate. "Mossadeq was quite stubborn," McGhee opined. "No matter how hard I tried, I could not make him understand the few basic facts of life I tried to teach him about the international oil business. At the end of my lessons on economic or technical matters, he would invariably say with a smile, 'I don't care about that. You don't understand. It's a political problem.'"

McGhee, of course, understood perfectly well that Iranian oil was above all a geo-political problem and that British and American Cold War strategists were seeking to block Soviet access to Iran's massive petroleum reserves. Mossadeq was a staunch nationalist, McGhee concluded, and was not about to replace British control of his country's oil deposits with Russian control. He would accept technical assistance from any quarter to help him operate the nationalized Anglo-Iranian Oil Company's wells and Abadan refinery, but not at the expense of Iranian sovereignty. "He was not will-ing," McGhee writes, "to sell Iran." McGhee opposed Mossadeq's subsequent CIA-orchestrated ouster from power, considering it ill-conceived and counterproductive.[74] He appears to have discussed Iran's political history at some length with Harrison and may have had something to do with Harrison's involvement in the Bel Air political views survey of Iranian students. Or perhaps the survey was a convenient happen-stance and Harrison was assigned to it because it concerned students, a category of political actors in which the agency had a growing interest. Either way the Bel Air experience would have fed into his conversations with McGhee and contributed to his long-standing interest in Iran.

George McGhee likely shared as well his thoughts about the CIA and the role of intelligence. He made a clear distinction between "covert intelligence" and "covert operations" (covert action). "No one questions the collection of information by gov-ernments, whether done openly or secretly," he writes. Covert operations, on the other hand, "which range from rigging an election to assassinating a head of state," were another matter altogether. From his own long experience, McGhee concluded that "almost all covert operations are eventually exposed, by accident or by self-seeking par-ties." And such exposure, he underscored, "is almost always more adverse . . . than an initial gain." This was exemplified by Operation Ajax, the joint Anglo-American over-throw of Mossadeq in 1953.

"I never questioned wartime use of covert operations," McGhee records, "and I could also make exceptions of certain projects during the Cold War." In peacetime, he was comfortable with such "innocent" methods as "secret CIA control of newspapers and magazines, as well as bribes to individuals and contributions to political parties." Once he joined the State Department, however, he was exposed to numerous covert operations he considered "neither useful nor moral." They struck him as "the product of minds still dominated by wartime operations," who fetishized "a secret, conspira-torial approach" to foreign affairs. Many targeted countries had not been "lost to com-munism," he writes, "and as a result of our own covert overreaction, as in Iran, they turned against us."[75]

This view of the CIA's role in the world seems to accord with, and probably rein-forced, Harrison's beliefs at the outset of his intelligence career. The Cold War was in many places a shooting war, and the historical moment when Harrison joined the CIA can hardly be described as "peacetime," so the kinds of lethal operations that his under-cover work supported were, at least abstractly, justifiable. But there was also an ethical thread that ran through McGhee's thinking about the clandestine side of American intelligence, and he was quite ready to deem a covert operation immoral if its human toll warranted it. This, too, would have resonated with Harrison's sense of morality and may have refined the setting of his own ethical compass, which ultimately would lead him to disillusionment and a traumatic break with the agency.

As noted by *New York Times* intelligence reporter Tim Weiner, at the time Harrison was being infiltrated into his deep cover role in Mexico, the CIA's influence "was felt in every nation in the Western Hemisphere, from the Texas border to Tierra del Fuego." In Mexico, according to Weiner, "the president dealt exclusively with the station chief, not the ambassador, and he received a personal New Year's Day briefing at his home from the director of central intelligence."[76] This is an extraordinary statement, one that Weiner neglects to document but that, at least in spirit, accords with the actual nature of CIA–Mexican government relations from the 1950s into the 1970s and probably beyond, as described in chapter 3. Political rhetoric for public consumption aside, within the inner sanctums of national power on both sides of the U.S.-Mexico border there was mutual comprehension of core geopolitical issues, and no CIA operative like Lorenzo Harrison could, or would, have been sent into the field without an explicit understanding on the part of those with a need to know in each country's national security bureaucracy. Although he was an agency illegal, Harrison went to and remained in Mexico by mutual bilateral consent.

14

Alien Terrain

It's terrible what they're doing down there [in Mexico]. It's terrible what they're doing up here. It's terrible! It's horrible! And believe me, the country is not going to be able to sustain itself on this path. This country is going to go down the tubes.
> —Lawrence Victor Harrison, interview with authors, Riverside, California (18 June 2009)

MORE THAN A NATIONAL GEOGRAPHY, the Mexico into which the CIA inserted Lorenzo Harrison was a historic moment of global dimensions whose long-term denouement could not be foreseen. And, as often happens, the primary documentary source for accessing that terrible Mexican time is itself the result of pure historical serendipity, to wit, the final report of a special prosecutor appointed in late November 2001 by Mexico's first opposition party president in seventy years, Vicente Fox Quesada, to establish the legal record of official political repression under previous PRI administrations from the later 1960s through the mid-1980s. Interestingly, although the Fox administration's investigation of past civil rights abuses, war crimes, and crimes against humanity was a judicial proceeding that could and did lead to criminal indictments (none of which resulted in prosecutions of major figures), its one palpable achievement was the production of a massive, albeit incomplete, historical record of how Cold War geopolitics played out in Mexico.

Numbering 742 pages plus subject, geographic, and name indexes, Special Prosecutor Ignacio Carrillo Prieto's final accounting of his five-year investigation was issued as a "Historical Report to Mexican Society."[1] This whole undertaking appears to have been an audacious political tactic intended to discredit the old guard, corporatist PRI and legitimate the private-sector-based National Action Party (PAN) as a transparent defender of civil society's most elementary collective rights. Some observers among Mexico's active human rights community lamented Carrillo Prieto's lack of professional stature, suggesting that his career as a law professor and government attorney (including in Gobernación, the federal secretariat responsible for state security) did not equip him with the requisite credibility and institutional weight to investigate former high-level officials known or suspected to have been complicit in crimes of political repression. Carrillo responded that, to the contrary, his lack of professional cachet freed him of the political taint that would likely attach to a more prominent appointee (as had occurred with Buendía case special prosecutor Miguel Ángel García Domínguez) and that he would not hesitate to call on the carpet key personages of past administrations, which he in fact did, including former president Luis Echeverría Álvarez.[2]

But, while there were indictments and attempted, albeit ultimately frustrated, prosecutions, as in the case of Miguel Nazar Haro,[3] Carrillo Prieto's deeper purpose clearly was to write a brief for the bar of history rather than a judicial bar. And this he did with consummate skill. Much of the groundwork had been accomplished over the previous decade by Mexico's National Human Rights Commission, whose massive report on dirty war disappearances came out in late 2001 and was the immediate stimulus for the Fox administration's appointment of Carrillo. The special prosecutor, Fox had announced, was to "shine light on parts of our past that are still covered in darkness," which PAN strategists likely anticipated would produce a historic indictment of the PRI.[4]

In a sublime twist of historic irony, however, Carrillo's final report indicts not just the PRI but the entire Mexican political class, including the PAN itself. "The period covering the events analyzed in the present Report," writes Carrillo, "lasts approximately half a century and, on a global level, has as its reference point the 'cold war' that arises following the Second World War and ends with hegemonized [U.S.] globalization." The principal conflicts of this period, according to Fox's special prosecutor, stemmed from "antioligarchic struggles to modify [Third World] peoples' conditions of exploitation and dependency, against which tyrannical governments embraced the interventionist policy of the United States and converted their own armies into 'armies of internal occupation.'" To justify this frontal assault on Mexico's constitutional order, successive "authoritarian" Mexican administrations invoked the American national security doctrine, which "employed counterinsurgency strategies that systematically perpetrated war crimes and crimes against humanity." The rationale for that doctrine ceased, Carrillo observes, with the fall of the Berlin Wall and the dissolution of the Soviet Union.[5]

But there were larger historical continuities that worked inexorably to denationalize Mexico's political class and mechanisms of governance, to which Carrillo alludes even as he pays lip service to the Fox administration's self-legitimating mantra of a "democratic" PAN replacing an "authoritarian" PRI. The process began, Carrillo notes, when following World War II "the Mexican government aligns itself with the capitalist bloc dominated by the United States." Control of capital and markets replaced landownership as the primary determinants of social relations, while the army now functioned as the arbiter of who would exercise effective political authority. This is the historical context in which the events of immediate concern to the special prosecutor for past social and political movements occurred.

The period that followed, however, witnessed the "hegemonic, unipolar domination of Mexico by the United States and the globalization of [Mexico's] economy, culture, communications, and data processing."[6] As we've been writing this book, an extraordinary trove of classified diplomatic traffic between the American embassy in Mexico City and the U.S. State Department has come to light, which documents the consummation under the two PAN administrations of presidents Vicente Fox and Felipe Calderón of what amounts to Mexico's vassal status vis-à-vis the United States. Released in December 2010 to the Mexico City daily newspaper *La Jornada* by the Internet hackers group WikiLeaks, the some three thousand secret cables revealed what veteran *La Jornada* journalist Blanche Petrich Moreno describes as "the astonishing degree to which the United States exercised its power and influence at the highest levels of the Mexican government."

In some cases, Moreno writes, "it appears that an essential part of the decision-making process on matters of internal security is actually designed not in Mexico City but in Washington." Mexico, she laments in reference to the country's political class, has been revealed not simply as a country that is being controlled "but as a country that has surrendered." The exposed diplomatic dispatches originating "behind the large windows of the imposing US Embassy building at 305 Paseo de la Reforma illustrated beyond a shadow of a doubt," Moreno concludes, "the degree to which the Mexican state has relinquished sovereign decisions [to the American government]."[7] They reflect the culmination of a decades-long process of effective power projection dating from the late 1940s (briefly described in chapter 3), whose inauspicious consequences for Mexico's cultural and political integrity as a sovereign nation Manuel Buendía foresaw and decried, a process already well advanced by the time Lawrence Harrison embarked on his covert assignments in support of that hegemonic project.

The prevailing mind-set of Mexico's political, national defense, and state security institutions during the Cold War years reflected a hemispherewide, U.S.-promoted, governing class consensus on the nature and provenance of threats to established institutional arrangements. In contrast to the World War II years, when the overriding threat to regional security was seen as the Axis powers' hostile operations against Western Hemisphere targets, in the postwar decades that threat was redefined as an ideologically inspired domestic menace nurtured and supported by the Soviet bloc, and most especially by revolutionary Cuba. "Those in charge of Mexican national security," observes intelligence historian Sergio Aguayo Quezada, "echoed the preoccupation with internal subversion and adopted some of the methods employed [by their counterparts]" in Chile, Argentina, and Uruguay, where in the name of "western civilization, Christian values, order, and economic growth," military regimes had set about mercilessly eliminating all who challenged existing governmental systems, "disappearing tens of thousands of people, while torturing and jailing many more during a reign of terror that enveloped the continent like a shroud."[8]

The individuals in charge of Mexico's national security in those years, writes Aguayo, "shared a vision of the world and national security and agreed on who constituted enemies of national security, as well as how best to fight them." As a group, they lacked a coherent concept of national security, he observed, and never bothered to study it seriously. One of the principal weaknesses of the Mexican security system, in Aguayo's view, was precisely its lack of intellectual content, which led "to a poverty of strategic thinking" and explains why, as neighbors of a great power, Mexicans "avoided discussing in depth the influence of the United States on [their] national security."[9]

Mexico's tight-knit coterie of state security officials believed themselves to be the possessors of political truth, and, as Aguayo recounts, "they gathered evidence to confirm it, not test it." In their view, nothing happened by accident, nor was anything ever a coincidence, and the only "facts" they would consider were those that fit their scheme of logic. The two Secretariat of Government intelligence branches with which Lawrence Harrison was associated, the DFS and IPS, according to Aguayo, "collected enormous quantities of information that was never analyzed, contextualized, or interpreted. They propounded conspiracy theories but did not document them. To justify their existence and methods, they self-servingly exaggerated domestic security threats and dedicated themselves to attacking supposed enemies without evaluating their real danger."[10]

The highest authorities of successive administrations, from the Adolfo Ruiz Cortines *sexenio* (1952–1958) through the presidency of Miguel de la Madrid Hurtado (1982–1988), concluded Special Prosecutor Ignacio Carrillo Prieto, "impeded, criminalized, and combated diverse sectors of the populace, whose members had organized themselves to demand fuller democratic participation in the decisions that affected their lives." The methods employed against these disaffected groups of Mexican nationals, perceived by the country's political class as "ideological enemies," grossly violated established and codified legal norms in an orgy of "massacres, forced disappearances, systematic torture, and genocide." The special prosecutor's final report documents "the excessive cruelty [*sevicia*]" with which the Mexican government proceeded against those citizens "who dared to pay the price of achieving a more just society with their suffering, their freedom, and their lives," clarifies Carrillo in the report's prefatory material, and consequently "is no less objective for having been issued in the spirit of bereavement for those who died and those who remain disappeared, which we share with their families and their friends, praying that this does not happen again." Special Prosecutor Carrillo himself had lost a family member in the scorched earth campaign against *subversivos*, a female cousin who joined one of the period's guerrilla groups, subsequently disappeared, and is presumed to have been killed.[11]

As one would expect in such circumstances, the number of political, police, and military officials involved in Mexico's dirty war was elevated, ranging from presidents and heads of federal secretariats to noncommissioned soldiers ordered to carry out executions. Key to the actual conduct of the antisubversive campaign, however, was a core group of military and national security officers, some of whom would become infamous, including several with whom Lawrence Harrison worked directly, notably, Javier García Paniagua, Miguel Nazar Haro, Florentino Ventura Gutiérrez, Col. Jorge Carranza Peniche, and Gen. Mario Arturo Acosta Chaparro. Acosta Chaparro, by way of an example, was emblematic of the unrestrained violence with which these individuals fought the dirty war.

Citing firsthand testimony published in the Mexico City daily newspaper *Reforma*, Carrillo Prieto recounts how during the presidency of Luis Echeverría (1970–1976) the Mexican army routinely executed captives in the State of Guerrero and dropped the bodies into the ocean from airplanes flying out of the Pie de la Cuesta military air base at Acapulco. Blindfolded men and women identified as "guerrillas" were brought to the base in groups of ten or twelve by military personnel in civilian dress driving civilian vehicles, taken to a small building with restricted access, registered in a black record book, then seated in chairs for what they were told would be their photo of record (*la foto del recuerdo*). Passing behind them, according to this account, Acosta Chaparro systematically executed the captives by firing a .38 caliber round into the base of their skulls, which he was alleged to have done "on at least two hundred occasions." The bodies were then placed in weighted canvas sacks, transferred to a military aircraft, flown off the coast at night, and dropped into the Pacific, a dozen victims per flight.[12]

Apparently, not all of those meant to disappear ended up on the ocean floor, however, and corpses frequently floated ashore around Acapulco. "The bodies came into a small inlet called Playa Angosta," Harrison told us. "I used to buy fish there every morning, and every morning I'd go there there'd be a fucking body floating there." He said he had not personally witnessed the night flights out of Pie de la Cuesta air base but had been told by one of the soldiers that they were putting people on airplanes and dropping them into the ocean. "When I tell you these things," he emphasized, "I tell you because I saw them, you know? And I felt sorry for all those people!"[13]

General (ret.) Acosta Chaparro was shot to death on a Mexico City sidewalk on 20 April 2012. The gunman escaped with an accomplice on a waiting motorcycle. The motive was not clear, but there were numerous possibilities stemming from the victim's sordid past. Two weeks later we telephoned Harrison to ask if he had known Acosta. "Mario Arturo?" he replied in immediate recognition. "He was a nice guy, the kind of guy you could talk to. He did me some favors." Harrison had not heard about Acosta's murder, and when we described how the assassin had approached the general on foot, then escaped on a waiting motorcycle, he guffawed and exclaimed incredulously, "Oh, my god! They're still using the same old tactic, just like with Buendía!"[14]

Mexico's "dirty war" was part and parcel of a hemispheric dirty war that for three decades engulfed the whole of Latin America and even reached into the continental United States, where one of its most prominent victims was the distinguished Chilean diplomat and former defense minister Orlando Letelier, assassinated on 21 September 1976 in a Washington, DC, car bombing.[15] While a few Americans of our generation who were politically engaged during the Vietnam and post-Vietnam decades knew about this massive orgy of state-sponsored violence, and even witnessed its terrible consequences themselves, most Americans had little or no idea that it was happening at all, much less its true nature and extent. Nor did they realize that their own country was in decisive measure responsible for propagating that violence. Now, three decades on and more than a decade into the post-9/11 world of extraordinary rendition, government-sanctioned torture, remotely targeted assassination, and the massive abuse of civilian populations across the globe, perhaps a majority of the U.S. citizenry is at least vaguely aware of how far we have in fact traveled down the "repugnant" road of "abandoned idealistic slogans" first recommended by George Kennan and James Doolittle more than half a century ago.[16]

While today many Americans are aware of the devastating toll taken by the militarization of Mexico's seemingly endless "drug war," for which the United States also bears major responsibility, few have (or had at the time) any notion of their southern neighbor's earlier and equally violent dirty war against civilian challenges to the country's established political order, a brutal conflict that would devolve into the now regionwide

war on drugs being utilized by American geopolitical strategists to reinforce U.S. hegemony throughout the United States' Mesoamerican flank. Mexico's dirty war of the
1960s, '70s, and '80s was a complex process deeply rooted in the country's own history, then infused with a toxic brew of global Cold War imperatives originating outside the country. Initially, it began as armed clashes between peasant bands and a
long-entrenched landed baronial caste that held much of Mexico's rural populace in
a perpetual state of feudal-type bondage.

Guerrilla groups appeared in various Mexican states but most prominently in the
northern State of Chihuahua and the southwestern State of Guerrero, where the peasantry's cause was joined by rural teachers, students, and a few university professors.
President Lázaro Cárdenas (1940–1934), most famously remembered for his sweeping land reform program and his 1938 nationalization of the Mexican oil industry,
had created rural defense forces known in Guerrero, Chiapas, and elsewhere as the
Guardias Rojas (Red Guards) and armed the peasants so they could defend their vital
interests against a notoriously predatory landed oligarchy. He would give the peasants
Mauser rifles, Cárdenas declared in a May 1934 presidential campaign speech delivered
at the Guerrero Tres Palos peasant collective (*ejido*), "the same Mauser with which they
made the [Mexican] Revolution, so they could [continue] to defend the Revolution,
as well as their *ejidos* and schools." With these words and actions, Cárdenas in effect
legitimated the Mexican peasantry's resort to armed revolt two decades later.[17]

Numerous rural guerrilla bands emerged across the Mexican countryside starting in
the 1950s, initially in response to local predations against peasant communities, then
increasingly on the initiative of university and polytechnic students politicized in the
various anticapitalist ideological currents originating with Karl Marx, Friedrich Engels,
and their subsequent interpreters, from Vladimir Lenin and Leon Trotsky to Antonio
Gramsci, Mao Tse-tung, and Fidel Castro. The Cuban Revolution had a major impact
on broad sectors of politically aware Mexicans, as it did throughout Latin America,
especially after Cuba's successful defeat of the U.S.-sponsored Bay of Pigs invasion in
April 1961 and Castro's subsequent embrace of socialism as the goal of Cuba's revolutionary government. The astonishing historical fact that Cuban revolutionaries,
having launched their armed struggle from remote mountain redoubts together with
strategic supporters in the island's principle cities, actually succeeded in overthrowing
an entrenched U.S.-imposed regime and then managed to survive in the shadow of a
hostile imperial superpower like the United States inspired many young Mexicans to
emulate the Cuban example.

The politicization of Mexican students occurred within a Latin America–wide tra-
dition of university autonomy dating from the 1918 Argentine university reform,
which established the principle of institutional inviolability to government interference. As early as during World War II, accused Buendía assassin Juan Rafael Moro
Ávila Camacho's great-grandfather, President Manuel Ávila Camacho (1940–1946),
launched the first government assault on the country's postsecondary educational
institutions as part of a strategy to reverse what were viewed as the socialist reforms and
policies of the preceding Cárdenas administration and to realign Mexico more closely
with the United States, both ideologically and strategically. Ávila Camacho attempted

to eliminate the rural normal schools that trained teachers supportive of the Cárdenas land reform project and rural workers' rights generally. He also sought to close down the National Polytechnic Institute (Politécnico), whose various vocational schools trained the skilled personnel needed to develop and operate Mexico's independent industrial base. And, as a judicial weapon to combat the anticipated resistance to these measures, the Ávila Camacho administration incorporated a new provision into the federal penal code criminalizing acts of "social dissolution," which in effect created a penal category of political offenses and formally institutionalized the incarceration of political prisoners.

Reductions in the Politécnico's budget and its proposed disaccreditation as an institution of postsecondary education produced a massive student protest march on 6 March 1942 through downtown Mexico City, which was violently dispersed by police two blocks from the capital's historic Plaza de la Constitución (Zócalo), the marchers' intended destination. Several students were fatally shot, and the authorities attempted to blame the confrontation on communist agitators. But the encounter had been witnessed by a number of elected officials, who declared that the lethal response by police had been unprovoked and defended the legitimacy of the protesters' demonstration. Ávila Camacho acquiesced to the students' demands and set aside his intention to dismantle the Politécnico. The first student blood had been spilled, however, and the Politécnico would remain at the center of the mounting confrontation between Mexico's politicized student population and the unyielding defenders of the country's established institutional order.[18]

The rural normal schools likewise survived their proposed dismantling by the Ávila Camacho administration and continued to play a decisive role in the defense of agricultural workers' rights in concert with the Mexico City–based Escuela Nacional de Maestros (National Teachers School, ENM), which launched a strike in 1949 demanding much-needed material support from the government and, most significantly, "ideological freedom" for teachers. The following year rural normal school students coordinated by the Federación de Estudiantes y Campesinos Socialistas de México (Mexican Federation of Socialist Students and Farmers) conducted a thirty-four-day strike demanding government attention to the severe material needs of teacher-training facilities in the countryside. While this strike was under way, Politécnico students struck to demand that the unfulfilled promises of former president Ávila Camacho be implemented. The Secretariat of Public Education threatened to close the Politécnico permanently, then relented and agreed to meet student demands. A second, forty-six-day, strike that same year by some twenty-two thousand students from both the Politécnico and the Escuela Nacional de Maestros forced the resignation of the Politécnico's director, Alejandro Guillot.

In 1954 the premier National Autonomous University of Mexico (UNAM) was relocated from its old facilities in central Mexico City to the new, architecturally impressive, University City campus in the Copilco district, six miles south of downtown. The lavish federal expenditures on UNAM compared to the meager resources allocated to the Politécnico and teacher-training schools provided an added element of contention between the student bodies of these latter institutions and the government. There was also antagonism between UNAM and the Politécnico rooted in the respective social class distinctions of the two institutions, with the UNAM serving the needs and interests of the more privileged sectors of Mexican society (only 10 percent of its student body came from working-class or peasant backgrounds), while the Politécnico's student body was overwhelmingly rural and working class in origin. These class differences in Mexico's postsecondary schools would in turn greatly complicate the country's radicalized political landscape during the Cold War decades.

A wave of student strikes swept Mexico between April and September 1956 involving the rural normal schools, agricultural vocational schools, the Escuela Nacional de Maestros, and the Politécnico. At its height, more than one hundred thousand students took part, moving government authorities to adopt a divide and conquer strategy of granting first virtually all the demands voiced by the rural normal and agricultural school students and subsequently most of the demands of the ENM, whose respective student bodies then abandoned the strike movement, leaving the Politécnico strikers in a much weakened position. By the third week of June, they, too, had ended their strike, but without having achieved any of their goals, although they continued to insist on the resignation of the Politécnico's director, whom the authorities did subsequently replace.

Then, on 23 September 1956, ostensibly in response to student displeasure over policies implemented by the institution's newly appointed director, three battalions of the Mexican army occupied the Politécnico, signaling the commencement of a qualitatively new stage in official tactics for combatting radicalized civilian challenges to Mexico's established institutional order. From this point forward, successive Mexican administrations would employ all the coercive resources at their disposal, including the military, to smash political dissent in the country's educational institutions. And they would do so with the active collaboration and encouragement of successive U.S. administrations, those of Dwight Eisenhower through Ronald Reagan.[19]

American readers old enough to remember the May 1969 Alameda County Sheriff's Department shooting of 110 student protesters and bystanders (1 fatally) and the subsequent seventeen-day occupation of the University of California's Berkeley campus by the California National Guard, followed a year later by the Ohio National Guard's shooting of Kent State University students (4 fatally) and the shooting of 18 Jackson State College students (2 fatally) by Jackson, Mississippi, police, may have some visceral appreciation of the psychological impact of the army's 1956 occupation of the Politécnico and the orgy of targeted violence unleashed thereafter against a plethora of radicalized antiregime movements and organizations. From this point forward, the Mexican government purposefully co-opted existing student organizations at all the country's postsecondary institutions, converting them into antisubversive vigilante groups (*porros*, from the Spanish word *porra*, meaning "club" or "blackjack"), whose members informed on politically active fellow students, disrupted their meetings, and physically assaulted individuals perceived to be playing key roles in organizing antigovernment movements. Where the authorities determined that additional coercion was required, they deployed the army and the police, which took an increasing toll of fatalities among the civilian population. This downward spiral of repressive violence spun fatally toward its ugly nadir and historical watershed in the 2 October 1968 Tlatelolco massacre at Mexico City's Plaza de las Tres Culturas.

MEXICO CITY, 3 OCTOBER 1968

In one savage display of firepower at the Plaza of the Three Cultures, the government wiped out the protest movement and probably several hundred lives. The massacre yesterday afternoon came as a surprise, because for almost a week both the government and the strike committee had been backing off from confrontation and nearly everyone believed that the crisis was passing. The Army had evacuated the UNAM and the Rector withdrew his resignation.

Nevertheless, yesterday about 5 p.m. some 3000 people—students, teachers, parents and some workers and peasants—gathered at the Plaza of the Three Cultures for a march in protest against continued government occupation of the Polytechnic Institute and several of its vocational schools.

The first speaker at the rally, however, called off the march because of a concentration of about 1000 troops with armoured vehicles and jeep-mounted machine-guns along the route. The rally continued peacefully but the military units surrounded the Plaza. Just after 6 p.m. the Army opened fire on the crowd and on the surrounding buildings believed to be sheltering sympathizers. Not until an hour later did the Army stop firing. Officially the toll is set at twenty-eight dead and 200 wounded, but several hundred were probably killed and many more wounded. Over 1500 were taken prisoner. Today mass confusion reigned as thousands of parents and relatives sought to find the bodies—already disappeared—of those unable to be located in hospitals or jails.[20]

Events had come to this fatal crossroads in a national as well as international context, where an accelerating civil challenge to an increasingly authoritarian Mexican state was further stimulated by historic examples of popular resistance to power abroad, most notably in Czechoslovakia (Prague Spring), France (the Paris student revolt), and the United States (the anti–Vietnam War movement and Democratic National Convention protests). As summarized by British historian Eric Hobsbawm, "1968 ended the era of General de Gaulle in France, the era of Democratic presidents in the USA, the hopes of liberal communism in communist central Europe and (through the silent after-effects of the student massacre of Tlatelolco) it marked the beginning of a new era in Mexican politics."[21] That post-Tlatelolco new era quickly devolved into a dark decade of spreading armed insurrection and the steady recrudescence of state repression, aided and abetted by the CIA.

Complicating Mexico's mounting political crisis was the fact that the 1968 Summer Olympics were slated to be held in October of that year in the Mexican capital, for which a massive Olympic Stadium was constructed on the grounds of UNAM's Ciudad Universitaria. It was the first time the Olympics had been sited in a "developing" country, and the Díaz Ordaz administration expended unprecedented sums, two hundred million U.S. dollars by one estimate,[22] to proclaim Mexican prominence in the "Free World." As with previous postwar games, Mexico was to host a Cold War Olympic event in which the U.S.-led "capitalist bloc" would contend with the Soviet-led "social-ist bloc" for medals of Olympian prestige hyped as manifestations of political superior-ity.[23] Fearful that the now radicalized student movement might sabotage the Olympic Games, in mid-September Díaz Ordaz ordered the army to occupy the UNAM cam-pus, then, in coordination with his secretary of government and eventual successor, Luis Echeverría Álvarez, authorized the Tlatelolco massacre on the second of October. As it was, the games came within a hairsbreadth of being canceled when, by a single vote on whether or not to hold them, the International Olympic Committee decided to proceed with the events.

Tlatelolco was the blow that caused significant numbers of students, teachers, and intellectuals to opt for armed resistance against Mexico's established political order. The change from what began as localized peasant confrontations with predatory land-owners to disciplined guerrilla organizations seeking the overthrow of the country's existing institutional system had begun prior to 1968 under the initial leadership of disaffected rural teachers, notably Arturo Gámiz García and Pablo Gómez Ramírez in the western Sierra Madre of Chihuahua and Genaro Vázquez and Lucio Cabañas in Guerrero. After 1968 armed insurrection became much more generalized, with guer-rilla groups operating in over half of the Mexican states. The primary revolutionary organization that would incorporate various preexisting armed bands under its cen-tralized command was the Liga Comunista 23 de Septiembre (September 23rd Com-munist League, or LC23S by its Spanish acronym), named after the date in 1965 when Gámiz and Gómez Ramírez's Grupo Popular Guerrillero attacked a military barracks in the Chihuahua mountain town of Madera, an episode replete with symbolism for its similarity to the 1953 attack on the Moncada Barracks in Santiago de Cuba that marked the beginning of the Cuban Revolution.

By the time Lawrence Harrison moved to Guadalajara in 1971, Jalisco had become a strategically situated state in Mexico's insurrectional geography. At the UAG, as described in chapter 13, student life was dominated by the Tecos-controlled Guadala-jara Student Federation (FEG by its Spanish acronym), renamed from its predecessor the FEJ. The FEG was utilized by the DFS as shock troops deployed against student body members engaged in antigovernment activities, much as the DFS resorted to violence-prone criminal elements (*madrinas*) to perform extralegal assignments on its behalf in other settings. The FEG enforcers conducted physical assaults on these groups, as well as carrying out assassinations of key activist leaders.

In response to the FEG assaults, students from various schools formed the Frente Estudiantil Revolucionario (Student Revolutionary Front, FER), which embarked on a course of armed confrontation that quickly ratcheted up the level of violence in Guadalajara and its environs. The FER initiated guerrilla warfare training in the Sierra del Tigre south of Lake Chapala, to which the army, police, and security forces responded without quarter. Soon insurgents' bodies began to appear floating in the lake. By 1973 a majority of the FER's membership had joined with other guerrilla groups to form the LC23S, which from that point on would coordinate the actions of armed rural and urban insurgents from Chihuahua to Chiapas.

INTENSE SHOOTOUT IN GUADALAJARA BETWEEN
DELINQUENTS AND POLICE

Excélsior—Jueves, 13 September 1984

By Eduardo Chimely Ch., Excélsior *correspondent*

Guadalajara, Jal., 12 September—An intense shootout between agents of the Judicial Police and some delinquents left a total of one dead, one wounded, and one arrested. These events took place at the intersection of Justo Sierra and General Coronado. The shooting erupted when three individuals attempted to retrieve three million pesos in an extortion plot.

According to information provided by State Judicial Police chief Carlos Aceves Fernández, agents surprised the subjects when they arrived at the intersection.

It all began when attorney Felipe Ceja Ángeles informed the police that three individuals had threatened to harm his family if he didn't pay them three million pesos. The agents instructed him to bring them the money in used bills of small denominations. When Ceja Ángeles arrived with the extorted amount, the agents were already there waiting for the delinquents.

The three delinquents arrived at the intersection in a pickup with license plates NZ-8904.

Lorenzo Harrison was shot three times in the upper body and Nicolás Ávila once in the leg; killed was Jesús Arce Sepúlveda. All three had a police record.

Jesús Arce Sepúlveda, known in the underworld as "El Arce," was found to be carrying an ID credential with his name and photograph from the Government Secretariat's Political Investigations Directorate.

"El Arce" had also reportedly taken part in an assault on a business called Carnes Asadas de la Torre, where three persons were killed.

And he had a record of bank robberies, car theft, and extortion. Years ago he participated in the Oblatos prison riot, in which there were nineteen deaths. On that occasion, the fight was over control of drugs within the prison.

The wounded man, Lorenzo Harrison, is in the Civil Hospital. His condition is serious.

Nicolás Ávila Meza has been detained by the Judicial Police and is undergoing intensive interrogation.

The State Justice Department has heightened security in and around its headquarters building in response to a telephone threat from someone claiming to be a member of the "September 23rd League," who said there would be an attempt to rescue the prisoner.

There have also been telephone warnings of bombs in the Civic Hospital. Riot police and military personnel have searched the building and found no explosive devices.

Nonetheless, the hospital is under tight security, as it is feared there may be confrontations between the supposedly revived "September 23rd League" and elements of the police.

When Harrison commenced his long-term assignment in Mexico, the DFS had no permanent facilities of its own in Guadalajara, but by middecade, in response to the country's deteriorating political situation, it would establish both office space and safe houses throughout the greater metropolitan area.[24] Piecing together the available circumstantial evidence, it seems apparent that the CIA had a good handle on the spreading insurgency in Mexico and the agency's placement of Harrison in Guadalajara was part of a collaborative effort to quash what both governments perceived as a mutual geopolitical threat. And *quash* was the operative verb. The Echeverría administration's antiguerrilla counteroffensive pursued a no-holds-barred strategy in which the United States was thoroughly complicit and respect for human rights had no part. Harrison's cover affiliation with a PRI law office, combined with his years of experience at Boalt Hall and in the volatile '60s student milieu on the Berkeley campus, allowed him to infiltrate the student body at the UAG, where he insinuated himself into the student federation and actually served as an FEG attorney, representing its members in the inevitable legal matters arising from their paramilitary activities against the FER and, subsequently, the LC23S.[25]

As the effective nationwide guerrilla coordinating organization, the LC23S became a primary target of the counterinsurgency campaign, and Harrison ran his own agents inside it, including Jesús Arce Sepúlveda, mentioned in the *Excélsior* article translated above. By his own account, repeated to us more than once, he also met with FEG operatives involved in paramilitary actions against LC23S members and was struck by how heavily armed they were, as well as by their ability to move about the greater Guadalajara area unchallenged by the authorities. Harrison's movements outside Guadalajara during the 1970s, especially in the Acapulco area, plus his interaction with key Mexican counterinsurgency officers—for example, Miguel Nazar Haro ("He was my *comandante*."), Jorge Carranza Peniche ("I was reporting to him in Cuernavaca."), and Mario Arturo Acosta Chaparro ("He did some favors for me.")—further confirm the depth of his, and the CIA's, involvement in Mexico's dirty war. During the 1970s, we conclude, he worked with senior Mexican security personnel to identify LC23S members for elimination.

With the advent of the Reagan administration in the United States, operational coordinates and channels of authority in the U.S. intelligence community were reconfigured in ways that disrupted established practices and command relationships in the field, most notably as a consequence of giving the National Security Council (NSC) an operational role it had not previously had. Combined with the imposing personalities of CIA director William Casey, national security adviser Adm. John Poindexter, and NSC assistant deputy director for political-military affairs Lt. Col. Oliver North, these changes occasioned dissension among veteran CIA covert operations personnel and negatively impacted the work of clandestine operatives like Harrison, who appears to have been retasked from primarily supporting Mexico's domestic counterinsurgency campaign to espionage assignments in support of renewed U.S. power projection in Central America. Over the period 1979–1981, Harrison became an operational, DFS-approved, electronic security specialist subordinate to the DFS's senior electronic surveillance officer, Alberto Guadalupe Estrella. He remained under the overall in-country command of DFS directors Javier García Paniagua (1977–1978), Miguel Nazar Haro (1978–1982), and José Antonio Zorrilla Pérez (1982–1985) and carried official ID credentials identifying him as a DFS and Secretariat of Government IPS electronics specialist.

Harrison began upgrading DFS and IPS communications systems in Guadalajara, then was assigned to do the same for DFS offices at various locations around the country.

In 1981 he was tasked by the DFS commandant in Guadalajara to do electronic communications upgrades for Jalisco narcotics boss Ernesto Fonseca. This assignment, which may or may not have originated with Harrison's home agency, resulted in an extraordinary three-year association with the principal figures of the Guadalajara drug cartel, during which Harrison personally confirmed the cartel's collaboration with the CIA in support of the Nicaraguan *contras*. He observed and interacted with CIA contract pilots flying narcotics and arms in and out of cartel-controlled landing strips in the State of Jalisco and elsewhere. He had conversations with cartel bosses about their material support for the *contras* and was warned by them not to concern himself with those activities because they were "political."

By 1984 U.S. covert operations in Mexico and Central America had become a tangle of often conflicting institutional and cohort agendas that hampered, even endangered, American intelligence agents on the ground. "It wasn't just CIA," Harrison explained. "Under [Director of Central Intelligence (DCI) William] Casey, for instance, Ollie North wasn't CIA. He wasn't DIA, either. It was a separate policy thing going on. You can't say CIA had much to do with that. CIA had a little to do with it."[26]

The figure of Oliver North and the personal chemistry between North and Casey are the two most elusive factors in this operational equation. Casey biographer Bob Woodward describes the two men as soulmates. "The DCI had evolved into a father figure, an intimate and adviser [for North]," Woodward has written. He was, in effect, "a case officer" for the younger man, whose whole life now went "off line" to become "the deniable link" in a "stand-alone, off-shore, self-financing entity that would operate independent of Congress and its appropriations," what Casey called "a full-service covert operation."[27]

Duane "Dewey" Clarridge, chief of the Latin America Division of the CIA's Directorate of Operations in the critical 1981–1984 period, did not view the way Casey and North interacted as "a father/son relationship," but rather one of deep mutual respect based on North's ability "to get things done." They each had an office on the third floor of the Old Executive Office Building, where North frequently sought Casey's advice and often consulted with the DCI informally. Meeting at the agency's Langley, Virginia, headquarters, Clarridge notes, always entailed the obligatory formalities of registration, security checks, and the issuance of a visitor's badge. It also created an official record of contact, we would add, which an unscheduled visit to Casey's Washington office just around the corner from his own did not.[28]

A third agency personage who interacted with North, Casey, and Clarridge during the *contra* years was career CIA lawyer John Rizzo. "I had never seen or dealt with anyone quite like Ollie North," Rizzo wrote in a recently published memoir. "He made a startling and vivid impression on me. Ramrod-straight in bearing (he was always in civilian clothes in those days . . .), he immediately set out to charm, flatter, and above all influence me in a way that I had never been 'worked' before, not even from any of the hardened and cynical DO [Directorate of Operations] operatives who were then my clients." Rizzo found North to be "very smart and always willing to listen." He exhibited an energy level that was "nothing short of phenomenal" and was always "churning out memos or talking on the phone . . . mostly with Dewey at first, but then with me and, I came to learn, with many other people inside and outside the intelligence community. He seemed to be everywhere, under the radar." North was, in Rizzo's judgment, "a full-fledged protégé, and surrogate, of Casey's."[29]

Those two singular individuals, in combination with an ideologically compatible executive branch and an operationally engaged NSC, created an out-of-the-box, off-the-shelf set of operational arrangements that allowed them to circumvent congressional constraints on their lethal response to what they perceived as a grave geopolitical threat in an adjacent sphere of long-standing American hegemony. Both men were inclined to employ direct action rather than diplomacy, and both disdained legislators who sought to oversee intelligence community operations. Casey, in particular, appears to have held an unnuanced Cold War view of the world, in which the "communist menace" literally threatened to sweep north from Nicaragua through Mexico and into the United States. He was not interested in hard intelligence that suggested otherwise, which was repeatedly brought to his attention by former Mexico City CIA station chief John Horton. He only expressed satisfaction, Woodward records, "when someone brought him intelligence that supported his preconceptions or Administration policy."[30]

The principal obstacles to the Reagan administration's planned overthrow of the Nicaraguan government were two successive amendments to the annual Defense Appropriations Act introduced by Massachusetts Democratic congressman Edward P. Boland in December 1982 and again in the fall of 1984. The first of the Boland Amendments, subsequently referred to as Boland I and Boland II, prohibited the CIA and the Department of Defense from expending any funds "for the purpose of overthrowing the Government of Nicaragua or provoking a military exchange between Nicaragua and Honduras." Boland II sought to close obvious loopholes in the initial restriction by prohibiting CIA, Defense, "or any other agency or entity of the United States involved in intelligence activities" from supporting "directly or indirectly military or paramilitary operations in Nicaragua by any nation, group, organization, movement or individual." While this second amendment had been drafted more broadly so it would apply to the NSC as well, Casey and other executive branch strategists chose to exempt the NSC from the latest legislative strictures on the dubious grounds that its purpose was to advise the president on defense and security matters, not to gather intelligence, and that it therefore was not a member of the "intelligence community." For the DCI, that was a loophole large enough to accommodate the administration's multifaceted covert offensive against Nicaragua's Sandinista government, which assured the NSC's unprecedented but now continuing operational role into the second Reagan administration. It also gave rise to competing agendas that blurred responsibilities on the ground.[31]

According to Harrison, by the time Ronald Reagan assumed the presidency of the United States, the CIA had become so compromised in Mexico that many of its operations, particularly those related to Nicaragua, were formally turned over to Israel's Mossad. (Manuel Buendía, he insisted, had played a major role in bringing about this operational change by publishing the names of CIA officers and agents in his Red Privada column.)[32] The covert supply of *contra* arms via Mexico, Harrison told us, was in large part handled by the Israelis. The Bravo family ranch in the State of Michoacán, where the bodies of DEA S/A Enrique Camarena and his Mexican pilot, Alfredo Zavala Avelar, were recovered, for example, was by his account a transfer point along an Israeli-run *contra* arms pipeline. That Israel had provided arms to the Somoza government prior to July 1979, and then subsequently to the *contras*, is well documented.[33] That they did so through Mexico as well is not widely known.

Former Israeli intelligence insider Ari Ben-Menashe confirms and adds to Harrison's assertions about Israeli operations in Mexico. Central to those operations, Ben-Menashe writes, was then Israeli defense minister Ariel Sharon, who earlier, as a private citizen with ties to the Israeli arms industry, had become a successful arms dealer in Central America. One of Sharon's associates was the ostensibly ex-Mossad agent Mike Harari, who had a close association with then Panamanian military intelligence chief Manuel Noriega. Prior to the Sandinistas' 1979 overthrow of Nicaraguan dictator Anastasio Somoza Debayle, Sharon and his associates had been providing Israeli military equipment to Somoza, as well as to other Central American countries "and even Mexico." They were running what amounted to an Israeli "off-the-shelf" operation analogous to Oliver North's Iran-Contra-related "enterprise," and both North and DCI Casey appear to have appreciated its utility for circumventing congressional prohibitions against providing arms to the Nicaraguan *contras*.

The Sharon network began supplying weapons to the *contras* in 1981 and soon was running what Mike Harari described as "more of a CIA network than an Israeli operation."[34] Sharon signed a security agreement with the Reagan administration in late 1981, which in effect made Israel a U.S. proxy "in situations where for political reasons the United States had to keep a low profile." A year later Sharon headed a high-level delegation to Tegucigalpa to discuss arms transfers with Honduran army chief Gen. Gustavo Álvarez Martínez. Among the other members of the delegation was Israel's principal arms dealer for Latin America, Mexico City–based David Marcos Katz, lending weight to Manuel Buendía's suggestion several years earlier that Israel was supplying arms "to governments with whom Washington [preferred] not to deal directly in such matters."[35]

Harrison repeatedly referred to the Israelis over the course of our conversations and to a meeting in Puerto Vallarta where the transfer of operational responsibilities supposedly took place. The changeover, he said, had been proposed by North and readily accepted by Casey, whom Harrison described as "a wheeler-dealer from outside the agency" who essentially had carried out a coup against his own shop of veteran covert operatives resistant to the renegade schemes favored by the Reagan administration.[36] According to Ben-Menashe, CIA deputy director Robert Gates and Israeli defense minister Ariel Sharon had a close working relationship at the time and were key players in the covert provision of lethal matériel to the *contras*, whom he bluntly characterizes as "narco-terrorists." With Gates's backing, Ben-Menashe writes, Sharon utilized his preexisting private network to procure and deliver weapons to the anti-Sandinista fighters, financing the whole operation by transporting "hundreds of tons of cocaine" from South America into the United States." The Sharon-Harari network, in other words, was a parallel shadow organization akin to Oliver North's "off-the-shelf" *contra*-support enterprise, both of which were linked to Latin American cocaine traffickers.[37]

By 1984 the Reagan administration's hardened Cold War approach to intelligence and national security matters had introduced a thorny mix of competing agendas into the Mexican theater of covert *contra*-related operations. Harrison concluded that North had orchestrated the reduction of CIA personnel in Mexico and their replacement with Mossad operatives in order to give him and the NSC freer rein in running the anti-Sandinista campaign. "As a matter of fact," he told us, "it was when they got CIA out that Ollie came down with his group, changed all the antennas at the consulates, and changed from the old long-wave system to the satellites. That was done on Ollie's watch. And he was there himself." Harrison described North as "a stupid fool" who wanted "a free hand to kill anybody who couldn't be compromised." It was North, he told us during our first interview, who ordered the assassination of Manuel Buendía. And it was North, he implied, who ordered the attempt on Harrison's own life.[38]

Further complicating matters was the simmering brew of evolving narco-geopolitical relationships. The Guadalajara cartel had come into being as a result of a vacuum created during the 1970s by the takedown of Mexico's principal narcotics traffickers, Sinaloa drug lord Pedro Avilés and the legendary Tijuana-based Cuban exile trafficker Alberto Sicilia Falcón. Combined with U.S. disruption of existing trans-Caribbean routes for the delivery of cocaine into the United States, second-tier Sinaloa traffickers decided to relocate their base of operations to Jalisco's strategically situated capital. The most senior member of the emergent Guadalajara cartel was Ernesto "Don Neto" Fonseca Carrillo, who brought to the new organization personal knowledge of the South American cocaine trafficking network, in which he had himself been involved in the early 1970s.[39]

Another problematic ingredient in this fetid brew were former FEG operatives who, with official authorization, had conducted armed attacks against antigovernment student activists during Mexico's dirty war and then, no longer useful and increasingly deemed a liability to the government, had joined the Guadalajara drug cartel as enforcers and traffickers. Three of those individuals had worked with Harrison: Gustavo Neri Delgado, Javier Barba Hernández, and Jesús "Chuy" Arce Sepúlveda. "All these people had been student leaders that I had worked with," Harrison told DEA debriefers. "While they needed them to combat the really dedicated ideological left-wing guerrillas . . . the government used them for that. They gave them many privileges. They gave them credentials that allowed them to have stolen cars, to drive all over the country and not have any problems . . . [and] to carry guns." Then, when they no longer needed these student operatives, "they began to send them messages, saying [they had] gotten out of hand. . . . They took away their credentials. They took away their privileges. They began to arrest them."[40]

And the same thing began to happen with the traffickers, Harrison said. "They began to have problems. . . . They began to get word from the government . . . that they were attracting too much attention." They were informed from Mexico City that the government was upset with them. "It's *puras broncas* with you guys," they were told. Nothing but problems. And that, Harrison explained, was a message "not to be misunderstood." Miguel Ángel Félix Gallardo, for his part, did understand and in late 1983 distanced himself from the other cartel bosses. He told Harrison that both

Fonseca and Caro Quintero were "too wild." They were "attracting too much attention," and he "didn't want to be around them any longer because they were too rowdy." "I could see that some kind of problem was coming," Harrison recalled. "I could see that they were having more and more trouble. I could see that the government was beginning to sometimes not recognize their credentials, not recognize the credentials that they themselves had given them." And there came a point when Harrison actually warned Fonseca. "I think you're going to have trouble with the government and I think you're going to have trouble with the Americans also," he told him, to which Fonseca replied that there couldn't be any trouble with the Americans because he and Caro Quintero "were together with the Americans."[41]

By 1984 Harrison's life in Guadalajara had become mired in a morass of competing demands and conflicting agendas. Most of the previous year he had been engaged in the development and monitoring of a radio communications system for the Guadalajara cartel while at the same time maintaining the communications systems of the local IPS and DFS offices. During the second half of 1983, he actually resided at Ernesto Fonseca's house and was on call twenty-four hours a day for whatever the cartel boss might order him to do. Harrison had taken a Mexican wife by then, had a baby daughter, and owned a home nearby, but he was allowed little time to be with his family. He moved out of Fonseca's house in January 1984, explaining that he could not remain there and still meet his obligations to the IPS and DFS. He continued to maintain and monitor Don Neto's radio system but now worked out of his own house.[42]

Matters were still further complicated by the private agendas of key people with whom Harrison was obliged to work. Two of his former UAG student operatives, "Chuy" Arce and Javier Barba Hernández, for example, had become Fonseca enforcers. Barba Hernández attained considerable notoriety as a cartel assassin, and by 1984 had become a boss in his own right. Together with another Fonseca enforcer, DFS agent Samuel "El Samy" Ramírez Razo, Barba was stealing from Don Neto even while conducting cartel business with him and other senior traffickers. The Guadalajara narco-political cabal was so shot through with criminality, according to Harrison, that virtually everyone associated with the cartel was involved in criminal activities beyond the immediate business of producing and marketing narcotics. Everyone had his price. Trust among this company was an illusory concept.

Increasingly frustrated by the inordinate demands on his time, Harrison finally sought to extricate himself from the cartel-Gobernación relationship altogether. He informed Fonseca that he no longer wanted to work for him and advised his IPS commandant, Sergio Espino Verdín, of his decision. Espino told him they needed to talk about it because things were getting very serious. Soon Harrison began receiving ominous messages over the traffickers' radio network saying that he was "dirty" and they were going to "give him a bath," which in the traffickers' argot meant "a bath of AK-47 bullets." Then Ramírez Razo accused Harrison of having talked to the DEA when he went to California in 1983 to purchase the VHF repeaters and related radio equipment for Ernesto Fonseca. Harrison denied that he had done any such thing but realized that "El Samy" had said as much to Fonseca and it was now a potentially lethal rumor. He tried unsuccessfully to arrange a meeting with Fonseca to talk things out face-to-face.[43]

Fonseca continued to give Harrison the silence treatment until, out of the blue one day, he called him in and announced, "I can help you now. I'll take care of everything, all your problems." To which Harrison replied that he had already taken care of his "problems." It was obvious to him, he later told us, that Fonseca "had made a deal with somebody." And that "somebody," he supposed, was the Americans, because "there were Americans [around Fonseca] all the time." Not long after this encounter, Fonseca asked him what he thought about the *contras*. Nonplused, Harrison thought to himself: "What the fuck do you care what I think about the Contras?" then quipped that they were "a bunch of thugs."

"Oh?" Fonseca replied. "You're not together with your people. You don't have the same commitment I do." He began to talk as if he were a secret agent, Harrison told us. "He was talking as if he was [the Americans'] secret source. And lecturing me! And I was trying to tell him to be careful, because I saw them running the people from Sinaloa off and putting all these other people in. And it was obvious that he was being taken for a ride."[44]

Then, on 11 September 1984, just three months and a few days after the Buendía assassination and five months before the Camarena killing, Fonseca ordered Harrison and "Chuy" Arce to retrieve some radios from an attorney in downtown Guadalajara. Harrison obeyed because Fonseca possessed a valid IPS investigator's credential, which made him Harrison's superior within the Secretariat of Government chain of command. When he, Arce, and a third cartel operative, Nicolás Ávila, arrived at the appointed location, they were met by a contingent of Jalisco State Judicial Police (PJJ) under the command of Víctor Manuel López Razón. The police opened fire on the three men, severely wounding Harrison and killing Arce. According to Harrison, López Razón executed Arce with a gunshot to the heart as he lay wounded on the ground. Why Harrison did not suffer the same fate is not clear, although he attributes it to the presence of too many witnesses by the time he was no longer able to resist his attackers.[45]

López Razón, for his part, was a co-opted PJJ commander in the pay of Ernesto Fonseca who would also take part in the kidnapping of DEA S/A Enrique Camarena the following February. The DFS agent "El Samy" Ramírez was in charge of Camarena's abduction in front of the U.S. consulate, while López Razón was one of two PJJ officers providing backup in the kidnap vehicle. Former Harrison UAG operative Javier Barba Hernández arrived on the scene after Camarena had been delivered to Caro Quintero's Lope de Vega residence and is said to have participated in the Camarena murder. He was subsequently shot and killed by members of the Federal Judicial Police.[46] While the web of complicity here is obscure and may never be fully untangled, the identifiable actors lend credibility to Harrison's conclusion that it was "the Americans" who ordered the attempt on his life.

The *Excélsior* account of the Guadalajara shootout by Eduardo Chimely Ch. translated above is based on carefully filtered information provided by the PJJ. It confirms the what, when, where, and who of the incident but obscures the why. While this press report reveals the intriguing detail that "Chuy" Arce was carrying a Gobernación IPS credential, it neglects to note that Harrison, too, was an IPS agent. The police version that described Harrison, Arce, and Ávila as "delinquents" attempting to extort three million pesos from a local attorney was a contrived cover story, which, in addition to its immediate purpose of concealing a premeditated ambush, would give Harrison a Mexican criminal record that six years later would be used to impugn his veracity as a U.S. government witness in the Los Angeles Camarena trials. Equally noteworthy is *Excélsior*'s reference to the LC23S, which Harrison and Arce had worked to subvert a decade earlier but by 1984 no longer existed, having fragmented into seven smaller groups unable to agree on a common political program.[47] Here again opaque messages ("tokens") and agendas were evidently in play.

Harrison's final five years in Mexico have proven frustratingly elusive compared to the preceding decade and a half. The thrust of what he has told us, only a minimal portion of which we have been able to corroborate, is that after he recovered from his nine gunshot wounds and was paroled from the Jalisco State Prison infirmary in June 1985, having declined U.S. offers of repatriation and decided to cease any further intelligence activity for the CIA, an arrangement was reached between the agency and the Mexican Secretariat of Government whereby he would be permitted to remain and work in Mexico under secretariat supervision. By the terms of this accord, Harrison could not leave Mexico but was allowed to be gainfully employed, including as a Gobernación agent.

One such assignment appears to have been the Buendía "investigation" he described to DEA debriefers and about which he testified in his voir dire hearing during the first Camarena (i.e., Zuno) trial.[48] While he testified that his Buendía inquiry had entailed "conducting interviews with friends of a group of Mexican newspaper reporters who had formed themselves into an informal group to investigate and push forward the police investigation into the assassination of Manuel Buendía," as well as "reading the books . . . and newspaper articles they had published," that appears not to have been the whole story. His court testimony about the journalists' oversight group, Harrison acknowledged, was inherently spurious. "I listened to them," he told us. "I had a listening post." In other words, he had tapped telephones and perhaps bugged meeting locations. This, he confirmed, he had done for Gobernación, not out of "personal interest" as he would testify in Judge Rafeedie's courtroom.[49]

This means that Secretary of Government Manuel Bartlett Díaz had assigned Harrison to monitor the very journalists' oversight group that Bartlett himself had authorized to monitor Buendía case special prosecutor Miguel Ángel García Domínguez. Operationally, it was a brilliant tactic. By assigning a disaffected CIA agent to spy on the group most able to disrupt government efforts to contrive a viable, self-serving resolution of the Buendía case, Bartlett assured plausible deniability should Harrison be exposed while providing a back channel to maintain the flow of Harrison-generated intelligence to the CIA. This arrangement also afforded the Mexicans an element of leverage against the Americans, as any operation in which Harrison was involved could, should circumstances warrant, be attributed to the CIA.

An especially puzzling detail in this final period of Harrison's time in Mexico is that within two months of his parole from prison in 1985 he set up a radio communications facility to assist with the landing and departure of Colombian drug flights at a clandestine airstrip in Jalisco. He personally guided two aircraft and helped transfer the cargoes from those flights to a ranch in the State of Durango. He performed these tasks, he testified, at the request of Antonio Gárate Bustamante, whom he had known since late 1980 as a PJJ officer complicit with Ernesto Fonseca and the Guadalajara cartel. According to Harrison's testimony, Gárate told him that what he was being asked to do was part of a "police investigation" and on completion of this assignment he was to report to Gárate, who then would prepare his own investigative report.

Neither prosecutors nor defense counsel chose to question Harrison further about this incident, which—at least for purposes of our investigation—is jarringly out of sync with Harrison's overall testimonial narrative. If he was indeed persuaded, as we have little doubt was the case, that he had been shot on 11 September 1984 because of what he had learned about clandestine CIA-sponsored drug and arms flights in support of the Nicaraguan *contras*, then why would he involve himself in such dangerous business again following his recovery and release from prison? Ernesto Fonseca and Rafael Caro Quintero had both been apprehended by then for the murder of Enrique Camarena, while Miguel Ángel Félix Gallardo was a fugitive, so on whose behalf was Gárate Bustamante facilitating the airlift of drug cargoes through Mexican territory? And why was Harrison so ready to follow orders from Gárate, whose ties to the DEA were not known in Mexico until August 1986, when he had to be extricated from the country and given asylum in the United States as an exposed DEA informant?[50]

In a second day of testimony during the 1990 Camarena trial, defense attorney Mary Kelly asked Harrison about the six-month period he had spent in the United States in 1983 purchasing radio communications equipment for Ernesto Fonseca. How, she inquired, was he employed during those six months? "I was a chief of security for the house of Antonio Gárate Bustamante," he stated. Gárate's house, he testified, was in Seal Beach, California, and he had performed those security duties the entire time he was in the United States.[51] There was no follow-up questioning about this extraordinary statement, which implied that there was much more to Harrison's association with Gárate and the DEA than met the eye. It suggests that Harrison may himself have been part of the CIA's penetration of the DEA. It also places the rumor of Harrison's having "talked to the DEA" circulated by Samuel Ramírez Razo prior to the Guadalajara shootout in a new light. Somebody had ratted on Harrison, it would seem, with the intent of getting him killed.

As for who might have been behind the covert flights Harrison helped guide into the clandestine Jalisco airstrip, Ari Ben-Menashe's account of Sharon network cocaine smuggling in support of the Nicaraguan *contras* opens the possibility that they were Israeli aircraft. Should that prove to be the case, we would have to wonder how Gárate came to be involved in the operation. Harrison, for his part, has remarked to us more than once that the Israelis were running guns to the *contras* through Mexico. He spoke with emotion about Israeli prime minister Shimon Peres's counterterrorism adviser and key Iran-Contra player, Amiram Nir, who died in a never fully resolved plane crash on 1 December 1988, roughly midway between Uruapan, Michoacán, and the Federal District. Nir, Harrison said, oversaw Israel's Mexican arms pipeline to Central America. The story that this particular Israeli was in Mexico on a private business venture to invest in avocado plantations, he scoffed, was thoroughly bogus. *Aguacate* (avocado), he laughed, was a euphemism for a soldier in a green uniform, and Nir had traveled to Mexico on that occasion to invest in uniformed *contra* guerrillas.

Amiram Nir seemed to occupy a special place in Harrison's Mexican universe. Harrison spoke about him in our initial telephone conversation and our first interview five weeks later, then again in our second interview the following year.[52] He indicated to us that he had met Nir; that the de la Madrid administration and the president personally were upset with Nir's presence in the country, as they were with Israeli gunrunning through Mexico; and that the Israelis had tried to conceal the identity of his remains after the plane crash. Nir's death, Harrison suggested, was not an accident, but rather had to do with Nir's pivotal role in the Iran-Contra affair.[53] (Israeli intelligence, according to Ari Ben-Menashe, "always believed it was a well-executed CIA operation" to prevent Nir from testifying at the trial of Oliver North.[54] Nir, Dewey Clarridge recalls in his CIA memoir, "was often described as the 'Ollie North of Israel.'"[55]) If Harrison indeed had occasion to meet Nir, as he indicated to us and his ready familiarity with Nir's activities in Mexico might suggest, it would have to have been in the post-1985 period when, ostensibly, he no longer reported to the CIA. As a Gobernación agent, he might well have been knowledgeable about the undercurrents of the Israeli-Mexican relationship. He once quipped to us, "I would rather have worked for Mossad than for our guys," his implication being that he considered Israel's Mossad a professional cut above the American CIA.[56]

By 1986 Harrison was working as a security specialist for a large Jalisco real estate company owned by former DFS chief and PRI heavyweight Javier García Paniagua. He worked directly under García Paniagua's personal secretary, who managed the firm, which developed and managed properties all over Mexico, including large tracts of land owned by the then imprisoned Ernesto Fonseca and Rafael Caro Quintero. His primary responsibility was to maintain radio communications between the firm's central office in Guadalajara and its outlying properties around the country. That he had access to García Paniagua in those years is apparent from the numerous color snapshots he has shared with us of the ex-DFS chief in a variety of settings, images he would not likely possess in the normal course of employment. At the same time, he continued to perform intelligence assignments for Gobernación, a relationship that would seem to have dovetailed perfectly with his work for García Paniagua.[57]

In the later part of 1988, Harrison formed his own communications consulting company, Comunicación Arboledas, located on Arboledas Street in Guadalajara's Zapopan district. He began to do PRI-related electronics work for Jalisco State government officials, as well as for private sector clients recommended to him by senior party officials. His office was located in the same building as the PRI's Electrocentro, where all the party's computerized rosters and other records were maintained. He installed radio systems, telephone systems, PBX systems, combined radio-PBX systems, fax machines, satellite dishes, and data transmission systems. His official clients included the Jalisco State finance secretary, the state secretary of urban renewal, and the Jalisco State Highway Patrol. He even served as the election campaign communications coordinator for Jalisco governor Guillermo Cosío Vidaurri (1989–1992), who was the uncle of Rafael

Caro Quintero's teenage paramour, Sara Cristina Cosío Martínez, and was in office at the time Harrison testified as a U.S. government witness during the first Zuno trial in the summer of 1990.[58] Whatever the precise nature of Harrison's relationship with the CIA was at this point, he was exceptionally well placed for the purposes of both Mexico's Secretariat of Government and U.S. intelligence, most immediately the DEA, with which he was now in communication.

> Not coincidentally, the issue of the Contras and drugs flared up during some of the 1991–92 criminal trials of Camarena's alleged killers. A longtime CIA operative in Mexico, Lawrence Victor Harrison, testified that the CIA was then collaborating with the Mexican intelligence service and cartel bosses who were providing money, arms, and training facilities for the Contras in exchange for the CIA's protection of their drug enterprises.
>   Both Harrison and his DEA overseer, Hector Berréllez, who headed an investigation into Camarena's murder, believe the agent was killed because his investigations into some "protected" marijuana plantations threatened to disrupt or expose this marriage of convenience. Based on his investigation—which discovered the audiotapes his killers had made during their torture sessions—Berréllez recommended that a federal grand jury be convened to examine the CIA's knowledge of Camarena's murder. Soon afterwards, Berréllez, one of the DEA's most decorated agents, was transferred to Washington and given a do-nothing desk job until his retirement.[59]

These two paragraphs do not appear in the original hardcover edition of Gary Webb's *Dark Alliance* because Webb had not yet talked to Harrison and Berréllez. Sometime between the release of the two editions, Harrison and Berréllez met with Webb in San Jose, California, and shared significant bits of information with him. At the time, Harrison was attending law school in Fullerton, California, while Berréllez had retired from the DEA and was developing a private security firm called The Mayo Group (incorporated November 1998) in San Bernardino. The most sensitive piece of information they shared with Webb on that occasion was their belief that Enrique Camarena had been killed to prevent his exposure of CIA collusion with Mexican drug traffickers in support of the Nicaraguan *contras*. Equally noteworthy for our own Buendía investigation is Webb's description of Harrison as "a longtime CIA operative in Mexico" and of Berréllez as Harrison's "DEA overseer." Webb may have surmised from a careful reading of Harrison's court testimony that he was with the CIA, but he could not state that as a fact unless either Harrison himself or Berréllez had confirmed it for him. Based on our own experience with both men, we suspect that Berréllez did so, as he would for us several years later. Harrison, in turn, probably described Berréllez to Webb as his "overseer," which he would also do (dismissively) in conversations with us. While initially this overseer label may have been applied with a sense of humor between two veteran government agents, it nonetheless reflected a coercive relationship that in time would turn viral. Webb, for his part, inserted these two paragraphs into the revised paperback edition of *Dark Alliance* but did not add Berréllez and Harrison to the book's index, which for a while may have served to conceal the real content of their San Jose meeting from government secrecy enforcers.

Gary Webb was an accomplished investigative reporter who was hired away from the *Cleveland Plain Dealer* in 1987 by the *San Jose Mercury News* of San Jose, California. In August 1996, the *Mercury News* published a three-part, fifteen-thousand-word series by Webb titled "Dark Alliance," which chronicled the introduction and distribution of crack cocaine by California-based, CIA-linked, Nicaraguan drug traffickers, who in the 1980s had channeled some of their profits to the Reagan administration's proxy army of *contra* "freedom fighters." The series sparked an immediate scandal, with outraged blacks claiming that the CIA had targeted their communities, political activists denouncing CIA collusion with international drug traffickers to fund illegal military actions in Central America, and the agency itself breaking with established policy to publicly deny Webb's accusations.

Executive branch damage controllers pulled out all the stops to discredit the "Dark Alliance" series and Gary Webb personally. Congresswoman Maxine Waters excoriated the agency for the devastating impact of its actions on her congressional district in South Central Los Angeles and applauded Webb for his *Mercury News* exposé, while then CIA director John Deutch took the unprecedented step of attempting to defuse public outrage by personally addressing a town hall meeting in a South Central high school auditorium. It was, as Webb biographer Nick Schou describes it, "the first time in American history that a journalist had forced the director of the world's most powerful spy agency to perform in-person, street-level damage control."[60] In a shameful display of subservience to power, the primary newspapers of record—the *New York Times*, *Washington Post*, and *Los Angeles Times*—abetted Reagan administration damage controllers by dismissing Webb's series as unsubstantiated, based on unreliable sources, or simply untrue. Most offensive of all was when Webb's own editors caved to the media attacks and abandoned their own well-proven star reporter, refusing to stand behind him, then pulling him from investigative assignments and exiling him to the paper's outlying Cupertino bureau in Silicon Valley.

To paraphrase a sixteenth-century bard, we thought the CIA protested too much and that all the furor over Gary Webb's *Mercury News* series linking the influx of crack cocaine to the CIA and the Nicaraguan *contras* only lent credence to what Webb was reporting. What he could not do in the limited space allotted by his editors, namely, share his evidence with his readers, he did in spades when he published his five-hundred-plus-page book two years later. We purchased the hardcover first edition as soon as it was released and were immediately struck by an opaque reference to Manuel Buendía within the first twenty pages. Webb there recounts a conversation he had with a San Francisco Bay Area businessman by the name of Denis Ainsworth, who had been a *contra* supporter until he discovered their ties to drug trafficking, at which point he alerted federal authorities and then, by his account, "had his life ruined."

Ainsworth was trying to dissuade Webb from pursuing his investigation. In response to Webb's assurance that he knew what he was doing, Ainsworth replied that he really had no idea at all. "Believe me," he insisted, "you don't understand. I almost got killed. I had friends in Central America who were killed. There was a Mexican reporter [Manuel Buendía] who was looking into one end of this, and he wound up dead. So don't pretend that you know."[61]

In August 1998, after reading *Dark Alliance*, we contacted Webb at his office in Sacramento, where he had secured a well-paying job as an investigator for the California Joint Legislative Audit Committee. In the course of a phone conversation, Gary suggested that Peter Dale Scott might be able to provide additional information about Ainsworth, then alerted us to an article by Charles Bowden about his own case in the latest issue of *Esquire* magazine.[62] The Bowden article, announced at the upper edge of the magazine's cover with the intriguing hook "Cocaine, the CIA, and a Good Man Destroyed," was a major piece illustrated with two dramatic black-and-white portraits by photographer Brad Wilson, one of Webb and the other of Héctor Berréllez, who, Bowden wrote, "had stumbled onto Gary Webb's story years before Gary Webb knew a thing about it." When Berréllez read the "Dark Alliance" series in the fall of 1996, his immediate reaction was "This shit is true." He knew it was true from his years as a DEA S/A and, above all, from his experience as G/S of the DEA's Camarena investigation, where to his surprise and consternation he discovered how deeply the CIA had penetrated the DEA. Webb, he concluded, was doomed. Gary "had hit a sensitive area, and for it he would be attacked and disbelieved."[63]

We wanted to talk to Héctor Berréllez, to which end Webb put us in touch with Chuck Bowden, who facilitated the contact. At that point, however, Berréllez was sorting out his life as a newly retired DEA agent and had too many things on his mind to talk with us. We traveled to Los Angeles the second week of November 1998 to meet with attorneys Ed Medvene and Michael Lightfoot and, while there, contacted Berréllez to see if we might meet with him as well. He tentatively agreed, then begged off, saying he was too busy just then to see us, that we should call him the next time we were in the Los Angeles area.

We met with Medvene and Lightfoot over lunch at the trendy Pinot Café in downtown Los Angeles—their invite. We updated them on our Buendía investigation and discussed various aspects of the case related to former Mexican government secretary Manuel Bartlett Díaz, whom Lightfoot was then representing. On the recommendation of former U.S. ambassador to Mexico John Gavin, Bartlett had retained Lightfoot to clear his name of allegations made by government witnesses in the 1990–1992 Camarena trials linking him to Camarena's 1985 death in Guadalajara.[64] Bartlett, Lightfoot confirmed, was going to seek the Mexican presidency in the 2000 elections and needed to remove the cloud of the Camarena affair from his candidacy. Lightfoot's strategy was to persuade the U.S. Attorney's Office for the Central District of California to pursue perjury charges against Jorge Godoy and René López Romero, the two witnesses who had implicated Bartlett. Given the time constraints and, perhaps most important, the political ends served by the Camarena trials, we thought that strategy unlikely to succeed.

We were struck, moreover, by what seemed to be Lightfoot's unmitigated naïveté about his celebrity client. While recognizing that people often deceive their attorneys, he told us, he had never before had a client "who so completely convinced him of his truthfulness." The same was true of Lightfoot's private investigator, John Brown, with whom we met the following day. Brown described to us how, when he arrived in Mexico City for meetings with Bartlett, he would be flown by helicopter to Puebla, where Bartlett was then serving as state governor. He had met with Bartlett perhaps a dozen times, he said, and had also witnessed interviews where journalists had asked the governor hard-hitting questions about his alleged role in the Camarena affair—questions, Brown told us, that Bartlett had answered "consistently and persuasively." Lightfoot's task on Bartlett's behalf did not relate directly to the Buendía case, but the governor's ability to beguile Lightfoot and his private investigator appealed to the same gullibility initially displayed by Ángel Buendía in his dealings with Bartlett.[65]

We asked Lightfoot if it would be possible for us to interview Bartlett. In light of the governor's pending presidential bid, he thought probably not. Might Bartlett consider responding to written questions about the Buendía case? Lightfoot said he would inquire and get back to us, which he never did.

Both Lightfoot and Medvene were surprised to learn that we were in touch with Héctor Berréllez, as they thought he had relocated to Florida or somewhere in the East following the Camarena trials. Curiously, Lightfoot asked that, "for his sake," we not mention our meeting to Berréllez. We, in turn, asked if either of them knew what had become of Lawrence Harrison. Lightfoot said he had heard that Harrison was studying law somewhere in Ventura County, California. We subsequently conducted a Ventura search for Harrison but failed to turn up any trace of him. Eventually, in the spring of 2004, it occurred to us that if Harrison had by chance earned a law degree in the intervening years, he might have been admitted to the California bar. A quick search of the CalBar website revealed that to be the case and gave us Harrison's contact information in San Dimas, California.

On April Fools' Day 2004, Russell mailed a letter to Harrison briefly explaining who we were, how we had come to be investigating the Buendía assassination, and our wish to discuss the case with him in person. Seven days later, at nine o'clock in the evening, he telephoned us at home. He was soft-spoken and polite, addressing Russell as "Mr. Bartley" and "Sir," but seemed pretty tightly wound. It was the first of many of what he would call "coded" conversations—seemingly disconnected, all but indecipherable, torrents of talk mixed with discrete bits of pertinent information. Speaking, no doubt, for what he had to assume were other ears on the line, Harrison launched into a boilerplate *Red Dawn*, "communist menace from the south" discourse about the Sandinistas seeking Soviet missiles, Mig-29s, and Hind helicopter gunships in Nicaragua, and the Reagan administration having correctly been concerned about a growing Soviet presence in Central America. He dismissed Manuel Buendía as "a sorry old man who made his living by publishing the names of CIA agents." Buendía was used, he said, and had been killed on orders of an intelligence service in reprisal for having so disrupted its operations in Mexico that Israel's Mossad had to take them over on the service's behalf.

"You say that Buendía's death was ordered by 'the intelligence service,'" Russell commented, plainly referring to the CIA.

"No, I did not say that."

"But you did," Russell insisted. "Which intelligence service?"

"I can't say. Are you kidding? I want to live!"

In this disconnected, all over the map, half-hour conversation, Harrison stated (presumably for the benefit of anyone listening in) that Buendía's assassination "wasn't about badges," "wasn't about drugs," and "wasn't about arms." In other words, it wasn't about the CIA, the *contras*, or Mexican drug traffickers. But in fact he had subtly linked these denials to specific hypotheses about possible motives for the assassination rather than ruling out the much thornier geopolitical motive some of us suspected from the outset, which Harrison would himself proceed to confirm for us over the next several years. His mention of "badges" referred to revelations that DFS chief Zorrilla Pérez had provided directorate credentials (*charolas*) to Guadalajara cartel kingpins, which fed the hypothesis that Buendía had been killed to prevent him from exposing the Zorrilla-trafficker connection. Harrison's assertion on the phone that Buendía's assassination "wasn't about drugs" implied that it wasn't about the Zorrilla-trafficker-DFS *charola* scandal, not that drug trafficking played no role at all.

Similarly, Harrison linked his assertion that the assassination "wasn't about arms" to an earlier statement that it "had nothing to do with German arms dealers in Guadalajara," that is, with Gerhard Mertins, leaving open the possibility that it had much to do with the covert flow of arms to the *contras* in collusion with major Mexican narcotics traffickers. In what at first might have been interpreted as a bit of disconnected storytelling but actually was a key piece of information, he described a diamond-studded pin depicting the official seal of the United States worn by Rafael Caro Quintero and recounted how Caro's cartel partner, Ernesto Fonseca, had flaunted his support of the Nicaraguan *contras*. Fonseca had even challenged Harrison about his own views on the *contra* operation, he remarked dismissively, while Caro's ostentatious display of the U.S. seal was offensive—as much for its reflection of a real relationship between the U.S. government and Mexican drug traffickers, he implied, as for Caro's delusional claim to American-guaranteed impunity.

In essence, although it would take us time to decipher his coded message, Harrison informed us in that initial conversation that the Buendía case had to do with narcotics trafficking, the Nicaraguan *contras*, and the CIA, as well as the DFS and Israel's Mossad. He had also made oblique reference to the Álvarez Macháin abduction, which seemed to suggest a link to the Kiki Camarena case, as both he and Operation Leyenda G/S Héctor Berréllez would soon confirm to us. Harrison concluded his call by saying he was willing to meet with us; that he would "tell us the story once, without a recorder, and not for attribution"; that "there were things that weighed on his mind"; and that "he wanted to tell someone the truth" about the Buendía killing. He had known Buendía's assassin personally, he remarked, "and had only recently sold one of the motorcycles used in the assassination." He gave us his phone number and e-mail address, and we said we would contact him as soon as we had made travel arrangements.[66]

15

Prohibited Conversations

I just cannot do the things I feel are right. I have, and had then, a duty to the country which conflicted with my greater duty to the truth. And I revere the truth. As I get older, I value the truth more than the other, but look where I am now: stubborn, broke, endangered for telling only a portion of the truth, and *pendejo*.

—Lawrence Victor Harrison, e-mail to Russell H. Bartley (23 January 2010)

ON FRIDAY, 14 MAY 2004, we drove the 160 winding miles across California's northern Coast Ranges from our home in Mendocino County to Sacramento International Airport, caught a Southwest Airlines flight to Ontario, California, and checked into the Airport Ramada Ltd. It was a little past 7:00 p.m. when we called Harrison, and he proposed that we meet that same evening at his San Dimas law office, a few miles west of Ontario via the San Bernardino Freeway and I-210. Downtown San Dimas had been gentrified into a pleasant tree-lined stretch of two-story buildings containing shops, restaurants, and professional offices typical of other upscale California communities. Harrison's office was located at 120 W. Bonita Avenue. It occupied a second-floor suite (no. 212) accessed from a common patio shared with an adjacent professional building. A directory board on the patio listed Suite 212 as The Mayo Group, Héctor Berréllez's private security and investigative agency, for which Harrison served as corporate attorney. No names were included on the board, but Harrison did have a law office listing in the San Dimas telephone directory. His home was forty highway miles away in Riverside.

Suite 212 comprised two interior rooms and a spacious outer office. There were two exterior doors, both open when we arrived. The number 212 was on a door leading to the suite's inner rooms, through which we entered. One room contained a few office furnishings, the other a large-screen television. On this occasion, they were occupied by two of Harrison's teenage daughters and his Mexican wife, Lorena. We entered Harrison's office through a door in the corner opposite his desk, where he was seated as we came in. He stood and greeted us with a full but reserved handshake, then invited us to occupy two upholstered chairs facing the desk. He wore a brown suit with a white polo shirt open at the neck. His overall physical appearance fit the descriptions we had heard and read in connection with the Camarena trials: tall, substantial build with some excess weight in the midsection, brown eyes, receding and graying brown hair.

The office was appointed with quality furniture and numerous items of decor reflective of Harrison's attachment to Mexico. He sat behind a finely crafted wooden desk in a high-backed, tapestry-upholstered, executive-style chair that comfortably accommodated his lanky frame. This primary work space was set apart in a recessed area of the office's interior wall, away from the windows, which opened onto the outside balcony and patio area below. The door to the suite's interior rooms was situated immediately to Harrison's left and could be quickly reached in one continuous motion from where he sat behind his desk, as we ourselves observed when, at one point during that initial interview, he suddenly decided to retrieve some photographs from one of the other rooms. These physical details—placement of the suite number, work area situated away from windows, ready exit close at hand—appeared to be elementary security precautions, although over the next several years we would observe puzzling lapses in Harrison's sensitivity to security issues that ultimately would bring him to a bad end.

On the wall immediately behind his desk were four framed legal documents, including his Western State University College of Law degree and his certificate of admission to the California State Bar (9 November 1999). On the recessed wall just to his left hung a large framed print of Pancho Villa and Emiliano Zapata; on the opposite wall hung a large framed print of Frida Kahlo's 1931 portrait of Diego Rivera and herself holding hands (a celebration of their marriage two years before), together with a second print from Rivera's "Woman with Calla Lilies" series.

A black nineteen-inch flat-screen monitor sat next to a silver and blue scanner on a computer table behind his desk. On another surface to his right and behind him were two framed photographs: one a close-up of himself and his wife at their Mexico City wedding; the second of their eldest daughter, Cristina, which he proudly handed to us for a closer look. Also on that surface was a ceramic figurine of the Virgin of Guadalupe.

Against the west wall of the office stood the obligatory lawyer's bookcase filled with legal tomes. On top of the bookcase were sundry artifacts and objets d'art. On the wall immediately to its left hung a framed print of Zapata with a rifle. Against the east wall behind us as we sat facing Harrison was a leather sofa. The two windows above the sofa were covered with closed white blinds. To one side of the adjacent office door stood a low, ornately carved, wooden table on which were a lamp and a large amethyst.

We spoke for two and a half hours that gentle spring evening. Rather than the one-time encounter that Harrison had intimated in our initial phone conversation, where he would tell us "off the record" what he knew about the Buendía case and then have no further contact with us, it proved to be but the first in an open-ended series of conversations and other communications spanning the next ten years. Much of the evening was spent in an intricate verbal dance of mutual evaluation, in which Harrison sought to gain a sense of how informed we were about Mexico and how serious our Buendía investigation was, while we took our own measure of him as a credible source. We would not gain any insight into his life story and the personality it had engendered for several years, but, in hindsight, we now can see clearly the underlying psychology of the discursive pattern he imposed on that first and subsequent conversations with us. It was a continuation of the confrontational attitude he had exhibited toward his school-teachers, where Russell's status as an academic immediately invited challenge. It quickly became apparent that he had read widely about history from ancient to modern times, that he had a special fascination with the exploits of prominent historical personages from Alexander the Great to Adolf Hitler, and that he held a traditional "great man" view of history conceived primarily as a continuum of political and military events.

This carried over to his view of Mexican history, as reflected by the iconic figures adorning his law office walls, although he did seem to have a more nuanced sense of history as social process in the case of Mexico. Harrison was keenly aware, for example, of the role played by family ties in determining the loyalties and actions of key Mexican figures during the twenty years he lived there. Two or three times in the course of our interview he digressed to probe "the professor's" knowledge of Mexican history—all part of his evaluation of us, we supposed, and of our ability to contextualize the information he was providing. But it also had the feel of "*el profe* and the spy," where the spy, not the professor, was the one who really knew what had transpired in Mexico—or indeed the world—as he would continue to engage Russell over the next several years in what amounted to an ongoing game of historical "trivial pursuit."

Still assuming that this might be our only opportunity to interview Harrison, we focused our questioning on three areas critical to our investigation: his personal background, who he knew in Mexico, and the Buendía assassination. He confirmed some of the biographical particulars he had recounted in his court testimony and added a few additional details for us. Among the individuals he had known or met while in Mexico, he named Manuel Bartlett Díaz, José Antonio Zorrilla Pérez, Florentino Ventura Gutiérrez, Miguel Aldana Ibarra, Jorge Carranza, Miguel Nazar Haro, Enrique Camarena, Ed Heath, Félix Rodríguez (aka "Dr." Max Gómez), Barry Seal, and Amiram Nir. As for Manuel Buendía, he assured us that the assassination had been planned more than a month in advance; that he had known beforehand it was going to happen, as did "many others" in Mexico's state security apparatus; and, most astonishing of all, that he personally had acquired one of the motorcycles used in the assassination, had shipped it to California when he returned to the United States in 1990, and only recently had disposed of it.

In response to that leading assertion, we asked Harrison directly who was behind the slaying of Manuel Buendía. "Forget Zorrilla," we posed. "Forget Bartlett. Who actually ordered the Buendía assassination?"

"Ollie North!" he exclaimed.

His reply came forcefully, unhesitatingly, with a steely gaze and suddenly hardened expression on his face. Col. Oliver North and his representatives, including veteran CIA operative Félix Rodríguez, Harrison averred, were the Reagan administration's primary channel to the Guadalajara cartel in its off-the-shelf, drugs-for-arms *contra* resupply operation. North, he believed, was also behind the September 1984 PJJ ambush that had nearly cost him his life.

At their first meeting on February 24, 1982, in Oklahoma City, Oliver North and [Terry] Reed had discovered they were cut from the same cloth. They had lived parallel lives, served their country in parallel ways and had been the victim of parallel lies from the nation's leaders who had sent men to die and then sat back to debate its morality. . . . Although neither realized it at the time, they were patriotic time bombs produced in the same Cold War factory.[1]

Harrison's mention of Félix Rodríguez and Barry Seal alludes to yet another *contra*-related operation that executive branch damage controllers were intent on covering up and that here requires a contextual digression in order to establish the significance of what Harrison was telling us, namely, that the CIA was using the Mena, Arkansas, Inter-Mountain Regional Airport and adjacent Ouachita National Forest as transshipment sites for arms, cocaine, and drug money, as well as the clandestine training of *contra* pilots.[2] Seal was a renowned aviator and drug smuggler turned government informant who had flown for the CIA since the 1960s and, in the early 1980s, appears to have combined agency assignments with profitable under-the-radar flights for the Medellín cartel. A 1963 posed photograph taken at a Mexico City nightclub places him in the company of Félix Rodríguez, Pentagon contract pilot William Robert "Tosh" Plumlee, and CIA clandestine service officer Porter J. Goss, together with six other men thought to be involved in joint CIA-Pentagon scheming to assassinate Fidel Castro and overthrow Cuba's revolutionary government.[3]

It appears to have been Seal who, in 1981, first scoped out the facilities at Inter-Mountain Regional Airport, then initiated the *contra* support operation at Mena. Two years later Col. Oliver North enlisted the services of Terry Kent Reed to assist Seal with the Mena operation. Reed was a former Air Force intelligence officer with a top security clearance, commercial pilot's license, and experience as a machine tool consultant. North, representing the CIA under the alias John Cathey, contracted Reed to develop and run the *contra* training facility at Nella, a dozen miles north of Mena. Reed would train two groups of Nicaraguan "freedom flyers" in the techniques of aerial resupply, precision airdrops, and night landings, then embark on a plan to create a CIA proprietary in Mexico that would move the core of the Arkansas operation out of the United States.

At the end of August 1985, on instructions from North, Reed met in Veracruz with Félix Rodríguez to discuss the proposed proprietary. In broad outlines, Reed was to develop a business plan for a foreign-owned firm to import machine tools for the de la Madrid administration's proposed modernization of Mexico's aging industrial infrastructure. At Reed's suggestion, it would be a joint venture with Japanese and Hungarian partners he knew from previous business dealings, who, in addition to enhancing the proposed proprietary's cover, offered the added benefit of access to Chinese and Soviet bloc arms suppliers. Rodríguez, for his part, assured Reed that, given Mexico's pressing need for high-tech machine tools, he would be able to secure an official waiver of the otherwise obligatory 51 percent Mexican ownership law.[4]

Three months later Barry Seal flew Reed to an out of the way airfield in Chagres, Panama, for a follow-up meeting with Seal's CIA case officer Leroy Tracta, Félix Rodríguez, and a fifth individual who, "for security reasons," was identified to Reed only as "a representative of another government who may wish to become involved in the

Mexico operation." The mystery person, it later developed, was Amiram Nir. The trip from Arkansas to Panama began with Reed and Seal, each flying identical twin-engine Cessnas, rendezvousing after midnight over Tennessee, then performing a dangerous precision maneuver that had the effect on air traffic control radar monitors of allowing Reed's Cessna to seamlessly replace Seal's aircraft, while Seal continued on undetected to Dallas, Texas. Reed followed Seal's original flight plan to Greenville, Mississippi, landed, and then flew back to Little Rock, Arkansas, where he caught a 6:00 a.m. Southwest Airlines flight to Dallas.

The point of this elaborate disappearing act was for Barry Seal to elude the FBI and other federal agencies monitoring his narcotics-trafficking activities so he could carry out an assignment for the CIA. It also served to conceal Reed's presence on the Panama trip. Reed caught up with Seal at Love Field in Dallas, where Seal kept a Lear Jet, and by 8:00 a.m. they were airborne again, with Reed at the controls. While en route to Brownsville, Texas, Seal handed Reed a pilot's license and voter registration card in the name of Emile Camp, an agency contract pilot recently killed in an aviation accident, and explained to him that when they landed to refuel, he was to use those documents to file a flight plan to Campeche, Mexico. Airborne again over the Gulf of Mexico, Reed was astonished to discover that Seal's Lear Jet was equipped with the most advanced avionics, which allowed them to fly to any destination without the assistance of air traffic controllers and even gave Seal the ability, in coordination with army intelligence personnel based at secret military tracking stations, to exit and enter U.S. air space undetected by American early warning satellites. With the assistance of one such secret facility at Guantánamo, Cuba, Seal and Reed vanished from the monitors of Mexican air traffic controllers just as they surreptitiously departed U.S. air space, proceeding below the radar to El Salvador's Ilopango Air Force Base for refueling, thence to Howard Air Force Base in Panama.[5]

Whatever doubts Terry Reed might have had about how highly connected Barry Seal actually was, they were quickly put to rest by the ease with which Seal accessed these restricted military air traffic communications channels and by what that implied about the level of authority approving his missions. "Seal got his flight plan authorizations not from someone on the ground, like most pilots," Reed observed, "but from satellites out in space." The same holds for our own appraisal of Reed as a witness to these extraordinary clandestine activities. His Air Force intelligence training and experience uniquely qualified him to observe, record, and report all that he witnessed as a CIA asset immersed in the Reagan administration's shadow *contra* war against Nicaragua's Sandinista government. As he himself expressed it, "I was a paid intelligence professional. I was recruited, selected, trained and compensated in great part for my ability to organize facts, events, analyze motives and mentally retain them." The complexity, coherence, and other internal evidence of his account make it a far more persuasive document than subsequent government efforts to discredit it.[6]

On Wednesday evening, 19 February 1986, Barry Seal was machine-gunned to death by two Colombian hit men outside a Salvation Army halfway house in Baton Rouge, Louisiana. Unbeknownst to Reed at the time, Seal had been performing a precarious juggling act with several agencies of the federal government whose respective agendas often conflicted. In 1983 he had been indicted for smuggling a load of Quaaludes into Florida and traded a ten-year suspended prison sentence for cooperation with the DEA in its operations against the Medellín cartel. This led to the elaborate plan to fabricate an ostensible link between Colombian cocaine traffickers and Nicaragua's Sandinista government, consummated on 25 June 1984 when Seal and his CIA copilot, Emile Camp, landed a camera-equipped C-123K cargo plane at a small airstrip outside Managua, snapped grainy photographs of more than half a ton of cocaine being loaded onto the plane, then flew the film and illicit cargo back to Homestead Air Force Base in Florida.

Although this had been a DEA operation, when, following Seal's return to Florida, the head of the DEA's cocaine desk, Ron Caffrey, met with Oliver North and Dewey Clarridge, head of the CIA's Latin America Division, to inform them of the Nicaraguan sting, he was surprised to learn that they already knew about it and had even seen copies of the photos Seal had taken. North wanted to publicize the sting in order to influence an upcoming congressional vote on support for the *contras*, which Caffrey strongly opposed, arguing that it would compromise DEA operations against the Medellín cartel and make Seal a cartel target for assassination. Details of the mission were nonetheless leaked to the media and Seal, now exposed, returned to flying for the CIA out of Mena.

In December 1984, he was arrested for smuggling marijuana into the state of Louisiana and agreed to serve as a government witness against Medellín cartel defendants in exchange for a guilty plea and light sentence. He testified in three separate trials during 1985, all the while free on bail and continuing to sandwich in his agency work, including the December flight to Panama with Terry Reed. While the understanding with the court had been that, in return for his testimony, Seal would not be incarcerated, he and his attorneys were stunned when the presiding judge ordered him to remain at the Salvation Army halfway house from 6:00 p.m. to 6:00 a.m. for the first six months of 1986. It was, they presciently protested, tantamount to a death sentence.[7]

The version of Seal's death circulated by the administration and carried in the media was that he had been killed by the Medellín cartel in reprisal for his undercover work and court testimony. But there has been much doubt about this scenario. Seal was an intelligence and law enforcement asset, and assets are expendable. While for an accountant, Reed notes, liabilities are red numbers on a spread sheet that can be offset, when an asset like Barry Seal becomes a liability, he cannot simply be "offset." He must be "erased." Seal knew too much, Reed and others have observed. "Four federal agencies, a governor, an attorney-general, at least two foreign governments, the Medellín Cartel and 50 or 60 individuals" had a motive to kill him.[8]

The big question remains. Why was he so blatantly exposed in Baton Rouge? Why did his executive branch handlers turn him into a "clay pigeon," as Seal referred to his court-imposed nighttime confinement to the Salvation Army halfway house? Similar questions arise about the aviation mishap that killed Seal's friend and CIA copilot, Emile Camp, six months after the two had flown the Nicaraguan sting operation. Camp, who was involved in Reed's "freedom flyer" training program at Nella, inexplicably struck a peak in the Ouachita Mountains near Mena while piloting a Seneca aircraft equipped with state-of-the-art navigational gear. Camp, close associates believed, had been the victim of sabotage. He was, they noted suggestively, a witness to Seal's secret activities for the CIA and DEA.[9]

There are striking similarities between the personalities of Barry Seal and Lawrence Harrison. Seal's ability "to handle his handlers," Reed observed, "had not gone unnoticed by his handlers," or "GS pukes," as Seal dismissively referred to them. Like Harrison, Seal appears to have thought he was more astute than his handlers and that his ultimate guarantee of personal immunity lay in the secrets he possessed. What you know can be power, he once remarked to Reed, just as Harrison seemed to think that information he had gleaned from his electronic espionage in Mexico amounted to his own life insurance policy. Although Seal seems to have been a self-serving opportunist, while Harrison appears to have been guided by an ethical compass, both men deluded themselves that they were smarter than their spymasters, and each suffered fatal consequences.[10]

One night in March 1986 Reed attended a critical meeting at Camp Joseph T. Robinson, a former World War II army base now serving as an Arkansas National Guard training facility in North Little Rock. Also present were Oliver North, Félix Rodríguez, Governor Bill Clinton, Clinton's chief economic adviser and liaison for local CIA operations Bob Nash, resident agency officer Akihide Sawahata, and William P. Barr (aka Robert Johnson),[11] previously identified to Reed as chief counsel for the CIA proprietary Southern Air Transport and, on this occasion, sent by the agency to chair what was to be an operational briefing for the pending Mexico operation, code-named Screw Worm. It was a clandestine gathering convened in an empty Camp Robinson ammunition storage bunker that would, as Reed describes it, "change the complexion of the secret American policy in Central America."[12]

With Clinton and Nash present (Nash was expected, Clinton apparently was not), the initial piece of business was to lay the groundwork for pulling CIA operations out of Arkansas and relocating them to Mexico. A particularly problematic aspect of those operations was the laundering of large sums of *contra*-related, cocaine-generated cash through the Arkansas Development Finance Authority, a Clinton-created, full-service, state financial body dealing in low-interest bonds that was managed from the governor's office with no legislative oversight. Legitimate loans, Reed and Cummings explain, were what Arkansas needed "to underwrite industrial development bonds at low interest rates to attract business to the state. If Arkansas allowed the CIA to guarantee its loans by collateralizing its industrial bonds with dirty, offshore money, the interest from the loan which is repaid in the form of clean money by the borrower, has in reality accomplished the goal of generating clean money from dirty money." Serious irregularities benefiting an entrenched coterie of Little Rock banking and political cronies, however, threatened to compromise covert agency activities to such a degree that it was deemed necessary to terminate them.[13]

After a testy discussion that put matters in their most pragmatic political perspective, Clinton and Nash were excused from the top secret, exclusively need-to-know meeting, whose remaining participants then reviewed details of Operation Screw Worm, a code name taken as an added layer of cover from a CIA operation run a dozen years earlier to covertly photomap Mexican territory from the air. Reed had already firmed up the participation of his Japanese and Hungarian business partners for the new CIA proprietary, Maquinaria Internacional, S.A., which would conduct its *contra* gunrunning cover business from a leased warehouse facility at the Guadalajara airport. The Mexicans had been persuaded to waive their majority national ownership requirement, agreeing in this instance to 100 percent foreign ownership. Fifty-five percent of the new company's stock was to be held by Southern Air Transport, 25 percent by Terry Reed, and 10 percent each by the Japanese and Hungarian investors.[14]

Having been described by North as a "star" agency asset, Reed was given the adolescent code name Señor Estrella. It was explained to him that he had now entered that gray zone where assets operate without a written contract and are purposely kept at arm's length for reasons of plausible deniability—their own and the agency's. Félix Rodríguez would be in charge of his and his family's personal security while they were in Mexico, with the caveat that in an emergency the agency would be unable to intervene overtly so as not to expose their cover. The only other in-country persons knowledgeable about Reed's undercover role would be his CIA handler, Mitch Marr, and the U.S. consul general in Guadalajara. Reed agreed to be in place by the first of July 1986.

Still troubled by Barry Seal's violent demise, however, and fully aware of his own vulnerability as a deniable agency asset ("illegals don't exist," in Lawrence Harrison's words), Reed had serious second thoughts about relocating to Mexico. He was most concerned about endangering his wife and two young sons and, not long after the Camp Robinson meeting, actually decided to back out of the Mexico venture altogether. He informed Clinton's assistant Bob Nash of his decision and the reasons for it. Nash promised to inform both Clinton and Oliver North. One evening a week later, by Reed's account, Nash approached Reed at a Little Rock restaurant and asked him to step outside for a word with the governor, who was sitting at the curb in his official security van. Clinton told Reed that North and the agency were "leaning on him" to persuade Reed to reconsider his decision and accept the Mexico assignment, that they were counting on him, and that it was a mistake to pass up the opportunity, an "attractive opportunity" that he, Clinton, wished he could accept in Reed's place. Clinton, apparently, was sufficiently persuasive on this occasion to change Reed's mind. By the end of June, he and his family had relocated to Lake Chapala, Jalisco.[15]

The next fourteen months were a roller coaster of unanticipated events, in the course of which Terry Reed became an asset who knew too much as the Iran-Contra scandal inexorably unraveled before congressional committees, in the U.S. press, and on American television. Three and a half months after Reed arrived in Mexico, an old friend and fellow CIA pilot, Bill Cooper, was shot down and killed while flying a *contra* resupply mission over Nicaragua. Cooper, whom Reed had known since their days together in Southeast Asia during the Vietnam War and who had also flown missions in and out of Mena while Reed was there training Nicaraguan "freedom flyers," had been piloting Barry Seal's former "Fat Lady" C-123K aircraft when his plane was brought down by a handheld surface-to-air missile. While Cooper and his copilot, Wallace "Buzz" Sawyer, both perished in the crash, their cargo kicker, Eugene Hasenfus, parachuted safely to the ground, was captured by Sandinista soldiers, and revealed the CIA link to the *contra* resupply flights. Back in Mexico, Operation Screw Worm was immediately put on hold, and Reed was instructed to take an extended vacation trip with his family.

By December 1986, it was decided that Screw Worm had not been compromised, and Reed received instructions to meet Félix Rodríguez at a hotel in Mexico City's Zona Rosa. When Reed arrived for the meeting, he found that Rodríguez was accompanied by the same unidentified individual who had been present at the Panama meeting he and Barry Seal had attended in November 1985, now introduced to him as "Pat Weber" but who in reality was Amiram Nir. Because of the fallout from the "Fat Lady" shootdown in Nicaragua and mounting congressional pressure in Washington, Rodríguez explained, it was essential that they bring the agency's proprietary facility at the Guadalajara airport into full operation immediately, as well as implementing the second phase of Operation Screw Worm, which entailed the covert manufacture of *contra* weapons. Given the sophistication of the machine tools required for such manufacture and the technical demands of setting up a viable assembly line, Reed thought it would take them at least a year to achieve actual production. That was why "Weber" had joined them, Rodríguez replied. "His people could make things happen fast in Mexico."

"His people," Nir now informed Reed, were the Israeli government. What Reed and the agency needed at that particular moment, he suggested, was a Mexican equivalent of the earlier arrangement they had worked out in Arkansas: a supportive state government "with a governor desperate to make things happen quickly for his impoverished state." That state, Nir proposed, was Michoacán. And that governor was none other than Cuahutémoc Cárdenas. Both he and Rodríguez, Nir added, "had friends in high places in Michoacán." As for Cárdenas, he had "high political ambitions" and could be counted on to cooperate. Indeed, in the coming months Cárdenas would promote a "democratic current" within the PRI to challenge the established practice of the *dedazo*, whereby the sitting president named the party's next official presidential candidate, at the time the seriously challenged PRI candidate Carlos Salinas de Gortari, in the 1988 presidential election as a breakaway contender under the banner of a newly formed "Democratic Front" coalition.

Cárdenas's six-year gubernatorial term had in fact ended by the time Nir, Rodríguez, and Reed met to discuss these matters in December 1986, but he remained the most influential political personage in Michoacán and was still able to deliver the kind of infrastructural support they required for Operation Screw Worm. Despite Rodríguez's characteristic bravado and offensively inflated sense of himself, Nir appeared to preside over their Zona Rosa meeting. He assured Reed that "his people" had experience with the technical requirements of military arms manufacture, could bring phase two of Screw Worm on line quickly, and proposed to do so at the Morelia airport. He, not Rodríguez, then instructed Reed to be at the remote Lake Zirahuén mountain resort twenty kilometers outside Pátzcuaro on 5 January 1987 for a clandestine meeting with "Cárdenas and others."

By Reed's remarkable yet plausible account, Cárdenas arrived at the appointed time and place aboard a white Bell HH-53 helicopter bearing the official Mexican insignia and escorted in close formation by four camouflaged Hughes-500D choppers, one of which was piloted by Félix Rodríguez. Accompanying Cárdenas was Barry Seal's former

CIA handler Leroy Tracta, Israeli agent Amiram Nir, and the mayor of Morelia, together with a retinue of aides and security personnel. The core group was transported by boat to Cárdenas's private retreat on a wooded island in the lake, where they were treated to a gourmet meal before turning to the primary purpose of that extraordinary gathering: the logistics of Operation Screw Worm. Reed briefed the group on the operation's technical requirements and infrastructural needs, including runway upgrades at the Morelia airport, a new electrical substation, and an earthquake-resistant structure in which to house the proposed arms-manufacturing facility.

To Reed's surprise, Cárdenas and Tracta appeared to be well acquainted. The two men had conversed easily and at length apart from the others when they first arrived at the governor's island retreat, and following the meal the CIA officer had actually moderated the Screw Worm discussion. Nir, too, it seemed to Reed, was a known quantity and had also interacted easily with Cárdenas. By afternoon's end, there appeared to be full accord on the immediate establishment of a major *contra* support facility in the state capital of Michoacán.[16]

Six months later a new eight-thousand-foot runway had been completed at Morelia's Gen. Francisco J. Mujica Airport, the new electrical substation had been installed, and construction was progressing apace on the building to house the arms factory, while the Israelis, who were in charge of actual production, had already custom designed a trial weapon that would test every facet of the sophisticated manufacturing process: a Striker short-barreled, twelve-round, semiautomatic 12-gauge shotgun for close combat situations. It was, Nir informed Reed, a weapon the Israeli military hoped to add to its own arsenal, implying that Nicaragua would provide a good place to field test it. Also in this same period, Reed completed the necessary paperwork for Maquinaria Industrial's Guadalajara International Airport facility and Southern Air Transport L-100 aircraft (the civilian version of the military C-130) had begun moving illicit *contra*-related cargoes through the Jalisco state capital.

By August 1987, CIA director William Casey had died of a brain tumor, Oliver North and Félix Rodríguez had both testified before the televised congressional Iran-Contra hearings, and Judge Lawrence E. Walsh had been appointed independent counsel to investigate the Iran-Contra affair, while on the ground in Mexico Operation Screw Worm was rapidly spiraling out of control. In March of that year, several crates inexplicably marked machine tools were shipped to Laredo, Texas, under the export license of Terry Reed's Hungarian associates in Mexico City but with the CIA proprietary Maquinaria Industrial's name on the shipping manifest. Neither Reed nor the Hungarians knew anything about the crates, as the purpose of their association was to import machine tools into Mexico, not export them to the United States. On closer examination, the crates were found to contain cocaine, which moved the Hungarians to terminate their business relationship with Maquinaria Industrial. Then, in July, Reed discovered a large, neatly packaged cocaine shipment concealed in Southern Air Transport cargo being moved through his Maquinaria Industrial warehouse at the Guadalajara airport. Appalled, disillusioned, and now seriously concerned for his own and his family's future, he parlayed carefully sequestered evidentiary samples from that shipment into a substantial severance payment from the agency and by October had dropped from sight in the United States. For the next several years, executive branch damage controllers conducted a full-bore campaign to discredit Reed as an eyewitness to their criminal activities in defense of "the national interest," first by prosecuting him (unsuccessfully) on fabricated charges of insurance fraud, then by means of a slanderous media attack qualitatively analogous to the one Gary Webb would suffer some years later.

Oral deposition by Richard J. Brenneke regarding Central America, drug trafficking and CIA activities in the State of Arkansas, taken in Little Rock on 21 June 1991 by Rep. William Alexander, Jr. and Chad Farris, Chief Deputy Attorney General for the State of Arkansas, as part of a joint investigation conducted by the U.S. Congress and the Arkansas State Attorney General's Office to develop evidence for Special Prosecutor Lawrence Walsh's Iran-Contra inquiry.[17]

. . .

WILLIAM ALEXANDER, JR.: So you were an independent contractor with the Central Intelligence Agency?

RICHARD J. BRENNEKE: That's correct.

Q: Beginning when and through what years?

A: 1968 through about 1986. Somewhere in 1985–'86 is when I called it off.

Q: So what services did you perform for the Central Intelligence Agency?

A: Specialized in two activities: I handled money for them [and] I handled East Bloc weapons purchases, primarily made in Yugoslavia and Czechoslovakia.

. . .

Q: And you said you performed other services, other than mutual fund consultant, for the CIA. What were those services?

A: I was a pilot for the CIA at several times.

. . .

Q: How many flights would you say that you made from the Mena, Arkansas airport for the CIA during the period of time you worked for them?

A: Ten to twelve.

Q: Ten to twelve flights. And you flew a C-130?

A: Generally flew a C-130. I did, however, on occasion come in . . . on one occasion specifically I recall coming in on a Lear Jet [and] on one occasion on a 400 Series Cessna.

. . .

Q: I see. So as I understand it, they would load the guns and munitions on the C-130 and you and a co-pilot, one of whom you've identified as Harry Rupp, would fly these munitions and equipment to locations in Central America. Where was the cargo destined for? Where did you fly it to?

A: We flew it to Panama City and off-loaded it there.

. . .

Q: Now, were these shipments met by people in Panama?

A: Yes, they were. They were met by military types who wore military uniforms and were easily identified as members of the Panamanian Defense Force, which is essentially the Palace Guard.

Q: All right, do you know any of the people? Did you recognize any of the PDF forces that met these shipments?

A: I recognized them. I did not know the names of all of them. However, I did know the name of the man who trained them, and he would frequently be there to meet the shipments. And he is a man by the name of Michael Harari.

Q: Who is Michael Harari?

A: Mike Harari was a Mossad agent. He's an Israeli national. My best understanding is he lives in Israel right now. He was Manuel Noriega's partner in a number of business deals in Panama. I know that firsthand because I had to deal with him.

. . .

Q: Now, you would stay a night or a couple of days and you returned [to Mena]. And would you return with cargo?

A: Yes, sir. We would. We would come back with individuals and, from time to time, unmarked boxes of items that were put in one aircraft along with the individuals. Now, being conservative by nature and not having a death wish, I opened the boxes on a number of occasions to find out what I was flying.

Q: And what did you discover the cargo to be?

A: I found the cargo to be cocaine, in some cases marijuana.

. . .

Q: And when you landed at Mena, what would be the disposition of the cargo?

A: On one or two occasions the cargo was taken off by people who were not residents of the Mena area and put into other aircraft, which departed from there. However, the most frequent activity was that the aircraft would be unloaded in front of Rich Mountain Aviation's hangar and it would be stored in the back of the hangar.

. . .

Q: . . . I am particularly interested in the identification of persons other than Freddie Hampton. You've talked about Freddie Hampton. You've identified him. Can you identify other people who might have received this cocaine?

A: Yes. I can identify people who in fact received the cocaine, not "might have."

Q: Can you tell us who they were?

A: I can tell you that they were members of John Gotti's family in New York. One of them was an individual known to me by the name of Sal Reale.

. . .

Q: Sal Reale?

A: Salvatore Reale.

Q: Salvatore Reale?

A: Correct.

Q: And how did you know Mr. Reale?

A: Mr. Reale at that time was the Director—I believe it was at that time—was the Director of Security of Kennedy International in New York City.

Q: In New York City. Speak to the subject of your knowledge of Mr. Reale and his activities as the head of security at Kennedy. Tell us what you know about him and what he did.

A: Okay. Mr. Reale was one of Mr. Gotti's lieutenants. I watched the two of them interact. Mr. Gotti would provide directions, Mr. Reale would carry them out. It was his job to make sure that cargo being shipped through Kennedy was not lost, but properly located, and in some cases avoided the customs procedures.

Q: Are you saying that you saw Mr. John Gotti, the famous head of the organized crime syndicate, in New York together with Mr. Reale?

A: Yes, sir. I did.

Q: Where did you see them?

A: That was in New York City.

Q: In New York City. What was the occasion that permitted you to see them together?

A: I don't recall the nature of it. I do recall it was a private club that I was taken to, and I had the opportunity to meet with them at that time.

. . .

Q: Was your notice of Mr. Gotti and Mr. Reale in any way connected with your contractural job with the Central Intelligence Agency?

A: Yes. As far back as 1968 and early '69 we had begun to launder money from organized crime families in New York. At that time, Mr. Gotti was an up-and-coming member of one of the families. I got to know them at that time. We used to wash their money out overseas and put it in Switzerland in nice, safe places for them.

Q: So you worked for Mr. Gotti as well as for the CIA?

A: Actually, the CIA told me to do that on their behalf.

Q: So the CIA was in, would you say, partnership or association with Mr. Gotti?

A: Yes, sir. I would say partnership.

. . .

Q: All right, now let's go back to Mena airport in Arkansas for a moment. At the time when you saw Mr. Reale there, did he receive any of the shipment, the cargo of drugs, that you brought back from Panama?

A: He did not personally take any of the drugs. He did, however, see that they were transferred into aircraft and vehicles so that they would be moved off the field. And that was his function. His function was not to load the vehicles, but to see that nothing got lost in transit.

Q: Are you saying that drugs that you brought back from Central America to Mena were for the purpose of delivery to Mr. Reale, who was in the employ of Mr. Gotti, the New York crime syndicate boss?

A: Yes, sir. I would say that.

. . .

Q: Now, did the Gotti organization, through Reale, pay money to the CIA for the drugs?

A: Yes, they did.

Q: Do you know how much money?

A: Firsthand knowledge, somewhere in the $50,000,000 bracket.

Q: How do you know how much money?

A: Because I banked the money for them in Panama City, and ultimately transferred it to other locations in Europe.

Q: Did they pay you in cash?

A: Yes, generally.

Q: And what do you mean: "generally"? What other forms did they pay you in?

A: I owned an aircraft in Mexico City for a while that was payment for some of the work I had done.

The fact that Harrison had introduced Amiram Nir into the discussion in our initial phone conversation and done so unprompted, then likewise volunteered the name Barry Seal during our first face-to-face interview, implied more than passing knowledge of their involvement in what we were seeing with increasing clarity as a Mexican

connection to the Reagan administration's proxy *contra* insurgency against the Sandinista government of Nicaragua. Was he familiar with Terry Reed? we asked him. Yes,
he was. Was Reed's account of the Arkansas link and subsequent agency activities in
Mexico accurate? Yes it was, he assured us. Twenty-four hours later, Héctor Berréllez
would also assure us that Reed's account was true.

By the time we wrapped up our San Dimas interview, Harrison had given us several
significant pieces of information: (1) he had personally met and collaborated with a
number of key personalities in Mexico's intelligence and national security apparatuses;
(2) he had known about the plot to assassinate Manuel Buendía weeks before it was
carried out; (3) Oliver North oversaw the *contra* drugs-for-arms arrangement with the
Guadalajara cartel; (4) Israel's Mossad had managed much of the *contra*-destined arms
flow through Mexico on behalf of the CIA because the agency had been compromised
by revelations about its Mexican operations; (5) the Federal Judicial Police raid on the
Bravo ranch where the bodies of Enrique Camarena and Alfredo Zavala were subsequently found had been conducted to cover up a Mossad arms depot; (6) both Camarena and Buendía had been killed to keep them from exposing the links among the
CIA, Mossad, the Guadalajara cartel, and the Mexican government in support of the
Nicaraguan *contras*; and (7) the September 1984 police ambush in which Harrison was
shot and nearly died had been conducted for the same reason.

After returning to the United States, Harrison told us, he feared that he might be
targeted for assassination to keep him from revealing what he knew about CIA operations in Mexico. He had been told not to talk to us, he said, but dismissed that advice
out of hand. No one was going to tell him who to talk to or not, he insisted with distinct bravado. Moreover, he added, he was willing to continue talking with us and
invited us to contact him again when next we had an opportunity to do so.

On Saturday, 15 May, Russell managed to reach Héctor Berréllez by phone a little
before noon. In contrast to previous attempts to get together with him starting in 1998,
he now seemed willing to talk to us about the Buendía case. He was busy just then, he
said. Would it be possible to meet on Sunday? When Russell informed him that we
had a morning flight back to Sacramento, he agreed to see us that evening and said we
should call him back around 7:00 p.m. to decide where. Russell phoned him around
five to let him know that we were going out for supper and would return in a couple
of hours. He asked where we were staying, then said he would meet us at the Ramada
in Ontario, as it would be simpler for us than locating him in Riverside.

Berréllez called our room from the Ramada lobby at quarter to eight. Russell invited
him up, then went out on the third-floor balcony to watch him walk across the
enclosed parking area below toward the elevator situated midway down the long,
three-story motel wing. It was a strange moment when, two or three minutes later, he
reappeared several rooms down the narrow balcony from where Russell was standing.
He started hesitantly toward us, instinctively evaluating what in his experience could
have been a dangerous situation, then inquired: "Mr. Bartley?"

"Héctor," Russell acknowledged.

Reassured, he approached, we shook hands, and he immediately handed us a copy of
the September 1998 *Esquire* magazine containing Chuck Bowden's Gary Webb article,

which included an account of Berréllez's dauntless career as a DEA agent enhanced by a full-page, tough-guy, black-and-white portrait of him by photographer Brad Wilson. "Hector was not fond of cops," Bowden wrote. "He remembered them slapping him around when he was a kid. He was a barrio boy from South Tucson, a square mile of poverty embedded in that booming Sun Belt city. His father was a Mexican immigrant. After serving in the Army in the late sixties, Berréllez couldn't find a job in the copper mines, so he hooked up as a temporary with the small South Tucson police force to finance his way through college." That, recounts Bowden, was when Berréllez "accidentally discovered his jones: He loved working the streets with a badge. The state police force hired him, and Hector, still green, managed to do a one-kilo heroin deal in the early seventies, a major score for the time. The DEA snapped him up, and suddenly the kid who had wanted to flee the barrio and become a lawyer was a federal narc. He loved the life."[18]

Our accommodations at the Ontario Airport Ramada consisted of a spacious bedroom with windows looking out on I-10 and the San Gabriel Mountains, plus a small sitting room with sofa, table, and chairs as one entered from the exterior balcony. Berréllez sat down on the sofa, Russell took a chair to his right, while Sylvia sat facing him. From the start there was a good rapport between us, and we conversed easily for the next three hours. We had two lines of questioning we wished to pursue with Berréllez: DEA interest in the Buendía case and Harrison's credibility as an informant. As the interview progressed, we also gained insight into the interpersonal relationship between

Decorated DEA veteran and former Operation
Leyenda supervisor Héctor G. Berréllez.
(Courtesy of Brad Wilson)

Harrison and Berréllez, as well as into Berréllez's personality and mental universe. These insights would later help us discern more clearly what was playing out when both men were subjected to a convoluted process of institutional reprisal for having shared with us (and perhaps others) confidential information about American covert activities in Mexico.

Berréllez confirmed for us that Harrison had been sent to Mexico by the CIA. When Harrison returned to the United States in September 1989 to testify before the Camarena case grand jury, Berréllez had run his fingerprints through the federal registry under the names Lawrence Victor Harrison and George Marshall Davis. The prints had matched those on file under both names, he told us, which can only happen in cases where a false identity has been assigned to a government agent. Then, following Harrison's initial debriefings and grand jury appearance, Berréllez had accompanied him to Washington, DC, where he was put through two days of lie detector questioning at DEA headquarters. Based on the polygraph results, Berréllez assured us, there could be no doubt that Harrison had worked for the CIA.

Berréllez gave us a thumbnail history of the Camarena investigation, describing how initially the DEA had assigned an "élite" East Coast team with French Connection experience to the case and how for the first three years they got nowhere because they had no understanding of the on-the-ground reality in Mexico. "They were all Italians," he remarked dismissively. In early 1989 DEA "suits" finally concluded that if their Camarena investigation was going to get anywhere they would have to replace the "Italians" with Mexico-savvy field agents. At that point, he recounted, they appointed him G/S for the Camarena case and by September he and his fellow agents had developed sufficient evidence to indict several high-profile individuals, including Rubén Zuno Arce, brother-in-law of former Mexican president Luis Echeverría Álvarez.

It seemed a self-serving account that overlooked what we increasingly saw as a continuous political thread woven throughout the Camarena case from beginning to end. Why, we asked, had they approached Rogelio Hernández and Octavio González back in 1986 with the offer of DEA documents purportedly implicating Manuel Bartlett Díaz in the Buendía assassination? Why was the DEA even interested in Manuel Buendía? Because, Berréllez replied, it appeared that Enrique Camarena had met with Buendía on at least one occasion and, more significantly, because both Buendía and Camarena had been killed for the same reason—to prevent them from exposing what they had learned about the CIA–drug trafficker connection. What sealed Camarena's fate, Berréllez told us, was that he had traced million-dollar sums of Guadalajara cartel money to agency bank accounts.

The fact that Camarena's torture interrogation was tape-recorded, he said, proved that the kidnapping was not a reprisal for damage done to cartel marijuana plantations, as alleged by American officials; rather, it was an intelligence operation meant to discover what Camarena knew about the CIA-trafficker link and then silence him. To our surprise, Berréllez stated that CIA operative Félix Rodríguez was present at the interrogation and had participated in the questioning of Camarena, an allegation not made to us by Harrison, nor, to our knowledge, by anyone else conversant with the case. Hypothetically, Rodríguez might be viewed as a plausible agency choice for such a black assignment, and his presence at the 881 Lope de Vega address on that occasion would constitute proof positive of CIA complicity in Camarena's death, but we have only Berréllez's statement to that effect and simply report it here for the record. Following up on Berréllez's mention of Rodríguez, we asked him about Terry Reed's account of having set up a CIA proprietary at the Guadalajara airport to handle arms and drug shipments for the *contras*. The account was true, he assured us.

Having no reason to anticipate that we would ask him about Reed, his ready response indicated to us that he was indeed familiar with Operation Screw Worm, which now, years later, he misremembered as "Fruit Fly." Reed had worked for Rodríguez, he correctly recalled, then informed us that Reed was living in the Los Angeles area and the two of them had met for lunch only the week before. Reed would probably be willing to talk to us, he thought, but subsequently declined to put us in touch. We had attempted unsuccessfully to contact Reed a dozen years earlier through his former Little Rock attorney, John Wesley Hall Jr., and were unable to arrange an interview with him thereafter. Like Richard J. Brenneke, who also declined to meet with us, Reed apparently felt it the better part of wisdom to avoid further exposure on the Mena, Arkansas, affair and the related matter of *contra*-linked arms, cocaine, and drug money passing through Mexico.

We also asked Berréllez about his and Gárate Bustamante's interest in Rafael Loret de Mola. Berréllez replied that while investigating the February 1986 murder of his father, Carlos, Rafael had developed information bearing on the Camarena case; that because of the Álvarez Macháin abduction, he and Gárate were unable to travel to Mexico to interview Loret in person but had managed to establish a fruitful relationship with him via telephone; and that typically either he or Gárate would initiate these long-distance phone conversations, although occasionally Loret would call them to volunteer some piece of information. In light of our own 1996 interview with Rafael, this seemed unlikely inasmuch as he had found the repeated calls sufficiently annoying that he began to record them. The investigative rationale for the calls escaped us, and Berréllez failed to offer any explanation beyond averring an institutional link between the deaths of Buendía, Camarena, and Carlos Loret de Mola. As with their earlier meddling in the Buendía case, this persistent intrusion into the Loret de Mola affair suggested a political purpose rather than a legitimate criminal investigation. Once again their target was Bartlett Díaz, now together with de la Madrid's defense secretary, Gen. Juan Arévalo Gardoqui.

Even before taking charge of Operation Leyenda, Berréllez had begun to realize that DEA operations were being compromised by the CIA whenever those operations interfered with agency priorities. Once he took over the Camarena investigation, he told us, he was stunned to discover just how deeply the agency had penetrated the DEA. Leyenda agents he had assumed were reporting directly to him were in fact reporting first to the CIA. He specifically named Dale Stinson, whom he blamed for frustrating DEA attempts to secure Harrison's cooperation while Harrison was still in Mexico. As Bowden recounts in his *Esquire* piece about Gary Webb, Berréllez's informants were reporting the existence of armed camps in Durango, Sinaloa, Baja, Veracruz, and elsewhere in Mexico transited by "American military planes" with cargoes of drugs.

"Hector wrote up these camps and the information he was getting on big drug shipments," Bowden recounted. "And each month, he would go to Mexico City to meet with his DEA superiors [including Ed Heath] and American-embassy staff and he started mentioning these reports." He was told, "Stay away from those bases; they're training camps, special operations." Like Mike Levene, like Cele Castillo, like Philip Agee and Lawrence Harrison and a long list of once deeply committed American law enforcement and intelligence agents who had believed in the professed high purposes of their country, Berréllez, too, became disillusioned. His initial reaction was anger at what looked increasingly like the sacrifice of a fellow narcotics officer by his own federal superiors in the interest of foreign policy priorities. He had learned about CIA-leased aircraft flying cocaine north into the United States and guns south to Mexico and Central America. "Everywhere he turned," Bowden wrote, Héctor "ran into dope guys who had CIA connections." He couldn't believe "the CIA [was] handling all this shit and [didn't] know what these pilots were doing."[19]

Following the Camarena-related prosecutions in Los Angeles, Berréllez requested a Justice Department criminal investigation of the CIA for aiding and abetting international drug traffickers. It was three and a half years before Gary Webb wrote his explosive exposé of CIA-linked *contra* supporters bringing crack cocaine into South Central Los Angeles—a case with which Berréllez was personally familiar, having himself participated in the compromised 27 October 1986 simultaneous, multiagency crack raids described by Webb at fourteen locations in Orange, Los Angeles, and San Bernardino counties. That law enforcement tour de force, Webb reported and Berréllez recalled well, appeared to have been sabotaged by the CIA.[20] Now that he was proposing that a grand jury be convened to investigate the CIA, Berréllez's superiors demanded that he provide hard evidence of agency complicity, then pulled him off the investigation altogether, transferred him to headquarters, and gave him a desk job with no tasks to perform. It quickly got to the point where he would spend his afternoons watching double features at DC-area cinemas until he was able to retire in September 1996. As Bowden expressed it, "The most decorated soldier in the war on drugs kind of faded out at the movies."[21]

Berréllez confirmed Bowden's *Esquire* account of events in both Gary Webb's case and his own. As we listened to and observed him that evening, he struck us as a no-nonsense, street-smart cop who was savvy about running the "bad guys" to ground but did not grasp the larger political and institutional parameters in which those bad guys operated across international frontiers, or even, on occasion, who the bad guys really were. He seemed to be a "straight shooter," literally and figuratively, "a gunslinger who had killed people," as Bowden described him.[22] He exhibited an essentially black-and-white sense of right and wrong rooted in the Mexican heritage and barrio values of his South Tucson upbringing.

In the final half hour of our interview, we discussed the increasingly evident social decay in the country and the societal upheaval looming on the American horizon. Berréllez talked to us about his family, his father's moral compass, and the life decisions facing his own teenage daughter. He railed against the stupidity of television, the failure of the schools, and the inability of today's youth to think. When we asked him rhetorically why those who govern in their own narrow interest would wish to promote a citizenry capable of thinking critically, he stared at us blankly for several moments, then nodded slowly and in a soft voice replied, "I think you're right. They want it that way. That's how they stay in power." We concluded the interview on that sober note, fully expecting to have a further opportunity to speak with him about the Buendía and Camarena cases, but it was not to be. It was, in fact, our sole in-person contact with Héctor Berréllez.

Eleven months passed before we were able to arrange a second interview with Harrison. When next we met with him, in mid-April of the following year, he had moved his law office from San Dimas to a landmark Victorian cottage at 4121 Mission Inn Avenue in a quiet residential neighborhood near downtown Riverside. He had terminated his professional relationship with Berréllez, he informed us, and no longer represented The Mayo Group. While we had no way of knowing it at the time, nor did he, Harrison's purchase of the Mission Inn Avenue building and subsequent exit from The Mayo Group after five years as the firm's corporate attorney were fateful steps in a prolonged process of personal decline that exhibited the distinctive earmarks of government coercive measures intended to silence him.

It gradually became apparent to us that Harrison and Berréllez had very different personalities and outlooks. Psychologically, both men were complex, deeply conflicted individuals who admired one another for their respective operational capabilities in the field yet readily challenged each other from obscure places within their competitive psyches—especially Berréllez, it seemed to us, who exhibited a distinct need to project an image as a supernarc. Part of his reason for leaving The Mayo Group, Harrison told us, was his inability to go along with Berréllez's determination to continue pursuing drug dealers and traffickers, knowing all the while that the ostensible "war on drugs" was a sham in which powerful political interests and corrupt officials assured a steady flow of cocaine and other narcotics into the United States. A second motive, he told us, was the personal offense he took at Berréllez's readiness to posture and dissemble for the benefit of his public persona.

Both Harrison and Berréllez presented their former government employers with an increasingly common postoperational problem: the disillusioned ex-agent who knows grave family secrets and whose silence needs to be assured. In Berréllez's case, the solution appears to have entailed a straightforward manipulation of his ego, first by designating him Harrison's "overseer" (DEA drug buster controlling a CIA spy), then by making him CEO of an ostensibly full-service private sector security firm with a license to operate internationally. The Mayo Group was incorporated in the state of California at the end of November 1998 as the parent company of a business called the Strategic Security Training Academy, organized two years earlier, as well as a succession of specialized entities with such suggestive names as 10-4 Patrol, the Security Private Investigative Group (SPI Group), and the International Institute of Forensic Science.

"When I retired from D.E.A.," Berréllez wrote in The Mayo Group's online mission statement, "my vision was twofold: First, to inject into the private security arena the high ideals, uncompromising honesty and solid professionalism of the United States Federal Service. That dream was accomplished with the founding of Strategic Security, which has become nationally known as a leader in the corporate security and investigations field." His second goal was "to make available to committed individuals, law enforcement, industry and foreign entities . . . ongoing advanced training in the new forensic technology and techniques of the 21st century." Advertised areas of specialized training included polygraph, personal and dignitary protection, private investigation, computer forensics, industrial espionage and sabotage, financial investigations and risk assessment, homicide and questionable death investigations, burglary and armed robbery investigations, money laundering investigations, forfeiture laws, DNA testing, and cell phone hacking. With the titles of president and CEO, Berréllez sought to give The Mayo Group corporate credibility by describing himself as the DEA's "most highly decorated agent for his handling and solving of the kidnap, torture and murder of DEA agent 'Kiki' Camarena."[23]

The ironies here say much about Héctor Berréllez as a personality, as well as about the private sector security thicket in which he, like many retired government agents, sought to reaffirm his former tough-guy persona in a second career on society's dark side. There seems to be little doubt that he was a man driven by appearances who, for the sake of his image, would compromise the traditional sense of right and wrong he so admired in his Mexican father. His evocation of "the high ideals, uncompromising honesty and solid professionalism of the United States Federal Service" (i.e., the Justice Department) in The Mayo Group's mission statement so contradicts the sentiments of professional disillusionment he expressed to us around the Camarena case that it sounds more like a mockery of government integrity than a statement of personal conviction.

So, too, does the image of Mayo's suit-and-tie CEO seated in an executive swivel chair in front of a large textile wall hanging a DEA S/A badge. Like other field agents, Berréllez had expressed nothing but contempt for "the suits," especially at the end of his career when he had been relegated to a headquarters desk assignment with nothing to do. Now he portrayed himself (or was portrayed) as a private sector suit, in striking contrast to the gunslinging agent image captured by Brad Wilson for *Esquire*. Subsequent photos of CEO Berréllez over the next several years seem to reveal a gradual decline of personal fortitude to the point where he was no longer even a shadow of his former self. He looked "corporate," Chuck Bowden remarked to us in the fall of 2010, "like they put him in a washing machine and rinsed all the street out of him."[24]

Bowden, who had known Berréllez for many years and dealt with him in connection with his own investigations of cross-border drug trafficking, viewed The Mayo Group as a device to keep Berréllez on a short leash. The U.S. government, he thought, had no need of such a dubious private firm to service security contracts with foreign governments but might well make use of it to keep problematic ex-agents like Berréllez and Harrison in line. The Mayo Group, in his view, served as Berréllez's "golden handcuffs." "He has always been afraid of saying what he really knows about the [Camarena] case," Bowden wrote us. Both he and Harrison wanted to talk, to tell what they knew, but they kept pulling back because they were scared. Both of them, Bowden said, were afraid of the CIA.[25]

When we met with Harrison for our second interview in April 2005, he explained that he had severed his ties to The Mayo Group because they interfered with his private practice and, above all, because he did not like Berréllez's cavalier management style or the direction in which he was taking the business. He was especially put off by Héctor's need to inflate his own professional image, starting with the way he hyped his ostensible expertise as a polygrapher and polygraphy as a Mayo Group specialization. Having himself been trained to defeat lie detectors, Harrison did not think much of polygraphy as an investigative tool and dismissed as hyperbole Héctor's claimed lie detection skills. Similarly, he told us, Berréllez wanted to obtain a law degree, not out of any commitment to the practice of law but simply for the sake of appearances, which Harrison found offensive, having himself actually made the effort to earn a law degree and done so honestly. Four years later Héctor Berréllez claimed to hold a Doctorate of International Law degree from the University of Michoacán,[26] while Harrison's law practice was in the process of being destroyed, apparently for talking to us about his undercover years in Mexico.

The two men possessed personalities virtually guaranteed to clash: both strong and self-centered, one (Berréllez) in a position of real or fancied authority over the other, and the second intellectually more developed and with a fuller sense of life purpose. Both, too, were emotionally damaged from their years of covert government work. Berréllez exhibited marked swings of attitude, from vindictiveness for perceived personal challenges by Harrison to a readiness to join Harrison in the revelation of state secrets concerning the Camarena case. Harrison, for his part, was distraught over the consequences and implications of his CIA service and morally moved to reveal what he knew yet constrained by his family's vulnerability and a conflicted sense of past secrecy oaths willingly given. He suffered from posttraumatic stress disorder and was seemingly possessed of the need to do penance for agency "sins" committed in Mexico. Charles Bowden, who also has interviewed Harrison, once described his law practice to us as one of "socially low-end drug cases rather than the gold-chain and bracelet dealers" he might have expected. Harrison, Bowden thought, was taking what were essentially poverty cases, which perhaps helped him "do penance for his sins as a CIA operative."[27]

Our April 2005 meeting at the new 4121 Mission Inn Avenue address in Riverside was a high point in our encounters with Harrison. We conversed in his private office from 1:30 in the afternoon to well past seven that evening, with one forty-minute interruption for him to attend to two Spanish-speaking clients who appeared to conform to the humble end of the socioeconomic spectrum noted by Bowden, although the legal matter at hand had nothing to do with narcotics. Harrison was very generous with his time and remained fully engaged in our marathon interview, giving not the slightest indication over the passing hours of a need or wish to wrap it up. This time he seemed more comfortable with us and there was none of the agenda testing that had characterized our initial interview eleven months earlier. As appeared to be his wont and we had previously observed, he occasionally lapsed into convoluted streams of consciousness or struck off on seeming tangents, which he explained as "wanting to make sure we saw the big picture."

In the course of that afternoon, Harrison talked to us about several matters bearing on our Buendía investigation, including Oliver North, William Casey, Gerhard Mertins, and the CIA–Israeli relationship; the importance of family ties among key Mexican officials; links among the WACL, the UAG, the *contras*, and the Guadalajara drug cartel; out-of-control corruption in the DFS; and the DFS–CIA relationship. He described how four motorcycles had been used in the Buendía assassination to cover the gunman and how subsequently he had been allowed to purchase one of them, had rebuilt it, and then had the U.S. consulate in Guadalajara crate it and ship it to the United States when he relocated to California in 1990.

Harrison spoke, too, about his youth, about having been hired as a teenager by the political consulting firm Spencer-Roberts to work as a motion picture cameraman for the 1960 Nixon presidential campaign, about his Berkeley years and CIA training, and about his association with Cold War diplomat George C. McGhee. Oliver North, he told us, oversaw the involvement of Mexican drug traffickers in the *contra* resupply network. Both Manuel Buendía and Enrique Camarena, he repeated, had been killed to keep them from exposing the Mexican connection to the *contras*.

As we wound down the afternoon's conversation, Russell mentioned the security concerns Harrison had expressed to us at the conclusion of our first interview the previous spring and now asked him how we should handle the information he had given us. "I've been to law school," he replied tersely. "I haven't placed any restrictions on you. You do what you need to do!" Russell reminded him that the concerns he had conveyed to us were for his physical safety and that we took those concerns seriously. "Yes, I'm scared!" he said. "But I'm an old man and don't care anymore. You do what you need to do!" Then he added as an afterthought, "They kill people. Nobody believes it, but they do. They really do kill people!"[28]

Ten days later Russell called Harrison to follow up on family background information that we had developed in Bakersfield, California, as well as to clarify two or three points from our most recent interview. His secretary Nallele answered the phone and put Russell briefly on hold. When Harrison came on the line, he was all business, launching straight into an intense monologue about various aspects of our investigation. He did not want us focusing on him, Berréllez, and Gárate Bustamante but rather on the larger implications of the Buendía case. We were dwelling unnecessarily, he said, on the fact that he had acquired one of the motorcycles used in the Buendía assassination, adding in seeming contradiction that had Manuel Buendía been killed on the initiative of the Mexican government, it never would have allowed a gringo to acquire one of the bikes used in the operation. His implication seemed to be that Buendía had been the victim of a U.S.-instigated hit and that he, Lorenzo Harrison, was viewed by the Mexicans as a trusted American agent. Only someone on the inside, he intimated, would be permitted to obtain such a compromising piece of evidence.

The more we have thought about this curious tale, the more significant we find it. We were able to confirm that it did in fact occur; that the bike was a red, 1200 cc Kawasaki with eleven hundred miles on it; that Harrison had rebuilt the engine; and that he had spilled it two or three times in the Los Angeles area, then given it to his brother-in-law Roy in Las Vegas, Nevada. Both Harrison's sister Kathleen and her husband remembered it well. "George had spilled it and banged it all up," Roy told us. Roy had not been into motorcycles much, he said, but he took the bike from Harrison, purchased new parts, and got it into running condition again. Eventually, he got rid of it because "it was too powerful" and would "rear up on him."[29]

The motorcycles used in the Buendía killing were a recurring topic in our conversations with Harrison. They had been procured by PRI president and former DFS chief Javier García Paniagua, he would tell us, and following the assassination were turned over to Guadalajara DFS commandant Federico Castell del Oro for disposal. Castell had offered to sell one to Harrison. That Harrison should have been moved to purchase that particular bike suggests that it had some personal significance for him. Why else would he want it? Why so quick to acquire it? (There was a narrow window of several weeks in which to do so.) He was not a biker, after all. Were it simply a matter of wanting a motorcycle, he could have picked one up easily anytime he chose. So why at that particular moment? Why did he hold on to it during his remaining years in Mexico, then have the U.S. consulate ship it to California? Why, in sum, did he make so much of it?

In light of the celebratory response of U.S. officials to the Manuel Buendía assassination noted by Matthew Rothschild, we detect a certain trophy quality in Harrison's "dirty" motorcycle—a token of recognition, perhaps, for a covert operation well executed. Charles Bowden expressed the opinion to us that Harrison himself had somehow been involved in the plot to kill Buendía, which we suspect may be true given the central place Buendía occupied in Harrison's recollections of those years. He kept coming back to the "motorcycles" the entire time we dealt with him and, on one occasion, even claimed that we had accused him of killing Buendía, which we had never so much as intimated and struck us as a reflection of some deeper emotional distress on his part around the Buendía assassination. "I haven't killed anybody!" he snapped in one of our conversations. "At least, no one you know."[30]

30 April 2005

Larry—

You indicated a wish to clarify perspectives on our Buendía investigation. I think that would be helpful.

First, I neither idealize Manuel Buendía nor attribute to him virtues he did not possess. Rather I view him as a marker of change in Mexican political history; of transition from nationalist *dinosaurios* to globalized *tecnócratas* in the governance of the country. . . .

Second, you worry that I will focus my account of the Buendía affair on you, Hector and Gárate. I've not spoken to Gárate nor do I intend to; he's peripheral to my purposes. Hector has been helpful, if not entirely forthcoming, and I hope to have another opportunity to do some follow-up with him. You, however, are key to my investigation. You are as close to a direct source as any investigator outside the cabal that committed and covered up the Buendía assassination is ever going to get and I need to press you for every piece of pertinent testimony you can give me. That said, you are a problematic source. As I noted on the phone, you have been effectively discredited in both countries—by Judge Rafeedie in the U.S.; by Rogelio Hernández in Mexico. On its face, your personal background could hardly be more improbable. While I am persuaded by what you have shared with us, I must find a way to make you credible to potential readers and that will necessarily entail a carefully crafted summary account of your life story. . . . A complicating factor in all of this is that your perception of what I need to know and my perception of what I need to know do not precisely coincide. For me to be persuasive in citing you as a source or otherwise drawing on the information you have provided, I need to be clear in my own mind as to who you really are. I need to know as many details of your life as I can elicit from you or am able to develop on my own, whether or not I actually use them in what I write about the Buendía case. . . .

Third, you insist that the key to the Buendía case is in the "public record" and that all I need to do is make the obvious connections. Would that it were so simple! Yes, there is a fair amount of relevant documentation in the public domain about the geopolitical context in which Manuel Buendía (and "Kiki" Camarena and Carlos Loret de Mola) were murdered but it all comes down to circumstantial evidence and circumstances can usually be read more than one way. Already in 1985 I read a much more limited "public record" and concluded that Buendía had been eliminated because of what he had learned about U.S.-Mexican collusion in the anti-Sandinista campaign. Others suspected as much but the circumstantial evidence wasn't sufficient to sustain the allegation. It was too easy to introduce plausible diversionary hypotheses that distracted public opinion and effectively neutralized "conspiracy theorists" like myself. While I enjoyed the respect and moral support of Mexico City press colleagues, I was myself dismissed by Renato Sales Gasque and other officials in the Procuraduría del DF because of my insistence in the pages of *Unomásuno* on the need to investigate a possible U.S. role in the Buendía killing. Gobernación, for its part, took our investigation quite seriously, as did the special prosecutor, and communicated their concern to us in unmistakable ways. What your information does now is allow me to surmount the inherent weaknesses of circumstantial evidence and, for the first time, to introduce a persuasive element of direct evidence.

This is important since I am making an historical case rather than a legal case. I am not arguing in a court of law nor am I constrained by the legal system's contrived, often arbitrary, rules of evidence. Indeed, the evidentiary requirements of historical argument are more rigorous than what is admissible in a court of law—which perhaps explains our differing perspectives on what I need to know. The very concept of "admissibility" is alien to the historian. Any and all elements of evidence bearing on an investigation, no matter how obtained or seemingly tangential, must be taken into full account. In the present instance, I now have a much clearer appreciation of the constraints on what you can and cannot tell me and am factoring them into the evidentiary equation.

. . .

Russell[31]

This letter followed Russell's having raised the need-to-know matter in a 25 April phone conversation. Harrison needed to understand the problem we confronted in trying to establish him as a credible source, since he had been publicly discredited in the United States by Judge Edward Rafeedie and in Mexico by *Excélsior* reporter Rogelio Hernández. Russell's mention of Judge Rafeedie elicited a surprisingly frank outburst on Harrison's part, surprising because they were conversing over an unsecure telephone connection: "I was instructed to sit up there [on the witness stand] and act like a clown!" he exclaimed. "They laid a mine field for me, and I didn't want to step on any mines!"

"Look," Russell elaborated, "I find what you've told us persuasive. I'm persuaded. But I have to find a way to make you credible to a broader audience. That's my problem."

"Everything I've told you is the truth," he replied. "I've moved some personal pieces around, because I'm not going to tell you I was somewhere I [testified] I wasn't. They told me to lie. I'm not going to open myself up to perjury!" "Don't make this about me, Hector, and Gárate," he repeated after some additional questioning about his background. "We're beside the point. The real story is in the public record. All anyone has to do is make the obvious connections."[32]

Berréllez, Harrison told us three and a half months later, "was upset with him for talking to us." In our next face-to-face conversation, we asked him why Berréllez was upset. It was, he replied, because Héctor "fancied himself" his controller. "But when he's not here," he insisted, "he's not my controller. I'll talk to anybody I choose!"

"Does anybody still care about any of this?" we asked.

"I don't know," he allowed. "I haven't talked about all this stuff before, so they leave me alone. It's a play: pretend this, pretend that. Go too far, you die."[33]

When we met with Harrison in March 2006 for our third interview, we asked him how he had gotten involved in intelligence work in the first place. He repeated that he had been "picked up" by Richard Nixon while still in high school to work on the 1960 presidential campaign as a cameraman. "I was on the Auricon," he remarked with pride, referring to the 16mm Auricon sound camera widely used for television production at the time. He went on to say that he was a patriot; he believed the Cold War myths of the day; and it was a perfectly natural transition for someone like him to make, implying that Nixon had something to do with it as well.

"So you were snookered?" Russell remarked.

"*You* were snookered!" he shot back defensively.

Indeed, Russell readily agreed. That was the point. Many of us had been "snookered" by the ideological mantra of the day. But Russell had stung him, and our explanation did little to mitigate the psychological bruise, although he made an effort to remain affable and responsive to our questions. After another hour or so, we decided we needed some time to digest the ground we had covered, and Russell asked if it might be possible to meet again in the next day or two. He agreed to see us Sunday afternoon, three days hence, but when we arrived at his office for the follow-up meeting, we were informed apologetically by his son that something had come up and "his parents were out of town." Since Harrison knew that we had to leave for home the next day, we wondered if perhaps he had decided it was best not to continue our conversation. Six months later it became apparent that he was being targeted for serious coercive measures.

16

Extreme Prejudice

My capability to think and function would be utterly ruined. I would be so doped up that I wouldn't be capable of exchanging ideas through conversation or the written word pretty much ever again. . . . This was "extreme prejudice," alright. The purpose was not only to discredit my reputation as an Asset, but to destroy me as a human being, physically and spiritually.

—Susan Lindauer, *Extreme Prejudice* (2010)

I get up in the morning, walk two blocks, then sit all day. That's all that's left in life—walk two blocks and sit.

—Lawrence Victor Harrison, telephone conversation with Russell H. Bartley (4 May 2012)

RUSSELL CALLED LAWRENCE HARRISON on Friday afternoon, 1 September 2006. We had not had any contact since March, although in the interim Russell had sent him a copy of an article he'd published five years earlier about the cultural Cold War in an effort to smooth any ruffled feathers from our previous encounter and to give him a clearer sense of how he saw the larger issues of the era in which they had each made comprehensible life choices.[1] We wanted to clarify several questions about his court testimony, as well as some details concerning his parents. When he came on the line, Russell asked him if he could have a few minutes of his time, to which he replied, "I've just been attacked and am still bleeding, but go ahead."

Russell's first thought was that he had been physically attacked, but he quickly realized that he was speaking metaphorically. Some government agency, perhaps the FBI, had supposedly launched a rumor campaign against him, including the accusation that he had killed Manuel Buendía. He had confronted his federal handlers about it, he said, but received no satisfaction. The attack sought to smear his professional reputation and had already hurt him. "I have no other income source outside of my law practice," he remarked presciently. "Hell, they obviously know that!"[2]

Influential local Mexican families had been involved, he thought, including the Guadalajara-linked Leaño clan and another family that he said owned a chain of Los Angeles–area supermarkets. When Russell asked him the reason for the attack, he replied, "I suppose it's because I've been talking to you." Then, for the benefit of presumed *pajaritos* on the line, he qualified his reply by stating that there were also "some

personality issues" involved and that his contact with us may simply have been a convenient pretext, because "he had not told us anything of consequence," which by then
was not true, as his federal overseers had to be perfectly aware.

In any event, Harrison was clearly upset and took advantage of that conversation
to drop a couple of "tokens" for the ears in between. "By the way," he said, "I have a
photograph I think you'll be interested in. It's two guys on motorcycles, in full uniform. They're Javier's people. I won't send it to you; you'll have to come down here and
get it." The "motorcycles" referred to the bikes used in the Buendía assassination, while
"Javier" alluded to former DFS chief, PRI head, and onetime presidential hopeful Javier
García Paniagua, whose name had not come up before in connection with the Buendía
case and, in Harrison's mind, apparently threatened to open a prohibited window on
U.S.-Mexico relations in the 1980s.

"Are you going to give me this photograph?" Russell asked him.

"Yes, I am!" he promised. "But you'll have to come down here and get it."

"That won't be tomorrow."

"I know," he said. "It'll be here when you come."

Seven months passed before we were able to travel to Southern California again. On
Wednesday, 28 March 2007, we checked into the Airport Sheraton in Ontario, had
some lunch, then set out for Riverside around 2:00 p.m. We exited State Highway 60
at Mission Inn Boulevard and followed it southeastward across the Santa Ana River,
where it becomes Mission Inn Avenue, continuing on to Harrison's law office in the
4100 block. His story-and-a-half, turn-of-the-century Victorian bungalow (built in
1898 and now designated a Riverside City Structure of Merit) sat on the north side
of the avenue, and as we approached we were surprised to catch sight of him sitting
in one of the wicker chairs on the building's small offset front porch. Just then he got
to his feet, his large, slightly stooped, six foot eight frame filling the partially enclosed
porch and, as though laboring under some great weight, slowly entered the house.

At the corner we turned north onto Brockton Ave., then west on Sixth, a quiet,
tree-lined residential street where we found an inconspicuous shaded space to park.
Walking back to 4121 Mission Inn, we found the gate in the property's white iron
picket fence ajar and a green notice from the local power company hanging from one
of its pickets. The notice informed the owner that unless an outstanding bill of over
two hundred dollars was promptly paid, electricity to that address would be turned off
the following week. We passed through the gate, mounted the porch steps, and, without ringing or knocking, entered the house. To our astonishment, we found Harrison
stretched out on the reception area's white Naugahyde couch, eyes closed, and yelling
in the throes of what we later concluded was some kind of posttraumatic stress episode. For the most part his yelling was incoherent, but at one point he demanded quite
clearly, "Why do you have to yell at me?"

Russell was standing closest to Harrison when he opened his eyes, focused on him
for a long moment while reorienting himself, and then said in a normal voice, "I'm
glad to see you. I want to tell you some things." Slowly getting to his feet, he looked
Russell in the eye and asked, "Why were you yelling at me that I killed Manuel
Buendía?

"Larry," Russell replied, "I have never yelled at you. Ever!"

"But why did you tell those people that I killed Buendía?" he insisted.

Incredulous, Russell told him he had the wrong person; that he had never accused him of killing Buendía; then reminded him that in a previous conversation he had told us that someone else had accused him of committing the Buendía homicide. He seemed confused, then asked if we would like a cold drink and invited us into his office. He sat behind his large executive-style desk, Russell on a chair to his right against the desk's outer edge, Sylvia facing him on a couch to the right of the doorway as one entered.

Harrison immediately began to rummage through his desk drawers, extracting a number of color snapshots and passing them to Russell across the desk. As he searched, he rambled on despondently about his recent troubles, saying that things had been made so bad for him that he thought he should leave the country. But where to go? he asked rhetorically. He had no real options abroad, certainly not in Mexico. He couldn't stand the intrigue anymore, he said. He feared he was going to be killed.

After going through the drawers on the right side of his desk, he started to look in the top left-hand drawer, mumbling as he did so that "it had been so long"—a reference to the seven months that had elapsed since he first informed us of the photo of "Javier's people" with the motorcycles. He had expected us to come sooner and implied that our delay was the cause of its having been misplaced. He soon found it buried beneath papers in the upper left-hand drawer and passed it across the desk to Russell. It was a soft-focus snapshot of two neatly attired men posing beside motorcycles. "This," he remarked, "is the piece you need. I would bet," he added, "that one of those guys is Castell del Oro," a reference to the DFS commandant responsible for Jalisco and the man who apparently conveyed orders to Harrison in Guadalajara. The second individual, according to the name penned on the back of the photo, was Agustín Morales Mejía, a man unfamiliar to us whom we have not been able to identify since.

Some of the other photos Harrison showed us were of Javier García Paniagua. It was García Paniagua, he told us, who had procured the motorcycles used in the Buendía assassination. The implications of that assertion were significant, inasmuch as it suggested a previously unknown chain of responsibility that bypassed the Secretariat of Government (Gobernación), leading instead to the executive committee of the PRI and even, perhaps, to President de la Madrid himself. He appeared to have taken these snapshots himself, which we thought noteworthy, inasmuch as it seemed to confirm his personal connection to García Paniagua.

It was clearly important to Harrison to have us see these photos and to pass this particular piece of the Buendía puzzle on to us. Yet all the while he was doing so, we could see that he was in a decidedly different frame of mind from that of our previous meetings. When we first sat down in his office following the apparent posttraumatic stress episode, he had indicated that this would be our last meeting, that he could not talk to us anymore. He told us he was not feeling well and, as we talked, kept shifting around uncomfortably in his chair. Gone were all the bravado and self-assurance that had typified his prior comportment with us. He was, he said, "at his wits' end."

Berréllez had shown up one day "with that *Esquire* guy," Harrison informed us, and proposed that the two of them tell Charles Bowden everything they knew. He had refused, he said, because he suspected that Héctor was trying to set him up. This was two or three months before our present meeting. Following his retirement from the DEA and subsequent involvement with The Mayo Group, Berréllez had embarked on a soaring ego trip, which transported him, according to a former Mayo Group employee, all the way to the saddle of a prancing steed in La Paz, Bolivia, on which he had pompously shown off in the company of mounted Bolivian National Police for whom he had been contracted to establish a polygraph unit.[3] By then, Bowden told us, Berréllez had left his wife and taken up with a pretentious blonde and was dreaming of books and a movie about his law enforcement exploits. Then, in May 2006, his eldest son committed suicide, dealing him a stunning emotional blow. When Bowden next saw him, Berréllez appeared to be a changed and sobered man, sans blonde, now devoted to raising two grandchildren and contemplating his own mortality. It was time, he told Bowden, to go see Harrison and together tell their Mexican secrets. Once before he had dropped by Bowden's Tucson home, "sat on the patio, talked for hours and laid out everything in the Camarena case that he would never say on the record."[4]

Now, apparently, he was ready to do just that, perhaps envisioning another *Esquire* feature like the one Bowden had done on Gary Webb. Harrison was having none of it, although it seemed clear to Bowden that he did, in fact, want to tell his story, just not that way. As Bowden put it, "Larry was not eager to die at CIA hands." He did show them the Castell del Oro motorcycle photo, made some opaque, even emotional statements about his Mexico experience, and above all stressed how dangerous it was to reveal anything about it. Bowden, for his part, understood that danger better than most people but "thought the truth of the Camarena murder [that the U.S. government had sacrificed its own agent] was—and still is—worth any risk." It was, as he expressed it, an earlier manifestation of today's drone culture, "where men in suits sacrifice those in the field and never miss dinner or their drinks." It was the true tale of American empire. He encouraged Harrison and Berréllez to think seriously about sharing with him what they knew, but he did not hear from them again.[5]

Russell now reminded Harrison that the last time they spoke by phone he told him that he had "just been attacked and was still bleeding." What was that about? It turned out, he explained, that all the papers related to his purchase of the 4121 Mission Inn Avenue property had been falsified and he was now being sued, which was going to have a negative impact on his law practice. The realtor who had handled the transaction for him, he said, worked out of Héctor Berréllez's Mayo Group. "You've been set up," we remarked in unison, to which he replied sharply, "Well, duh!" There comes a time, he added bitterly, "when you're all alone with the pigs. Even your false friends are gone!" He was clearly referring here to Berréllez, whom he blamed in large part for his current tribulations.

In another of his stream-of-consciousness monologues, Harrison went on incoherently about Pope John Paul, Archbishop Romero, the bishops of Chiapas and Mexico City, "Jungle FedEx," Terry Reed under the radar, guerrilla recruits from Central America trained on "El Güero's" Chihuahua ranch,[6] drug overdoses induced by third parties, contrived "suicides," the Vatican Bank, and the Vatican banker Roberto Calvi, "who liked to hang around under London bridges."[7] His point seemed to be that he was not sanguine about his future and he, too, might turn up as an apparent suicide. We asked him how his family figured in all this, wanting to know if he thought they, too, might be in danger, but he interpreted this to mean "Did your family afford you some measure of personal protection?" "They don't care about family!" he exclaimed. "They just shut you up!"

And with that, he indicated that our meeting was over. "I've been telling you the fucking truth!" he said, referring to our numerous conversations over the previous three years. "I don't dare say anything else. I may be dead the next time you come by!" Despite having promised to give us the Castell del Oro motorcycle snapshot, it was clear that he was now too intimidated to do so. He promised to send us a scan of it, which we doubted he would do, and in fact he never did. Did he have our address? we asked, knowing that he did.

"Oh, yes. I even have a satellite photo of your house," he added, with just a hint of the playful bravado we had come to expect in our relationship with him.

"Anybody can do that," we countered.

"Not just anyone."

"Well, it can't be very interesting," we remarked, referring to the rusticity of our place.

"Oh, I think it might be pleasant living in the woods," he said, implying that it would be an attractive escape from his present troubles.

"But you're not a country boy."

"Oh, yes I am," he insisted with just the suggestion of a twinkle in his eye. "But which country?"

With that he gave us a fleeting smile and a full parting handshake. In all we had been there less than three-quarters of an hour. We would not see him again for another two years.

On October 19, 1995, I walked into a roomful of DEA agents in the National City regional office, squirreled away in an industrial complex south of San Diego. Two of the agents I recognized from court and reading their names in the court files: [Danilo] Blandón's handlers, the immaculately coiffed Chuck Jones and his worried-looking sidekick, Judy Gustafson. The other four I didn't know. The agent behind the desk, a tall man with an easy smile, got up and shook my hand warmly. Craig Chretien, he said, special agent in charge.

"This is a little awkward for us," Chretien began. They knew generally the story I was working on, he said, and unfortunately I was getting into some rather sensitive areas. . . . "What's your angle, here?" Chretien asked. "Is it that the DEA sometimes hires scumbags to go after people?"

"No. It's about Blandón and Norwin Meneses and the Contras," I said. "And their dealings with Ricky Ross."

. . .

"That whole Central American thing," Chretien said dismissively. "I was down there. You heard all sorts of things. There was never any proof that the Contras were dealing drugs. If you're going to get involved in that, you'll never get to the truth. No one ever will."

"I think that's been pretty well established," I said. "Your informant was one of the men doing it."

Chretien gave Jones a sidelong glance and Jones came to life. "I can tell you that I have never, *ever* heard anything about Blandón being involved with that," he said firmly. "Not once. His only involvement with the Contras was that his father was a general or something down there."

. . .

I could not quite believe what I was hearing. What kind of scam was this?

"Have you ever asked him about it?" I asked Jones.

"I've already said more than I should."

"Did you ever ask him about doing it with Norwin Meneses?"

"You'd better go check your sources again," Jones snapped.

"My source is Blandón," I said. "He testified to it under oath, before a grand jury. You're telling me you don't know about that?"

Jones threw up his hands. "Oh, listen, he understands English pretty well, but sometimes he gets confused, and if you ask him a question the wrong way he'll say yes when he means no."

I shook my head. "I've got the transcripts. These weren't yes or no questions. He gave very detailed responses."

"Jones's face and forehead grew beet red and his voice rose. "You're telling me that he testified that he sold cocaine for the Contras in *this* country? He sold it in *this* country?"

"That's exactly what I'm telling you. You want to see the transcripts? I've got them right here."

"I cannot believe that those two U.S. attorneys up there, if they had him saying that before a grand jury, that they would ever, ever, ever put him on a witness stand!" Jones fumed. "They'd have to be insane! They'd have to be total idiots!"

"They didn't put him on the witness stand," I reminded him. "They yanked him at the last minute."[8]

We eventually concluded that Héctor Berréllez was not Harrison's primary nemesis but rather a susceptible gull exploited by executive branch damage controllers for their own coercive purposes, including restraint of Berréllez himself. Over the course of the next two years, various figures emerged from the shadows who seemed to be part of a concerted effort to silence Harrison, among them that same Charles "Chuck" Jones who had so clumsily challenged Gary Webb in the testy verbal exchange quoted above. The first of these shadowy individuals we identified was one Peter Cimino, whose name turned up on the deeds to both Harrison's Riverside residence (4367 Emerson Street) and his 4121 Mission Inn Avenue law office. The Mission Inn property had been sold directly to Cimino in November 2004, while ownership of the Emerson Street residence (originally offered as collateral) had been transferred to Cimino the following February, ostensibly by Harrison and his wife Lorena, although their signatures on the recorded grant deed appear to have been forged.[9]

Peter Cimino, Harrison would tell us, was a man he had known in Mexico in the 1970s who also had been involved in some capacity with the CIA. He now lived in Watsonville, California, where he speculated in real estate. When Harrison wanted to purchase the Mission Inn Avenue property, he did not have sufficient funds to cover the down payment and so turned to Cimino for help, proposing what he envisioned as a mutually beneficial business arrangement based on a "gentlemen's understanding" that, despite the formal paperwork, both properties would actually belong to him. He had turned to Cimino because Peter "used to be a friend," he told us. "When I came back up here, I didn't know anybody. All I knew was Héctor and his people. I mean, it was like being in the middle of a bunch of black widow spiders!"[10]

Financing of the Harrison–Cimino real estate deal had been handled by Horizon Realty, a firm opaquely associated with The Mayo Group and one of whose staff, Delia Ann Rodríguez, was a business associate of Héctor Berréllez. By his own account, Harrison had arranged for Horizon to handle all paperwork concerning loan applications, title transfers, and related formalities because he was not himself sufficiently familiar with the technicalities of such matters. Due to a prior negative experience in which Delia Rodríguez had allegedly made fraudulent use of his name and California State Bar Association number, Harrison had demanded, and Horizon agreed, that she would have no hand in the Cimino transactions. It subsequently developed, however, that signatures had been forged and papers falsely executed with the apparent notarization of Delia Rodríguez, resulting in foreclosure on both Harrison's law office and his Emerson Street home of more than a decade.[11]

What actually transpired behind the scenes we do not know, but by the time we decided to visit Harrison again, in mid-February 2008, he had been evicted from the Mission Inn Avenue property. We had intended to drop in on him unannounced so as to better evaluate his current circumstances by not alerting him or his handlers beforehand. As we approached along Mission Inn Avenue from the west, we immediately noted that his distinctive professional sign had been removed from the front lawn and 4121's windows were now covered over on the inside with brown paper. We circled the block for a second look, then parked around the corner on Brockton Avenue and walked up the alley behind the house. The missing law office sign was leaning against the back of the building.

As Sylvia was photographing the sign and rear area of the house, a black Jeep Cherokee approached slowly down the alley and pulled up next to us. The driver, a portly balding man perhaps in his later seventies who identified himself as the owner of the adjacent apartment building, lowered the passenger side window and asked what was going on. "What became of Mr. Harrison?" Russell inquired. "You mean the attorney? Well, there was a bankruptcy is all I know," he replied, then went on to recount how we "wouldn't believe the money they poured into that place" before Harrison moved in. "There were crews in there day and night for weeks!" he remarked. He had chatted with Harrison once and thought him "a pleasant enough fellow" but could not understand how he managed to have a law office in that particular neighborhood, which was zoned residential. As far as he had been able to determine, he told us, Harrison had not been granted a zoning variance, yet there he was conducting business and no one from City Hall came to challenge him about it.

We had had no contact with Harrison for almost a year at that point, wishing to give him the space he seemed to need to sort out his recent difficulties. Following our visit to Riverside, we drove to Tucson to discuss what we had learned with Charles

Bowden, who thought that Harrison, while scared, really did want to talk and encouraged us to keep trying to get him to open up. A month later Russell phoned him. "Law office," answered a woman's voice. Russell identified himself, and she put him on hold with an overly modulated rap track. After a short pause, Harrison came on the line. "Hello, how are you?" he greeted him in a subdued voice. Russell told him that we had just been in Riverside and seen that he was no longer at the Mission Inn address. "They took it away from me," he stated matter-of-factly. "They were very upset with me for talking about what we were talking about. *Very* upset."

"So, now you're practicing out of your home?" Russell asked.

"Yup, as long as they let me have a home," he replied laconically.

"I sent you an e-mail a while back asking you some questions about that. Maybe you can't answer them, but tell me how that worked, how they took it away from you."

"They were upset because of what I was talking about with you."

"No, no. I mean the mechanics of it," Russell clarified.

"I can't say anything. I can't talk to you about it. I'm glad to hear from you. Maybe we can get together sometime, but I can't talk to you now." And he hung up.[12]

From: "Lawrence Harrison"
To: "Russel H. Bartley"
Sent: Tuesday, June 09, 2009 6:43 PM
Dear Russel and Sylvia,
    You might have known it, I need you now. You are the witnesses to the truth of why I am going through an attack which has now begun to overwhelm me. If you do not want to become further involved, I will understand. But if you help me now, I will not withhold my help to you or any other researcher you recommend. I am sending you with this email an urgent S.O.S.
    Sincerely,
    Lawrence V. Harrison

We received the above e-mail communication from Harrison on Tuesday evening, 9 June 2009, along with the following message on our home phone answering machine: "This is Lawrence Harrison, and I'm looking for Russell or Sylvia Bartley. My telephone number is . . . . You will have to dial 'o' to ring through. Please call me as soon as possible. Thank you."

We were dumbfounded, as this was the first time in five years of contact that Harrison had sent us an e-mail or communicated with us in any written form. Moreover, it was a stunning attitudinal change from his characteristic self-assurance and bravado, and later his panicked termination of contact, to a desperate personal plea for help. We forwarded Harrison's e-mail to Charles Bowden for his thoughts on how best to reply. Bowden was at a loss as to "what might have sent Larry around the bend" but insisted that we ought to follow up. "I would immediately respond to Larry," he wrote, "even if his reaching out is simply the result of being addled. He knows things, and any scrap is worth getting down."[13]

Russell telephoned Harrison the next morning. In a ten-minute conversation, he explained that the attack on him was now targeting his law practice, that charges had been filed against him with the California State Bar Association, and that he was fighting it but was facing an uphill battle. Things had become so perverse, he said, that "it was time to pull the lid off it all." It had to be exposed. "I need to talk to you," he said. Russell indicated to him that we were willing to do so but he should know that it would not be easy for us to make the trip. He understood, he said, and was grateful. Russell asked if he wished us to meet him at his Emerson Street residence. "Yes," he replied, "if I am still here. I may have to move out." He then gave us a cell phone number where we could reach him in the event he should be evicted before we arrived.[14]

We canceled prior commitments for the next two weeks, rented a discreet vehicle from a local body shop, and on Saturday, 13 June, set out for a two-day drive to Southern California, with an overnight stopover in the San Francisco Bay Area. That first evening on the road, we met for supper with Berkeley friends Bill Roller and Vivian Nelson, family therapists with whom we had discussed Harrison and our Buendía investigation previously and whose advice we now sought on how best to approach him in his current agitated state. Bill had a special interest in cross-generational manifestations of posttraumatic stress in the children of government agents, a malady he had experienced personally, and wondered how it might have manifested itself in Harrison's son and daughters.

We had grappled for some time with the question of whether anyone was paying attention. Did anybody at the CIA or elsewhere in the U.S. intelligence apparatus really care about what may have happened in Mexico two decades or more ago? By now all but convinced that someone out there in the secret world actually did care and that Lawrence Harrison was being subjected to extreme measures for violating official secrecy oaths, we raised it yet again with Bill and Vivian. "Of course they care!" Bill exclaimed. "CIA involvement in drug running and arms trafficking in Mexico during the time Harrison was there relates to what they are doing today."

On Monday morning Russell phoned Harrison from Santa Barbara. Would the next day, Tuesday the sixteenth, work for him? He said it would. At the Emerson Street address? "Yes," he replied, then repeated, "If I'm still here. They're trying to throw me out." Later that Monday we drove to Ontario and took a room at the Airport Sheraton, a convenient location for dealing with Harrison thirty or forty minutes away in Riverside. We arrived at his place at midmorning the following day.

Harrison's Emerson Street residence was located near the west end of a quiet tree-lined cul-de-sac in a working-class neighborhood between the Riverside Freeway and the Santa Ana River, an easy two-mile drive via Brockton Avenue from his now foreclosed 4121 Mission Inn Avenue law office. There were several cars parked at the curb and in the driveway as we drove up. The house was an early 1950s single-story, three-bedroom, 2,344 square-foot ranch-style residence set on a quarter-acre lot. It was shaded by a large magnolia tree in the front yard and was in need of paint and repair. The windows were covered with what appeared to be soiled drapery liners. A partially open garage door revealed the attached garage to be crammed full of boxed items, suggesting preparations to vacate.

Harrison's son Daniel intercepted us before we reached the front door and instructed us to go around to the gate at the side of the house, then went back inside. He reappeared from behind the house, opened the gate, and motioned us toward the backyard, a small, unkempt, fence-enclosed area containing three lemon trees and a 14 × 20 cinder block structure in the yard's northwest corner that may once have been an in-law apartment but now served as Harrison's home law office. Its outward appearance was rather forbidding, more like a predator's lair than a place in which to conduct one's private law practice. Daniel ushered us into the blockhouse's dim interior, informed us that his dad was in the shower but would be along shortly, then left.

This distinctly seedy structure in the unattended backyard of an unremarkable working-class neighborhood set amid the sprawling urban blight of an environmentally toxic Riverside Basin seemed the perfect metaphor for a sly fox run to ground by his mounted pursuers and their baying hounds. Our first face-to-face meeting with Harrison five years earlier had been in a spacious second-floor suite in tony downtown San Dimas. The following year, and for another two years after that, we would meet with him in the pleasant Victorian bungalow he had acquired on Mission Inn Avenue, where he was the happiest we had seen him during our four-year association. Now he had been reduced to this sorry bunker hidden from view in an unremarkable, out-of-the-way, residential neighborhood unlikely to be visited by paying clients in need of legal services, the law career he had worked so diligently to achieve reduced to shambles.

The bunker's interior was dominated by the same hardwood executive desk we had observed previously in Harrison's San Dimas and Mission Inn law offices, together with the now familiar pair of high-backed, upholstered chairs for clients or, in our case, interviewers. Toward one side of the desktop sat a tall lamp with a fringed fabric shade, turned wooden stem, and ornately carved camel base. At the desk's outer edge rested an elaborate brass pen and ink holder of probable Middle Eastern origin. It was supported by four knobbed feet and backed by an ornate arch with two polished hooks for holding a pen, in place of which we noted a silver rifle cartridge with brass base and pointed, metal-jacketed bullet—"a sniper round" according to an old friend who served in the U.S. Marine Corps. The other side of the desktop was occupied by a covered cut glass bowl and large flat-screen computer monitor.

Behind and to one side of the desk stood a lawyer's bookcase with glass pull-up doors. On the north wall hung Harrison's law degree, his certificate of admission to the California bar and the elegantly framed iconic rendering of Saint George slaying the dragon. The same array of family photos we had observed at his other offices was there, too, arranged on a small mahogany table and watched over by an imposing carved and painted, bronze-skinned, golden-winged, avenging angel. There were two ceiling fans and an air conditioner and, against the east wall opposite the desk, a well-used brown Naugahyde couch.

Harrison filled the doorway as he came in. He moved slowly, painfully it seemed, slightly stooped, looking very poorly. He deposited an armful of files on his desk, sank heavily into his chair, gathered his wits, and thanked us for coming. He immediately launched into a tangled account of ostensibly collusive relations between Héctor Berréllez, Peter Cimino, Delia Rodríguez, Horizon Realty, and The Mayo Group. His own secretary, María Ibáñez, he told us, had been reporting everything she heard and observed in his law office to Héctor Berréllez, although she had denied the allegation in a signed declaration taken by Harrison two years earlier when his troubles first began to metastasize.[15]

As he talked, a clean-shaven man with light brown hair, probably in his midthirties, appeared at the door. Harrison explained that he had asked him to sit in on this session because he was a former Mayo Group employee whom Héctor Berréllez was trying to destroy professionally, just as he was doing to him. He introduced the man as Jeffrey Guy, a former police officer who had been hired by Berréllez to head The Mayo Group's security training program. By Guy's account, his problems had begun when he started noticing irregularities and improper conduct and refused to ignore it. A sexual molestation incident involving Berréllez's younger son Chris in which he had summoned the police, Guy told us, had led Berréllez to frame him on felony charges, which prevented him from working as a security specialist. The case had now gone to court, and Harrison was serving as Guy's attorney, a situation we thought likely to exacerbate existing tensions between him and Berréllez. Harrison in fact stated to us that Berréllez had recently told him to his face that he would destroy his law practice.

Guy expressed the view that Berréllez had lost his compass and was "totally out of control."[16] He had behaved in a similar fashion with two other employees, Guy told us, both of them former DEA agents who were now taking legal action against Berréllez. Because of the pending lawsuits, he said, Berréllez had created several other corporate entities as business covers for The Mayo Group, among them the SPI Group and 10-4 Patrol, both with the same address as The Mayo Group in an out-of-the-way San Bernardino business park (1814 Commercenter Plaza West, Suite H).

In a photograph on the contact page of a website created specifically for the SPI Group, someone in Berréllez's shop not very skilled at computer graphics had superimposed the words SECURITY/INVESTIGATIONS/INTERNATIONAL TRAINING & PROTECTION SERVICES across the upper facade of the building housing the SPI/Mayo Group corporate offices. As we were able to confirm on the ground, however, none of the buildings in the Commercenter business park exhibited corporate names or logos on its exterior facade. Clearly, this was a deception for promotional purposes, an inexpert one that further evidenced the low level of professionalism in Berréllez's private security ventures that Jeff Guy was describing to us.[17]

Toward the end of that day's interview, we recounted our experience in February 2008 when we had gone to the 4121 Mission Inn address and discovered that the building had been repossessed. Harrison listened intently as we described our conversation with the owner of the apartment units behind his previous law office. As for the work crews that had been there "day and night" before he had occupied the premises, Harrison said simply that they "had been doing some renovation work in the bathrooms and kitchen." We were suggesting that they might have been doing a good deal more, such as wiring the place for sound and perhaps video. When we asked him directly if he had ever "swept" the place for electronic devices, Jeff Guy endorsed our question with a knowing nod. "No," Harrison replied flatly, he had not. For an experienced electronics espionage operative, we thought, he had become inattentive to his own surveillance vulnerabilities since returning to the United States.[18]

As we were wrapping up this session, both Guy and Harrison insisted that we should talk to Chuck Jones, the ex-DEA agent who had crossed words with Gary Webb and now turned out to be assisting Harrison with some investigative work related to the charges that had been lodged against him at the state bar. We knew nothing about Jones at the time but would soon come to suspect that rather than helping Harrison he was involved in the effort to silence him. Jones had known Kiki Camarena, they told us, and was also familiar with Héctor Berréllez's private security business. He was now a private investigator based in San Diego.

Harrison also wanted us to speak with Paul Virgo, an attorney who had been assisting him with his state bar defense. He gave us a copy of Virgo's professional resume and contact information and tried unsuccessfully several times to reach him by phone while we were there. "I am begging you on my knees to help me pull the lid off this thing!" he pleaded. He also said he would photocopy the Cimino-related legal documents and mail them to us, which he did following our return home.

The next day, Wednesday the seventeenth, we arrived at Harrison's Emerson Street address around 10:30 a.m. Jeff Guy was again present, he and Harrison having just returned from an early morning court appearance. They had to be back in court at one o'clock that afternoon, Harrison informed us, but we could talk for an hour or so and then continue on Thursday. He repeated that he had been reduced to a desperate situation. "They've taken away everything I have," he lamented. "I don't owe them anything anymore. I'm going to tell you what I know. Fuck them!" We asked if we could record him, which he had not permitted before. "Don't you take notes?" he asked, then relented and said yes, we could record. While we were positioning the recorder on his desk, he remarked to Guy, "You'd better cover your ears. What you're about to hear can ruin your life." Sylvia offered that we could do the interview in Spanish if he preferred, which he did, giving us an insightful glimpse of the fully acculturated Lorenzo Harrison mentally immersed once again in the Mexican milieu of his undercover years.

He launched into a now familiar, seemingly disconnected discourse of names, places, events, and relationships that in actuality was an integrated summary of Mexican history from the late 1960s to the present. It would not seem so to the uninitiated, but we were struck once again by his easy recall of key names and associations that only someone who had himself been deeply involved could possibly possess. In our judgment, it authenticated him as a credible witness and source for events that are otherwise difficult to document. He went on at length about drug trafficking and the collusive cross-border understandings that make it possible. While a San Bernardino, California, prosecutor had recently touted a twenty-kilo cocaine conviction as a major achievement, he scoffed, a thousand kilos were entering California every week from Mexico. It came across in tractor trailers, he marveled, hundreds of kilos in a single load.

Ernesto Fonseca, he recounted, would deposit loads of cocaine at points near the border on the Mexican side, and six days later it was being distributed in Imperial Valley, Riverside, San Bernardino, Los Angeles, and even Long Beach, by a Chino Hills trucking firm. And it wasn't simply a matter of a few corrupt border patrol and customs officers, Harrison insisted. "No, no, no, no! It went way beyond the border. It was a global arrangement!" An arrangement from Chiapas to Chicago, as he explained it, a bilateral arrangement made at the top not the bottom. Viewed from the inside where he had been, he said, it was all too obvious. That is what he told Gary Webb, he added. What Webb had alleged in his "Dark Alliance" series in the *San Jose Mercury News*, he underscored, was all too obvious.

Switching back to English, Harrison referred again to Chuck Jones. "He's the guy that wants to talk to you," he said. "A friend of Camarena's. He doesn't think that Camarena might have been set up. . . . He just doesn't believe that anything like that could happen. But it can, and it did!"[19]

Here we turned off the recorder, as it was getting to be time for him and Guy to return to court. Before leaving, Harrison made the surprising statement that Javier García Paniagua had been present at Camarena's interrogation. He had previously told us that García Paniagua procured the motorcycles used in the Buendía assassination. While we could not judge the veracity of these assertions at the time, Harrison's personal association with García Paniagua at least made them plausible. Before leaving, we reminded him that we very much wished to contact his sister Kathleen in Las Vegas. He gave us her married name, said he didn't have her phone number at hand and wasn't remembering it, but promised to get it for us. We agreed to meet again the following day at 10:00 a.m., then drove back to Ontario.

Ex-CIA agent Lawrence Victor Harrison in conversation with the authors, June 2009. Note the sniper round in the ornate penholder on Harrison's desk. (Sylvia E. Bartley)

The next morning we spent two hours talking, recording, and photographing. It was the first time in our five-year association that Harrison had allowed Sylvia to take his picture, a reflection, we thought, of his decision to throw fate to the winds and share with us what he knew. The core of this third session, now without the presence of Jeff Guy, was a lengthy tape-recorded interview in English, which included, among others, the following salient points.

(1) Mossad took over some of the CIA's Mexican operations in 1984 as a consequence of press exposure of agency operatives, for which Manuel Buendía was blamed.

(2) Manuel Buendía was killed because "he had learned about the airstrips," that is, about the CIA-trafficker-*contra* connection.

(3) Zorrilla Pérez, while chief of the DFS, told Harrison that he (Zorrilla) "had to take care of Manuel Buendía" because Buendía "had learned something very important," which wasn't Zorrilla's involvement with the Guadalajara cartel and wasn't about German arms dealer Gerhard Mertins.

(4) Harrison was ambushed by the PJJ in September 1984 "on orders of the Americans" because of what he had learned about the CIA-trafficker-*contra* connection. "I was shot because I was told to stay out of it, and I didn't stay out of it," he told us. "That was on orders of the Americans. They shot me! . . . I was outside of their control, and they knew I saw things all the time. They knew that they couldn't hide them any longer. They knew that I [had] put it together."

(5) Ed Heath "was DEA but wasn't DEA," that is, he was a CIA officer operating under DEA cover.

(6) "Jungle FedEx" was a system whereby cocaine was transported across Guatemala to Chiapas by Kaibiles, that is, Guatemalan special forces. It was part of a larger narcotics network that has been overseen since World War II by elements of the U.S. government.

Former DFS director, PRI Executive Committee president, and Mexican presidential hopeful Javier García Paniagua, who has been implicated in the Buendía assassination by former CIA agent Lawrence Harrison. (Courtesy of L. V. Harrison)

(7) Peter Cimino worked with Rubén Zuno Arce in the 1970s moving drugs through Guerrero. Zuno, Harrison told us on another occasion, "was our guy," implying that he had cooperated with the CIA and, by extension, that Cimino had as well. Harrison now stated that he had "kicked Cimino out" of his asset network "because he had done very little and he was making a lot of noise and didn't seem to be very reliable."

And what, we asked him, was his explicit understanding with the U.S. government when he and his family were resettled in the United States? "That I wouldn't write any books and they wouldn't kill me."

Now fearing that his law practice would be sabotaged, Harrison mused bitterly about Héctor Berréllez's readiness to cheat on law course exams in pursuit of a bogus degree merely to enhance his professional image. "I'm not a cheater," he declared. "I don't have to cheat. I wanted to be a real lawyer. I was sincere, and they're not," he insisted, alluding to Berréllez's security associates and the assistant U.S. attorneys who had directed him to give perjured testimony in the Zuno trials. "They don't like sincerity," he emphasized. "Sincerity scares them!"

Harrison then segued into an emotional lament about the perversion of traditional American ideals and the nation's advanced state of political rot. "This country is full of the most terrible, damning, sinful, horrible contradictions that you can imagine!" he exclaimed. "It's hanging over us like a cloud. It's terrible what they're doing. It's terrible what they're doing down there [in Mexico]. It's terrible what they're doing up here. It's terrible! It's horrible! And believe me," he predicted, "the country is not going to be able to sustain itself on this path. This country is going to go down the tubes. And it hurts! It's outrageous! And nobody's telling the truth. Nobody will stand up and say, 'This is the truth!'"

As we were leaving, Harrison gave us his sister's phone number in Las Vegas, thanked us for coming, and repeated that he wanted "to pull the lid off" the whole mess. All we could promise was that we would try to help. He said he understood and that he was grateful for our efforts on his behalf. His parting handshake was firm. On some deeper level, our relationship had changed.

Three weeks later to the day he telephoned us at home. Sylvia answered, said she would have to call Russell in from outside, then listened as he recounted his latest travails. He was desperate, actually on the verge of tears. He and his family were being evicted and had to vacate by the following afternoon. He had money to rent another place but had not been able to find a landlord willing to accept their three dogs—two mixed Chihuahua toys and a larger mongrel. Harrison seemed especially attached to the dogs. Aside from his immediate family, his sister and brother-in-law in Las Vegas, and now the two of us, they were his only friends in the world. "I'm at the end of my rope!" he whimpered. "I have no place to go. I'll be on the street." It was a pathetic personal denouement for a man of his background and government service. "I don't know why I called you," he remarked. "Just to whine, I guess." We didn't know what to say. He didn't either, he said, and repeated that he guessed he had called "just to whine." We urged him to stay in touch however things worked out for them, and he assured us he would.

Two and a half weeks later Russell sent Harrison an e-mail to see if he was reachable and, if so, to let him know that we had been unable to contact his attorney, Paul Virgo, nor had we gotten through to either Chuck Jones or Jeff Guy. He replied the following day. "Dear Russ," he wrote. "Thank you for sticking. I enjoyed whining with (at) you the other day.:) Two hours later Jeff called with a house and I now live in beautiful downtown Hemet (sigh). . . . I have much to tell you. Once again, thanks for being there. Sincerely, Crybaby."[20]

He had won Jeff Guy's court case, the judge having dismissed Berréllez's charges against Guy, who now, somehow, had managed to locate a house for Harrison and his family to rent in the San Jacinto Valley retirement community of Hemet, thirty straight-line miles southeast of downtown Riverside. It was an emotional reprieve that buoyed Harrison for the immediate struggle to save his law practice and opened a new stage in our relationship with him. Russell had been making an effort for some time to cultivate their mutual passion for history, having given him several books on the subject, including one of his own, another that Russell and Sylvia had done together, and one in Spanish by the remarkable Uruguayan author Eduardo Galeano.[21] Whereas initially in our relationship Harrison would commit nothing to writing, he now began to communicate openly with us via e-mail about his legal problems and our Buendía investigation, as well as engaging Russell in wide-ranging historical discourses contrived to display his own uncommon knowledge and, in the competitive spirit of his youth, to challenge "the professor."

"You must know I have always had this sadness inside for the country," he wrote in a January 2010 e-mail that began: "Querido Profe" (Dear Prof). "So much sin hanging over us all and so little done to make it right." He was "on the brink of madness," he said, "the madness of telling the truth." But first, he had some "homework" for Russell: "Who first freed the slaves on our continent? And when? And more important, why? And where? When you have answered that," he explained, "you will understand what little tidbits keep me going in the midst of all this crap."[22]

"I gave you some homework two emails ago, and you have not turned it in," he reproached Russell when he failed to take his bait. "This is especially galling in an ex-teacher. You have been given five demerits. Please write me back with the answer."[23]

"Lord Dunmore, royal governor of Virginia, 14 November 1775, from the deck of HMS *Fowey* in the James River," Russell replied. "Edict applied to all slaves who would agree to bear arms on behalf of the Brits against the colonists."[24]

The answer Harrison wanted was the parish priest and father of Mexican independence Miguel Hidalgo y Costilla (1753–1811), who in the first months of the 1810 uprising against Spanish rule had declared the abolition of slavery in Mexico. In a conflated, creative rejoinder of chronologically disconnected historical events and actors (e.g., Hidalgo publishing his edict abolishing slavery in Reform-era journalist Francisco Zarco's newspaper *El Libertador* a decade after Zarco's execution, the fabled eleventh-century Castillian warrior El Cid championing the liberal Spanish Cortes of 1823, and Benito Juárez supposedly refusing the advances of Emperor Maximilian's widow the "Encueratriz" [Carnal Empress] Carlota), he made the lawyerly argument that Hidalgo was the first to outlaw slavery as a matter of universal human rights.[25]

Russell replied that, while he understood Harrison's admiration for Father Hidalgo, his question had asked who first freed the slaves in the Americas, when, why, and where. And the answer, Russell insisted, was not "the noble Mexican priest, rather the ignoble British governor of Virginia" forty-six years earlier. Moreover, "the why of Dunmore's edict is as historically significant as Hidalgo's edict is inspirational."

Russell called him on his careless presentation of historical facts, then noted that the only "homework" he related to was what he assigned himself. In high school, Russell told him, "I hated history because it was always reduced to a litany of names, dates and events that somebody else decided were important and that I should know but which had no meaningful connection to me." It was not until he went to live and study in Argentina as a young man, Russell explained, that history had become deeply personal. Now he decided for himself what could most helpfully be gleaned from the past.[26]

Harrison responded with a six-page, single-spaced, electronic missive arguing, first, that the legends of Santiago (St. James) and El Cid—not the men themselves—inspired popular support for parliamentary government (Cortes) in early nineteenth-century Spain, then detailing the history of the antislavery movement and further developing his legalistic argument that Fr. Miguel Hidalgo was the first to effectively abolish the institution of slavery in the Americas.

We marveled at the breadth of his interest in and familiarity with the historical record, Russell replied. But he had missed Russell's point. He did not have to prove himself to Russell, nor did Russell feel any need to prove himself to him. Russell did not care for games of "one-upsmanship," he clarified, and had no wish to play intellectual "gotcha." He had only sought to convey to him some sense of what history meant to us and what we find meaningless in so much of what passes for history. That said, Russell urged him to stay focused on the immediate issues before us, as time was pressing in on both of them. Three weeks later Harrison suffered a medical crisis that plunged him into a final downward spiral from which he would not fully recover.

By now we had made contact with his sister Kathleen and traveled to Las Vegas for an initial interview with her during the second week of November 2009. We explained to her that the book we were writing was not about her brother George per se but rather about the Mexican journalist Manuel Buendía and the circumstances surrounding his assassination. In order for us to be able to evaluate the information her brother was providing us about Buendía, however, it was essential that we learn as much as possible about him as a person, about his family background, his youth, his interests and education, and the experiences that ultimately led him into the CIA.

To give Kathleen a sense of how we perceived her brother, as well as to test our perceptions of him, we first remarked that George's IQ appeared to be "off the chart." She processed that statement for a moment, then nodded her agreement. George was exceptionally smart, we elaborated, but did not always think clearly. She studied us intently, then assented with a nod. And he was not particularly savvy in his choice of friends. She pondered this last assertion a little longer, then with a slow nod indicated her agreement. By that point in our association with George, we explained, we had concluded that having been obliged to return to the United States after two decades in Mexico, he was like the proverbial fish out of water, now unable to move comfortably in his birth culture. He had become so thoroughly acculturated to Mexican society and Mexican ways of doing things that back in his own country he missed cultural cues and sometimes violated American customs of comportment, which in turn may have compromised his law practice and left him vulnerable to the kind of institutional reprisal he now seemed to be experiencing.

George's contentious temperament, hardened by his and Kathleen's difficult upbringing, added a complicating layer of behavioral factors to his current situation, which, we repeated, was why we had come to Las Vegas to speak with her. During that first meeting, Kathleen detailed their family history, described their experiences growing up in Bakersfield, and then told us what she recalled of her brother's disappearance into the CIA and sudden reappearance two decades later. She warmed to us as we talked, and, when we finished, there were parting hugs all around. We agreed to remain in touch and did so for the next two years and eight months, meeting twice more in Nevada and once in California. We also spoke on numerous occasions by phone.[27]

Following our initial Las Vegas meeting with Kathleen, we drove to Hemet to meet with Harrison about his pending California Bar Association issues, which dated from the summer of 2006 when he had been "attacked and bloodied," as he put it, by unidentified parties intent on sabotaging his law practice. The most visible of those parties was Peter Cimino, who, together with two other former clients, had filed professional misconduct complaints against Harrison at the state bar. In August 2006, the bar opened formal investigations of those complaints, which culminated three years later in the filing of disciplinary charges (nine counts) at the State Bar Court.[28] By the fall of 2009, Harrison had been deposed by and was in ongoing communication with Brandon K. Tady, the deputy trial counsel assigned to present his case to the court. On learning of our association with Harrison, Tady expressed interest in discussing the case with us. At Harrison's request, we had contacted him and scheduled a meeting at the bar's Los Angeles offices for Friday, 13 November.

We had phoned Harrison the previous Tuesday evening on our arrival from Las Vegas and he immediately invited us to come by his house, but, tired from the day's long drive, we demurred until the next morning. We now found him in an upscale, nicely landscaped, gated development of Spanish-style stucco homes with red tile roofs, a significant number of them exhibiting foreclosure notices, which no doubt explains the circumstances in which he and his family had managed to rent their latest place, a two-story house with a four-column street-side arcade on Bee Balm Road. The interior of the house had tile floors, seemed relatively spacious, and was well lit. Entering through the front door, we moved down a corridor to Harrison's new office space, set off in a small alcove to our right. The corridor continued on into the main living area and a set of stairs accessing the second floor. To the right of the front entrance was a bathroom and, next to it, a room occupied by Harrison's son Daniel. On the corridor wall just outside the alcove office hung the iconic representation of Saint George slaying the dragon that we had observed in his previous offices as well.

Harrison had organized his new work space in roughly the same manner as before. His large oak desk dominated the alcove, and on its surface sat the black flat-screen computer monitor, the camel base desk lamp with fringed fabric shade, and the ornate

Middle Eastern brass pen holder, now without the mysterious rifle round we had observed in his Emerson Street bunker. (Asked about the missing cartridge, he feigned not to recall, then digressed into a discussion of ballistics, saying the bullet was probably .22 caliber, whatever the size of the cartridge, because it "was a subsonic bullet that could be easily silenced.") His bookcases of law tomes were in place, and on top of one of them rested the oval-framed family portrait of a younger, fitter Harrison ringed by his wife Lorena and their five children. Against the opposite corridor wall stood a vintage Philco floor radio, one of the many radios, we learned from his sister Kathleen, that he had repaired as a boy.

We met for two hours at midday on Wednesday to discuss our upcoming meeting with the State Bar Court attorney, then for another two and a half hours on Thursday afternoon clarifying details of our Buendía investigation. Harrison was feeling very poorly on Wednesday and in a great deal of pain, apparently occasioned by a combination of advanced diabetes and an untreated strangulated hernia. It was all he could do to raise his arms to rotate the computer monitor on his desk for us to view. After we had been talking for some time, there came a point when he lowered his head and, barely above a whisper, remarked plaintively, "I may not make it." We agreed to break until the next morning.

When we returned a little past 11:00 a.m. on Thursday, he was not home, having neglected to inform us that he had a morning court appointment. His son Daniel said he would be back within an hour, but, familiar with Harrison's fluid sense of time, we decided not to wait, saying we would check in with him later. Back at our motel, Russell placed a call to Chuck Jones in San Diego and was surprised when he actually answered the phone. Harrison had been urging us to get in touch with Jones and had himself tried unsuccessfully to contact him during our meeting the day before. Jones recognized Russell's name when he introduced himself and seemed interested in speaking with him. Russell explained briefly our interest in Harrison, Berréllez, The Mayo Group, Kiki Camarena, and Manuel Buendía, and Jones gave him the highlights of his own background as a retired DEA agent and now private investigator.

Jones had known Camarena, he said, and had heard of Berréllez but only met him after he retired. Jeff Guy had introduced them, he explained, and Berréllez then persuaded him to help find qualified staff for The Mayo Group. By his account, he had brought in "a couple dozen of the best professionals to be found," all of them security experts and former government employees. And they had all become disillusioned by the mediocrity of Berréllez's operation, he said. He himself had no respect for Berréllez and even less for his son Chris, who also worked for The Mayo Group and whom Jones described as "a convicted felon."

As Russell pursued his questioning about Berréllez and The Mayo Group, Jones interrupted to say that he didn't really know Russell or anything about him and that he was only speaking with him "because Lawrence had asked him to." He trusted Lawrence, he assured Russell, and "Lawrence's recommendation was good enough for him." It was an oddly dissonant remark, perhaps made to allay any doubts we might harbor about him but which had the opposite effect. Together with Harrison's earlier observation that Jones did not share his view of Camarena's fate, it raised a cautionary red flag.

Russell further explained that we were looking closely at Berréllez and his private security firm because there appeared to be some connection between The Mayo Group and Harrison's current difficulties. He mentioned the legal problems Jeff Guy had told us Berréllez was having and recounted the incident in which someone had utilized computer graphics software to insert the name "SECURITY/INVESTIGATIONS/ INTERNATIONAL TRAINING & PROTECTION SERVICES" across the facade of The Mayo Group's Commercenter headquarters building on a newly created SPI Group website. It was a thoroughly amateurish job, Russell remarked, of a piece with the hangdog image of SPI Group CEO Berréllez in the executive suit and tie he had once so despised as a gunslinging field agent. Russell repeated Charles Bowden's thought that these security firms served as "golden handcuffs" by means of which "they" could control a potentially rogue Berréllez. "Who are 'they'?" Jones asked with a distinct edge to his voice. "Presumably some agency of the U.S. government," Russell replied.

Russell's mention of Bowden's association with Berréllez, the September 1998 *Esquire* article, and Gary Webb elicited an unexpectedly caustic response from Jones. "Gary Webb was an out-of-control asshole who blew three major DEA operations by shooting off his mouth to the wrong people!" he fumed. Jones seemed especially exercised by Webb's assertion that Danilo Blandón had been trafficking cocaine in support of the Nicaraguan *contras*. To our astonishment, he described Blandón as "a fine person" with whom he personally had had "business dealings." (As noted earlier, by Gary Webb's account Jones had served as Blandón's "handler," which in the context of the 1980s could also have meant his CIA "case officer.") Jones expressed total disdain for both Webb and U.S. congresswoman Maxine Waters, who, based on Webb's "Dark Alliance" series in the *San Jose Mercury News*, had excoriated the CIA for allegedly facilitating the introduction of crack cocaine into her South Central Los Angeles district through its association with Blandón and his trafficker associates.

Jones added that he had a box of legal documents concerning Gary Webb at his Chula Vista office, which he was willing to share with us. They were "legal," he curiously clarified, in the sense that he possessed them legitimately. He then talked to Russell at some length about his private investigator's business, noting that it was typically feast or famine, that he worked out of his home to save on overhead, and that at the moment he was very busy with a major case in Atlanta, which was the reason he had not been able to give Lawrence Harrison the assistance he needed to prepare his State Bar Court defense. He went on to tell Russell about "a genuinely high-powered" private security firm (as compared to Berréllez's Mayo/SPI Group) with which he was associated that specialized in computer-based security-screening technology and had contracts "from Jordan to Timbuktu." He encouraged us to take a look at the firm's website, and we agreed to stay in touch.[29]

We returned to Harrison's Bee Balm Road rental that afternoon and found him feeling much better than the day before. He had good days and bad days, he explained, and this was one of his better days. With the exception of a bitter reference to Berréllez having threatened to destroy his law practice ("I made you a lawyer, and I can take it away from you anytime I want!") and, in response to a direct question, his statement that following the Camarena trials he had been given a onetime, half-million-dollar government severance payment, we talked exclusively about matters related to our Buendía investigation. We wrapped up around 4:30, promised to call him after our meeting with Brandon Tady the next day, and took our leave.

We met with Tady from 11:00 a.m. to 1:00 p.m. in a windowless, fourth-floor conference room in the AT&T Building in downtown Los Angeles, where the California State Bar has its local offices. By then Tady had three decades of lawyering behind him, and he impressed us as an exceptionally competent attorney. As deputy trial counsel, he was a prosecutor for the State Bar Court but made clear to us that he had no wish to prosecute the charges against Harrison simply for the sake of prosecution. His purpose, he explained, was to determine the truth of the matter insofar as that was possible and then to proceed appropriately. He methodically reviewed for us the nine counts against Harrison, speaking nonstop and without notes for approximately forty-five minutes, after which we shared with him what we knew about the case and the impinging circumstances of Harrison's situation as a disillusioned former CIA agent.

The most serious charges were those made by Peter Cimino, who alleged that Harrison had fraudulently involved him in the scheme to purchase the 4121 Mission Inn Avenue property, had forged Cimino's signature on loan papers and related real estate documents, had surreptitiously placed Delia Rodríguez's notary stamp on documents containing Cimino's forged signature, and had forged Rodríguez's signature on the bogus notarizations of Cimino's signature.[30] These were felony counts, which, if upheld by the State Bar Court, almost certainly would have led to criminal prosecution and the likelihood of long-term incarceration, effectively eliminating Harrison as a discloser of state secrets and discrediting him as a source for any secrets already compromised.

Tady seemed to have a reasonable grasp of Harrison's version of what was behind his bar problems but understood that the coercive measures scenario could never be proven in a court of law. The complicating factor, he noted, and we acknowledged, was that Harrison had pursued a career of inherent deception and was himself a practiced prevaricator, which made it exceedingly difficult to distinguish truth from falsehood in his account of events. That said, Tady could not dismiss the possibility that what Harrison alleged might actually be true. That possibility, combined with the fact that Tady was unable to establish a coherent train of events to prove the fraud and forgery charges, plus the additional information that we were able to provide about the case, moved him to drop the felony charges and press only the remaining malpractice infractions. After we left, Harrison later informed us, Tady had called to tell him that we had been helpful and he had been favorably impressed with what we had to say. Harrison's case would be heard the following Wednesday, 18 November.[31]

It all ended "with a whimper rather than a bang," Harrison e-mailed us a week later. "All charges alleging moral turpitude or client damage [i.e., the felonies] were dismissed, leaving only failure to cooperate, failure to pay sanctions, and failure to perform competently." He had been given a two-month suspension, would be back in practice in sixty days, and was "still on [Cimino's] tail." In the end, he wrote, "Tady didn't know what to do. All of the facts seemed to show what you and Sylvia had told him." Harrison now intended to sue the parties who had filed the charges against him, Peter Cimino in the first instance.[32]

On Sunday evening, 27 December 2009, Harrison e-mailed us that Delia Rodríguez's daughter Melissa had supposedly been arrested by the FBI for loan modification fraud. Héctor Berréllez had called to tell him, saying that the feds had investigated him as well but cleared him of any wrongdoing. Jeff Guy had dropped from sight, and no one seemed to know where he was. Harrison wondered if he might be in cahoots with Berréllez. He would try to find out if Melissa Rodríguez had in fact been arrested. If so, he speculated, she would be vulnerable and might be persuaded to expose what her mother, Berréllez, and others had confabulated against him. Berréllez was scared, he thought, and would do whatever he could to cover up. "For my part," Harrison wrote in Spanish, "I pray to God that the truth comes out. Please advise me. I'm your friend and am treading on uncertain ground."[33]

Russell got back to him the following morning. Why would the FBI conduct an investigation of alleged loan fraud in California? he asked Harrison. What was the potential federal infraction? Or was this perhaps a "national security" matter? And why did he suppose Berréllez had called him? What did Héctor expect from him if he'd been screwing him these past years? As for Jeff Guy, we found his behavior stranger with each passing day.[34]

An hour after sending this electronic communication to Harrison, we received what we quickly determined to be a spurious e-mail from lawhyer@yahoo.com, Harrison's address. The only message appeared in the subject line. It read, "Heya, long time no news" and had been sent to forty different addresses, ours first on the list. After puzzling over it briefly, we replied, "Heya, back. What's this all about?" Harrison's reply came four days later: "Russ, I don't know, I didn't send it but it has all my recent email recipients. Some kind of hack? Nothing there I'm trying to hide."[35]

It was the beginning of an electronic assault on Harrison's credibility and a simultaneous attempt to intimidate us. Hackers had accessed Harrison's computer address book and were now blanket-mailing nonsensical electronic messages in his name to all listed parties, which included law associates and county, state, and federal judicial personnel with whom he had professional attorney relations. A second spurious e-mail went out on Saturday, 2 January 2010, with a subject line that read, "Be ready at the right moment" and a line of faux code in the text space: ^C/y*41C7)/r&z]d; ^C/y*41C7)r&z]d; ^C/y*41C7)/r&z]d;.[36] We assumed it was more of the same. Harrison replied two days later that it was, that he had no idea what "be ready at the right moment" meant, and that he wished they would stop "their childish crap" as it was quite tiresome.[37]

On Sunday, 3 January, Russell e-mailed Harrison some calculated comments about what was by then an obvious hacking incident. It was a good example of why one ought not use the computer address book feature, and Russell suggested that he delete all the entries from his. The attack was surprisingly amateurish, he noted. As Markus Wolf, the legendary East German spymaster, might have remarked, "Sehr interesant. . . . Und dumm!" Dumb, indeed. It had the same quality of incompetence we had observed in Héctor Berréllez's SPI Group website.

What we found most puzzling about the whole thing, Russell wrote, was that the hackers had made a point of revealing their hand. Why? To what practical end? Any halfway savvy person knew that no electronic communication system was entirely secure and any computer can be hacked, so it seemed unlikely that this was their message. Was he supposed to be intimidated by their pulp novel "coded" messages? It seemed unlikely. If, however, any recipients of those messages were to accept them at face value, then Harrison's emotional stability would be placed in doubt, which in turn would negatively impact his law practice.

We did note with interest, Russell wrote, that the hackers had taken pains to insert his e-mail address into his own address book, thereby assuring that he would receive the bogus communications as well. It struck us as an obvious attempt to unnerve him. He was clearly dealing with "dirt balls," Russell remarked, who never outgrew adolescence and desperately needed to get a life, because theirs served no socially redeeming purpose. Unfortunately, they probably would or could not, which made them potentially dangerous. It wouldn't surprise us, Russell closed, if the party or parties behind the hacking assault were in the compromised address book. Russell named no one, but among the possible candidates we placed Chuck Jones and Jeff Guy high on our list of primary suspects.[38]

Within the next two hours there came another spurious e-mail, ostensibly from Harrison but clearly from the hackers. While broadcast, like the previous ones, to the entire address book, this message was unmistakably addressed to us: "Take and dip your stick," read the subject line. Below, in a bold, 36-point, Times New Roman font, were the words

US DRUGSTORE ONLINE!
GO GO GO

Our e-mail address again appeared first in the compromised address book list.[39]

Harrison took immediate measures to secure his e-mail and Internet connections, and by the third week in January the bogus messages appeared to have stopped. Recognizing that online communications could never be 100 percent secure, however, he suggested that we take additional precautions for any sensitive messages. He had been feeling very poorly, he informed us—"ill, alone, and depressed that they were shooting at me again"—an allusion to the September 1984 PJJ ambush in which he had almost been killed. Jeff Guy, he told us, was the only person outside his immediate family who might have known his computer password.[40]

Following these initial e-mail exchanges about the hacker attack, we suddenly found our access to Héctor Berréllez's SPI Group website blocked. We had been monitoring the SPI site since our March 2009 conversations with Jeff Guy about Berréllez's private security activities. Then one day in early February 2010, having decided to revisit the site, we unexpectedly found ourselves greeted by an animated, pitchfork-wielding, red, white, and blue devil thrusting a middle digit in our general direction. Incongruously, small red letters beneath the little devil's feet read, "United Arab Emirates." In a larger font below that were the words "Go To Hell IRAN," with "Go To Hell" in black bold type and "IRAN" in red. At the top of the screen in red and black were the words "Own3d By Team Emirates." Strung out in two lines across the bottom of the screen was an apparently coded series of credits: "Greetz: Red Devils Crew

[Saudi | x] o xOOmxOOm o ZombiE_KsA o aBO mOh4mM3d o V4 Team o Group XP o Islamic Ghosts Team o ByLenis."

It had the distinctive stamp of cyberwarriors infused with hallmark American arrogance toward nonwestern societies. It also suggested the possibility of private security contractors and immediately brought to mind the firm Chuck Jones had described to Russell—the one with contracts "from Jordan to Timbuktu." That firm, in which Jones served as director, was a high-tech security company specializing in the development and marketing of psycho-physiological stress analysis devices for security-screening purposes. It was headquartered in Las Vegas on West Sahara Avenue, not far from where we'd met with Harrison's sister Kathleen, and no doubt employed web-savvy personnel familiar with cyberwar techniques.[41] At the time, Jones told us, they were "in negotiations with high-level officials in Mexico" who were "very much interested" in the stress analysis screening systems. "Talk about cleaning house in Mexico!" he had remarked facetiously. "Nobody would be left to run the country."[42]

After the middle-digit-thrusting little devil block had been in place at the SPI Group website for a while, Russell informed Harrison about it and e-mailed him an attached file of the "Go To Hell IRAN" screen. Within days the anomalous animation

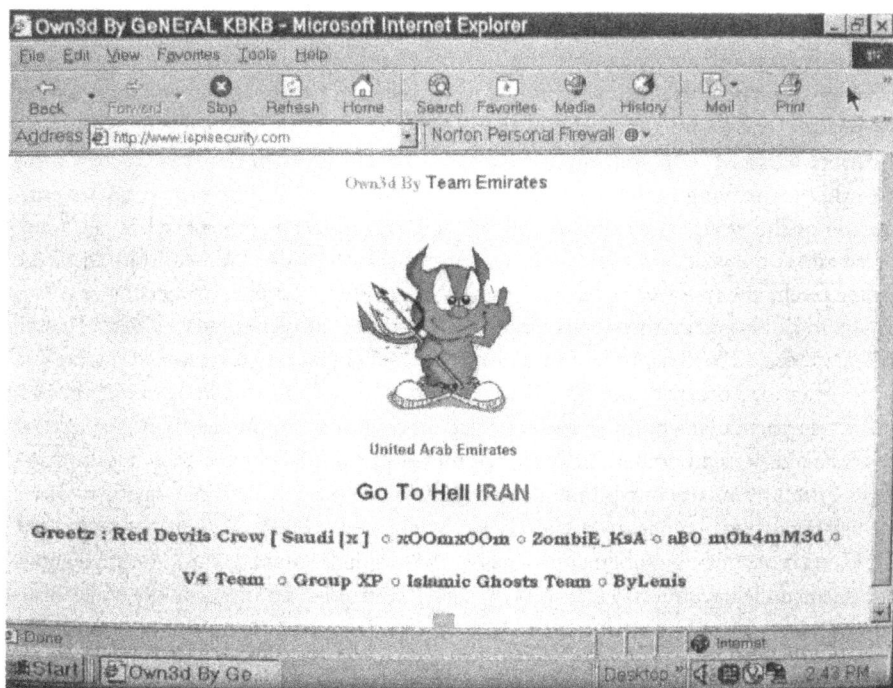

The authors' compromised computer monitor showing an animated, pitchfork-wielding, middle-digit-thrusting devil denying access to the website of the SPI Group, Héctor Berréllez's private security firm in San Bernardino, California. The references to the United Arab Emirates, Iran, and Saudi Arabia suggest a National Security Agency link, either direct or through a private contractor. (Sylvia E. Bartley)

disappeared, replaced with six capital letters in bold type: "NOJODA." The unseparated Spanish words *No joda* mean "Don't fuck with us."

"This has the fingerprints of ex-S/A Cojones all over it," Russell told Harrison, using a double-entendre sobriquet we had given Chuck Jones derived from his e-mail user name (cjonesinv).[43] We had expressed our doubts about Jones to Harrison three weeks earlier. "I don't know how you came to know this Cojones dude, nor why you confided in him," Russell wrote in Spanish, "but let me tell you, in my view he's not to be trusted, not at all. Be very careful with him." It was Jones, we thought, who was behind Jeff Guy.[44]

Harrison replied that his suspicions had already been raised. When his State Bar Court problems developed, he wrote us, Guy disappeared and Jones was nowhere to be found. During the discovery period, neither of them showed up to help, despite past promises. "Thank God I had my own sources and evidence, as well as your help," he expressed. In the end, Jones failed to assist him at all, yet a month after Harrison's state bar case had concluded, Jones reassured us, "I'm looking forward to meeting with you and Lawrence in the future to help you in any way I can with your investigation." We imagined he was indeed, for his own ulterior purposes.[45]

The harassment went on for some time after we had reestablished a modicum of Internet security. (We, too, had been hacked and were obliged to upgrade our hardware, software, and server connection.) On our end, we now began receiving e-mails inviting us to click on links we assumed were designed to breach the enhanced security measures we had taken, some of those messages ostensibly sent by Harrison. We also were harassed with spurious phone calls, sometimes with the same recognizable live caller identifying herself or himself as a representative of different corporate entities. He or she would typically ask for "Russell," claim to be "returning his call," and, for whatever purpose, attempt to engage him in conversation. We would listen to the callers' pitch, always given against a background of room sounds, then hang up.

The most blatant of these calls came late one afternoon in September 2010. Russell had telephoned Harrison to let him know that we had just sent him some Gravenstein apples from our orchard, the first of the season. We had talked briefly about the fact that those particular apples were "historic," having been produced by a tree grafted from the old Russian orchard at Fort Ross on California's Sonoma Coast. Ten minutes after Russell hung up, our phone rang and Sylvia answered. Without saying a word, the caller noisily bit into an apple. Twice Sylvia said, "Hello?" There was no reply, just the audible chewing of an apple against the ambient sounds of an office. The message seemed clear enough: Harrison's overseers continued to monitor the three of us closely.

Who, precisely, those overseers were we could not positively establish, although we assumed they were most likely Los Angeles–based CIA operatives working in concert with former federal agents now employed as private security contractors. Suggestive documentation of such practice has come to our attention in the form of a John Doe civil complaint filed in August 2013 against the CIA in U.S. District Court for the District of Columbia. Because of the plaintiff's covert status, neither his true name nor his whereabouts could be revealed. He is described in the filing as "a senior covert paramilitary officer" who carried out overseas assignments for the agency during the period 2003–2011, was "wrongfully accused of participating in, committing and/or possessing information about war crimes," and had been subjected to an "unreasonably and intentionally delayed" internal investigation by the CIA's Office of the Inspector General (OIG) so as to "discredit or otherwise cause harm to his career." The purpose of the complaint was to compel the OIG to expeditiously conclude its investigation of the plaintiff, to cover court costs and attorney's fees, and to provide such additional relief to the plaintiff as the court deemed just and proper.[46]

Of particular relevance to the present account of measures taken against Lawrence Victor Harrison and collaterally against the authors is paragraph nine of John Doe's complaint, under the rubric "Facts." "In connection with internal investigations of John Doe," that paragraph reads, "CIA employees, either with or without authority, initiated physical and electronic surveillance of him. . . . The surveillance included harassment tactics undertaken by local law enforcement who were cooperating with the CIA. Other tactics involved corruption of electronic devices such as computers and cell phones." A subsequent paragraph under the "Facts" rubric alleges that "the CIA OIG is aware that there is no evidentiary basis for the allegations against John Doe and is purposefully refusing to administratively close its investigation *in order to discredit or otherwise cause harm to his career*" (emphasis added). The same objectives were pursued against Harrison, albeit with greater prejudice to the target. Qualitatively, however, the two cases are similar, as is the punitive mind-set behind them. The main operational difference seems to be that in John Doe's case the CIA utilized local law enforcement, whereas in Harrison's it apparently employed private contractors.[47]

For our part, we continued to communicate by e-mail without overt hacker interference from mid-January through February 2010. In addition to our history exchanges about Hidalgo, Lord Dunmore, El Cid, and the Cortes de Cádiz, Russell offered Harrison further thoughts about his conflicted conscience around violating CIA secrecy oaths. Picking up on his statements about "the madness of telling the truth," of being "soul-torn" by having to weigh his family against a "clear duty to tell the truth," and of having "a duty to the country [i.e., the CIA] which conflicted with [his] greater duty to tell the truth," Russell acknowledged that telling the truth could have dire consequences, especially where one's family was involved. "Duty to the country," however, posed a different set of issues.

"Duty," Russell offered, is an ethical concept, while "country" is not. Nor is "government" synonymous with "country"; rather it is the coercive instrumentality of those in society who wield decisive influence. "One who serves the ends of a government agency," he suggested, "is ethically bound by the terms and conditions of that agency only so long as s/he chooses to continue serving those ends." Should one come to decide that such ends are "inimical to the ethical precepts inculcated from childhood and on which civilized life depends," then "duty" to that agency ceases. "Dans le domaine de la Divinité régit la Vérité, n'est pas?" In the realm of the Divine, Truth reigns, does it not?[48]

"Oui," he responded. "Mais oui. But you still die, and it's hard to get your story across when you're in that state."[49] It was a circular argument without a satisfactory resolution, yet one he still could not bring himself to abandon.

A month later we returned home one day to find a message on our answering machine from Kathleen: "George is in the hospital. Call me." When we did, she informed us that her brother had been admitted to the Hemet Valley Medical Center (HVMC). He required surgery for his untreated strangulated hernia, but surgical intervention was problematic because of advanced diabetes and what doctors had tentatively diagnosed as congestive heart failure. His condition "was very serious," she said, implying that he might not live. We had already been planning to meet again with Kathleen in Las Vegas the following week and now agreed to modify those plans as required by Harrison's evolving medical crisis.

It was in these circumstances that the true insidiousness of Harrison's situation and the coercive measures being taken against him came into full focus. When he was admitted to the HVMC in a life-threatening emergency, he immediately confronted the cost and payment bane of American hospital care, though in a more sinister manner than most. Harrison had turned sixty-five the previous fall and was technically eligible for Medicare. *Harrison*, however, was a false CIA identity whose faux Social Security number made him two years younger than he really was and thus ineligible. There was nothing he or his family could do in the immediate circumstances to remedy that official deception, and they had no savings of their own to cover what promised to be major medical expenses. He was, in effect, indigent.

After twenty-four hours of tests and observation, HMVC medical staff concluded that he required further coronary evaluation before the surgical repair of his hernia could be performed and decided to send him to the Riverside County Regional Medical Center (RCRMC) in Moreno Valley some thirty miles away. Rather than arrange for the ambulance transfer his delicate condition seemed to warrant, HVMC medicated him, then had his son Daniel drive him to Moreno Valley. Russell had spoken briefly with Harrison by phone the previous day and could barely make out what he was saying. "It doesn't look good," Harrison managed to whisper. But when Russell tried to call Daniel the following afternoon for an update on his father's status, Harrison himself answered in a surprisingly strong voice. Where was he? Russell asked. "I checked out! Well, not all the way," he clarified with hallmark sardonicism. "I'm eternal," he added. "They can't kill me. I'm a weed!" It was an apt metaphor, we thought, but also a searing indictment of a social system run amuck.

At the RCRMC, a large public facility that accepts indigent patients, staff repeated the tests that had been done in Hemet, prescribed a course of medication to strengthen Harrison's heart function in preparation for an eventual angiogram and possible arterial stent, and stabilized his diabetes. Repair of the hernia was postponed pending treatment of his coronary problems. Unable to resolve Harrison's Medicare eligibility, RCRMC staff managed to enroll him in MediCal, the California state health care program for residents below the poverty line. MediCal coverage would provide him with the basic care he had previously been unable to afford, the lack of which had gravely compromised his health.

During a lunch break while visiting Harrison at the RCRMC, we discussed his situation with Kathleen and his brother-in-law Roy, who were still trying to grasp what exactly had been happening to George since he'd begun talking to us in 2004. Roy, in particular, was concerned for Kathleen's safety, fearing that, because of what her brother had been doing in Mexico and now our involvement with him, she might be in some kind of danger. George had, after all, told all four of us that he thought he might be killed for not remaining silent. Did we have any concerns, they wanted to know. "Were we scared?" as Kathleen expressed it.

No, we assured them, we were not, with the qualifying observation that no matter how sober one's judgment it was always possible to misread a situation. Our circumstances differed from George's, we explained, in that we were independent investigators seeking information from him about an important historical event, whereas he had been involved in highly sensitive covert operations that remain classified and whose exposure could have a negative impact on certain aspects of U.S. foreign relations. Additionally, he had been a member of the intelligence fraternity and was still subject to its coercive code of secrecy, no matter his personal disillusionment with the CIA's practices and purposes. For our part, we were not bound by the intelligence code but rather by the journalistic ethic of discovery and revelation. What we could anticipate as a consequence of our investigation were government attempts to intimidate and thwart us and then a concerted effort to discredit our book, as well as the two of us personally.

George, on the other hand, had good reason to fear that he might actually be killed to prevent him from talking further about Mexico. That might well be what was happening to him now, we suggested: death from compromised health aggravated by worry, tension, and penury rather than a bullet to the mastoid, as he had once explained to us was the prescribed way to assassinate someone with a small-caliber subsonic round that could be silenced. Were this indeed the case, it would mean that the primary objective of silencing him was to be accomplished with a perverse element of reprisal for violating the intelligence fraternity's secrecy code. George's punishment would thus be doubly enhanced: certain knowledge that he was going to die within a proximate future yet sufficient time to dwell on the emotional and material tribulations he had visited on his family. While we reviled the covert tasks he had performed in Mexico, we understood that he had carried them out in good faith as a true patriot persuaded by the political rhetoric of his day, only to be discarded by the government he had served at great personal sacrifice. George's tragedy, we told Roy and Kathleen, was that now, at the end of his life, when he most needed and deserved his country's support, he had found himself to be a government throwaway.

A further complicating factor derived from the settlement terms of Harrison's recent bar case. In addition to his sixty-day suspension from the practice of law, he was required to attend a session of the State Bar Ethics School, as well as pass the Multistate Professional Responsibility Examination (MPRE) administered by the National Conference of Bar Examiners, which his deteriorating health now prevented him from doing. On 26 September 2011, he was suspended from the practice of law until such time as he could provide proof of having passed the MPRE to the state bar's Office of Probation, thus effectively terminating his law career.[50]

When next we met with him, three days after he returned home from the RCRMC, we found him alert but visibly weak and now connected to a large green oxygen bottle on a wheeled dolly, which had to be towed around with him wherever he went. It was apparent that he would not be returning to a courtroom anytime soon, even if he could somehow muster the strength to fulfill the state bar's ethics and professional responsibility requirements. Despite the relatively favorable outcome of the State Bar Court proceedings, Harrison's overseers had managed to destroy him professionally. "I keep looking down the road, and there's no road," he remarked in a brief phone conversation two weeks later. He didn't care anymore who his persecutors were or what their plans for him might be. He didn't have that much time left, he said, and did not care to spend whatever he did have fighting them. In the end, he thought, they would fail as a result of their own contradictions.

By June 2010, Harrison and his family were on food stamps. In July, they were evicted from their Hemet residence. Over the next two years they would live vagabond-like, moving from cramped quarters with a daughter to cramped quarters with an in-law to a remote rental property on the southern outskirts of Riverside, all to the continued detriment of Harrison's precarious health. In March 2012, he suffered a repeat hernia crisis and was taken to Riverside Community Hospital, where a staff surgeon managed to repair the abdominal rupture without precipitating the feared coronary crisis that earlier had kept doctors in Hemet and Moreno Valley from performing the needed surgery. His limited MediCal health coverage had forced him into a health maintenance organization (HMO) arrangement, which effectively kept him from receiving the priority coronary care he required. During a twenty-minute phone conversation at the beginning of May 2012, he commented resignedly that his daily routine had been reduced to getting up in the morning, walking two blocks, then sitting all day. It was as much as he could physically endure. "That's all that's left in life," he lamented. "Walk two blocks and sit."

That July Harrison's sister Kathleen died suddenly of undiagnosed cancer, and he took her death very hard. Later that year he suffered two heart attacks and a stroke, which landed him back in RCRMC, where doctors finally performed the angiogram and inserted the arterial stent that had been discussed and debated over the previous two and a half years. His Medicare conundrum had resolved itself when the age recorded in his false identity records reached sixty-five. "When they give you an identity," Harrison explained, "they tell you to remember your original Social Security number. I couldn't remember mine."[51]

He'd had to surrender all his personal documentation to the CIA when he was given his Lawrence Victor Harrison identity so as to keep any of it from surfacing inconveniently to compromise his government cover. Now, when he had emergency need of Medicare coverage, the agency would not reinstate his original number, ostensibly because to do so would have confirmed his false identity as a former undercover CIA operative. It was an institutional decision likely intended to hasten his demise. If this was in fact the result of premeditated measures taken to silence a recalcitrant former spy, as the progression of events over the previous four years seemed to suggest, then indeed the guardians of U.S. government secrets had proceeded against Lawrence Victor Harrison "with extreme prejudice."

We last visited Harrison in mid-March 2013. His family had managed to rent a pleasant house near the RCRMC, where he was at last receiving regular outpatient care and had immediate access to emergency hospitalization if needed. He was now receiving a monthly Social Security payment, and three of his children were helping to meet expenses. "I've given up on life," he had commented during a phone conversation the previous month, still in pain from his arterial stent surgery. On entering their new residence, however, it was apparent that, while he recognized and accepted his approaching mortality, he had not given up on himself.

The framed representation of Saint George that we had observed in San Dimas, Riverside, and Hemet watched over the front entryway, while the carved avenging angel from those earlier sites, now with a broken right hand damaged in transit, kept vigil over the small ground-floor sitting room that doubled as Harrison's personal work space. In its mahogany stand on top of a replica Victorian desk sat the ever-present oval family portrait of a younger Harrison surrounded by wife and children. Next to it stood the familiar figurine of the Virgin of Guadalupe, while on a nearby Victorian cabinet were arrayed photographs of his father and paternal grandmother and a group shot of Davis and Cummings ancestors.

We had brought Harrison a copy of the present book's table of contents together with the first two chapters, which he read in their entirety while we sat there with him. "Interesting chapter titles," he offered as he started to read. "Where's the rest of it?" he wanted to know as soon as he finished. We promised to send him additional chapters after we returned home. Neither he nor we had expected he would live to see the completed manuscript. Even his RCRMC doctors were incredulous that he had survived his most recent spate of medical crises. Yet there he was, still engaged in the historic events that had brought us together nine years earlier, clarifying questions, confirming significant details, offering us new information. Yes, he had dealt with Barry Seal in Mexico and helped him replace an engine on a DC-3. Yes, he knew Robert Baer but declined to tell us how, when, or where they had met. Yes, he had dealt personally with Rafael Loret de Mola and considered him a "friend." It was the DEA (Justice Department), not the CIA, that had paid him the half-million-dollar witness fee for testifying in the Camarena trials. Manuel Buendía was killed because of what he had learned about guns, drugs, Central America, and the CIA.

17

Parsing the Evidence

It's like a Russian novel with its cast of characters meshing together into a world where the murder is never perfectly solved but finally understood.

—Charles Bowden, e-mail to Russell H. Bartley (8 August 2012)

The most audacious aspect of Manuel Buendía's columns was that the national security topics he analyzed publicly were seamlessly interlinked, although few readers appeared to notice. But those in the know could see that he was connecting the dots.

—Rogelio Hernández López, *Zorrilla* (1989)

STATE-PERPETRATED ASSASSINATIONS are inherently more difficult to expose than premeditated civilian homicides, especially when they involve more than one state, as we conclude occurred in the murder of Manuel Buendía. Exposure of such crimes is further complicated by a government's ability to cover up its felonious activities. While civilian felons contrive alibis and frame innocent parties, such ruses typically fail to hold up under close police investigation. Only, perhaps, in the corporate world might one find a comparable capacity to cover up criminal activity. No specifically business-linked hypothesis has yet been advanced to explain the Buendía killing, however.

The single greatest obstacle confronting members of the public who seek to investigate suspected crimes of state is the state's ability to define the terms and parameters of inquiry. Public skepticism of government notwithstanding, majorities in most national societies grant at least a modicum of institutional legitimacy to their respective political systems, which absent blatant malfeasance in office imbues senior government officials with privileged authority not easily challenged by private citizens. Independent special prosecutors and "blue ribbon" commissions appointed to definitively resolve crimes of potentially system-disrupting consequence are emergency measures designed to repair compromised institutional credibility and assuage dangerously disabused public opinion. Within the prevailing political ethos of modern states, the verdict of such personages is typically deemed unassailable. As a matter of logic, however, that premise is fallacious.

The twentieth-century American iconoclast I. F. Stone once famously quipped, "All governments are run by liars and nothing they say should be believed." While clearly an exaggeration to make a valid point, namely, that no government official's word should be accepted simply because of its source, little of what Mexican authorities have had to say over the years about the Buendía assassination in fact warrants credence. The same holds for official American assertions about Buendía, as well as the related abduction, torture interrogation, and murder of DEA S/A Enrique Camarena Salazar.

A corollary to the empirical fact of mendacity as a tactical instrument of government is the equally well-established executive practice of pursuing active measures against any individual, group, or other nongovernmental entity that seriously challenges official policies or threatens to expose state secrets. Such measures range from the impugning of critics' evidence to personal and professional harassment and, in especially sensitive cases, even physical assault. The professional crucifixion of *San Jose Mercury News* investigative reporter Gary Webb following his 1996 exposé of CIA ties to *contra*-linked cocaine traffickers is an emblematic example. The savaging of Lawrence Harrison's personal life for what he threatened to reveal about U.S. complicity in the Buendía and Camarena killings is another. Mexican authorities, for their part, have employed the full range of active measures to mask their own involvement in the Buendía and Camarena affairs.

To date scant attention has been paid to the evidentiary logic of the Buendía case. Early on this could be explained by the pressing need to develop a body of evidence, a process in which Mexican reporters and other independent investigators, including ourselves, became so deeply immersed that we failed to consider fully the larger perspective wherein the accumulating evidence acquired meaning. Three decades later we at last begin to gain that perspective, and, while we are still unable to "perfectly solve" the Buendía murder, as Charles Bowden has expressed it, we believe we now begin to understand it.

A helpful element of logic in sorting out the seeming imponderables of the Buendía case is what scholars and scientists refer to as "Occam's Razor," an analytical principle attributed to the fourteenth-century English Franciscan monk William of Ockham (ca. 1285–1349), which holds that the fewest number of factors required to explain a problem fully most likely provides the actual explanation. Known in the philosophical literature as "the principle of parsimony" or "unnecessary plurality," it posits that in attempting to solve a problem one should discard superfluous hypotheses and not introduce unnecessary elements of proof. It is a principle used to reach evidence-based conclusions.

The logic of the investigative method, however, is governed by several principles in addition to Occam's Razor, which only serves to winnow and sift the working hypotheses that drive an investigation. In the present instance, our methodology has been that of the historian, which theoretically should be the methodology of criminal investigators as well but in practice tends to be compromised by the often arbitrary imperatives of state judicial and criminal justice systems. The logic of historical thought, David Hackett Fischer notes in a now classic treatise on the subject, "consists neither in inductive reasoning from the particular to the general, nor in deductive reasoning from the general to the particular" but rather is "a process of *adductive* reasoning in the simple sense of adducing answers to specific questions, so that a satisfactory 'fit' is obtained." History, Fischer stresses, is a problem-solving discipline, and the historical investigator is anyone "who asks an open-ended question about past events and answers it with selected facts," which must always be presented in the form of a reasoned argument.[1]

If conclusions are to be persuasive, they must be reasonably argued, and the way that occurs is via a progression of reasoned arguments investigators have with themselves about the key questions on which final conclusions necessarily rest. As Fischer describes in great detail, however, ostensibly reasoned historical argument is all too often vitiated by fallacies of logic, especially in the framing of questions, the positing of factual significance, the verification of facts, and the attribution of motivation. Much of what has been written about the slaying of Manuel Buendía, including Special Prosecutor Miguel Ángel García Domínguez's final report and summary of investigation, exemplifies those fallacies. To avoid them ourselves, it is well to summarize what we can now state as unequivocal fact about the Buendía case.

(1) The victim, Manuel Buendía Tellezgirón, was a politically influential Mexican newspaper columnist whose views often clashed with powerful domestic, as well as foreign, interests.

(2) Given Buendía's professional stature, it could be anticipated that his assassination would produce a public clamor.

(3) The Buendía homicide occurred in a peculiar coincidence of circumstances that heightened its impact on diverse sectors of the populace: a blatantly visible shooting during the evening rush hour on one of Mexico City's busiest thoroughfares on the day of an annular solar eclipse.

(4) The crime scene was immediately secured by the DFS, Mexico's secret police, in violation of established jurisdictional authority.

(5) Agents of the DFS violated crime scene protocols as they searched the victim and his adjacent office for what some presumed to be compromising evidence; DFS personnel also sequestered witnesses, whom they interrogated for days and weeks before releasing them to the proper investigative authorities, that is, the PJDF and the capital city's Public Ministry.

(6) Neither the DFS nor the PJDF searched Buendía's home, nor did they question more than perfunctorily any of the victim's professional colleagues.

(7) Despite presidential assurances that no effort would be spared to identify and prosecute the perpetrators of the Buendía assassination, Mexican authorities failed to conduct a sound and proper investigation to that end.

(8) For the better part of four years, various investigative bodies concerned themselves with the Buendía case, at least three of them separately and at seeming cross-purposes from the official lead agency, that is, the Federal District Public Ministry under the direction of three successive district attorneys general.

(9) Mexican president Miguel de la Madrid personally authorized DFS chief José Antonio Zorrilla Pérez to take charge of the initial Buendía investigation; previously, Secretary of Government Manuel Bartlett Díaz had instructed Zorrilla to secure the crime scene, in effect assuring the compromise of evidence and laying the groundwork for a subsequent cover-up.

(10) The DFS, Mexico's leading national security agency, was disbanded less than two years after the Buendía slaying as a consequence of rampant corruption and exposure of institutional links to organized crime, most notably Mexican drug traffickers.

(11) From the outset, DFS chief Zorrilla was a prime suspect in the Buendía case, but for more than three years the authorities sought to protect him from possible indictment.

(12) Over that same period, the official handling of the Buendía case was driven by unrelenting pressure from the media, in response to which Federal District Public Ministry officials offered fatuously optimistic progress reports and distractive hypotheses at conveniently scheduled press conferences, which had little or no bearing on a substantive resolution of the crime.

(13) After three years and eight months of failing to mitigate relentless media criticism, President de la Madrid took the unprecedented step of appointing an ostensibly independent special prosecutor to take overall charge of the Buendía investigation for the express purpose of providing a credible resolution of the case by the end of his presidential term eleven months hence. Given the arbitrary time constraints, this amounted to a political decision with virtually no possibility of success.

(14) The special prosecutor for the Buendía case was primarily concerned with his own reputation (he explicitly told us so in two separate interviews) and accordingly was not disposed to pursue his investigation "wherever it might lead" nor to dwell on politically inconvenient hypotheses. When the special prosecutor concluded his investigation, his final report and summation of charges were flawed by various fallacies of logic rooted in the extrajudicial imperatives imposed on him by political circumstances.

(15) Presidential politics materially influenced decisions made by Secretary of Government Manuel Bartlett Díaz regarding the conduct of the Buendía investigations.

(16) The assassination of Manuel Buendía occurred in a conflictive geopolitical context that necessarily raised the hypothesis of foreign involvement. Mexican officials responsible for the Buendía investigations, however, refused to consider that hypothesis, especially the possibility of CIA involvement.

(17) There was a long-standing institutional relationship between the DFS and the CIA dating from the creation of both organizations in 1947.

(18) Manuel Buendía was outspokenly hostile to the CIA, had exposed some of the agency's in-country personnel and covers, and could be expected to reveal covert agency operations should he become aware of them.

(19) At the time of Buendía's death, the CIA was actively engaged in several covert operations in Mexico aimed at subverting the revolutionary government of Nicaragua, as well as combating other Central American insurgencies. Despite regional foreign policy positions that ran counter to U.S. geopolitical interests, some Mexican officials covertly collaborated with U.S. administrations in the furtherance of American strategic objectives. A threat to expose those covert relationships and operations would be a plausible motive for state-sponsored assassination.

(20) American court records, declassified law enforcement and intelligence records, and the testimony of former U.S. agents establish a connection between the murders of Manuel Buendía and DEA S/A Enrique Camarena. Those same sources link both homicides to covert U.S. activities on Mexican soil in support of the Nicaraguan *contras*.

(21) The Buendía case was treated as a national security matter in both Mexico and the United States. Thirty years later it is still considered a national security matter in the United States, while in Mexico case files have been declassified and opened to public scrutiny.

Though lengthy, this is not an exhaustive list of objective statements we can make about the Buendía case, but it does bring together a core of empirical facts that refutes the official version of events and suggests the likely involvement of the United States.

A number of contextual factors argue against the Mexican government's resolution of the Buendía case, starting with the failure of local and federal authorities to conduct a proper criminal investigation. Attempts to attribute manifestly improper police conduct and poor investigative oversight to a prevailing lack of professionalism in Mexican law enforcement are not persuasive. Many, if not most, senior police officials and criminal investigators had received specialized training abroad, about which some actually bragged, as did Florentino Ventura Gutiérrez when we interviewed him in 1987. "I've trained with all of the principal U.S. law enforcement bodies," he wanted us to know, "as well as in other countries." Ventura emphasized the strides that had been made in recent years to modernize Mexico's police, "especially the Federal Judicial Police," which he had come to head as a consequence of "thirty-seven years of professionalism."[2] Even Special Prosecutor García Domínguez, who denigrated the Mexican police for their ostensible lack of professionalism, boasted to us about firearms instruction he had received at the FBI's Quantico, Virginia, training facility and made a special point to us of his own extensive contacts with American officials.[3]

The issue here is determination, not professional qualifications. What was lacking in the Buendía case, the victim's widow bitterly observed, was "political will." Had the authorities wished to solve her husband's murder, they would have done so expeditiously. "When the [Mexican] police want to clear up a case," she emphasized, "they can. In this instance, they did not want to do so."[4] The empirical evidence, in sum, confirms beyond all reasonable doubt that from the outset official decisions were taken to investigate the Buendía assassination not for the purpose of identifying and prosecuting its perpetrators but rather to contrive a plausible resolution of the crime that eclipsed Buendía's true assassins from public view.

Authorities made much of the large pool of individuals and organizations with possible motives for homicide in the Buendía case, for all of them at one time or another had been objects of acerbic commentary in the victim's Red Privada columns. District attorneys general Victoria Adato and Renato Sales Gasque, as well as Special Prosecutor García Domínguez, all cited the many hypotheses as a primary reason for the dilatory pace of the official Buendía investigation. They also floated hypotheses in periodic statements to the press that they intimated might eventually lead to a resolution of the case but meanwhile served to keep their media critics at bay.

Barely two and a half months after the event, Adato made the improbable statement to reporters that the Buendía homicide was not a political killing, even as she recognized that investigators confronted the widest range of possible motives behind the columnist's slaying. What precisely she meant by "political" was unclear, but her categorical dismissal of the term implied that the Buendía case had nothing to do with matters of state. In a Shakespearean vein ("The lady doth protest too much, methinks."), her adamant denial suggested official prevarication.

Adato followed her rejection of a political motive with the dubious suggestion that the Buendía homicide might have been a "crime of passion" rooted in an extramarital liaison or homosexual affair. Buendía's closest friends and associates dismissed that notion as spurious, viewing it as a cynical tactic employed to defame the victim and distract public attention from more likely scenarios in which government officials themselves were complicit. Although the crime of passion hypothesis failed to gain judicial traction, it initiated an assault on Manuel Buendía's character that sought to diminish him as a figure of political consequence.

Shortcomings in the official resolution of the Buendía affair notwithstanding, Special Prosecutor García Domínguez established the falsehood of alleged dishonesty, deviousness, and moral turpitude in Buendía's personal comportment. He assured us in our 1990 interview with him that no evidence had surfaced to support allegations of sexual dalliances, blackmail, or, most preposterous of all, a covert relationship with the CIA, as charged by various character assassins who sought to diminish the deceased columnist's importance.[5] As recently as February 2013, he described Manuel Buendía as "the most honest journalist one could find anywhere in the world, incapable, absolutely incapable, of receiving compensation of any kind that might oblige him to alter his views." In the course of his investigation, he told an interviewer, he confirmed that Buendía "was a guy who never had more than modest means despite the [privileged] circles in which he moved."[6] Having neither the intention nor the desire to romanticize Manuel Buendía, we find no empirical evidence to indicate that he was anything but the ethically exemplary individual his closest associates portray him to have been. The fact that the crime of passion hypothesis did not advance beyond an initial moment of unsubstantiated speculation argues strongly against its ever having had any merit.

Similarly, we find it significant that of the numerous individual and corporate suspects with potential motives to do Buendía physical harm, only one, German arms dealer Gerhard Mertins, was ever presented to the public as a party of serious official interest, and then only until Mertins led Mexican authorities into the shadows of foreign intelligence, where they let him slip quietly away. Moreover, documented efforts by the Federal District's Public Ministry to force confessions of complicity from ex-DFS agents and others suggest strongly that none of the individuals with grievances occasioned by Buendía's Red Privada columns was in fact a viable suspect.[7]

The public's widely held suspicion that the Mexican government itself had a hand in the Buendía assassination, perhaps in concert with the Americans, raised institutionally untouchable hypotheses that Friar Ockham nonetheless would have deemed meritorious. The figure of DFS chief José Antonio Zorrilla posed an especially thorny challenge for the de la Madrid administration, given the DFS's historical ties to the CIA and Zorrilla's personal role in the initial stages of the government's Buendía investigation. Empirically, for more than three years a concerted effort was made by Mexican authorities to distance Zorrilla from the case, but when, in the final year of the de la Madrid *sexenio*, it was decided to appoint a special prosecutor who would have sufficient authority among the public to give effective closure to the politically delicate affair, the former DFS chief could no longer be spared.

García Domínguez's credibility virtually rested on his indictment of Zorrilla, so questionable was the ex-DFS director's presence in the months leading up to and immediately following the Buendía assassination. The only feasible way for the special prosecutor to indict Zorrilla, however, was to adduce a personal motive that did not involve Zorrilla's professional relationship with the CIA or his own superiors in Mexico's national security apparatus. And the only motive that could be sustained with a modicum of plausibility before public opinion was Manuel Buendía's alleged intention to expose Zorrilla's ties to Mexican drug traffickers.

Whether Buendía might have been inclined to reveal the DFS chief's cartel links solely as a matter of official corruption and whether a supremely arrogant and self-assured Zorrilla might have been moved to homicide to prevent Buendía from doing so, both in detriment to a mutually beneficial relationship, remain open questions to which only speculative answers can be offered. It seems unlikely, however, that Zorrilla's superiors in the Secretariat of Government would have been unaware of his involvement with the traffickers (as DEA country attaché Edward Heath assured they were not),[8] or that he would have committed such a politically portentous act on his own account. He was, after all, "a man of the system," as he insistently reiterated following his June 1989 arrest.

Had Buendía instead intended to expose a broader collusive relationship of illicit enrichment between various government officials and the drug traffickers, which indisputably would have constituted a motive for murder? That is not what Special Prosecutor García Domínguez alleged. The motive for the murder of Manuel Buendía, he averred in his final report of investigation, was "the deceased's knowledge of José Antonio Zorrilla Perez's links to drug trafficking."[9] Were that actually the case, it is difficult to conceive that Mexican authorities would have made the concerted effort they in fact did to protect Zorrilla from prosecution. The more plausible conclusion is that Zorrilla did not act alone but rather in concert with other parties of greater weight and influence, whose motivation in plotting Buendía's carefully choreographed assassination extended well beyond issues of corruption in high places.

As detailed in chapters 7 and 8, the political circumstances in which Special Prosecutor García Domínguez conducted his Buendía investigation tainted the entire inquiry, its results, and the indictments it sustained. The artificial time constraints imposed on him by virtue of his presidential appointment made it improbable that he could accomplish in eleven short months what judicial and law enforcement authorities had failed to do in more than three and a half years. Nor was the special prosecutor truly independent, inasmuch as he ultimately answered to the president and consequently did not have the freedom to take his investigation "wherever it might lead," should doing so implicate the president himself or otherwise compromise presidential agendas. García Domínguez saw little likelihood, he told us shortly after his appointment, that the Buendía murder would in fact be solved.[10]

His reappointment as special prosecutor by President Carlos Salinas de Gortari, in turn, further complicated the political constraints under which he was obliged to conduct his high-profile inquiry. Judging from Ángel Buendía's account of having persuaded de la Madrid's successor to reappoint the special prosecutor, Salinas would have preferred to consign the still unresolved Buendía case to the tarnished legacy of his predecessor. Deciding at the last possible moment to retain de la Madrid's appointee and continue the Buendía investigation into the new *sexenio*, Salinas then gave clear signs of manipulating García Domínguez for his own political purposes. This was seen most blatantly in the choreographed cinematic finale given to the Buendía case just seven months into the Salinas presidency, together with García Domínguez's erratically contradictory status assessments in the final weeks of the investigation, the improbable sequence of events he alleged to have occurred on the day of the assassination, and his slipshod final report on which the Buendía case indictments rested.

He had accomplished as much as he feasibly could within the constraints of the country's political reality, he expressed to us nine months later. He had produced a mastermind, a gunman, and three accomplices, as well as a motive. While the motive he adduced was to prevent the victim from exposing the mastermind's links to drug traffickers, it was quite possible, García Domínguez acknowledged, that other interests were involved in the Buendía assassination as well, but he could not realistically pursue that hypothesis and therefore chose to confine his inquiry to the immediate players on the ground.[11] It was a significant admission, which vitiates the motive for which Zorrilla, Moro, Prado, Pérez Carmona, and Naya Suárez were convicted and imprisoned. Indeed, nothing about the final conduct of the special prosecutor's inquiry, nor the resultant judicial proceedings that officially closed the Buendía case, suggests integrity on the part of the responsible Mexican authorities.

Drug production and trafficking were central to the Buendía case, which brings us to two Red Privada columns on the subject that appeared in May 1984—the first, twenty-six days before the columnist's assassination, the second ten days later. The initial column referred to a pastoral letter issued on 19 March of that year by nine Mexican bishops about the dangers of mafia-controlled marijuana and opium poppy production in the southern states of Oaxaca and Chiapas. Given their ideological differences ("two notable progressives alongside rancid conservatives"), it was unusual, Buendía noted, for all nine prelates to place their signatures on the same document, which only highlighted the urgency of the situation they had been moved to denounce. The bishops' alarm contrasted sharply with the upbeat reports of Attorney General Sergio García Ramírez about the government's ostensible successes in combating the drug trade. A profoundly alarmed citizenry, he remarked pointedly, "would be interested to know if someone is lying."

The remainder of Buendía's 4 May column comprised eighteen paragraphs excerpted from the bishops' pastoral letter, in which the prelates expressed their concern over a spreading cycle of violence among the region's impoverished rural population occasioned by an influx of domestic and foreign drug mafias. Lacking the fertilizers and farm machinery required to produce commercially viable food crops, growing numbers of peasants and Indians were easily enticed to plant marijuana and opium poppies. Once they had produced a crop, the bishops observed, they found themselves trapped in a trafficking network from which they could not escape. The traffickers provided seed, fertilizer, credit, and technical supervision, then oversaw harvesting, packaging, storage, and distribution. They also maintained an elaborate transportation system of pickup trucks, tractor trailers, and clandestine airstrips for moving their product to market, all of which gave local growers the impression of a legitimate business. And they protected their investments with ready recourse to force and violence.

"With the power of money and, above all, the firepower of guns," wrote the bishops, "the *patrón* and the mafia he represents take practical control of people's lives. They manipulate local authorities, or frequently replace them with their own people, and establish a reign of terror throughout the region. . . . The mafias that control the drug trade are thoroughly organized, domestically as well as internationally. Nor do they hesitate to deceive, bribe, threaten, or kill if their interests so require. The planting of marijuana and opium poppies in our region is only explicable," the bishops underscored, "if one takes into account the enormous power that these domestic and international mafias possess." And that power, which allows them to defy the law brazenly and with total impunity, "is itself inexplicable unless one assumes the direct or indirect complicity of senior public officials at both the state and federal levels." President de la Madrid had committed himself to a "moral renovation" campaign against corruption in government, the bishops observed with evident intention, "a campaign that no one would take seriously if it failed to confront drug trafficking, which was a primary source of corruption in Mexico's justice system."

Not insignificantly, Buendía chose to close his 4 May column with a paragraph from the pastoral letter linking the drug trade to the worsening geopolitical crisis in Central America. "Mexico has gained an image abroad of which Mexicans can justly be proud," the nine prelates noted, "one of defending peaceful coexistence among nations through democratic political means rather than by force. This image, currently demonstrated by the efforts of the Contadora, can be compromised," they warned, "if, as a nation, we make room for international drug mafias, who in the end are going to compromise all of our national affairs."[12]

In his follow-up Red Privada column on Monday, 14 May 1984, Buendía drew on the bishops' pastoral letter to give his own trenchant appraisal of drug trafficking via Mexican territory as a national security issue. Attorney General Sergio García Ramírez and Secretary of National Defense Gen. Juan Arévalo Gardoqui should not ignore the Church leaders' warning about the political implications of drug trafficking in Mexico, he began, for "as they lay out—and can also be inferred from other news reports—this matter involves [our] national security." Moreover, he emphasized, the prelates "coincide with what other observers know [to be true]," namely, that senior public officials were directly or indirectly complicit "at both the state and federal levels."

Most worrisome, Buendía expressed, was the bishops' well-founded concern that with the spread of international drug trafficking would come increased foreign interference in Mexico's internal affairs, as had occurred in other countries "where these trafficker networks have come to exert decisive political influence." Colombia and Bolivia were two obvious examples, he wrote, but it was in the United States that this phenomenon had developed most dangerously, "not only for its own populace but for other countries of the region as well, especially Mexico." The commingling of politics and organized crime, "including the clandestine drug trade," was a long-standing feature of the U.S. system and "a pillar of continuous market growth," which stimulated the production of illicit narcotics beyond its borders. In Mexico the associated corruption of public officials had reached unprecedented levels during the López Portillo *sexenio* (1976–1982) under the influence of the president's close friend, Mexico

City police chief Arturo "El Negro" Durazo Moreno. "But with or without Durazo," Buendía concluded his 14 May column, "the international drug mafia has evidently increased its activities in Mexico from 1982 to the present. And this, as the nine bishops note, cannot happen without inside complicity."[13]

These two columns raised eyebrows when they appeared, as drug trafficking was a taboo topic that most Mexican journalists preferred to avoid. While both were mentioned following the assassination as possibly offering clues to Buendía's killers, the consensus among the victim's associates and other members of the press was that the 4 and 14 May columns were too recent to have occasioned such a major crime. Moreover, there was no evidence that Buendía had made a concerted effort to investigate drug trafficking. His assistant Luis Soto, who organized and maintained the columnist's extensive reference files, dismissed as "pure imagination" the notion that Buendía had been preparing an exposé of links between government officials and drug traffickers. Although there were occasions when Buendía preferred not to share information with him, Soto acknowledged, he usually could figure it out by correlating related material Buendía would request from his files with the columns he wrote. A year before the assassination, Soto told *The Progressive* magazine editor Matthew Rothschild, he had compiled an index of Buendía's published columns, and the drug trade did not figure among the fifteen hundred subjects listed.[14]

They did make a point of collecting information about traffickers, Soto noted, along with many other topics. And in the two weeks prior to the assassination, he recalled, Buendía met twice with Defense Secretary Juan Arévalo Gardoqui to discuss the bishops' pastoral letter, but he was "very reserved" about what had transpired on those two occasions.[15] Arévalo himself confirmed to Special Prosecutor García Domínguez that he and another senior officer had met privately with Buendía on 25 May 1984 and that Buendía had told them he intended to pursue the subject of drug trafficking as "a grave threat to Mexico's national security." Other sources had told García Domínguez the same thing.[16]

A close reading of the 4 and 14 May Red Privada columns themselves provides the strongest evidence that Manuel Buendía had embarked on an analysis of drug trafficking in Mexico not as a matter of official corruption but as a regional geopolitical problem driven by strategic foreign policy objectives of the United States that compromised Mexico's legitimate national interests. All of his primary concerns were carefully woven together in those columns: the United States as the single greatest threat to the integrity of the Mexican nation, the collusion of Mexican officials and vested private interests with agents of the U.S. government, the international drug trade as a subversive instrument of American power projection, and U.S. covert operations throughout the Mesoamerican region. Conscious of the treacherous ground on which he was treading, Buendía took care to have the nine Catholic bishops state his main points first, then in his own words reiterated the dangers they implied.

Explicit reference to the Contadora Group, in which Mexico played a central role, plus concerns he had expressed in previous columns about threats to the country's national security posed by U.S. efforts to topple Nicaragua's Sandinista government, leave no doubt that Buendía here alluded to an operational arrangement between drug traffickers and Nicaraguan *contras* sustained by the Americans in collusion with Mexican officials. What Buendía was in fact doing in these and other Red Privada columns, *Excélsior* reporter Rogelio Hernández perceptively noted, was to seamlessly interweave key national security topics that bore materially on Mexico's subservient relationship with the United States. Although few of his readers seemed to notice, "those in the know could see that he was connecting the dots."[17] And that, Ockham would have to agree, was a clear and present motive for murder.

The evidence for U.S. complicity in that murder is circumstantial and informant based. With a judicious application of Occam's Razor, however, it is also persuasive. Here, again, we note a number of relevant empirical facts.

(1) The U.S. government considered the Buendía assassination a national security matter and, except where obliged by federal court order, has withheld from public access all executive branch records pertaining to the case.

(2) Links between the murders of Manuel Buendía and DEA S/A Enrique Camarena Salazar have been established by agents and officials of the U.S. government.

(3) U.S. Drug Enforcement Administration agents ostensibly investigating the Camarena case sought to influence the outcome of the Buendía case by implicating in Buendía's murder then government secretary Manuel Bartlett Díaz, which was an act of political subversion rather than a legitimate investigative task.

(4) At the time of the Buendía assassination, the CIA had a deep-cover agent, Lawrence Victor Harrison, embedded in Mexico's national security apparatus. Harrison knew about the planned attack on Buendía more than a month before it was carried out.

(5) Two former U.S. agents knowledgeable about the Buendía and Camarena homicides, one CIA (Harrison) and the other DEA (Héctor Berréllez), have stated that both Buendía and Camarena were killed to keep them from exposing American collusion with Mexican drug traffickers in support of the Reagan administration's proxy *contra* war against the Sandinista government of Nicaragua.

(6) Former DEA G/S Héctor Berréllez has stated that S/A Enrique Camarena traced Guadalajara drug cartel money to U.S. and offshore CIA bank accounts, that Camarena was interrogated under torture to learn who his sources were, and that Camarena was killed to prevent him from revealing what he had discovered. Berréllez has also stated that Camarena had been in contact with Manuel Buendía.

(7) Former CIA agent Lawrence Harrison has stated that Lt. Col. Oliver North, in his capacity as White House NSC deputy director for political-military affairs, ordered the assassination of Manuel Buendía. In light of what is now known about Reagan-era covert operations, the personalities involved, and the anomalous CIA–NSC relationship in those years, the allegation is plausible, albeit unlikely ever to be proven. If it should indeed be true, we must assume that North sought and received DCI Casey's prior authorization to proceed.

(8) Lawrence Harrison was sufficiently distraught following his CIA service in Mexico that he was moved to share some of his privileged knowledge with us in violation of agency secrecy regulations. When he failed to heed warnings to cease talking to us, he suddenly experienced a series of grave disruptions in his professional and personal life, which he interpreted as measures undertaken to silence him.

Harrison seemed obsessed with Manuel Buendía, to the point that, like Charles Bowden, we wonder if he might not have been more involved in the assassination plot than he has ever acknowledged. What we know for certain is that it was Harrison who introduced the Buendía affair into the now declassified portions of official U.S. government records concerning the Camarena case, and thus it was Harrison who first linked the Buendía and Camarena homicides.

He did this in the 20 September 1989 recorded debriefing conducted by DEA S/As Martínez and Morales while en route from Los Angeles to Nogales, Arizona. In response to a question by S/A Morales about DFS electronics specialist Alberto Guadalupe Estrella, Harrison volunteered that Estrella "was one of the people arrested for the Buendía killing." Farther along in that debriefing Harrison explained that he and Estrella knew each other "because [Estrella] was the head of special electronics operations . . . in Mexico City" and, he repeated, "was one of the people arrested with the Buendía investigation." Also arrested as accessories to the Buendía homicide, he added, were "[Juventino] Prado and [Raúl Pérez] Carmona and all those who'd been assistants to Javier García Paniagua" and previously, "during '84 and '83 and parts of '82, [had been] assistants to Antonio Zorrilla."[18]

Harrison was offering this information to his debriefers five years after the Buendía slaying and just three months after the Estrella, Prado, and Pérez Carmona arrests, which suggests a long-standing and continuing personal interest in the case. At that moment, he was preparing to slip back into Mexico to perform various intelligence tasks for the Drug Enforcement Administration while making final arrangements for his own and his family's permanent relocation to the United States.[19] On his return to the United States four and a half months later, he was debriefed by DEA S/A Wayne Schmidt "concerning intelligence information related to the murder of Manuel Buendía Tellezgirón, an investigative reporter; narcotics trafficking information relating to Ruben Zuno Arce; arms trafficking by Gerhard Mertins; and other related intelligence concerning corrupt Mexican Police Officers and elected Mexican officials."[20]

The DEA-6 Report of Investigation prepared by S/A Schmidt on this occasion exemplifies the inaccuracies and erroneous information that insinuate themselves into the official record as a consequence of faulty reporting by government agents. We know from our own experience just how difficult it was to note down fully and accurately everything Lawrence Harrison said in an unrecorded conversation, because of the way he spoke, as well as the complexity of the topics he discussed. "I was constantly making corrections," Harrison explained during the first Zuno trial, "because I felt [S/A Schmidt] was constantly [condensing] all my remarks and changing the meaning of them."[21]

Harrison was responding here to questioning by Zuno defense attorney Ed Medvene about an assertion Schmidt had attributed to him to the effect that CIA operatives were training "Guatemalan guerrillas" on a ranch in the State of Veracruz owned by Guadalajara drug kingpin Rafael Caro Quintero. Special Agent Schmidt, Harrison told the court, had conflated two separate events: the Mexican government's response to the influx of Guatemalans ("guerrillas") into the southern border State of Chiapas, and the alleged training of Nicaraguan *contras* on a trafficker-owned ranch in Veracruz.

In response to a direct question by Medvene as to whether he had stated to S/A Schmidt that the CIA had been training *contras* in Veracruz, Harrison avoided a direct answer but implied that this was the case.

MEDVENE: "Did you indicate to [S/A Schmidt] that the training place was at a ranch owned by Caro Quintero?"

HARRISON: "Yes, I did."

MEDVENE: "And that it was used for operations training?"

HARRISON: "Yes, I did."

MEDVENE: "And that the operations and training were conducted by the C.I.A. at that ranch?"

HARRISON: "I indicated to him that the operations and training were conducted by members of the Mexican government under some type of a fiat or contract from our government. I did not specifically say that it was the C.I.A."[22]

What Harrison in essence reported to S/A Wayne Schmidt was (1) that Manuel Buendía had been investigating collusion between high-level Mexican officials, Mexican drug traffickers, and the American CIA in support of the Nicaraguan *contras*; (2) that Buendía had learned from a newspaper reporter in Veracruz (Javier Juárez Vásquez) that the CIA was training *contras* on a ranch owned by Rafael Caro Quintero; (3) that the CIA maintained clandestine airfields in Mexico for the use of aircraft transporting arms to the *contras*; (4) that CIA-trafficker collusion facilitated the flow of arms south to the *contras* and narcotics north to the United States; (5) that Juárez Vásquez had been murdered in Veracruz an hour after Buendía was slain in Mexico City; (6) that *contra* southern front commander Edén Pastora (aka "Commander Zero") had also provided Buendía with information about CIA arms smuggling and himself suffered an agency-sponsored bombing attempt on his life the night of the Buendía assassination; (7) that German arms dealer Gerhard Mertins had a relationship with the CIA, was shipping arms to Central America via Mexico, and was expelled from Mexico because of revelations Buendía had published about him; (8) that DEA country attaché Edward Heath was behind the attempt to pass to *Excélsior* reporter Rogelio Hernández a file of suspect documents implicating Secretary of Government Manuel Bartlett Díaz in the Buendía killing; and (9) that Buendía had obtained information linking high-ranking PRI members to the CIA–*contra*–drug trafficker nexus.[23]

The operative questions here concerned, precisely, what Harrison stated about the Buendía homicide and the covert side of U.S.-Mexico relations more broadly and how we are to judge the veracity of those assertions. The evidentiary value of DEA-6 reports based on a debriefer's notes is not the same as the verbatim transcription of a recorded interview, where the investigator can determine exactly what the informant said, as well as the nuances with which he or she said it. An illustrative example of the analytic pitfalls in this kind of documentation is provided by Mexican investigative journalist Anabel Hernández, who in an often insightful but occasionally flawed historical account of Mexico's drug cartels accepts at face value S/A Schmidt's 13 February 1990 DEA-6 report of the Harrison debriefing.[24]

Hernández fails to note, for example, Schmidt's misidentification of Javier Juárez Vásquez as "(FNU) Velasco," who allegedly informed Manuel Buendía about "Guatemalan guerrillas" being trained by the CIA "at a ranch owned by Rafael CARO-Quintero in Vera Cruz." Nor does she note that Schmidt mistakenly cites 1985 as the year of Buendía's assassination, or that he erroneously reports German arms dealer Gerhard Mertins to have been living in Mexico City during the early 1980s while running "a company identified as Mermex [sic] located in Guadalajara." As recounted in chapter 5, Mertins founded a German export company in 1963 called Merex and three years later established a U.S. branch in Bethesda, Maryland. When he eventually established a business presence in Mexico, it was through a joint silver-mining venture in the northern State of Durango called Minera Romer, S.A., which served as a cover for the supply of arms to the Nicaraguan *contras* and other Central American clients.[25]

At one point, Hernández takes the unacceptable liberty of condensing multiple pieces of information into a single abbreviated statement, which she then attributes verbatim to Harrison by putting words in his mouth that he never uttered. "Based on the investigation I did, I believe there was a *contra* training camp on [Rafael Caro Quintero's] ranch," she misquotes him as saying. "My impression is that the operation was there by order of the American government."[26] The "investigation" Harrison mentions had to do with the Buendía assassination, and in the court testimony where he discusses it he does not mention Caro's Veracruz ranch. In response to subsequent questioning about *contra* leader Edén Pastora, he clarifies that the point of his mentioning Pastora to S/A Schmidt was that the attempt on Pastora's life had coincided with the Buendía assassination and the murder of "the investigative reporter" Juárez Vásquez in Veracruz, whose name he mistakenly remembered as "Velasco."[27] Harrison's unstated implication was that the coincidence of those three events could only have occurred as a consequence of a coordinated effort by elements of the Mexican government and U.S. intelligence.

These editorial liberties and imprecisions aside, Anabel Hernández gets the essence of Harrison's testimony right and even corroborates key elements of it from her own primary sources. She gained access, for example, to the transcript of the Federal Judicial Police interrogation of Ernesto Fonseca conducted by Florentino Ventura Gutiérrez following Fonseca's April 1985 arrest for involvement in the Camarena kidnapping, in which "Don Neto" confirmed Harrison's relationship with the Guadalajara cartel five years before Harrison described it in U.S. federal court. Drawing on official Mexican and American records, as well as key published sources, she reasonably concludes that Harrison's version of events surrounding the Buendía and Camarena killings is true, that is, that Mexican government authorities, PRI officials, and influential business interests conspired with international narcotics traffickers and the CIA to facilitate the illicit supply of arms via Mexican territory to the Nicaraguan *contras*; that Manuel Buendía and DEA S/A Enrique Camarena Salazar had discovered and threatened to expose that collusion; and that both men were slain to prevent them from doing so.

Hernández further expands on information provided to American authorities by Lawrence Harrison (or "Torre Blanca," as she prefers to call him) about the Guadalajara-based Leaño and Aviña Bátiz families, their alleged links to drug and arms traffickers, and their political influence in certain PRI circles.[28] Rubén Zuno Arce, Harrison told

DEA S/A Schmidt, had been a heroin trafficker in the 1970s and was himself a licensed pilot who "had access to numerous air strips thru an individual identified as Juan AVINA-Batiz." (Zuno, Schmidt noted from his own sources, possessed both a Mexican pilot's license [no. 5747] and a U.S. pilot's license [no. 0022 78454].) Juan Aviña Bátiz's brother Eduardo, Harrison adds, was head of the Jalisco branch of the PRI, a state and federal deputy, and a strong contender for governor. He was also alleged to have been Zuno's former heroin-trafficking partner.[29]

Juan and Eduardo Aviña's parents, Hernández recounts, had moved from Sinaloa to Guadalajara, where they made a fortune in real estate and rose to social prominence. Eduardo "belonged to García Paniagua's political circle" and was "very close" to Jalisco governor Guillermo Cosío Vidaurri, who, as mentioned in chapter 14, was the uncle of Rafael Caro Quintero's paramour Sara Cosío—and, we note, in whose 1989 election campaign Lawrence Harrison served as communications coordinator. Harrison implicated not only the Aviña Bátiz family in cartel-related activities, Hernández writes, but also the high command of the Fifth Military Region, which corresponded to the State of Jalisco.

Brig. Gen. Vinicio Santoyo Feria, a member of Mexico's political class who chaired the Joint Chiefs of Staff in the initial years of the de la Madrid administration and was close to Secretary of Defense Gen. Juan Arévalo Gardoqui, she recounts, assumed command of Region Five one month after the Camarena murder. Except for the arrests of Caro Quintero and Fonseca Carrillo, however, "there was no change in the privileged position of the Guadalajara cartel bosses." General Santoyo Feria, according to Harrison and Hernández, had an association with Guadalajara attorney Everardo Rojas Contreras, who had done "extensive legal work for Ernesto Fonseca and Caro Quintero." Together with Santoyo, they aver, Rojas was involved in large-scale, less than transparent real estate transactions effected in part with protection money extorted from Miguel Ángel Félix Gallardo and other local traffickers. Harrison reported to S/A Schmidt that in November 1988 he had visited Félix Gallardo's Guadalajara residence, where Félix's employees had informed him that they lacked sufficient funds to cover household expenses because their boss had just paid General Santoyo a million-dollar bribe.[30]

The September 1989 and February 1990 DEA-6 debriefing reports are key to a resolution of the Buendía and Camarena cases. This is confirmed, in effect, by the U.S. government's concerted effort to prevent them from surfacing in the 1990 Camarena trial proceedings, then, once Judge Rafeedie ordered those documents introduced into evidence, to discredit Harrison's testimony about CIA collusion with Mexican drug traffickers on behalf of the Nicaraguan *contras*. That, in turn, obliged both the prosecuting assistant U.S. attorneys and Judge Rafeedie himself to adopt the untenable position that the portion of Harrison's testimony required to indict and prosecute Rubén Zuno Arce was credible, while what he had to say about the CIA was not.

The pertinent trial transcripts of relevance to our Buendía investigation are likewise problematic due to procedural constraints governing the presentation of evidence and the specific ends to which that evidence was developed. This is especially so with regard to Lawrence Harrison's 6 July 1990 voir dire examination, which was conducted for the purpose of determining what direct personal knowledge, if any, Harrison possessed about CIA activities in Mexico that might have had a bearing on the Camarena case. As noted in chapter 11, Judge Rafeedie used the voir dire proceeding to block further defense counsel probing into possible agency links to the Camarena and Buendía homicides by dismissing Harrison's CIA-related testimony as "incompetent" evidence "based entirely on hearsay, supposition, rumors, gossip, [and] speculation." Harrison had no personal knowledge of what he reported, Rafeedie declared. "He was simply reporting what was in the air and what was being said and discussed and what he heard from various people."[31]

The fallacy in Judge Rafeedie's blanket categorization of Harrison's voir dire testimony as "hearsay," and thus inadmissible in a court of law, lies in the failure of American jurisprudence to recognize the potential evidentiary value of secondhand information. There is, after all, a substantive difference between what the casual witness may claim to have heard about a particular defendant, or the crime with which that defendant has been charged, and what an experienced intelligence operative may determine to be actual fact based on information gleaned from his or her operational milieu. In this regard, Harrison's presence in Judge Rafeedie's courtroom had a distinctly contrived and delusory quality to it. Listening closely to what he told the court, one would have to suspect that he was an American intelligence agent, most likely CIA, which in turn would (and does) cast a very different light on the "hearsay, supposition, rumors, gossip [and] speculation" that allowed Rafeedie to dismiss Harrison's agency-related testimony as "incompetent."[32]

At least three of the defense attorneys suspected as much, and one, Martin R. Stolar, lead counsel for defendant Juan Ramón Matta Ballesteros, asked Harrison directly, "Have you ever had any formal relationship with any American intelligence agency in Mexico?"

"Formal relationship?" Harrison replied evasively. "No, I haven't."

"How about an informal relationship?" Stolar pressed him.

"I don't think so," he prevaricated.[33]

While Harrison has never stated explicitly that he was a CIA agent, in the same way that he knew Dale Stinson was CIA he let us know that he, too, had been with the agency. "You're going to ask, and I'm not going to tell you," was the way he acknowledged as true what he had denied on the witness stand.[34] Moreover, DEA G/S Héctor Berréllez, the man primarily responsible for bringing him back to the United States to serve as a government witness, explicitly confirmed Harrison's CIA affiliation when we interviewed him in May 2004.

For us the most persuasive evidence that Harrison was an American intelligence operative and actually did the things he claims to have done is his encyclopedic knowledge of the sordid underbelly of post–World War II Mexico and above all his uncanny ability to identify without prior prompting and then place in their respective relationships all of the key Mexican players of the 1970s and 1980s, few of whom would be familiar names to most foreigners. Harrison, as Anabel Hernández puts it, "was not a character out of some spy novel; he was real."[35] And the supreme irony of his voir dire testimony about CIA collusion with Mexican drug traffickers being disallowed by Judge Rafeedie as "hearsay, supposition, rumors" is that he himself was proof of that collusion.

While defense attorneys suspected that Harrison had been sent to Mexico by the CIA, the prosecuting attorneys likely knew that to be the case, and Rafeedie should have suspected as much if he was not already witting. Neither the judge nor defense counsel pressed Harrison on his transparently perjured denial of links to American intelligence.

Harrison was instructed by his federal handlers to lie about such matters, he told us. And agency personnel were present to monitor his testimony, among them Ed Heath and Dale Stinson. At one point in the proceedings, a CIA attorney actually met with Rafeedie in the judge's chambers. Defense counsel Ed Medvene attempted to join them, but Rafeedie refused to admit him. When court reconvened, the judge prohibited any further questioning of Harrison about his intelligence activities in Mexico.[36] The lies he'd been coached to tell, moreover, served a double purpose: to befog the facts of CIA activities in Mexico; and, equally important, to gag a disillusioned ex-operative who might expose them. Asked in cross-examination toward the end of the second Zuno trial if the government's attorneys had rehearsed his testimony with him, Harrison acknowledged that to have been the case. Had he deviated from the approved testimonial line, he told the court, "they would have prosecuted me for perjury."[37]

This was a statement of double entendre, implying (falsely) that in the courtroom his testimony was perforce truthful, but also signifying that threatened prosecution for perjury was a Sword of Damocles with which the government could enforce his silence outside the courtroom. A decade and a half later he would confirm as much to us. "Everything I've told you is the truth," he emphasized. "I've moved some personal pieces around, because I'm not going to tell you I was somewhere I [testified] I wasn't. They told me to lie. I'm not going to open myself up to perjury!"[38]

The final proof of Harrison's bona fides is what happened to him once he began talking to us. Due, we suppose, to the prolonged nature of our investigation and the fact that nothing he was telling us had yet been made public, federal secrecy enforcers did not play the perjury card. They opted instead to so disrupt his life and livelihood that he would either desist from further disclosure or be reduced to such a broken state that he lost any semblance of credibility. As described in chapter 16, the warnings and accompanying train of events became so ominous that at one point he seriously thought he might be killed.

As we write this concluding chapter, the extraordinary unfolding case of National Security Agency whistleblower Edward Snowden adds serendipitous perspective to the fate of Lawrence Harrison. While Snowden's revelations have been more far-reaching and have inflicted much greater damage on U.S. global power projection than Harrison's, both men have exposed what they consider to be crimes of state and in doing so opened themselves to a predictable, no-holds-barred, punitive response on the part of the American government. In both cases, that official response is the ultimate proof of who these two men are and what they have done.

Just as Lawrence Harrison feared for his life and, above all, for his family, Snowden's primary fear was "that they will come after my family, my friends, my partner, anyone I have a relationship with." The authorities, he foresaw, would "act aggressively against anyone who had known him." He himself could be snatched from a foreign refuge by the CIA and "rendered" back to the United States—or simply "disappeared." The prevailing attitude among his former colleagues in American intelligence, he told interviewers, was that "it's better to kick someone out of a plane than let [him] have a day in court." One could not challenge "the world's most powerful intelligence agencies" and ignore the risk, he stressed. "If they want to get you, over time they will."[39]

Motive is the final element of proof that Friar Ockham would want to consider here. What moves whistleblowers and disillusioned spies entrusted with state secrets to risk prosecution, or worse, by violating confidentiality oaths to reveal what they know? We stress *disillusionment* as a crisis of conscience distinct from the more typical ego-driven pursuit of self-interest that moves people to break the rules, defy the law, or otherwise violate established norms of conduct. Testimony given out of ethical principle is inherently more trustworthy than dissenting assertions made in defense of vested interests, be they personal, corporate, or institutional. Edward Snowden exemplifies the principled integrity that has motivated so many before him, including Lawrence Harrison.

Like Harrison, Snowden was drawn to intelligence work by a deeply instilled belief in the righteousness of his country's national purpose. "I believed in the nobility of our intentions to free oppressed people overseas," he told the *Guardian* of London, only to discover in the course of his work for the CIA and NSA that it wasn't so. "We were actually involved in misleading the public and misleading all the publics, not just the American public," he explained, "in order to create a certain mindset in the global consciousness and I was actually a victim of that." ("Snookered," is how we put it to Harrison, who had been similarly motivated to join the CIA.) Contrary to the way he was immediately portrayed as a "traitor" by media pundits and government damage controllers, Snowden was moved to expose CIA and NSA criminality as an assault on his fellow citizens and the bedrock values of the country he had been raised to esteem. "America is a fundamentally good country," he elaborated. "We have good people with good values who want to do the right thing. But the structures of power that exist are working to their own ends to extend their capability at the expense of the freedom of all publics." Snowden decided to expose the NSA's global collection of Internet and other electronic communications, he said, because "I don't want to live in a world where everything that I say, everything I do, everyone I talk to, every expression of creativity or love or friendship is recorded." That was not something he could abide, much less help build or live under.[40]

"This country is full of the most terrible, damning, sinful, horrible contradictions that you can imagine!" Harrison lamented in that same vein. "It's terrible what [the U.S. government] is doing down there [in Mexico]. It's terrible what they're doing up here!" In other words, an unbridled quest for power at the expense of the citizenry and the vaunted patriotic ideals we have been indoctrinated to hold, noble, altruistic ideals of social solidarity cynically vitiated by the country's governing overseers and their ideological gatekeepers to whom both Harrison and Snowden allude. "It hurts! It's outrageous! And nobody's telling the truth," Harrison decried. "Nobody will stand up and say, 'This is the truth!'"[41]

Individuals of strong moral fiber have in fact emerged from the shadow world of intelligence to reveal government transgressions against civil society and the sovereignty of other states, invariably at great personal risk. Edward Snowden is but the latest, albeit the most noteworthy for the scope of his revelations, as well as the seeming care he took not to expose American agents to personal harm. Like Harrison, he had no illusions about the personal consequences of "pulling the lid" from the malodorous brew of national intelligence operations. "The moral decision to tell the public about spying that affects all of us has been costly," he told the media while stranded at Sheremetevo Airport in Moscow, "but it was the right thing to do and I have no regrets." He believed in the Nuremberg principle that "individuals have international duties which transcend the national obligations of obedience," he said, and that individual citizens therefore "have the duty to violate domestic laws to prevent crimes against peace and humanity."[42]

Dans le domaine de la Divinité régit la Vérité, Harrison agreed, but here on earth he was torn between his sworn duty to the government and his greater duty to the truth. Those who shape, govern, and impose their will on society tend not to be encumbered by such ethical conundrums, nor do they let appeals to principle thwart their purposes; rather they throw moral principle to the winds whenever their material interests are challenged. Such objectively self-serving political conduct obtains as well in the judicial realm, where submission to the prevailing societal order is coerced through inequitable adjudication of law. This, Friar Ockham reminds us, is a fact of human comportment that must be taken into account when weighing evidence of criminal intent.

Reduced to its essential elements, we conclude, the assassination of Manuel Buendía is not persuasively explained by Special Prosecutor García Domínguez's official resolution of the case. To the contrary, the objective circumstances surrounding the special prosecutor's appointment, the political constraints compromising his independence, the manner in which his inquiry unfolded, and his own admission that it was not feasible for him to pursue certain hypotheses, as well as the poorly argued indictments he ultimately issued, all support the conclusion that García Domínguez in fact served to obscure the actual motive behind the assassination on behalf of two successive Mexican administrations. Lawrence Harrison, in turn, proved to be a far more credible source for deconstructing the Buendía case than any of the witnesses presented by García Domínguez. Like Snowden, he felt morally compelled to expose government criminality. But, whereas the classified information that Snowden revealed was undeniably authentic and American authorities could only cajole foreign governments after the fact to extradite him as a fleeing felon, in Harrison's case the state secrets he possessed could be plausibly denied, leaving him vulnerable to the full range of coercive measures at the government's disposal to discredit and silence him. De facto resort to those measures, coupled with Harrison's determination to resist them and share with us what he knew about the Buendía case anyway, in effect authenticates his revelations, just as his very presence in Judge Rafeedie's courtroom confirmed the truth of his testimony about CIA collusion with Mexican drug traffickers.

The preponderance of evidence now available in the public record, confirmed and further nuanced by our own cited sources and most especially by Lawrence Victor Harrison, persuades us beyond a reasonable doubt that Manuel Buendía was slain on behalf of the United States because of what he had learned about U.S.-Mexico collusion with narcotics traffickers, international arms dealers, and other governments in support of Reagan administration efforts to overthrow the Sandinista government of Nicaragua. The evidence we have developed also leads us to conclude that DEA S/A Enrique Camarena Salazar was abducted, interrogated, and killed for the same reason and that the two cases are therefore related. The import of this latter conclusion is that, contrary to the hero status accorded Camarena as an ostensible casualty of the "war on drugs," he was sacrificed by his own government in order to prevent exposure of a covert operation against the legitimate authorities of another country.

The implications of our conclusions about these two cases are sobering. What emerges from the evidence we have developed over the course of our Buendía investigation is an unflattering portrait of members of Mexico's governing class inimical to the nationalist sensibilities of many of their fellow citizens: a political culture of institutionalized collusion with the country's historically hegemonic northern neighbor. Power co-opts, and, for the better part of the past century, key actors in the Mexican state have been effectively co-opted by the power of the United States. The historical interface between the CIA and the highest echelons of the Mexican government is a documented fact.[43] As noted in chapter 14, U.S. domination extends to Mexico's economy, culture, and mass media and even determines basic national security policy, all issues of primary concern to Manuel Buendía. So effective is American hegemony over Mexico, lamented one local commentator after studying a trove of recently revealed secret diplomatic communications, "that an essential part of the decision-making process on matters of internal security is actually designed not in Mexico City but in Washington." Mexico, she decried, has been revealed not simply as a country that is being controlled, "but as a country that has surrendered."[44]

The reality of this historic relationship makes all the more plausible the evidence we cite of collusion on the part of Mexican officials with their American counterparts in providing material support to the Nicaraguan *contras*, even as the de la Madrid administration was voicing opposition to U.S. interventionist policy in the region. Despite the overriding weight and influence of the United States on Mexican affairs, however, the maintenance of that hegemonic relationship is far from frictionless, as reflected in the readiness of those same Mexican authorities who collude and collaborate with their American counterparts to frustrate U.S. objectives whenever that can be done without provoking a bilateral crisis with potentially intolerable consequences. Leaving aside the corrupt, criminal, and opportunistic elements of Mexican society, not even virtuous Mexican nationalists can afford to expose the extent of CIA involvement in Mexico, for they themselves have been complicit.

Applying Occam's principle of parsimony against this backdrop of Mexico's satellite relationship with the United States, we arrive at a tenable reconstruction of the Buendía homicide that accounts for the unaddressed gaps in the official resolution of the case. We have not perfectly solved Buendía's murder, as Charles Bowden observes, but we believe we have explained it. What remains to be done is for other researchers to study the original case files generated by the Federal District Public Ministry and Special Prosecutor Miguel Ángel García Domínguez, which in May 2011 were ordered released to the public,[45] as well as any surviving investigative records created by the DFS, by

Miguel Nazar Haro in concert with District Attorney General Victoria Adato Green, by Attorney General Sergio García Ramírez and the Federal Judicial Police, and by presumed presidential investigators.

It appears that this has now begun to happen, as evidenced by a recent article based on the Buendía and related case files in which investigative journalist Humberto Padgett offers new insights into the DFS–Guadalajara cartel relationship, the personal relationship between cartel kingpin Rafael Caro Quintero and former DFS director José Antonio Zorrilla Pérez, Manuel Buendía's relationship with Zorrilla, and Buendía's preoccupation with government-cartel collusion as a threat to the integrity of the Mexican state. Moreover, Padgett writes, the documentary record shows that "the murder of DEA agent Enrique Camarena in 1985 has as its precedent the assassination of journalist Manuel Buendía in 1984." In the end, "the Mexican justice system sentenced [Zorrilla] for committing a murder to protect a drug-trafficking network, yet refused to charge him as a trafficker." Zorrilla, Padgett emphasizes, "was not just anyone, rather a cofounder of the Mexican Narcostate."[46]

Barring end-of-life confessions by assassination principals, we think it unlikely that the Buendía case will ever be "perfectly" solved in the sense of being able to positively identify the primary culprits and establish the precise sequence of events. At the very least, we anticipate that, properly interrogated, the surviving case files will give up significant substantiating clues in support of the case we make. In time researchers may also gain access to currently classified U.S. government files concerning Buendía, which we are certain will only strengthen our deconstruction of this historic crime. Manuel Buendía, in sum, was felled by mercenaries of power who dared not confront him face-to-face because of the man he was and the virtues he defended. They and their hired executioner could only strike him down from behind, for figuratively, as well as literally, he was armed and dangerous.

EPILOGUE

Three Decades On

IN THE MONTHS LEADING UP to the thirtieth anniversary of the Buendía slaying, a remarkable sequence of events brought that historic assassination, together with the subsequent murder of DEA S/A Enrique "Kiki" Camarena Salazar, back into public focus. It began on 9 August 2013 when former Mexican drug kingpin Rafael Caro Quintero was unexpectedly released from the Jalisco State Penitentiary in Puente Grande, where he had been serving a forty-year sentence for ordering the Camarena homicide. "Rafa," as Caro is familiarly known, walked out of the Puente Grande prison at 1:30 a.m., boarded a waiting Land Rover, and disappeared into the darkness. Authorities made a halfhearted effort to follow, but he easily evaded the tail, and, as we write this epilogue more than a year later, he has not been seen since. The U.S. Justice Department expressed immediate outrage, as did a number of former DEA officials and agents who had known and worked with Camarena.[1]

Five weeks after Caro's release, convicted Buendía assassination mastermind José Antonio Zorrilla Pérez was likewise released from the Federal District's Eastside Men's Prison (Reclusorio Preventivo Varonil Oriente) to serve out the remainder of his twenty-nine-year sentence under house arrest. Zorrilla had been briefly paroled in February 2009, but so great was the media outcry against his release that he was returned to prison. In September 2013, authorities avoided a repeat public challenge by justifying Zorrilla's transfer to home detention on the grounds of declining health. By then the other ex-DFS agents convicted in the Buendía killing had all been released from prison.[2]

Although virtually no one, least of all the Mexican authorities, had previously suggested a link between the Camarena and Buendía homicides, that connection was now made explicit. The day following Caro Quintero's release, independent narcotics investigator Bill Conroy asserted in an online blog posting that Mexico's DFS had been involved in both murders. Citing Charles Bowden's groundbreaking book *Down by the River*, Conroy noted that senior DFS officers had been trained by the CIA and the DFS "was functionally a unit of the CIA." It also functioned as "the eyes and ears of the cartels." If the DFS was in league with Mexican drug traffickers, Conroy concluded,

Former DEA S/A Enrique Camarena Salazar on the cover of the 13 October 2013 issue of the Mexican newsweekly *Proceso*, in which feature articles link the CIA to Camarena's murder and allege U.S. government collusion with Mexico's drug cartels.

then so, too, was the CIA. Likewise, DFS complicity in the Camarena and Buendía killings suggested that the CIA was complicit as well.[3]

Then, in early October 2013, two retired DEA veterans and a former CIA contract pilot—Héctor Berréllez, Phil Jordan, and Robert "Tosh" Plumlee—publicly accused the CIA of having been behind the Camarena killing. Their sensational accounts were first reported, albeit incompletely, by the Fox News television network on 10 October. Three days later the Mexican weekly *Proceso* appeared on newsstands with Camarena on its cover and a banner headline announcing the "End of a Myth," followed by a highlighted tag proclaiming that "28 years later the official story is refuted: DEA agent 'Kiki' Camarena was tortured and murdered by the CIA." That issue's feature article by reporter Luis Chaparro and Washington correspondent Jesús Esquivel led off with a color close-up of Camarena standing in a seized marijuana field and an overlapping black-and-white photo of six U.S. Marines in dress uniform carrying Camarena's flag-draped casket. Immediately beneath the photos, the article's bolded title declared, "Camarena was executed by the CIA, not Caro Quintero."

Proceso's editors introduced the explosive feature with a highlighted white-on-black summary, which read, "A story seemingly out of a complex spy novel has just exploded on U.S. television: Enrique *Kiki* Camarena, the DEA police officer murdered in Mexico in February 1985, apparently was not the victim of Mexican capo Rafael Caro Quintero, but rather of an obscure CIA operative. This individual was ordered to silence the [American] narcotics agent for a pivotal reason: he had discovered that Washington was associating with [Caro Quintero] and using the profits from drug trafficking to finance the activities of the Nicaraguan counterrevolutionaries."[4] The ostensible CIA operative named by *Proceso* was Cuban exile and Bay of Pigs veteran Félix Rodríguez.

The simultaneity of the *Proceso* and Fox News exposés, as well as the particulars and conclusions of their respective reports, raises several questions. Both were the result of interviews with Berréllez, Jordan, and Plumlee, but each appears to have pursued different ends: *Proceso* to indict the U.S. government and Fox to diminish the damage of the whistleblowers' revelations. While all three men had long been troubled by what they had learned about U.S. covert operations in Mexico and Central America during the 1980s, it remains unclear what motivated them to go public at this precise point in time and who took the initiative to make it happen. Chaparro and Esquivel write at the beginning of their article that Jordan, Berréllez, and Plumlee "confided their explosive information simultaneously" to the two media outlets, yet given the elaborate nature of *Proceso*'s Camarena feature and the comparatively garbled Fox News coverage of those same revelations, we wonder if the Mexican newsweekly was not already working on its exposé when Fox learned of it and in reaction hurried to defuse what promised to be a sensational scoop.

Whatever the case, the initiative for the whistleblowers' public statements to Fox News, they have told us, came from the network, not themselves. Fox approached Plumlee first, presumably because he provided a direct link to the CIA. Plumlee, however, was reluctant to be interviewed because the Fox people were vague about exactly what they wanted from him. But they were insistent, calling him repeatedly until he finally relented, at which point they flew a camera crew to Colorado Springs, Colorado, where they shot a forty-five-minute interview with him, barely eleven seconds of which were ultimately used in Fox's televised report. The network next interviewed Berréllez, who named Félix Rodríguez as the CIA asset allegedly involved in Camarena's interrogation. Jordan, the last of the trio to be interviewed, corroborated Plumlee's and Berréllez's accounts from his own inside knowledge of the Camarena case.[5]

The interviews with Plumlee, Berréllez, and Jordan were ostensibly intended to provide testimonial evidence for the Fox News Network's evening *Kelly File* report with anchor Megyn Kelly, but when the program aired it was little more than a sensationalized rehash of the Camarena affair, together with a blistering attack on the Mexican government for having released Caro Quintero and on the Obama administration for doing nothing about it. The only fleeting item of controversy was an out-of-context statement by Berréllez that "it was an American pilot" who flew Caro out of Mexico, followed by a five-shot clip of Tosh Plumlee in and next to a Cessna aircraft, confirming Berréllez's statement. Asked by the interviewer in voice-over, as shots two, three, and four streamed by, if that American pilot "had any regrets about flying Caro Quintero out," Plumlee, looking directly at the camera, replied matter-of-factly, "Yes, he does." What Fox neglected to tell its viewers was that Plumlee himself claimed to be that pilot.[6]

As Plumlee subsequently elaborated for us, there were two or three CIA-trafficker-related pilots involved in Caro Quintero's evasion of arrest immediately following the Camarena murder. The first, thought by Plumlee to have been Werner Lotz, apparently flew Caro from Guadalajara to Caborca, 150 miles northwest of Hermosillo, Sonora, where Caro lay low for three weeks before fleeing to Costa Rica. (Peter Dale Scott and Jonathan Marshall identify Lotz as Guadalajara cartel kingpin Miguel Ángel Félix Gallardo's personal pilot.[7]) In late February, Caro flew to his Veracruz ranch, where he was picked up by Plumlee and flown in a Cessna 310 to an airfield on the Mexico-Guatemala border. There, Plumlee recounted, Caro was met by the same Falcon aircraft that three weeks earlier had flown him out of Guadalajara, which now transported him to Costa Rica. Plumlee stated to us that he had been ordered by his CIA handler to fly Caro to Guatemala "before the Mexican and US authorities closed in on him." He did not know who flew Caro to Costa Rica but later heard it was a SETCO pilot and thought that pilot might have been Werner Lotz.[8]

Fox's *Kelly File* segment further distorted events at the Guadalajara airport based on Héctor Berréllez's embellished secondhand account of what had transpired there. "Upon arrival we were confronted by over fifty DFS agents pointing machine guns and shotguns at us, the DEA. They told us we were not going to take Caro Quintero," Berréllez stated to Fox interviewer William La Jeunesse behind a network artist's dramatic depiction of Caro's plane surrounded by numerous armed DFS agents confronting a much smaller number of DEA agents. It was a stunning piece of political propaganda, subliminally suggesting to viewers that the United States had a right to make arrests on Mexican soil and had been arbitrarily prevented from doing so by Mexico's rogue intelligence agency. Berréllez, for his part, did not personally witness the events in Guadalajara and now, almost twenty-nine years later, spun an illusory account based on his flawed recollection of what others had reported to him at the time.

There was, in fact, a standoff at the Guadalajara airport on 9 February 1985, but it was between the Mexican Federal Judicial Police and a dozen of Caro Quintero's personal security guards, at least some of whom appear to have been DFS agents. Once notified of Camarena's disappearance by DEA country attaché Edward Heath, Federal Judicial Police director Manuel Ibarra Herrera dispatched a large contingent of heavily armed officers to Guadalajara under the command of First Comandante Armando Pavón Reyes. It was, in the estimation of the DEA's Guadalajara resident agent in charge James "Jaime" Kuykendall, "the largest group of judicial police comandantes ever assembled for anything except pictures."[9] While neither DEA nor the Federal Judicial Police knew at that point who had ordered Camarena's abduction, they assumed the Guadalajara cartel was behind it, and when a DEA scanner picked up a radio communication between Miguel Félix Gallardo and his office requesting that a large sum of cash be delivered to the airport because he was about to leave town, Pavón Reyes and about twenty of his officers, together with three or four DEA agents, set out for the airport to intercept the drug lord's private plane.

On their arrival they encountered a Falcon executive jet idling on a taxiway and quickly surrounded the aircraft, together with the dozen armed men guarding it. Preparing to depart on that plane was Caro Quintero, not Félix Gallardo. The four DEA agents present at the Guadalajara airport that day were little more than interested spectators, inasmuch as the DEA had no independent operational authority in Mexico and could only take part in such actions together with and subordinate to the Federal Judicial Police, or "Mex-Feds," as the Americans called them. After some initial posturing on the part of both groups, Pavón Reyes approached Caro Quintero and the head of Caro's security detail, each of whom handed him DFS credentials (*charolas*), which he then carried into an adjacent hangar reserved for the country's attorney general and

Fox News Network's Megyn Kelly and William La Jeunesse presenting the 10 October 2013 *Kelly File* segment about the early release from prison of Mexican drug lord Rafael Caro Quintero. (Sylvia E. Bartley)

placed a call to Mexico City. When he returned, Pavón handed the ID badges back to the two men, then walked with Caro to the other side of the aircraft for a private conversation. When they reappeared, Pavón conspicuously embraced Caro and his head of security, shook hands with other members of the capo's security group, and allowed the plane to depart. The men's DFS credentials, he informed his Federal Judicial Police officers and the accompanying DEA agents, were valid, and he had been ordered to let Caro leave.[10]

Other key pieces of information omitted from the *Kelly File* broadcast were reported in an online Fox News article by William La Jeunesse and Lee Ross, who had conducted the original interviews with Plumlee, Berréllez, and Jordan. Headlined "US Intelligence Assets in Mexico Reportedly Tied to Murder of DEA Agent," the article reported the three ex-agents' allegations that the CIA had colluded with Mexican drug traffickers and had actually played a role in the abduction, torture interrogation, and murder of Kiki Camarena. La Jeunesse and Ross quoted Phil Jordan's assertion that "CIA operatives were in [the room where Camarena was interrogated]. Actually conducting the interrogation. Actually taping Kiki." One of them, they quote Héctor Berréllez as saying, "was a Cuban who worked as a CIA operative, who helped run guns and drugs for the Contras."

According to Tosh Plumlee, Ross and La Jeunesse wrote, the U.S. government played both ends against the middle. "We were running guns," Plumlee told them. "We were running drugs. We were using drug money to finance the gun running operation." The various entities engaged in those covert activities, he emphasized, "were cutouts financed and operated by the Central Intelligence Agency. Our operations were sanctioned by the federal government, controlled out of the Pentagon. The CIA acted in some cases as our logistical support team."[11]

A Fox News Network artist's inaccurate depiction of the 9 February 1985 Guadalajara airport standoff between Caro Quintero and supposed DEA agents. The standoff was actually between Caro's security guards and members of the Mexican Federal Judicial Police, accompanied by four DEA observers. (Sylvia E. Bartley)

Whereas the televised *Kelly File* report on Caro Quintero's early release from prison was neutered infotainment devoid of coherent factual content, the expanded La Jeunesse and Ross online article did make the eyebrow-raising revelation of CIA complicity in Camarena's fatal ordeal, as well as implying that it was somehow related to the Reagan administration's illicit support of the Nicaraguan *contras*. It also mentioned, but did not name, a Cuban CIA operative who, according to Berréllez, "helped run guns and drugs for the Contras." That operative, as would be revealed by *Proceso* three days after FoxNews.com posted the La Jeunesse and Ross article, was Félix Ismael Rodríguez (aka Max Gómez), whose central role in Reagan administration support of the *contras* was overseen by Lt. Col. Oliver North.

Plumlee, Berréllez, and Jordan each told us that North, now a program host and regular commentator for the Fox News Network, was allowed to preview the raw interview footage and remove all references to the CIA from the *Kelly File* broadcast. According to Plumlee, who angrily protested the way Fox had misused its videoed interview with him, Fox's own reporters La Jeunesse and Ross were sufficiently upset with the way their material had been distorted for broadcast that they were allowed to be more explicit in their online article about CIA involvement with Mexican drug traffickers, the *contras*, and the murder of Kiki Camarena. Even there, however, La Jeunesse and Ross were not allowed to name Félix Rodríguez as the "Cuban CIA operative" allegedly present during Camarena's interrogation.

On this point, Phil Jordan surmised, North's primary concern likely was that "there is no statute of limitations for murder." Were Rodríguez's participation in the Camarena affair to be established, Jordan implied, responsibility for the American agent's death would ultimately come to rest with North himself.[12] Inasmuch as North did not recruit Rodríguez until seven months after Camarena's abduction, however, we think it more likely that he would have been acting on CIA orders, and if so, responsibility for Camarena's death lies with DCI Casey.[13] We e-mailed North requesting his comment on the allegation that he had censored Fox's whistleblower reportage but received no reply.

Over the next eight months, a steady stream of developments cast new light on the Buendía and Camarena slayings of three decades earlier.

13 October 2013. *Proceso* publishes a Camarena cover story alleging CIA complicity in the DEA agent's abduction. Based on interviews with Berréllez, Jordan, and Plumlee, the newsweekly places Cuban exile and CIA agent Félix Rodríguez at the scene of Camarena's fatal interrogation.

19 October 2013. The *El Paso Times*, based on its own interviews with Berréllez, Jordan, and Plumlee, as well as former DEA agent Celerino "Cele" Castillo III, reports in more detail the allegations of CIA involvement in the Camarena abduction. Castillo, who was stationed in Central America from 1985 to 1990, confirms the truth of those allegations from his own investigations of the *contra*-drug-trafficker relationship.

20 October 2013. *Proceso* publishes a second Camarena feature based on an exclusive interview with Berréllez that links the Buendía and Camarena cases and alleges CIA complicity in both.

27 October 2013. *Proceso* publishes a cover story based on an interview with former senior Mexican intelligence official Jorge Carrillo Olea, which details the CIA–DFS

DEA veteran Héctor Berréllez on the 20 October 2013 cover of the Mexican newsweekly *Proceso*. In this issue, Berréllez implicates the CIA in the Buendía and Camarena homicides.

relationship in the mid-1980s; links both agencies to the Buendía and Camarena slayings, as well as the Guadalajara cartel and Nicaraguan *contras*; and asserts that then government secretary Manuel Bartlett Díaz and Mexican attorney general Sergio García Ramírez were aware of these links at the time. A second feature in this issue provides additional details about Mexican government collusion with the Guadalajara cartel, the *contras*, and the CIA.

Also on this date, Bill Conroy posts a lengthy *Narcosphere* blog, based on his own interviews with Berréllez, Jordan, and Plumlee, in which he links the Buendía and Camarena murders and attributes both to the CIA. He also reports for the first time a late 1984 meeting in Phoenix, Arizona, ostensibly attended by Plumlee and Camarena, where, according to Plumlee, Camarena revealed what he had learned about CIA collusion with the Guadalajara cartel and Nicaraguan *contras*. Conroy suggests that Plumlee reported this information to the CIA and thus influenced the agency's decision to have Camarena killed.

29 October 2013. The Drug Enforcement Administration Museum hosts a public panel at its Arlington, Virginia, headquarters to counter and discredit the public statements made by former agents Berréllez and Jordan about alleged CIA involvement in the Camarena abduction, interrogation, and murder. It is a transparent exercise in damage control streamed live on the Internet, which only serves to increase Berréllez and Jordan's credibility.

5 January 2014. Proceso publishes an issue with former government secretary Manuel Bartlett Díaz on its cover and an accompanying feature article alleging that both Bartlett and former defense secretary Juan Arévalo Gardoqui were present during the torture interrogation of Enrique Camarena. The article repeats the allegation that the CIA was involved in Camarena's abduction and that "Cuban" CIA operative Félix Rodríguez personally participated in the DEA agent's interrogation.

22 February 2014. Joaquín "El Chapo" Guzmán Loera, famed head of Mexico's Sinaloa cartel, is captured in Mazatlán by a detachment of Mexican marines without a shot being fired. Published close-up photographs show Guzmán being handled gently by his masked captors with no visible concern on his face. Observers quickly conclude that El Chapo was complicit in his own capture and that his arrest served larger agendas on both sides of the U.S.-Mexico border.

6 April 2014. Proceso publishes an issue with Manuel Buendía on its cover and a lead feature story linking the Buendía and Camarena cases based on the 13 February 1990 DEA-6 report of investigation summarizing information provided by ex-CIA operative Lawrence Victor Harrison.

This sequence of events three decades after the fact places the Buendía and Camarena killings in their larger historical moment. The assassination of Buendía on 30 May 1984, writes Buendía acolyte Carlos Ramírez, "not only opened the cycle of [Mexico's] national instability but also initiated the [current] phase of organized crime as an autonomous power group." Buendía was killed when he was investigating "the protection of criminals by civil servants, politicians, and police officials." A year later "drug traffickers murdered a DEA agent in Mexico, Enrique Camarena Salazar, exposing for the first time the organic relationship between organized crime and political power." That relationship, Ramírez suggests, extends to the United States as well and binds the power structures of both countries together.[14]

There is an important difference, however, in how that relationship functions on the U.S. side of the border, where established mechanisms of political power far outweigh the power of the drug cartels and thus allow those who govern American society to utilize organized crime for their own geopolitical ends. While the antecedents of narco-politics as an instrument of U.S. power projection date from the post–World War II decades, in Mexico it is during the crushing economic crisis of the 1980s that the United States fully utilizes the international drug trade as part of a long-term strategy to further co-opt the Mexican political system.

American-sponsored opium poppy eradication efforts in the 1970s, conducted jointly with the Mexican government under an aerial spraying program ominously dubbed Operation Condor,[15] moved key Sinaloa traffickers to relocate their bases of operations to the state of Jalisco, where they created what came to be known as the Guadalajara cartel and began trafficking cocaine together with cannabis and reduced amounts of heroin. The Reagan administration, in turn, used the Guadalajara cartel for its own covert purposes, then took down Caro Quintero, Fonseca Carrillo, and, belatedly, Félix Gallardo, the principal kingpins of those years, which resulted in the violent fragmen-tation of the Guadalajara-dominated trafficking network into a number of competing cartels based in Tijuana, Ciudad Juárez, Tamaulipas, and Sinaloa.

The reconstituted Sinaloa cartel assumed a position of decisive power and influence under the astute leadership of "Joaquín El Chapo" Guzmán, who had been mentored in the 1970s by the Sinaloa cartel's founder, Pedro Avilés Pérez, then in the 1980s by Avilés's protégé and eventual godfather of the Guadalajara cartel, Miguel Ángel Félix Gallardo. El Chapo's business savvy earned him a place on *Forbes* magazine's list of the world's billionaires, while his political acumen and keen sense of tactics and strategy permitted him to establish a Mexican version of the Sicilian *pax mafiosa*, which co-opted government and law enforcement officials and regulated relations among some, though not all, of Mexico's proliferating drug cartels. It also appears to have led the DEA to work out a hands-off arrangement with El Chapo's organization, whereby the Sinaloa cartel would supply intelligence about its competitors in return for noninter-ference in its operations.[16]

The relevance of these and subsequent developments to the Buendía and Camarena cases lies in the evidence they provide of a continuing history of U.S. government col-lusion with organized crime in pursuit of foreign policy objectives. When to every-one's surprise El Chapo Guzmán was arrested on 22 February 2014, some observers speculated that he had calculated he would be safer in government custody than out-side, where he was a target of Zeta paramilitaries, former members of the Mexican army's Airborne Special Forces Group who initially provided security for the Gulf cartel (of Tamaulipas), then formed their own criminal organization with firepower unmatched by any of Mexico's other cartels. The operation that culminated in El Chapo's capture seemed too neat not to have been choreographed, and it was widely suspected that Guzmán and the authorities had worked out the details in advance. The Sinaloa cartel, *Guardian* columnist Ed Vulliamy wrote suggestively, "has enough lieu-tenants on the outside to easily continue its formidable global operation, answerable to Guzmán on the inside."[17]

The lieutenant slated to replace El Chapo was Ismael "El Mayo" Zambada García, whose son and former logistics coordinator for the Sinaloa cartel, Jesús Vicente "El Vicentillo" Zambada Niebla, was extradited to the United States in February 2010 by the Felipe Calderón administration (2006–2012) and was still awaiting trial in Chicago as we were completing this book. In late February 2014, *Proceso* reported that the U.S. Justice Department had negotiated an agreement with El Vicentillo whereby, in exchange for information on Sinaloa's rival cartels, he would be given a fifteen-to twenty-year prison sentence rather than the life term he otherwise faced on eight counts of drug trafficking and money laundering. "There will be no trial," an anonymous Justice Department official confided. A trial would be too costly because it threatened to reveal "various agreements between federal agencies (like the DEA) and the Mexican drug trade." It also risked having to identify informants in Mexico, "including traffickers, members of the military, police, and politicians."[18]

Based on information emerging from pretrial maneuvering by federal prosecutors and defense attorneys in the Chicago case, the U.S. government had developed a special relationship with the Sinaloa cartel, considered by some observers to be the most powerful drug trafficking organization in the world. That arrangement, according to publicly available court documents, appears to have given the Sinaloa traffickers unimpeded access to the U.S. drug market in return for intelligence on rival cartels. "Sometime prior to 2004," reads a pretrial discovery petition filed in the Chicago case, "the United States government entered into an agreement with [cartel lawyer Humberto Loya Castro] and the leadership of the Sinaloa Cartel, including Mayo and Chapo. Under that agreement, the Sinaloa Cartel, through Loya, was to provide information accumulated by Mayo, Chapo, and others, against rival Mexican Drug Trafficking Organizations to the United States government. In return, the United States government agreed to dismiss the prosecution of the pending case against Loya, not to interfere with his drug trafficking activities and those of the Sinaloa Cartel, to not actively prosecute him, Chapo, Mayo, and the leadership of the Sinaloa Cartel, and not to apprehend them."[19] As described by Fernando X. Gaxiola, one of Zambada Niebla's Chicago defense attorneys, the U.S. government strategy was "to eliminate all the smaller groups, concentrate all the power in one place, and then go back and hit that one place."[20]

The accumulated evidence of the past three decades leaves little doubt that the United States has and continues to use its antinarcotics operations worldwide as an instrument of power projection rather than law enforcement. While the origins of this policy can be traced to the 1960s and '70s in Southeast Asia and the 1970s in Latin America, it was during the final Cold War decade of the 1980s that it emerged as a fully developed foreign policy stratagem for the pursuit of U.S. interests in Mexico and other countries of the Mesoamerican region. What began in the early 1980s with the Guadalajara cartel as a useful pawn for combating socialist-oriented popular insurrections in Central America transitioned through a violent proliferation of competing cartels, precipitated by the withdrawal of U.S. support for the Guadalajara traffickers, to a new collusive relationship with the reconstituted Sinaloa cartel, whose principal figures had mastered their trade under the tutelage of Félix Gallardo, Fonseca Carrillo, and Caro Quintero.

Considering those antecedents, Phil Jordan speculates, El Chapo may have been behind Caro Quintero's August 2013 release from prison. "Chapo began his drug career under these capos," Jordan notes, "and owes his current status as the new 'boss of bosses' to them. They mentored him, and Chapo has the power and money to help them."[21] Even in custody he continues to wield power and influence.

The cynicism of executive branch collusion with organized crime elements in Mexico and elsewhere, while hardly unique to the United States and justified by its apologists as a real world necessity ("realpolitik" in the euphemistic jargon of political science), is nonetheless stunning. Most recently it appears to have been exposed yet again in the Operation Fast and Furious (OFF) scandal, wherein between 2009 and 2011 as many as two thousand AK-47s and other military-type assault rifles supposedly monitored by the U.S. Bureau of Alcohol, Tobacco, Firearms, and Explosives (ATF) were sold by licensed Arizona gun dealers to proxy buyers, who then facilitated their transfer across the Arizona-Sonora border and into the hands of the Sinaloa cartel. "If you're selling guns in Arizona, and they're gonna go south," remarked Zambada Niebla defense attorney Gaxiola, "the first place they go is to Sinaloa. Doesn't take a genius [to figure that out]. If you want them to go to the Gulf cartel, you send them through Laredo; if you want to send them to Juárez, you send them through El Paso. They want to fortify the Sinaloa cartel to take out all the other cartels."[22]

"The United States government considered the arrangements with the Sinaloa Cartel an acceptable price to pay," asserted Zambada Niebla's attorneys in their "Memorandum of Law," "because the principal objective was the destruction and dismantling of rival cartels by using the assistance of the Sinaloa Cartel—without regard for the fact that tons of illicit drugs continued to be smuggled into Chicago and other parts of the United States and consumption continued virtually unabated." Justification for such arrangements, Zambada's attorneys aver, rests on the proposition that the "end justifies the means" and "it is more important to receive information about rival drug cartels' activities from the Sinaloa Cartel in return for being allowed to continue their criminal activities, including and not limited to their smuggling of tons of illegal narcotics into the United States."

This same Machiavellian approach informed OFF, they note, which was authorized "at the highest levels of the Justice Department" and "included agents from ATF, DEA, FBI, ICE [Immigration and Customs Enforcement], and the IRS [Internal Revenue Service]."[23] That multiple executive branch agencies are named here as witting participants in this lethal operation is noteworthy, as is the omission from this list of the one agency most concerned and experienced with such covert schemes, the CIA. *Washington Times* reporters Robert Farago and Ralph Dixon had already linked the CIA to OFF in the summer of 2011. According to a "CIA insider," they wrote, the agency "had a strong hand in creating, orchestrating and exploiting Operation Fast and Furious."[24]

In light of what has long been known about CIA collusion with drug traffickers and other organized crime figures, the revelation attributed to that anonymous agency source is perfectly plausible. It is yet another piece of the now well-documented history of such covert operations that lends perspective to the Buendía and Camarena homicides and, above all, to the links between them. In both cases, the alleged motives were smoke screens meant to obscure their shared political motive: in the Buendía case, the victim's threatened exposure of DFS director Zorrilla Pérez's ties to the Guadalajara cartel; and in the Camarena case, reprisal for the disruption of a major cartel cannabis operation in southern Chihuahua.

The initial furor produced by Caro Quintero's unexpected release from prison in August 2013, together with the provocative allegations of CIA complicity it moved two retired DEA veterans to make, has introduced compelling new evidence of U.S. involvement in both killings. The first indication of a cover-up was the insistent repetition of reprisals for the destruction of a massive marijuana production and packaging operation at a place called El Búfalo as the motive for the abduction, torture, and murder of Kiki Camarena. El Búfalo, a small community in southern Chihuahua named after American "Wild West" showman "Buffalo Bill" Cody (1846–1917), was the geographic reference used by the Guadalajara cartel to distinguish it from other large-scale cannabis plantations in Sonora, Zacatecas, and San Luis Potosí. When in early November 1984 the de la Madrid administration was pressured by the U.S. Justice Department to launch a joint military and Federal Judicial Police raid on the main Búfalo operation (there were untouched outlying feeder plantations as well), it was touted as the largest such raid ever.

Mexican authorities subsequently claimed to have confiscated and destroyed between five and ten thousand tons of marijuana at El Búfalo, with an estimated street value of 2.5 billion dollars according to an inflated DEA estimate. While there may have been that amount if one includes the outlying feeder fields untouched by the raid, together with immature plants still in the ground and drying cannabis, the fully processed, ready-for-market marijuana seized on that occasion was substantially less. And there was also the matter of government collusion. According to Caro associate Michael Hooks, within two weeks of the Búfalo raid at least one hundred tons of confiscated marijuana were returned to the Caro brothers. Hooks knew this for a fact, he told *Fort Worth Weekly* reporter Peter Gorman, "because I moved that much of it myself between December [1984] and January [1985]." Hooks's bona fides as a major marijuana smuggler and close associate of Rafael and Miguel Caro Quintero are amply documented by published photographic evidence, as well as his 1988 seventeen-count federal indictment.[25]

As significant as marijuana may have been for Rafael Caro Quintero and his trafficker associates in the 1980s, cocaine was incomparably more so as a revenue generator on the seemingly insatiable American narcotics market. Two of the Guadalajara cartel's three founding capos, Ernesto Fonseca Carrillo and Miguel Ángel Félix Gallardo, were primarily cocaine traffickers, while cocaine profits were also invested in Caro Quintero's expanding marijuana plantations. "It was the cocaine," Hooks remarked years later. "They were going crazy," he said, referring to Fonseca, Caro, and Félix Gallardo. "They thought they were bigger than the government of Mexico. They bragged about owning the government."[26] Cocaine, Elaine Shannon recognized in *Desperados*, "was far more lucrative than marijuana and heroin combined" and was, in fact, transforming the nature of the Mexican drug trade. Fonseca, the eldest of the three Guadalajara capos, had begun trafficking cocaine from Ecuador in the early 1970s, while Félix Gallardo was beginning to move cocaine "on a scale that had been accomplished only by Colombia's Medellín cartel."[27] All of this objectively diminished the significance of the November 1984 Búfalo raid.

In this light, the linking of DEA S/A Camarena and his brutal demise to the Búfalo raid is puzzling, all the more so because there is no credible evidence that Camarena had anything to do with it. His immediate superior at the time, Jaime Kuykendall, states as much in his own published memoir of the Camarena case. "The Guadalajara DEA office had not been involved in [the] enormous marijuana bust in the state of Chihuahua in November of 1984," Kuykendall wrote in reference to the Búfalo operation.[28] Moreover, Camarena himself confirmed this in considerable detail to his interrogators before succumbing to their physical abuse. We know this from a partial transcription of Camarena's recorded interrogation produced in less than transparent circumstances by the CIA. Camarena repeatedly told one of his interrogators that he had not been personally involved in either the Búfalo investigation or the raid and that he only knew about Chihuahua matters from internal reports shared with the various DEA field offices. The basic intelligence on Búfalo had been obtained by the Hermosillo office from an on-site informant and was then passed on to DEA country attaché Edward Heath in Mexico City, who persuaded Mexican authorities to conduct the raid. What they actually found at the Búfalo location, according to Camarena, was considerably less than what was subsequently reported. Illustrative fragments of his interrogation went as follows.

CAMARENA: The one who informed us about Chihuahua worked at the Búfalo ranch.
INTERROGATOR: Go on. Don't stop.
CAMARENA: The information came from the Hermosillo agent, who'd received a call from an informant in Chihuahua. He and one of his agents went to interview him . . . [groans] . . . When they met with this informant in Chihuahua, he told them that there was a place near Búfalo where they were packaging a lot of marijuana, that he was working there as a cook, and that he had pretended to get sick so he could go to Chihuahua to report this information to agent Miguel Grozos.
INTERROGATOR: What else?
CAMARENA: They tried to coordinate with the [government's antinarcotics] campaign coordinator for Chihuahua, but he didn't want to overfly that area to verify if the encampment was actually there.
INTERROGATOR: Who was the coordinator for Chihuahua who didn't want to overfly the area?
CAMARENA: I don't recall.
INTERROGATOR: Go on.
CAMARENA: They tried various times. They went back to him again and requested that he fly over that zone but he refused. So, the DEA agent contacted the DEA's Mexico City office.
INTERROGATOR: Who?
CAMARENA: Miguel Grozos. He spoke with our chief about it, and he passed the information on to Ibarra. Then they planned the Chihuahua raid.
  . . .
INTERROGATOR: Who led the [Búfalo raid]?

CAMARENA: I understand that it was [Miguel] Aldana.

INTERROGATOR: Couldn't you see?

CAMARENA: I didn't take part in the operation.

INTERROGATOR: I'm supposed to know that? Fill me in.

CAMARENA: Comandante Aldana was in charge. They made a fool of him . . . [*moans*]
. . . The people . . . [*coughs*] . . . they arrested told them that there were guards there
who worked for the Mexican government. Those guards were from the [Federal
Security] Directorate. They were always armed and kept people from entering or
leaving.

. . .

INTERROGATOR: Talk to me about the Chihuahua operation.

CAMARENA: Sure . . . [*moans*] . . . They got to the place and from there began
searching for more planted fields and encampments and found one or two. They'd
also found others from the air. There was a big field of young marijuana plants,
about eighty hectares [two hundred acres]. According to the [postraid] report, the
workers said there was a pickup that came around with a person they thought was
Rafael Caro Quintero. The report doesn't indicate who exactly said this, as there were
many detainees in the encampment.

. . .

INTERROGATOR: Lie still!

CAMARENA: [*Moans*] . . . At first they said they had seized 10,000 tons, but in their
final reports they calculated it was between 2,000 and 4,000 tons, which wasn't that
much. They had exaggerated the weight and volume. They said there were some
trucks there carrying away the marijuana. They didn't know where it was being taken
but said two or three truckloads left every day.

INTERROGATOR: Who was the report for? What names did you learn?

CAMARENA: I have no reason to conceal names from you. You already see that I am
telling you what I read in the report . . . [*groans*] . . . I don't remember any names.
I only recall that some people commented that the plantation was Caro Quintero's.
No one said they had seen him. No one said they had met him, rather that this had
come from the guards . . . that the guards had given them to understand that it
belonged to Rafael Caro Quintero. [The government people] spent a week there
searching, analyzing and asking questions. Many of the laborers were hired in
Chihuahua, the state of Sonora and in Sinaloa. They had come because of the lack of
jobs. They needed the work.

INTERROGATOR: No, no. You're not telling me anything hijo de la chingada! [*He hits
Camarena several times.*] . . . What else do you know about the Chihuahua operation?
But there, on the ground!

CAMARENA: I have no knowledge of things on the ground, señor. Only what's in the
report.

INTERROGATOR: Who coordinated the operation?

CAMARENA: An agent from Mexico City.

INTERROGATOR: What's his name?

CAMARENA: Carlos Lugo.

INTERROGATOR: What's his position?

CAMARENA: He's an agent. There was no group supervisor then.

INTERROGATOR: How long has he been there?

CAMARENA: About eight years. He dealt directly, or deals directly, with Aldana. They're very good friends. They got to know each other through their work. Carlos Lugo was the one who dealt with our chief, Edward Heath, in coordinating the operation. All this was done in Mexico City in the offices of the Federal Judicial Police.

INTERROGATOR: All right. Now tell me who is named in your report as the contact between Rafa and the federal authorities?

CAMARENA: There's a report they've told us about. . . . I heard the person say Rafael is in contact with a general . . . Gen. Arévalo Gardoqui.

INTERROGATOR: Who gave you that report?

CAMARENA: A person by the name of Juan García gave us that report. . . . I doubt that's his real name. . . . He was working in El Paso, Texas, before.

INTERROGATOR: What's his name?

CAMARENA: Juan García. He was working in El Paso, Texas.

INTERROGATOR: What does this person do?

CAMARENA: He's an informant.

INTERROGATOR: For whom?

CAMARENA: For the DEA. . . . For us.

INTERROGATOR: I'm asking you about Rafa's contact with the federal authorities.

CAMARENA: I'm getting to that, señor. He told us that one time he was there in Zacatecas when a Mexican Air Force plane came in with one of Gen. Gardoqui's daughters.

INTERROGATOR: Who brought her?

CAMARENA: An Army plane. It had been arranged for the young lady to introduce the general, who was in Zacatecas at the time, to Rafael Caro.[29]

Investigators have long puzzled over this transcription, as indeed they have over the existence of two tape cassettes containing recorded portions of the interrogation. Drug Enforcement Administration officials had learned of the recordings' existence from the CIA ten weeks after Camarena's abduction, and four weeks after that it was again the CIA that delivered this forty-three-page transcript to DEA headquarters in Washington, DC. The transcription, however, does not correspond to material recorded on the two cassettes, nor has the actual recording from which the transcription was made ever materialized. The official version has been that the interrogation tapes were made by elements of the Mexican government for their own nefarious purposes and altered copies of those tapes were made available to U.S. officials only after the CIA discovered their existence and informed the DEA.[30]

The problem with this version has always been that the CIA itself was the agency that first brought the interrogation tapes to light and then provided a partial transcription of Camarena's interrogation, which could not be verified against an actual recording. Jaime Kuykendall had read that forty-three-page document "many, many times" and had no doubt that it was "a legitimate transcript of an interrogation of DEA agent Enrique Camarena." He accepted, seemingly without question, that the Mexican government possessed the original recording and that it was the Mexican government that chose not to provide a dubbed copy to the DEA. Reference to Mexico's former defense secretary Gen. Juan Arévalo Gardoqui as having provided protection for marijuana plantations in the State of Zacatecas, Kuykendall noted, could have been dismissed easily enough as uncorroborated informant speculation. There must have been something else on that tape "damaging enough, or embarrassing enough," he concluded, for the Mexicans not to release it to the Americans.[31]

Kuykendall also calls attention to another potentially significant detail: whereas the interrogation tapes were entered into evidence at the Los Angeles Camarena trials, "the transcript was ruled inadmissible because its source could not be substantiated."[32] Kuykendall appears to have accepted the CIA's account of having learned about the tapes and acquired the copy of the transcript from Mexican authorities, then turned the information over to the DEA as a matter of institutional collaboration, although he readily acknowledges that the two agencies' respective priorities of law enforcement versus foreign intelligence often put the DEA and CIA at odds. He clearly recognized as well the CIA's lack of institutional transparency in the conduct of its undercover operations. According to Elaine Shannon, he even questioned whether Rafael Caro Quintero and Ernesto Fonseca had in fact been the key players in Camarena's abduction, interrogation, and murder. The crime was too well planned, he concluded, and was likely carried out by DFS operatives, perhaps in coordination with the Federal Judicial Police—both of which agencies, we would add, were compromised by the CIA. It was possible, Kuykendall thought, that Caro and Fonseca "were being hung out to dry because they were the usual suspects." Had the traffickers been behind Camarena's abduction, he told Shannon, "we would have known about it. We had *very* good informants."[33]

"Somewhere within the interrogations," Kuykendall believed, "lay the information as to the motive for the [Camarena and Zavala] kidnappings and the identity of the mastermind or masterminds."[34] If so, then presumably it was in a segment excised from the cassettes or transcript turned over to the DEA. In this light, we find the point where the CIA-provided transcript abruptly ends potentially significant.

CAMARENA: Let me explain how it was. [Federal Judicial Police Comandante] Lorrobaquio bugged the telephone of a guy who has a ranch in Veracruz. . . . Give me a second to remember. . . . I'm going to tell you the whole story, Comandante.
INTERROGATOR: No problem. Go ahead.
CAMARENA: A man who had a ranch with an airstrip in Veracruz. . . . [end of transcript][35]

We suspect that the ranch with the airstrip Camarena mentions here was Caro Quintero's Veracruz ranch, where Nicaraguan *contras* were alleged to be training under CIA auspices and the airstrip was being used to refuel agency contract aircraft flying arms south to the *contras* and cocaine north to the United States. Contract pilot Robert "Tosh" Plumlee flew to the Veracruz ranch on *contra*-related missions and on one occasion in 1984 recalls meeting agency electronics technician Lawrence Harrison, although no one used his real name in those situations and he did not know Harrison's true identity at the time. They talked briefly, and Harrison informed him that he was working on the strip's navigational beacon. "That part of the operation," Plumlee tells us, "would have been CIA, not Mexican."[36] Camarena, it seems, was entering prohibited terrain. The information might have interested his interrogators, but, we can suppose, the Reagan administration's national security apparatus would not want to see it shared with the Justice Department or, potentially, the public via open-court criminal proceedings.

The public allegations of U.S. government collusion with Mexican drug traffickers and CIA complicity in the Buendía and Camarena killings made by Héctor Berréllez, Phil Jordan, and Tosh Plumlee resulted in several months of renewed investigation on our part, now joined by Charles Bowden and border affairs specialist Molly Molloy. Bowden had known Berréllez and Jordan for many years, and, intrigued that after years of silence they had suddenly gone public, he began talking with them about their decision to do so. He had had only sporadic contact with Berréllez for some time but now found him willing to talk about the sensation he, Jordan, and Plumlee had caused with their explosive allegations. He also facilitated our direct communication with Berréllez and Jordan, who in turn put us in touch with Plumlee.

In this flurry of sensational revelations and allegations, the most significant disclosures for contextualizing the Buendía and Camarena homicides came not from the three American whistleblowers but from veteran, now retired, senior Mexican intelligence official Jorge Carrillo Olea, who in *Proceso*'s 27 October 2013 cover story revealed previously unknown details about the CIA's relationship with its Mexican counterpart, the DFS. Carrillo Olea served as undersecretary of government in the de la Madrid administration and, following the dissolution of the DFS, played a central role in the reorganization of Mexico's intelligence service. He was, in the estimation of Mexican intelligence historian Sergio Aguayo Quezada, as influential in national security matters as the legendary Fernando Gutiérrez Barrios and "enjoyed the political confidence of [both] Miguel de la Madrid and Carlos Salinas de Gortari."[37]

As a government undersecretary during the de la Madrid *sexenio*, it normally would have been Carrillo Olea's responsibility to oversee DFS operations, but, breaking with established bureaucratic custom, Secretary of Government Manuel Bartlett Díaz retained that responsibility in his own hands, which implies that in all likelihood he would have been apprised of DFS director Zorrilla Pérez's multifarious criminal activities, as well as the directorate's close relationship with the CIA and, by extension, their joint involvement in both the Buendía and Camarena homicides. If Bartlett did not have that information, Carrillo asked rhetorically, then who would? "Assuming it wasn't the undersecretary of agrarian reform," he remarked caustically to his *Proceso* interviewer, "then it was the secretary of government."[38]

"The Federal Security Directorate was entirely at the service of the CIA," Carrillo assured *Proceso*. It even had some of its agents assigned to the agency full time. "There was a house in the Ansures district where [those agents] lived," he explained. "The Americans paid them, dressed them, and gave them their orders. There were ten of them on duty twenty-four hours a day, directly with the CIA. They were paid in dollars." The DFS, *Proceso* emphasized in bold type, "was literally at the service of the CIA, and both [agencies] collaborated with the Guadalajara cartel."[39]

What the DEA's Leyenda investigation discovered, *Proceso* elaborated, just as Kiki Camarena and Manuel Buendía had done earlier, was "the collusion of the security

services of Mexico and the United States in support of the Nicaraguan counterrevolution, in an international operation to purchase arms and traffic in drugs that also
involved Iran and Israel. The purpose [of that operation] was to provide arms to the
Contras for the overthrow of the Sandinista regime, *but money from the Iran-Contra
operation was also used to establish training camps in Mexico for the so-called Freedom
Fighters.*"[40] This last detail, the training of Nicaraguan *contras* on Mexican soil, was
perhaps the most delicate of all, at least at the time and from the perspective of the
Mexican government, whose ostensible commitment to a negotiated settlement of
regional conflicts (the Contadora Initiative) those clandestine facilities would have
exposed as a cynical deception had their existence been revealed.

Even now, a quarter century later, Carrillo Olea tiptoes cautiously around his revelation of the training camps. He did not know, he professed, how the decision to establish them had been taken nor whether anyone in the Mexican government was
involved. Then defense secretary Gen. Juan Arévalo Gardoqui was well aware of Caro
Quintero's Búfalo operation, he noted suggestively, while Manuel Bartlett Díaz's claim
that he had no knowledge of how the CIA operated in Mexico was patently absurd.
"Of course Bartlett knew that the DFS was at the service of the CIA," Carrillo insisted.
"He knew it perfectly well." But, he qualified, "It's a big stretch to allege that the for-
mer secretaries of defense and government took part in the Camarena murder, as the
Americans have so crudely done."[41]

Héctor Berréllez is the primary source for these latest allegations of CIA collusion
with the Guadalajara cartel in support of the Nicaraguan *contras* and agency responsibility for the death of Kiki Camarena. He made virtually the same assertions to us
when we interviewed him in 2004, specifically that Camarena was murdered because
he had discovered the trafficker-CIA-*contra* nexus and that Félix Rodríguez was present during Camarena's interrogation. He also told us on that occasion that he had
been ordered to leave the CIA out of his Leyenda investigation and should do the
same with former Mexican government secretary Bartlett as well.[42] It is clear to us that
Berréllez has long wished to speak out about what he believes to be the CIA's role in
the Camarena affair but until now was sufficiently intimidated by official warnings,
explicit or intimated, not to do so. We suspect that the private security firm he founded
following his retirement (The Mayo Group) was predicated on his continued silence,
in effect constituting what Charles Bowden once described to us as "Héctor's golden
handcuffs."

That Berréllez spoke to us about these matters, knowing that we were writing a
book, is an indication of his compulsion to reveal what he knew; that he declined to
speak further with us following our interview suggests either nervous second thoughts
about having done so or that someone had perhaps tightened his golden handcuffs.
When two years later, following his eldest son's suicide, he tried unsuccessfully to persuade Lawrence Harrison to join him and together reveal what they knew about CIA
operations in Mexico to Bowden, no doubt envisaging an exposé similar to Bowden's
1998 *Esquire* article about Gary Webb,[43] that was another sign of his continuing wish
to speak out. (Curiously, this latter approach to Harrison appears to have occurred at
a point in time when he was pressuring the ex-CIA operative to terminate his contact

with us.) When in October 2013 he finally did go public, now accompanied by Phil Jordan and Tosh Plumlee, it was, he told *Proceso*, because he had "carried this information stuck inside him like a thorn" since his retirement from the DEA in 1996 and "wanted to get it off his chest."[44] Lawrence Harrison had said something similar to us about himself when we first spoke to him in the spring of 2004.

In broad outline, the thrust of what Berréllez, Jordan, and Plumlee have alleged meshes well with our own investigations as developed in the present book. Two of the more surprising allegations, however, pose evidentiary questions not easily resolved, to wit: (1) that veteran CIA operative Félix Rodríguez participated in the interrogation of Kiki Camarena and (2) that senior members of the de la Madrid administration were also present during Camarena's interrogation. The primary sources on which the alleged complicity of senior government officials in the Camarena affair is based are four ex-Mexican police officers who served as bodyguards and enforcers for the Guadalajara cartel and were brought to this country in the early 1990s as protected Justice Department witnesses to testify in the Los Angeles Camarena case prosecutions. One of these witnesses actually took part in Camarena's abduction yet was granted immunity and asylum in return for his testimony on behalf of federal prosecutors. The other three were likewise granted immunity and asylum in return for their testimony, despite having worked for Mexico's leading drug lords. In their preliminary DEA debriefings, and then on the witness stand, they testified that numerous senior government and military officials participated in the planning of Camarena's abduction and were present in the exclusive residence where Camarena was tortured to death while being interrogated.

The inherent problem with this kind of witness testimony as a basis for determining historical fact is the difficulty, or perhaps impossibility, of establishing the veracity of the self-interested party who provides it. All four of these witnesses faced precarious futures in Mexico because of the criminal lives they had led and thus viewed cooperation with U.S. authorities as their only assurance of survival and personal security. They were vulnerable, in other words, to manipulation by their American handlers, and there is no sound reason to assume they were not coached and rehearsed by the assistant U.S. attorneys who prosecuted the two Camarena-related Zuno trials for which they were granted immunity and asylum. As with the Buendía case, so, too, in the Camarena case: both were politically compromised and had little to do with imparting justice.

The U.S. administrations of Ronald Reagan (1981–1989) and George H. W. Bush (1989–1993) sought to effect a change of political actors in Mexico, in terms of both governing style (from nationalist PRI corporatism to a globalist technocracy) and specific individuals, among whom PRI presidential hopeful Manuel Bartlett Díaz was a primary target. As noted in chapter 16 and recounted previously by Rogelio Hernández López,[45] the DEA had been involved in an attempt to implicate Bartlett Díaz in the Buendía assassination, which, had it succeeded, would have prevented him from running in the 1988 presidential election. As it happened, President Miguel de la Madrid did so himself by unexpectedly naming his budget and planning secretary, Carlos Salinas de Gortari, as the PRI's official candidate. Bartlett remained a major figure in Mexican politics, however, and a decade later let it be known that he still had presidential ambitions. By then, as we recounted in chapter 14, Bartlett had retained a prominent Los Angeles attorney to clear his name of allegations linking him to the Camarena homicide, allegations made during the second Zuno trial by two of the four witnesses on whom Berréllez now relies for his most recent statements about Félix Rodríguez and the CIA.

The waters have been muddied by *Proceso*'s sensationalization of the American ex-agents' allegations and its editorial decision to treat the Camarena and Buendía cases as media "thrillers," which in effect trivializes these historic events. A majority of that newsweekly's coverage has been produced by its Washington-based correspondent, J. Jesús Esquivel, who in addition to having interviewed Berréllez and Jordan also interviewed three of the former Jalisco police officers on whose testimony their allegations of CIA and Mexican government complicity rest. Although the identities of those now protected witnesses can be discovered in publicly available trial and investigative records (see www.reneverdugo.org/docs.html), a condition of Esquivel's access to them was that he only refer to them as José 1, José 2, and José 3.

When several months later Charles Bowden and Molly Molloy conducted their own interviews with José 2, José 3, and a fourth Mexican source also in the Justice Department's witness protection program, they, too, were asked not to reveal their names. Given the relative ease with which the identities of all four witnesses can be discovered, we suspect that their identification as José 1, 2, 3, and 4 was more for dramatic effect than protection of their anonymity. They did not assume new identities when they relocated to the United States and have long been known to those on either side of the border who might wish to do them harm. They are, in order of appearance, Enrique Plascencia Aguilar, Jorge Godoy López, Ramón Lira, and René López Romero, all former police officers who served as bodyguards and enforcers for Guadalajara cartel kingpin Ernesto Fonseca Carrillo and his associates.

Plascencia Aguilar testified in the first Zuno Arce trial, together with the later discredited Héctor Cervantes Santos, discussed in chapter 11. Neither Plascencia nor Cervantes were called as witnesses in Zuno's 1992 retrial. Godoy López and López Romero testified in the second Zuno trial, while Lira only served as a DEA source and was never called to testify. Esquivel interviewed Plascencia, Godoy, and Lira (Josés 1, 2, and 3), while Bowden and Molloy interviewed Godoy, Lira, and López Romero (Josés 2, 3, and 4).

Esquivel's interviews with three of the four Josés were arranged by Héctor Berréllez, no doubt to reinforce his own allegation of CIA complicity in the martyrdom of Kiki Camarena, which Esquivel has done fully in the pages of *Proceso*. But Esquivel also makes erroneous statements that complicate our evaluation of what he reports these protected witnesses to have said. He misinformed *Proceso* readers, for example, when he wrote that what the three Josés told him about Félix Rodríguez and the CIA was a "repeat" of what they testified in the 1990–1992 Camarena trials.[46] That is false, inasmuch as Judge Edward Rafeedie did not allow testimony about the CIA after Lawrence Harrison's 6 July 1990 voir dire examination, nor did any of these prosecution witnesses ever testify about the alleged presence of Félix Rodríguez (aka Max Gómez) at the Camarena interrogation. And, as noted, José 3 (Ramón Lira) never testified at all.

José 1 (Plascencia) is the first of these protected witnesses cited by Esquivel to substantiate the presence and involvement of CIA operative Félix Rodríguez in the interrogation of Kiki Camarena. Plascencia told Esquivel that "eight to ten days before Camarena's abduction" he had attended a planning session in one of Ernesto Fonseca's Guadalajara residences and that Rodríguez (using the pseudonym "Max") had taken part in that meeting together with Fonseca, Caro Quintero, Félix Gallardo, Manuel "El Cochiloco" Salcido Uceta, and a Mexican army colonel he did not know. Plascencia may have been at such a meeting as part of Fonseca's security detail and in that capacity could have observed the other participants, as well as learned the name of an unfamiliar attendee, but he would not have attended the meeting itself. The same holds for Godoy, Lira, and López Romero and their accounts of Camarena abduction planning sessions.

These three witnesses struck Bowden as credible, albeit with obligatory caveats. "The only known evidence of the presence of [Félix Rodríguez], Bartlett Díaz and the generals comes from disreputable Mexican cops," Bowden remarked to us after interviewing them. "I am inclined to believe the disreputable cops but that hardly changes their reputations. . . . They are also careful not to say they know things beyond their own experience." Assertions that senior government officials were present during Camarena's interrogation, Bowden adds, were made by Godoy, Lira, and López Romero without the slightest suggestion that the presence of such personalities was in any way out of the ordinary. "They assume the big guys have immunity and get away with things," he observed.[47] The problem with this for us is that we cannot conceive a plausible reason why Bartlett, Arévalo Gardoqui, or other senior federal or state officials would want to be at the residence where Camarena was being interrogated. Their presence would have served no practical purpose, certainly not their own.

Jesús Esquivel has further muddied the waters by rushing a book into print based on his late 2013 interviews with Berréllez, Plascencia, Godoy, and Lira. Titled *La CIA, Camarena y Caro Quintero: La historia secreta* (The CIA, Camarena and Caro Quintero: The Secret History), it is a 190-page sensationalist paperback written and produced in only nine months, with all the errors, inaccuracies, and lack of perspective to be expected in such hasty treatment of a major historic event. He clearly did not have control of his facts. Nor did he seem to grasp the geopolitical continuities running throughout the Buendía and Camarena cases.

Esquivel's book is episodic, not analytical, with emphasis on the sensational aspects of Mexican drug trafficking, the efforts of American narcotics agents to combat it ("white hats"), collusion with the traffickers on the part of the CIA ("black hats"), and above all his own inside access to netherworld informants on the U.S. side of the border. Even its title is misleading, as it suggests, and Esquivel avers as much, that Rafael Caro Quintero was the capo of capos in the Guadalajara cartel, which was not in fact the case. Nor does the book recount "the secret history" of that dark chapter of U.S.-Mexico relations.

The bulk of the book consists of lengthy transcriptions from Esquivel's recorded interviews with Berréllez and the three "Josés," no doubt a dramatic device to authenticate the author's reportorial credentials. The result is a series of voyeuristic windows

on the debased comportment of cartel members but no insight into the criminal enterprise that took the lives of Kiki Camarena and Manuel Buendía. Of greatest interest
to us, and the book's one significant contribution, is what these transcribed segments
reveal about the testimony of Esquivel's informants: a confusion of both persuasive
and improbable accounts, factual error and faulty recollection.

"José 2" (Godoy), for example, mistakenly recounts that Lawrence Harrison was
shot in Puerto Vallarta in reprisal for having threatened a man who made advances
to one of Ernesto Fonseca's female favorites, rather than in Guadalajara where he was
in fact ambushed by Jalisco State Police in a failed assassination attempt.[48] Héctor
Berréllez, in turn, exhibits strikingly compromised recall when he recounts his recruitment of Harrison as a DEA informant and government witness. He first learned of
Harrison's existence in 1990, he tells Esquivel, which is patently untrue since by then
Harrison and his family had already been relocated to southern California.

Berréllez then states that he had dispatched Leyenda agents to Guadalajara to locate
and approach Harrison, that a meeting was arranged with Harrison at a local hotel,
and that the DEA's Mexico City office intervened to prevent the Leyenda agents
from interviewing him until S/A Dale Stinson arrived from the American embassy to
speak with him first. (Esquivel consistently misspells Stinson's name as "Steinson."
He likewise misidentifies Harrison as "Victor Lawrence" instead of Lawrence Victor,
and inexplicably refers to Federal Judicial Police legend Florentino Ventura Gutiérrez
as "Ventura Anaya.") Stinson, according to Berréllez, persuaded Harrison not to cooperate with the DEA's Leyenda agents, although Harrison supposedly had assured
them previously that he was willing to serve as a DEA informant and protected witness
and two months after the Stinson encounter would allow Leyenda operatives to bring
him out of Mexico to Los Angeles. The problem with this version is that, as recounted
above in chapter 11, the Stinson incident occurred in 1987, when Berréllez was serving
as resident agent in charge of the DEA's Mazatlán station and would not be appointed
to take charge of Operation Leyenda for another two years.[49]

Berréllez further misrepresents Harrison to Esquivel by describing him as a CIA
contract agent who had been recruited by the agency in Mexico, initially to identify
radical students who, once he fingered them, were killed by Mexican security forces;
then subsequently to infiltrate the Guadalajara cartel. From Berréllez's own confirmation to us of Harrison's false identity it is apparent that he was not merely an expedient
contract operative but rather a fully trained agency "illegal," as we describe in chapter
13. Assets and contractors are not given false identities with all of the elaborately contrived supporting documentation such identities require. In describing Harrison to
Esquivel as a CIA contract agent, Berréllez in effect diminishes him with respect to
himself, an apparent psychological need we have noted over the years we've been aware
of his strained relationship with Harrison.

The final picture Berréllez paints of Harrison for Esquivel's book is that he was "over
80 years of age," lived in California, and was "completely out of touch with police
matters and the mysteries and covert ways of U.S. intelligence agencies." At the time
Berréllez made this statement, Harrison was sixty-nine, very well informed about
developments in Mexico, and not talking to Berréllez but discussing the underbelly of

American intelligence with us. Berréllez, we suspect, did not want Jesús Esquivel to seek
an interview with Harrison and sought to discourage him from doing so by portraying
Harrison as irrelevant for his book—all of which calls into question the reliability of
Berréllez's own recent testimony.[50]

For purposes of the present investigation, the alleged presence of one or more CIA
operatives during the interrogation of Kiki Camarena is the most significant and plausible element of Berréllez's assertions. Even before taking charge of the official Camarena
investigation in 1989, he had become aware of CIA links to Mexican drug traffickers.
As head of the DEA's Mazatlán office in 1986–1987, he had learned of a Sinaloan camp
with an airstrip from which American planes were flying loads of cocaine into the
United States. When he reported this to his superiors at the U.S. embassy in Mexico
City, he was told that it was "a *contra* training camp" and to "leave it alone."[51] When
he subsequently took charge of Operation Leyenda, he was stunned to discover the
extent to which the CIA had penetrated the DEA; agents he had assumed were reporting directly to him, he told us, were actually reporting to the Central Intelligence
Agency.[52]

Berréllez did not hear about Félix Rodríguez participating in the Camarena interrogation until after the Los Angeles trials had concluded. It was the notorious Federal
Judicial Police commander Guillermo González Calderoni who first alerted Berréllez
to the involvement of the CIA and its infamous Cuban operative. He also informed
Phil Jordan.[53]

Calderoni, who preferred and is best known by his mother's family name, apparently ran afoul of the Salinas administration over its alleged links to the Sinaloa cartel
and, through the personal intervention of Héctor Berréllez, fled Mexico in 1993 for
the United States, where he served for a decade as a Justice Department informant
until an assassin killed him in McAllen, Texas, in early February 2003.[54] As Berréllez
recounts it, "He said to me, 'Hector, drop it, because you're gonna get screwed ["Te
van a chingar"]. The CIA's involved in the *Kiki* matter. It's very dangerous for you to
pursue this.' He gave me names, among them Félix [Rodríguez], and details and everything, but when my superiors found out, they pulled me from the case and sent me
to Washington."[55] It was only after receiving this information from Calderoni that
Berréllez had Plascencia, Godoy, Lira, and López Romero look at the photo lineups
from which they each, separately, are said to have identified Félix Rodríguez.

In attempting to evaluate this testimonial evidence, we have been confronted with
inconsistencies and seeming improbabilities regarding what these witnesses have stated,
when and to whom they stated it, and the precise circumstances in which they were
moved to make their respective statements. As we were writing these final pages and
after a ten-year hiatus, we managed to reestablish communication with Berréllez.
"There were a total of four witnesses that identified Félix Rodríguez," he now tells us.
"Two of them . . . actually saw Félix Rodríguez interrogating Kiki Camarena at the 881
Lope de Vega residence. . . . The other two witnesses . . . knew Rodríguez as Max
Gómez, who they saw arrive at Fonseca's residence accompanied by Manuel Bartlett
Díaz and numerous DFS Agents on numerous occasions." The four witnesses were
brought to the United States separately, he notes, and were isolated from one another

to avoid contamination of the evidence. "It would be inconceivable," he insists, "for all four to be mistaken or untruthful regarding Rodríguez."[56]

Just when we thought we could conclude this epilogue, Charles Bowden, who had been reading the 1990–1992 Camarena trial transcripts, called our attention to a connection between Enrique Plascencia (José 1) and Antonio Gárate Bustamante, the former Guadalajara riot squad officer, drug trafficker associate, and DEA informant who, after being exposed in August 1986, was brought to the United States by the DEA to work with Berréllez on the Leyenda investigation.[57] Gárate apparently had himself been present at one of the meetings where Camarena's abduction was discussed and by all rights should have been indicted. Instead, quipped one of the defense attorneys in the 1990 trial, "he turned himself into a witness factory and produced a bunch of bought witnesses."[58] Those witnesses included the four Josés.

It immediately occurred to us that if Plascencia, who had worked under and for Gárate in Guadalajara, had observed Félix Rodríguez at the Fonseca residence, how was it that Gárate himself had not confirmed the Cuban's presence there as well? We now put that question to Berréllez, and his reply was enlightening. "Antonio Gárate Bustamante, one of my paid informants, was never put on the [witness] stand due to credibility issues," he explained. "He was found not to be credible on numerous serious issues and for that reason the prosecutors chose not to use him." He did, nonetheless, "recall the one meeting attended by Rodríguez in which Camarena's picture was passed around."

Even as a highly paid informant, Berréllez elaborated, Gárate "kept close ties with the drug lords" and "was always loyal to [Ernesto] Fonseca," who had been best man at his wedding. "DEA did not trust him as far as we could throw him," Berréllez told us. "Gárate, as a lot of informants that we had, played both sides against the middle, taking money from the DEA and also from the drug lords. We knew their game and we used them as we needed." Gárate, for his part, "was very useful in locating and recruiting witnesses, and was a walking encyclopedia of who was who in the drug world." After he relocated to the United States, Berréllez kept a permanent wiretap on his phone.[59]

The connection between Plascencia and Gárate Bustamante brought to mind a remarkable snippet of testimony offered by Lawrence Harrison while he was being cross-examined on 7 June 1990 by defense attorney Mary Kelly. Kelly's questioning concerned the six-month period in 1983 when Harrison had been assigned to upgrade Guadalajara cartel radio communications and was in the United States purchasing the necessary components. "During the time period that you returned to the United States in 1983 for six months, what employment did you have?" Kelly asked.

"I was a chief of security for the house of Antonio Gárate Bustamante," Harrison replied.

"In the United States?"

"Yes."

"Where was that house?"

"It was in Seal Beach [California]. I don't remember the address."

"And that was for the entire time you were in the United States?"

"Yes."[60]

Our puzzlement was over what Gárate was doing in the United States at that time, how it was that he possessed a house in Seal Beach, why that house required security, and what Harrison was doing there in a security capacity. At the time we came across this testimony, we were not in regular communication with Harrison, so we posed these questions to Héctor Berréllez. The Seal Beach house, Berréllez told us, was a Guadalajara cartel stash house where large quantities of cocaine were stored. Gárate apparently had overseen the place for the cartel, and, we realized, it was only natural that Fonseca would have Harrison stay there while he was in California on cartel business. A CIA operative providing security for a stash house in Seal Beach in 1983, as Chuck Bowden wryly commented to us, leads one to wonder if there might have been a connection there to the Nicaraguan *contras*.[61]

Asked about this, Berréllez replied that the DEA was not aware of the Seal Beach house at the time and he had no information linking it to the *contras*. "We raided 14 *contra* stash houses in the southern California area in the early '80s," he said, "and none were connected to the Seal Beach stash house." The known *contra* cocaine connection in California, he noted, was the one described by Gary Webb through the Nicaraguan traffickers Danilo Blandón and Norwin Meneses. "The link of the *contras* with the Guadalajara drug cartel is Félix Rodríguez," Berréllez insisted. That connection was through Honduran Juan Ramón Matta Ballesteros's SETCO airline, which Rodríguez contracted to resupply the *contras*, and Rodríguez himself, who had direct access to the Mexican traffickers through Secretary of Government Manuel Bartlett Díaz and the DFS. "This," he assured us, "is the information that Manuel Buendía had which resulted in his murder."[62]

On 30 August 2014, Charles Bowden died suddenly of heart failure. He had been working for more than a year on a manuscript about the Camarena case and two weeks before his death had completed a first draft.[63] Ten weeks later a richly illustrated version of that draft, titled *Blood on the Corn*, was published electronically by Medium .com, coauthored by Molly Molloy with illustrations by New York artist Matt Rota. Numbering sixteen chapters divided into three parts, *Blood on the Corn* draws on recent interviews with Héctor Berréllez and three of the protected witnesses (Godoy, Lira, and López Romero), a January 2007 interview with Lawrence Harrison, documentary research in the René Verdugo digital archive of court and investigative records (www.reneverdugo.org/docs.html), and a thorough familiarity with our research for the present book.[64]

While not the flawless, fully developed work that Bowden surely envisioned, *Blood on the Corn* does contribute new information and additional insights to what we already know about CIA complicity with the Guadalajara cartel and, through the cartel, its involvement in the Camarena and Buendía murders. It has also resulted in new information coming to light as a consequence of its varied effect on interested parties. Harrison, for example, experienced an adrenaline spike on reading it that gave him a heightened energy level and clarity of thought we had not observed in years. He thought Bowden's treatment obscured rather than clarified the truth of the Camarena case, which for him was the CIA, not the dramatized thuggery of the drug traffickers or the alleged complicity of corrupt government officials, and Félix Rodríguez, not Bartlett Díaz, Arévalo Gardoqui, or Jalisco governor Enrique Álvarez del Castillo.

Harrison even agreed to be interviewed by Molly Molloy, Bowden's collaborator and coauthor. He wanted to take her measure, then give her a clearer perspective on what from his unique vantage point had actually occurred. Berréllez proposed the interview, apparently by phone, then sent Jorge Godoy to Harrison's residence to work out the details. Harrison family members' deep animosity toward Berréllez because of the role they believe he played in Lawrence's earlier professional tribulations make him unwelcome in their home. That Lawrence himself remains on speaking terms with Berréllez despite his family's strong negative feelings seems to be for reasons of personal intelligence rather than out of civility or a sense of obligation. He does not trust Berréllez.

He does recognize the importance of Berréllez's recent public allegations of CIA complicity in the Camarena and Buendía homicides, however, and wishes to add his own informed voice to the discussion—above all to focus attention on the CIA and away from diversionary accounts of high-level Mexican government collusion with cartel kingpins. Harrison's determination to set the record straight as he observed it unfold on the ground is reflected in his willingness to meet with Molloy at a location other than his own home, which, given his seriously compromised health, presupposed an element of personal risk. That meeting took place on Wednesday, 17 December 2014, at the residence of Jorge Godoy, who picked Harrison up in the early afternoon, then drove him home again several hours later.[65]

It was a strange gathering: Harrison, Berréllez, and the departed Charles Bowden in the person of his mate Molly Molloy come together with a shared purpose but differing motives while being hosted by two Camarena case protected witnesses, José 2 (Godoy) and José 3 (Ramón Lira). Molloy describes her encounter with Harrison as more of a conversation than a structured interview. Seated on opposite ends of an L-shaped living room couch, they talked for about two hours while the others prepared a meal. Harrison was weak, Molloy noted, and spoke so softly that at times she had difficulty making out what he said. Nonetheless, "he was completely alert and communicative." Now and then he had to use an inhaler. He required assistance getting to his feet, as well as moving about, and used a cane to steady himself. His exceptional height and large frame, Molloy thought, made his systemic weakness more of a problem than it might have been for a smaller person.

After talking for some time, Molloy and Harrison joined the others for a meal of grilled chicken with tortillas, guacamole, and salsa. They sat together around a kitchen table, all speaking Spanish. Harrison ate well, showed a good sense of humor, and, Molloy thought, exhibited a normal range of emotions "under the circumstances." Considering those circumstances, she added, the gathering "was friendly and pleasant." Harrison and Berréllez, for their part, conversed quite a bit with no apparent animosity or tension between them. Both men, it appears, have reconciled themselves to whatever came down between them in the past.[66]

Asked why Ramón Lira was there that day, Molloy thought it was because he and Godoy were friends. "These men see each other," she wrote us, "because of their long

and unusual acquaintance and the fact that they form [part of] a very small group with
such shared experiences." There are, Molloy supposed, "few people in their lives with
whom they can talk about these things." Both Godoy and Lira knew Harrison when
all three worked for Ernesto Fonseca and on this occasion were "very solicitous and
kind" to him.[67]

Berréllez, too, is part of this group, albeit for different reasons. He saved their lives
and assured their future by bringing them out of Mexico to serve as protected witnesses
in the 1992 retrial of Zuno Arce. We find it noteworthy that Berréllez sent Godoy to
talk to Harrison about doing the Molloy interview and that, by Harrison's account,
Godoy had pitched the interview to him with an implied enticement of "money to be
made from *Blood on the Corn*."[68] (We note in passing that Godoy is identified by his
real name in *Blood on the Corn*, which suggests that he has little concern about preserving his anonymity and may, in fact, be pleased to receive a bit of literary notoriety.)
Berréllez, for his part, has long sought recognition for having solved the Camarena
case and, we suspect, has his own thoughts about how he might utilize Bowden's name
to further that recognition. Both he and Phil Jordan, Bowden wrote us in early 2014,
"clearly want to return to the spotlight. Ex agents are like a lot of ex athletes, they find
it hard to let go of their glory days. And of course Hector has personal needs."[69]

However that may be, there can be little doubt that Héctor Berréllez sorely wants to
indict the CIA, as does Lawrence Harrison, though each for subtly different reasons.
Berréllez passionately resents the agency for having destroyed his career, as well as caus-
ing the martyrdom of a fellow law enforcement agent and, more broadly, injuring the
American public by allowing the flood of cocaine and other illicit drugs reaching U.S.
markets to continue virtually unimpeded. Harrison, in turn, wants to hold the agency
accountable for its crimes against the Mexican public and the mockery it has made
of professed American ideals, as well as for the tribulations it has visited on him and
his family. *Blood on the Corn* has proved a ready catalyst for both men, each of whom
is now providing new information and insights on CIA involvement in the Camarena
and Buendía murders.

The most significant new datum that Berréllez gave Bowden and Molloy is that after
Guillermo Calderoni informed him in 1993 that the CIA was behind the Camarena
murder and agency operative Félix Rodríguez had been present during Camarena's
interrogation, and after he had Plascencia, Godoy, Lira, and López Romero separately
identify Rodríguez from photo lineups and passed that information to his superiors,
a CIA official flew to Los Angeles to dissuade him from pursuing that aspect of the
Leyenda investigation. He was, the man said, "jeopardizing national security." When
it became apparent that Berréllez would not back off, the DEA reined him in on the
agency's behalf. This incident constitutes a persuasive piece of circumstantial evidence
that Félix Rodríguez did, in fact, have something to do with the abduction, interrogation, and murder of Kiki Camarena and that the cover-up of CIA-managed cartel
support for the Nicaraguan *contras* was the motive.[70]

We had been talking with Harrison by phone over the three weeks preceding his
meeting with Molly Molloy and were struck by the renewed vigor in his voice, his facile
recall of detail, and the clarity of his thinking. He had been animated by *Blood on the*

El caso **Buendía,** ligado al de "Kiki" Camarena

J. JESÚS ESQUIVEL

WASHINGTON.- La Agencia Central de Inteligencia (CIA), varios políticos mexicanos, un traficante alemán de armas y el asesinato del periodista Manuel Buen-día forman parte de una trama que, de una u otra manera, involucra también al Cártel de Guadalajara, el cual dirigía en los años ochenta Rafael Caro Quintero, de acuerdo con un expediente del gobierno de Estados Unidos elaborado por su Departamento de Justicia y clasificado como de máximo secreto.

Fechado el 13 de febrero de 1990, el documento -con una etiqueta en la cual se estampó el sello de "top secret"- contiene las declaraciones del ciudadano estadunidense Víctor Lawrence Harrison, subcontratista y operador de la CIA en México, quien en los ochenta colaboraba con el Cártel de Guadalajara, con la desaparecida Dirección Fede-

Three decades after their deaths, a cover story in the 6 April 2014 issue of *Proceso* links the 1984–1985 murders of Manuel Buendía and Enrique Camarena. (Courtesy of Molly Molloy)

Corn, about which he had a number of misgivings, and seemed anxious to set the record straight as he saw it. Berréllez's allegation that Félix Rodríguez had participated in the interrogation of Camarena, he told us, was true. While he himself was not there, he said, he knew for a fact from his own sources that Rodríguez was in the interrogation room, although he doubted that he had inflicted any of the torture. Harrison likewise doubted that Secretary of Government Bartlett Díaz or Secretary of Defense Arévalo Gardoqui would have been there. It simply was not the way they operated, he insisted. They would have sent trusted subordinates to deal with Fonseca and the other drug capos, not gone themselves.[71]

When Russell called Harrison the day after his visit with Molloy, Berréllez, Godoy, and Lira, it was once again the weak-voiced, health-compromised man we had become accustomed to hearing over the previous two or three years. The visit to Godoy's house appeared to have taken its toll on his energy reserves. He was tired, he said, and thought that he probably would not live out the new year, but he had wanted "to make a last stand" against Félix Rodríguez, whom he clearly despised. Even in this subdued state, however, Harrison remained thoughtful and clearheaded. He had been favorably impressed by Molly Molloy and felt he had managed to give her a new perspective on the Camarena case and the political context in which it had occurred.

Struck by the visceral animosity Harrison exhibited toward Félix Rodríguez, Russell asked him why the CIA would have assigned a Cuban operative to oversee Camarena's abduction and interrogation when the agency had Mexican assets in place who were perfectly capable of carrying out that task. He replied that Rodríguez's presence was a message to the Mexicans that this was a priority CIA operation and the Americans wanted Camarena eliminated. Rodríguez, he noted, was well known in Mexican intelligence and leadership circles, above all for his role in the capture and execution of revolutionary icon "Che" Guevara but also as a key agency operative in the *contra* resupply effort. He had, Harrison told us, advised *contra* southern front commander Edén Pastora, meeting with the renowned "Commander Zero" in Guadalajara during the same period he appears to have been in contact with Harrison. His presence, Harrison emphasized, assured full Mexican backing for the Camarena operation.[72]

These final details and insights provided by Héctor Berréllez and Lawrence Harrison effectively close the evidentiary circle that indicts the U.S. government under the administration of President Ronald Reagan for the 1984 assassination of Mexican political columnist Manuel Buendía and the 1985 murder of DEA S/A Enrique Camarena Salazar—both historic crimes committed in the furtherance of a much larger criminal enterprise: the U.S. government's proxy *contra* war against the Sandinista government of Nicaragua.[73]

GLOSSARY OF NAMES

Ábalos Lebrija, María Dolores (viuda de Buendía)—widow of Manuel Buendía.

Acosta Chaparro, Col. Mario Arturo—apparent link between the Mexican military, Guadalajara cartel boss Miguel Ángel Félix Gallardo, and the CIA.

Adato Green (viuda de Ibarra), Victoria—Federal District attorney general (1982–1985).

Aguilar Camín, Héctor—prominent editor, journalist, and media commentator; member of Manuel Buendía's inner circle; formulated the "Ides of May" hypothesis suggesting that the Buendía assassination was part of a U.S. destabilization strategy.

Aguilar Zínser, Adolfo—prominent journalist and political figure; colleague of Manuel Buendía; Mexican ambassador to the United Nations (2002–2003).

Aldana Ibarra, Miguel—head of Mexico's INTERPOL office (1982–1985).

Álvarez del Castillo, Enrique—governor of Jalisco; Mexican attorney general (1988–1994).

Anaya Suárez, Sofia—former DFS officer convicted of coconspiracy in the Manuel Buendía assassination.

Aranda Zorrivas, Luis—PJDF commandant who conducted an early police investigation of the Buendía assassination.

Arévalo Gardoqui, Gen. Juan—Mexican secretary of defense (1982–1988).

Arista Jiménez, Tizoc—reporter for the Mexico City newsweekly *Quehacer Político*.

Avirgan, Tony—American freelance journalist based in Costa Rica during the 1980s; together with his wife Martha Honey (q.v.), he was among the first to expose CIA links to the Nicaraguan *contras* and international narcotics traffickers.

Bartlett Díaz, Manuel—Mexican secretary of government (1982–1988).

Bautista Ortiz, Juan Manuel—young office assistant to Manuel Buendía who witnessed the columnist's assassination.

Becerra Acosta, Manuel—founding editor of the Mexico City daily newspaper *unomásuno* (1977–1989).

Berréllez, Héctor G.—veteran DEA S/A; supervisor of Operation Leyenda, the official DEA investigation of the 1985 abduction and torture slaying in Guadalajara, Mexico, of S/A Enrique Camarena Salazar (q.v.).

Brenneke, Richard J.—Oregon businessman, arms dealer, pilot, and CIA money launderer who, among numerous other tasks, appears to have served as an intermediary between the agency and the John Gotti mafia family in New York, which allegedly paid some fifty million dollars for CIA-supplied cocaine, the money then being used to purchase congressionally prohibited arms for the Nicaraguan *contras*; Brenneke personally flew *contra*-related transport missions between Mena, Arkansas, and Panama; he dealt directly with DCI William Casey (q.v.), as well as with Vice President George H. W. Bush's national security adviser, Donald P. Gregg, himself a veteran CIA officer.

Brumel Álvarez, Héctor Manuel—ostensibly a member of PRI presidential candidate Carlos Salinas de Gortari's security detail, as well as an intermediary for Mexican Gen. Juan Poblano Silva in negotiations with DEA undercover agent Michael Levine (q.v.) for the supposed transshipment of Bolivian cocaine through Mexico as part of a major DEA sting operation ultimately sabotaged by the CIA.

Buendía Tellezgirón, Ángel—younger brother of Manuel Buendía (q.v.).

Buendía Tellezgirón, Manuel—the most prominent and influential newspaper columnist in 1970s and early 1980s Mexico, assassinated in 1984.

Camacho Solís, Manuel—Federal District regent (1988–1994) and PRI notable with presidential ambitions.

Camarena Salazar, Enrique "Kiki"—DEA special agent abducted, tortured, and murdered in February 1985 by Mexican narcotics traffickers in collusion with U.S. and Mexican officials.

Cárdenas, Cuauhtémoc—son of former Mexican president Lázaro Cárdenas (q.v.), leader of a PRI dissident movement and breakaway PRD; opposition presidential candidate in 1988.

Cárdenas, Lázaro—Mexican president (1934–1940)

Caro Quintero, Rafael—one of the principal Guadalajara drug cartel bosses; imprisoned in Mexico for the murder of DEA S/A Enrique Camarena Salazar (q.v.).

Carranza Peniche, Jorge—Mexican military intelligence operative with links to the CIA; entrapped in a DEA/Customs Service sting operation, convicted of conspiracy to import Bolivian cocaine into the United States, and imprisoned.

Carrillo Olea, Jorge—senior Mexican intelligence official; undersecretary of government at the time of the Buendía and Camarena homicides.

Casares Cámara, Hernán—reporter for the Mexico City daily newspaper *unomásuno* and the newsweekly *Punto*.

Castell del Oro, Federico—commandant in charge of the DFS's Guadalajara regional office.

Castillo, Celerino "Cele"—veteran DEA special agent assigned to Guatemala and El Salvador from 1985 to 1990; documented and exposed CIA–NSC collusion with cocaine traffickers in support of the Nicaraguan *contras*.

Cervantes Santos, Héctor—former Jalisco State Judicial Police officer and Guadalajara cartel bodyguard; key U.S. Justice Department paid witness in the 1990 prosecution of Rubén Zuno Arce (q.v.) for complicity in the 1985 murder of DEA S/A Enrique Camarena Salazar (q.v.).

Chávez Almanza, Rosa Elvia—eyewitness to the Buendía assassination.

Cimino, Peter—suspected CIA asset in Mexico during the 1970s, who more than two decades later appears to have played a role in destroying the livelihood of former agency operative Lawrence Victor Harrison (q.v.) in reprisal for talking to the authors of this book.

Cruz Sandoval, Roberto—Costa Rican journalist who linked the 30 May 1984 La Penca bombing attempt against *contra* commander Edén Pastora (q.v.) and the assassination of Manuel Buendía, attributing both incidents to the American CIA.

Davis, George Marshall—birth name of CIA agent Lawrence Victor Harrison (q.v.).

Díaz Redondo, Regino—editor of the Mexico City daily *Excélsior* during the period when Manuel Buendía was publishing his Red Privada column in that newspaper.

Durazo Moreno, Arturo "El Negro"—Mexico City police chief (1976–1982); a legendary López Portillo administration enforcer and exemplar of unbridled institutional corruption; briefly a suspect in the Buendía assassination.

Durruty Castillo, Fernando—former DFS agent falsely accused of being the gunman in the Buendía homicide.

Echeverría Álvarez, Luis—president of Mexico (1970–1976).

"Eko" (Héctor Estanislao de la Garza Batorski)—socially and politically mordant caricaturist affiliated with the Mexico City daily newspaper *unomásuno*; married to Buendía intimate Susana Fisher (q.v.) and briefly a suspect in the "crime of passion" hypothesis promoted by Federal District attorney general Victoria Adato Green (q.v.) to explain the Buendía homicide.

Espino Verdín, Sergio—commandant of the Guadalajara regional office of the Mexican Secretariat of Government's IPS directorate.

Esqueda Gutiérrez, José Luis— Secretariat of Government investigator murdered by DFS agents nine months after the Buendía killing; he had been reporting directly to Secretary of Government Manuel Bartlett Díaz (q.v.) about DFS director José Antonio Zorrilla Pérez (q.v.) and other internal DFS matters, including the Buendía case.

Estrella, Alberto Guadalupe—deputy to DFS director José Antonio Zorrilla Pérez (q.v.); DFS wiretap and electronic surveillance specialist.

Félix Gallardo, Miguel Ángel—one of the top Guadalajara drug cartel bosses, apparent CIA asset, and supplier of arms and money to the Nicaraguan *contras*.

Félix Gutiérrez, Jesús—associate of Guadalajara drug cartel boss Rafael Caro Quintero, with businesses in Costa Rica and Southern California; codefendant with René Verdugo (q.v.) and Raúl López Álvarez (q.v.) in the first Enrique Camarena Salazar (q.v.) murder trial (Los Angeles, 1988).

Fernández Menéndez, Jorge—Mexican investigative journalist, columnist for the Mexico City daily newspaper *El Financiero*, and the first media professional to conclude in print that Manuel Buendía and Enrique Camarena Salazar (q.v.) had both been killed for the same reason: to prevent them from exposing CIA collusion with Mexican narcotics traffickers in support of the Nicaraguan *contras*.

Ferrat, Valentín—Argentine journalist instrumental in the formation of the independent Latin American news service SIPE, based in Mexico City; murdered in Guatemala in 1981.

Fisher, Susana—longtime intimate of Manuel Buendía; married to *unomásuno* caricaturist "Eko" (q.v.), briefly making her a focus of the "crime of passion" hypothesis promoted by Federal District attorney general Victoria Adato Green (q.v.) to explain the Buendía slaying.

Fonseca Carrillo, Ernesto—one of the Guadalajara drug cartel bosses and a Nicaraguan *contra* supporter; imprisoned in Mexico for complicity in the 1985 abduction and murder of DEA S/A Enrique Camarena.

Fox Quesada, Vicente—president of Mexico (2000–2006); member of the PAN and the first non-PRI candidate to win the presidency in more than half a century.

Gárate Bustamante, Antonio "Tony"—former Jalisco State Judicial Police riot squad commander and Guadalajara drug cartel security operative; long-term DEA asset exposed in 1986 and forced to seek refuge in the United States; played a central role in securing Mexican witnesses for the U.S. government in its various Camarena prosecutions.

García Cuéllar, Samuel—attorney for German arms dealer Gerhard Mertins's (q.v.) Durango-based Compañía Minera Romer.

García Domínguez, Miguel Ángel—special prosecutor for the Manuel Buendía case; the first such judicial appointment in Mexican history.

García Paniagua, Javier—former DFS head (1977–1978), deputy government secretary, and president of the ruling PRI; alleged to have had a hand in both the Manuel Buendía assassination and the Enrique Camarena Salazar (q.v.) murder.

García Ramírez, Sergio—Mexican attorney general (1982–1988).

Gehlen, Reinhard—head of Nazi Eastern Front intelligence during World War II; recruited by U.S. Army Intelligence at war's end; subsequently made head of West German intelligence; facilitated the recruitment of numerous former Nazi intelligence operatives and military officers into the netherworld of Cold War covert operations, among them Gerhard Georg Mertins (q.v.); worked closely with the CIA and DIA, as well as with other Allied secret services.

Girón Ortiz, Pablo—alleged ex-DFS agent with connections to corrupt high-level Mexican government officials and military officers; utilized in the joint Customs-DEA sting dubbed Operation Trifecta (1987–1988).

Godoy López, Jorge—former Jalisco State Judicial Police officer and Guadalajara drug cartel security operative; one of two key prosecution witnesses in the 1992 retrial of Rubén Zuno Arce (q.v.).

González, Octavio—ex-DFS agent who worked as an investigator for the independent journalists' Buendía case oversight group coordinated by Ángel Buendía (q.v.).

González Calderoni, Guillermo—legendary senior Mexican Federal Judicial Police commander who took down major narcotics traffickers while accepting protection money from others; sought asylum in the United States in 1993; served for a decade as a DEA, FBI, and Justice Department informant; revealed CIA involvement in the Camarena homicide; assassinated in McAllen, Texas, in February 2003.

Granados Roldán, Otto—presidential press secretary during the Salinas de Gortari administration (1988–1994).

Gregg, Donald P.—national security adviser to former CIA director (1976–1977) and Reagan administration vice president George H. W. Bush; thirty-year CIA veteran; regional chief of station (Bien Hoa) in Vietnam, where one of his deputy field advisers was Félix Rodríguez (q.v.), an agency and personal relationship that would extend through the Iran-Contra affair; both men played key roles in the Reagan administration's proxy *contra* war against Nicaragua's Sandinista government.

Gregory, Patrick—onetime CIA officer turned DEA agent; suspected of never having left the agency.

Gutiérrez Barrios, Fernando—"godfather" of Mexico's intelligence and national security apparatus; DFS director (1965–1970); deputy secretary of government (1970–1976); secretary of government (1988–1994).

Gutiérrez Rodríguez, Luis—general manager of the Mexico City daily *unomásuno*; replaced founding editor Manuel Becerra Acosta (q.v.) in March 1989 when the Salinas de Gortari administration forced Becerra to sever his ties to the paper and go into foreign exile.

Gutiérrez Sánchez, José Trinidad—chief of the PJDF at the time of the Buendía homicide.

Guy, Jeffrey—private security operative employed for a time by the San Bernardino, California, security firm The Mayo Group, founded by retired DEA veteran Héctor G. Berréllez (q.v.).

Harrison, Lawrence Victor—cover name assumed by George Marshall Davis (q.v.) when he was given a new identity by the CIA in the mid-1960s; served as a CIA "illegal" (deep-cover agent) in Mexico; has personal knowledge of the Manuel Buendía assassination, as well as agency collusion with Mexican drug traffickers and government officials in support of the Nicaraguan *contras*.

Hasenfus, Eugene—American contract "cargo kicker" captured in October 1986 by Sandinista soldiers after parachuting from a stricken C-123 aircraft while on a *contra* resupply mission; exposed CIA involvement in *contra* campaign to overthrow Nicaraguan government.

Heath, Edward—Drug Enforcement Administration's Mexico attaché (1983–1989); oversaw in-country handling of the Enrique Camarena Salazar (q.v.) murder investigation; alleged to have been a CIA officer under DEA cover.

Hernández López, Rogelio—investigative reporter for the Mexico City daily newspaper *Excélsior*; member of the independent journalists' Buendía case oversight group; author of first book about the Buendía case, *Zorrilla: El imperio del crimen* (1989).

Hernández Martínez, Judge Roberto—Mexican magistrate who presided over trials of Buendía case defendants.

Honey, Martha—American freelance journalist based in Costa Rica during the 1980s; together with her then husband Tony Avirgan (q.v.), she was among the first to expose CIA links to the Nicaraguan *contras* and international narcotics traffickers.

Hooks, Michael Keith—American marijuana smuggler who worked for the Caro Quintero organization in the Mexican states of Sonora and Chihuahua at the time of the Manuel Buendía and Enrique Camarena Salazar (q.v.) killings.

Ibarra Herrera, Manuel—director of the PJDF (1982–1985).

Jones, Charles "Chuck"—retired DEA agent and private investigator based in Chula Vista, California; appears to be part of the network of former federal agents who contract out their professional skills and experience to both private sector firms and the U.S. government.

Jordan, Phillip (given name Felipe)—thirty-year DEA veteran; personal friend of S/A Enrique Camarena Salazar (q.v.); head of the DEA's Dallas bureau, then director of the El Paso Intelligence Center; one of several whistleblowers who have revealed CIA links to the Camarena Salazar homicide.

Juárez Vásquez, Javier—editor of the Coatzacoalcos, Veracruz, newsweekly *Primera Plana*, shot to death the same night as Manuel Buendía and left by the side of a road, his mouth sewn shut with baling wire.

Katel, Peter—Newspaper *Arizona Republic*'s Mexico City bureau chief; suspected Israeli Mossad agent.

Kennedy, William H.—U.S. attorney (San Diego) who in 1982 attempted to prosecute Mexican DFS director Miguel Nazar Haro (q.v.) for operating a cross-border car theft ring and was fired by the Reagan administration for revealing that Nazar was an important CIA asset.

King, James Lawrence—federal judge (Southern District of Florida, Miami) who in June 1988 dismissed as "frivolous" the Christic Institute's civil suit against alleged members of the Nicaraguan *contra* support network.

Kuykendall, James "Jaime"—resident agent in charge of the DEA's Guadalajara station at the time of the Camarena homicide.

Levine, Michael—veteran undercover agent for the DEA; outspoken critic of the "war on drugs."

Lightfoot, Michael J.—Los Angeles attorney retained by former Mexican secretary of government Manuel Bartlett Díaz to refute allegations of complicity in the murders of Manuel Buendía and Enrique Camarena Salazar.

López Álvarez, Raúl—codefendant with René Verdugo Urquídez (q.v.) and José Félix Gutiérrez (q.v.) in the first Enrique Camarena Salazar (q.v.) murder trial (Los Angeles, 1988).

López Portillo, José—president of Mexico (1976–1982).

López Romero, René—former Jalisco State Judicial Police officer and Guadalajara drug cartel security operative; admitted participant in the 1985 abduction of DEA S/A Enrique Camarena Salazar (q.v.); a key paid prosecution witness against Rubén Zuno Arce (q.v.).

Loret de Mola, Carlos—former governor of Yucatán, prominent journalist, and outspoken PRI critic of the de la Madrid administration (1982–1988); perished in early February 1986 in a single-car accident on an isolated road in the State of Guerrero, which many suspect was not an accident but rather a political assassination.

Loret de Mola, Rafael—son of Carlos Loret de Mola (q.v.), attorney, combative journalist, and political commentator; persuaded that his father's death was a political killing; contacted by DEA's Operation Leyenda G/S Héctor Berréllez (q.v.) and DEA asset Antonio Gárate Bustamante (q.v.) because of averred links between the deaths of Manuel Buendía and Carlos Loret de Mola.

Luellen, Jack R.—Los Angeles defense attorney who represented Rubén Zuno Arce (q.v.) in the U.S. Supreme Court appeal (1995) of his conviction for complicity in the 1985 abduction and torture murder of DEA S/A Enrique Camarena Salazar (q.v.).

Madrid Hurtado, Miguel de la—president of Mexico (1982–1988).

Matta Ballesteros del Pozo, Juan Ramón—Honduran narcotics trafficker convicted in U.S. District Court (Los Angeles) of complicity in the abduction and homicide of DEA S/A Enrique Camarena Salazar (q.v.); alleged intermediary between Colombian cocaine traffickers and the Guadalajara cartel; owner of SETCO Aviation, which was utilized by the CIA for covert *contra*-related missions.

McFarlane, Lt. Col. (ret.) Robert C.—deputy U.S. national security adviser (1982–1983); national security adviser (1983–1985).

McGhee, George C.—key figure in U.S. Cold War diplomacy who administered Truman Doctrine funds in Turkey and Greece, promoted American oil interests in the Middle East, led and participated in numerous diplomatic missions, and served as U.S. ambassador to Turkey (1951–1953) and the Federal Republic of Germany (1963–1968); apparently played an influential role in the CIA career of Lawrence Victor Harrison (q.v.).

Medvene, Edward M.—lead defense attorney for Rubén Zuno Arce (q.v.) in the 1990–1992 Enrique Camarena Salazar (q.v.) case prosecutions.

Meléndez Preciado, Jorge—reporter for the Mexico City daily *Excélsior*; key figure, together with Rogelio Hernández López (q.v.), in the independent journalists' oversight group for the Buendía case.

Méndez Dueñas, Efrén—Mexican intermediary between Bolivian cocaine producers and Mexican traffickers; targeted by the DEA's Operation Trifecta and arrested in January 1988 in La Jolla, California; charged with conspiring to import cocaine into the United States, convicted, and sentenced to thirty years in prison.

Mertins, Gerhard Georg—decorated Nazi war hero; major postwar arms dealer and U.S. intelligence asset; supplied arms to Nicaraguan *contras* through a business front in the Mexican State of Durango; exposed by Manuel Buendía and expelled from Mexico; for a time a prime suspect in the Buendía assassination.

Miyazawa Álvarez, Jesús—chief of the Federal District Judicial Police (1986–1988).

Monsiváis, Carlos—distinguished Mexican cultural historian, journalist, and essayist; member of Manuel Buendía's inner circle.

Morales Lechuga, Ignacio—Federal District attorney general (1988–1994).

Moro Ávila Camacho, Juan Rafael—Mexican playboy and TV soap opera (*telenovela*) star; rock musician, motorcyclist, and DFS agent; convicted and imprisoned as the gunman who assassinated Manuel Buendía.

Munguía, Mario—police reporter with the Mexico City evening newspaper *Ovaciones*.

Murphy, Kim—Los Angeles Times staff writer who covered the 1988 Enrique Camarena Salazar (q.v.) murder trial of Mexicali businessman and marijuana smuggler René Verdugo Urquídez (q.v.).

Nazar Haro, Miguel—veteran Mexican state security operative; DFS chief (1978–1982); major CIA asset; conducted an extraofficial, never explained investigation of the Buendía slaying under the institutional umbrella of Federal District Attorney General Victoria Adato Green (q.v.).

Nicolaysen, Gregory—Los Angeles defense attorney for 1990 Enrique Camarena Salazar (q.v.) murder trial defendant Javier Vásquez Velasco (q.v.).

Nir, Amiram—key Israeli covert operative in the Iran-Contra affair; thought to have been involved in the movement of arms through Mexico to the Nicaraguan *contras*; killed in Mexico on 1 December 1988 in an unexplained plane crash considered by Israeli intelligence insiders to have been a CIA operation intended to prevent Nir from testifying in the Iran-Contra inquiries.

Noriega, Manuel—Panamanian head of state (1981–1989); CIA asset since the 1960s; supporter of the Reagan administration's proxy *contra* war against Nicaragua's Sandinista government but not an unconditional supporter; defended Panamanian sovereignty; refused to readmit U.S. School of the Americas into the Panama Canal Zone following the death of Omar Torrijos (q.v.); shared intelligence with regional insurgents and the Cubans; a significant player in narcotics trafficking and money laundering. His activities figured opaquely in the George H. W. Bush administration's decision to launch a military invasion of Panama on Christmas Eve, 1989.

North, Lt. Col. Oliver L.—career Marine Corps officer, decorated Vietnam veteran, temporarily assigned to NSC staff in August 1981; a chance sequence of circumstances prolonged his stint at the NSC through the end of 1986, during which time, as deputy director for political-military affairs, he had direct responsibility for two major covert operations that normally would have been handled by the CIA but, due to political obstacles and congressional prohibitions, had to be conducted outside normal institutional channels: arms for American hostages in Iran and the proxy *contra* campaign to topple Nicaragua's revolutionary Sandinista government. North became DCI William Casey's (q.v.) proxy field operative at the CIA, learning covert ops (for which none of his previous military training and experience had prepared him) from the old master himself; through North and the organization he created, Casey's CIA was able to do in Central America and the Middle East what it was otherwise prohibited from doing.

Ochoa Alonso, José Luis "El Chocorrol"—suspected killer of Manuel Buendía; murdered by DFS agents several weeks after the Buendía assassination.

Pastora, Edén—Sandinista *comandante* turned *contra*; commander of the *contra* southern front, based in Costa Rica; accepted CIA support but not direction; refused to coordinate actions with ex-Somoza National Guard–dominated northern front based in Honduras; suffered suspected CIA-instigated bombing attempt on his life while holding a news conference at his La Penca jungle camp just inside Nicaragua on the same evening as the Buendía assassination in Mexico City.

Paz Horta, René—Federal District deputy prosecutor under District Attorney General Victoria Adato Green (q.v.).

Pazienza Donato, Francesco—Italian SISMI intelligence agent in Mexico City at the time of the Enrique Camarena Salazar (q.v.) abduction; learned of Camarena's whereabouts, flew to New York to report what his Mexican contacts had told him, and was arrested by the Americans and extradited to Italy; in a published memoir, he writes that Camarena "was killed twice: once by Mexicans, and once by someone in Washington." Camarena, he implied, had been murdered on orders from his own government.

Pérez Carmona, Raúl—former DFS agent convicted of complicity in the Buendía assassination.

Plumlee, William Robert "Tosh"—veteran U.S. government covert operations contract pilot who flew *contra*-related missions via Mexico and has testified about those activities; exposed the CIA link to Mexican narcotics traffickers in support of the Reagan administration's clandestine operations against the Sandinista government of Nicaragua.

Poblano Silva, Gen. Juan—Mexican army general in charge of the Puebla military zone; target of the joint Customs/DEA Operation Trifecta sting (1987–88); allegedly agreed to facilitate the refueling of an aircraft transporting a shipment of cocaine from Colombia to the United States; avoided being ensnared by timely warning passed down from the Mexican Attorney General's Office.

Poindexter, Admiral John M.—Deputy national security adviser (1983–1985); national security adviser (1985–1986).

Prado Hurtado, Juventino—former DFS agent convicted of complicity in the assassination of Manuel Buendía.

Quintero, Rafael "Chi Chi"—Cuban exile Bay of Pigs veteran and longtime CIA asset; involved with the transport of arms to the Nicaraguan *contras*; defendant in the Christic Institute's 1986–1988 civil suit on behalf of American freelance journalists Martha Honey (q.v.) and Tony Avirgan (q.v.).

Rafeedie, Judge Edward—conservative Reagan-appointed federal judge in the U.S. District Court for the Southern District of California (Los Angeles), who presided over all trials heard in that court during the later 1980s and early 1990s in which alleged CIA collusion with drug traffickers and the Nicaraguan *contras* was an issue, including the 1988, 1990, and 1992 trials of defendants charged with complicity in the 1985 abduction, torture interrogation, and murder in Guadalajara of DEA S/A Enrique Camarena Salazar (q.v.).

Ramírez de Aguilar, Fernando—police reporter for the Mexico City daily *unomásuno*; key collaborator with the authors of this book.

Ramírez Hernández, Carlos—investigative reporter for the Mexico City dailies *El Día* and *El Financiero*; lifelong family friend of Manuel Buendía; one of the most knowledgeable investigators of the Buendía assassination.

Reed, Terry—former CIA asset turned whistleblower; involved in *contra* pilot training and other *contra* support activities in Mena, Arkansas; enlisted in 1986 by Oliver North to establish a fictitious business at the Guadalajara airport to be used for the covert transshipment of arms to the *contras*. Reed's handler in Mexico was longtime CIA operative Félix Rodríguez (q.v.), aka Max Gómez. Having discovered that cocaine was moving north through Guadalajara as arms were shipped south, Reed walked away from the Mexico operation and immediately became a target of U.S. government reprisals.

Reyes Heroles, Jesús—Mexican secretary of government (1976–1982).

Riding, Alan—*New York Times* Mexico City bureau chief (1979–1985) and veteran Latin American correspondent.

Riva Palacio, Raymundo—foreign affairs reporter for the Mexico City daily *Excélsior*; assigned to the Buendía story for several weeks following the assassination.

Rocha Díaz, Salvador—Mexican Secretariat of Government legal director; worked with Ángel Buendía on the appointment of a special prosecutor for the Manuel Buendía assassination case.

Rodríguez, Félix (aka Max Gómez)—infamous Cuban exile and CIA agent with personal links to senior Reagan administration officials, including Vice President George H. W. Bush and Bush's national security adviser, veteran CIA officer Donald P. Gregg (q.v.); coordinated *contra* supply operations from Ilopango airfield in El Salvador; involved in establishing the covert *contra* arms pipeline through Mexico; had contact in Guadalajara with CIA "illegal"

Lawrence Victor Harrison (q.v.); accused by former DEA agents Héctor G. Berréllez (q.v.) and Phillip Jordan (q.v.) of having been present at the torture interrogation of Enrique Camarena Salazar (q.v.).

Rodríguez, Remberto—Panama-based money launderer for Bolivian cocaine producers (La Corporación) and other major narcotics traffickers; alleged CIA asset.

Rodríguez Santillán, Col. Jesús—named as a second Buendía shooter by Sergio Von Nowaffen (q.v.), implying a Mexican army connection to the Buendía assassination.

Román Salas, Jorge—representative of Bolivian cocaine producers entrapped in the DEA Operation Trifecta sting (1987–1988).

Rosales Moreno, Enrique—Durango business partner of German arms dealer Gerhard Georg Mertins (q.v.).

Ross, John—one of a kind journalist and author; veteran Mexico hand; reporter for the *San Francisco Examiner* and *San Francisco Bay Guardian*.

Rothschild, Matthew—managing editor of the monthly political affairs magazine *The Progressive* (Madison, Wisconsin); author of the first investigative piece about the slaying of Manuel Buendía to appear in a U.S. publication.

Sales Gasque, Renato—Federal District attorney general (1986–1988).

Salinas de Gortari, Carlos—president of Mexico (1988–1994).

Sánchez de Armas, Miguel Ángel—founding director of the Fundación Manuel Buendía; founding editor of the professional mass communications journal *Revista mexicana de comunicación* (Mexico City); member of the Buendía investigation's independent journalists' oversight group; member of Manuel Buendía's inner circle; considered Buendía his professional mentor.

Scherer García, Julio—founding editor of the Mexico City newsweekly *Proceso*.

Scott, Peter Dale—former Canadian diplomat; Canadian-trained political scientist; professor emeritus of English, University of California, Berkeley; one of the most perspicacious students of political praxis in the Cold War era; has written extensively on matters central to our own inquiry into the assassination of Manuel Buendía.

Scott, Winston McKinley—Mexico City CIA station chief (1956–1969).

Secord, Air Force Maj. Gen. (ret.) Richard V.—former commander of the U.S. Air Force's Mission to Iran (1975–1978); head of U.S. Air Force International Programs office at the Pentagon (1978–1981); deputy secretary of defense for the Middle East, Africa, and Southern Asia (1981–1983). Alleged to have colluded with ex-CIA agent Edwin P. Wilson in the illicit sale of arms to Libya, as a consequence of which he lost his security clearance and retired from the Air Force; subsequently partnered with Iranian American businessman Albert Hakim, who figured prominently in the Iran-Contra affair. At CIA director William Casey's (q.v.) suggestion, Oliver North (q.v.) enlisted Secord's services as point man in the acquisition of congressionally prohibited arms for the Nicaraguan *contras*.

Shannon, Elaine—award-winning investigative reporter whose 1988 book *Desperados* provided some of the first insights into the Enrique Camarena kidnap/murder case.

Sheehan, Daniel—flamboyant lead attorney for the Christic Institute's 1986–1988 civil suit on behalf of freelance journalists Tony Avirgan (q.v.) and Martha Honey (q.v.) against twenty-nine defendants accused of complicity in a criminal enterprise to supply arms purchased with drug money to the Nicaraguan *contras*.

Sicilia Falcón, Alberto—Cuban exile narcotics boss whose Tijuana-based organization dominated the flow of marijuana, cocaine, and heroin into the United States following the 1972 takedown of the French Connection; allegedly protected for a time by the CIA; enjoyed protection of senior Mexican officials as well, including Miguel Nazar Haro (q.v.). The

Sicilia network is said to have been taken over by Miguel Ángel Félix Gallardo (q.v.) after Sicilia was prosecuted and imprisoned by Mexican authorities in the mid-1970s. Honduran trafficker Juan Ramón Matta Ballesteros (q.v.) served as the intermediary between Colombian cocaine traffickers and both the Sicilia and Félix Gallardo organizations.

Somoza Debayle, Anastasio—last of the U.S.-supported Somoza dynasty Nicaraguan dictators (1934–1979), overthrown in July 1979 by a popular armed insurgency under the leadership of the FSLN. His ouster from power constituted a sea change in Mesoamerican geopolitics, precipitating a new era of U.S. interventionism and what came to be known as the Iran-Contra scandal.

Sosa Ortiz, Alejandro—Federal District deputy prosecutor involved with the Buendía case.

Soto Olguín, Luis Pablo—assistant to Manuel Buendía; organizer and keeper of Buendía's reference archive.

Spadafora, Hugo—Panamanian medical doctor, close associate of Gen. Omar Torrijos (q.v.) and enemy of Torrijos's successor, Manuel Noriega (q.v.); renowned internationalist guerrilla fighter who participated in the armed insurrection against Nicaraguan dictator Anastasio Somoza Debayle (q.v.), then joined *contra comandante* Edén Pastora in the U.S.-supported campaign against Nicaragua's Sandinista government. He obtained evidence of Noriega's dealings with *contra*-related drug traffickers, passed that evidence to the DEA in the hope of exposing Noriega, and was brutally tortured and decapitated in September 1985 by unidentified parties near the Panama–Costa Rica border.

Suárez, Luis—Spanish Civil War (1936–1939) refugee, naturalized Mexican citizen, and prominent journalist and foreign affairs commentator; columnist for the Mexico City newsweekly *Siempre!*

Torrijos, Gen. Omar—Panamanian head of state (1968–1981); concluded the Panama Canal Treaty of 1978, which established Panamanian sovereignty over the Canal Zone by the year 2000 and required the removal of U.S. bases and military training facilities from Panama; supporter of the Contadora peace process and significant obstacle to American regional hegemony; killed on 31 July 1981 in a plane crash suspected by many to have been an assassination.

Tort, José "Pepe"—Federal District Judicial Police deputy director of operations; one of DEA country attaché Edward Heath's (q.v.) links to the Mexican military and narcotics traffickers.

Tulsky, Fredric N.—*Los Angeles Times* staff writer who a decade and a half after the 1990–1992 Enrique Camarena Salazar (q.v.) murder trials reported new information that raised doubts about the veracity of prosecution witness testimony.

Valle, Eduardo "El Buho"—outspoken investigative reporter nicknamed "The Owl" for his thick eyeglasses; president of the UPD; active in pressuring Mexican authorities to resolve the Buendía assassination; audacious (some would say foolhardy) reporter of drug-related matters. For a time in the mid-1990s, he was an adviser to Mexican attorney general Jorge Carpizo on combating the country's major narcotics traffickers, but he was subsequently forced to seek refuge in the United States.

Ventura Gutiérrez, Florentino—infamous Mexican law enforcement officer; acting director of the PJDF (1985–1988); head of Mexico's INTERPOL office (1985–1988); claimed to have received training from all the main U.S. law enforcement agencies and is presumed to have been an American intelligence asset. He met a violent death in September 1988 when, following a heated argument with his wife (twenty-five years younger and Mexico's first female PJDF officer), he shot her and a woman friend dead, then ostensibly turned his gun on himself. Rumors persist that his death was not self-inflicted.

Verdugo Urquídez, René—major Mexicali-based marijuana smuggler partnered with Guadalajara cartel boss Rafael Caro Quintero; abducted by the Baja California Judicial Police in concert with U.S. marshals, pushed through a hole in the border fence near Mexicali and arrested by waiting U.S. Border Patrol officers; charged with complicity in the Enrique Camarena Salazar (q.v.) murder, tried, and convicted in federal District Court in 1988 (Judge Edward Rafeedie [q.v.] presiding) and given a life sentence; vehemently professes his innocence of complicity in the Camarena homicide and maintains an elaborate Internet website calling for a reconsideration of his murder conviction. That site contains an invaluable archive of official court and law enforcement records, which we have utilized for the present volume.

Victoria Zepeda, Felipe—investigator in the Federal District Attorney General's Office (Ministerio Público) at the time of the Buendía assassination; subsequently turned to journalism; conducted himself as a disinformation agent around the Buendía case, disseminating patently false assertions about Manuel Buendía's professional and personal life.

Villar, Samuel del—presidential aide to Miguel de la Madrid (q.v.); headed secret presidential investigative group appointed to inquire into the Buendía assassination.

Von Nowaffen, Sergio—reporter with the Mexico City evening newspaper *Ovaciones*.

Walsh, Lawrence E.—independent counsel appointed in December 1986 to conduct a criminal investigation of the Iran-Contra affair.

Webb, Gary—investigative reporter with the *San Jose Mercury News* (San Jose, California), who in 1996 published a three-part exposé titled "Dark Alliance: The Story Behind the Crack Explosion," which linked the CIA to Nicaraguan cocaine traffickers and the crack cocaine epidemic in the predominantly poor black neighborhoods of South Central Los Angeles, all in support of the Reagan administration's proxy *contra* war against Nicaragua's revolutionary Sandinista government. Webb's journalism career was ruined and he was ultimately driven to suicide by a mainstream media defamation campaign prompted by the CIA.

Weinstein, Henry—*Los Angeles Times* staff writer who covered the 1990–1992 Enrique Camarena Salazar (q.v.) murder trials.

Wheeler, David Laird—U.S. Customs Service informant who played a central role in the joint Customs/DEA Operation Trifecta sting (1987–1988) against Bolivian and Mexican cocaine traffickers.

Zorrilla Pérez, José Antonio—head of the DFS (1982–1985); convicted of masterminding the assassination of Manuel Buendía but widely believed to have been sacrificed as a cover for more senior officials, both domestic and foreign.

Zuno Arce, Rubén—prominent Mexican businessman; brother-in-law of Mexican president Luis Echeverría Álvarez (1970–1976, q.v.); charged, tried, and convicted in U.S. District Court of complicity in the 1985 abduction, torture interrogation, and murder of DEA S/A Enrique Camarena Salazar (q.v.). Zuno's prosecution appears to have been politically motivated, and his conviction is unsubstantiated by the evidence.

NOTES

INTRODUCTION

All translations are by the authors unless otherwise indicated.

1. Manuel Buendía, *El humor*, preface by José Joaquín Blanco (Xalapa, Mexico: Universidad Veracruzana, 1986).

2. Miguel Cabildo, Raúl Monge, and Ignacio Ramírez, "Cada pista en el caso Buendía señala a Zorrilla y sus hombres: Inactividad oficial, según todas las apariencias, para protegerlo," *Proceso*, 22 May 1989, 19–20; Rogelio Hernández López, *Zorrilla: El imperio del crimen* (Mexico City: Planeta, 1989), 27.

3. Hernández López, *Zorrilla*, 46, 77; Fernando Ramírez de A. and Héctor Cruz López, "Lo torturó la Judicial, dice Juventino Prado," *unomásuno*, 26 June 1989, 14; David Romero Ceyde and Alfonso Moraflores, "El plan para desaparecer a Buendía lo reveló Prado y hundió a Moro A.," *Ovaciones*, 26 June 1989, 10; Ignacio G. Almanza, "Prado hunde a Zorrilla: 'él planeó el asesinato,'" *El Nacional*, 26 June 1989, 12.

4. For a history of Mexico's national security apparatus, see Sergio Aguayo Quezada, *La charola: Una historia de los servicios de inteligencia en México* (Mexico City: Grijalbo, 2001); and Aaron W. Navarro, *Political Intelligence and the Creation of Modern Mexico, 1938–1954* (University Park: Pennsylvania State University Press, 2010).

5. Miguel Ángel Granados Chapa, *Buendía: El primer asesinato de la narcopolítica en México* (Mexico City: Grijalbo, 2012), 13–14.

6. This narrative of the assassination has been drawn from a multiplicity of sources. For a detailed account by a Mexican investigative journalist, see Hernández López, *Zorrilla*. For crime scene reports, see Ignacio Ramírez, "El homicidio, tal como aparece en las actas judiciales: La muerte de Buendía, según tres testigos," *Proceso*, 24 July 1989, 24–27.

7. On the *Excélsior* affair and its impact on the Mexican press, see Manuel Becerra Acosta, *Dos poderes* (Mexico City: Grijalbo, 1985); Héctor Minués Moreno, *Los cooperativistas: El caso Excélsior* (Mexico City: EDAMEX, 1987); Julio Scherer García, *Los presidentes* (Mexico City: Grijalbo, 1986); Jorge Hernández Campos, ed., *Unomásuno: Diez años (1977–1987)* (Mexico City: Editorial Uno, 1987). For a historical overview of the Mexican press from the perspective of the period, see Leopoldo Borrás, *Historia del periodismo mexicano: Del ocaso porfirista al derecho a la información* (Mexico City: Dirección General de Información, National Autonomous University of Mexico, 1983); and Miguel Ángel Granados Chapa, *Examen de la comunicación en México* (Mexico City: Ediciones El Caballito, 1983).

8. U.S. Congress, Church Committee, *Alleged Assassination Plots Involving Foreign Leaders: Interim Report of the Select Committee to Study Government Operations with Respect to Intelligence Activities* (New York: W. W. Norton, 1976).

9. An essential reference work on the underside of American foreign policy is Michael McClintock's *Instruments of Statecraft: U.S. Guerrilla Warfare, Counterinsurgency, and Counterterrorism, 1940–1990* (New York: Pantheon, 1992).

10. Ibid., 53–55, 92–93, 150–151, 435–437.

11. Statement made to Bill Moyers in documentary film *The CIA's Secret Army* (New York: Carousel Films, 1977).

CHAPTER 1. KNIGHT ERRANT

1. For earlier accounts of the Buendía killing, see "¿Quién mató a Manuel Buendía?," a summary of known facts surrounding the Buendía assassination prepared as an internal reference document by Manuel Buendía Foundation staff coordinated by Carlos Ramírez (1985, 37 pages) (hereafter Fundación, "¿Quién mató a Manuel Buendía?"), Bartley Buendía Case Files (BBCF), press binder 1; Matthew Rothschild, "Who Killed Manuel Buendía? A Mexican Mystery," *The Progressive*, April 1985, 18–23; and Hernández López, *Zorrilla*.

2. For detailed accounts of the Polk slaying, see Kati Marton, *The Polk Conspiracy: Murder and Cover-Up in the Case of CBS Correspondent George Polk* (New York: Times Books, 1992); and Elias Vlanton, with Zak Mettger, *Who Killed George Polk? The Press Covers Up a Death in the Family* (Philadelphia: Temple University Press, 1996). A useful companion volume that provides an additional perspective on Marton's account is Edmund Keeley's *The Salonika Bay Murder: Cold War Politics and the Polk Affair* (Princeton, NJ: Princeton University Press, 1989).

3. Quoted in Marton, *Polk Conspiracy*, 317. One of the accused partisans, Adam Mouzenidis, was apparently dead at the time of Polk's murder, while the other, Vangelis Vasvanas, was in exile; both were sentenced to death, but neither was ever apprehended. See Keeley, *The Salonika Bay Murder*, 188, 316, 369.

4. Manuel Buendía, *La CIA en México* (Mexico City: Océano, 1984).

5. Manuel Buendía, "CIA vs. Torrijos: Crimen y motivo," Red Privada, *Excélsior*, 21 August 1981, 15. The CIA also had an institutional relationship with the Mexican government, Buendía noted, through the DFS within the all-powerful Secretariat of Government. But, he observed with characteristically sardonic wit, "The CIA operates on two levels, and what transpires on the level open to Mexican officials is the least interesting of all." Buendía, *La CIA en México*, 24.

6. Marton, *Polk Conspiracy*, vii.

7. For accounts of the attempted assassination of Pastora, see Tony Avirgan and Martha Honey, eds., *La Penca: On Trial in Costa Rica; The CIA vs. the Press*, 2nd ed. (San José, Costa Rica: Editorial Porvenir, 1988); and Martha Honey and Tony Avirgan, *La Penca: Reporte de una investigación*, 2nd ed. (San José, Costa Rica: Editorial Porvenir, 1989). An earlier edition of this latter volume was published in Lima, Peru, by the publishing house El Gallo Rojo (n.d.). All citations are from the Editorial Porvenir edition. For an account of the bombing and the larger context in which it occurred, see Martha Honey, *Hostile Acts: U.S. Policy in Costa Rica in the 1980s* (Gainesville: University Press of Florida, 1994).

8. "El Director de 'Primera Plana' de Coatzacoalcos muerto también a tiros," *Proceso*, 4 June 1984, 14.

9. Honey and Avirgan, *La Penca: Reporte de una investigación*, 15–16.

10. Theodore Draper, *A Very Thin Line: The Iran-Contra Affairs* (New York: Simon & Schuster, 1991), 51.

11. See McClintock, *Instruments of Statecraft*. On the domination of mass media by the major powers, see Anthony Smith, *The Geopolitics of Information: How Western Culture Dominates the World* (New York: Oxford University Press, 1980). For a broader historical discussion of the relationship between power and ideology, see Edward W. Said, *Culture and Imperialism* (New York: Vintage, 1994).

12. For a now classic firsthand account of covert media manipulation in Latin America, see Philip Agee, *Inside the Company: CIA Diary* (New York: Stonehill, 1975).

13. Omar Raúl Martínez et al., "Un período sombrío para el periodismo mexicano," *Revista mexicana de comunicación* 7, no. 40 (May–July 1995): 6–10.

14. Alejandro Olmos, "La marea de la crisis económica arrastra a los medios mexicanos," *Revista de comunicación mexicana* 7, no. 40 (May–July 1995): 27–29.

15. "Mensaje de Ana Lorena Cartín Leiva, directora de Radio Noticias del Continente, minutos antes de la suspensión provisional de las emisoras" (6 March 1981), Radio Noticias del Continente, press packet (Mexico City, 9 March 1981), BBCF, carton 2, folder: SIPE/Radio Noticias del Continente. See also Honey, *Hostile Acts*, 245–246, 296, 377, 558–559n19.

16. Edgar Chamorro, *Packaging the Contras: A Case of CIA Disinformation*, Monographs, no. 2. (New York: Institute of Media Analysis, 1987), appendix A, "Excerpts from Transcript of November 6, 1982, Interview with Héctor Francés," 65.

17. Valentín Ferrat to Russell H. Bartley, Mexico City, 11 July 1981, a three-page form letter on SIPE letterhead outlining its organizational goals, premises, and procedures, BBCF, carton 2, folder: SIPE/Radio Noticias del Continente.

18. For an unsympathetic account of the Managua event, see Shirley Christian, "Pro-Sandinista Journalists Link U.S. Press to CIA," *Miami Herald*, 4 May 1981.

19. The preceding account draws on Russell H. Bartley's personal knowledge as a SIPE collaborator and former associate of Valentín Ferrat.

20. Quoted in Saul Landau, *The Dangerous Doctrine: National Security and U.S. Foreign Policy* (Boulder, CO: Westview, 1988), 1.

21. Matthew Rothschild, "La CIA vs. Manuel Buendía," *Revista mexicana de comunicación* 1, no. 5 (May–June 1989): 18.

22. Andrea Fernández, "Encuentro por escrito," in Fundación Manuel Buendía, *Los días de Manuel Buendía: Testimonios* (Mexico City: Océano, 1984), 49.

23. Quoted in Leopoldo H. Mendoza, *El asesinato de un periodista* (Mexico City: Editorial Diana, 1984), 21; and also in Granados Chapa, *Buendía*, 122.

24. For a concise account of Nazar Haro's CIA connection, see Elaine Shannon, *Desperados: Latin Drug Lords, U.S. Lawmen, and the War America Can't Win* (New York: Viking, 1988), 180–184.

25. Manuel Buendía, "Por una Comisión Defensora de la Libertad de Prensa: Principios elementales para su constitución" (1980), reprinted in *Revista mexicana de comunicación* 7, no. 40 (May–July 1995): 11.

26. Manuel Buendía, "El Estado pelea en reversa: Buendía en 82," interview by Carlos Landeros, *Excélsior*, 31 May 1989, 38. This interview was conducted in 1982 and published for the first time in its entirety on the fifth anniversary of Buendía's assassination.

27. Manuel Buendía, "Memorándum presidencial," *Nexos*, August 1984, 47.

28. Ibid., 48–49, 53.

29. Ibid., 51.

30. Manuel Buendía, "El Ejército y la comunicación social," Tema presentado en la Secretaría de la Defensa el 25 de mayo de 1984 [Topic addressed at the Secretariat of Defense on 25 May 1984], in *Ejercicio periodístico* (Mexico City: Océano, 1985), 183–184.

31. Ibid., 186.

32. Manuel Buendía, "Comunicación, seguridad y democracia," in *Ejercicio periodístico* (Mexico City: Océano, 1985), 178.

33. Ibid., 177; Buendía, "El Ejército y la comunicación social," 186.

34. McClintock, *Instruments of Statecraft*, 185–196.

35. Sanjuana Martínez, "El Ejército mexicano ha enviado a 440 oficiales a especializarse en la Escuela de las Américas: Por lo menos tres actúan en Chiapas," *Proceso*, 3 April 1995, 26–27.

36. See, for example, Laura Carlsen, "Mexico's Oil Privatization Risky Business: Mexico's Oil Privatization Scheme Will Hurt the Environment, Scar the Landscape, and Leave Mexico at the Mercy of Transnational Firms," *Foreign Policy in Focus*, 27 May 2014, http://fpif.org/mexicos-oil-privatization-risky-business/; and Adam Williams, Eric Martin, and Nacha Cattan, "Mexico Passes Oil Bill Seen Luring $20 Billion a Year," Bloomberg Business, 13 December 2013, http://www.bloomberg.com/news/2013-12-12/mexico-lower-house-passes-oil-overhaul-to-break-state-monopoly.html.

37. Quoted in Héctor Aguilar Camín, "El monstruo que vendrá," in *El desafío mexicano*, 2nd ed. (Mexico City: Océano, 1985), 99. For a broader historical analysis of Mexico's changing political order, see Héctor Aguilar Camín, *Después del milagro*, 2nd ed. (Mexico City: Cal y Arena, 1989); and Miguel Ángel Centeno, *Democracy within Reason: Technocratic Revolution in Mexico*, 2nd ed. (University Park: Pennsylvania State University Press, 1997). In this same vein, six months before Miguel de la Madrid won the 1982 presidential election, the prominent Mexican sociologist and presidential adviser Jorge Bustamante suggested to us that de la Madrid might well be Mexico's last duly elected president. Sufficient generational and ideological changes had taken place within the Mexican military's officer corps, Bustamante observed, to warrant concern that the established ground rules of civilian authority might be contravened by a disaffected military. Jorge Bustamante, conversation with authors, Mexico City, 24 December 1981.

38. For an insightful overview of these developments and their geopolitical context, see John Ross, *The Annexation of Mexico: From the Aztecs to the I.M.F.; One Reporter's Journey through History* (Monroe, ME: Common Courage Press, 1998). See also John Ross, *Rebellion from the Roots: Indian Uprising in Chiapas* (Monroe, ME: Common Courage Press, 1995).

39. Brian Latell, *Mexico at the Crossroads: The Many Crises of the Political System*, Hoover Monographs Series 6 (Stanford, CA: Hoover Institution, 1986), 3–5.

40. Ibid., 12–13. For a lucid historical account of this process, see Centeno, *Democracy within Reason*.

41. For a concise overview of the Mexican military, see Otto Granados Roldán, "¿Regreso a las armas?," in *El desafío mexicano*, 2nd ed., edited by Héctor Aguilar Camín (Mexico City: Océano, 1985), 125–135.

42. Aguilar Camín, "El monstruo que vendrá," 100.

43. Buendía, "Comunidad, seguridad y democracia," 180.

44. Manuel Buendía, "Fut y Política: TV 'Contra,'" Red Privada, *Excélsior*, 3 May 1984, 1, 20.

45. Ibid., 20. Edén Pastora had been a prominent figure in the insurrectionary movement that overthrew the Anastasio Somoza Debayle dictatorship and for a time served in the Sandinista Government of National Reconstruction (GNR) as chief of the People's Militia and deputy minister of defense. He then broke with his former comrades and in 1982 took up arms against them, ostensibly because of their embrace of Marxism but actually, according to former acquaintances, out of his own political ambition: he felt slighted by the posts he had been given in the GNR and thought he deserved a position of greater importance. Pastora formed an anti-Sandinista guerrilla organization called the Democratic Revolutionary Alliance (ARDE by its Spanish acronym) based in Costa Rica. For a time, ARDE received material support and encouragement

from the CIA, which sought to create a second, southern, anti-Sandinista front subordinate to its main Honduran-based *contra* force, the so-called Fuerza Democrática Nicaragüense (FDN). Pastora, however, refused to collaborate with the former Somoza National Guard officers who occupied the FDN's command structure, and by early 1984 he was seen increasingly as an impediment to Reagan administration objectives. Hence, his attempted assassination at La Penca on the same day as the Buendía homicide.

46. Ibid., 1, 20.

47. Buendía is referring to the Tlatelolco Square student massacre of 2 October 1968 in Mexico City and subsequent actions by the Echeverría administration (1970–1976), which precipitated a major institutional crisis in which there was even talk of a possible military coup.

48. Buendía, "El Estado pelea en reversa," 38, 41.

49. See, e.g., Hernández López, *Zorrilla*, 40; Fundación, "'¿Quién mató a Manuel Buendía?,'" 29; and Luis Suárez, "Más que una mera coincidencia, los atentados contra Buendía y Pastora," *Excélsior*, 16 August 1989, 5, 37.

CHAPTER 2. UNDER THE CARPET

1. See, e.g., *El Comercio* (Lima, Peru), 1 June 1984, international section; *El Mercurio* (Santiago, Chile), 1 June 1984, A1, 12; *La Prensa* (Buenos Aires, Argentina), 1 June 1984, 2; *El Tiempo* (Bogotá, Colombia), 1 June 1984, A11; *Presencia* (La Paz, Bolivia), 1 June 1984, 5; and *O Estado do São Paulo* (São Paulo, Brazil), 1 June 1984, 6.

2. Richard J. Meislin, "Noted Mexican Journalist Shot Dead," *New York Times*, 1 June 1984, 3.

3. Jean-Claude Buhrer, "Manuel Buendia: A Man Who Knew Too Much," *The Guardian Weekly* (London), 29 July 1984, BBCF, archival ring binder 1, Buendía assassination news reports & *Red Privada* columns.

4. José G. González, *Lo negro del Negro Durazo* (Mexico City: Posada, 1983).

5. Buendía, *La CIA en México*.

6. Russell H. Bartley, "CIA behind Journalist's Murder? Agency Implicated in Mexican Writer's Assassination," *People's World*, 7 July 1984, 3.

7. We experienced the disconnect between White House assertions and reality on the ground in a particularly visceral way later the same day of our encounter with NBC cameraman John Kechele. We had accompanied the press corps to a Managua dance school being used for security checks prior to covering the opening session of a Non-Aligned Nations meeting. While we awaited transfer to the meeting site, we listened on a shortwave radio to a broadcast from Washington, DC, in which President Ronald Reagan denounced Sandinista tyranny and promised support for Nicaraguan "freedom fighters." As the president's hostile words wafted through the soft tropical evening, even representatives of U.S. mainstream media shook their heads in wonder. There was no correlation at all between what the president alleged and what we were observing on the ground. The Nicaragua he described was a complete fiction. Surreal was the only way to describe it.

8. Matthew Rothschild, interview with authors, Madison, Wisconsin, 29 March 1985, original English transcript in BBCF, carton 1, folder: Rothschild, Matthew. Subsequent quotations of Rothschild are from this interview.

9. Russell H. Bartley, "¿Quién mató a Manuel Buendía? Hay cuatro grupos merecedores de sospecha; Entrevista con Matthew Rothschild, autor de una pesquisa periodística sobre el caso," *páginauno*, 19 May 1985, 1–3.

10. See Rothschild, "Who Killed Manuel Buendía?"

11. Jack Anderson, "Pressure on the Press in Mexico," *Washington Post*, 5 August 1984.

12. Aguayo Quezada, *La charola*, 96.

13. Ibid., 107.

14. Fundación, "¿Quién mató a Manuel Buendía?," 33.

15. Rothschild, "Who Killed Manuel Buendía?," 20.

16. Matthew Rothschild, phone conversation with Russell Bartley, 28 January 2008.

17. Juan María Aponte, "Dos textos: Uno sobre Buendía; Otro sobre el Papa," *El Día*, 25 May 1985, BBCF, clippings binder 1.

18. E. Howard Hunt, with Greg Aunapu, *American Spy: My Secret History in the CIA, Watergate, and Beyond*, foreword by William F. Buckley Jr. (Hoboken, NJ: Wiley, 2007), 199. In his history of the CIA, Tim Weiner describes Hunt as a "relentlessly mediocre" operative. See Weiner's *Legacy of Ashes: A History of the CIA* (New York: Doubleday, 2007), 156.

19. Héctor Aguilar Camín, "Manuel Buendía y los idus de mayo," in *Los días de Manuel Buendía: Testimonios*, ed. Fundación Manuel Buendía (Mexico City: Océano, 1984), 7–18.

20. Rothschild, "Who Killed Manuel Buendía?," 20.

21. Quoted in *unomásuno*, 19 March 1985, 24.

CHAPTER 3. LEGWORK

1. For an overview of the paper's first ten years, see Hernández Campos, *Unomásuno*.

2. Manuel Buendía, Red Privada, *Excélsior*, 1 February 1978, reprinted in Miguel Bonasso, *Recuerdo de la muerte* (Mexico City: Ediciones Era, 1984), 209.

3. Ibid., 208–210.

4. Ibid., 201–208.

5. For an insightful examination of the historical linkages between U.S. policies toward Latin America in these years and post-9/11 force-based policies elsewhere in the world, see Greg Grandin, *Empire's Workshop: Latin America, the United States, and the Rise of the New Imperialism* (New York: Metropolitan Books, 2006).

6. On Operation Condor and Chile's role in transnational state terrorism, see Peter Kornbluh, *The Pinochet File: A Declassified Dossier on Atrocity and Accountability* (New York: New Press, 2003).

7. Heinz Dieterich, *Nicaragua: La construcción de la sociedad sin clases*, interview with Noam Chomsky, preface by Gregorio Selser (Mexico City: Editorial Uno, 1986), 125.

8. Philip Agee, interview with authors, Chicago, 10 November 1991. When we met with Agee for this interview, he was being tailed by three strikingly well-dressed agents, presumably CIA, whose appearance and demeanor spoke as forcefully as the histrionic comportment of their Mexican counterparts at the Café París. We spoke with Agee about the Buendía case in our car while driving on the Kennedy Expressway between downtown Chicago and O'Hare International Airport.

9. See, e.g., James Mills, *The Underground Empire: Where Crime and Governments Embrace* (Garden City, NY: Doubleday, 1986), 543. Mills describes Ventura as "arguably the most powerful police officer in Latin America."

10. Ibid., 526, 535–536. See also Enrique Maza, "Florentino Ventura 'es el hombre más brutal y el más eficiente,'" *Proceso*, 2 May 1988, 20–23. For doubts regarding the official version of Ventura's death, see reportage in *Excélsior*, 20–24 September 1988.

11. Aguayo Quezada, *La charola*, 237–246; Hernández López, *Zorrilla*, 49–52.

12. Aguayo Quezada, *La charola*, 144–160.

13. There is an abundant literature that examines these issues. See, e.g., Weiner, *Legacy of Ashes*. For an especially insightful discussion of Casey's role in intelligence matters, see Peter Dale Scott, *The Road to 9/11: Wealth, Empire, and the Future of America* (Berkeley: University

of California Press, 2007), chap. 6, "Casey, the Republican Countersurprise, and the Bank of Credit and Commerce International, 1980."

14. Aguayo Quezada, *La charola*, 260. On Israel's regional involvements, see Jane Hunter, *No Simple Proxy: Israel in Central America; A Report*, ed. Jane Power and James Zogby (Washington, DC: Washington Middle East Associates, 1987); Jonathan Marshall, Peter Dale Scott, and Jane Hunter, *The Iran-Contra Connection: Secret Teams and Covert Operations in the Reagan Era* (Boston: South End Press, 1987), chap. 5, "Israel and the Contras"; and Ari Ben-Menashe, *Profits of War: Inside the Secret U.S.-Israeli Arms Network* (New York: Sheridan Square Press, 1992).

15. On one occasion Russell had taken what he thought was a discreet photograph of the exterior of PJDF headquarters on a congested downtown street off the Alameda, only to be confronted by a stern plainclothes officer who materialized out of the passing pedestrians and demanded his camera. Not wishing to reveal the previous images he had taken that day, Russell opened the camera, stripped out the film, and handed him the film cartridge with its trailing tail of exposed Tri-X. The officer glared at him but was not of a mind to make further issue of the encounter.

16. Luis Suárez, *La otra cara de Afganistán: Reportaje en el corazón de Asia* (Barcelona: Grijalbo, 1983).

17. Rafael Rodríguez Castañeda, *Prensa vendida: Los periodistas y los presidentes; 40 años de relaciones* (Mexico City: Grijalbo, 1993), 236–237, 252.

18. Aguilar Camín, "Manuel Buendía y los idus de mayo," 16.

19. Jefferson Morley, *Our Man in Mexico: Winston Scott and the Hidden History of the CIA* (Lawrence: University Press of Kansas, 2008), 101–150.

20. Agee, *Inside the Company*, 524, 526.

21. Ibid., 524–526.

22. The best, most fully documented account of CIA operations in Mexico to date is Morley's *Our Man in Mexico*.

23. Ibid., 94.

24. Buendía, *La CIA en México*, 48.

25. Eduardo Valle, "Fábula de mayo," *El Universal*, 30 May 1985.

26. Eduardo Valle, "Castigo a la torpeza," *El Universal Gráfico*, 29 May 1985; "Azorrillados," *El Universal Gráfico*, 15 June 1985. See also Eduardo Valle, "Crónica de un atentado," *Proceso*, 26 June 1989, 16–17.

Chapter 4. Coordinates of Power

Chapter epigraphs: see McClintock, *Instruments of Statecraft*, 8; Weiner, *Legacy of Ashes*, 108–109.

1. See Héctor Cárdenas, *Las relaciones mexicano-soviéticas: Antecedentes y primeros contactos diplomáticos (1789–1927)*, preface by Roque González Salazar (Mexico City: Secretaría de Relaciones Exteriores, 1974); and William Harrison Richardson, *Mexico through Russian Eyes, 1806–1940* (Pittsburgh: University of Pittsburgh Press, 1988), especially chapter 3, "The Nineteen-Twenties: A Shared Revolutionary Experience."

2. Committee of Santa Fe, *A New Inter-American Policy for the Eighties* (Washington, DC: Council for Inter-American Security, 1980), 3, 5, 39, 43–44.

3. Ibid., 19.

4. The standard chronological reference for the Iran-Contra affair is National Security Archive, *The Chronology: The Documented Day-by-Day Account of the Secret Military Assistance to Iran and the Contras*, foreword by Seymour Hersh (New York: Warner Books, 1987). See also Brown University, "Understanding the Iran-Contra Affairs: Nicaragua and Iran Timeline," http://www.brown.edu/Research/Understanding_the_Iran_Contra_Affair/timeline-n-i.php#headertop.

5. Russell Bartley, "Cuba Solidly Backs the New Nicaragua," *Milwaukee Journal*, 6 September 1979, 13.

6. Russell H. Bartley, "Nicaraguan Images: Leaders Hold Media Events to Try to Change Hostile Attitudes in US," *Milwaukee Journal*, 31 May 1981, 1, 3. Citing this article six days later, the *Milwaukee Journal* editorialized, "What is happening in Nicaragua is representative of the economic, political and social change that is blowing through Central America today. The Reagan administration needs to ask itself how extreme it wants those winds to become."

7. That film was *Five Months That Changed a Nation* (Milwaukee: Educational Communications Division, University of Wisconsin–Milwaukee, 1982). It was awarded a Silver Medal at the twenty-sixth annual International Film and TV Festival of New York, 9–11 November 1983.

8. Russell H. Bartley to *unomásuno*, Mexico City, Telex: 01777255 UNOME/01777495 (Managua, TELCOR, 12 May 1984).

9. Russell H. Bartley, "Costa Rica: Un proyecto *made in USA*," *unomásuno*, 3 May 1984, 11; Buendía, "Fut y Política."

10. Alan Riding, *Distant Neighbors: A Portrait of the Mexicans* (New York: Vintage, 1986), 219.

11. Gil Green, *Cold War Fugitive: A Personal Story of the McCarthy Years* (New York: International Publishers, 1984), 99–100.

12. Riding, *Distant Neighbors*, 522–527.

13. The preceding thumbnail narrative of Mexico's role in the Sandinista Revolution follows that of Alan Riding's *Distant Neighbors* (ibid., 509–512) but rests on an abundant literature, as well as personal knowledge. For fuller details in English, see Robert A. Pastor and Jorge G. Castañeda, *Limits to Friendship: The United States and Mexico* (New York: Vintage, 1989), 177–181; Robert Kagan, *A Twilight Struggle: American Power and Nicaragua, 1977–1990* (New York: Free Press, 1996); and Anthony Lake, *Somoza Falling: The Nicaraguan Dilemma; A Portrait of Washington at Work* (Boston: Houghton Mifflin, 1989).

14. Luis Méndez Asensio, *Contadora: Las cuentas de la diplomacia* (Mexico City: Plaza y Valdés, 1987), 30.

15. William Blum, *Killing Hope: U.S. Military and CIA Interventions since World War II* (Monroe, ME: Common Courage Press, 1995), 306; John Perkins, *The Secret History of the American Empire* (New York: Plume, 2007), 152, 241–242.

16. Perkins, *Secret History*, 241–242. Roldós's daughter Marta, who was married to a nephew of Omar Torrijos, was very moved by her father's death and fully expected to be killed in the same way. According to her account, her father's plane had been piloted by a close personal friend and one of the best pilots in the Ecuadorian Air Force. The crash site had immediately been sealed off, local police were denied access, and "only Ecuadorian and U.S. military personnel were allowed in." Two key witnesses mysteriously died in automobile accidents shortly before they were to testify at an official inquiry into the crash, while press accounts differed materially from the established facts of the incident (quoted in ibid., 152).

17. Méndez Asensio, *Contadora*, 38–39.

18. Riding, *Distant Neighbors*, 513.

19. *Guía del Tercer Mundo, 1981* (Mexico City: Cuadernos del Tercer Mundo, 1981), 416. This is an annual supplement to the periodical *Cuadernos del Tercer Mundo*.

20. See chapter 2, p. 20.

21. Pastor and Castañeda, *Limits to Friendship*, 160–161, 179–181; Riding, *Distant Neighbors*, 509–515.

22. Pastor and Castañeda, *Limits to Friendship*, 183, 187–189.

23. Ibid., 189.

24. Eduardo Valle, phone interview with authors, 3 April 1996.

25. John Womack to Russell H. Bartley, e-mail, 25 October 2010.

26. Adolfo Aguilar Zínser, interview with authors, Milwaukee, 2 February 1988.

27. Ibid.

28. Anthony DePalma, "Adolfo Aguilar Zinser, Blunt Mexican Envoy, Dies at 55," *New York Times*, 7 June 2005; Jo Tuckman, "Adolfo Aguilar Zínser: Acute Mexican Politician with a Reputation for Integrity," obituary, *Guardian*, 8 June 2005; Phil Davison, "Adolfo Aguilar Zínser," obituary, *Independent*, 7 June 2005.

29. Miguel Ángel Sánchez de Armas to Russell H. Bartley, e-mail, 29 July 2008.

30. Aguilar Zínser, interview with authors, Milwaukee, 2 February 1988; Jorge A. Bustamante, conversations with authors, South Bend, Indiana, 7–8 April 1989.

31. As it developed, a mercurial operative of Italian Military Intelligence (SISMI) by the name of Francesco Pazienza Donato was present in Mexico when U.S. DEA agent Enrique "Kiki" Camarena Salazar and his Mexican pilot, Alfredo Zavala Avelar, were kidnapped by members of the Guadalajara drug cartel in early February 1985. Pazienza claimed to have a source with access to the kidnappers and flew to New York to inform the U.S. authorities, where he was arrested on an outstanding Italian warrant and subsequently extradited to Italy, no action having been taken on the information he had sought to provide regarding the Camarena affair. Kiki Camarena, Pazienza later wrote, "was murdered twice: by Mexicans and by someone in Washington." See chapter 16 of Pazienza's memoir, *Il disubbidiente* (Milan: Longanesi, 1999).

32. Manuel Buendía, "Private Line: The Jalisco Branch," op-ed, *New York Times*, 5 November 1979.

33. Manuel Buendía, "Armas en México: 'Preguntas a Roel,'" Red Privada, *El Porvenir* (Monterrey, Nuevo León), 10 November 1978.

34. Manuel Buendía, "Sicópatas en Oferta: Bello Sueño Americano," Red Privada, *Excélsior*, 11 July 1979.

35. Manuel Buendía, "Amanecer en Panamá: Colonialismo en Serio," Red Privada, *Excélsior*, 4 October 1979.

36. Buendía, "CIA vs. Torrijos," 1, 15.

37. Gabriel García Márquez, "Torrijos," *El País* (Madrid), 12 August 1981.

38. Buendía, "CIA vs. Torrijos," 1, 15.

39. Manuel Buendía, "Torrijos: Por qué; La CIA Ejecutora," Red Privada, *Excélsior*, 25 August 1981.

40. Manuel Buendía, "CIA vs. Torrijos."

41. María Dolores Ábalos Lebrija, interview with authors, Mexico City, 9 March 1990.

42. María Dolores Ábalos Lebrija, interview with authors, Mexico City, 7 March 1990.

43. John H. Wright, Information and Privacy Coordinator, Central Intelligence Agency, to Professor Russell H. Bartley, letter, 27 November 1992.

CHAPTER 5. BALLET FOLKLÓRICO, ACT I

1. Rothschild, "Who Killed Manuel Buendía?," 21; Ángel Buendía, interviews with authors, Guadalajara, Mexico, 11 March 1992 and 10 March 1996; Ángel Buendía Téllez Girón, *Mi testimonio sobre el asesinato de mi hermano Manuel Buendía*, 2nd ed. (Guadalajara: Amate Editor, 1999), 24 (hereafter Á. Buendía, *Mi testimonio*). Russell's personal copy of *Mi testimonio* is inscribed by the author, "Para el Sr. Russell H. Bartley con todo el respeto y cariño que siento para todos aquellos que se arriesgaron y se preocuparon igual que yo para que el crimen en contra de mi hermano Manuel no quedara impune."

2. Á. Buendía, *Mi testimonio*, 24.

3. Ibid., 55–56.

4. Hernández López, *Zorrilla*, 44–45.

5. The Mexican judicial system differs significantly from the U.S. legal establishment. At the state and Federal District (Mexico City) levels, the maximum prosecutorial body is the Ministerio Público, which should not be confused with public defenders' offices in the United States. The head of a Public Ministry has the administrative title *procurador general de justicia*, literally "general procurator of justice" but usually rendered in English as "attorney general." His or her immediate subordinates are designated *subprocuradores*, here translated as "deputy prosecutors." As in the United States, Mexico's chief judicial authorities at both the state and national levels are "attorneys general." Where contextually unclear, we identify them respectively as District attorney general, referring to the Federal District, and federal attorney general, referring to the national government.

6. Aguayo Quezada, *La charola*, 234–236; Hernández López, *Zorrilla*, 52, 88, 90.

7. Fundación, "¿Quién mató a Manuel Buendía?," 34.

8. Teresa Gil, "No hay hipótesis concreta sobre el asesinato de Buendía: Sales Gasque," *unomásuno*, 28 February 1986, 8; Francisco Ortiz Pinchetti, "Desde hace seis meses, de hecho no investigaban ya el asesinato de Buendía," *Proceso*, 10 March 1986, 6–9.

9. Á. Buendía, *Mi testimonio*, 58.

10. Ibid., 57–59.

11. Ibid., 62–64.

12. Ibid., 65–66.

13. Conferencia de prensa que dio el C. Procurador General de Justicia del D.F., Licenciado Renato Sales Gasque en torno al caso del periodista Manuel Buendía Tellezgirón, 25 January 1988, 12, 13, BBCF, archival ring binder 2, Oficios & Other Buendía-related Documents.

14. Russell H. Bartley, "15 cables sobre Manuel Buendía: Se sigue la pista," parts 1–5, *unomásuno*, 25–29 November 1987.

15. Ibid., 25 October 1987, 1, 11.

16. Procuraduría General de Justicia del Distrito Federal (PGJDF), Texto de la entrevista del C. Procurador al término de la toma de posesión del nuevo Subdirector Técnico-Administrativo de la Policía Judicial [27 May 1987], 5, BBCF, archival ring binder 2, Oficios & Other Buendía-related Documents. See also Fernando Ramírez de Aguilar L. and Jorge Reyes Estrada, "Avance sustancial en las pesquisas sobre el asesinato de Manuel Buendía: La Procuraduría," *unomásuno*, 28 May 1987, 12.

17. PGJDF, "Información sobre el caso Buendía," Mexico City, 29 May 1987; PGJDF, "Lista de las personas que han sido investigadas con relación al caso de Manuel Buendía," 29 May 1987, BBCF, archival ring binder 2, Oficios & Other Buendía-related Documents; Jorge Reyes Estrada and Fernando Ramírez de Aguilar, "Un alemán, traficante de armas, principal sospechoso de la muerte de Manuel Buendía," *unomásuno*, 30 May 1987, 7.

18. For the fullest available account in English of Mertins's role as an international arms merchant and intelligence asset, see Ken Silverstein, *Private Warriors*, research by Daniel Burton-Rose (New York: Verso, 2000), 109–140.

19. Mary Ellen Reese, *General Reinard Gehlen: The CIA Connection* (Fairfax, VA: George Mason University Press, 1990), ix. See also Peer de Silva, *Sub Rosa: The CIA and the Uses of Intelligence* (New York: Times Books, 1978), 37–43; John Ranelagh, *The Agency: The Rise and Decline of the CIA, from Wild Bill Donovan to William Casey* (New York: Simon & Schuster, 1986), 91–92, 137–138, 748–749; David Wise and Thomas B. Ross, *The Invisible Government* (New York: Random House, 1964), 124–128; and Markus Wolf, with Anne McElvoy, *Man without a Face: The Autobiography of Communism's Greatest Spymaster* (New York: Public Affairs, 1997), 52–53.

20. Silverstein, *Private Warriors*, 109, 113.

21. Ibid., 116–117.

22. Ibid., 131.

23. Ibid., 122–131.

24. Manuel Buendía, "Vende Armas," Red Privada, *Excélsior*, 2 March 1983, reprinted in Manuel Buendía, *La ultraderecha en México* (Mexico City: Océano, 1984), 136–138; Manuel Robles, "El socio de Mertins, acusado de haberlo delatado ante Manuel Buendía," *Proceso*, 21 March 1988, 20–23.

25. Buendía, "Vende Armas"; Manuel Buendía, "'Western' orolesco," Red Privada, *Excélsior*, 17 February 1984, reprinted in Buendía, *Los empresarios*, 204–206; PGJDF, Palabras del Subdirector de Averiguaciones Previas de la Procuraduría General de Justicia del D.F., Licenciado Alejandro Sosa, durante la conferencia de prensa que ofreció el Procurador General de Justicia del D.F. Licenciado Renato Sales Gasque sobre el caso Manuel Buendía, 29 May 1987, 1, BBCF, archival ring binder 2, Oficios & Other Buendía-related Documents.

26. PGJDF, Palabras del Subprocurador de Averiguaciones Previas de la Procuraduría General de Justicia del D.F., Licenciado Alejandro Sosa; Manuel Buendía, "Traficante protegido," Red Privada, *Excélsior*, 29 February 1984, reprinted in Manuel Buendía, *Los empresarios* (Mexico City: Océano, 1986), 206–209; Silverstein, *Private Warriors*, 110.

27. Á. Buendía, *Mi testimonio*, 75–76. "Píquele por otro lado" was the Mexican idiom used by García Domínguez.

28. Ibid., 76–82.

29. Ibid., 83–85.

30. Ibid., 102.

Chapter 6. Ballet Folklórico, Act II

Chapter epigraphs: see Jesús Blancornelas, comments made at the Autonomous University of Baja California (Mexicali) on 22 October 1988; Sergio García Domínguez, "El asesinato de Buendía, visto por extranjeros," *Novedades de Baja California*, 23 October 1988, 1, 12; Russell H. Bartley, "El affaire Buendía: ¿La CIA involucrada?," *unomásuno*, Sunday political supplement *páginauno*, 4 June 1989, 11; Luis Suárez, "Buendía: Credibilidad recuperada," *Excélsior*, 15 June 1989, 7.

1. Á. Buendía, *Mi testimonio*, 95.

2. Ibid., 97.

3. PGJDF, Conferencia de prensa que dio el C. Procurador General de Justicia del D.F., Licenciado Renato Sales Gasque en torno al caso del periodista Manuel Buendía Tellezgirón, 25 January 1988, transcript, BBCF, archival ring binder 2, Oficios & Other Buendía-related Documents.

4. Miguel Ángel Sánchez de Armas, "Caso Buendía: Respuesta a una demanda de la opinión pública," *Punto* (Mexico City), 1 February 1988, 7.

5. Á. Buendía, *Mi testimonio*, 100–102.

6. Ibid., 102–105.

7. Fernando Ramírez de Aguilar L., "500 millones de pesos de recompensa a quien aporte datos que conduzcan a atrapar al asesino de Buendía," *unomásuno*, 25 February 1988, 12.

8. PGJDF, "Fiscal especial para el caso Buendía" (work plan, 23 February 1988); Rafael Croda, "Negligencia e interferencia policiacas en el caso Buendía: García Domínguez," *La Jornada*, 25 February 1988, 1, 12; Ramírez de Aguilar, "500 millones," 12.

9. PGJDF, "Informe que rinde el fiscal especial sobre la investigación del homicidio de Manuel Buendía," 29 May 1988, BBCF, archival ring binder 2, Oficios & Other Buendía-related Documents.

10. José Antonio Zorrilla Pérez, "A la opinión pública," *Excélsior*, 1 March 1988, 20; "Soy ajeno al homicidio de Buendía: Zorrilla; En un texto que envió al subprocurador García Domínguez, dice que no ha sido citado formalmente," *Excélsior*, 1 March 1988, 5, 45.

11. PGJDF, "Homicidio de Manuel Buendía Tellezgirón: Boletín," 11 March 1988, BBCF, archival ring binder 2, Oficios & Other Buendía-related Documents; Fernando Ramírez de Aguilar L., "Zorrilla Pérez se presentará a declarar ante el MP *en algún lugar* de la capital," *unomásuno*, 4 March 1988, 10.

12. See, e.g., Russell H. Bartley, *Imperial Russia and the Struggle for Latin American Independence, 1808–1828* (Austin: Institute of Latin American Studies, University of Texas, 1978); and Russell H. Bartley, ed. and trans., *Soviet Historians on Latin America: Recent Scholarly Contributions* (Madison: University of Wisconsin Press, 1978).

13. Manuel Buendía, *Ul'trapravye v Meksike* [La ultraderecha en México] (Moscow: Progress Publishers, 1987).

14. Hernández López, *Zorrilla*, 67.

15. Ángel Buendía, interviews with authors, Guadalajara, Mexico, 11 March 1992 and 10 March 1996.

16. PGJDF, "Informe del viaje a Suecia," n.d., BBCF, archival ring binder 2, Oficios & Other Buendía-related Documents.

17. Ibid., 6–7.

18. Robles, "El socio de Mertins."

19. Carlos Marín, "Casi cuatro años después, Gobernación se abre a la investigación del caso Buendía," *Proceso*, 21 March 1988, 20–21.

20. Tizoc Arista Jiménez, "Zorrilla no es el culpable, dice la viuda de Buendía," *Quehacer Político*, 21 March 1988, 6–9.

21. Tizoc Arista Jiménez, "Narcos involucrados en el asesinato de Buendía," *Quehacer Político*, 14 March 1988, 12–15.

22. Russell H. Bartley, "¿Intereses políticos internacionales en el asesinato de Buendía?," *unomásuno*, Sunday political supplement *páginauno*, 17 April 1988, 1, 3–4.

23. Ibid., 3.

24. PGJDF, A.P. 7a./2358/84, "Homicidio de Manuel Buendía Tellezgirón, Boletín," 11 March 1988, BBCF, archival ring binder 2, Oficios & Other Buendía-related Documents.

25. Bartley, "¿Intereses políticos internacionales en el asesinato de Buendía?," 4.

26. Á. Buendía, *Mi testimonio*, 127.

27. Ibid., 133.

28. Ibid., 133–136.

29. "Informe del fiscal especial: Aún no aparece el autor de la muerte de Buendía," *unomásuno*, 28 November 1988, 13.

30. Á. Buendía, *Mi testimonio*, 137–138; Hernández López, *Zorrilla*, 141–142; Ross, *Annexation of Mexico*, 180–181.

31. Hernández López, *Zorrilla*, 142–143.

CHAPTER 7. GRAND FINALE

1. Aurora Berdejo Arvizu, "Frentes políticos," *Excélsior*, 1 February 1989, 30.

2. Fernando Ramírez de Aguilar L., "Podría pasar el sexenio sin aclararse la muerte de Buendía, dice García Domínguez," *unomásuno*, 7 December 1988, 12.

3. Miguel Badillo et al., "Sobre los cambios en *unomásuno*," *Revista mexicana de comunicación* 1, no. 6 (July–August 1989): 20–22; Luis Gutiérrez Rodríguez, conversation with authors, Milwaukee, 28 September 1989.

4. Luis Gutiérrez Rodríguez, "¿Qué más quiere Becerra Acosta?," *unomásuno*, 2 October 1989, 9.

5. Hernández López, *Zorrilla*, 144–149; "Resucitan a Nazar: No importaron las acusaciones de represor, de torturador, de informante de la CIA," *Proceso*, 26 December 1988, 6–13; Raúl Monge, "Inútiles los reclamos de la oposición: Nazar se encargará de 'la inteligencia' en la capital," *Proceso*, 26 December 1988, 6–8; Luis García Rojas, Roberto Santiago, and Ernesto Zavaleta, "Nassar atribuye su salida a los cargos en EU: Intentan desacreditar al gobierno, afirma," *unomásuno*, 25 February 1989, 12; Gustavo Hirales and José Domínguez, "Presentan denuncia formal contra Miguel Nazar Haro," *La Jornada*, 18 March 1989, 13.

6. John Womack Jr., personal communication, 6 December 2010.

7. Raúl Monge and Ignacio Ramírez, "Es muy probable que el autor intelectual de la muerte de Buendía sea un político: El fiscal especial; Zorrilla Pérez alteró el escenario del crimen," *Proceso*, 15 May 1989, 14–17; Raúl Monge and Ignacio Ramírez, "Funcionarios que obstruyeron la investigación y substrajeron pruebas, a punto de quedar impunes," *Proceso*, 15 May 1989, 14–15.

8. Hernández López, *Zorrilla*, 162–164.

9. Á. Buendía, *Mi testimonio*, 143–146.

10. Quoted in Hernández López, *Zorrilla*, 163–166.

11. Ibid., 166–167.

12. Whether or not Adato's judicial immunity as a Supreme Court justice protected her from criminal charges related to acts allegedly committed prior to her appointment to the Supreme Court is unclear.

13. Cabildo, Monge, and Ramírez, "Cada pista en el caso Buendía," 18–21.

14. Hernández López, *Zorrilla*, 167–168; José Quintero Arias, "Hay sólo 24 posibles autores intelectuales y 7 presuntos materiales: García Domínguez," *unomásuno*, 25 May 1989, 6.

15. Hernández López, *Zorrilla*, 166, 168; Roberto Santiago, "Acuerdo de la Permanente para conocer el estado de la investigación sobre Buendía," *unomásuno*, 25 May 1989, 6.

16. Russell H. Bartley, "Evidencias de un posible involucramiento de intereses foráneos en el asesinato de MB: El caso visto desde el exterior," *Revista mexicana de comunicación* 1, no. 5 (May–June 1989): 11–17; Rothschild, "La CIA vs. Manuel Buendía."

17. Manuel Roque, "Esperanzas de resolver el caso, dice Angel Buendía," *unomásuno*, 25 May 1989, 6. This report was filed from Zitácuaro, Michoacán, Manuel Buendía's hometown, where a statue of the slain journalist had just been dedicated and Ángel Buendía spoke to the press.

18. Raúl Monge and Ignacio Ramírez, "Zorrilla Pérez se contradice sobre lo que hizo en el caso Buendía: Durante 22 horas declaró ante el fiscal especial," *Proceso*, 29 May 1989, 16–19.

19. Miguel Ángel García Domínguez, interview with authors, Mexico City, 12 March 1990.

20. Antonio Hernández Montoya, "Elena Poniatowska: Buendía, buscar el gato escondido, en el caso," *El Día*, 29 May 1989, 1, 6.

21. Manú Dornbierer, "El negocio Buendía," *Excélsior*, 29 May 1989, 7.

22. Fernando Ramírez de Aguilar L., "A 5 años de la muerte de Buendía, todo indica que no se resolverá a corto plazo," *unomásuno*, 29 May 1989, 10.

23. Hernández López, *Zorrilla*, 170.

24. Manú Dornbierer, "El negocio Buendía," *Excélsior*, 30 May 1989, 8.

25. Fernando Ramírez de Aguilar L., "Caso Buendía: No puede desecharse la hipótesis de un crimen político; Acepta García Domínguez," *unomásuno*, 30 May 1989, 11.

26. "Manuel Buendía: Cinco años después; Cronología de las investigaciones desde 1984 hasta el día de ayer," *El Día*, 30 May 1989, 10.

27. Hernández López, *Zorrilla*, 170–173.

28. Our article was Bartley, "El affaire Buendía."

29. Miguel Cabildo and Raúl Monge, "Decepcionada, la viuda de Buendía no cree que se quiera aclarar el crimen," *Proceso*, 5 June 1989, 26–27.

30. Jorge Fernández Menéndez, "Ante el periodismo del futuro," *unomásuno*, 8 June 1989, 8.

31. The address is transcribed in Héctor Aguilar Camín, "La prensa mexicana, factor claro de la modernización política: Aguilar Camín," *unomásuno*, 8 June 1989, 7.

32. "La libertad de expresión, básica para el funcionamiento de un sistema democrático: Palabras de CSG al conmemorar el Día de la Libertad de Prensa," *unomásuno*, 8 June 1989, 6.

33. Fernando Ramírez de Aguilar L. and Héctor Cruz López, "Acusa la PJDF a Zorrilla Pérez del homicidio de Manuel Buendía," *unomásuno*, 12 June 1989, 1, 12.

34. Hernández López, *Zorrilla*, 173.

35. Estados Unidos Mexicanos, PGJDF, "Informe del Subprocurador Dr. Miguel Angel García Domínguez, Fiscal Especial para el esclarecimiento del homicidio de Manuel Buendía Tellezgirón," 30 June 1989, Anexo no. 2 (enriquecimiento ilícito), 31–33, BBCF, archival ring binder 2, Oficios & Other Buendía-related Documents.

36. He was a scapegoat in the sense that he was being sacrificed to provide cover for higher-ups and other powerful interests, not that he was himself an innocent with clean hands.

37. "El día de la aprehensión Zorrilla estuvo en riesgo de perder la vida: Camacho," *unomásuno*, 16 June 1989, 13; Xavier Rojas, "Claro que sentí miedo, pero hay que cumplir con el deber, señaló el procurador Morales Lechuga," *El Heraldo*, 17 June 1989, 1; Sergio von Nowaffen, "Estaba abatido . . . la sonrisa desapareció," *Ovaciones*, 14 June 1989, 1.

38. Rigoberto López, "Procuraduría de Justicia: ¿Acuerdos con Zorrilla?," *unomásuno*, 18 June 1989, 18; Jorge Reyes Estrada, "Trasladaron a Zorrilla Pérez al Reclusorio Norte: Hermetismo total," *unomásuno*, 15 June 1989, 14; Jorge Reyes Estrada and Fernando Ramírez de Aguilar L., "El asesino fue visto en la DFS: Aún no lo aprehenden," *unomásuno*, 17 June 1989, 1, 11.

39. "Mexico: The Cop and the Newsman," *Time*, 26 June 1989, 46.

40. Reyes Estrada and Ramírez de Aguilar L., "El asesino fue visto en la DFS," 11.

41. Miguel Cabildo, Raúl Monge, and Ignacio Ramírez, "Zorrilla pretende prolongar la protección que le dio el gobierno anterior," *Proceso*, 19 June 1989, 8.

42. Miguel Cabildo, Raúl Monge, and Ignacio Ramírez, "El caso Buendía se vuelve embrollo: Resiste Zorrilla, niega todo y en respuesta le acumulan cargos," *Proceso*, 19 June 1989, 14.

43. "El día de la aprehensión Zorrilla estuvo en riesgo de perder la vida," 13.

44. Jorge Reyes Estrada and Héctor Cruz López, "Cuatro ex jefes de la DFS, aprehendidos," *unomásuno*, 20 June 1989, 1, 11.

45. "Cuestión de horas la captura del asesino material de Manuel Buendía," *El Nacional*, 20 June 1989, 1.

46. Jorge Reyes Estrada and Héctor Cruz López, "Cayó el asesino de Buendía: Es Juan R. Moro Avila Camacho, un ex agente," *unomásuno*, 21 June 1989, 1, 13; "Las lecciones del caso Zorrilla," *unomásuno*, 21 June 1989, 3.

47. Héctor Cruz López and Jorge Reyes Estrada, "Nunca fui autónomo; siempre mantuve informados a mis superiores: Zorrilla," *unomásuno*, 21 June 1989, 13.

48. Rubén Chavarría Balleza, "Fueron 'dos o más' matones," *Ovaciones*, 21 June 1989, 8.

49. Jorge Reyes Estrada and Héctor Cruz López, "Acusa Moro Ávila Camacho del homicidio de Buendía a un ex *madrina* asesinado," *unomásuno*, 22 June 1989, 1, 13.

50. Ricardo Blanco Velázquez, "Moro recibió entrenamiento de la DEA: Siete veces campeón de motociclismo y rockero," *El Nacional*, 21 June 1989, 1, 10; Reyes Estrada and Cruz López, "Acusa Moro Ávila Camacho," 13.

51. Fernando Ramírez de Aguilar L., "Han desertado 350 agentes de la Dirección de Inteligencia: Está acéfala en su mando," *unomásuno*, 27 June 1989, 11.

52. Ignacio Ramírez, "Caso Buendía: Confusión y contradicciones en una investigación que no termina; No fue un crimen político dijeron Adato y Sales Gasque," *Proceso*, 26 June 1989, 6–7.

53. "El autor material del asesinato de Manuel Buendía, identificado: PGJDF," *unomásuno*, 13 June 1989, 11; Roberto Gómez Villarreal, "La Operación Noticia: La distancia entre el poder y la sombra," *El Nacional*, 29 June 1989, 3; Á. Buendía, *Mi testimonio*, 148.

54. "Moro asesinó a Buendía: La PGJDF," *unomásuno*, 1 July 1989, 1, 11.

CHAPTER 8. AFTER THE CURTAIN

1. Manuel Alonso Enríquez, "'Informaba periódicamente a mi jefe Bartlett: No era autónomo'; Zorrilla," *El Universal*, 21 June 1989, 1, 17.

2. Chavarría Balleza, "Fueron 'dos o más' matones," 1, 8; Hernández López, *Zorrilla*, 54–55.

3. Six years later, virtually to the day (19 June 1995), Polo Uscanga would be shot to death in a ninth-floor suite of an aging office building just a few blocks from Manuel Buendía's old office, also on South Insurgentes Avenue. The motive behind Polo Uscanga's murder, however, does not appear to be related to the Buendía case.

4. Xavier Rojas, "Moro Ávila-Camacho, admitió haber ayudado al asesino del periodista: Para cubrir a los criminales, se desató una ola de muertes; El autor material, acribillado un mes después del homicidio," *El Heraldo*, 22 June 1989, 1.

5. Héctor Cruz López, "Cae Moro en innumerables contradicciones al rendir su declaración preparatoria ante el juez 34 penal," *unomásuno*, 23 June 1989, BBCF, clippings binder 2.

6. H. Adorno and L. Segura, "Vi en la DFS papeles de Buendía que relacionaban a Zorrilla con narcos: Moro," *Excélsior*, 23 June 1989, 1, 10.

7. Ignacio G. Almanza, "Prado hunde a Zorrilla: 'Él planeó el asesinato,'" *El Nacional*, 26 June 1989, 1, 12; Fernando Ramírez de Aguilar L. and Héctor Cruz López, "Lo tortuó la Judicial, dice Juventino Prado: Niega haber confesado que participó en el homicidio de Buendía," *unomásuno*, 26 June 1989, 1, 14; David Romero Ceyde and Alfonso Moraflores, "El plan para desaparecer a Buendía lo reveló Prado y hundió a Moro A.," *Ovaciones*, 26 June 1989, 1, 10.

8. Almanza, "Prado hunde a Zorrilla," 1, 12; Ramírez de Aguilar L. and Cruz López, "Lo tortuó la Judicial," 1, 14.

9. Ramírez de Aguilar L. and Cruz López, "Lo torturó la Judicial," 1, 14.

10. Ibid.; Almanza, "Prado hunde a Zorrilla," 1, 12.

11. "La DFS investigó el caso Buendía sólo tres semanas," *unomásuno*, 27 June 1989, 1, 10–11.

12. Héctor Cruz López and Jorge Reyes Estrada, "Acusaciones mutuas de Juventino Prado, Raúl Pérez, Sofía Naya y Moro Ávila," *unomásuno*, 28 June 1989, 10.

13. Estados Unidos Mexicanos, PGJDF, "Informe del Subprocurador Dr. Miguel Ángel García Domínguez, Fiscal Especial para el esclarecimiento del homicidio de Manuel Buendía Tellezgirón," 30 June 1989, BBCF, archival ring binder 2, "Oficios & Other Buendía-related Documents."

14. Ibid., 14–17, 25–26. Only portions of these pages concern the Buendía homicide.

15. Lawrence Victor Harrison, interview with authors, San Dimas, California, 15 May 2004.

16. Carlos Ramírez, "La muerte de Buendía, una investigación policiaca inconclusa," *El Financiero*, 10 July 1989, 4.

17. Guillermo Correa, Manuel Robles, and Ignacio Ramírez, "Pese a las confusiones, García Domínguez da por cerrada la investigación y se va: La Procuraduría del Distrito y el Fiscal Especial del caso Buendía se contradicen," *Proceso*, 3 July 1989, 16–21, 23–25.

18. Ibid., 16, 25; Ignacio Ramírez, "Se difundirá una filmación de la reconstrucción del asesinato de Buendía," *Proceso*, 6 June 1988, 26–28; Fundación, "¿Quién mató a Manuel Buendía?," 10.

19. Antonio Arrellano, "Borran el caso del Chocorrol," *El Universal Gráfico*, 26 June 1989, 1, 3; Renato Dávalos and Héctor Adorno, "Desaparece de los archivos del Forense el expediente de 'El Chocorrol' Ochoa," *Excélsior*, 30 June 1989, 28, 43.

20. "Desde hace cuatro años las autoridades sabían que la DFS estaba involucrada en el asesinato: Un informe de agentes y el jefe de la judicial," *Proceso*, 26 June 1989, 12–16, 18–19.

21. Miguel Cabildo and Raúl Monge, "El periodista que en 1986 dio a conocer al 'Chocorrol' dice que sus datos apuntan más alto que Zorrilla," *Proceso*, 26 June 1989, 14–15.

22. Héctor Cruz López, "Ni Moro ni *El Chocorrol* son los asesinos de Manuel Buendía," *unomásuno*, 2 July 1989, 11.

23. Raúl Monge, "Con sus declaraciones, Moro enturbió más el caso Buendía," *Proceso*, 10 September 1990, 28–29.

24. John Ross, "The Nota Roja's Notoriety Is Paying Off for Mexico's President," photocopied typescript of article submitted to the *San Francisco Examiner*, July 1989, 7–8, BBCF, carton 1, Informants and sources: Ross.

25. John Ross, "Mexico's Blood-Stained Pens: Mexico Has Trumpeted the Arrest of a Suspect in the Killing of Journalist Manuel Buendía, but What the Government Doesn't Say Is the Epidemic of Journalists' Killings Continues Unabated," *San Francisco Bay Guardian*, 28 June 1989, 20–22, 26.

26. John Ross to Russell H. Bartley, Mexico City, 26 July 1989.

27. PGJDF, "Informe que rinde el Fiscal Especial sobre la investigación del homicidio de Manuel Buendía," 29 May 1988, 22, BBCF, archival ring binder 2, "Oficios & Other Buendía-related Documents."

28. Alfredo Jiménez and Luis Segura, "Gerhardt Mertins no participó en el asesinato de Buendía: Morales L.," *Excélsior*, 25 July 1989, 1, 36; Patricia Dávila and Ignacio Ramírez, "Mertins, exonerado en el caso Buendía, vendió ya sus propiedades en Durango," *Proceso*, 9 October 1989, 31–33.

29. Luis Suárez, "Más que una mera coincidencia, los atentados contra Buendía y Pastora," *Excélsior*, 16 August 1989, 5, 37.

30. United States District Court, Southern District of Florida, Civil Action no. 86-1146-CIV-KING: *Tony Avirgan, Martha Honey, Plaintiffs, v. John Hull, René Corbo et al., Defendants*; and Civil Action no. 87-1545-CIV-KING, *Tony Avirgan, Martha Honey, Plaintiffs, v. Felipe Vidal Santiago, Raúl Villaverde et al., Defendants*, Declaration of Plaintiffs' Counsel, 159.

31. For background on La Penca and the Christic Institute's lawsuit, see Rod Holt, ed., *Assault on Nicaragua: The Untold Story of the U.S. "Secret War"* (San Francisco: Walnut Publishing, 1987), which includes speeches by Daniel Sheehan and Daniel Ortega, an essay by Jeff Mackler and Nat Weinstein, and an introduction by Rod Holt; Honey, *Hostile Acts*; Marshall, Scott, and Hunter, *The Iran-Contra Connection*; Peter Dale Scott and Jonathan Marshall, *Cocaine Politics: Drugs, Armies, and the CIA in Central America*, updated paperback ed. (Berkeley: University of California Press, 1998); and Holly Sklar, *Washington's War on Nicaragua* (Boston: South End Press, 1988).

32. Russell H. Bartley, "¿Vínculos mexicanos con los contras? Caro Quintero no fue," *unomásuno*, 17 March 1987, 18.

33. Hernán Casares Cámara, interviews with authors, Mexico City, 8 May 1987 and 27 November 1987.

34. Hernán Casares Cámara, "Revelación del Instituto Christic: Caro Quintero abastecía de armamento a la contra; El narco mexicano tenía la simpatía de la DEA y la CIA," *Punto*, 9 March 1987, 16–17.

35. Lawrence Victor Harrison, interview with authors, Riverside, California, 15 April 2005.

36. Mills, *Underground Empire*, 525–526.

37. Shannon, *Desperados*, 126–127.

38. Marta Anaya, "Falsificado, el informe sobre Buendía: DEA: Ni siquiera se parece a los nuestros; Heath: 'No ligamos su muerte con el narcotráfico,'" *Excélsior*, 30 June 1989, 1, 28; Alberto Carbot, "Reconoce Heath logros de la campaña hecha por México," *unomásuno*, 30 June 1989, 10.

39. Rogelio Hernández López, "'Seguro: No seremos extraditados'; Confía la DEA en nosotros; Gárate y Héctor Berréllez," *Excélsior*, 25 October 1990, 22.

40. Hernández López, *Zorrilla*, 82–83.

41. Héctor Berréllez, interview with authors, Ontario, California, 15 May 2004.

42. Lawrence Victor Harrison, phone conversation with Russell H. Bartley, 1 September 2005; Lawrence Victor Harrison, interview with authors, Riverside, California, 23 March 2006; Charles Bowden to Russell H. Bartley, e-mail, 12 February 2013.

43. Shannon, *Desperados*, 126–127.

44. Mills, *Underground Empire*, 543–547.

45. At one point during our interview, Ventura excused himself briefly and left us seated alone in his office as he exited through a side door into an adjacent room. Some moments later he suddenly flung open the door, scrutinized us with a steely glare, then withdrew again, closing the door behind him. We had not stirred from our chairs while he was out of the room, nor would we have been so foolish, but Ventura clearly wished to reassure himself that we were up to no mischief in his absence, as well as to convey to us with a bit of melodrama his suspicions about our ulterior purposes.

46. Florentino Ventura Gutiérrez, interview with authors, Mexico City, 25 November 1987.

47. Mills, *Underground Empire*, 74–75, 534–535.

48. Ibid., 534–535. See also Shannon, *Desperados*, 283; and Arguayo Quezada, *La charola*, 64–65.

49. Mills, *Underground Empire*, 535–541.

50. Among the extensive news reports of Ventura's violent death, see, e.g., Alfonso Millares García and Juan Rivas, "Se suicidó Florentino Ventura tras matar a su esposa y otra mujer," *Excélsior*, 18 September 1988, 1, 30–31; Héctor Adorno, Jorge Espinosa, and Héctor Cruz, "Hermetismo en el caso de F. Ventura," *Excélsior*, 19 September 1988, 5, 38; Héctor A. González and Ernesto Zavaleta, "La muerte de Ventura y esposa, por líos conyugales," *unomásuno*, 19 September 1988, 12; and Marjorie Miller, "Scandal Spurs Fears over Violence: Death of 'the Tiger' Puts Mexico Police in Spotlight," *Los Angeles Times*, 28 September 1988. Ventura's remains lay in state in the same Gayosso mortuary as those of Manuel Buendía had four years earlier.

51. Fernando Ortega Pizarro, "*Proceso* tiene la razón: El director de la DEA en México; 'Se provocó una reacción del Gobierno y hablaron a la Embajada,' dice Edward Heath," *Proceso*, 10 June 1985, 6–8, 11; "El boletín de la embajada de los Estados Unidos," *Proceso*, 10 June 1985, 6–7; Carlos Marín, "Gobernación exonera a Zorrilla, corre a 427 y afirma que la DFS es legal," *Proceso*, 10 June 1985, 8–10.

52. Shannon, *Desperados*, 283.

53. Ibid., 284–285.

54. Mills, *Underground Empire*, 1156.

55. DEA-6 Report of Investigation, transcription of recorded debriefing of Cooperating Individual [Lawrence Victor Harrison] by Special Agents Manuel R. Martinez and [first name not recorded] Morales, approved by Group Supervisor Hector G. Berréllez, 25 September 1989, 54, BBCF, archival ring binder 3.

56. Shannon, *Desperados*, 297.

57. Héctor Berréllez, interview with authors, Ontario, California, 15 May 2004.

58. Shannon, *Desperados*, chapter 15, "The Camarena Tapes," 282–301.

59. Florentino Ventura Gutiérrez, interview with authors, Mexico City, 25 November 1987; Anaya, "Falsificado."

CHAPTER 9. BACK ON THE PAVEMENT

1. Cabildo and Monge, "Decepcionada," 26.

2. María Dolores Ábalos Lebrija, interviews with authors, Mexico City, 7 and 9 March 1990. Subsequent statements by Doña Dolores are from these interviews.

3. Arista Jiménez, "Zorrilla no es el culpable, dice la viuda de Buendía," 9.

4. Hernández López, *Zorrilla*, 17–27.

5. Ibid., 22.

6. See, e.g., Arista Jiménez, "Zorrilla no es el culpable," 7; and Erendira Estrada, "Siento asco por Zorrilla: La viuda de Buendía," *El Nacional*, 6 July 1989, 10.

7. Hernández López, *Zorrilla*, 25.

8. Ibid., 23–24.

9. Ibid., 39.

10. Miguel Cabildo et al., "Las actuaciones de la fiscalía especial y la Procuraduría, en entredicho," *Proceso*, 17 July 1989, 24–25; Estados Unidos Mexicanos, PGJDF, "Informe del Subprocurador Dr. Miguel Ángel García Domínguez."

11. Miguel Ángel García Domínguez, interview with authors, Mexico City, 15 March 1990. Subsequent statements by García Domínguez are from this interview.

12. Molly Molloy and Charles Bowden, eds., *El Sicario: The Autobiography of a Mexican Assassin* (New York: Nation Books, 2011).

13. Felipe Victoria Zepeda, *El caso del periodista asesinado: Una pista segura para atrapar a los asesinos* (Mexico City: EDAMEX, 1988), 90–92.

14. Felipe Victoria Zepeda, interview with authors, Mexico City, 25 March 1989.

15. J. Jesús Esquivel, *La CIA, Camarena y Caro Quintero: La historia secreta* (Mexico City: Grijalbo, 2014), 71–73.

16. Lawrence Victor Harrison, interview with authors, Riverside, California, 28 March 2007.

17. Octavio Colmenares, interview with authors, Mexico City, 9 March 1990.

18. Luís Gutiérrez Rodríguez, interview with authors, Milwaukee, 28 September 1989.

19. Ibid.; Russell H. Bartley, "Cuba: La revolución y el narcotráfico," *unomásuno*, 30–31 August and 1 September 1989, 21, 26, 19, respectively.

20. Sergo Mikoyan, interview with authors, Arlington, Virginia, 12 March 1994.

21. This interview would have been in connection with the appearance in Russian translation of a posthumous collection of Buendía columns on the Mexican Far Right first published in 1984 (Buendía, *La ultraderecha en México*). The Russian volume is Buendía, *Ul'trapravye v Meksike*.

22. Anatoly Borovkov and Viktor Volsky, personal conversation with authors, Mexico City, 14 March 1990. Volsky died on 18 November 1999. According to Sergo Mikoyan, Borovkov remained in Mexico following the collapse of the Soviet Union, apparently as a Russian intelligence operative, but we have had no further contact with him. Mikoyan also indicated to us that Volsky and Borovkov had a close working relationship in which Borovkov would facilitate Volsky's visits to Mexico and Volsky would cover Borovkov's to Moscow. Sergo Mikoyan, interview with authors, Arlington, Virginia, 12 March 1994.

23. Miguel Ángel Sánchez de Armas, interview with authors, Mexico City, 15 March 1990.

24. Miguel Ángel Sánchez de Armas to Russell H. Bartley, e-mail, 8 June 2011.

25. Carlos Ramírez to Russell H. Bartley, e-mails, 9 and 14 June 2011.

26. Miguel Ángel Sánchez de Armas, "En defensa de la palabra: 'El caso Buendía nos debe llevar a examinar toda la cuestión de la prensa, en México y en EU'; Russell Bartley," *Revista mexicana de comunicación* 2, no. 11 (May–June 1990): 30–31.

27. Nedda G. de Anhalt, "¿Quién es Eko?," *unomásuno*, cultural supplement *sábado*, 17 March 1990, 3.

28. Miguel Ángel Sánchez de Armas, interview with authors, Mexico City, 17 March 1990.

29. Ramírez, "La muerte de Buendía," 74.

30. Miguel Ángel Sánchez de Armas, "Caso Buendía: Precisiones," *El Financiero*, 17 July 1989; BBCF, clipping binder 3.

Chapter 10. secret, noforn

1. Fernando Ramírez de Aguilar, personal conversation, Mexico City, 15 March 1990.

2. "Proceedings had before the Grand Jury of the United States of America, in and for the Central District of California, at United States District Courthouse, 312 North Spring Street, Los Angeles, California, on Thursday, September 7, 1989," court reporter's transcript.

3. Ibid., 16–19.

4. United States Court of Appeals, Ninth Circuit, Case No. 93-50311 (C.D. Cal. No. CR-87-422 ER): *United States of America, Plaintiff-Appellee, v. Rubén Zuno-Arce, Defendant-Appellant*, Appeal from the United States District Court for the Central District of California, the Honorable Edward Rafeedie presiding; Appellant's Opening Brief (Edward M. Medvene, James E. Blancarte & Jack R. Luellen, Attorneys for Defendant-Appellant Rubén Zuno-Arce), 2–6.

5. The designation FNU signifies "first name unknown." In this case, the individual in question was Alfredo del Mazo, ex-governor of the state of Mexico and a former cabinet member who unsuccessfully sought the nomination as PRI presidential candidate in the 1988 election. Manuel Buendía was slain in 1984 and could not, therefore, have supported del Mazo's candidacy. Berréllez and Schmidt, it would seem, were not very knowledgeable about Mexico's recent political history.

6. Aldana Ibarra was the former director of Mexico's INTERPOL office. Ibarra Herrera was the head of Mexico's Federal Judicial Police and had never served as head of the DFS.

7. "El informe de la DEA en el juicio a Zuno habla de los federales muertos en Veracruz, la CIA, Buendía, Bartlett, y el narco," *Proceso*, 16 July 1990, 18–20.

8. Russell H. Bartley to FOIA/Privacy Act Unit of the Drug Enforcement Administration, letter, 16 September 1988, BBCF, carton 2, subject files: Freedom of Information request.

9. Russell H. Bartley to Assistant Attorney General, Office of Legal Policy, United States Department of Justice, letter, 27 April 1989, BBCF, carton 2, subject files: Freedom of Information request.

10. Russell H. Bartley to H. Lee Halterman, District Counsel for Ronald V. Dellums, letter, 7 March 1991, BBCF, carton 2, subject files: Freedom of Information request.

11. Affidavit of Daniel P. Sheehan, The Christic Institute, 1324 North Capitol Street, NW, Washington, D.C. Filed on December 12, 1986 (Minor Revisions, 12/18/86); United States District Court, Southern District of Florida, Civil Action No. 86–1146-CIV-KING, TONY AVIRGAN, MARTHA HONEY, Plaintiffs, v. JOHN HULL, RENE CORBO, et al., Defendants; Civil Action No. 87–1545-CIV-KING, TONY AVIRGAN, MARTHAN HONEY, Plaintiffs, v. FELIPE VIDAL SANTIAGO, RAUL VILLAVERDE, et al., Defendants. Declaration of Plaintiffs' Counsel, 25 March 1988.

12. Russell H. Bartley to Edward M. Medvene, letter, 2 October 1992; Bartley to Medvene, letter, 4 March 1993; Wendilyn Hufnagel-Giba, Paralegal Assistant, Law Offices of Mitchell,

Silberberg & Knupp, to Russell Bartley, 6 April 1993, BBCF, carton 1, Informants and sources: Medvene.

13. Russell H. Bartley to Assistant Attorney General, Office of Legal Policy, United States Department of Justice, letter, 7 October 1991; Richard L. Huff, Co-Director, Office of Information and Privacy, to Russell H. Bartley, letter, 5 November 1991, BBCF, carton 2, subject files: Freedom of Information request.

14. Russell H. Bartley to Edward M. Medvene, letter, 28 April 1993, BBCF, carton 1, Informants and sources: Medvene.

15. Michael Levine, *Deep Cover: The Inside Story of How DEA Infighting, Incompetence, and Subterfuge Lost Us the Biggest Battle of the Drug War* (New York: Delacorte Press, 1990), 184.

16. Lawrence Victor Harrison, interview with authors, San Dimas, California, 14 May 2004.

17. Levine, *Deep Cover*, 26–27, 32–33.

18. Ibid., 53.

19. Ibid., 102–104; Rick Szykowny, "A Funny, Dirty Little Drug War" (interview with Michael Levine), *Humanist* 50, no. 5 (September–October 1990): 16–18.

20. Levine, *Deep Cover*, 98.

21. Ibid., 155–158, 165–166, 169, 179, 203–204, 207–208, 266–267.

22. Ibid., 277.

23. Michael Levine, "The Emperor Is Butt Naked," Expert Witness Radio, 1997, http://www.expertwitnessradio.org/site/the-emperor-is-butt-naked/.

24. See Alfred W. McCoy, *The Politics of Heroin: CIA Complicity in the Global Drug Trade* (Chicago: Lawrence Hill Books, 1991), a revised and expanded edition of McCoy's *The Politics of Heroin in Southeast Asia*; and Scott and Marshall, *Cocaine Politics*.

25. Daniel Ellsberg, *Secrets: A Memoir of Vietnam and the Pentagon Papers* (New York: Viking, 2002); Daniel Ellsberg, *The Pentagon Papers: The Defense Department History of United States Decision-Making on Vietnam*, 4 vols. (Boston: Beacon, 1971); Victor Marchetti and John D. Marks, *The CIA and the Cult of Intelligence*, introduction by Melvin L. Wulf (New York: Knopf, 1974); Agee, *Inside the Company*; John Stockwell, *In Search of Enemies: A CIA Story* (New York: W. W. Norton, 1978); Blum, *Killing Hope*; Luke Harding, *The Snowden Files: The Inside Story of the World's Most Wanted Man* (New York: Vintage, 2014).

26. Charles Bowden to Russell H. Bartley, e-mail, 27 April 2007. Among Bowden's numerous books, see his *Down by the River: Drugs, Money, Murder, and Family* (New York: Simon & Schuster, 2004); and *A Shadow in the City: Confessions of an Undercover Drug Warrior* (New York: Harcourt, 2005).

27. Levine, *Deep Cover*, 11.

28. Ibid., 7–9, 11.

29. Former CIA consultant Chalmers Johnson and retired career U.S. Army officer Andrew J. Bacevich are two sober voices that have articulated dissenting views of American power projection and the national security apparatus that supports it. See, e.g., Andrew J. Bacevich, *Washington Rules: America's Path to Permanent War* (New York: Metropolitan Books, 2010), especially "Introduction: Slow Learner"; and Chalmers Johnson, *Dismantling the Empire: America's Last Best Hope* (New York: Metropolitan Books, 2010).

30. Philip Taubman, "Objection by C.I.A. Blocks Indictment: Prosecution of Mexican Could Curb Spying, Agency Says," *New York Times*, 28 March 1982, 1, 14; Dana Littlefield, "Senior Judge Is Retiring after 25 Years on Bench," *San Diego Union-Tribune*, 29 December 2008, http://www.utsandiego.com/news/2008/dec/29/1m29kennedy21194; Szykowny, "A Funny, Dirty Little Drug War," 26.

31. Quoted in Mills, *Underground Empire*, 873.

32. Robert F. Jones, "Marlin Lover of Mazatlán," *Sports Illustrated*, 31 March 1969, 42.

33. Levine, *Deep Cover*, 305–306.

34. Lawrence Victor Harrison, interviews with authors, San Dimas, California, 14 May 2004, and Riverside, California, 15 April 2005.

35. Levine, *Deep Cover*, 293.

36. Ibid., 293–297.

37. Ibid., 300.

38. Aguayo Quezada, *La charola*, 201–203.

39. "Memorias de Miguel Félix Gallardo," 23 July 2009, in Miguel Félix Gallardo, *Diarios del Jefe de Jefes*, written in Mexico's Almoloya maximum security prison and excerpted via the Internet by the Mexican daily *Milenio*, BBCF, carton 2, personality files.

40. Levine, *Deep Cover*, 311; Levine, "The Emperor Is Butt Naked," 2.

41. Michael Levine, interviews with authors, Stone Ridge, New York, 20–21 May 1995.

42. Celerino Castillo III and Dave Harmon, *Powderburns: Cocaine, Contras, and the Drug War*, foreword by Michael Levine (Buffalo: Mosaic Press, 1994), 8–9.

43. Peter Gorman, "Big-Time Smuggler's Blues," *Cannabis Culture*, 16 June 2006,; United States District Court, District of Arizona, "Indictment," *United States of America, Plaintiff, v. Rafael Caro-Quintero, Miguel Caro-Quintero, Michael Keith Hooks, et al., Defendants*, 14 July 1988.

44. Levine, *Deep Cover*, 184, 266.

45. Mike Levine to Russ Bartley, letter, 16 November 1995; Russell H. Bartley to Mike Levine, letter, 14 February 1996, BBCF, carton 1, Informants and sources: Levine.

46. Mike Levine to Russ Bartley, letter, 25 June 1995, BBCF, carton 1, Informants and sources: Levine.

47. Gorman, "Big-Time Smuggler's Blues."

48. Mike Gallagher, "Trafficker-Turned-Informant Hides in N.M. and Waits for Reward from Feds," *Albuquerque Journal*, 15 January 2006.

49. Gorman, "Big-Time Smuggler's Blues."

50. Michael Hooks, with Herbert Johnson, "Kingpin," forty-five-page typescript précis of a proposed book or movie, n.d., 1–2, BBCF, carton 1, Informants and sources: Hooks.

51. Russell H. Bartley to Michael Hooks, letter, 20 July 1995; Michael Hooks to Russell H. Bartley, letter, 19 September 1995; Russell H. Bartley to Michael Hooks, letter, 28 October 1995; Michael Hooks to Russell H. Bartley, letter, 5 November 1995, BBCF, carton 1, Informants and sources: Hooks.

52. Gallagher, "Trafficker-Turned-Informant Hides in N.M."

CHAPTER 11. ATTORNEYS IN WONDERLAND

1. Avirgan and Honey, *La Penca: On Trial in Costa Rica*; Honey and Avirgan, *La Penca: Reporte de una investigación*; Honey, *Hostile Acts*.

2. Honey and Avirgan, *La Penca: Reporte de una investigación*, 92–100.

3. Avirgan and Honey, *La Penca: On Trial in Costa Rica*, 9–10.

4. Central Intelligence Agency, Office of the Inspector General, Investigations Staff, *Allegations of Connections between the CIA and the Contras in Cocaine Trafficking to the United States*, vol. 2, *The Contra Story*, Reports: "Other Individuals Involved in the Contra Program: John Floyd Hull," 11, https://www.cia.gov/library/reports/general-reports-1/cocaine/contra-story/other.html.

5. Quoted in Honey, *Hostile Acts*, 566n90.

6. Ibid., 273.

7. Draper, *A Very Thin Line*, 352–354, 362–363, 443, 530–534.

8. Robert Parry, *Lost History: Contras, Cocaine, the Press, and "Project Truth"* (Arlington, VA: Media Consortium, 1999), 133.

9. Lawrence E. Walsh, *Firewall: The Iran-Contra Conspiracy and Cover-Up* (New York: W.W. Norton, 1997), 531.

10. Honey, *Hostile Acts*, 25–46; Scott and Marshall, *Cocaine Politics*, 137–139, 157–159. A significant part of the blame, in Honey and Avirgan's view, lay with lead prosecution attorney Daniel Sheehan, who insisted on arguing a sensational but more difficult to prove RICO case rather than focusing on the Reagan administration's illegal proxy war against Nicaragua. Honey, *Hostile Acts*, 44–45.

11. Edward J. Boyer, "Drug Trafficker Gets Life Plus 240 Years in U.S. Agent's Killing," *Los Angeles Times*, 27 October 1988; Kim Murphy, "Contra-Drugs Link Called 'Fantasy,'" *Los Angeles Times*, 31 August 1988; "Trial Opens in Death of Tortured Drug Agent," *New York Times*, 31 July 1988.

12. "Edward Rafeedie, 1929–2008," obituary, *Los Angeles Times*, 30 March 2008; Hon. Edward Rafeedie, United States District Court, Central California, FindLaw/Lawyer Profile, 28 April 2007, http://pview.findlaw.com/view/2427065_1.

13. Henry Weinstein, "Opening Volleys in Camarena Case Trial: Prosecutors Say They Will Show Agent's Murder Was Part of a Campaign to 'Intimidate the DEA,'" *Los Angeles Times*, 16 May 1990.

14. United States District Court for the Central District of California, Case No. CR 87-422(F)-ER, vol. 13, Reporters' Transcript of Proceedings, 6 June 1990, 136–137.

15. Henry Weinstein, "Official Mexico Corruption Blasted: Drug Cartel Called 'Beyond Reach of Law,'" *Press Democrat* (Santa Rosa, California), 12 July 1990, B4; Carlos Puig, "Según la fiscalía de Los Angeles, García Paniagua estuvo en una junta en que se decidió secuestrar a Camarena," *Proceso*, 7 May 1990, 26–27; Carlos Puig, "La DEA se anima a extender el juicio a acusados del caso Camarena," *Proceso*, 24 September 1990, 31; Lawrence Victor Harrison, interviews with authors, Riverside, California, 28 March 2007 and 17 June 2009.

16. Henry Weinstein, "Judge Is Asked to Turn Over Papers or Quit Case: Lawyers for a Mexican Businessman Accused of Plotting to Kill Drug Agent Enrique Camarena Say They Have a Right to See Secretly Filed Documents," *Los Angeles Times*, 12 February 1990.

17. Mitchell, Silberberg & Knupp, Interoffice Memorandum, File No. 22958-1-8, Document No. BMC_M010, BMC, 4 June 1990, Brian M Colligan to Zuno Team re. Interview Tape of Victor [sic] Lawrence Harrison, 2 pp. plus attachment.

18. Henry Weinstein, "Judge Overrules Bid to Link CIA, Drug Lords in Camarena Trial," *Los Angeles Times*, 8 June 1990; Henry Weinstein, "Witness Who Tied CIA to Traffickers Must Testify Anew," *Los Angeles Times*, 6 July 1990.

19. United States District Court for the Central District of California, Case No: CR 87-422(F)-ER, vol. 14, Reporters' Transcript of Proceedings, 7 June 1990, 213–238.

20. Lawrence Victor Harrison, interviews with authors, Riverside, California, 23 March 2006, and Hemet, California, 11 March 2010.

21. Lawrence Victor Harrison, interview with authors, Riverside, California, 18 June 2009.

22. United States District Court for the Central District of California, Case No. CR 87-422(F)-ER, vol. 26, Reporter's Transcript of Proceedings, 6 July 1990, 114–115.

23. Ibid., 116, 144–145.

24. Lawrence Victor Harrison, phone conversation with Russell H. Bartley, 25 April 2005; Lawrence Victor Harrison, interview with authors, Hemet, California, 11 March 2010.

25. Lawrence Victor Harrison, interview with authors, Riverside, California, 23 March 2006.

26. Henry Weinstein, "Witness Says Drug Lord Told of Contra Arms," *Los Angeles Times*, 7 July 1990. See also, e.g., "Witness Testifies Drug Lord Supplied Arms to Contras," *Oakland Tribune*, 7 July 1990, A4; and Henry Weinstein, "'Everyone I Met' Is Corrupt: Informant Tells Drug Tales at Camarena Trial," *Press Democrat* (Santa Rosa, California), 7 June 1990, B7.

27. William Branigin, "Trial in Camarena Case Shows DEA Anger at CIA," *Washington Post*, 16 July 1990, A1.

28. Ibid., A1, A16.

29. Lawrence Victor Harrison, interview with authors, Riverside, California, 23 March 2006.

30. Edward M. Medvene and Kenneth M. Miller, joint interview with authors, West Lake, California, 14 February 2008.

31. Jesús Blancornelas, "Autoridades mexicanas: Se hacen como que no oyen," *Zeta* online, Edición 1690, photocopy in BBCF, carton 2, Personality files: Blancornelas.

32. Fredric N. Tulsky, "Evidence Casts Doubt on Camarena Case Trials," *Los Angeles Times*, 26 October 1997, A23; Michael J. Lightfoot, interview with authors, Los Angeles, California, 10 November 1998. Lightfoot confirmed in this interview that then Puebla governor Manuel Bartlett Díaz intended to seek nomination as the PRI presidential candidate in the 2000 elections.

33. Names in brackets are redacted in the copy of the document from which these excerpts were taken.

34. United States Department of Justice, Drug Enforcement Administration, DEA-6 Report of Investigation by S/A Salvador Leyva and G/S Hector G. Berrellez, Los Angeles, California, 9 April 1992, http://reneverdugo.org/pdf/RelatedCases/ZunoArce/ZunoTrialWitnesses.pdf.

35. United States District Court for the Central District of California, Case No: CR 87-422(F)-ER, vol. 13, Reporters' Transcript of Proceedings, 6 June 1990, p. 191, and Reporter's Partial Transcript of Proceedings, 7 December 1992, 55–56.

36. Jim Newton, "Camarena's Abduction and Torture Described: Former Bodyguard Says Ranking Mexican Officials Were at the House Where U.S. Drug Agent Was Killed," *Los Angeles Times*, 10 December 1992; Jim Newton, "Testimony Links Mexican Officials to Agent's Death: Trial; Cabinet Members Helped Plot Camarena Murder, Informant Says; Mexico Denounces Accusation," *Los Angeles Times*, 9 December 1992.

37. Quoted in Tulsky, "Evidence Casts Doubt on Camarena Case Trials," A22.

38. Quoted in ibid.

39. Ibid., A23.

40. David Rosenzweg, "Camarena Case Witness Recants Allegations, U.S. Says," *Los Angeles Times*, 6 February 1998.

41. Hernández López, *Zorrilla*, 81–83.

42. "Passings: Ruben Zuno Arce," *Los Angeles Times*, 20 September 2012.

CHAPTER 12. ON DOWN THE RABBIT HOLE

1. For a fully documented account of these events, see Gary Webb, *Dark Alliance: The CIA, the Contras, and the Crack Cocaine Explosion*, rev. paperback ed., foreword by U.S. congresswoman Maxine Waters (New York: Seven Stories Press, 1999).

2. Ibid., 384–385.

3. Ibid., 385–386.

4. Ibid., 386–387.

5. Victor Merina, "Judge Slaps Gag Order on Trials of 7 Deputies," *Los Angeles Times*, 24 October 1990.

6. Webb, *Dark Alliance*, rev. ed., 387.

7. Marjorie Miller and Jim Newton, "Defendant Freed in Camarena Case: Efforts to Keep Dr. Humberto Alvarez Machain in Los Angeles Fail; Mexican Officials Hail His Release," *Los Angeles Times*, 16 December 1992; Henry Weinstein, "DEA Operative Details His Role in Kidnaping: He Says He Arranged the Abduction of Mexican Doctor with U.S. Agent's Approval," *Los Angeles Times*, 28 April 1990.

8. Miller and Newton, "Defendant Freed in Camarena Case"; Carlos Salinas de Gortari, *México: Un paso difícil a la modernidad* (Barcelona: Plaza & Janés Editores, 2000), 62–63.

9. Salinas de Gortari, *México*, 62–63, 140–141, 358–370. Like virtually all political memoirs, this account of the Salinas *sexenio* is self-serving. In recounting the Álvarez Machín affair, Salinas presents himself as a steadfast defender of Mexico's national interest. "The attitude we adopted in this delicate matter," he writes, "proved empirically that there was nothing to the supposed subordination of our country's policy decisions to the wishes of Washington. During my administration, when Americans at any level sought to violate basic principles, we responded accordingly, no matter how significant the negotiations nor the possible repercussions of our actions" (141). More significantly, Salinas recognizes the recurrent problem of Mexican officials pursuing agendas counter to presidential policy, often in collusion with their American counterparts or other agents of the U.S. government.

10. Rafael Loret de Mola, *Las entrañas del poder: Secretos de campaña* (Mexico City: Grijalbo, 1991), 157–158.

11. Rafael Loret de Mola, *Denuncia: Presidente sin palabra*, rev. ed. (Mexico City: Grijalbo, 1995), 35–78.

12. For discussion of the history of the military-civilian relationship in Mexican politics, see Navarro, *Political Intelligence*, 79–120. See also Centeno, *Democracy within Reason*, 47–51. For an account of later-twentieth-century military-civilian tensions by an informed, well-connected Mexican journalist, see Rafael Loret de Mola, *Los escándalos: Un ensayo donde los culpables de los desórdenes políticos tienen nombre y apellido* (Mexico City: Grijalbo, 1999), 91–99.

13. His son Rafael posthumously published the book, based on a second copy of the manuscript recovered from Loret's personal papers, as Carlos Loret de Mola, *Que la nación me lo demande* (Mexico City: Grijalbo, 1986). It appeared just two months after the author's unresolved death, with a final chapter by the son recounting the circumstances of his father's violent demise and the blatant inconsistencies in the official account of a single-vehicle accident.

14. Rafael Loret de Mola, "El 'accidente,'" chapter 10 of Carlos Loret de Mola, *Que la nación me lo demande*, 2nd ed. (Mexico City: Grijalbo, 1986), 204. All citations are to the 2nd edition (published in the same year as the 1st edition). The following account of Carlos Loret's demise is drawn from both this chapter and Rafael Loret's later book *Denuncia: Presidente sin palabra*.

15. Had his father's Mercedes driven off the road, Rafael Loret reasoned, it would have become momentarily airborne and, attaining greater velocity, proceeded farther down the steep slope. A seventy-kilogram boulder that he and Antonio Nogueda rolled off the edge of the precipice came to a rest in virtually the same spot as the wrecked automobile.

16. Aguayo Quezada, *La charola*, 244–246.

17. Ibid.; Rafael Loret de Mola, *Denuncia: Presidente sin palabra*, 233.

18. Rafael Loret de Mola, *Denuncia: Presidente sin palabra*, 233.

19. Lawrence Victor Harrison, interview with authors, Riverside, California, 23 March 2006. Manuel Buendía and Enrique Camarena, Harrison told us, were killed because of what they had learned about the Nicaraguan *contras*, the CIA, and Mexican drug traffickers; Carlos Loret de Mola was killed "because he had challenged President Miguel de la Madrid." As Harrison summarized it, "The army kills on behalf of the president. DFS [Gobernación] kills for reasons of national security."

20. Rafael Loret de Mola, *Denuncia: Presidente sin palabra*, 35–38.

21. Mexican sociologist and former presidential adviser Jorge Bustamante recounted for us an occasion a few weeks prior to Rafael Loret de Mola's meeting with the ex-president in which, at a small dinner affair in his honor offered by former close associates, de la Madrid lamented in similar terms his administration's failure to resolve the Manuel Buendía case. Jorge A. Bustamante, interview with authors, South Bend, Indiana, 7 April 1989.

22. Rafael Loret de Mola, *Denuncia: Presidente sin palabra*, 218.

23. Ibid., 219–220.

24. Ibid., 217–218, 220–221.

25. Rafael Loret de Mola, *Manos sucias: Crónicas verdaderas del poder* (Mexico City: Océano, 1996), 191. On Loret's 1991 Spanish exile, see 192–205.

26. Rafael Loret de Mola, *Denuncia: Presidente sin palabra*, 231–232.

27. Ibid., ten-image photographic section between pages 214 and 215.

28. Ibid., 74–75, 229.

29. José Francisco Ruiz Massieu served as governor of Guerrero from 1987 to 1993, then moved back into the federal government and, as former brother-in-law and continuing close associate of President Salinas, quickly rose to positions of influence within the PRI, serving simultaneously as general secretary of the party's National Executive Committee and coordinator of the majority PRI representation in the national Chamber of Deputies. On 28 September 1994, as he was about to start his parked vehicle following a meeting with his congressional colleagues, he was shot and killed by a lone gunman. The previous March, PRI presidential candidate Luis Donaldo Colosio had been gunned down at an open-air campaign event in Tijuana, Baja California, which opened the door to Colosio's campaign manager, Ernesto Zedillo, who would in turn oversee the PRI's final spiral from political hegemony and, for the first time since the Mexican Revolution, admit an opposition party to the presidency.

30. Rafael Loret de Mola, *Denuncia: Presidente sin palabra*, 229–230.

31. Ibid., 231–232.

32. Ibid., 226–227.

33. Loret de Mola, *Los escándalos*, 174. There were multiple phone conversations between Berréllez, Gárate Bustamante, and Rafael Loret de Mola, all of them apparently recorded by Loret and turned over to Mexican federal judicial authorities. This particular conversation has been reproduced, with some editorial modification but essentially identical content, in two other books by the same author: *Denuncia: Presidente sin palabra*; and, in its most complete version, *Manos sucias*, 85–89.

34. Ángel Buendía Téllez Girón, interview with authors, Guadalajara, Mexico, 11 March 1992; Russell H. Bartley, "El asesinato de Manuel Buendía Tellezgirón (Ciudad de México, 30/V/84): Síntesis de una investigación," February 1992, BBCF, Carton 1, folder: Buendía case, Miscellaneous background & contextual materials (hereafter Bartley, "Síntesis de investigación").

35. Sergio René de Dios, "Ángel Buendía acusa: 'Estoy convencido de que fue la CIA la que ordenó el asesinato de mi hermano,'" *Jalisco Hoy*, 24 May 1993, 6–9.

36. Ángel Buendía, phone conversation with Russell H. Bartley, 13 April 1994; Á. Buendía, *Mi testimonio*, 186.

37. Lionel Martin, *The Early Fidel: Roots of Castro's Communism* (Secaucus, NJ: Lyle Stuart, 1978), 9.

38. Russell H. Bartley to Ivan Jaksič, Director, Center for Latin America, University of Wisconsin–Milwaukee, Final Report on Center-supported research trip, 13 April 1992; Sylvia E. Bartley, 1991–92 calendar book notes.

39. Russell H. Bartley to Fidel Castro Ruz, letter, 7 November 1995, BBCF, Carton 2, folder: Castro Ruz, Fidel; Lawrence Victor Harrison, phone conversation with Russell H. Bartley, 1 September 2005.

40. Miguel Ángel Sánchez de Armas, interview, Mexico City, 23 March 1992.

41. Bartley, "El caso Buendía," 12–17.

42. Á. Buendía, *Mi testimonio*, 7–8.

CHAPTER 13. BY MUTUAL CONSENT

Chapter epigraph: L. Fletcher Prouty, *The Secret Team: The CIA and Its Allies in Control of the United States and the World* (New York: Skyhorse Publishing, 2008), xxiii, 212. As a colonel in the U.S. Air Force, Prouty served from 1955 to 1963 as liaison officer between the Pentagon and the CIA, in which capacity he was responsible for coordinating operations between the agency and the military.

1. Russell H. Bartley to Edward M. Medvene, letter, 28 April 1993.

2. Rogelio Hernández López, "Protege la DEA a los secuestradores de Macháin," *Excélsior*, 23 October 1990, 1, 17; "Preparan en la DEA la tercera fase de la Operación Leyenda," *Excélsior*, 24 October 1990, 1, 26, 39; "'Seguro: No seremos extraditados'; Confía la DEA en nosotros; Gárate y Héctor Berréllez," *Excélsior*, 25 October 1990, 1, 22; "Planea la DEA detener a más mexicanos," *Excélsior*, 26 October 1990, 1, 28, 43.

3. Hernández López, "'Seguro,'" 22.

4. Ibid.

5. While there was ample reason to suspect that Lawrence Harrison was an ex-CIA agent, at the time Rogelio Hernández wrote his *Excélsior* series there was no available documentary or testimonial evidence on which to base that assertion. Two decades later Lawrence Harrison continued to hold Hernández in the deepest, most abiding contempt. We were never able to pin him down as to precisely why he was so negatively disposed toward Hernández but must assume that, at least in part, it was owing to Hernández's uninformed defaming of his character in *Excélsior*. In a puzzling twist we have not been able to clarify, Harrison repeatedly insisted to us that Rogelio Hernández was in league with Miguel Aldana Ibarra, a former Mexican Federal Judicial Police commander and director of Mexico's INTERPOL office and one of two senior Mexican officials indicted by a U.S. federal grand jury as coconspirators in the Camarena case. (The other was Manuel Ibarra Herrera, a former Federal Judicial Police director.) Harrison assured us that Hernández was Aldana's point man in the latter's unsuccessful attempt to purchase *Excélsior* in 2003. On the *Excélsior* sale, see Gerardo Israel Montes, "Liquidaciones pendientes en Excélsior: Desacuerdo interno por los montos de las indemnizaciones," *Revista Zócalo*, January 2003.

6. Eduardo "El Buho" Valle, phone conversation with Russell H. Bartley, 3 April 1996.

7. Ibid.

8. Mylène Sauloy and Yves Le Bonniec, *À qui profite la cocaïne?* (Mesnil-sur-l'Estrée, France: Calmann-Lévy, 1992), 211.

9. Ibid., 212; Branigin, "Trial in Camarena Case Shows DEA Anger at CIA," A16.

10. Sauloy and Le Bonniec, *À qui profite la cocaïne?*, 212–213.

11. Rogelio Hernández López, "Ellos, nos escondieron la verdad," in Á. Buendía, *Mi testimonio*, 15–40.

12. Jorge Fernández Menéndez, *Narcotráfico y poder* (Mexico City: Rayuela Editores, 1999).

13. Ibid., 24.

14. Russell H. Bartley to Edward M. Medvene, letter, 14 February 1995.

15. BBCF, carton 3, folder: Harrison-related documents from MS&K.

16. Mitchell, Silberberg & Knupp, Interoffice Memorandum, File No. 22958-1-8 (27 November 1990), Debra Robins to Zuno Team re. Conversation with Congressman McCandless' Administrative Aide, BBCF, carton 3, folder: Harrison-related documents from MS&K.

17. Mitchell, Silberberg & Knupp, Interoffice Memorandum, File No. EMM_M004.ZUN, Document No. 22958-1-8 (3 September 1992), Edward Medvene to File, cc. Jim Blancarte, Mary Fulginiti, Ron DiNicola, Jack Luellen, Mary Fitzgerald, re. Zuno—status of various tasks, BBCF, carton 3, folder: Harrison-related documents from MS&K.

18. Mary Fulginiti, Jeffer, Mangels, Butler & Marmaro (Los Angeles, California), Memorandum to Zuno Team re. Lorenzo Harrison (10 October 1992), 1, BBCF, carton 3, folder: Harrison-related documents from MS&K.

19. Lawrence Victor Harrison, interviews with authors, Riverside, California, 15 April 2005 and 17 June 2009.

20. Mitchell, Silberberg & Knupp, Interoffice Memorandum, File No. 22958-1-8, Document No. BMC_M010, BMC (4 June 1990), Brian M. Colligan to Zuno Team re. Interview Tape of Victor [sic] Lawrence Harrison, BBCF, carton 3, folder: Harrison-related documents from MS&K.

21. Ibid.

22. Lawrence Victor Harrison DEA debriefings, BBCF, archival ring binder 3.

23. Manú Dornbierer, *La guerra de las drogas: Historia y testimonios de un negocio político*, 4th ed. (Mexico City: Grijalbo, 1993); Loret de Mola, *Denuncia: Presidente sin palabra*; Loret de Mola, *Manos sucias*; Loret de Mola, *Secretos de Estado: Narcotraficantes, narcopolicías . . . y una narcoguerra avivada por un tratado comercial y unas elecciones* (Mexico City: Grijalbo, 1994); Francisco Martínez de la Vega, *Personajes* (Mexico City: Océano, 1986); Julio Scherer García, *Estos años: Con una cierta mirada* (Mexico City: Océano, 1995); Eduardo Valle, *El segundo disparo: La narcodemocracia mexicana* (Mexico City: Océano, 1995); Felipe Victoria Zepeda, *Lo que me dijo Abraham Polo Uscanga: Confidencias antes de su muerte* (Mexico City: EDAMEX, 1995).

24. Rafael Loret de Mola, interview with authors, Mexico City, 17 March 1996.

25. Ángel Buendía, interview with authors, Guadalajara, 10 March 1996.

26. Á. Buendía, *Mi testimonio*, 68–70.

27. Universidad Autónoma de Guadalajara, *Reseña Histórica de la Universidad Autónoma de Guadalajara*, http://campusdigital.uag.mx/varios/resena.php (the official online history of the UAG); Scott Anderson and Jon Lee Anderson, *Inside the League: The Shocking Exposé of How Terrorists, Nazis, and Latin American Death Squads Have Infiltrated the World Anti-Communist League* (New York: Dodd, Mead, 1986), 71–81.

28. Universidad Autónoma de Guadalajara, "La Educación y la Justicia Social en la Filosofía de la UAG," *Reseña Histórica de la Universidad Autónoma de Guadalajara*, http://campusdigital.uag.mx/varios/laeduca.php.

29. Universidad Autónoma de Guadalajara, "Principales logros del Plan Maestro de Desarrollo," *Reseña Histórica de la Universidad Autónoma de Guadalajara*, 3, http://www.uag.mx/201/principales.htm.

30. Manuel Buendía, "Los secreteros," *Excélsior*, 5 April 1984; "Los juramentados," *Excélsior*, 6 April 1984; and "Dios, ¿fascista?," *Excélsior*, 9 April 1984; all reprinted in Buendía, *La ultraderecha*, 159–167.

31. Manuel Buendía, "Lo que pasa en la UAG," *El Día*, 31 May 1976, reprinted in Buendía, *La ultraderecha*, 61–62.

32. Manuel Buendía, "Colima, Fuhrer," *Excélsior*, 18 November 1983, reprinted in Buendía, *La ultraderecha*, 153.

33. Manuel Buendía, "Sucia intriga," *Excélsior*, 24 January 1984, reprinted in Buendía, *La ultraderecha*, 157–159.

34. Anderson and Anderson, *Inside the League*, 78–79.

35. Raymundo Guerrero Guerrero's ideological influence on the UAG is reflected by the fact that he figures prominently in the list of sources provided at the end of its official online history, where two tracts of political philosophy by him are cited: "Pensamiento y acción de la Universidad Autónoma de Guadalajara" (1954) and "El pensamiento político de la U.A.G." (n.d.), both in *Reseña Histórica de la Universidad Autónoma de Guadalajara*, http://campusdigital.uag.mx/varios/bibliogr.php.

36. Anderson and Anderson, *Inside the League*, 79.

37. Ibid., xv–xvi, 79.

38. Manuel Buendía, "Quintacolumnistas," *Excélsior*, 7 October 1983; "Somocistas, aquí," *Excélsior*, 14 November 1983, both reprinted in Buendía, *La ultraderecha*, 145–146.

39. Buendía, "Quintacolumnistas," 144.

40. Ibid., 143–144.

41. Ibid., 143–145.

42. Lawrence Victor Harrison, interview with authors, Riverside, California, 17 June 2009.

43. Russell H. Bartley to Edward M. Medvene, memo re. Antonio Gárate Bustamante et al., 24 March 1996, BBCF, carton 1, folder: Medvene, Edward M.

44. Ibid.; Terry Reed and John Cummings, *Compromised: Clinton, Bush, and the CIA* (New York: S.P.I. Books, 1994), 237–326.

45. Bartley to Medvene, memo re. Antonio Gárate Bustamante et al., 6.

46. Prouty, *Secret Team*, xxiii–xxiv.

47. Lawrence Victor Harrison, phone conversation with Russell H. Bartley, 25 April 2005.

48. Lawrence Victor Harrison, phone conversation with Russell H. Bartley, 1 September 2006.

49. Kathleen Anne Henson (née Davis), interview with authors, Las Vegas, Nevada, 9 November 2009.

50. Lawrence Victor Harrison, interview with authors, Riverside, California, 18 June 2009.

51. Lawrence Victor Harrison to Querido Profe [Russell H. Bartley] , e-mail, 23 January 2010. Some of Harrison's recollections of his Cummings ancestors' contributions to the Church of the Nazarene in Pasadena and elsewhere in Southern California are embellished; e.g., his maternal grandfather did not found either the Pasadena Nazarene College or the Bresee Avenue Nazarene Church. What is significant here, however, is not misremembered facts but rather the emotion with which Harrison recalls a qualitatively real experience from his formative childhood years.

52. Roy Henson, conversation with authors, Riverside County Regional Medical Center, Moreno Valley, California, 7 March 2010.

53. Robert Baer, *See No Evil: The True Story of a Ground Soldier in the CIA's War on Terrorism* (New York: Three Rivers Press, 2003), 13–23.

54. Henry A. Crumpton, *The Art of Intelligence: Lessons from a Life in the CIA's Clandestine Service* (New York: Penguin, 2012), 21–23.

55. Lawrence Victor Harrison, interview with authors, Hemet, California, 12 November 2009.

56. Kathleen Anne Henson, interview with authors, Las Vegas, Nevada, 9 November 2009.

57. Tom Wolfe, *The Electric Kool-Aid Acid Test* (1968; repr., New York: Picador, 2004).

58. William Benemann, archivist, Law School Archives, University of California, Berkeley, interview with authors, Berkeley, California, 1 March 2012; William Benemann to Russell and Sylvia Bartley, letter, 12 March 2012. Benemann wrote, "As promised, I checked the facebooks for both Lawrence Victor Harrison and George Marshall Davis, and—as expected—I found

nothing. If he merely audited classes, he would not under normal circumstances show up in official records such as the facebook." The facebook collection is restricted and not open to the public. Had it existed, Benemann reiterated, "I would not have been able to supply a copy of his photograph—but in any event, the issue is moot."

59. Lawrence Victor Harrison, interview with authors, Riverside, California, 15 April 2005.

60. Robert Sanders, "Memorial service Jan. 25 for the late Kenneth Pitzer, former chemistry dean at UC Berkeley and past president of Rice and Stanford Universities," news release, 8 January 1998, http://www.berkeley.edu/news /media/releases/98legacy/01_08_98a.html.

61. United States Department of Justice, Federal Bureau of Investigation, Identification Division, Master File 3276/brb 8-3-9, p. 2, BBCF, carton 3, Harrison-related documents from MS&K (Zuno Arce).

62. Agee, *Inside the Company*, 44–45.

63. Lawrence Victor Harrison, interview with authors, Riverside, California, 23 March 2006; George C. McGhee, *On the Front Line of the Cold War: An Ambassador Reports* (Westport, CT: Praeger, 1997), 114.

64. Agee, *Inside the Company*, 49–97.

65. Lawrence Victor Harrison, interviews with authors, Riverside, California, 15 April 2005 and 23 March 2006.

66. Lawrence Victor, interview with authors, San Dimas, California, 14 May 2004.

67. Baer, *See No Evil*, 30–31.

68. Lawrence Victor Harrison, interview with authors, Riverside, California, 23 March 2006.

69. Crumpton, *Art of Intelligence*, 27–28.

70. McGhee, *On the Front Line*; Truman Presidential Museum and Library, "Oral History Interview with George C. McGhee," http://www.trumanlibrary.org/oralhist/mcgheeg.htm; Society of Exploration Geophysicists Virtual Geoscience Center, Biographies: George C. McGhee, http://www.mssu.edu/SEG-VM/bio_george_c_mcghee.html.

71. Lawrence Victor Harrison, phone conversation with Russell H. Bartley, 31 March 2010.

72. McGhee, *On the Front Line*, 183; Ranelagh, *The Agency*, 288–296.

73. Lawrence Victor Harrison, interview with authors, Riverside, California, 23 March 2006.

74. McGhee, *On the Front Line*, 114.

75. Ibid., 143–144.

76. Weiner, *Legacy of Ashes*, 306.

Chapter 14. Alien Terrain

1. Mexico, Procuraduría General de la República, Fiscalía Especial para Movimientos Sociales y Políticos del Pasado, *Informe Histórico a la Sociedad Mexicana* (Mexico City: Procuraduría General de la República, 2006).

2. Kevin Sullivan, "Mexican Vows Investigation into 'Dirty War': Military to Be Focus of Probe of Killings, Disappearances," *Washington Post*, 27 January 2002, A25.

3. Gustavo Castillo García and Javier Valdez, "Hay suficientes pruebas para consignar a Nazar Haro, afirma Carrillo Prieto: La fiscalía sobre desaparecidos políticos lo cita a declarar para el seis de febrero," *La Jornada*, 1 February 2003, http://www.jornada.unam.mx/2003/feb03/030201/015n1pol.php?printver=1; Olga R. Rodriguez, "Mexico Arrests Ex-Spy Chief in '75 Kidnapping: Former Official Accused in 'Dirty War' Disappearance of Leftist," *San Francisco Chronicle*, 20 February 2004, A2; Associated Press, "Security Chief during Mexico's 'Dirty War' Dies," *Miami Herald*, 27 January 2012.

4. Sullivan, "Mexican Vows Investigation into 'Dirty War'"; Sue Fox, "Mexico Moves on Rights Probe," *Chicago Tribune*, 6 January 2002.

5. Mexico, "Informe Histórico a la Sociedad Mexicana," 19.

6. Ibid., 19–20.

7. Blanche Petrich Moreno, "The Long Arm of the War on Drugs: WikiLeaks Cables Reveal How Much Washington Drives Mexico's Counternarcotics Policies," *The Nation*, 13 August 2012, 17–22.

8. Aguayo Quezada, *La charola*, 93–94.

9. Ibid., 91.

10. Ibid., 92–94.

11. Mexico, "Informe Histórico a la Sociedad Mexicana," 6. See also Sullivan, "Mexican Vows Investigation into 'Dirty War.'"

12. Mexico, "Informe Histórico a la Sociedad Mexicana," 427–428.

13. Lawrence Victor Harrison, interview with authors, Riverside, California, 18 June 2009.

14. Lawrence Victor Harrison, phone conversation with Russell H. Bartley, 4 May 2012.

15. Kornbluh, *The Pinochet File*, 341–346.

16. From the now extensive literature on the United States' role in state-sponsored terrorism in Latin America and elsewhere around the world, the following references provide a basic introduction: Grandin, *Empire's Workshop*, especially chapter 3, "Going Primitive: The Violence of the New Imperialism," 87–120; A. J. Langguth, *Hidden Terror* (New York: Pantheon, 1978); Penny Lernoux, *Cry of the People: United States Involvement in the Rise of Fascism, Torture, and Murder and the Persecution of the Catholic Church in Latin America* (Garden City, NY: Doubleday, 1980); McClintock, *Instruments of Statecraft*; and Theodore Shackley, *The Third Option: An American View of Counterinsurgency Operations* (New York: Dell, 1981).

17. Mexico, "Informe Histórico a la Sociedad Mexicana," 282.

18. Ibid., 44–45.

19. Ibid., 46–48.

20. Agee, *Inside the Company*, 556–557.

21. Eric Hobsbawm, *The Age of Extremes: A History of the World, 1914–1991* (New York: Pantheon, 1994), 298.

22. John Ross, *El Monstruo: Dread and Redemption in Mexico City* (New York: Nation Books, 2009), 242.

23. A decade later, mired in another theater of the hemisphere's "dirty war," Argentina's military junta would stage a similar event for identical reasons when it hosted the 1978 World Cup soccer championship. "How can you play soccer in a concentration camp?" asked a protest poster ironically displayed in a Mexico City store window. The pointed question was illustrated with a soccer ball in the form of a human skull.

24. Mexico, "Informe Histórico a la Sociedad Mexicana," 457.

25. United States Department of Justice, Drug Enforcement Administration, DEA-6 Report of Investigation by S/A Manuel R. Martínez and G/S Hector Berréllez, transcript of recorded interview, 25 September 1989, 3.

26. Lawrence Victor Harrison, interview with authors, Riverside, California, 18 June 2009.

27. Bob Woodward, *Veil: The Secret Wars of the CIA, 1981–1987* (New York: Simon & Schuster, 1987), 466–467.

28. Duane R. Clarridge, with Digby Diehl, *A Spy for All Seasons: My Life in the CIA* (New York: Scribner, 1997), 311.

29. John Rizzo, *Company Man: Thirty Years of Controversy and Crisis in the CIA* (New York: Scribner, 2014), 104–106.

30. Woodward, *Veil*, 345.

31. Draper, *A Very Thin Line*, 15–26; Clarridge, *Spy for All Seasons*, 279–280.

32. Manuel Buendía, "CIA: Directorio," Red Privada, *Excélsior*, 19 January 1981, in Buendía, *La CIA en México*, 146–150. Ex-CIA officer Philip Agee was the first to expose agency personnel in his book *Inside the Company*, and others followed. The seventy-nine names published by Buendía dated from 1968 and were taken from a *Who's Who in the CIA* sent to him by someone with the German news agency Deutsche Presse-Agentur (DPA) as "a gift from Father Noel" (Santa Claus).

33. See, e.g., Hunter, *No Simple Proxy*.

34. Ben-Menashe, *Profits of War*, 104–105.

35. Hunter, *No Simple Proxy*, 44–48.

36. Lawrence Victor Harrison, interview with authors, Riverside, California, 15 April 2005.

37. Ben-Menashe, *Profits of War*, 105, 161. See also Sauloy and Le Bonniec, *À qui profite la cocaïne?*, 195.

38. Lawrence Victor Harrison, interviews with authors, Riverside, California, 15 April 2005 and 18 June 2009, and San Dimas, California, 14 May 2004.

39. Aguayo Quesada, *La Charola*, 222; Shannon, *Desperados*, 112–114.

40. Lawrence Victor Harrison, testimony in United States Department of Justice, Drug Enforcement Administration, DEA-6 Report of Investigation, 25 September 1989, 11–12. See also Aguayo Quesada, *La charola*, 216–223.

41. Lawrence Victor Harrison, testimony in United States Department of Justice, Drug Enforcement Administration, DEA-6 Report of Investigation, 25 September 1989, 12.

42. Ibid., 10–11, 18–19.

43. Ibid., 17–19.

44. Lawrence Victor Harrison, interview with authors, Riverside, California, 18 June 2009.

45. Ibid.; Lawrence Victor Harrison, testimony in United States Department of Justice, Drug Enforcement Administration, DEA-6 Report of Investigation, 25 September 1989, 20–22.

46. Shannon, *Desperados*, 235, 260; Aguayo Quesada, *La charola*, 223.

47. Mexico, "Informe Histórico a la Sociedad Mexicana," 486.

48. S/A Wayne Schmidt, testimony in United States Department of Justice, Drug Enforcement Administration, DEA-6 Report of Investigation, 25 September 1989, 13 February 1990; United States District Court for the Central District of California, *United States of America, Plaintiff, v. Juan Ramon Matta-Ballesteros, Ruben Zuno Arce* et al., *Defendants*, Case No. CR 87-422(F)-ER, vol. 26, 6 July 1990, 66–68.

49. Court Reporter's Transcript of Proceedings, United States District Court for the Central District of California, *United States of America, Plaintiff, v. Juan Ramon Matta-Ballesteros, Ruben Zuno Arce* et al., *Defendants*, Case No. CR 87-422(F)-ER, vol. 26, 6 July 1990, 67, 85–86; Lawrence Victor Harrison, interviews with authors, Riverside, California, 18 June 2009, and Hemet, California, 11 March 2010.

50. Shannon, *Desperados*, 386–389.

51. Court Reporters' Transcript of Proceedings, United States District Court for the Central District of California, *United States of America, Plaintiff, v. Juan Ramon Matta-Ballesteros, Ruben Zuno Arce* et al., *Defendants*, Case No. CR 87-422(F)-ER, vol. 14, 7 June 1990, 62.

52. Lawrence Victor Harrison, phone conversation with Russell H. Bartley, 7 April 2004; Lawrence Victor Harrison, interviews with authors, San Dimas, California, 14 May 2004, and Riverside, California, 15 April 2005.

53. Amiram Nir was killed on the same day that Carlos Salinas de Gortari assumed the presidency of Mexico. For anyone inclined to find symbolism in significant events, Nir's death

could be viewed as the closing act of the de la Madrid administration or the inaugural act of the Salinas *sexenio*.

54. Ben-Menashe, *Profits of War*, 290.

55. Clarridge, *Spy for All Seasons*, 342.

56. Lawrence Victor Harrison, interview with authors, Riverside, California, 23 March 2006.

57. Lawrence Victor Harrison, interview with authors, Riverside, California, 28 March 2007; Lawrence Victor Harrison, phone conversation with Russell H. Bartley, 6 May 2010.

58. Court Reporters' Transcript of Proceedings, United States District Court for the Central District of California, *United States of America, Plaintiff, v. Juan Ramon Matta-Ballesteros, Ruben Zuno Arce* et al., *Defendants*, Case No. CR 87-422(F)-ER, vol. 13, 136–137; vol. 14, 71–72.

59. Webb, *Dark Alliance*, rev. ed., 205.

60. Nick Schou, *Kill the Messenger: How the CIA's Crack-Cocaine Controversy Destroyed Journalist Gary Webb*, introduction by Charles Bowden (New York: Nation Books, 2006), 118–119.

61. Webb, *Dark Alliance*, 1st ed., 17.

62. Charles Bowden, "The Pariah," *Esquire*, September 1998, 150–159, 180, 182.

63. Ibid., 159, 180.

64. Tulsky, "Evidence Casts Doubt on Camarena Case Trials."

65. Michael J. Lightfoot and Edward M. Medvene, luncheon meeting with authors, Los Angeles, 10 November 1998; John Brown, luncheon meeting with authors, Los Angeles, 11 November 1998.

66. Lawrence Victor Harrison, phone conversation with Russell H. Bartley, 7 April 2004.

CHAPTER 15. PROHIBITED CONVERSATIONS

1. Reed and Cummings, *Compromised*, 11.

2. For an excellent, well-documented summary account of the Mena affair and its subsequent cover-up, see Alexander Cockburn and Jeffrey St. Clair, *Whiteout: The CIA, Drugs, and the Press* (London: Verso, 1998), 317–346.

3. Barry Seal biography, *Spartacus Educational*, http://www.spartacus.schoolnet.co.uk/JFKseal.htm. Porter Goss served in the CIA's Latin America division during the 1960s, left the agency in the early 1970s to recover from a nearly fatal bacterial infection, and eventually gained a seat in Congress, as well as what *New York Times* reporter Tim Weiner has described as "a viceroy's dominion over the CIA as chairman of the House intelligence committee." Post-9/11 he became an outspoken critic of agency intelligence failures and, in 2004, was himself appointed DCI by President George W. Bush, only to be fired by Bush nineteen months later. Weiner, *Legacy of Ashes*, 499.

4. Reed and Cummings, *Compromised*, 183–187.

5. Ibid., 200–212.

6. Ibid., 10, 205.

7. Ibid., 220–222; Cockburn and St. Clair, *Whiteout*, 320–328.

8. Reed and Cummings, *Compromised*, 221, 240–241.

9. Ibid., 145–147; Cockburn and St. Clair, *Whiteout*, 327.

10. Reed and Cummings, *Compromised*, 221.

11. This was the same William P. Barr who replaced Richard Thornburgh as Attorney General during the George H. W. Bush administration (1989–1993). Barr had joined the CIA in 1973 and, although subsequently holding various executive branch appointments, remained an Agency man throughout his career in the federal government. It was Barr who in the first year of the Bush Sr. presidency drafted the legal opinion justifying the December 1989 invasion of Panama and the arrest of Panamanian president Manuel Noriega, a paid CIA asset. Reed, professionally

knowledgeable about and experienced in the dark world of intelligence and covert action, seriously wondered if the American invasion of Panama might not have been to cover up the CIA's narcotics trail from Colombia via the Isthmus, Central America, and Mexico to Arkansas, Florida, and other points in the continental United States.

12. Reed and Cummings, *Compromised*, 227.

13. Ibid., 149.

14. Ibid., 227–240, 278.

15. Ibid., 258–274.

16. Ibid., 318–327.

17. Richard J. Brenneke, Oral Deposition, taken on 21 June 1991 at the Arkansas State Attorney General's Office, 323 Center Street, Little Rock, Arkansas, to develop evidence for the use of independent counsel Lawrence E. Walsh in the Iran-Contra investigation, taken before Jeff Bennett, of Bushman Court Reporting, Inc., by Congressman William Alexander and Chief Deputy Attorney General for the State of Arkansas Chad Farris, http://www.idfiles.com/rbde po.htm.

18. Bowden, "Pariah," 154, 155.

19. Ibid., 157–158.

20. Webb, *Dark Alliance*, rev. ed., 317–327.

21. Bowden, "Pariah," 158.

22. We note with amusement the differing preferences for personal handguns expressed by Héctor Berréllez and Félix Rodríguez, two men with inflated images of themselves as intrepid fighters against the forces of evil. Whereas Rodríguez "felt naked" without his customized, black, polymer-housed, Glock 9 mm pistol with nickel-plated slide, "a gift from the *Presidente* of El Salvador" (Reed and Cummings, *Compromised*, 228), Berréllez considered the Glock "a sissy gun that only girls carried." They were made of "plastic," he said dismissively. "You can't hit anyone over the head with a Glock" (Bowden, "Pariah," 154).

23. The Mayo Group, International Forensic Investigations, Training and Security, 2005, 2007, http://www.themayogroup.net. As of mid-2012, this website was no longer active and The Mayo Group, Inc.'s corporate rights and privileges as a California domestic corporation had been suspended (http://california.14thstory.com/the-mayo-group-inc.html).

24. Charles Bowden to Russell H. Bartley, e-mail, 5 November 2010.

25. Ibid.; Charles Bowden, interview with authors, Tucson, Arizona, 18 February 2008. "You know [Héctor] and I were both raised in Tucson in the same era and pretty much have the same haunts in our past," Bowden wrote us. "The barrio that sent him into law enforcement also creates marines like a factory." Charles Bowden, e-mail to Russell H. Bartley, 27 April 2007.

26. IMDbPro, Biography for Hector Berrellez, 10 December 2009, http://www.imdb.com/name/nm3171195/bio.

27. Charles Bowden, interview with authors, Tucson, Arizona, 18 February 2008.

28. Lawrence Victor Harrison, interview with authors, Riverside, California, 15 April 2005.

29. Lawrence Victor Harrison, interview with authors, Riverside, California, 23 March 2006; Roy Henson, conversation with authors, Riverside County Regional Medical Center, Moreno Valley, California, 7 March 2010.

30. Charles Bowden, interview with authors, Tucson, Arizona, 18 February 2008; Lawrence Victor Harrison, phone conversation with Russell H. Bartley, 1 September 2006.

31. Russell Bartley to Lawrence Victor Harrison, letter, 30 April 2005.

32. Lawrence Victor Harrison, phone conversation with Russell H. Bartley, 25 April 2005.

33. Lawrence Victor Harrison, interview with authors, Riverside, California, 23 March 2006.

CHAPTER 16. EXTREME PREJUDICE

Chapter epigraph: Susan Lindauer, *Extreme Prejudice: The Terrifying Story of the Patriot Act and the Cover-Ups of 9/11 and Iraq* (Lexington, KY: Creative Space, 2010). This is an appalling account that was never supposed to have come to light of an American intelligence asset, run jointly by the CIA and the Pentagon's Defense Intelligence Agency, who was subsequently disavowed because of what she had learned about the run-up to 9/11 and the U.S. invasion of Iraq, then indicted as an alleged foreign agent and threatened with forced medication for purported mental illness as a means of permanently silencing her. Ultimately, a vigorous legal defense led to her acquittal on all charges, although the ad hominem assault to which she was subjected has effectively erased her story from public memory.

1. Russell H. Bartley, "The Piper Played to Us All: Orchestrating the Cultural Cold War in the USA, Europe, and Latin America," *International Journal of Politics, Culture, and Society* 14, no. 13 (Spring 2001): 571–619.

2. Lawrence Victor Harrison, phone conversation with Russell H. Bartley, 1 September 2006.

3. Jeff Guy, interview with authors, Riverside, California, 16 June 2009. This interview took place in Harrison's presence at his Riverside residence.

4. Charles Bowden to Russell H. Bartley, e-mail, 4 January 2013.

5. Charles Bowden, interviews with authors, Tucson, Arizona, 18 February 2008, and Yuma, Arizona, 14 April 2011.

6. El Güero is Héctor Luis Palma Salazar, a Sinaloa cartel kingpin.

7. On Calvi, see Rupert Cornwell, *"God's Banker"* (New York: Dodd, Mead, 1983).

8. Webb, *Dark Alliance*, rev. ed., 433–434.

9. L. V. Harrison–related real estate and California Bar Association matters, collected documents, BBCF, archival ring binder 4 (hereafter Harrison property/CalBar records).

10. Lawrence Victor Harrison, interviews with authors, Riverside, California, 16–17 June 2009.

11. California State Bar Court, Hearing Department-Los Angeles, Verified Answer of Lawrence V. Harrison to State Bar Charges, Case No. 06-0-13692, 06-0-13797, 06-0-14825 (21 July 2009); Superior Court of the State of California, County of San Diego, North County Division, *Lawrence V. Harrison* et al., *Plaintiffs, v. Peter Cimino* et al., *Defendants*, Case: RIC448947, Telephonic Deposition of Delia Rodriguez, Tuesday, 29 May 2007; Declaration of María Ibáñez, Riverside, California (7 April 2007); Declaration of Sandy Ibáñez, Riverside, California (7 April 2007), all in Harrison property/CalBar records.

12. Lawrence Victor Harrison, phone conversation with Russell H. Bartley, 14 March 2008.

13. Charles Bowden to Russell H. Bartley, e-mail, 10 June 2009.

14. Lawrence Victor Harrison, phone conversation with Russell H. Bartley, 10 June 2009.

15. Declaration of María Ibáñez, Riverside, California (7 April 2007), Harrison property/CalBar records.

16. Jeff Guy, interview with authors, Riverside, California, 16 June 2009.

17. SPI Security, http://ispisecurity.com/index2.php?option=com_contact&task=view&contact_id=1&Itemid=3&pop=1 (no longer active).

18. Lawrence Victor Harrison, interview with authors, Riverside, California, 16 June 2009.

19. Lawrence Victor Harrison, interview with authors, Riverside, California, 17 June 2009.

20. Lawrence Victor Harrison to Russell H. Bartley, e-mail, 28 July 2009.

21. Bartley, *Imperial Russia*; Allan Nelson, *The Nelson Brothers: Finnish-American Radicals from the Mendocino Coast*, edited and introduced by Russell Bartley and Sylvia Bartley (Ukiah, CA: Mendocino County Historical Society, 2005); Eduardo Galeano, *Espejos: Una historia casi*

universal (Madrid: Siglo XXI de España, 2008). We also shared with Harrison a short study we had produced on some northern California coal deposits as an example of our special interest in geology and paleontology, or what we described to him as "deep history." On one occasion earlier on in our relationship, when he was still trying to figure out who we really were, he told us that he had had a dream about Russell, that in it he "was a captain marching up a mountain with a compass." "Well," Russell had replied, "I am a geologist and I do have a compass and I do climb hills, but I have never held rank of any kind outside the academic world."

22. Lawrence Victor Harrison to Russell H. Bartley, e-mail, 23 January 2010.

23. Lawrence Victor Harrison to Russell H. Bartley, e-mail, 6 February 2010.

24. Russell H. Bartley to Lawrence Victor Harrison, e-mail, 6 February 2010.

25. Lawrence Victor Harrison to Russell H. Bartley, e-mail, 6 February 2010.

26. Russell H. Bartley to Lawrence Victor Harrison, e-mail, 8 February 2010.

27. Kathleen Anne Henson, interview with authors, Las Vegas, Nevada, 9 November 2009.

28. State Bar of California, State Bar Court, Hearing Department—Los Angeles, In the Matter of: Lawrence Victor Harrison, No. 202689, a member of the State Bar, Case Nos. 06-O-13792, 06-O-13797, 06-O-14825, filed 29 June 2009.

29. Charles "Chuck" Jones, phone conversation with Russell H. Bartley, 12 November 2009.

30. State Bar of California, State Bar Court, Hearing Department—Los Angeles, In the Matter of: Lawrence Victor Harrison, No. 202689, a member of the State Bar, Case Nos. 06-O-13792, 06-O-13797, 06-O-14825, Filed 29 June 2009, pp. 3–5.

31. Notes on meeting re. California State Bar disciplinary charges against Lawrence Victor Harrison, AT&T Bldg., 1149 S. Hill Street, Los Angeles, 13 November 2009, BBCF, carton 3, folder: Harrison, L. V. State Bar of California.

32. Lawrence Harrison to Russell H. Bartley, e-mail, 20 November 2009.

33. Lawrence Harrison to Russell H. Bartley (Lorenzo to Roselio), e-mail, 27 December 2009. The Spanish text reads, "De mi parte, estoy rezándole a Dios que la verdad [salga]. Aconséjame, por favor. Soy tu amigo y estoy pisando territorio no probado."

34. Russell H. Bartley to Lawrence Harrison (Roselio to Lorenzo), e-mail, 28 December 2009.

35. Lawrence Harrison to Russell H. Bartley, e-mail, 1 January 2010.

36. Lawrence Harrison [*sic*] to Address Book, e-mail, 2 January 2010.

37. Lawrence Harrison to Russell H. Bartley, e-mail, 4 January 2010.

38. Russell H. Bartley to Lawrence Harrison, e-mail, 3 January 2010.

39. Lawrence Harrison [*sic*] to Address Book, e-mail, 3 January 2010.

40. Lawrence Harrison to Russell H. Bartley, e-mail, 20 January 2010.

41. Chuck Jones to Russell H. Bartley (Russ Bartley/Lawrence), e-mail, 16 December 2009.

42. Chuck Jones to Russell H. Bartley (Russ Bartley), e-mail, Thursday, 17 December 2009.

43. Russell H. Bartley to Lawrence Harrison, e-mail, 14 February 2010. The Spanish word *cojones* is a colloquial term signifying "testicles."

44. Russell H. Bartley to Lawrence Harrison, e-mail, 21 January 2010. Russell's precise words were "No sé cómo fue que conociste al vato Cojones, ni por qué le tomaste confianza, pero yo te digo, a mi ver no es de confiar, ni mucho menos. Mucho ojo con él."

45. Lawrence Harrison to Russell H. Bartley, e-mail, 23 January 2010; Chuck Jones to Russell H. Bartley, e-mail, 17 December 2009.

46. United States District Court for the District of Columbia, John Doe, c/o 1250 Connecticut Avenue, N.W., Suite 200, Washington, D.C. 20036, Plaintiff v. Central Intelligence Agency, Washington, D.C. 20505, Defendant, Case No. 1:13-cv-01231, assignment date: 9 August 2013, http://cryptome.org/2013/09/doe-v-cia.pdf.

47. Ibid., 3. There is now a substantial literature on the role of private contractors in U.S. intelligence and paramilitary operations. See, e.g., Jim Hougan, *Spooks: The Haunting of America; The Private Use of Secret Agents* (New York: William Morrow, 1978); Jeremy Scahill, *Blackwater: The Rise of the World's Most Powerful Mercenary Army*, rev. and updated ed. (New York: Nation Books, 2008); and Tim Shorrock, *Spies for Hire: The Secret World of Intelligence Outsourcing* (New York: Simon & Schuster, 2008).

48. Russell H. Bartley to Lawrence Harrison, e-mail, 28 January 2010.

49. Lawrence Harrison to Russell H. Bartley, e-mail, 28 January 2010.

50. State Bar of California, Hearing Department, Los Angeles, Counsel for the State Bar Brandon K. Tady (Bar # 83045), in pro per respondent Lawrence Victor Harrison (Bar # 202689), in the matter of: Lawrence Victor Harrison (Bar # 202689), Case Nos. 06-O-13792-DFM, 06-O-13797-DFM, and 06-O-14825-DFM, Stipulation re facts, conclusions of law and disposition and order approving *actual suspension*, filed 21 December 2009, State Bar Court Clerk's Office, Los Angeles; Attorney Search: Lawrence Victor Harrison, 3 February 2013, State Bar of California, http://members.calbar.ca.gov/fal/Member/Detail/202689.

51. Lawrence Victor Harrison, phone conversation with Russell H. Bartley, 7 February 2013.

Chapter 17. Parsing the Evidence

1. David Hackett Fischer, *Historians' Fallacies: Toward a Logic of Historical Thought* (New York: Harper Torchbooks, 1970), xv.

2. Florentino Ventura Gutiérrez, interview with authors, Mexico City, 25 November 1987.

3. Miguel Ángel García Domínguez, interview with authors, Mexico City, 12 March 1990.

4. Cabildo and Monge, "Decepcionada," 27.

5. Miguel Ángel García Domínguez, interview with authors, Mexico City, 12 March 1990.

6. Quoted in Soledad Jarquín Egar, "Mujeres y política: Manuel Buendía, periodista incomparable," *Las Caracolas: Periodismo de la condición social de las mujeres*, 10 March 2013, http://caracolasfem.blogspot.com/2013/03/mujeres-y-politica-manuel-buendia.html.

7. See, e.g., Fundación, "¿Quién mató a Manuel Buendía?," 26–35; Héctor A. González, "La Procuraduría quiere fabricar al asesino de Buendía, dice un agente de la Federal de Seguridad inculpado," *unomásuno*, 31 May 1985, 24; and "Formal prisión a 3 agentes de la Federal de Seguridad," *unomásuno*, 1 June 1985, 27.

8. Fernando Ortega Pizarro, "Para la DEA, Zorrilla es clave para descifrar el narcotráfico en México," *Proceso*, 3 June 1985, 6, 8–9 Ortega Pizarro, "*Proceso* tiene la razón," 6–8, 11.

9. Estados Unidos Mexicanos, Procuraduría General de Justicia del Distrito Federal, "Informe del Subprocurador Dr. Miguel Ángel García Domínguez," 15.

10. Miguel Ángel García Domínguez, interview with authors, Mexico City, 17 March 1988.

11. Miguel Ángel García Domínguez, interview with authors, 12 March 1990.

12. Manuel Buendía, "Obispos denuncian.: ¿Y el procurador?," Red Privada, *Excélsior*, 4 May 1984, photocopy of original typescript, Fundación Manuel Buendía, 1–2, BBCF, archival ring binder 1, Buendía assassination news reports & *Red Privada* columns.

13. Manuel Buendía, "Seguridad nacional: Concreta amenaza," Red Privada, *Excélsior*, 14 May 1984, photocopy of original typescript, Fundación Manuel Buendía, BBCF, archival ring binder 1, Buendía assassination news reports & *Red Privada* columns.

14. Rafael Rodríguez Castañeda, "Buendía sabía su riesgo, pero no calculó el asesinato, dice su secretario," *Proceso*, 3 June 1985, 9–10, 12–15; Rothschild, "Who Killed Manuel Buendía?," 21.

15. Rodríguez Castañeda, "Buendía sabía su riesgo," 15.

16. Miguel Ángel García Domínguez, interview with authors, Mexico City, 12 March 1990.

17. Hernández López, *Zorrilla*, 25.

18. Lawrence Victor Harrison, testimony in United States Department of Justice, Drug Enforcement Administration, Report of Investigation, 25 September 1989, 30, 43 (transcript signed by S/A Manuel R. Martínez and G/S Hector Berrellez).

19. United States District Court for the Central District of California, United States of America, plaintiff, v. Juan Ramon Matta-Ballesteros, Ruben Zuno-Arce, Juan Jose Bernabe-Ramirez, and Javier Vasquez-Velasco, defendants, Case No. CR 87-422 (F)-ER, Reporter's transcript of proceedings, vol. 26, 6 July 1990, 110–112.

20. Lawrence Victor Harrison, testimony in United States Department of Justice, Drug Enforcement Administration, DEA-6 Report of Investigation, 13 February 1990, 1 (transcript signed by S/A Wayne Schmidt and Special Agent in Charge John M. Zienter).

21. Court Reporter's Transcript of Proceedings, United States District Court for the Central District of California, United States of America, plaintiff, v. Juan Ramon Matta-Ballesteros, Ruben Zuno-Arce, Juan Jose Bernabe-Ramirez, and Javier Vasquez-Velasco, defendants, Case No. CR 87-422 (F)-ER, vol. 26, 6 July 1990, 103.

22. Ibid., 61–62.

23. Lawrence Victor Harrison, testimony in United States Department of Justice, Drug Enforcement Administration, DEA-6 Report of Investigation, 13 February 1990, 1–3.

24. Anabel Hernández, *Los señores del narco* (Mexico City: Grijalbo, 2011), 94–101.

25. Manuel Robles, "El socio de Mertins, acusado de haberlo delatado ante Manuel Buendía," *Proceso*, 21 March 1988, 20–23.

26. Hernández, *Los señores del narco*, 106.

27. Court Reporter's Transcript of Proceedings, United States District Court for the Central District of California, United States of America, plaintiff, v. Juan Ramon Matta-Ballesteros, Ruben Zuno-Arce, Juan Jose Bernabe-Ramirez, and Javier Vasquez-Velasco, defendants, Case No. CR 87-422 (F)-ER, vol. 26, 6 July 1990, 66–69.

28. Hernández states that Harrison was given this nickname by Ernesto Fonseca Carrillo, the Guadalajara cartel kingpin with whom he associated most closely. Meaning "White Tower," the sobriquet referred to Harrison's exceptional height (6 foot 8). In a typed page that Hernández reproduces from the transcription of Fonseca's 1985 interrogation by PJF chief Florentino Ventura, Fonseca refers to Harrison as "Torre Blanca." See Hernández, *Los señores del narco*, 104–105.

29. Lawrence Victor Harrison, testimony in United States Department of Justice, Drug Enforcement Administration, DEA-6 Report of Investigation, 13 February 1990, 4–5.

30. Hernández, *Los señores del narco*, 100–101; Lawrence Victor Harrison, testimony in United States Department of Justice, Drug Enforcement Administration, DEA-6 Report of Investigation, 13 February 1990, 5–6.

31. Court Reporter's Transcript of Proceedings, United States District Court for the Central District of California, United States of America, plaintiff, v. Juan Ramon Matta-Ballesteros, Ruben Zuno-Arce, Juan Jose Bernabe-Ramirez, and Javier Vasquez-Velasco, defendants, Case No. CR 87-422 (F)-ER, vol. 26, 6 July 1990, 115.

32. Ibid., 115, 143.

33. Ibid., 70.

34. Lawrence Victor Harrison, interview with authors, San Dimas, California, 14 May 2004.

35. Hernández, *Los señores del narco*, 104.

36. Edward M. Medvene, interview with authors, together with Zuno attorney Ken Miller, Westlake Village, California, 14 February 2008.

37. United States District Court for the Central District of California, *United States of America, plaintiff, v. Rafael Caro-Quintero et al., defendants*, Case No. CR-87-422-ER, court reporter's partial transcript of proceedings, 7 December 1992, 78.

38. Lawrence Victor Harrison, phone conversation with Russell H. Bartley, 25 April 2005.

39. Ewen MacAskill, "Edward Snowden, NSA Files Source: 'If They Want to Get You, in Time They Will,'" *Guardian*, 10 June 2013; Glenn Greenwald, Ewen MacAskill, and Laura Poitras, "Edward Snowden: The Whistleblower behind the NSA Surveillance Revelations," *Guardian*, 9 June 2013.

40. Glenn Greenwald, Laura Poitras, and Ewen MacAskill, "Edward Snowden: US Surveillance 'Not Something I'm Willing to Live Under,'" *Guardian*, 8 July 2013.

41. Lawrence Victor Harrison, interview with authors, Riverside, California, 18 June 2009.

42. "Edward Snowden Statement: 'It Was the Right Thing to Do and I Have No Regrets,'" *Guardian*, 12 July 2013.

43. Morley, *Our Man in Mexico*. See also Aguayo Quezada, *La charola*.

44. Petrich Moreno, "Long Arm of the War on Drugs," 17–22.

45. Alberto Aguirre M., "El expediente Buendía," *El Economista*, 3 June 2011, http://elecono mista.com.mx/columnas/columna-especial-politica/2011/06/03/expediente-buendia; María Idalia Gómez, "México: Abren al público expediente del crimen de Manuel Buendía," *Sociedad Interamericana de Prensa*, no. 70 (1 June 2011); Carlos Gutiérrez, "Harán público expediente sobre el asesinato del periodista Manuel Buendía," *Milenio*, 16 May 2011.

46. Humberto Padgett, "Reportaje: Caro Quintero, el hombre que compró al Estado," *ZonafrancaMX*, 3 September 2013, http://zonafranca.mx/reportaje-caro-el-hombre-que-compro-al -estado/.

EPILOGUE

1. Randal C. Archibold and Karla Zabludovsky, "Mexican Tied to Killing of D.E.A. Agent Is Freed," *New York Times*, 9 August 2013, 4; "Mexican Drug Lord Transferred to State Prison," Borderland Beat: Reporting on the Mexican Cartel Drug War, 2 June 2010, http://www.border landbeat.com/2010/06/mexican-drug-lord-transferred-to-state.html; Adriana Gómez Licón and Mark Stevenson, "US Angry over Release of Mexican Drug Lord," Associated Press, 10 August 2013; "Libre, Caro Quintero: EU lo busca," 10 August 2013, Informador, www.informador.com .mx/mexico/2013/477668/6/libre-caro-quintero-eu-lo-busca.htm; Michael Weissenstein, "Rafael Caro Quintero Released: U.S. Angry Mexico Sets Free Drug Lord Who Killed DEA Agent Kiki Camarena," Huffington Post, 10 August 2013, http://www.huffingtonpost.com/2013/08/10/ rafael-caro-quintero-released_n_3736511.html; Bill Conroy, "Release of DEA Agent Kiki Camarena's 'Murderer' Is Game Changer for CIA," *Narcosphere*, 10 August 2013, http://narcosphere .narconews.com/notebook/bill-conroy/2013/08; "Una cadena de fallas puso en la calle a Caro Quintero," *Proceso*, 11 August 2013.

2. Alejandro Cruz Flores, "Liberan al autor intelectual del asesinato de Buendía: Zorrilla Pérez, en prisión domiciliaria," *La Jornada*, 11 September 2013, 16; "Liberan a Zorrilla y Moro, homicidas de Buendía," *Milenio*, 19 February 2009; "Reaprehenden a José Antonio Zorrilla," *Milenio*, 15 June 2009; Miguel Ángel Granados Chapa, "Respuesta a Zorrilla," *Reforma*, 7 September 2009, http://www.etcetera.com.mx/articulo/respuesta_a_zorrilla/1372/.

3. Conroy, "Release of DEA Agent Kiki Camarena's 'Murderer'"; Bowden, *Down by the River*, 147–148.

4. Luis Chaparro and J. Jesús Esquivel, "A Camarena lo ejecutó la CIA, no Caro Quintero," *Proceso*, 13 October 2013, 6–9.

5. Robert Plumlee to Russell H. Bartley, e-mails, 22 and 25 November 2013; Robert Plumlee, phone conversation with Russell H. Bartley, 24 December 2013; Héctor Berréllez to Russell H. Bartley, e-mail, 5 December 2013; Phil Jordan, phone conversation with Russell H. Bartley, 19 December 2013.

6. "Mexico Releases Killer of DEA Special Agent 'Kiki' Camarena," reported by William la Jeunesse, *Kelly File*, Fox News, 10 October 2013; Robert Plumlee to Russell H. Bartley, e-mail, 22 November 2013.

7. Scott and Marshall, *Cocaine Politics*, 41.

8. Robert Plumlee to Russell H. Bartley, e-mails, 22 November and 3 December 2013; Robert Plumlee, phone conversation with Russell H. Bartley, e-mail, 20 June 2014; Hooks and Johnson, "Kingpin," 41–42; James Kuykendall, *¿O plata o plomo? Silver or Lead? The Abduction and Murder of DEA Agent Kiki Camarena* (San Bernardino, CA: Xlibris, 2005), 43–49.

9. Kuykendall, ¿O plata o plomo? Silver or Lead?, 44

10. Kuykendall, *Silver or Lead?*, 43–49; Shannon, *Desperados*, 13–16.

11. William La Jeunesse and Lee Ross, "US Intelligence Assets in Mexico Reportedly Tied to Murdered DEA Agent," FoxNews.com, 10 October 2013, http://www.foxnews.com/poli tics/2013/10/10/us-intelligence-assets-reportedly-played-role-in-capture-dea-agent-in-mexico/.

12. Robert Plumlee to Russell H. Bartley, e-mail, 22 November 2013; Héctor Berréllez to Russell H. Bartley, e-mail, 5 December 2013; Phil Jordan, phone conversation with Russell H. Bartley, 19 December 2013.

13. Lawrence E. Walsh, *Final Report of the Independent Counsel for Iran/Contra Matters*, vol. 1, *Investigations and Prosecutions* (Washington, DC: U.S. Court of Appeals for the District of Columbia Circuit, 4 August 1993), 489.

14. Carlos Ramírez, "Manuel Buendía y el huevo de la serpiente," editorial, *Revista indicador político*, 26 May 2014, 2.

15. We say "ominously" because the operation was easily confused with the contemporaneous collaboration of South American intelligence services in a multilateral "dirty war" campaign against opponents of the region's authoritarian regimes, also known as Operation Condor. As described in chapter 14, that same dirty war was being waged in Mexico with U.S. support and in its human costs differed little from the wanton violence visited in those years on the opium poppy growers of the western Sierra Madre.

16. "El Chapo: Crimen y poder," special issue, *Proceso*, January 2012; Ed Vulliamy, "Joaquín 'Chapo' Guzmán: The Mexican Drug Lord Adept at Playing the System," *Guardian*, 22 February 2014.

17. Vulliamy, "Joaquín 'Chapo' Guzmán."

18. J. Jesús Esquivel, "El proceso contra El Vicentillo, asunto de 'seguridad nacional' para EU," *Proceso*, 27 February 2014.

19. United States District Court for the Northern District of Illinois, Eastern Division, "Memorandum of Law in Support of Motion for Discovery Regarding Defense of Public Authority," *United States v. Zambada-Niebla*, Case No. 1:09-cr-00383, Document No.: 94, Filed: 07/29/11, http://narcosphere.narconews.com/userfiles/70/Pleadings.Sinaloa.Zambada.pdf.

20. Quoted in Douglas Lucas, "A Deal with the Right Devil," WhoWhatWhy, 10 March 2014, http://whowhatwhy.com/2014/03/10/deal-right-devil/. See also Doris Gómora, "La guerra secreta de la DEA en México," *El Universal*, 6 January 2014, http://www.eluniversal.com.mx/ nacion-mexico/2014/impreso/la-guerra-secreta-de-la-dea-en-mexico-212050.html; United States District Court for the Northern District of Illinois, Eastern Division, "Affidavit of Manuel Castanon," *United States v. Zambada-Niebla*, Case No. 1:09-cr-00383, Document No.: 148-1, Filed: 12/02/11, http://narcosphere.narconews.com/userfiles/70/148-1.pdf.

21. Diana Washington Valdez and Daniel Borunda, "Mexican Kingpin Rafael Caro Quintero's Release Fuels Anger," *El Paso Times*, 18 August 2013.

22. Quoted in Lucas, "Deal with the Right Devil."

23. United States District Court for the Northern District of Illinois, Eastern Division, "Memorandum of Law," 10–11.

24. Robert Farago and Ralph Dixon, "Farago: Was CIA behind Operation Fast and Furious?," *Washington Times*, 11 August 2011.

25. Peter Gorman, "Smuggler's Run," *Fort Worth Weekly*, 26 April 2006, 7–9. See also Shannon, *Desperados*, 195; Hooks and Johnson, "Kingpin," 35–36; Gorman, "Big-Time Smuggler's Blues"; and United States District Court for the District of Arizona, "Indictment," *United States of America, Plaintiff, v. Rafael Caro Quintero, Miguel Caro Quintero, Michael Keith Hooks, aka Jesse Bishop, aka Jesse Livingston*, et al., 14 July 1988.

26. Gallagher, "Trafficker-Turned-Informant Hides in N.M."

27. Shannon, *Desperados*, 113–116.

28. Kuykendall, *¿O plata o plomo?*, 14.

29. Camarena interrogation transcript, obtained by the CIA (in Spanish, 43 pages), downloaded from http://reneverdugo.org/docs.html, 1–8.

30. Kuykendall, *¿O plata o plomo?*, 11–15; Shannon, *Desperados*, 282–301.

31. Kuykendall, *¿O plata o plomo?*, 118–119.

32. Ibid., 119.

33. Shannon, *Desperados*, 261.

34. Kuykendall, *¿O plata o plomo?*, 15.

35. Camarena interrogation transcript, 43.

36. Robert Plumlee to Russell H. Bartley, e-mails, 25 November 2013.

37. Aguayo Quezada, *La charola*, 243.

38. Jorge Carrasco Araizaga, "La Federal de Seguridad y la CIA colaboraban con Caro Quintero," *Proceso*, 27 October 2013, 8.

39. Ibid., 10.

40. Ibid., 11 (emphasis added).

41. Ibid.

42. Héctor Berréllez, interview with authors, Ontario, California, 15 May 2004.

43. Bowden, "Pariah," 150–159, 180, 182.

44. J. Jesús Esquivel, "El 'thriller' Camarena," *Proceso*, 20 October 2013, 6–7.

45. Hernández López, *Zorrilla*, 81–83.

46. J. Jesús Esquivel, "Expolicías mexicanos exhiben a Bartlett y a Arévalo Gardoqui," *Proceso*, 5 January 2014, 8.

47. Charles Bowden to Russell H. Bartley, e-mails, 8–9 July 2014.

48. Esquivel, *La CIA, Camarena y Caro Quintero*, 149–150.

49. Ibid., 174–177.

50. Ibid. Inasmuch as Esquivel's book effectively serves the interests of CIA damage controllers by distracting readers' attention from the seminal elements of the Camarena and Buendía killings, and in light of what is now known about agency utilization of corporate enterprises for its covert purposes, we can only wonder about the role of the book's publishers in fast-tracking its production and release. While the book appears under the imprimatur of the well-known Spanish-language publishing house Grijalbo, the first edition copyright is held by Penguin Random House, a combined corporate entity whose two multinational British and American firms have long-standing reputations for quality book publication strikingly at odds with the sloppily produced Esquivel volume. In a similar vein, Harrison has suggested that Berréllez the whistleblower likewise serves the interests of government damage controllers with his garbled accounts and misstatements of fact. "DEA loves Héctor," he remarked in a recent phone conversation, "because he's so full of crap." Lawrence Victor Harrison, phone conversation with Russell H. Bartley, 30 March 2015.

51. Esquivel, "El 'thriller' Camarena," 9.

52. Berréllez, interview with authors, Ontario, California, 15 May 2004.

53. Esquivel, "El 'thriller' Camarena," 10.

54. Former CIA agent Lawrence Harrison assured us (interview with authors, Riverside, California, 18 June 2009) that González Calderoni had been a key figure in the overland transport of Colombian cocaine from the Guatemalan border north to the U.S. border. He is alleged to have had ties to both the Gulf and the Juárez cartels and, Berréllez believes (Chaparro and Esquivel, "A Camarena lo ejecutó la CIA," 8), had he been apprehended by the Salinas administration he likely would have been killed. As it was, a hired gunman did eventually catch up to him. "Two guys got out of a car with Louisiana plates and popped him in the noggin," Harrison embellished the story with intended reference to the February 1986 Baton Rouge murder of master pilot, drug smuggler, and CIA asset Barry Seal (interview with the authors, Riverside, California, 17 June 2009). Calderoni's obligatory epitaph, a Spanish reporter observed, was "He knew too much." Juan Jesús Aznárez, "La caída del comandante," *El País*, 20 February 2003.

55. Chaparro and Esquivel, "A Camarena lo ejecutó la CIA," 8.

56. Héctor Berréllez to Russell H. Bartley, e-mail, 15 July 2014.

57. Charles Bowden to Russell H. Bartley, e-mail, 7 August 2014.

58. Henry Weinstein, "Now-DEA Operative Heard Camarena Killing Discussed, Witness Says," *Los Angeles Times*, 23 June 1990.

59. Héctor Berréllez to Russell H. Bartley, e-mail, 7 August 2014.

60. Court Reporter's Transcript of Proceedings, United States District Court for the Central District of California, United States of America, plaintiff, v. Juan Ramon Matta-Ballesteros, Ruben Zuno-Arce, Juan Jose Bernabe-Ramirez, and Javier Vasquez-Velasco, defendants, Case No. CR 87-422 (F)-ER, vol. 14, 7 June 1990, 14–62.

61. Héctor Berréllez to Russell H. Bartley, e-mail, 7 August 2014; Charles Bowden to Russell H. Bartley, e-mail, 7 August 2014.

62. Héctor Berréllez to Russell H. Bartley, e-mail, 8 August 2014.

63. Molly Molloy to Russell H. Bartley, e-mail, 21 December 2014.

64. Charles Bowden and Molly Molloy, *Blood on the Corn*, illustrated by Matt Rota, Medium .com, part 1, https://medium.com/matter/blood-on-the-corn-52ac13f7e643; part 2, https://medium .com/matter/blood-on-the-corn-part-ii-b4f447d70a8c; part 3, https://medium.com/matter/blood -on-the-corn-part-iii-b13f100cbf32.

65. Lawrence Victor Harrison, phone conversation with Russell H. Bartley, 18 December 2014; Molly Molloy to Russell H. Bartley, e-mails, 19, 22, and 23 December 2014.

66. Molly Molloy to Russell H. Bartley, e-mail, 22 December 2014.

67. Molly Molloy to Russell H. Bartley, e-mail, 23 December 2014.

68. Lawrence Victor Harrison, phone conversation with Russell H. Bartley, 9 December 2014.

69. Charles Bowden to Russell H. Bartley, e-mail, 27 February 2014.

70. Bowden and Molloy, *Blood on the Corn*, part 3, 26–27.

71. Lawrence Victor Harrison, phone conversation with Russell H. Bartley, 26 November 2014.

72. Lawrence Victor Harrison, phone conversation with Russell H. Bartley, 18 December 2014.

73. Russell H. Bartley, "No por el motivo aducido murió Manuel Buendía," *Indicador Político* (Mexico City), 26 May 2014, 14–15. This solicited article summarizing key conclusions of this book was published on the thirtieth anniversary of the Buendía assassination.

SOURCES

Iɴᴛᴇʀᴠɪᴇᴡᴇᴇs ᴀɴᴅ Iɴꜰᴏʀᴍᴀɴᴛs

María Dolores Ábalos Lebrija
Philip Agee
Héctor Aguilar Camín
Adolfo Aguilar Zínzer
Manuel Becerra Acosta
Héctor G. Berréllez
Jesús Blancornelas
Anatoly Borovkov
Charles Bowden
Ángel Buendía Tellezgirón
Jorge A. Bustamante
Hernán Casares Cámara
Octavio Colmenares
Miguel Ángel García Domínguez
Luis Gutiérrez Rodríguez
Jeffrey Guy
Lawrence Victor Harrison
Kathleen Anne Henson
Rogelio Hernández López
Michael Keith Hooks
Charles "Chuck" Jones
Phil Jordan
Michael Levine
Lionel Martin
Rafael Loret de Mola
Edward M. Medvene
William Robert "Tosh" Plumlee
Carlos Ramírez
Jorge Fernando Ramírez de Aguilar
John Ross

Matthew Rothschild
Miguel Ángel Sánchez de Armas
Peter Dale Scott
Luis Suárez
Frederic N. Tulsky
Eduardo "El Buho" Valle
Florentino Ventura Gutiérrez
Felipe Victoria Zepeda
Viktor V. Volsky
Gary Webb
John Womack Jr.

DOCUMENTARY SOURCES

Bartley Buendía Case Files, 1984–2013 (hereafter BBCF), five cartons, fourteen ring binders.
Brenneke, Richard J. Oral Deposition taken on 21 June 1991 at the Arkansas State Attorney General's Office, 323 Center Street, Little Rock, Arkansas, to develop evidence for the use of independent counsel Lawrence E. Walsh in the Iran-Contra investigation. Taken before Jeff Bennett, of Bushman Court Reporting, Inc., by Congressman William Alexander and Chief Deputy Attorney General for the State of Arkansas Chad Farris, http://www.idfiles.com/rbdepo.htm.
Camarena interrogation transcript. Obtained by the CIA. http://reneverdugo.org/docs.html. In Spanish, authors' translation.
Committee of Santa Fe [L. Francis Bouchey, Roger Fontaine, David C. Jordan, and Lt. General Gordon Sumner]. *A New Inter-American Policy for the Eighties*. Edited by Lewis Tambs. Washington, DC: Council for Inter-American Security, 1980.
Estados Unidos Mexicanos, Procuraduría General de Justicia del Distrito Federal (PGJDF). "Informe del Subprocurador Dr. Miguel Ángel García Domínguez, Fiscal Especial para el esclarecimiento del homicidio de Manuel Buendía Tellezgirón," 30 June 1989.
Fundación Manuel Buendía. "¿Quién mató a Manuel Buendía?" Summary of known facts surrounding the Buendía assassination prepared as an internal reference document by Manuel Buendía Foundation staff coordinated by Carlos Ramírez, 1985.
Mexico, Procuraduría General de la República, Fiscalía Especial para Movimientos Sociales y Políticos del Pasado. *Informe Histórico a la Sociedad Mexicana*. Mexico City: Procuraduría General de la República, 2006.
National Security Archive. *The Chronology: The Documented Day-by-Day Account of the Secret Military Assistance to Iran and the Contras*. Foreword by Seymour Hersh. New York: Warner Books, 1987.
United States Central Intelligence Agency, Office of Inspector General Investigations Staff. "Managing a Nightmare: CIA Public Affairs and the Drug Conspiracy Story." Approved for Release: 2014/07/29 C01372115. www.foia.cia.gov/sites/default/files/DOC0001372115.pdf.
———. *Report of Investigation Concerning Allegations of Connections between CIA and the Contras in Cocaine Trafficking to the United States* (96-0143-IG), 29 January 1998. *Overview: Report of Investigation*. Vol. 1, *The California Story*; vol. 2, *The Contra Story*. https://www.cia.gov/library/reports/general-reports-1/cocaine/overview-of-report-of-investigation-2.html.
United States Court of Appeals, Ninth Circuit. Case No. 93<HT>50311 (C.D. Cal. No. CR-87-422 ER): *United States of America, Plaintiff-Appellee, v. Rubén Zuno-Arce, Defendant-Appellant*. Appeal from the United States District Court for the Central District of California, the

Honorable Edward Rafeedie presiding. Appellant's Opening Brief (Edward M. Medvene, James E. Blancarte & Jack R. Luellen, Attorneys for Defendant-Appellant Rubén Zuno-Arce).

United States Department of Justice, Drug Enforcement Administration. DEA-6 Report of Investigation by S/A Manuel R. Martínez and G/S Hector Berréllez. Transcript of recorded interview, 25 September 1989.

———. DEA-6 Report of Investigation by S/A Salvador Leyva and G/S Hector G. Berrellez, Los Angeles, California, 9 April 1992. http://reneverdugo.org/pdf/RelatedCases/ZunoArce/ ZunoTrialWitnesses.pdf.

United States District Court for the Central District of California. *United States of America, Plaintiff, v. Juan Ramon Matta-Ballesteros, Ruben Zuno Arce et al., Defendants*. Case No. CR 87-422(F)-ER.

———. *United States of America, Plaintiff, v. Rafael Caro-Quintero et al., Defendants*. Case No. CR-87-422-ER.

United States District Court for the District of Arizona. "Indictment." *United States of America, Plaintiff, v. Rafael Caro Quintero, Miguel Caro Quintero, Michael Keith Hooks, aka Jesse Bishop, aka Jesse Livingston, et al.* 14 July 1988.

United States District Court for the District of Columbia. *John Doe, c/o 1250 Connecticut Avenue, N.W., Suite 200, Washington, D.C. 20036, Plaintiff, v. Central Intelligence Agency, Washington, D.C. 20505, Defendant*. Case No. 1:13-cv-01231. Assignment date: 9 August 2013. http://cryp tome.org/2013/09/doe-v-cia.pdf.

United States District Court for the Northern District of Illinois, Eastern Division. "Affidavit of Manuel Castanon." *United States v. Zambada-Niebla*. Case No. 1:09-cr-00383. Document No. 148-1. Filed: 12/02/11. http://narcosphere.narconews.com /userfiles/70/148-1.pdf.

———. "Memorandum of Law in Support of Motion for Discovery Regarding Defense of Public Authority." *United States v. Zambada-Niebla*. Case No. 1:09-cr-00383. Document No. 94. Filed: 07/29/11. http://narcosphere.narconews.com/userfiles/70/Pleadings.Sinaloa.Zam bada.pdf.

United States District Court, Southern District of Florida. Civil Action No. 86-1146-CIV-KING. *Tony Avirgan, Martha Honey, Plaintiffs, v. John Hull, Rene Corbo et al., Defendants*.

———. Civil Action No. 87-1545-CIV-KING. *Tony Avirgan. Martha Honey, Plaintiffs, v. Felipe Vidal Santiago, Raul Villaverde et al., Defendants*. Declaration of Plaintiffs' Counsel, 159.

United States Senate, Select Intelligence Committee. Prepared statement of Jack A. Blum, Esq., former Special Counsel to the Senate Foreign Relations Committee, on drug trafficking and the Contra War, 23 October 1996. http://www1.sjmercury.com/drugs/library/47.htm.

———. Transcript of hearing on alleged CIA drug trafficking to fund Nicaraguan Contras in the 1980s. Chaired by Senator Arlen Specter (R-PA). Witnesses: Jack Blum, former Special Council to the Senate Foreign Relations Committee; Frederick Hitz, CIA Inspector General; and Michael Bromwich, Justice Department Inspector General. http://www1.sjmercury.com/ drugs/library/48.htm.

Verdugo Urquídez, René. *René Verdugo: Information on His 24 years of Injustice*. http://renever dugo.org. This website challenges Verdugo's 1988 conviction in U.S. federal court as an accessory to the abduction, torture, interrogation, and murder of U.S. DEA S/A Enrique Camarena Salazar, for which Verdugo was sentenced to life in prison. It includes an extensive digital archive of downloadable court records and other legal documents bearing not only on the Verdugo Urquídez trial but also on the Camarena case more broadly, including the 1990–1992 Rubén Zuno Arce trials (http://reneverdugo.org/Zuno.html). We have retrieved fifty-two files from this source, printed copies of which are in the BBCF.

Walsh, Lawrence E. *Final Report of the Independent Counsel for Iran/Contra Matters.* 3 vols. Washington, DC: United States Court of Appeals for the District of Columbia Circuit, Division for the Purpose of Appointing Independent Counsel, Division no. 86-6, August (vols. 1–2) and December (vol. 3) 1993.

Zorrilla Pérez, José Antonio. "A la opinión pública." Texto del Documento enviado al señor doctor Miguel Ángel García Domínguez, Subprocurador de Justicia del Distrito Federal, encargado de la investigación del homicidio del periodista Manuel Buendía Tellezgirón. Averiguación Previa no. 7a/2358/84, 26 February 1988. Published in *Excélsior*, 1 March 1988, 20.

ARTICLES AND PUBLISHED INTERVIEWS

Acosta, Carlos. "En la modernización, motor del sexenio, ha cabido hasta el ajuste de cuentas: Once meses de carrera en afán de legitimidad." *Proceso*, 30 October 1989, 7–13.

Adorno, Héctor, Jorge Espinosa, and Héctor Cruz. "Hermetismo en el caso de F. Ventura." *Excélsior*, 19 September 1988, 5, 38.

Adorno, H., and L. Segura. "Vi en la DFS papeles de Buendía que relacionaban a Zorrilla con narcos: Moro." *Excélsior*, 23 June 1989, 1, 10.

Aguilar Camín, Héctor. "Manuel Buendía y los idus de mayo." In Fundación Manuel Buendía, *Los días de Manuel Buendía: Testimonios*, 7–18. Mexico City: Océano, 1984.

———. "El monstruo que vendrá." In *El desafío mexicano*, edited by Héctor Aguilar Camín, 87–101. 2nd ed. Mexico City: Océano, 1985.

———. "La prensa mexicana, factor claro de la modernización política." *unomásuno*, 8 June 1989, 7. Address delivered to the presidential banquet marking Press Freedom Day, 1989.

Aguirre M., Alberto. "El expediente Buendía." *El Economista*, 3 June 2011. http://eleconomista.com.mx/columnas/columna-especial-politica/2011/06/03/expediente-buendia.

Almanza, Ignacio G. "Prado hunde a Zorrilla: 'Él planeó el asesinato.'" *El Nacional*, 26 June 1989, 1, 12.

Alonso Enríquez, Manuel. "'Informaba periódicamente a mi jefe Bartlett: No era autónomo'; Zorrilla." *El Universal*, 21 June 1989, 1, 17.

Anaya, Marta. "Falsificado, el informe sobre Buendía: DEA: Ni siquiera se parece a los nuestros; Heath: 'No ligamos su muerte con el narcotráfico.'" *Excélsior*, 30 June 1989, 1, 28.

Anderson, Jack. "Pressure on the Press in Mexico." *Washington Post*, 5 August 1984.

Anderson, Jack, and Dale Van Atta. "A Mexican Journalist's Fatal Scoop." *Washington Post*, 21 August 1990.

Anhalt, Nedda G. de. "¿Quién es *Eko*?" *unomásuno*, cultural supplement *sábado*, 17 March 1990, 3.

Aponte, Juan María. "Dos textos: Uno sobre Buendía; Otro sobre el Papa." *El Día*, 25 May 1985.

Archibold, Randal C., and Karla Zabludovsky. "Mexican Tied to Killing of D.E.A. Agent Is Freed." *New York Times*, 9 August 2013, 4.

Arellano, Antonio. "Borran el caso del Chocorrol." *El Universal Gráfico*, 26 June 1989, 1, 3.

Arista Jiménez, Tizoc. "Narcos involucrados en el asesinato de Buendía." *Quehacer Político*, 14 March 1988, 12–15.

———. "Zorrilla no es el culpable, dice la viuda de Buendía." *Quehacer Político*, 21 March 1988, 6–9.

Armstrong, Scott, and Jeff Nason. "Company Man." *Mother Jones*, October 1988, 20–25, 42–47.

Associated Press. "Security Chief during Mexico's 'Dirty War' Dies." *Miami Herald*, 27 January 2012.

Aznárez, Juan Jesús. "La caída del comandante." *El País*, 20 February 2003.

Badillo, Miguel, Juan Becerra, Raúl Correa, Maribel Gutiérrez, Eduardo Huchim, Rebeca Lizá-
rraga, and Alicia Ortiz. "Sobre los cambios en *unomásuno*." *Revista mexicana de comunicación*
1, no. 6 (July–August 1989): 20–22.

Bartley, Russell H. "15 cables sobre Manuel Buendía: Se sigue la pista." Parts 1–5. *unomásuno*,
25–29 November 1987.

———. "Caro Quintero no fue: ¿Vínculos mexicanos con los contras?" *unomásuno*, 17 March
1987, 18.

———. "CIA behind Journalist's Murder? Agency Implicated in Mexican Writer's Assassination." *People's World*, 7 July 1984, 3.

———. "Costa Rica: Un proyecto made in USA." *unomásuno*, 3 May 1984, 11.

———. "Cuba: La revolución y el narcotráfico." *unomásuno*, 30–31 August and 1 September
1989, 21, 26, 19, respectively.

———. "Cuba Solidly Backs the New Nicaragua." *Milwaukee Journal*, 6 September 1979, 13.

———. "El affaire Buendía: ¿La CIA involucrada?" *unomásuno*, Sunday political supplement
páginauno, 4 June 1989, 11.

———. "El caso Buendía: ¿cerrado sin resolver? ¿Involucradas la CIA y la DEA?" *Revista mexicana de comunicación* 6, no. 32 (November–December 1993): 12–17.

———. "En defensa de la palabra: 'El caso Buendía nos debe llevar a examinar toda la cuestión
de la prensa, en México y en EU.'" *Revista mexicana de comunicación* 2, no. 11 (May–June
1990): 30–31. Interview conducted by Miguel Ángel Sánchez de Armas.

———. "Evidencias de un posible involucramiento de intereses foráneos en el asesinato de MB:
El caso visto desde el exterior." *Revista mexicana de comunicación* 1, no. 5 (May–June 1989):
11–17.

———. "¿Intereses políticos internacionales en el asesinato de Buendía?" *unomásuno*, Sunday
political supplement *páginauno*, 17 April 1988, 1, 3–4.

———. "Nicaraguan Images: Leaders Hold Media Events to Try to Change Hostile Attitudes
in US." *Milwaukee Journal*, 31 May 1981.

———. "No por el motivo aducido murió Manuel Buendía." *Indicador Político* (Mexico City),
Supplement 1, 26 May 2014, 14–15.

———. "The Piper Played to Us All: Orchestrating the Cultural Cold War in the USA, Europe,
and Latin America." *International Journal of Politics, Culture, and Society* 14, no. 13 (Spring
2001): 571–619.

———. "¿Quién mató a Manuel Buendía? Hay cuatro grupos merecedores de sospecha; Entrevista con Matthew Rothschild, autor de una pesquisa periodística sobre el caso." *unomásuno*,
Sunday political supplement *páginauno*, 19 May 1985, 1–3.

———. "¿Vínculos mexicanos con los contras? Caro Quintero no fue." *unomásuno*, 17 March
1987, 18.

Berdejo Arvizu, Aurora. "Frentes políticos." *Excélsior*, 1 February 1989, 30.

Blancornelas, Jesús. "Autoridades mexicanas: Se hacen como que no oyen." *Zeta* online, Edición
1690. Photocopy in BBCF, carton 2, Personality files: Blancornelas.

Blanco Velázquez, Ricardo. "Moro recibió entrenamiento de la DEA: Siete veces campeón de
motociclismo y rockero." *El Nacional*, 21 June 1989, 1, 10.

Bloice, Carl. "Murder Stalks Col. North's 'French Connection.'" *People's Daily World*, 24 February 1987, A4.

———. "New Reports Shed Light on Israel's Arms Deals." *People's Daily World*, 3 February
1987, A3.

Bowden, Charles. "The Pariah." *Esquire*, September 1998, 150–159, 180, 182.

Boyer, Edward J. "Drug Trafficker Gets Life Plus 240 Years in U.S. Agent's Killing." *Los Angeles Times*, 27 October 1988.

Branigin, William. "Trial in Camarena Case Shows DEA Anger at CIA." *Washington Post*, 16 July 1990, A1, 16.

Brown University. "Understanding the Iran-Contra Affairs: Nicaragua and Iran Timeline." http://www.brown.edu/Research/Understanding_the_Iran_Contra_Affair/timeline-n-i.php#head ertop.

Buendía, Manuel. "Amanecer en Panamá: Colonialismo en Serio." Red Privada. *Excélsior*, 4 October 1979.

———. "Armas en México: 'Preguntas a Roel.'" Red Privada. *El Porvenir* (Monterrey, Nuevo León), 10 November 1978.

———. "CIA: Directorio." Red Privada. *Excélsior*, 19 January 1981. Reprinted in Manuel Buendía, *La CIA en México*, 146–150. Mexico City: Océano, 1984.

———. "CIA vs. Torrijos: Crimen y Motivo." Red Privada. *Excélsior*, 21 August 1981.

———. "Colima, Fuhrer." *Excélsior*, 18 November 1983.

———. "Comunicación, seguridad y democracia." Reprinted in Manuel Buendía, *Ejercicio periodístico*, 169–181. Mexico City: Océano, 1985.

———. "Dios, ¿fascista?" Red Privada. *Excélsior*, 9 April 1984.

———. "El Ejército y la comunicación social." Tema presentado en la Secretaría de la Defensa el 25 de mayo de 1984 [Topic addressed at the Secretariat of Defense on 25 May 1984]. Reprinted in Manuel Buendía, *Ejercicio periodístico*, 183–189. Mexico City: Océano, 1985.

———. "El Estado pelea en reversa: Buendía en 82." Interview by Carlos Landeros. *Excélsior*, 31 May 1989, 1, 38, 41.

———. "Ese arte misterioso: Apuntes inéditos sobre el estilo." *Revista mexicana de comunicación* 6, no. 34 (April–May 1994): 5–6.

———. "Fut y Política: TV 'Contra.'" Red Privada. *Excélsior*, 3 May 1984, 1, 20.

———. "Hablar y escribir bien: Cuidar el estilo oral, tarea intransferible." *Revista mexicana de comunicación* 6, no. 34 (April–May 1994): 7.

———. "Lo que pasa en la UAG." *El Día*, 31 May 1976.

———. "Los juramentados." Red Privada. *Excélsior*, 6 April 1984.

———. "Los secreteros." Red Privada. *Excélsior*, 5 April 1984.

———. "Memorándum presidencial." *Nexos*, August 1984, 47–53.

———. "Obispos denuncian: ¿Y el procurador?" Red Privada. *Excélsior*, 4 May 1984. Photocopy of original typescript, Fundación Manuel Buendía.

———. "Por una Comisión Defensora de la Libertad de Prensa: Principios elementales para su constitución." 1980. Reprinted in *Revista mexicana de comunicación* 7, no. 40 (May–July 1995): 11–12.

———. "Private Line: The Jalisco Branch." Op-ed. *New York Times*, 5 November 1979.

———. "Quintacolumnistas." *Excélsior*, 7 October 1983.

———. "Seguridad nacional: Concreta amenaza." Red Privada. *Excélsior*, 14 May 1984. Photocopy of original typescript, Fundación Manuel Buendía.

———. "Sicópatas en Oferta: Bello Sueño Americano." Red Privada, *Excélsior*, 11 July 1979.

———. "Sólo es digno de llamarse libre quien cumple honestamente con sus responsabilidades: No tenemos libertad para mentir, calumniar, injuriar o desinformar." *Revista mexicana de comunicación* 5, no. 29 (May–June 1993): 17–22.

———. "Somocistas, aquí." *Excélsior*, 14 November 1983.

———. "Sucia intriga." *Excélsior*, 24 January 1984.

———. "Torrijos: Por qué; La CIA Ejecutora." Red Privada. *Excélsior*, 25 August 1981.

———. "Traficante protegido." Red Privada. *Excélsior*, 29 February 1984. Reprinted in Manuel Buendía, *Los empresarios*, 206–209. Mexico City: Océano, 1986.

———. "Vende Armas." Red Privada. *Excélsior*, 2 March 1983. Reprinted in Manuel Buendía, *La ultraderecha en México*, 136–138. Mexico City: Océano, 1984.

Buhrer, Jean-Claude. "Manuel Buendia: A Man Who Knew Too Much." *Manchester Guardian/Le Monde*, weekly English ed., 29 July 1984.

Cabildo, Miguel, Guillermo Correa, Raúl Monge, Fernando Ortega, and Ignacio Ramírez. "Las actuaciones de la fiscalía especial y la Procuraduría, en entredicho." *Proceso*, 17 July 1989, 24–25.

Cabildo, Miguel, and Raúl Monge. "Decepcionada, la viuda de Buendía no cree que se quiera aclarar el crimen." *Proceso*, 5 June 1989, 26–27.

———. "El periodista que en 1986 dio a conocer al 'Chocorrol' dice que sus datos apuntan más alto que Zorrilla." *Proceso*, 26 June 1989, 14–15.

Cabildo, Miguel, Raúl Monge, and Ignacio Ramírez. "Cada pista en el caso Buendía señala a Zorrilla y sus hombres: Inactividad oficial, según todas las apariencias, para protegerlo." *Proceso*, 22 May 1989, 18–21.

———. "El caso Buendía se vuelve embrollo: Resiste Zorrilla, niega todo y en respuesta le acumulan cargos." *Proceso*, 19 June 1989, 12, 14–16.

———. "Zorrilla pretende prolongar la protección que le dio el gobierno anterior: Bartlett y García Ramírez le dieron público aval." *Proceso*, 19 June 1989, 6–11.

Cabildo, Miguel, and Ignacio Ramírez. "Los tortuosos caminos de la investigación." *Proceso*, 22 February 1993, 20–21.

Cabildo, Miguel, and Rodrigo Vera. "La investigación del caso Buendía llevaba más allá de Zorrilla, pero el Subprocurador Paz Horta la detuvo." *Proceso*, 3 July 1989, 20–21.

Carbot, Alberto. "Reconoce Heath logros de la campaña hecha por México." *unomásuno*, 30 June 1989, 1, 10.

Carlsen, Laura. "Mexico's Oil Privatization Risky Business: Mexico's Oil Privatization Scheme Will Hurt the Environment, Scar the Landscape, and Leave Mexico at the Mercy of Transnational Firms." *Foreign Policy in Focus*, 27 May 2014. http://fpif.org/mexicos-oil-privatization-risky-business/.

Carrasco Araizaga, Jorge. "La Federal de Seguridad y la CIA colaboraban con Caro Quintero." *Proceso*, 27 October 2013, 8–11.

———. "Mártir, con verdades a medias." *Proceso*, 20 October 2013, 10–13.

Casares Cámara, Hernán. "Revelación del Instituto Christic: Caro Quintero abastecía de armamento a la contra; El narco mexicano tenía la simpatía de la DEA y la CIA." *Punto*, 9 March 1987, 16–17.

Castillo García, Gustavo, and Javier Valdez. "Hay suficientes pruebas para consignar a Nazar Haro, afirma Carrillo Prieto: La fiscalía sobre desaparecidos políticos lo cita a declarar para el seis de febrero." *La Jornada*, 1 February 2003.

Cervantes, Abigail. "Manuel Buendía: El deber ser en el periodismo; Un esbozo biográfico." *Revista mexicana de comunicación* 5, no. 29 (May–June 1993): 5–9.

Chaparro, Luis. "La versión del piloto Plumlee: La Casa Blanca protegió a Caro Quintero." *Proceso*, 10 November 2013, 10–12.

Chaparro, Luis, and J. Jesús Esquivel. "A Camarena lo ejecutó la CIA, no Caro Quintero." *Proceso*, 13 October 2013, 6–9.

Chaparro, Luis, and Jesús Salas. "Visitamos el rancho de Caro Quintero en Chihuahua." *Animal Político*, 17 August 2013. http://www.animalpolitico.com/2013/08/visitamos-el-rancho-de-caro-quintero-en-chihuahua/#axzz2mijoUaOS.

Chavarría Balleza, Rubén. "Fueron 'dos o más' matones." *Ovaciones*, 21 June 1989, 1, 8.

Christian, Shirley. "Pro-Sandinista Journalists Link U.S. Press to CIA." *Miami Herald*, 4 May 1981.

Cockburn, Andrew. "The Kingpin Strategy: Assassination as Policy in Washington and How It Failed, 1990–2015." TomDispatch, 28 April 2015.

Colhoun, Jack. "Contra Arms Scandal: Israeli Handwriting All Over Iran-Contra Scandal." *Guardian*, 4 November 1987, 3.

———. "Israel in Central America: Arms to the Contras." *CovertAction*, Summer 1988, 46–48.

Conroy, Bill. "Release of DEA Agent Kiki Camarena's 'Murderer' Is Game Changer for CIA." *Narcosphere*, 10 August 2013. http://narcosphere.narconews.com.

Correa, Guillermo. "Los jueces de los presuntos delincuentes célebres se dicen libres para decidir." *Proceso*, 3 July 1989, 22–23.

Correa, Guillermo, Manuel Robles, and Ignacio Ramírez. "Pese a las confusiones, García Domínguez da por cerrada la investigación y se va: La Procuraduría del Distrito y el Fiscal Especial del caso Buendía se contradicen." *Proceso*, 3 July 1989, 16–21, 23–25.

Croda, Rafael. "Negligencia e interferencia policiacas en el caso Buendía: García Domínguez." *La Jornada*, 25 February 1988, 1, 12.

Cruz Flores, Alejandro. "Liberan al autor intelectual del asesinato de Buendía: Zorrilla Pérez, en prisión domiciliaria." *La Jornada*, 11 September 2013, 16.

Cruz López, Héctor. "Cae Moro en innumerables contradicciones al rendir su declaración preparatoria ante el juez 34 penal." *unomásuno*, 23 June 1989.

———. "Ni Moro ni *El Chocorrol* son los asesinos de Manuel Buendía, asegura Zorrilla Pérez." *unomásuno*, 2 July 1989, 11.

"Cuestión de horas la captura del asesino material de Manuel Buendía." *El Nacional*, 20 June 1989, 1.

Cruz López, Héctor, and Jorge Reyes Estrada. "Acusaciones mutuas de Juventino Prado, Raúl Pérez, Sofía Naya y Moro Ávila." *unomásuno*, 28 June 1989, 10.

———. "Nunca fui autónomo; siempre mantuve informados a mis superiores: Zorrilla." *unomásuno*, 21 June 1989, 13.

Dávalos, Renato, and Héctor Adorno. "Desaparece de los archivos del forense el expediente de 'El Chocorrol' Ochoa." *Excélsior*, 30 June 1989, 28, 43.

Dávalos, Renato, Héctor Adorno, and Mario Peralta. "'Moro lo mató: Zorrilla lo ordenó; móvil, el narcotráfico'; MM y Bartlett cumplieron siempre; Informe de García Domínguez." *Excélsior*, 1 July 1989, 1, 10.

Davison, Phil. "Adolfo Aguilar Zínser." Obituary. *Independent*, 7 June 2005.

Dávila, Patricia, and Ignacio Ramírez. "Mertins, exonerado en el caso Buendía, vendió ya sus propiedades en Durango." *Proceso*, 9 October 1989, 31–33.

DePalma, Anthony. "Adolfo Aguilar Zinser, Blunt Mexican Envoy, Dies at 55." *New York Times*, 7 June 2005.

"Desde hace cuatro años las autoridades sabían que la DFS estaba involucrada en el asesinato: Un informe de agentes y el jefe de la Judicial." *Proceso*, 26 June 1989, 12–16, 18–19.

Devereaux, Ryan. "Managing a Nightmare: How the CIA Watched Over the Destruction of Gary Webb." *Intercept*, 25 September 2014. https://firstlook.org/theintercept/2014/09/25/managing-nightmare-cia-media-destruction-gary-webb.

Dornbierer, Manú. "El negocio Buendía." *Excélsior*, 29 May 1989, 7.

———. "El negocio Buendía." *Excélsior*, 30 May 1989, 8.

"Edward Rafeedie, 1929–2008." Obituary. *Los Angeles Times*, 30 March 2008.

"Edward Snowden Statement: 'It Was the Right Thing to Do and I Have No Regrets.'" *Guardian*, 12 July 2013.

"El autor material del asesinato de Manuel Buendía, identificado: PGJDF." *unomásuno*, 13 June 1989, 11.

"El boletín de la embajada de los Estados Unidos." *Proceso*, 10 June 1985, 6–7.

"El Chapo: Crimen y poder." Special issue, *Proceso*, January 2012.

"El día de la aprehensión Zorrilla estuvo en riesgo de perder la vida: Camacho." *unomásuno*, 16 June 1989, 13.

"El director de 'Primera Plana' de Coatzacoalcos muerto también a tiros." *Proceso*, 4 June 1984, 14.

"El informe de la DEA en el juicio a Zuno habla de los federales muertos en Veracruz, la CIA, Buendía, Bartlett y el narco." *Proceso*, 16 July 1990, 18–20.

Esquivel, J. Jesús. "El proceso contra El Vicentillo, asunto de 'seguridad nacional' para EU." *Proceso*, 27 February 2014.

———. "El secuestro de Álvarez Machain, ordenado por la Casa Blanca." *Proceso* 30 March 2014, 18–20.

———. "El 'thriller' Camarena." *Proceso*, 20 October 2013, 6–9.

———. "Expolicías mexicanos exhiben a Bartlett y a Arévalo Gardoqui." *Proceso*, 5 January 2014, 6–11.

Estrada, Erendira. "Siento asco por Zorrilla: La viuda de Buendía." *El Nacional*, 6 July 1989, 10.

"Expediente Buendía: La impunidad es lo normal." *Revista mexicana de comunicación* 1, no. 2 (November–December 1988): 30–32. Commentary and excerpts from interview with Buendía case special prosecutor Miguel Ángel García Domínguez.

Farago, Robert, and Ralph Dixon. "Farago: Was CIA behind Operation Fast and Furious?" *Washington Times*, 11 August 2011.

Félix Gallardo, Miguel. "Memorias de Miguel Félix Gallardo." 23 July 2009. In *Diarios del Jefe de Jefes*, excerpted in *Milenio*. BBCF, carton 2, Personality Files: Félix Gallardo.

Fernández, Andrea. "Encuentro por escrito." In Fundación Manuel Buendía, *Los días de Manuel Buendía: Testimonios*, 45–50. Mexico City: Océano, 1984.

Fernández Menéndez, Jorge. "Ante el periodismo del futuro." *unomásuno*, 8 June 1989, 8.

Ferreira, Argemiro (Prensa Latina). "Oscuro pasado de Bush y el mundo del narcotráfico: Visión cubana." *Excélsior*, 17 March 1990, 1, 6.

"Formal prisión a 3 agentes de la Federal de Seguridad." *unomásuno*, 1 June 1985, 27.

Fox, Sue. "Mexico Moves on Rights Probe." *Chicago Tribune*, 6 January 2002.

Gallagher, Mike. "Trafficker-Turned-Informant Hides in N.M. and Waits for Reward from Feds." *Albuquerque Journal*, 15 January 2006.

García, Arturo Rodríguez. "Los ochenta, cuando se impuso la narcopolítica." *Proceso*, 27 October 2013, 12–14.

García Domínguez, Sergio. "El asesinato de Buendía, visto por extranjeros." *Novedades de Baja California*, 23 October 1988, 1, 12.

García Márquez, Gabriel. "Torrijos." *El País* (Madrid), 12 August 1981.

Gerth, Jeff. "C.I.A. Shedding Its Reluctance to Aid in Fight against Drugs: The C.I.A. and the Drug War; A Special Report." *New York Times*, 25 March 1990, 1, 10.

Gil, Teresa. "No hay hipótesis concreta sobre el asesinato de Buendía: Sales Gasque." *unomásuno*, 28 February 1986, 8.

Gómez Licón, Adriana, and Mark Stevenson. "US Angry over Release of Mexican Drug Lord." Associated Press, 10 August 2013.

Gómez Villarreal, Roberto. "La Operación Noticia: La distancia entre el poder y la sombra." *El Nacional*, 29 June 1989, 3.

Gómora, Doris. "La guerra secreta de la DEA en México." *El Universal*, 6 January 2014. http:// www.eluniversal.com.mx/nacion-mexico/2014/impreso/la-guerra-secreta-de-la-/dea-en-mexico.

González, Héctor A. "La Procuraduría quiere fabricar al asesino de Buendía, dice un agente de la Federal de Seguridad inculpado." *unomásuno*, 31 May 1985, 24.

González, Héctor A., and Ernesto Zavaleta. "La muerte de Ventura y esposa, por líos conyugales." *unomásuno*, 19 September 1988, 12.

González Ruiz, Edgar. "Manuel Buendía: Su legado para la BUAP, a 25 años de su asesinato." *Tiempo Universitario. Gaceta histórica de la Benemérita Universidad Autónoma de Puebla* 12, no. 3 (January 2009).

Gorman, Peter. "Big-Time Smuggler's Blues." *Cannabis Culture*, 16 June 2006.

———. "Smuggler's Run." *Fort Worth Weekly*, 26 April 2006, 7–9.

Granados Chapa, Miguel Ángel. "Plaza Pública: Aprehendan a Zorrilla; Una culpabilidad anunciada." *La Jornada*, 12 June 1989, 1.

———. "Respuesta a Zorrilla." Reforma, 7 September 2009. http://www.etcetera.com.mx/arti culo/respuesta_a_zorrilla/1372/.

Granados Roldán, Otto. "¿Regreso a las armas?" In *El desafío mexicano*, edited by Héctor Aguilar Camín, 125–135. 2nd ed. Mexico City: Océano, 1985.

Greenwald, Glenn, Ewen MacAskill, and Laura Poitras. "Edward Snowden: The Whistleblower behind the NSA Surveillance Revelations." *Guardian*, 9 June 2013.

Greenwald, Glenn, Laura Poitras, and Ewen MacAskill. "Edward Snowden: US Surveillance 'Not Something I'm Willing to Live Under.'" *Guardian*, 8 July 2013.

Gutiérrez, Carlos. "Harán público expediente sobre el asesinato del periodista Manuel Buendía." *Milenio*, 16 May 2011.

Gutiérrez Rodríguez, Luis. "¿Qué más quiere Becerra Acosta?" *unomásuno*, 2 October 1989, 9.

Hallinan, Conn. "The Iran-Contragate Drug Connection." *People's Daily World*, 30 January 1987, A14.

Hernández López, Rogelio. "Ahora es más fácil desnudar los excesos del poder." *Revista mexicana de comunicación* 2, no. 10 (April 1990): 21–23. Interview conducted by Omar Raúl Martínez.

———. "El caso Buendía, razón de Estado: ¿Fue un crimen con intención política?" *Excélsior*, 29 May 1986, 1, 16.

———. "Ellos, nos escondieron la verdad." In Ángel Buendía Téllez Girón, *Mi testimonio sobre el asesinato de mi hermano Manuel Buendía*, 15–40. 2nd ed. Guadalajara, Jalisco: Amate Editor, 1999.

———. "Planea la DEA detener a más mexicanos." *Excélsior*, 26 October 1990, 1, 28, 43.

———. "Preparan en la DEA la tercera fase de la Operación Leyenda." *Excélsior*, 24 October 1990, 1, 26, 39.

———. "Protege la DEA a los secuestradores de Macháin." *Excélsior*, 23 October 1990, 1, 17.

———. "'Seguro: No seremos extraditados'; Confía la DEA en nosotros; Gárate y Héctor Berréllez." *Excélsior*, 25 October 1990, 1, 22.

Hernández Montoya, Antonio. "Elena Poniatowska: Buendía, buscar el gato escondido, en el caso." *El Día*, 29 May 1989, 1, 6.

Hirales, Gustavo, and José Domínguez. "Presentan denuncia formal contra Miguel Nazar Haro." *La Jornada*, 18 March 1989, 13.

Hooks, Michael, with Herbert Johnson. "Kingpin." Forty-five-page typescript précis of a proposed book or movie, n.d. BBCF, carton 1, Informants and sources: Hooks.

Hunter, Jane. "Harari, el asesor israelí de Noriega, apareció en Tel Aviv." *unomásuno*, 12 January 1990, 1, 19.

Idalia Gómez, María. "México: Abren al público expediente del crimen de Manuel Buendía." *Sociedad Interamericana de Prensa*, no. 70 (1 June 2011).

"Informe del fiscal especial: Aún no aparece el autor de la muerte de Buendía." *unomásuno*, 28 November 1988, 13.

Israel Montes, Gerardo. "Liquidaciones pendientes en Excélsior: Desacuerdo interno por los montos de las indemnizaciones." *Revista Zócalo*, January 2003.

Jarquín Egar, Soledad. "Mujeres y política: Manuel Buendía, periodista incomparable." *Las Caracolas: Periodismo de la condición social de las mujeres*, 10 March 2013. http://caracolasfem .blogspot.com/2013/03/mujeres-y-politica-manuel-buendia.html.

Jiménez, Alfredo, and Luis Segura. "Gerhardt Mertins no participó en el asesinato de Buendía: Morales L." *Excélsior*, 25 July 1989, 1, 36.

Johnston Hernández, Beatriz. "El gran acusado en el juicio por el asesinato de Camarena, el gobierno mexicano: Fiscal y defensa, en lucha por su propio prestigio." *Proceso*, 16 July 1990, 18, 20–21.

Jones, Robert F. "Marlin Lover of Mazatlán." *Sports Illustrated*, 31 March 1969, 42.

Juárez, Fernando A. "¿Fiscalías para delitos contra periodistas? Expertos advierten sobre las contradicciones del sistema judicial que enfrentan los fiscales especiales y las fiscalías especiales." *Los Periodistas* (Órgano oficial de la Fraternidad de Reporteros de México, A.C.), no. 10 (June 2005).

"Judge Throws Out Testimony on CIA." *Press Democrat* (Santa Rosa, CA), 7 July 1990, B3.

"La DFS investigó el caso Buendía sólo tres semanas." *unomásuno*, 27 June 1989, 1, 10–11.

La Jeunesse, William, and Lee Ross. "US Intelligence Assets in Mexico Reportedly Tied to Murdered DEA Agent." FoxNews.com, 10 October 2013. http://www.foxnews.com/politics /2013/10/10/us-intelligence-assets-reportedly-played-role-in-capture-dea-agent-in-mexico/.

"La libertad de expresión, básica para el funcionamiento de un sistema democrático: Palabras de CSG al conmemorar el Día de la Libertad de Prensa." *unomásuno*, 8 June 1989, 6.

"Las lecciones del caso Zorrilla." *unomásuno*, 21 June 1989, 3.

Levine, Michael. "The Emperor Is Butt Naked." Expert Witness Radio, 1997. http://www.expert witnessradio.org/site/the-emperor-is-butt-naked/.

"Liberan a Zorrilla y Moro, homicidas de Buendía." *Milenio*, 19 February 2009.

"Libre, Caro Quintero: EU lo busca." Informador, 10 August 2013. www.informador.com.mx/ mexico/2013/477668/6/libre-caro-quintero-eu-lo-busca.htm.

"Libres, los verdaderos asesinos de Buendía: El defensor de Zorrilla." *El Universal*, 12 July 1989, 12.

Littlefield, Dana. "Senior Judge Is Retiring after 25 Years on Bench." *San Diego Union-Tribune*, 29 December 2008.

López, Rigoberto. "Procuraduría de Justicia: ¿Acuerdos con Zorrilla?" *unomásuno*, 18 June 1989, 18.

Lucas, Douglas. "A Deal with the Right Devil." WhoWhatWhy, 10 March 2014. http://who whatwhy.com/2014/03/10/deal-right-devil.

MacAskill, Ewen. "Edward Snowden, NSA Files Source: 'If They Want to Get You, in Time They Will.'" *Guardian*, 10 June 2013.

"Manuel Buendía: Cinco años después; Cronología de las investigacions desde 1984 hasta el día de ayer, versiones oficiales." *El Día*, 30 May 1989, 10.

Marín, Carlos. "Casi cuatro años después, Gobernación se abre a la investigación del caso Buendía." *Proceso*, 21 March 1988, 20–21.

———. "Gobernación exonera a Zorrilla, corre a 427 y afirma que la DFS es legal." *Proceso*, 10 June 1985, 8–10.

Martínez, Omar Raúl, Juan Antonio Barrera, Fabiola N. Perafín, and Verónica T. Martínez. "Un período sombrío para el periodismo mexicano." *Revista mexicana de comunicación* 7, no. 40 (May–July 1995): 6–10.

Martínez, Sanjuana. "El Ejército mexicano ha enviado a 440 oficiales a especializarse en la Escuela de las Américas: Por lo menos tres actúan en Chiapas." *Proceso*, 3 April 1995, 26–27.

Martínez M., José. "Buendía, crimen desde el poder." *La Crítica*, 6 June 2004.

Maza, Enrique. "Florentino Ventura 'es el hombre más brutal y el más eficiente.'" *Proceso*, 2 May 1988.

Meislin, Richard J. "Noted Mexican Journalist Shot Dead." *New York Times*, 1 June 1984, 3.

Merina, Victor. "Judge Slaps Gag Order on Trials of 7 Deputies." *Los Angeles Times*, 24 October 1990.

"Mexican Drug Lord Transferred to State Prison." Borderland Beat: Reporting on the Mexican Cartel Drug War, 2 June 2010. http://www.borderlandbeat.com/2010/06/mexican-drug-lord -transferred-to-state.html.

"Mexico: The Cop and the Newsman." *Time*, 26 June 1989, 46.

Meyer, Lorenzo. "El Zorrillagate: Presidencialismo y patología del sistema." *Excélsior*, 30 June 1989, 1, 10.

"Michael Harari: Israeli Agent Avenged Athletes." Obituary. *San Francisco Chronicle*, 29 September 2014, C3.

Millares García, Alfonso, and Juan Rivas. "Se suicidó Florentino Ventura tras matar a su esposa y otra mujer." *Excélsior*, 18 September 1988, 1, 30–31.

Miller, Marjorie. "Ex-Chief of Mexico Police Group Accused as Mastermind of '84 Killing of Journalist." *Los Angeles Times*, 13 June 1989.

———. "Scandal Spurs Fears over Violence: Death of 'the Tiger' Puts Mexico Police in Spotlight." *Los Angeles Times*, 28 September 1988.

Miller, Marjorie, and Jim Newton. "Defendant Freed in Camarena Case: Efforts to Keep Dr. Humberto Alvarez Machain in Los Angeles Fail; Mexican Officials Hail His Release." *Los Angeles Times*, 16 December 1992.

Monge, Raúl. "Con sus declaraciones, Moro enturbió más el caso Buendía." *Proceso*, 10 September 1990, 28–29.

———. "Inútiles los reclamos de la oposición: Nazar se encargará de 'la inteligencia' en la capital." *Proceso*, 26 December 1988, 6–8.

Monge, Raúl, and Ignacio Ramírez. "Es muy probable que el autor intelectual de la muerte de Buendía sea un político: El fiscal especial; Zorrilla alteró el escenario del crimen." *Proceso*, 15 May 1989, 14–17.

———. "Funcionarios que obstruyeron la investigación y substrajeron pruebas, a punto de quedar impunes." *Proceso*, 15 May 1989, 14–15.

———. "Zorrilla Pérez se contradice sobre lo que hizo en el caso Buendía: Durante 22 horas declaró ante el fiscal especial." *Proceso*, 29 May 1989, 16–19.

Morales Lechuga, Ignacio. "'Hay elementos absolutamente suficientes para demostrar la culpabilidad de Zorrilla Pérez': PJDF; Hubo voluntad política para *desterrar* la impunidad." *Revista mexicana de comunicación* 3, no. 17 (May–June 1991): 19–20. Interview conducted by Miguel Ángel Sánchez de Armas.

Morley, Jefferson. "The Spy Who Loved Him." *Washington Post*, 17 March 1996, F1, 5.

"Moro asesinó a Buendía: La PGJDF." *unomásuno*, 1 July 1989, 1, 11.

Murphy, Kim. "Contra-Drugs Link Called 'Fantasy.'" *Los Angeles Times*, 31 August 1988.

Newton, Jim. "Camarena's Abduction and Torture Described: Former Bodyguard Says Ranking Mexican Officials Were at the House Where U.S. Drug Agent Was Killed." *Los Angeles Times*, 10 December 1992.

————. "Testimony Links Mexican Officials to Agent's Death: Trial; Cabinet Members Helped Plot Camarena Murder, Informant Says; Mexico Denounces Accusation." *Los Angeles Times*, 9 December 1992.

Olmos, Alejandro. "La marea de la crisis económica arrastra a los medios mexicanos." *Revista de comunicación mexicana* 7, no. 40 (May–July 1995): 27–29.

Ortega Pizarro, Fernando. "Para la DEA, Zorrilla es clave para descifrar el narcotráfico en México." *Proceso*, 3 June 1985, 6, 8–9.

————. "*Proceso* tiene la razón: El director de la DEA en México; 'Se provocó una reacción del Gobierno y hablaron a la Embajada,' dice Edward Heath." *Proceso*, 10 June 1985, 6–8, 11.

————. "Washington cedió un peón, Mullen, pero acusó a autoridades mexicanas de complicidad con cabezas del narcotráfico." *Proceso*, 4 March 1985, 18–20.

Ortiz Pinchetti, Francisco. "Desde hace seis meses, de hecho no investigaban ya el asesinato de Buendía." *Proceso*, 10 March 1986, 6–9.

Padgett, Humberto. "Reportaje: Caro Quintero, el hombre que compró al Estado." *Zona FrancaMX*, 3 September 2013. http://zonafranca.mx/reportaje-caro-el-hombre-que-compro -al-estado/.

————. "Reportaje: Cuando los tigres del narco se soltaron." *ZonaFrancaMX*, 6 September 2013. http://zonafranca.mx/reportaje-cuando-los-tigres-del-narco-se-soltaron/.

————. "Reportaje: La gran traición: la Inteligencia en manos del narco." *ZonaFrancaMX*, 7 September 2013). http://zonafranca.mx/reportaje-la-gran-traicion-la-inteligencia-en-manos -del-narco/.

Parry, Robert. "The CIA/MSM Contra-Cocaine Cover-Up." 26 September 2014. https://con sortiumnews.com/2014/09/26/the-ciamsm-contra-cocaine-cover-up/.

"Passings: Ruben Zuno Arce." *Los Angeles Times*, 20 September 2012.

Petrich Moreno, Blanche. "The Long Arm of the War on Drugs: WikiLeaks Cables Reveal How Much Washington Drives Mexico's Counternarcotics Policies." *The Nation*, 13 August 2012, 17–22.

Puig, Carlos. "La DEA se anima a extender el juicio a acusados del caso Camarena." *Proceso*, 24 September 1990, 31.

————. "Según la fiscalía de Los Angeles, García Paniagua estuvo en una junta en que se decidió secuestrar a Camarena." *Proceso*, 7 May 1990, 26–27.

Quintero Arias, José. "Hay sólo 24 posibles autores intelectuales y 7 presuntos materiales: García Domínguez." *unomásuno*, 25 May 1989, 6.

Ramírez, Carlos. "La muerte de Buendía, una investigación policiaca inconclusa." *El Financiero*, 10 July 1989, 4.

————. "Manuel Buendía y el huevo de la serpiente." Editorial. *Revista indicador político*, 26 May 2014, 2.

Ramírez, Ignacio. "Buendía, caso cerrado: Quedan dudas, contradicciones, hilos sueltos." *Proceso*, 22 February 1993, 21–24.

————. "Caso Buendía: Confusión y contradicciones en una investigación que no termina; No fue un crimen político dijeron Adato y Sales Gasque." *Proceso*, 26 June 1989, 6–8, 10.

————. "'Dije lo que querían, me jugaron chueco; me había presentado amparado': Moro Ávila Camacho." *Proceso*, 10 July 1989, 20, 22–25.

————. "El homicidio, tal como aparece en las actas judiciales: La muerte de Buendía, según tres testigos." *Proceso*, 24 July 1989, 24–27.

————. "Los testimonios revelan nuevos datos sobre el asesinato de Buendía: Coincidencias en que hubo alguien que cubrió al asesino." *Proceso*, 21 August 1989, 22–24.

————. "Se difundirá una filmación de la reconstrucción del asesinato de Buendía." *Proceso*, 6 June 1988, 26–28.

Ramírez de Aguilar L., Fernando. "500 millones de pesos de recompensa a quien aporte datos que conduzcan a atrapar al asesino de Buendía." *unomásuno*, 25 February 1988.

———. "A 5 años de la muerte de Buendía, todo indica que no se resolverá a corto plazo." *unomásuno*, 29 May 1989, 10.

———. "Caso Buendía: No puede desecharse la hipótesis de un crimen político; Acepta García Domínguez." *unomásuno*, 30 May 1989, 11.

———. "Han desertado 350 agentes de la Dirección de Inteligencia: Está acéfala en su mando." *unomásuno*, 27 June 1989, 11.

———. "Podría pasar el sexenio sin aclararse la muerte de Buendía, dice García Domínguez." *unomásuno*, 7 December 1988, 12.

———. "Un grupo de agentes de la DEA busca pruebas contra Zuno Arce." *unomásuno*, 12 March 1989, 12.

———. "Zorrilla Pérez se presentará a declarar ante el MP *en algún lugar* de la capital." *unomásuno*, 4 March 1988.

Ramírez de Aguilar L., Fernando, and Héctor Cruz López. "Acusa la PJDF a Zorrilla Pérez del homicidio de Manuel Buendía." *unomásuno*, 12 June 1989, 1, 12.

———. "Lo torturó la Judicial, dice Juventino Prado: Niega haber confesado que participó en el homicidio de Buendía." *unomásuno*, 26 June 1989, 1, 14.

Ramírez de Aguilar L., Fernando, and Jorge Reyes. "Avance sustancial en las pesquisas sobre el asesinato de Manuel Buendía: La Procuraduría." *unomásuno*, 28 May 1987, 12.

"Reaprehenden a José Antonio Zorrilla." *Milenio*, 15 June 2009.

René de Dios, Sergio. "Ángel Buendía acusa: 'Estoy convencido de que fue la CIA la que ordenó el asesinato de mi hermano.'" *Jalisco Hoy*, 24 May 1993.

"Resucitan a Nazar: No importaron las acusaciones de represor, de torturador, de informante de la CIA." *Proceso*, 26 December 1988, 6–13.

Reyes Estrada, Jorge. "Trasladaron a Zorrilla Pérez al Reclusorio Norte: Hermetismo total." *unomásuno*, 15 June 1989, 14.

Reyes Estrada, Jorge, and Héctor Cruz López. "Acusa Moro Ávila Camacho del homicidio de Buendía a un ex *madrina* asesinado." *unomásuno*, 22 June 1989, 1, 13.

———. "Cayó el asesino de Buendía: Es Juan R. Moro Avila Camacho, un ex agente." *unomásuno*, 21 June 1989, 1, 13.

———. "Cuatro ex jefes de la DFS, aprehendidos." *unomásuno*, 20 June 1989, 1, 11.

Reyes Estrada, Jorge, and Fernando Ramírez de Aguilar L. "El asesino fue visto en la DFS: Aún no lo aprehenden." *unomásuno*, 17 June 1989, 1, 11.

———. "Un alemán, traficante de armas, principal sospechoso de la muerte de Manuel Buendía." *unomásuno*, 30 May 1987, 7.

Robles, Manuel. "El socio de Mertins, acusado de haberlo delatado ante Manuel Buendía." *Proceso*, 21 March 1988, 20–23.

Robinson, Deborah. "Unsolved Mysteries in Clinton Country." *In These Times*, 12–18 February 1992, 9, 11.

Rodriguez, Olga R. "Mexico Arrests Ex-Spy Chief in '75 Kidnapping: Former Official Accused in 'Dirty War' Disappearance of Leftist." *San Francisco Chronicle*, 20 February 2004.

Rodríguez Castañeda, Rafael. "Buendía sabía su riesgo, pero no calculó el asesinato, dice su secretario." *Proceso*, 3 June 1985, 9–10, 12–15.

———. "La intromisión de agentes de Washington en México vulnera la Constitución: De la legal Operación Janos, a la delictuosa Operación Padrino." *Proceso*, 4 March 1985, 16, 21–23.

Rohter, Larry. "Nir's Fatal Visit to Mexico Called a Business Trip to Buy Avocados." *New York Times*, 6 December 1988, 8.

Rojas, Luis García, Roberto Santiago, and Ernesto Zavaleta. "Nassar atribuye su salida a los cargos en EU: Intentan desacreditar al gobierno, afirma." *unomásuno*, 25 February 1989, 12.

Rojas, Xavier. "Claro que sentí miedo, pero hay que cumplir con el deber, señaló el procurador Morales Lechuga." *El Heraldo*, 17 June 1989, 1.

———. "Moro Ávila-Camacho, admitió haber ayudado al asesino del periodista: Para cubrir a los criminales, se desató una ola de muertes; El autor material, acribillado un mes después del homicidio." *El Heraldo*, 22 June 1989, 1.

Romero Ceyde, David, and Alfonso Moraflores. "El plan para desaparecer a Buendía lo reveló Prado y hundió a Moro A." *Ovaciones*, 26 June 1989, 1, 10.

Romero Jacobo, César. "'La diferencia con Salinas es que él juega a cuatros y yo no': El Buho Valle." *unomásuno*, Sunday political supplement *páginauno*, 2 July 1989, 3–4.

Roque, Manuel. "Esperanzas de resolver el caso, dice Angel Buendía." *unomásuno*, 25 May 1989, 6.

Rosenzweg, David. "Camarena Case Witness Recants Allegations, U.S. Says." *Los Angeles Times*, 6 February 1998.

Ross, John. "Mexico's Blood-Stained Pens: Mexico Has Trumpeted the Arrest of a Suspect in the Killing of Journalist Manuel Buendía, but What the Government Doesn't Say Is the Epidemic of Journalists' Killings Continues Unabated." *San Francisco Bay Guardian*, 28 June 1989, 20–22, 26.

———. "The Nota Roja's Notoriety Is Paying Off for Mexico's President." Photocopied typescript of article submitted to the *San Francisco Examiner*, July 1989, 7–8. BBCF, carton 1, Informants and sources: Ross.

Rothschild, Matthew. "La CIA vs. Manuel Buendía." *Revista mexicana de comunicación* 1, no. 5 (May–June 1989): 18–20.

———. "¿Quién mató a Manuel Buendía? Hay cuatro grupos merecedores de sospecha." Entrevista realizada por Russell H. Bartley. *unomásuno*, Sunday political supplement *páginauno*, 19 May 1985, 1–3.

———. "Who Killed Manuel Buendía? A Mexican Mystery." *The Progressive*, April 1985, 18–23.

Sánchez de Armas, Miguel Ángel. "Caso Buendía: Precisiones." *El Financiero*, 17 July 1989, 11.

———. "Caso Buendía: Respuesta a una demanda de la opinión pública." *Punto*, 1 February 1988.

———. "En defensa de la palabra: 'El caso Buendía nos debe llevar a examinar toda la cuestión de la prensa, en México y en EU'; Russell Bartley." *Revista mexicana de comunicación* 2, no. 11 (May–June 1990): 30–31.

———. "Zorrilla y Moro presos: Otras preguntas quedan." *Revista mexicana de comunicación* 1, no. 6 (August 1989): 9.

Santiago, Roberto. "Acuerdo de la Permanente para conocer el estado de la investigación sobre Buendía." *unomásuno*, 25 May 1989, 6.

"Soy ajeno al homicidio de Buendía: Zorrilla; En un texto que envió al subprocurador García Domínguez, dice que no ha sido citado formalmente." *Excélsior*, 1 March 1988, 5, 45.

Suárez, Luis. "Buendía: Credibilidad recuperada." *Excélsior*, 15 June 1989, 7.

———. "Más que una mera coincidencia, los atentados contra Buendía y Pastora." *Excélsior*, 16 August 1989, 5, 37.

Sullivan, Kevin. "Mexican Vows Investigation into 'Dirty War': Military to Be Focus of Probe of Killings, Disappearances." *Washington Post*, 27 January 2002, A25.

Szykowny, Rick. "A Funny, Dirty Little Drug War." *Humanist* 50, no. 5 (September–October 1990): 16–18. Interview with Michael Levine.

Taubman, Philip. "Objection by C.I.A. Blocks Indictment: Prosecution of Mexican Could Curb Spying, Agency Says." *New York Times*, 28 March 1982, 1, 14.

"Trial Opens in Death of Tortured Drug Agent." *New York Times*, 31 July 1988.

Tuckman, Jo. "Adolfo Aguilar Zínser: Acute Mexican Politician with a Reputation for Integrity." Obituary. *Guardian*, 8 June 2005.

Tulsky, Fredric N. "Evidence Casts Doubt on Camarena Case Trials." *Los Angeles Times*, 26 October 1997, A23.

Uhlig, Mark A. "American's Jailing Revives Contra Issue." *Milwaukee Journal*, 12 February 1989, A6.

"Una cadena de fallas puso en la calle a Caro Quintero." *Proceso*, 11 August 2013.

Universidad Autónoma de Guadalajara. *Reseña Histórica de la Universidad Autónoma de Guadalajara.* http://campusdigital.uag.mx/varios/resena.php. Official online history of the Autonomous University of Guadalajara. Photocopy in BBCF, carton 2: subject files.

———. "La Educación y la Justicia Social en la Filosofía de la UAG." *Reseña Histórica de la Universidad Autónoma de Guadalajara.* http://campusdigital.uag.mx/varios/laeduca.php.

———. "Principales logros del Plan Maestro de Desarrollo." *Reseña Histórica de la Universidad Autónoma de Guadalajara.* http://campusdigital.uag.mx/varios/principales.php.

Valle, Eduardo. "Azorrillados." *El Universal Gráfico*, 15 June 1985.

———. "Castigo a la torpeza." *El Universal Gráfico*, 29 May 1985.

———. "Crónica de un atentado." *Proceso*, 26 June 1989.

———. "Fábula de mayo." *El Universal*, 30 May 1985.

Vera, Rodrigo. "Ni narcos ni campesinos: Fueron contras entrenados por la CIA, los que asesinaron a 22 judiciales en Veracruz; Cinco años después, un informe de la DEA contradice la versión que dio la Procuraduría." *Proceso*, 9 July 1990, 23–24.

Von Nowaffen, Sergio. "El Secreto de Buendía: Líderes en tráfico de armas pedían cabeza de un alemán." *Ovaciones*, 14 June 1989, 1, 6.

———. "Estaba abatido . . . la sonrisa desapareció." *Ovaciones*, 14 June 1989, 1.

Vulliamy, Ed. "Joaquín 'Chapo' Guzmán: The Mexican Drug Lord Adept at Playing the System." *Guardian*, 22 February 2014.

Washington Valdez, Diana, and Daniel Borunda. "Mexican Kingpin Rafael Caro Quintero's Release Fuels Anger." *El Paso Times*, 18 August 2013.

Watrous, Steve. "What the Contra Hearings Didn't Tell." *Shepherd Express* (Milwaukee), 4–18 March 1988, 5.

Weinstein, Henry. "DEA Operative Details His Role in Kidnaping: He Says He Arranged the Abduction of Mexican Doctor with U.S. Agent's Approval." *Los Angeles Times*, 28 April 1990.

———. "'Everyone I Met' Is Corrupt, Informant Tells Drug Tales at Camarena Trial." *Press Democrat* (Santa Rosa, CA), 7 June 1990, B7.

———. "Judge Is Asked to Turn Over Papers or Quit Case: Lawyers for a Mexican Businessman Accused of Plotting to Kill Drug Agent Enrique Camarena Say They Have a Right to See Secretly Filed Documents." *Los Angeles Times*, 12 February 1990.

———. "Judge Overrules Bid to Link CIA, Drug Lords in Camarena Trial." *Los Angeles Times*, 8 June 1990.

———. "Now-DEA Operative Heard Camarena Killing Discussed, Witness Says." *Los Angeles Times*, 23 June 1990.

———. "Official Mexico Corruption Blasted: Drug Cartel Called 'Beyond Reach of Law.'" *Press Democrat* (Santa Rosa, CA), 12 July 1990, B4.

———. "Opening Volleys in Camarena Case: Trial; Prosecutors Say They Will Show Agent's Murder Was Part of a Campaign to 'Intimidate the DEA.'" *Los Angeles Times*, 16 May 1990.

———. "Witness Says Drug Lord Told of Contra Arms." *Los Angeles Times*, 7 July 1990.

———. "Witness Who Tied CIA to Traffickers Must Testify Anew." *Los Angeles Times*, 6 July 1990.

Weissenstein, Michael. "Rafael Caro Quintero Released: U.S. Angry Mexico Sets Free Drug Lord Who Killed DEA Agent Kiki Camarena." Huffington Post, 10 August 2013. http://www.huffingtonpost.com/2013/08/10/rafael-caro-quintero-released_n_3736511.html.

Williams, Adam, Eric Martin, and Nacha Cattan. "Mexico Passes Oil Bill Seen Luring \$20 Billion a Year." Bloomberg Business, 13 December 2013. http://www.bloomberg.com/news/2013-12-12/mexico-lower-house-passes-oil-overhaul-to-break-state-monopoly.html.

"Witness Testifies Drug Lord Supplied Arms to Contras." *Oakland Tribune*, 7 July 1990, A4.

Zorrilla Pérez, José Antonio. "A la opinión pública." *Excélsior*, 1 March 1988, 20.

Books

Agee, Philip. *Inside the Company: CIA Diary*. New York: Stonehill, 1975.

———. *On the Run*. Secaucus, NJ: Lyle Stuart, 1987.

Aguayo Quezada, Sergio. *La charola: Una historia de los servicios de inteligencia en México*. Mexico City: Grijalbo, 2001.

Aguilar Camín, Héctor. *Después del milagro*. 2nd ed. Mexico City: Cal y Arena, 1989.

Anderson, Scott, and Jon Lee Anderson. *Inside the League: The Shocking Exposé of How Terrorists, Nazis, and Latin American Death Squads Have Infiltrated the World Anti-communist League*. New York: Dodd, Mead, 1986.

Article 19. *In the Shadow of Buendía: The Mass Media and Censorship in Mexico*. Introductory essay by Carlos Monsiváis. London: International Centre on Censorship, 1989.

Arvide, Isabel, and Dora Herrera. *La verdadera historia de Camarena según Hilda Vázquez*. Mexico City: Ediciones Argrami, 1990.

Avirgan, Tony, and Martha Honey, eds. *La Penca: On Trial in Costa Rica; The CIA vs. the Press*. 2nd ed. San José, Costa Rica: Editorial Porvenir, 1988.

Bacevich, Andrew J. *Washington Rules: America's Path to Permanent War*. New York: Metropolitan Books, 2010.

Baer, Robert. *See No Evil: The True Story of a Ground Soldier in the CIA's War on Terrorism*. New York: Three Rivers Press, 2003.

Bartley, Russell H. *Imperial Russia and the Struggle for Latin American Independence, 1808–1828*. Austin: Institute of Latin American Studies, University of Texas, 1978.

Bartley, Russell H., ed. and trans. *Soviet Historians on Latin America: Recent Scholarly Contributions*. Madison: Conference on Latin American History, University of Wisconsin, 1978.

Becerra Acosta, Manuel. *Dos poderes*. Mexico City: Grijalbo, 1985.

Beck, Melvin. *Secret Contenders: The Myth of Cold War Counterintelligence*. Introduction by Thomas Powers. New York: Sheridan Square Press, 1984.

Ben-Menashe, Ari. *Profits of War: Inside the Secret U.S.-Israeli Arms Network*. New York: Sheridan Square Press, 1992.

Blum, William. *America's Deadliest Export: Democracy; The Truth about US Foreign Policy and Everything Else*. London: Zed Books, 2013.

———. *Killing Hope: U.S. Military and CIA Interventions since World War II*. Monroe, ME: Common Courage Press, 1995.

———. *Rogue State: A Guide to the World's Only Superpower*. Monroe, ME: Common Courage Press, 2000.

Bonasso, Miguel. *Recuerdo de la muerte*. Mexico City: Era, 1984.

Borrás, Leopoldo. *Historia del periodismo mexicano: Del ocaso porfirista al derecho a la información*. Mexico City: Dirección General de Información, National Autonomous University of Mexico, 1983.

Bowden, Charles. *Down by the River: Drugs, Money, Murder, and Family*. New York: Simon & Schuster, 2004.

———. *A Shadow in the City: Confessions of an Undercover Drug Warrior*. New York: Harcourt, 2005.

Bowden, Charles, and Molly Molloy. *Blood on the Corn*. Illustrated by Matt Rota. Medium.com. Part 1, https://medium.com/matter/blood-on-the-corn-52ac13f7e643; part 2, https://medium.com/matter/blood-on-the-corn-part-ii-b4f447d70a8c; part 3, https://medium.com/matter/blood-on-the-corn-part-iii-b13f100cbf32.

Brewton, Pete. *The Mafia, CIA, and George Bush*. New York: S.P.I. Books, 1992.

Buendía, Manuel. *Ejercicio periodístico*. Mexico City: Océano, 1985.

———. *El fútbol y la TV: Apuestas, derrotas y vicios deportivos*. Mexico City: Cuadernos de las Horas Extras, 1988.

———. *El humor*. Preface by José Joaquín Blanco. Xalapa: Universidad Veracruzana, 1986.

———. *El oficio de informar*. Preface by Rogelio Hernández. Guadalajara: Universidad de Guadalajara, 1988.

———. *Instantáneas del poder*. Preface by Oscar Hinojosa. Mexico City: Fundación Manuel Buendía, 1988.

———. *La CIA en México*. Mexico City: Océano, 1984.

———. *La Santa Madre*. Mexico City: Océano, 1985.

———. *La ultraderecha en México*. Mexico City: Océano, 1984.

———. *Los empresarios*. Mexico City: Océano, 1986.

———. *Los petroleros*. Mexico City: Océano, 1985.

———. *Pensamiento y acción de la derecha poblana*. Puebla: Universidad Autónoma de Puebla, 1987.

———. *Ul'trapravye v Meksike*. Moscow: Progress Publishers, 1987. Translation of Buendía's *La ultraderecha en México*.

Buendía Téllezgirón, Ángel. *Mi testimonio sobre el asesinato de mi hermano Manuel Buendía*. 2nd ed. Guadalajara: Amate Editor, 1999.

Cárdenas, Héctor. *Las relaciones mexicano-soviéticas: Antecedentes y primeros contactos diplomáticos (1789–1927)*. Preface by Roque González Salazar. Mexico City: Secretaría de Relaciones Exteriores, 1974.

Castañeda, Jorge G. *México: El futuro en juego*. Mexico City: Joaquín Mortiz, 1987.

Castillo, Celerino, III, and Dave Harmon. *Powderburns: Cocaine, Contras, and the Drug War*. Buffalo: Mosaic Press, 1994.

Centeno, Miguel Ángel. *Democracy within Reason: Technocratic Revolution in Mexico*. 2nd ed. University Park: Pennsylvania State University Press, 1997.

Chamorro, Edgar. *Packaging the Contras: A Case of CIA Disinformation*. Monographs, no. 2. New York: Institute for Media Analysis, 1987.

La CIA en América Latina. Cuadernos 2. Bogotá, Colombia: Alternativa, 1975.

Clarridge, Duane R., with Digby Diehl. *A Spy for All Seasons: My Life in the CIA*. New York: Scribner, 1997.

Cockburn, Alexander, and Jeffrey St. Clair. *Whiteout: The CIA, Drugs, and the Press*. London: Verso, 1998.

Cockburn, Leslie. *Out of Control: The Story of the Reagan Administration's Secret War in Nicaragua, the Illegal Arms Pipeline, and the Contra Drug Connection*. New York: Atlantic Monthly Press, 1987.

Committee of Santa Fe. *A New Inter-American Policy for the Eighties.* Washington, DC: Council for Inter-American Security, 1980.

Corn, David. *Blond Ghost: Ted Shackley and the CIA's Crusades.* New York: Simon & Schuster, 1994.

Cornwell, Rupert. *"God's Banker."* New York: Dodd, Mead, 1983.

Crumpton, Henry A. *The Art of Intelligence: Lessons from a Life in the CIA's Clandestine Service.* New York: Penguin, 2012.

deHaven-Smith, Lance. *Conspiracy Theory in America.* Austin: University of Texas Press, 2013.

Dieterich, Heinz. *Nicaragua: La construcción de la sociedad sin clases.* Interview with Noam Chomsky, preface by Gregorio Selser. Mexico City: Editorial Uno, 1986.

de la Madrid Hurtado, Miguel, with Alejandra Lajous. *Cambio de Rumbo: Testimonio de una Presidencia, 1982–1988.* Mexico City: Fondo de Cultura Económica, 2004.

De Silva, Peer. *Sub Rosa: The CIA and the Uses of Intelligence.* New York: Times Books, 1978.

Dornbierer, Manú. *La guerra de las drogas: Historia y testimonios de un negocio político.* 4th ed. Mexico City: Grijalbo, 1993.

———. *Los periodistas mueren de noche.* Mexico City: Grijalbo, 1993.

Draper, Theodore. *A Very Thin Line: The Iran-Contra Affairs.* New York: Simon & Schuster, 1991.

Ellsberg, Daniel. *The Pentagon Papers: The Defense Department History of United States Decision-Making on Vietnam.* 4 vols. Boston: Beacon, 1971.

———. *Secrets: A Memoir of Vietnam and the Pentagon Papers.* New York: Viking, 2002.

Englehardt, Tom. *Shadow Government: Surveillance, Secret Wars, and a Global Security State in a Single-Superpower World.* Chicago: Haymarket Books, 2014.

Esquivel, J. Jesús. *La CIA, Camarena y Caro Quintero: La historia secreta.* Mexico City: Grijalbo, 2014.

———. *La DEA en México: Una historia oculta del narcotráfico contada por los agentes.* Mexico City: Grijalbo, 2013.

Fernández Menéndez, Jorge. *Narcotráfico y poder.* Mexico City: Rayuela Editores, 1999.

Fischer, David Hackett. *Historians' Fallacies: Toward a Logic of Historical Thought.* New York: Harper Torchbooks, 1970.

Fundación Manuel Buendía. *Los días de Manuel Buendía: Testimonios.* Mexico City: Océano, 1984.

Galeano, Eduardo. *Espejos: Una historia casi universal.* Madrid: Siglo I de España, 2008.

García Ibarra, Abraham. *Los bárbaros del Norte: La contra mexicana.* Mexico City: Comunicación Meridiana, 1988.

Goldman, Francisco. *The Art of Political Murder: Who Killed the Bishop?* New York: Grove Press, 2008.

González, José G. *Lo negro del Negro Durazo.* Mexico City: Posada, 1983.

Granados Chapa, Miguel Ángel. *Buendía: El primer asesinato de la narcopolítica en México.* Mexico City: Grijalbo, 2012. Volume edited posthumously by Tomás Granados Salinas, with an appended documentary analysis by Tomás Tenorio Galindo titled "El crimen de Estado."

———. *Examen de la comunicación en México.* Mexico City: Ediciones El Caballito, 1983.

Grandin, Greg. *Empire's Workshop: Latin America, the United States, and the Rise of the New Imperialism.* New York: Metropolitan Books, 2006.

Green, Gil. *Cold War Fugitive: A Personal Story of the McCarthy Years.* New York: International Publishers, 1984.

Greenwald, Glenn. *No Place to Hide: Edward Snowden, the NSA, and the U.S. Surveillance State.* New York: Metropolitan Books, 2014.

Guía del Tercer Mundo, 1981. Mexico City: Cuadernos del Tercer Mundo, 1981. Annual supplement to *Cuadernos del Tercer Mundo.*

Harding, Luke. *The Snowden Files: The Inside Story of the World's Most Wanted Man.* New York: Vintage, 2014.

Helms, Richard, with William Hood. *A Look over My Shoulder: A Life in the Central Intelligence Agency.* Foreword by Henry A. Kissinger. New York: Random House, 2003.

Hernández, Anabel. *Los señores del narco.* Mexico City: Grijalbo, 2011.

———. *Narcoland: The Mexican Drug Lords and Their Godfathers.* Foreword by Roberto Saviano. Translated by Iain Bruce. London: Verso, 2013.

Hernández Campos, Jorge, ed. *Unomásuno: Diez años (1977–1987).* Mexico City: Editorial Uno, 1987.

Hernández López, Rogelio. *Zorrilla: El imperio del crimen.* Mexico City: Planeta, 1989.

Hitz, Frederick P. *The Great Game: The Myths and Reality of Espionage.* New York: Vintage, 2004.

Hobsbawm, Eric. *The Age of Extremes: A History of the World, 1914–1991.* New York: Pantheon, 1994.

Holt, Rod, ed. *Assault on Nicaragua: The Untold Story of the U.S. "Secret War."* San Francisco: Walnut Publishing, 1987. Includes speeches by Daniel Sheehan and Daniel Ortega, an essay by Jeff Mackler and Nat Weinstein, and an introduction by Rod Holt.

Honey, Martha. *Hostile Acts: U.S. Policy in Costa Rica in the 1980s.* Gainesville: University Press of Florida, 1994.

Honey, Martha, and Tony Avirgan. *La Penca: Reporte de una investigación.* Lima, Peru: El Gallo Rojo, n.d.

———. *La Penca: Reporte de una investigación.* 2nd ed. San José, Costa Rica: Editorial Porvenir, 1989.

Hougan, Jim. *Spooks: The Haunting of America; The Private Use of Secret Agents.* New York: William Morrow, 1978.

Hunt, E. Howard, with Greg Aunapu. *American Spy: My Secret History in the CIA, Watergate, and Beyond.* Foreword by William F. Buckley Jr. Hoboken, NJ: Wiley, 2007.

Hunter, Jane. *No Simple Proxy: Israel in Central America; A Report.* Edited by Jane Power and James Zogby. Washington, DC: Washington Middle East Associates, 1987.

Johnson, Chalmers. *Dismantling the Empire: America's Last Best Hope.* New York: Metropolitan Books, 2010.

Kagan, Robert. *A Twilight Struggle: American Power and Nicaragua, 1977–1990.* New York: Free Press, 1996.

Keeley, Edmund. *The Salonika Bay Murder: Cold War Politics and the Polk Affair.* Princeton, NJ: Princeton University Press, 1989.

Kornbluh, Peter. *Nicaragua: The Price of Intervention; Reagan's Wars against the Sandinistas.* Washington, DC: Institute for Policy Studies, 1987.

———. *The Pinochet File: A Declassified Dossier on Atrocity and Accountability.* New York: New Press, 2003.

Kuykendall, James. *¿O plata o plomo? "Silver or Lead?" The Abduction and Murder of DEA Agent Kiki Camarena.* San Bernardino, CA: Xlibris, 2005.

Kwitny, Johnathan. *The Crimes of Patriots: A True Tale of Dope, Dirty Money, and the CIA.* New York: W. W. Norton, 1987.

Lake, Anthony. *Somoza Falling: The Nicaraguan Dilemma; A Portrait of Washington at Work.* Boston: Houghton Mifflin, 1989.

Landau, Saul. *The Dangerous Doctrine: National Security and U.S. Foreign Policy.* Boulder, CO: Westview, 1988.

Langguth, A. J. *Hidden Terror.* New York: Pantheon, 1978.

Latell, Brian. *Mexico at the Crossroads: The Many Crises of the Political System.* Hoover Monograph Series 6. Stanford, CA: Hoover Institution Press, 1986.

Lemus, J. Jesús. *Los malditos: Crónica negra desde Puente Grande.* Mexico City: Grijalbo, 2013.

Lernoux, Penny. *Cry of the People: United States Involvement in the Rise of Fascism, Torture, and Murder and the Persecution of the Catholic Church in Latin America.* Garden City, NY: Doubleday, 1980.

Levine, Michael. *Deep Cover: The Inside Story of How DEA Infighting, Incompetence, and Subterfuge Lost Us the Biggest Battle of the Drug War.* New York: Delacorte Press, 1990.

Levine, Michael, with Laura Kavanau-Levine. *The Big White Lie: The CIA and the Cocaine/ Crack Epidemic.* New York: Thunder's Mouth Press, 1993.

Lindauer, Susan. *Extreme Prejudice: The Terrifying Story of the Patriot Act and the Cover Ups of 9/11 and Iraq.* Lexington, KY: Creative Space, 2010.

Loret de Mola, Carlos. *Que la nación me lo demande.* 2nd ed. Mexico City: Grijalbo, 1986.

Loret de Mola, Rafael. *Denuncia.* Mexico City: Grijalbo, 1987.

———. *Denuncia: Presidente sin palabra.* Rev. ed. Mexico City: Grijalbo, 1995.

———. *Las entrañas del poder: Secretos de campaña.* Mexico City: Grijalbo, 1991.

———. *Los escándalos: Un ensayo donde los culpables de los desórdenes políticos tienen nombre y apellido.* Mexico City: Grijalbo, 1999.

———. *Manos sucias: Crónicas verdaderas del poder.* Mexico City: Océano, 1996.

———. *Secretos de Estado: Narcotraficantes, narcopolicías . . . y una narcoguerra avivada por un tratado comercial y unas elecciones.* Mexico City: Grijalbo, 1994.

Marchetti, Victor, and John D. Marks. *The CIA and the Cult of Intelligence.* Introduction by Melvin L. Wulf. New York: Knopf, 1974.

Marshall, Jonathan, Peter Dale Scott, and Jane Hunter. *The Iran-Contra Connection: Secret Teams and Covert Operations in the Reagan Era.* Boston: South End Press, 1987.

Martin, Lionel. *The Early Fidel: Roots of Castro's Communism.* Secaucus, NJ: Lyle Stuart, 1978.

Martínez de la Vega, Francisco. *Personajes.* Mexico City: Océano, 1986.

Marton, Kati. *The Polk Conspiracy: Murder and Cover-Up in the Case of CBS News Correspondent George Polk.* New York: Times Books, 1992.

McClintock, Michael. *Instruments of Statecraft: U.S. Guerrilla Warfare, Counterinsurgency, and Counterterrorism, 1940–1990.* New York: Pantheon, 1992.

McCoy, Alfred W. *Policing America's Empire: The United States, the Philippines, and the Rise of the Surveillance State.* Madison: University of Wisconsin Press, 2009.

———. *The Politics of Heroin: CIA Complicity in the Global Drug Trade.* Brooklyn, NY: Lawrence Hill Books, 1991. Revised and expanded edition of *The Politics of Heroin in Southeast Asia.*

McCoy, Alfred W., Josep M. Fradera, and Stephen Jacobson, eds. *Endless Empire: Spain's Retreat, Europe's Eclipse, America's Decline.* Madison: University of Wisconsin Press, 2012.

McGhee, George C. *On the Front Line of the Cold War: An Ambassador Reports.* Westport, CT: Praeger, 1997.

Méndez Asensio, Luis. *Contadora: Las cuentas de la diplomacia.* Mexico City: Plaza y Valdés, 1987.

Mendoza, Leopoldo H. *El asesinato de un periodista.* Mexico City: Editorial Diana, 1984.

Menges, Constantine C. *Inside the National Security Council: The True Story of the Making and Unmaking of Reagan's Foreign Policy.* New York: Simon & Schuster, 1988.

Menjívar, Cecilia, and Néstor Rodríguez, eds. *When States Kill: Latin America, the U.S., and Technologies of Terror.* Austin: University of Texas Press, 2005.

Mills, James. *The Underground Empire: Where Crime and Governments Embrace.* Garden City, NY: Doubleday, 1986.

Minués Moreno, Héctor. *Los cooperativistas: El caso Excélsior.* Mexico City: EDAMEX, 1987.

Molloy, Molly, and Charles Bowden, eds. *El Sicario: The Autobiography of a Mexican Assassin.* New York: Nation Books, 2011.

Morley, Jefferson. *Our Man in Mexico: Winston Scott and the Hidden History of the CIA.* Foreword by Michael Scott. Lawrence: University Press of Kansas, 2008.

National Security Archive. *The Chronology: The Documented Day-by-Day Account of the Secret Military Assistance to Iran and the Contras.* Foreword by Seymour Hersh. New York: Warner Books, 1987.

Navarro, Aaron W. *Political Intelligence and the Creation of Modern Mexico, 1938–1954.* University Park: Pennsylvania State University Press, 2010.

Nelson, Allan. *The Nelson Brothers: Finnish-American Radicals from the Mendocino Coast.* Edited with an introduction and afterword by Russell and Sylvia Bartley. Ukiah, CA: Mendocino County Historical Society, 2005.

Neuberger, Günter, and Michael Opperskalski. *La CIA en Centroamérica y el Caribe.* Havana: Editorial José Martí, 1985.

O'Neil, Shannon K. *Two Nations Indivisible: Mexico, the United States, and the Road Ahead.* New York: Oxford University Press, 2013.

Parry, Robert. *Lost History: Contras, Cocaine, the Press, and "Project Truth."* Arlington, VA: Media Consortium, 1999.

Pastor, Robert A., and Jorge G. Castañeda. *Limits to Friendship: The United States and Mexico.* New York: Vintage, 1989.

Pazienza Donato, Franceso. *Il disubbidiente.* Milan: Longanesi, 1999.

Perkins, John. *The Secret History of the American Empire.* New York: Plume, 2007.

Poniatowska, Elena. *Fuerte es el silencio.* Mexico City: Era, 1988.

Powers, Thomas. *The Man Who Kept the Secrets: Richard Helms and the CIA.* New York: Knopf, 1979.

Prouty, L. Fletcher. *The Secret Team: The CIA and Its Allies in Control of the United States and the World.* New York: Skyhorse Publishing, 2008.

Ramírez, Carlos. *Operación Gavin: México en la diplomacia de Reagan.* Mexico City: El Día en Libros, 1987.

Ranelagh, John. *The Agency: The Rise and Decline of the CIA, from Wild Bill Donovan to William Casey.* New York: Simon & Schuster, 1986.

Reed, Terry, and John Cummings. *Compromised: Clinton, Bush, and the CIA.* New York: S.P.I. Books, 1994.

Reese, Mary Ellen. *General Reinhard Gehlen: The CIA Connection.* Fairfax, VA: George Mason University Press, 1990.

Richardson, William Harrison. *Mexico through Russian Eyes, 1806–1940.* Pittsburgh: University of Pittsburgh Press, 1988.

Riding, Alan. *Distant Neighbors: A Portrait of the Mexicans.* New York: Vintage, 1986.

Risen, James. *Pay Any Price: Greed, Power, and Endless War.* Boston: Houghton Mifflin Harcourt, 2014.

Rizzo, John. *Company Man: Thirty Years of Controversy and Crisis in the CIA.* New York: Scribner, 2014.

Robles, Manuel. "El socio de Mertins, acusado de haberlo delatado ante Manuel Buendía." *Proceso*, 21 March 1988, 20–23.

Rodriguez, Felix I., and John Weisman. *Shadow Warrior: The CIA Hero of a Hundred Unknown Battles*. New York: Simon & Schuster, 1989.

Rodríguez Castañeda, Rafael. *Prensa vendida: Los periodistas y los presidentes; 40 años de relaciones*. Mexico City: Grijalbo, 1993.

Ross, John. *The Annexation of Mexico: From the Aztecs to the I.M.F.; One Reporter's Journey through History*. Monroe, ME: Common Courage Press, 1998.

———. *El Monstruo: Dread and Redemption in Mexico City*. New York: Nation Books, 2009.

———. *Rebellion from the Roots: Indian Uprising in Chiapas*. Monroe, ME: Common Courage Press, 1995.

Said, Edward W. *Culture and Imperialism*. New York: Vintage, 1994.

Salinas de Gortari, Carlos. *México: Un paso difícil a la modernidad*. Barcelona: Plaza & Janés Editores, 2000.

Sauloy, Mylène, and Yves le Bonniec. *À qui profite la cocaïne?* Mesnil-sur-l'Estrée, France: Calman-Lévy, 1992.

Scahill, Jeremy. *Blackwater: The Rise of the World's Most Powerful Mercenary Army*. Rev. and updated ed. New York: Nation Books, 2008.

Scherer García, Julio. *Estos años: Con una cierta mirada*. Mexico City: Océano, 1995.

———. *Historias de muerte y corrupción: Calderón, Mouriño, Zambada, El Chapo, La Reina del Pacífico* . . . Mexico City: Grijalbo, 2011.

———. *Los presidentes*. Mexico City: Grijalbo, 1986.

Schou, Nick. *Kill the Messenger: How the CIA's Crack-Cocaine Controversy Destroyed Journalist Gary Webb*. Introduction by Charles Bowden. New York: Nation Books, 2006.

Scott, Peter Dale. *The Road to 9/11: Wealth, Empire, and the Future of America*. Berkeley: University of California Press, 2007.

Scott, Peter Dale, and Jonathan Marshall. *Cocaine Politics: Drugs, Armies, and the CIA in Central America*. Updated paperback ed. Berkeley: University of California Press, 1998.

Shackley, Theodore. *The Third Option: An American View of Counterinsurgency Operations*. New York: Dell, 1981.

Shannon, Elaine. *Desperados: Latin Drug Lords, U.S. Lawmen, and the War America Can't Win*. New York: Viking, 1988.

Shorrock, Tim. *Spies for Hire: The Secret World of Intelligence Outsourcing*. New York: Simon & Schuster, 2008.

Silverstein, Ken. *Private Warriors*. Research by Daniel Burton-Rose. New York: Verso, 2000.

Sklar, Holly. *Washington's War on Nicaragua*. Boston: South End Press, 1988.

Smith, Anthony. *The Geopolitics of Information: How Western Culture Dominates the World*. New York: Oxford University Press, 1980.

Stevens, Evelyn P. *Protest and Response in Mexico*. Cambridge, MA: MIT Press, 1974.

Stockwell, John. *In Search of Enemies: A CIA Story*. New York: W. W. Norton, 1978.

Suárez, Luis. *La otra cara de Afganistán: Reportaje en el corazón de Asia*. Barcelona: Grijalbo, 1983.

Thomas, Gordon. *Gideon's Spies: The Secret History of the Mossad*. Updated ed. New York: St. Martin's Press, 2012.

U.S. Congress, Church Committee. *Alleged Assassination Plots Involving Foreign Leaders: Interim Report of the Select Committee to Study Government Operations with Respect to Intelligence Activities*. New York: W. W. Norton, 1976.

Valdés Castellanos, Guillermo. *Historia del narcotráfico en México*. Mexico City: Aguilar, 2013.

Valle, Eduardo. *El segundo disparo: La narcodemocracia mexicana*. Mexico City: Océano, 1995.

Victoria Zepeda, Felipe. *El caso del periodista asesinado: Una pista segura para atrapar a sus asesinos*. Mexico City: EDAMEX, 1988.

———. *Lo que me dijo Abraham Polo Uscanga: Confidencias antes de su muerte*. Mexico City: EDAMEX, 1995.

Vlanton, Elias, with Zak Mettger. *Who Killed George Polk? The Press Covers Up a Death in the Family*. Philadelphia: Temple University Press, 1996.

Walsh, Lawrence E. *Final Report of the Independent Counsel for Iran/Contra Matters*. Vol. 1, *Investigations and Prosecutions*. Washington, DC: U.S. Court of Appeals for the District of Columbia Circuit, 4 August 1993.

———. *Firewall: The Iran-Contra Conspiracy and Cover-Up*. New York: W. W. Norton, 1997.

Webb, Gary. *Dark Alliance: The CIA, the Contras, and the Crack Cocaine Explosion*. Foreword by U.S. congresswoman Maxine Waters. New York: Seven Stories Press, 1998.

———. *Dark Alliance: The CIA, the Contras, and the Crack Cocaine Explosion*. Rev. paperback ed. Foreword by U.S. congresswoman Maxine Waters. New York: Seven Stories Press, 1999.

———. *"The Killing Game": Selected Writings by the Author of "Dark Alliance."* Edited by Eric Webb, foreword by Tom Loftus, afterword by Robert Parry. New York: Seven Stories Press, 2011.

Weiner, Tim. *Legacy of Ashes: The History of the CIA*. New York: Doubleday, 2007. Winslow, Don. *The Power of the Dog*. New York: Vintage, 2005.

Wise, David, and Thomas B. Ross. *The Invisible Government*. New York: Random House, 1964.

Wolf, Markus, with Anne McElvoy. *Man without a Face: The Autobiography of Communism's Greatest Spymaster*. New York: Public Affairs, 1997.

Wolfe, Tom. *The Electric Kool-Aid Acid Test*. 1968. Repr., New York: Picador, 2004.

Woods, Randall B. *Shadow Warrior: William Egan Colby and the CIA*. New York: Basic Books, 2013.

Woodward, Bob. *Veil: The Secret Wars of the CIA, 1981–1987*. New York: Simon & Schuster, 1987.

INDEX

Page numbers in bold refer to illustrations and captions.

Radio Noticias del Continente (RNC), 19
Rafeedie, Judge Edward, 221, 247; and
Álvarez Macháin kidnapping, 252; and
Harrison (Lawrence Victor), 231, 238, 398–
399, 425; and Los Angeles County sheriff's
deputies cocaine shakedown case, 247–
249; and media, 238–240; and Zuno Arce
trials, 231, 232
Ramírez, Ignacio, 128, 133
Ramírez de Aguilar, Fernando, 111; and
Buendía case, 134, 135, 195; and García
Domínguez (Miguel Ángel), 134
Ramírez Faz, Rosalino, 138
Ramírez Hernández, Carlos, 150, 157; and
Buendía (Manuel), 193–194; on organized
crime and political power, 413; and
Sánchez de Armas (Miguel Ángel),
193–194
Ramírez Razo, Samuel "El Samy," 319, 322
Reagan, Ronald, 23, 48, 51, 221, 310; and
Cold War, 20; and contras, 66; and pursuit
of U.S. global preeminence, 60, 65; and
reassertion of U.S. hegemony, 19
Reagan administration, 19, 67; and Buendía
(Manuel), 20; Caribbean basin strategizing, 84; and Mexico, 424; and neo–cold
warriors, 73, 74; and Nicaragua, 33, 451n7;
and "plausibly deniable" covert operatives,
163–164, 220; and Soviet challenge, 75
Reale, Salvatore "Sal": and CIA–mafia
collusion, 340–341; and Mena (Arkansas),
341; and Nicaraguan contra-related cocaine
trafficking, 341
Red Guards (Guardias Rojas), 308
Reed, Terry Kent: authors' unsuccessful
attempt to interview, 345; and CIA proprietary Maquinaria Internacional, S.A.,
332, 336, 338; and clandestine Chagres
(Panama) meeting, 332–333, 337; and
Clinton (William "Bill" Jefferson), 335,
336; and Cooper (Bill), 336; executive
branch damage controllers and, 339; and
North (Oliver L.), 331–332; and Mena
(Arkansas), 332; and Nir (Amiram), 332–
333; and relocation to Jalisco (Mexico),
336; and Rodríguez (Félix, pseud. Max
Gómez), 332, 337; and Seal (Alder
Barriman "Barry"), 332–333, 337; severance

of ties to Operation Screw Worm, 338;
and training of Nicaraguan contra pilots,
332
Reforma (Mexico City), 306
Revista mexicana de comunicación (Mexico
City), 132, 268
Reyes Heroles, Jesús, 98
Reyes Zurita, Antonio, 273
Riding, Alan, 71; and Distant Neighbors
(1986), 168
Riva Palacio, Raymundo, 37
Riviello Bazán, Gen. Antonio: and Loret de
Mola homicide, 259–260
Rizzo, John: and North (Oliver L.),
315–316
Rocha Díaz, Salvador, 101; and appointment
of special prosecutor for Buendía case,
101–102
Rodríguez, Delia Ann, 360, 374
Rodríguez, Félix (pseud. Max Gómez): and
alleged interrogation of Enrique
Camarena, 424, 426; and Berréllez (Héctor
G.), 424; and Harrison (Lawrence Victor),
332; and Iran-Contra hearings, 338; and
Mexico, 332, 337; and Reed (Terry Kent),
331–332, 337
Rodríguez, Melissa, 375
Rodríguez, Remberto, 206, 207
Rodríguez Santillán, Col. Jesús, 161
Roldós Aguilera, Jaime: suspected assassina-
tion of, 74, 453n16
Roller, William Lloyd, 362
Román Salas, Jorge, 204, 205, 206, 207, 209
Rosales Moreno, Enrique, 98
Ross, John: and Buendía case, 160–162; and
CIA, 161; and Mertins (Gerhard Georg),
162; and Moro Ávila Camacho (Juan
Rafael), 160–161; and Zorrilla Pérez (José
Antonio), 161
Ross, Lee, 410, 411
Rothschild, Matthew, 20, **35**, 52, 92–93, 120,
132, 351, 393; and authors, 34, 36–37,
38–40; and "Who Killed Manuel
Buendía?" article, 33–34, **35**
Ruiz Cortines, Adolfo, 15, 53, 306
Ruiz Massieu, José Francisco, 262, 471n29
Russian Revolution, 62; and Mexican Revo-
lution of 1910, 62–63

Zambada García, Ismael "El Mayo," 415
Zambada Niebla, Jesús Vicente "El
  Vicentillo," 415
Zapata, Emiliano, 25, 63
Zapatistas, 25
Zarco, Francisco, 138
Zavala Avelar, Alfredo, 117
Zea, Leopoldo, 20
Zetas, 414
Zona Rosa (Pink Zone, Mexico City), 3, 55,
  57, 79
Zorrilla Pérez, José Antonio, 36, 51, 129, 132,
  151, 314; and Bartlett Díaz (Manuel), 48,
  59, 150; and Buendía (Manuel), 3–4, 113–
  114, 404; and Buendía assassination, 5, 8,
  59, 99–100, 156, 157, 389–390; and Caro

Quintero (Rafael), 404; detention and
  incarceration of, 142–144; government
  protection of, 124, 389; and Harrison
  (Lawrence Victor), 196, 224, 240, 397–398;
  and impending arrest, 135–136; and Moro
  Ávila Camacho (Juan Rafael), 152; post-
  arrest testimony, 150–151; and release to
  house arrest, 405; removal from DFS, 48;
  and rescinded parole, 405; as scapegoat,
  142, 460n36; special prosecutor García
  Domínguez (Miguel Ángel) and, 108, 117,
  130
Zuno Arce, Rubén, 149, 195, 196–197; and
  Harrison (Lawrence Victor), 196, 224, 240,
  397–398; U.S. prosecution of, 224, 240

www.ingramcontent.com/pod-product-compliance
Lightning Source LLC
Chambersburg PA
CBHW050231270326
41914CB00033BA/1874/J